W9-CKF-992

MANAGEMENT

THE NATURE AND SCOPE OF ··WADIA·· SCOTT, FORESMAN

ATE

E

California Western University   **Maneck S. Wadia**

The Nature
and Scope
of MANAGEMENT

SCOTT, FORESMAN AND COMPANY · Chicago · Atlanta · Dallas · Palo Alto · Fair Lawn, N. J.

To my parents

Preface

It is often said that most professors write or edit books to impress their colleagues. A readings book produced for this purpose will contain either so many articles that the student cannot possibly study them all or such esoteric articles that he is rarely able to understand them. The present volume has been compiled to aid in the instruction of undergraduate and graduate students who are about to be initiated into the challenging field of management. Its objective is neither to present a new approach to the field nor to support an existing one; rather, it is to provide the reader with a well-rounded view of the subject and to lay the groundwork for advanced study. This is done by bringing together systematically the most appropriate articles from the various approaches to management, as well as from other disciplines, that have contributed to a better and fuller understanding of the subject. The primary criterion for selecting the articles and for the taxonomy of those selected was the degree to which the articles and their classification contributed to this objective. *The Nature and Scope of Management* can be used independently or as a supplement to basic textbooks, cases, and/or lectures. A correlation chart at the end of the book indicates how the readings can be integrated with a number of textbooks.

Over the past three years I have discussed the possibilities of a book based on such objectives with a number of my American colleagues, as well as with professors from abroad who were studying at the International Center for Advancement of Management Education at Stanford University. The consensus was that there is an increasing interest, among faculty and students, in the newer concepts of management and that the functional approach is the most appropriate and widely utilized means of introducing students to the field. This book is therefore concerned with two basic themes. First, from the taxonomic point of view, it utilizes the functional approach; second, it includes articles on areas in which there is a growing interest—not only those within the functional framework but especially those contained in the last three sections of the book on the behavioral sciences, international management, and new developments.

The first article in each section gives the general background of the area under consideration, and the articles that follow cover the major topics in that area. It is hoped that this approach will give the reader a wide view of the subject without sacrificing depth. The articles have been selected in an attempt to maintain an appropriate balance among the classics, the various approaches to management, the results of empirical research, and the latest developments in the field. Management is becoming so dynamic and diversified that it brings to mind the myth of Proteus, who kept changing his shape and taking on new characteristics. Yet, just as Proteus was regarded as but one person, so management is considered here as but one field.

One of the great pleasures of writing the preface to a book is the opportunity to thank, in print, the many persons who have contributed to its completion. Dean Ernest C. Arbuckle of the Graduate School of Business, Stanford University, provided an environment that not only facilitated my progress on this project but also allowed me to undertake many other activities that contributed to my understanding of administration. While this project was still in the embryonic stage, Associate Dean Samuel A. Pond of Stanford University of-

fered encouragement by providing opportunities for me to discuss it with professors at various universities, as well as by his own interest in the subject. My teachers and colleagues, both at Stanford University and at Indiana University, have contributed much to my understanding of management, and I gratefully acknowledge their contributions.

My students at the International Center for Advancement of Management Education and the Graduate School of Business, Stanford University, bore the initial brunt of many of the articles in this book; I thank them for their patience and their valuable suggestions. I thank Professor Charles E. Summer of Columbia University and the editors of Scott, Foresman and Company for their assistance in shaping the content of the book. And no one helped more in the preparation of the manuscript than my secretary, Mrs. Lynette Sweet; it is a pleasure to acknowledge her always cheerful assistance.

All the readings in this book have been reprinted with the permission of the publishers and, wherever possible, by permission of the authors. The source of each reading and the affiliation of its author at the time of its original publication are cited in the footnotes. I am grateful to the publishers and authors for their kind cooperation.

Finally, I would like to thank my wife for accepting with charm the inevitable irregular and late hours that go with the preparation of a manuscript.

Maneck S. Wadia

Contents

Functions

PART ONE

Introduction

*Where there is much desire to learn, there of necessity
will be much arguing, much writing, many opinions; for
opinion in good men is but knowledge in the making.*
John Milton

A study of the history of management thought shows that a variety of disciplines have contributed to the ever increasing knowledge of management.[1] Engineers, economists, physical scientists, mathematicians, behavioral scientists, soldiers, politicians, professors, practitioners, and priests have all played a role in the development of administration,[2] both as a science and as an art. Perhaps it is this varied genesis that has led to the development of various schools of thought in management. This variety, in turn, has led scholars, especially in the past decade, to engage in a controversy over which school of thought has the right approach to management, which disciplines can contribute to management, what the proper scheme of classification is, and what should be included in and what excluded from the study of the nature and scope of management. This controversy, in turn, has often led to the attitude that "If I have the right approach, then others may have the wrong approach." What is worse, it has sometimes led to the attitude that "*Since* I have the right approach, others *must* have the wrong approach." "Disagreement and controversy have almost reached the point where any theoretical light that has been generated has been overwhelmed by emotional heat."[3]

Much of the controversy has been concerned with the different approaches rather than with the objectives of these approaches. Each approach has made, and will continue to make, important contributions to management. "One system is better or worse than another only because it has more use in achieving the purpose intended. This gets down to whether it helps or hinders insight, verification and communication."[4] The present text is in substantial agreement with Herbert Simon, who believes that scholars and practitioners of administration should take all facets of the field into consideration.

We are all concerned with human behavior in organizations; hence our work is, whether we call it so or not, behavioral science. We are particularly concerned with managerial behavior—hence with management functions. Since most of the behavior that occurs in organizations involves the choice of courses of action, we all take a decision-making approach. Several of us use quantitative techniques from time to time, although not exclusively; hence we represent the mathematical approach. Human behavior in organizations produces complex interactions and indirect consequences; hence all of us, in striving to understand that behavior, represent a management systems ap-

1. John F. Mee, *Management Thought in a Dynamic Economy* (New York: New York University Press, 1963).
2. The terms *management* and *administration* are used synonymously throughout.
3. Waino W. Suojanen, "Management Theory: Functional and Evolutionary," *Academy of Management Journal,* VI (March 1963), 7.
4. Paul J. Gordon, "Transcend the Current Debate on Administrative Theory," *Academy of Management Journal,* VI (December 1963), 290.

proach. . . . There is nothing antithetical about being interested, at one and the same time, in management functions, behavioral science, decision-making, systems and mathematics. Indeed, I recommend such a combination of interests to anyone who wants to take part in the exciting task of advancing the science and art of management.[5]

Management is a vast and challenging field, and a scholar need not find the various schools of thought mutually exclusive. To a large extent, the approach one takes will depend upon the way he defines the field and estimates its scope.

Before defining management, it seems appropriate to see what types of collectivities can be administered. Scholars at the Administrative Science Center, University of Pittsburgh, by a process of elimination, have "narrowed the search for administration to certain kinds of collectivities: those which exhibit sustained activity; are part of a larger system; have specialized purposes; and are dependent upon interchange with the larger system."[6] These characteristics are essential to the organizations that have administrative activity. Without such organizations, there can be no administrative activities, and without such activities, organizations would find it difficult to survive, since administrative activity is "related to the creation, maintenance or operation of an organization as an organization."[7] Hence, *administered organizations* give us a basis for hypothesizing that administration is concerned with both a short-range and a long-range point of view, with the environment, with purposes or objectives, and with certain administrative activities, often referred to as management functions or subfunctions.[8] We can now define management, both as art and as science, as the process of achieving desired results by influencing human behavior within a suitable environment.

Four major aspects of management emerge from this definition. First, management is a process—that is, a series of interrelated functions[9] leading to a definite goal. The functions may vary from expert to expert, and some managers may not be conscious of any specific process, but the fact remains that managers do perform definite functions. Second, management can be practiced only where an objective or a goal has to be achieved. The objectives of an organization may vary over a wide range, and they may not be properly stated; but in order to have management, as the term is defined here, there must be goal-oriented behavior. Third, management involves influencing people, directly or indirectly; even in a one-man business, other people are involved—suppliers, landlords, customers—whose behavior must be channeled toward a goal. Finally, management involves the establishment of the environment best suited to efficiency and effectiveness for applying the process to achieve the desired results by influencing behavior.[10]

This definition of management is universally applicable and reflects on the vast scope of the field. From the President of the United States to the chief of a Zulu tribe, from the man who runs a global electric firm to the guy who runs the corner hot dog stand, from the madam of a brothel to the administrator of a hospital, from the professor to the great prophet—the definition applies to them all. Each one is an administrator.

---

5. Herbert A. Simon, "Approaching the Theory of Management," in Harold Koontz, ed., *Toward a Unified Theory of Management* (New York: McGraw-Hill Book Co., 1964), pp. 77–78.

6. James D. Thompson, *et al.*, *Comparative Studies in Administration* (Pittsburgh: University of Pittsburgh Press, 1959), p. 6.

7. *Ibid.*, p. 7.

8. Not to be confused with business functions, such as finance, distribution (marketing), and creation (production).

9. The concepts of process and function will be examined in greater detail in Part 2.

10. See Herbert A. Simon, *Administrative Behavior* (New York: The Macmillan Co., 1959), p. 24, and Koontz, *Toward a Unified Theory of Management*, p. 248.

SECTION *I*

THE FIELD OF MANAGEMENT

As noted in the Introduction, various schools of thought have developed in management, and the defense of pet theories has led to semantic, pedagogical, and theoretical conflicts. In his article (#1), Koontz succinctly presents the different schools of thought, the jungle they have created, and steps that might be taken to untangle the jungle.

The avenues of thought opened by Koontz provoked a number of responses, among them the article by Urwick (#2), which discusses the roots of the controversy, evaluates other articles on the subject, and suggests some guidelines to follow in seeking a resolution of the conflict.

Litchfield's article (#3) is an attempt to develop a general theory of management. He presents a number of propositions concerning administration, with the hope that they will be tested and eventually help in the development of a universal theory of management.

What will this universal theory be like? Wadia's article (#4) presents a broad preview of administrative science. It also indicates in a conceptual chart the present approach to administration, which can serve as a take-off point for the development of an administrative science.

1 — The Management Theory Jungle

HAROLD KOONTZ

Although students of management would readily agree that there have been problems of management since the dawn of organized life, most would also agree that systematic examination of management, with few exceptions, is the product of the present century and more especially of the past two decades. Moreover, until recent years almost all of those who have attempted to analyze the management process and look for some theoretical underpinnings to help improve research, teaching, and practice were alert and perceptive practitioners of the art who reflected on many years of experience. Thus, at least in looking at *general* management as an intellectually based art, the earliest meaningful writing came from such experienced practitioners as Fayol, Mooney, Alvin Brown, Sheldon, Barnard, and Urwick. Certainly not even the most academic worshipper of empirical research can overlook the empiricism involved in distilling fundamentals from decades of experience by such discerning practitioners as these. Admittedly done without questionnaires, controlled interviews, or mathematics, observations by such men can hardly be accurately regarded as *a priori* or "armchair."

The noteworthy absence of academic writing and research in the formative years of modern management theory is now more than atoned for by a deluge of research and writing from the aca-

"The Management Theory Jungle," *Academy of Management Journal*, IV (December 1961), 174-188. Reprinted by permission of the author and the publisher. **Harold Koontz**: Graduate School of Business Administration, University of California, Los Angeles.

demic halls. What is interesting and perhaps nothing more than a sign of the unsophisticated adolescence of management theory is how the current flood has brought with it a wave of great differences and apparent confusion. From the orderly analysis of management at the shop-room level by Frederick Taylor and the reflective distillation of experience from the general management point of view by Henri Fayol, we now see these and other early beginnings overgrown and entangled by a jungle of approaches and approachers to management theory.

There are the behavioralists, born of the Hawthorne experiments and the awakened interest in human relations during the 1930's and 1940's, who see management as a complex of interpersonal relationships and the basis of management theory the tentative tenets of the new and undeveloped science of psychology. There are also those who see management theory as simply a manifestation of the institutional and cultural aspects of sociology. Still others, observing that the central core of management is decision-making, branch in all directions from this core to encompass everything in organization life. Then, there are mathematicians who think of management primarily as an exercise in logical relationships expressed in symbols and the omnipresent and ever revered model. But the entanglement of growth reaches its ultimate when the study of management is regarded as a study of one of a number of systems and subsystems, with an understandable tendency for the researcher to be dissatisfied until he has encompassed the entire physical and cultural universe as a management system.

With the recent discovery of an ages-old problem area by social, physical, and biological scientists, and with the supersonic increase in interest by all types of enterprise managers, the apparent impenetrability of the present thicket which we call management theory is not difficult to comprehend. One can hardly be surprised that psychologists, sociologists, anthropologists, sociometricists, economists, mathematicians, physicists, biologists, political scientists, business administration scholars, and even practicing managers, should hop on this interesting, challenging, and profitable band wagon.

This welling of interest from every academic and practicing corner should not upset anyone concerned with seeing the frontiers of knowledge pushed back and the intellectual base of practice broadened. But what is rather upsetting to the practitioner and the observer, who sees great social potential from improved management, is that the variety of approaches to management theory

has led to a kind of confused and destructive jungle warfare. Particularly among academic disciplines and their disciples, the primary interests of many would-be cult leaders seem to be to carve out a distinct (and hence "original") approach to management. And to defend this originality, and thereby gain a place in posterity (or at least to gain a publication which will justify academic status or promotion), it seems to have become too much the current style to downgrade, and sometimes misrepresent, what anyone else has said, or thought, or done.

In order to cut through this jungle and bring to light some of the issues and problems involved in the present management theory area so that the tremendous interest, intelligence, and research results may become more meaningful, it is my purpose here to classify the various "schools" of management theory, to identify briefly what I believe to be the major source of differences, and to offer some suggestions for disentangling the jungle. It is hoped that a movement for clarification can be started so at least we in the field will not be a group of blind men identifying the same elephant with our widely varying and sometimes viciously argumentative theses.

THE MAJOR "SCHOOLS" OF MANAGEMENT THEORY

In attempting to classify the major schools of management theory into six main groups, I am aware that I may overlook certain approaches and cannot deal with all the nuances of each approach. But it does seem that most of the approaches to management theory can be classified in one of these so-called "schools."

THE MANAGEMENT PROCESS SCHOOL

This approach to management theory perceives management as a process of getting things done through and with people operating in organized groups. It aims to analyze the process, to establish a conceptual framework for it, to identify principles underlying it, and to build up a theory of management from them. It regards management as a universal process, regardless of the type of enterprise, or the level in a given enterprise, although recognizing, obviously, that the environment of management differs widely between enterprises and levels. It looks upon management theory as a way of organizing experience so that practice can be improved through research, empirical testing of principles, and teaching of fundamentals involved in the management process.[1]

Often referred to, especially by its critics, as the "traditional" or "universalist" school, this school can be said to have been fathered by Henri Fayol, although many of his offspring did not know of their parent, since Fayol's work was eclipsed by the bright light of his contemporary, Frederick Taylor, and clouded by the lack of a widely available English translation until 1949. Other than Fayol, most of the early contributors to this school dealt only with the organization portion of the management process, largely because of their greater experience with this facet of management and the simple fact that planning and control, as well as the function of staffing, were given little attention by managers before 1940.

This school bases its approach to management theory on several fundamental beliefs:

(1) that managing is a process and can best be dissected intellectually by analyzing the functions of the manager;

(2) that long experience with management in a variety of enterprise situations can be grounds for distillation of certain fundamental truths or generalizations — usually referred to as principles — which have a clarifying and predictive value in the understanding and improvement of managing;

(3) that these fundamental truths can become focal points for useful research both to ascertain their validity and to improve their meaning and applicability in practice;

(4) that such truths can furnish elements, at least until disproved, and certainly until sharpened, of a useful theory of management;

(5) that managing is an art, but one like medicine or engineering, which can be improved by reliance on the light and understanding of principles;

(6) that principles in management, like principles in the biological and physical sciences, are nonetheless true even if a prescribed treatment or design by a practitioner in a given case situation chooses to ignore a principle and the costs involved, or attempts to do something else to offset the costs incurred (this is, of course, not new in medicine, engineering, or any other art, for art is the creative task of compromising fundamentals to attain a desired result); and

(7) that, while the totality of culture and of the physical and biological universe has varying effects on the manager's environment and subjects, as indeed they do in every other field of science and art, the theory of management does not need to encompass the field of all knowledge in order for it to serve as a scientific or theoretical foundation.

The basic approach of this school, then, is to look, first, to the functions of managers. As a second step in this approach, many of us have taken the functions of managers and further dissected them by distilling what we see as fundamental truths in the understandably complicated practice of management. I have found it useful to classify my analysis of these functions around the essentials involved in the following questions:

(1) What is the nature of the function?
(2) What is the purpose of the function?
(3) What explains the structure of the function?
(4) What explains the process of the function?

Perhaps there are other more useful approaches, but I have found that I can place everything pertaining to management (even some of the rather remote research and concepts) in this framework.

Also, purely to make the area of management theory intellectually manageable, those who subscribe to this school do not usually attempt to include in the theory the entire areas of sociology, economics, biology, psychology, physics, chemistry, or others. This is done not because these other areas of knowledge are unimportant and have no bearing on management, but merely because no real progress has ever been made in science or art without significant partitioning of knowledge. Yet, anyone would be foolish not to realize that a function which deals with people in their various activities of producing and marketing anything from money to religion and education is completely independent of the physical, biological, and cultural universe in which we live. And, are there not such relationships in other "compartments" of knowledge and theory?

THE EMPIRICAL SCHOOL

A second approach to management I refer to as the "empirical" school. In this, I include those scholars who identify management as a study of experience, sometimes with intent to draw generalizations but usually merely as a means of teach-

---

1. It is interesting that one of the scholars strongly oriented to human relations and behavioral approaches to management has recently noted that "theory can be viewed as a way of organizing experience" and that "once initial sense is made out of experienced environment, the way is cleared for an even more adequate organization of this experience." See Robert Dubin in "Psyche, Sensitivity, and Social Structure," critical comment in Robert Tannenbaum, I. R. Weschler, and Fred Massarik, *Leadership and Organization: A Behavioral Science Approach* (New York: McGraw-Hill Book Co., 1961), p. 401.

ing experience and transferring it to the practitioner or student. Typical of this school are those who see management or "policy" as the study and analysis of cases and those with such approaches as Ernest Dale's "comparative approach."[2]

This approach seems to be based upon the premise that, if we study the experience of successful managers, or the mistakes made in management, or if we attempt to solve management problems, we will somehow understand and learn to apply the most effective kinds of management techniques. This approach, as often applied, assumes that, by finding out what worked or did not work in individual circumstances, the student or the practitioner will be able to do the same in comparable situations.

No one can deny the importance of studying experience through such study, or of analyzing the "how-it-was-done" of management. But management, unlike law, is not a science based on precedent, and situations in the future exactly comparable to the past are exceedingly unlikely to occur. Indeed, there is a positive danger of relying too much on past experience and on undistilled history of managerial problem-solving for the simple reason that a technique or approach found "right" in the past may not fit a situation of the future.

Those advocating the empirical approach are likely to say that what they really do in analyzing cases or history is to draw from certain generalizations which can be applied as useful guides to thought or action in future case situations. As a matter of fact, Ernest Dale, after claiming to find "so little practical value" from the principles enunciated by the "universalists," curiously drew certain "generalizations" or "criteria" from his valuable study of a number of great practitioners of management.[3] There is some question as to whether Dale's "comparative" approach is not really the same as the "universalist" approach he decries, except with a different distiller of basic truths.

By the emphasis of the empirical school on study of experience, it does appear that the research and thought so engendered may assist in hastening the day for verification of principles. It is also possible that the proponents of this school may come up with a more useful framework of principles than that of the management process school. But, to the extent that the empirical school draws generalizations from its research, and it would seem to be a necessity to do so unless its members are satisfied to exchange meaningless and structureless experience, this approach tends to be and do the same as the management process school.

THE HUMAN BEHAVIOR SCHOOL

This approach to the analysis of management is based on the central thesis that, since managing involves getting things done with and through people, the study of management must be centered on interpersonal relations. Variously called the "human relations," "leadership," or "behavioral sciences" approach, this school brings to bear "existing and newly developed theories, methods, and techniques of the relevant social sciences upon the study of inter- and intrapersonal phenomena, ranging fully from the personality dynamics of individuals at one extreme to the relations of cultures at the other."[4] In other words, this school concentrates on the "people" part of management and rests on the principle that, where people work together as groups in order to accomplish objectives, "people should understand people."

The scholars in this school have a heavy orientation to psychology and social psychology. Their primary focus is the individual as a socio-psychological being and what motivates him. The members of this school vary from those who see it as a portion of the manager's job, a tool to help him understand and get the best from people by meeting their needs and responding to their motivations, to those who see the psychological behavior of individuals and groups as the total of management.

In this school are those who emphasize human relations as an art that the manager should advantageously understand and practice. There are those who focus attention on the manager as a leader and sometimes equate management to leadership, thus, in effect, tending to treat all group activities as "managed" situations. There are those who see the study of group dynamics and interpersonal relationships as simply a study of socio-psychological relationships and seem, therefore, merely to be attaching the term "management" to the field of social psychology.

That management must deal with human behavior can hardly be denied. That the study of human interactions, whether in the environment of management or in unmanaged situations, is important and useful one could not dispute. And it would be a serious mistake to regard good leadership as unimportant to good managership. But whether the field of human behavior is the equiv-

2. *The Great Organizers* (New York: McGraw-Hill Book Co., 1960), pp. 11–28.

3. *Ibid.*, pp. 11, 26–28, 62–68.

4. R. Tannenbaum, I. R. Weschler, and F. Massarik, *Leadership and Organization* (New York: McGraw-Hill Book Co., 1961), p. 9.

alent of the field of management is quite another thing. Perhaps it is like calling the study of the human body the field of cardiology.

THE SOCIAL SYSTEM SCHOOL

Closely related to the human behavior school and often confused or intertwined with it is one which might be labeled the social system school. This includes those researchers who look upon management as a social system, that is, a system of cultural interrelationships. Sometimes, as in the case of March and Simon,[5] the system is limited to formal organizations, using the term "organization" as equivalent to enterprise, rather than the authority-activity concept used most often in management. In other cases, the approach is not to distinguish the formal organization, but rather to encompass any kind of system of human relationships.

Heavily sociological in flavor, this approach to management does essentially what any study of sociology does. It identifies the nature of the cultural relationships of various social groups and attempts to show these as a related, and usually an integrated, system.

Perhaps the spiritual father of this ardent and vocal school of management theorists is Chester Barnard.[6] In searching for an answer to fundamental explanations underlying the managing process, this thoughtful business executive developed a theory of cooperation grounded in the needs of the individual to solve, through cooperation, the biological, physical, and social limitations of himself and his environment. Barnard then carved from the total of cooperative systems so engendered one set of interrelationships which he defines as "formal organization." His formal organization concept, quite unlike that usually held by management practitioners, is any cooperative system in which there are persons able to communicate with each other and who are willing to contribute action toward a conscious common purpose.

The Barnard concept of cooperative systems pervades the work of many contributors to the social system school of management. For example, Herbert Simon at one time defined the subject of organization theory and the nature of human organizations as "systems of interdependent activity, encompassing at least several primary groups and usually characterized, at the level of consciousness of participants, by a high degree of rational direction of behavior toward ends that are objects of common knowledge."[7] Simon and others have subsequently seemed to have ex-

panded this concept of social systems to include any cooperative and purposeful group interrelationship or behavior.

This school has made many noteworthy contributions to management. The recognition of organized enterprise as a social organism, subject to all the pressures and conflicts of the cultural environment, has been helpful to the management theorist and the practitioner alike. Among some of the more helpful aspects are the awareness of the institutional foundations of organization authority, the influence of informal organization, and such social factors as those Wight Bakke has called the "bonds of organization."[8] Likewise, many of Barnard's helpful insights, such as his economy of incentives and his theory of opportunism, have brought the power of sociological understanding into the realm of management practice.

Basic sociology, analysis of concepts of social behavior, and the study of group behavior in the framework of social systems do have great value in the field of management. But one may well ask the question whether this *is* management. Is the field of management coterminous with the field of sociology? Or is sociology an important underpinning like language, psychology, physiology, mathematics, and other fields of knowledge? Must management be defined in terms of the universe of knowledge?

THE DECISION THEORY SCHOOL

Another approach to management theory, undertaken by a growing and scholarly group, might be referred to as the decision theory school. This group concentrates on rational approach to decision—the selection from among possible alternatives of a course of action or of an idea. The approach of this school may be to deal with the decision itself, or to the persons or organizational group making the decision, or to an

5. *Organizations* (New York: John Wiley & Sons, Inc., 1958).

6. *The Functions of the Executive* (Cambridge, Mass.: Harvard University Press, 1938).

7. "Comments on the Theory of Organizations," 46 *American Political Science Review*, No. 4 (December, 1952), p. 1130.

8. *Bonds of Organization* (New York: Harper & Brothers, 1950). These "bonds" or "devices" of organization are identified by Bakke as (1) the functional specifications system (a system of teamwork arising from job specifications and arrangements for association); (2) the status system (a vertical hierarchy of authority); (3) the communications system; (4) the reward and penalty system; and (5) the organization charter (ideas and means which give character and individuality to the organization, or enterprise).

analysis of the decision process. Some limit themselves fairly much to the economic rationale of the decision, while others regard anything which happens in an enterprise the subject of their analysis, and still others expand decision theory to cover the psychological and sociological aspect and environment of decisions and decision-makers.

The decision-making school is apparently an outgrowth of the theory of consumer's choice with which economists have been concerned since the days of Jeremy Bentham early in the nineteenth century. It has arisen out of such economic problems and analyses as utility maximization, indifference curves, marginal utility, and economic behavior under risks and uncertainties. It is, therefore, no surprise that one finds most of the members of this school to be economic theorists. It is likewise no surprise to find the content of this school to be heavily oriented to model construction and mathematics.

The decision theory school has tended to expand its horizon considerably beyond the process of evaluating alternatives. That point has become for many only a springboard for examination of the entire sphere of human activity, including the nature of the organization structure, psychological and social reactions of individuals and groups, the development of basic information for decisions, an analysis of values and particularly value considerations with respect to goals, communications networks, and incentives. As one would expect, when the decision theorists study the small, but central, area of decision *making*, they are led by this keyhole look at management to consider the entire field of enterprise operation and its environment. The result is that decision theory becomes no longer a neat and narrow concentration on decision, but rather a broad view of the enterprise as a social system.

There are those who believe that, since management is characterized by its concentration on decisions, the future development of management theory will tend to use the decision as its central focus and the rest of management theory will be hung on this structural center. This may occur and certainly the study of the decision, the decision process, and the decision maker can be extended to cover the entire field of management as anyone might conceive it. Nevertheless, one wonders whether this focus cannot also be used to build around it the entire area of human knowledge. For, as most decision theorists recognize, the problem of choice is individual, as well as organizational, and most of what has been said that is pure decision theory can be applied to the existence and thinking of a Robinson Crusoe.

THE MATHEMATICAL SCHOOL

Although mathematical methods can be used by any school of management theory, and have been, I have chosen to group under a school those theorists who see management as a system of mathematical models and processes. Perhaps the most widely known group I arbitrarily so lump are the operations researchers or operations analysts, who have sometimes anointed themselves with the rather pretentious name of "management scientists." The abiding belief of this group is that, if management, or organization, or planning, or decision making is a logical process, it can be expressed in terms of mathematical symbols and relationships. The central approach of this school is the model, for it is through these devices that the problem is expressed in its basic relationships and in terms of selected goals or objectives.

There can be no doubt of the great usefulness of mathematical approaches to any field of inquiry. It forces upon the researcher the definition of a problem or problem area, it conveniently allows the insertion of symbols for unknown data, and its logical methodology, developed by years of scientific application and abstraction, furnishes a powerful tool for solving or simplifying complex phenomena.

But it is hard to see mathematics as a truly separate school of management theory, any more than it is a separate "school" in physics, chemistry, engineering, or medicine. I only deal with it here as such because there has appeared to have developed a kind of cult around mathematical analysts who have subsumed to themselves the area of management.

In pointing out that mathematics is a tool, rather than a school, it is not my intention to underestimate the impact of mathematics on the science and practice of management. By bringing to this immensely important and complex field the tools and techniques of the physical sciences, the mathematicians have already made an immense contribution to orderly thinking. They have forced on people in management the means and desirability of seeing many problems more clearly, they have pressed on scholars and practitioners the need for establishing goals and measures of effectiveness, they have been extremely helpful in getting the management area seen as a logical system of relationships, and they have caused people in management to review and occasionally reorganize information sources and systems so that mathematics can be given sensible quantitative meaning. But with all this meaningful contribution and the greater sharpness and sophistication of planning which is resulting, I cannot see that mathematics is management theory any more than it is astronomy.

THE MAJOR SOURCES OF MENTAL ENTANGLEMENT IN THE JUNGLE

In outlining the various schools, or approaches, of management theory, it becomes clear that these intellectual cults are not drawing greatly different inferences from the physical and cultural environment surrounding us. Why, then, have there been so many differences between them and why such a struggle, particularly among our academic brethren to obtain a place in the sun by denying the approaches of others? Like the widely differing and often contentious denominations of the Christian religion, all have essentially the same goals and deal with essentially the same world.

While there are many sources of the mental entanglement in the management theory jungle, the major ones are the following:

THE SEMANTICS JUNGLE

As is so often true when intelligent men argue about basic problems, some of the trouble lies in the meaning of key words. The semantics problem is particularly severe in the field of management. There is even a difference in the meaning of the word "management." Most people would agree that it means getting things done through and with people, but is it people in formal organizations, or in all group activities? Is it governing, leading, or teaching?

Perhaps the greatest single semantics confusion lies in the word "organization." Most members of the management process school use it to define the activity-authority structure of an enterprise and certainly most practitioners believe that they are "organizing" when they establish a framework of activity groupings and authority relationships. In this case, organization represents the formal framework within an enterprise that furnishes the environment in which people perform. Yet a large number of "organization" theorists conceive of organization as the sum total of human relationships in any group activity; they thus seem to make it equivalent to *social* structure. And some use "organization" to mean "enterprise."

If the meaning of organization cannot be clarified and a standard use of the term adopted by management theorists, understanding and criti-

cism should not be based on this difference. It hardly seems to me to be accurate for March and Simon, for example, to criticize the organization theories of the management process, or "universalist," school for not considering the management planning function as part of organizing, when they have chosen to treat it separately. Nor should those who choose to treat the training, selecting, guiding or leading of people under staffing and direction be criticised for a tendency to "view the employee as an inert instrument" or a "given rather than a variable."[9] Such accusations, proceeding from false premises, are clearly erroneous.

Other semantic entanglements might be mentioned. By some, decision-making is regarded as a process of choosing from among alternatives; by others, the total managerial task and environment. Leadership is often made synonymous with managership and is analytically separated by others. Communications may mean everything from a written or oral report to a vast network of formal and informal relationships. Human relations to some implies a psychiatric manipulation of people, but to others the study and art of understanding people and interpersonal relationships.

DIFFERENCES IN DEFINITION OF MANAGEMENT AS A BODY OF KNOWLEDGE

As was indicated in the discussion of semantics, "management" has far from a standard meaning, although most agree that it at least involves getting things done through and with people. But, does it mean the dealing with all human relationships? Is a street peddler a manager? Is a parent a manager? Is a leader of a disorganized mob a manager? Does the field of management equal the fields of sociology and social psychology combined? Is it the equivalent of the entire system of social relationships?

While I recognize that sharp lines cannot be drawn in management any more than they are in medicine or engineering, there surely can be a sharper distinction drawn than at present. With the plethora of management writing and experts, calling almost everything under the sun "management," can one expect management theory to be regarded as very useful or scientific to the practitioner?

THE A PRIORI ASSUMPTION

Confusion in management theory has also been heightened by the tendency for many newcomers

9. March, J. G., and H. A. Simon, *Organizations* (New York: John Wiley & Sons, Inc., 1958), pp. 29–33.

in the field to cast aside significant observations and analyses of the past on the grounds that they are *a priori* in nature. This is an often-met accusation made by those who wish to cast aside the work of Fayol, Mooney, Brown, Urwick, Gulick, and others who are branded as "universalists." To make the assumption that the distilled experiences of men such as these represent *a priori* reasoning is to forget that experience in and with managing *is* empirical. While the conclusions that perceptive and experienced practitioners of the art of management are not infallible, they represent an experience which is certainly real and not "armchair." No one could deny, I feel sure, that the ultimate test of accuracy of management theory must be practice and management theory and science must be developed from reality.

THE MISUNDERSTANDING OF PRINCIPLES

Those who feel that they gain caste or a clean slate for advancing a particular notion or approach often delight in casting away anything which smacks of management principles. Some have referred to them as platitudes, forgetting that a platitude is still a truism and a truth does not become worthless because it is familiar. (As Robert Frost has written, "Most of the changes we think we see in life are merely truths going in or out of favor.") Others cast away principles of Fayol and other practitioners, only to draw apparently different generalizations from their study of management; but many of the generalizations so discovered are often the same fundamental truths in different words that certain criticized "universalists" have discovered.

One of the favorite tricks of the managerial theory trade is to disprove a whole framework of principles by reference to one principle which the observer sees disregarded in practice. Thus, many critics of the universalists point to the well-known cases of dual subordination in organized enterprise, coming to the erroneous conclusion that there is no substance to the principle of unity of command. But this does not prove that there is no cost to the enterprise by designing around, or disregarding, the principle of unity of command; nor does it prove that there were not other advantages which offset the costs, as there often are in cases of establishing functional authorities in organization.

Perhaps the almost hackneyed stand-by for those who would disprove the validity of all principles by referring to a single one is the misunderstanding around the principle of span of management (or span of control). The usual source of authority quoted by those who criticize is Sir Ian

Hamilton, who never intended to state a universal principle, but rather to make a personal observation in a book of reflections on his Army experience, and who did say, offhand, that he found it wise to limit his span to 3 to 6 subordinates. No modern universalist relies on this single observation, and, indeed, few can or will state an absolute or universal numerical ceiling. Since Sir Ian was not a management theorist and did not intend to be, let us hope that the ghost of his innocent remark may be laid to deserved rest!

What concerns those who feel that a recognition of fundamental truths, or generalizations, may help in the diagnosis and study of management, and who know from managerial experience that such truths or principles do serve an extremely valuable use, is the tendency for some researchers to prove the wrong things through either misstatement or misapplication of principles. A classic case of such misunderstanding and misapplication is in Chris Argyris' interesting book on *Personality and Organization*.[10] This author, who in this book and his other works has made many noteworthy contributions to management, concludes that "formal organization principles make demands on relatively healthy individuals that are incongruent with their needs," and that "frustration, conflict, failure, and short-time perspective are predicted as results of this basic incongruency."[11] This startling conclusion—the exact opposite of what "good" formal organization based on "sound" organization principles should cause, is explained when one notes that, of four "principles" Argyris quotes, one is not an organization principle at all but the economic principle of specialization and three other "principles" are quoted incorrectly.[12] With such a postulate, and with no attempt to recognize, correctly or incorrectly, any other organization and management principles, Argyris has simply proved that wrong principles badly applied will lead to frustration; and every management practitioner knows this to be true!

THE INABILITY OR UNWILLINGNESS OF MANAGEMENT THEORISTS TO UNDERSTAND EACH OTHER

What has been said above leads one to the conclusion that much of the management theory jungle is caused by the unwillingness or inability of the management theorists to understand each other. Doubting that it is inability, because one must assume that a person interested in manage-

---

10. New York: Harper & Brothers, 1957.
11. *Ibid.*, p. 74.
12. *Ibid.*, pp. 58−66.

ment theory is able to comprehend, at least in concept and framework, the approaches of the various "schools," I can only come to the conclusion that the roadblock to understanding is unwillingness.

Perhaps this unwillingness comes from the professional "walls" developed by learned disciplines. Perhaps the unwillingness stems from a fear that someone or some new discovery will encroach on professional and academic status. Perhaps it is fear of professional or intellectual obsolescence. But whatever the cause, it seems that these walls will not be torn down until it is realized that they exist, until all cultists are willing to look at the approach and content of other schools, and until, through exchange and understanding of ideas some order may be brought from the present chaos.

DISENTANGLING THE MANAGEMENT THEORY JUNGLE

It is important that steps be taken to disentangle the management theory jungle. Perhaps, it is too soon and we must expect more years of wandering through a thicket of approaches, semantics, thrusts, and counter-thrusts. But in any field as important to society where the many blunders of an unscientifically based managerial art can be so costly, I hope that this will not be long.

There do appear to be some things that can be done. Clearly, meeting what I see to be the major sources of the entanglement should remove much of it. The following considerations are important:

1. *The Need for Definition of a Body of Knowledge.* Certainly, if a field of knowledge is not to get bogged down in a quagmire of misunderstandings, the first need is for definition of the field. Not that it need be defined in sharp, detailed, and inflexible lines, but rather along lines which will give it fairly specific content. Because management is reality, life, practice, my suggestion would be that it be defined in the light of the able and discerning practitioner's frame of reference. A science unrelated to the art for which it is to serve is not likely to be a very productive one.

Although the study of managements in various enterprises, in various countries, and at various levels made by many persons, including myself, may neither be representative nor adequate, I have come to the conclusion that management is the art of getting things done through and with people in *formally organized groups,* the art of creating an environment in such an organized

group where people can perform as individuals and yet cooperate toward attainment of group goals, the art of removing blocks to such performance, the art of optimizing efficiency in effectively reaching goals. If this kind of definition of the field is unsatisfactory, I suggest at least an agreement that the area should be defined to reflect the field of the practitioner and that further research and study of practice be done to this end.

In defining the field, too, it seems to me imperative to draw some limits for purposes of analysis and research. If we are to call the entire cultural, biological, and physical universe the field of management, we can no more make progress than could have been done if chemistry or geology had not carved out a fairly specific area and had, instead, studied all knowledge.

In defining the body of knowledge, too, care must be taken to distinguish between tools and content. Thus mathematics, operations research, accounting, economic theory, sociometry, and psychology, to mention a few, are significant *tools* of management but are not, in themselves, a part of the *content* of the field. This is not to mean that they are unimportant or that the practicing manager should not have them available to him, nor does it mean that they may not be the means of pushing back the frontiers of knowledge of management. But they should not be confused with the basic content of the field.

This is not to say that fruitful study should not continue on the underlying disciplines affecting management. Certainly knowledge of sociology, social systems, psychology, economics, political science, mathematics, and other areas, pointed toward contributing to the field of management, should be continued and encouraged. And significant findings in these and other fields of knowledge might well cast important light on, or change concepts in, the field of management. This has certainly happened in other sciences and in every other art based upon significant science.

2. *Integration of Management and Other Disciplines.* If recognition of the proper content of the field were made, I believe that the present crossfire of misunderstanding might tend to disappear. Management would be regarded as a specific discipline and other disciplines would be looked upon as important bases of the field. Under these circumstances, the allied and underlying disciplines would be welcomed by the business and public administration schools, as well as by practitioners, as loyal and helpful associates. Integration of management and other disciplines would then not be difficult.

3. *The Clarification of Management Semantics.* While I would expect the need for clarification and uniformity of management semantics would largely be satisfied by definition of the field as a body of knowledge, semantics problems might require more special attention. There are not too many places where semantics are important enough to cause difficulty. Here again, I would suggest the adoption of the semantics of the intelligent practitioners, unless words are used by them so inexactly as to require special clarification. At least, we should not complicate an already complex field by developing a scientific or academic jargon which would build a language barrier between the theorist and the practitioner.

Perhaps the most expeditious way out of this problem is to establish a commission representing academic societies immediately concerned and associations of practicing managers. This would not seem to be difficult to do. And even if it were, the results would be worth the efforts.

4. *Willingness to Distill and Test Fundamentals.* Certainly, the test of maturity and usefulness of a science is the sharpness and validity of the principles underlying it. No science, now regarded as mature, started out with a complete statement of incontrovertibly valid principles. Even the oldest sciences, such as physics, keep revising their underlying laws and discovering new principles. Yet any science has proceeded, and more than that has been useful, for centuries on the basis of generalizations, some laws, some principles, and hypotheses.

One of the understandable sources of inferiority of the social sciences is the recognition that they are inexact sciences. On the other hand, even the so-called exact sciences are subject to a great deal of inexactness, have principles which are not completely proved, and use art in the design of practical systems and components. The often-encountered defeatist attitude of the social sciences, of which management is one, overlooks the fact that management may be explained, practice may be improved, and the goals of research may be more meaningful if we encourage attempts at perceptive distillation of experience by stating principles (or generalizations) and placing them in a logical framework. As two scientists recently said on this subject:

The reason for this defeatist point of view regarding the social sciences may be traceable to a basic misunderstanding of the nature of scientific endeavor. What matters is not whether or to what extent inexactitudes in procedures and predictive capability can eventually be removed . . . : rather it is *objectivity*, i.e., the intersubjectivity of findings independent of any one person's intuitive judgment, which distinguishes science from intuitive guesswork however brilliant. . . . But once a new fact or a new idea has been conjectured, no matter how intuitive a foundation, it must be capable of objective test and confirmation by anyone. And it is this crucial standard of scientific objectivity rather than any purported criterion of exactitude to which the social sciences must conform.[13]

In approaching the clarification of management theory, then, we should not forget a few criteria:

1) The theory should deal with an area of knowledge and inquiry that is "manageable"; no great advances in knowledge were made so long as man contemplated the whole universe;

2) The theory should be *useful* in improving practice and the task and person of the practitioner should not be overlooked;

3) The theory should not be lost in semantics, especially useless jargon not understandable to the practitioner;

4) The theory should give direction and efficiency to research and teaching; and

5) The theory must recognize that it is a part of a larger universe of knowledge and theory.

2 – The Tactics of Jungle Warfare

LYNDALL F. URWICK

Professor Harold Koontz' paper on *The Management Theory Jungle*[1] called attention to a tendency in the academic study of management in the U.S.A. which has troubled outside observers for some years. "Inky warfare" is both an occupational disease and the favourite hobby of some professors. Through practice they become extremely

13. Helmer, O., and N. Rescher, "On the Epistemology of the Inexact Sciences," (Santa Monica, California: The Rand Corporation, P-1513, 1958), pp. 4–5.

"The Tactics of Jungle Warfare," *Academy of Management Journal*, VI (December 1963), 316–329. Reprinted by permission of the author and the publisher. Lyndall F. Urwick: Management consultant and visiting professor, Department of Business Administration, University of New South Wales, Australia.

skilled at the gentle art of verbal in-fighting. For an outsider who, having been prevented by the demands of more lethal warfare from proceeding beyond a first degree, is not even a passable academic, to venture into the area of hostilities, is therefore a hazardous step. But, on the other hand, an outside view may be helpful.

Perhaps a good starting point is Von Clausewitz' famous distinction between tactics and strategy . . . "The Art of War divides itself into tactics and strategy. The former occupies itself with the form of the separate combat, the latter with its use."[2]

That there is a combat, both Professor Koontz and Professor Suojanen are agreed. To quote the latter "To-day it is almost impossible to find two people who share more than a very general agreement as to what should be included, and what excluded, in the definition and study of management theory. Disagreement and controversy have almost reached the point where any theoretical light that has been generated has been overwhelmed by emotional heat."[3]

It has certain obvious roots. Perhaps the principal of these is the fact that the United States is a very large country. In the last half-century this continent has developed academic apparatus for the study of management at a speed and on a scale which are, as far as the writer is aware, unparalleled in the history of education anywhere in the world. Inevitably much of the communication between individuals is in written, and often published, form. It is difficult, if not often impossible, for the holders of opposing views to meet personally and learn to laugh with and at each other as human beings. The temptation to score "debating points" is frequently irresistible.

The danger of such a situation has been emphasized by David Lilienthal: "making decisions from papers has a dehumanizing effect. Much of man's inhumanity to man is explained by it."[4] In the British Infantry Division with which the writer served in World War I one of the standing orders to the General Staff was "Never enter into an argument on paper. Go and see the man."[5]

From one point of view this particular combat is extremely comic. Here are two groups of people, one of which has been engaged quite seriously in trying to teach rising generations the art of managing for the last half-century. And the art of managing is primarily and fundamentally the art of arranging for human cooperation in the pursuit of objectives. The other group is drawn from what are described broadly as "the behavioural sciences." That is to say it specializes in knowledge about human behaviour. And here are two of them faced with what is, after all, a fairly elementary management problem—how to arrange for reasonable cooperation between people of the same occupation, of the same level of education and intellectual ability, of the same nationality—putting up about as big a "black" in elementary human relations as it is possible to imagine.

Of course they are not unique. In 1959, in the University of Cambridge, England, Sir Charles Snow delivered the Rede Lecture on the subject of "The Two Cultures and the Scientific Revolution."[6] This moved Dr. F. R. Leavis to entitle his Richmond Lecture, delivered in the Hall of Downing College in the same University in 1962, "The Significance of C. P. Snow."[7] It was about as barbed an attack on the thinking of a not uneminent colleague as the writer has ever read. In a sense the combat between the established teachers of management and the behavioural scientists is merely an extension to the management field of the sharper conflict between those educated in science and those educated in the humanities which was the theme of Snow's lecture, as of Dr. Leavis' retort.

As it is incumbent on anyone discussing such a subject publicly to declare his "interest" the writer would add that he secured his university degree in Modern History. Subsequently he had some brief instruction from the late Sidney and Beatrice Webb on the application of scientific method to sociological enquiry. Since 1934 he has been a management consultant.

But while the tactics of the combat, its form, is not without interest and amusement, its strategy, its use, is more questionable. Those who are likely to laugh longest at it are those, and they are a considerable number, perhaps more than the "behavioural scientists" realize, perhaps more than anyone in the United States realizes, who still think that "there's not much in all this management stuff anyway." They do not believe that human government can be made the subject of knowledge, whether exact or less exact. It's just a

1. Harold Koontz, "The Management Theory Jungle," *Journal of the Academy of Management*, December 1961, p. 175.

2. General Carl von Clausewitz, *On War,* English Translation by Colonel J. J. Graham, London, Kegan Paul, 1940, Bk. II, Cp. 2, V. I. p. 94.

3. Waino W. Suojanen, "Management Theory: Functional & Evolutionary," *Journal of the Academy of Management*, V. 6, No. 1, March 1963, p. 7.

4. David E. Lilienthal, *TVA—Democracy on the March,* Penguin Books, London, 1944, p. 126.

5. 11th British Division, Standing Orders, Office Orders, 1917. Ms. copy in the author's possession.

6. C. P. Snow, *The Two Cultures and the Scientific Revolution,* Cambridge (England), The University Press, 1959.

7. F. R. Leavis, *The Significance of C. P. Snow,* full text printed in *The Spectator*, London, March 9, 1962.

power struggle, a matter of experience and political agility. And the spectacle of the American universities, who have led the world in the study of the subject, sharply divided on what the subject is about, will cause this group of reactionaries immense satisfaction. There is a very real danger of yet another instance of "What is truth? said jesting Pilate; and would not stay for an answer."[8]

It is therefore constructive and helpful to find Professor Suojanen making suggestions designed to reduce "the management theory jungle" to "an orderly tree farm, in which theorists of many different persuasions will be able to plant and prune in harmony, thereby advancing the state of the art on all relevant fronts."[9] His strategy is correct. It is essential that at least "the emotional heat" should be turned off discussion of the subject. But his article fails to suggest to the writer that he has any conception of the causes of this "emotional heat." "Emotional heat" is not an abstraction. The phrase means that some human being, a person, feels hot and hurt and angry because of what some other person has written or said or done.

He will no doubt agree with the writer that the initiative has come from the "behavioural scientists." For the last fifty years the universities of the United States have been steadily building up Departments or Faculties of Business Administration; today there are some 500 of them. They have developed from various angles, administratively speaking. Some of them have hived off from existing faculties of engineering, economics or, more rarely, political science. Some have tended to replace the older subject of Commerce, which may perhaps be defined as teaching the business leaders of tomorrow the bad practices of yesterday. Some have been started up quite independently by a combination of younger men from various faculties.

The Heads of these Departments have had a difficult row to hoe. On the one side they have had to face up to the scepticism of their colleagues in charge of established subjects. They have been "upstarts," newcomers in the academic fold. On the other hand they have had to make headway against a widespread tendency among business men to fail to understand what university education is about, to demand professional training in techniques rather than basic study of theory, the pursuit of knowledge of immediate practical utility rather than of knowledge for its own sake. Thirdly, and perhaps most important of all, they have been discovering that management is a field of study in which it is particularly difficult to train and keep competent instructors because of the competing claims of business which can afford to pay much higher salaries than can the universities for young men of real initiative and ability. It is no accident that proportionately fewer third degrees are taken by students in business management than by those in any other subject.

Management is also a difficult subject to teach. In the first place it is new as a recognized discipline and was, at the beginning, uncertain as to its pattern and content. In the second place managing is a practical art. The activity is in itself a synoptic or integrating function. It is engaged in uniting the contributions of quite a large variety of specialized bodies of knowledge and special skills in the service of a common objective. And the disciplines which underlie these special skills belong to different categories of knowledge, which, traditionally, are assigned to independent faculties in University organization.

Thus the body of knowledge known generically as management includes a large contribution from:

1. Engineering and its underlying body of physical sciences such as mathematics, physics, mechanics and so on. This has enabled it to attain a much higher degree of precision in analyzing and measuring the tasks, especially the tasks using mechanical help, which it asks individuals to perform. It has issued in the applied body of knowledge usually described as Production or Industrial Engineering.

2. Individual Physiology and Psychology and the underlying sciences in the biological group on which they are based. While Psychology is a much newer recruit to the body of inductive disciplines than the physical sciences — till within the last decades of the XIX Century it was usually regarded as a branch of speculative philosophy — it is, of course, an extremely interesting and challenging development. Interest in it was also stimulated by the two World Wars which occurred in the first half of the XX Century, both by the possibilities which it uncovered of greater accuracy in the assignment of individuals to tasks and by its contribution, through the special branch of medicine known as psycho-pathology, to the problem of dealing with the special neuroses developed by the strains of war. But, since it was a young science and its methodologies not wholly reliable, it had to be supplemented by reliance on practical experience and responsible judgment. These two elements in combination have been built up into the body of knowledge usually known as Personnel Management. Its function is to assist the manager to greater accuracy in adjusting each individual to the task he/she may be asked to perform.

8. Francis Bacon, *Essays*, 1621, "Of Truth."
9. *Op. Cit. N.* (3), p. 16.

3. Economics and the sciences underlying economic theory and practice, such as Statistical Method, Accounting, Commercial Geography and Law. These have enabled management to attain greater precision in the task of arranging and correlating the different tasks which members of a group are called upon to perform and in developing the methodologies of functions other than production and personnel, such as transportation, marketing and so on. They have issued in a number of applied bodies of knowledge such as Cost Accounting, Management Accounting and Organization and Methods.

4. Political Science and the more modern studies underlying it such as Sociology, Social Psychology and Anthropology. In addition a great deal of special study has been devoted to what is described broadly as "The Industrial Problem," i.e., the failure of Employers and Managers on the one side and of employed persons, represented by Trade Unions, on the other, to arrive at any agreed view as to the purpose and organization of economic life. The writer's own instructors, Sidney and Beatrice Webb, produced, of course, a shelf-full of weighty volumes on this and kindred subjects. These contributed to the manager's understanding of the behaviour of human beings in groups, just as 2. contributes to his understanding of the behaviour of the individual as an isolated individual. They tend to correct one of the cardinal weaknesses of orthodox economics, namely that it is strongly biased towards the assumption that the relations between the individual and the institution in which he works should be regarded purely from the standpoint of his reactions as an individual. The influence on those reactions of social conditioning should be ignored. Their difficulty lies, of course, in the fact that their content is extremely close to what are commonly described as ideologies, the theories which men hold as to political and social organization. Men cling to these theories with passionate conviction; currently conflicting ideas on the subject are the foundation of what is known as the "cold war." They are the most common basis of what are described as "value judgments."

But the manager is concerned most of his time with the reactions of human beings *in groups*, though he should be equally concerned with the reactions of individuals as isolated individuals. And at the present time there is virtually no technique known to man for forming concepts as to group behaviour other than observation of the behaviour of persons as individuals. If therefore Psychology, regarded as the study of individual behaviour, is as yet a long way from being an exact science, the prospect of an exact science of group psychology is much more remote. At the same time managers are compelled by practical necessity every day to numerous actions based on their estimate of what group reactions are likely to be. And such estimates are particularly prone to bias due to the social and political background of the individual.

Nevertheless a considerable volume of effort has been devoted to building up techniques in this area under such titles as Publicity, Marketing, Consumer Studies, Public-Customer-Stockholder- & Industrial Relations, Group Dynamics and the like. Much research has centered around terms such as Leadership, Morale and Entrepreneurship.

In addition to the difficulty of unifying these very different disciplines—different in origin, in outlook, in methodology, in degree of development—into a single balanced course covering three or four years of undergraduate study, Heads of Departments of Business Administration have been faced by a limiting time factor. The generations pass quickly. The undergraduate they are teaching today may be an up-and-coming young President of an industrial undertaking within ten to fifteen years of leaving the university. Attractive though it may be to the academic mind to contemplate the gradual evolution of more exact knowledge, the student who is going out into practical life will probably never again have such an opportunity of continuous whole-time study. The kind of outlook on life which he takes with him from the university determines the mental equipment with which he will probably face the gravest practical problems, involving often the lives of many thousands of his fellow-citizens, within ten to fifteen years.

It is no use teaching him what exact science may be able to do in 20 or 30 years' time. It is much more important to teach him a healthy scepticism as to premature conclusions which seem to carry the authority of science. For nothing is more dangerous than scientific knowledge which claims complete accuracy prematurely. The bio-chemist Professor J. B. S. Haldane has made the point neatly. "A hundred and fifty years ago one of Napoleon's armies was put on a cheap and portable diet drawn up by the best physiologists of that day. Some essential ingredients were left out with disastrous results." But in World War I British politicians took the advice of some very competent biochemists "and rationing was a success."[10]

About twenty years ago, in the midst of all these preoccupations, Heads of Schools of Busi-

---

10. J. B. S. Haldane, "Science and Politics" in *Possible Worlds*, London, Chatto and Windus, 1928, p. 186.

ness Administration were faced with a rather sudden outbreak of claims by "behavioural scientists," chiefly sociologists and social psychologists, that they should play a larger part in the teaching of management. Curiously enough this "take-over bid," and it was of the nature of a "take-over bid," really originated in a variety of influences which were not strictly sociological.

Some of it stemmed from the work of Elton Mayo and the group associated with him in the famous Hawthorne experiments. Elton Mayo was not himself a sociologist. He was by training and inclination a psychiatrist. He was preeminently a clinician with a genius for helping unhappy people. His devotion to "any human being who needed help"[11] was his most pronounced characteristic. In his earlier clinical work he seems to have thought that most social problems were basically individual. But his experience at Hawthorne convinced him that many of the stresses and strains to be encountered in modern industry are social in origin.

He did not think, however, that Sociology as it was being taught in the United States in the first half of this century was likely to provide a remedy. "The so-called social sciences do not seem to equip students with a single skill that is usable in ordinary human situations. Sociology is highly developed, but mainly as an exercise in the acquisition of scholarship. Students are taught to write books about each other's books. . . . The equivalent of the clinic, or indeed of the laboratory, are still to seek. . . . The social sciences are impressed by the achievement (of the physical sciences); but the unfortunate effect has been to encourage too much jerry-building of imposing facades in the social area. . . . Those graduates of brilliant achievement who lead the procession out of the universities are not well equipped for the task of bringing order into social chaos."[12]

Obviously the sociologists were going to take up the cudgels. One relatively impartial observer has suggested that "attention might be drawn to some of the critics' own failings. They have subjected the putative motivation and the level of professional integrity of the human relations researchers to a form of unfriendly public scrutiny which must be quite rare in the literature of the social sciences."[13] One of Mayo's own colleagues, whose findings accord fairly closely with those with which Professor Suojanen appears to agree, has commented "To have to admit that this war was waged by intellectuals and academics and by men called political and social scientists makes me still blush with shame for my 'reference group.' That men who called themselves 'scientists' should un-

derstand so little the nature of scientific questions and evidence appalled me."[14]

Sociology itself, quite apart from its bearing on management, was somewhat rent by faction. One fairly recent book identifies two of the warring "schools" as "The Grand Theorists" and "The Abstracted Empiricists."[15]

Another influence was the possibility of using mathematical theory, greatly encouraged by the development of the computer, to short-circuit the necessarily more prolonged evolution of exact knowledge in the sciences of individual and social psychology. Much of the most recent work in the management field consists of somewhat elaborate exercises in the application of statistical method. Two difficulties present themselves:

1. Men grow and change. Whatever results may be obtained from statistics bearing on a group of human beings on Monday will no longer be absolutely valid on Tuesday, even with the same group of human beings. They will be different human beings. There is some danger that the ardent pursuit of statistical method may lead management into much the same error which Veblen attributed to the orthodox economists. "The hedonistic conception of man is that of a lightning calculator of pleasures and pains, who oscillates like a homogeneous globule of desire of happiness under the impulse of stimuli that shift him about the area, but leave him intact. . . . Spiritually the hedonistic man is not a prime mover. He is not the seat of a process of living."[16]

2. Much of this mathematical proof is based on questionnaires addressed to workers and/or managers. The writer's father used to tell a story which illustrates the limitations involved. An acquaintance of his, a former Indian administrator, had written an elaborate book on famine in India. It was a weighty tome in two volumes containing hundreds of statistical tables. Another Indian administrator spoke slightingly of it. The writer's father, being an amiable person, pointed out its apparent authority. "My dear fellow," came the reply, "every figure in that book is based on statements made by the ryot or Indian peasant. The

11. Personal statement to the author by T. N. Whitehead, who worked with Mayo at Hawthorne.
12. Elton Mayo, *The Social Problems of an Industrial Civilization with an appendix on the Political Problem*, London, Routledge & Kegan Paul, 1949, p. 19.
13. Henry A. Landsberger, *Hawthorne Revisited*, Ithaca, New York, Cornell University Press, 1958, pp. 50, 51.
14. Foreword to the paperback edition of Mayo's *Human Problems of an Industrial Civilization*, New York, Viking Press, by F. J. Roethlisberger.
15. C. Wright Mills, *The Sociological Imagination*, New York, Oxford University Press, 1959, cpp. 2 & 3.
16. Thorstein Veblen, "Economics and Evolution" in *The Place of Science in Modern Civilization*, New York, 1919, p. 73.

ryot, when asked a question by a British official, invariably lies."[17]

These comments are not advanced in any spirit of controversy, but merely to illustrate the kind of difficulties which faced the heads of established university faculties of business administration when approached, and it was sometimes reproached, with the "take-over bid" by the behavioural scientists. A "take-over bid" is a delicate matter to negotiate in the most favourable circumstances. It is no more than an amusing accident that one of the standard books on the subject in Great Britain should have been written by two authors named Bull and Vice.[18] "Bull," of course, is a British Army colloquialism for the over-elaboration of "spit and polish"; vice is a well-recognized term. Recently in Great Britain the Board of Directors of the largest chemical corporation attempted to "take over" the largest corporation making artificial silk. The attempt having failed, the Directors of the silk company held a thanksgiving service in one of London's most famous churches. In any such operation, human emotions at their most sensitive are inevitably involved.

These considerations point up some of the difficulties in Professor Suojanen's "olive branch" – difficulties which he has not, perhaps, sufficiently considered.

From the practical point of view it appears to the writer an essential preliminary precaution if a negotiation of this kind is in prospect, and he is assuming with Professor Suojanen, "values of freedom, democracy and the dignity of the individual," that the parties to controversy should avoid calling each other names. New bodies of knowledge need, of course, new technical terms for precise communication between peers. But in constructing these technical languages care is necessary if terms are to be avoided which, in popular usage, carry a defamatory implication when applied to the work of others. Professor Herbert Simon, for example, has applied the terms "classical" and "traditional," (and he has printed them in quotation marks) to the work of many of his predecessors.[19] In the climate of American popular opinion, with its rejection of the past, love of novelty and optimism as to the speed of progress, these epithets are freely translated into "obsolete" and "out-of-date." He is compounding with the notorious denial of the values of scholarship – Henry Ford's "History is bunk."[20]

Professor Suojanen tends to fall into this tactical error. On the first page of his paper he describes the work of many earlier management theorists as the "principles" or "management process" school, the universalistic approach, the traditional – or Newtonian – school of management and the "functional" school.[21] The latter is his final choice in pursuit of the biological analogy which is the subject of his paper.

Many students of management would question whether the analogy with biology is viable. As has been pointed out above, management is not a single discipline. It is the body of knowledge bearing on the art of managing which draws on many disciplines. Managing has been defined as "getting things done with and through people." And while knowledge about people is, of course, an essential component of the art, it is also necessary for the manager to have some knowledge of the things, that is, of the objectives of the undertaking, whatever it is.

On this basis the "discipline" of an established kind which most nearly resembles management is medicine. And biology is only one of the many "sciences" on which medicine draws in training practitioners. The analogy with biology does, however, allow Professor Suojanen to suggest that the views of the earlier management theorists are *functional*, while those of the behavioural scientists are *evolutionary*.

The last epithet assumes that the future is with "the behavioural scientists." This assumption is in its very nature open to the Scottish verdict "not proven."

As for *functional* as descriptive of the ideas of earlier management theorists it is, on Professor Suojanen's own showing, misleading. For, later on in his paper, he identifies these earlier theories with hierarchy and authority. It is true that F. W. Taylor emphasized "functional foremanship." But what he meant by that phrase was exactly the opposite of the theories to which Professor Suojanen applies the epithet "functional." In fact, he was very close to Professor Suojanen who would discard military experience as "crisis-oriented." Taylor wrote "throughout the whole field of management the military type of organization

17. Author's recollection. If, for instance, the technique of "sampling" where human beings are concerned or the technique of questioning, were wholly reliable, why should the United States continue the very expensive procedure of holding Presidential and other elections to political office? The statistical results of a sample, properly selected and controlled, would be equally effective. The activities of "pollsters" to-date do not suggest that either of these techniques is wholly reliable.

18. George Bull and Anthony Vice, *Bid for Power*, London, Elek Books, Ltd., 1958.

19. James G. March & Herbert A. Simon, *Organizations*, New York, John Wiley & Sons, 1958, Cp. 2, pp. 12 – 33.

20. Henry Ford, Libel Suit v. The Chicago Tribune, July 1919.

should be abandoned, and what may be called 'the functional type' substituted in its place."[21]

It is a feature of Taylor's philosophy with which many later theorists, including the writer, have disagreed. They feel that Taylor overlooked a very simple principle, namely that the more you specialize functions, the more ample and intricate must be your machinery for coordinating actions, assuming of course, that the object of the exercise is to secure cooperative action from a larger or smaller group of people. But it is surely to make confusion worse confounded to employ the epithet "functional" in the exactly opposite meaning to that which it has hitherto been used in the literature of management.

To be sure the terminology, the semantics, of management are in a sorry state of confusion, as the writer has pointed out elsewhere.[22] He has had it demonstrated to him on a number of occasions that any serious attempt to resolve these misunderstandings would be a challenge to that freedom of the individual which is at the core of American political philosophy. But if "freedom" is translated as the right of any individual to affix any label to any object which he pleases, an enormous amount of intellectual luggage is bound to be sent to the wrong address. Words become inevitably bludgeons or beatitudes instead of instruments of communication.

To quote J. B. S. Haldane once again, "Mechanics became a science when physicists had decided what they meant by such words as weight, velocity and force, *but not till then.*"[22] It may be, for the reasons stated, impossible to initiate any serious effort to clean up this confusion. But so long as it persists there is a special obligation on all those who value management as a subject to avoid epithets liable to generate "emotional heat."

A second claim by the "behavioural scientists" which has a similar effect, is that they have a peculiar responsibility for the maintenance of the intellectual standards of science. Here again Professor Suojanen in discussing the loss of love between what the writer would call the "practical" (Koontz' "Management Process") School and "the more recent settlers in the management jungle" asserts "To ignore the results (of the latter) constitutes a rejection of the scientific method itself. Management, the discipline can (not) afford to reject the concept that research increases the sum total of human knowledge."[23]

Let us turn back to F. W. Taylor again. On this subject he remarked "There is another type of scientific investigation which has been referred to several times in this paper, and which should receive special attention, namely the accurate study of the motives which influence men."[24] It is the

writer's conviction that, were Taylor alive today, he would welcome many of the researches of "the behavioural scientists." And the writer knows of no instance of any sincere and authoritative worker in the management field who does not so welcome them.

What they do reject, where they have practical responsibilities, is that they should attempt to teach "principles" founded on inadequate or irrelevant measurement, or which are at odds with the facts of situation after situation, in which they were not involved personally, but which they have encountered in real life. If the writer is correct in using the medical analogy with management, medicine does just that. No research work, no treatment however well supported by laboratory experiments, is accepted and incorporated into general medical teaching and practice, until it has been through the fire of "clinical experience." And any enthusiasm for "results" which leads to light-heartedness or carelessness in this respect is properly regarded as quasi-criminal. Recent press controversy about "thalidomide babies" is an illustration. Human lives and human happiness are at stake. So they are in management.

As for the generalization that "research increases the sum total of human knowledge" that is only true in the sense that all genuine research at least increases the area in which men are aware of their ignorance. And that is a gain. But that *all* the research work that is at present being carried out in any country adds positively to the "sum total of human knowledge" is not a tenable proposition. Quite a large proportion of the research work undertaken leads to "dead ends." The writer has never seen figures on this subject. It is not the kind of figure which research institutions and workers are anxious to publicize. But the broad fact is well-known to all serious workers in the sciences.

A third assumption inherent in Professor Suojanen's exposition is that there are only two kinds of knowledge, (1) Knowlege like that developed by the physical sciences and, (2) Knowledge developed from "personal experience, personal observation and resort to authority." This is a very large assumption. It rules out completely all those 'disciplines' which preceded the modern scientific age such as philosophy, history, political

21. F. W. Taylor, *Scientific Management,* New York, Harper & Brothers, 1947, "Shop Management" (1903), p. 99.
22. Lyndall F. Urwick, "The Problem of Management Semantics," *California Management Review,* Vol. II, No. 2, Spring 1960, pp. 77–83, Quotation from Haldane, *Ibid.,* p. 77, Note 2.v. also *Op. Cit. N.* (10), p. 185. Italics added.
23. Suojanen, *Op. Cit. N.* (3), p. 13.
24. Taylor, *Op. Cit. N.* (21), "The Principles of Scientific Management" (1911), p. 119.

science, and the whole of man's recorded experience of administrative problems.

Moreover, it is an assumption which is bound to cause "emotional heat" in any "knowledge-oriented" undertaking, because it challenges the "colleague authority" of quite a large number of established 'disciplines'. It is an assumption with which it is extremely dangerous to initiate negotiations for a "take-over bid." To quote Professor Suojanen himself "In the truly evolutionary organization the basis of authority, or better yet, influence, is individual reputation as determined by professional achievement." Does he not appreciate that this assumption calls in question as no-knowledge the whole of the professional achievement of those among his colleagues who do not adhere to the methodologies developed by that group of "behavioural scientists" described by a fellow-sociologist as "the abstracted empiricists?"[25]

Finally, on the subject of assumptions, Professor Suojanen quotes, apparently with approval, the dictum that "the behavioural science theory of organization advocates the decision premise viewpoint."[26] In the opinion of many students of management this premise is not only untenable, but is distorting the study of management. It is an attractive, but extremely dangerous oversimplification. And it is misleading students who are unaware of its ambiguous character all over the world. For instance, "management is a decision-making process."[27] Its use in management has been analogous to saying "man is a two-legged animal" and thus confining the study of human anatomy, physiology and psychology exclusively to the legs.

It is attractive because it is flattering to managers. As Mary Parker Follett has observed: "I have seen an executive feel a little self-important over a decision he had made, when that decision had really come to him ready-made. An executive decision is a moment in a process. The growth of a decision, the accumulation of authority, not the final step, is what we need most to study."[28]

It is dangerous because it represents the process of management as consisting almost exclusively of this momentary act and therefore, even when the growth leading up to it is studied, of placing much too much emphasis on the processes by which those concerned in carrying out decisions participate in making them. This derives from our preoccupation with the *forms* of political democracy, and our identification of democracy itself with the forms to which we are accustomed. The writer is just as concerned as is Professor Suojanen with the values of democracy. But he believes that those values can be most effectively preserved, by giving to all those concerned in any activity a satisfying sense of participation in the activity as a whole rather than by copying political models as to the forms and procedures for recording decisions.

It also ignores all that part of the management process which is concerned with communicating downwards. Professor Suojanen may be pleased to know that the writer agrees with him that, at an earlier stage, students of management, including the writer himself, have placed too much emphasis on *authority* as the key to organization theory. He concurs with the late Chester Barnard that authority is accorded to a communication by the recipient. That is to say, it moves upwards. What moves downwards is communication. "The need of a definite system of communication creates the first task of the organizer and is the immediate origin of executive organization."[29] Barnard has some trenchant things to say about the difficulties of democratic process on the political model where what men are aiming at is integrated action.[30]

Finally come Professor Suojanen's proposals for resolving these difficulties. These are briefly that we should abandon the attempt at an integrated theory of management altogether. We should regard management as an "open-ended function of three factors: (1) the orientation of the organization: (2) the participants in the organization, and (3) the cultural environment."[31] With regard to (1) he proposes to classify human institutions into three groups. a. Those that are crisis-oriented, b. Those that are routine-oriented, and c. Those that are knowledge-oriented.

This seems to the writer a very curious proposition to originate with an advocate of the "behavioural and social sciences." Because if these sciences have an integrating principle it is that they deal with man and his behaviour. In fact it is to deny the possibility of any coherent theory of human behaviour at all. We can only hope for a theory of man as a soldier (crisis-oriented), of man as a business executive (routine-oriented) and of the same man as a member of a Board of

25. V. N. (15).

26. *Op. Cit. N.* (3), quoting from Edward G. Koch "Three Approaches to Organization," *Harvard Business Review,* March−April 1961, p. 162.

27. Australian Institute of Management, Melbourne Division, *Management Diary,* V. 3, No. 4, June 1963, "Decision Making by Management," p. 1.

28. M. P. Follett, "The Illusion of Final Authority" in *Freedom and Coordination,* London, Pitmans, 1949, p. 1.

29. Chester I. Barnard, *The Functions of the Executive,* Cambridge, Mass., Harvard University Press, 1938, p. 217.

30. Barnard, *Organization and Management-Selected Papers,* Cambridge, Mass., Harvard University Press, 1949, "Dilemmas of Leadership in the Democratic Process," pp. 24−50.

31. Suojanen, *Op. Cit. N.* (3), p. 15.

Directors (knowledge-oriented). Moreover, if the writer follows the argument correctly, we shall have to have separate studies of human behaviour in all these contexts for every different national and social environment—for American man and Russian man and Chinese man.

When the formal study of management was first proposed, rather more than half-a-century ago, and it was first proposed in connection with business undertakings, there was a chorus of criticism from men of different trades, "my business is different." Because managing had always been learned empirically, by experience, men were unable to distinguish between knowledge-of-acquaintance with a particular trade and knowledge about managing *per se*. The man who made boots was quite unable to convince himself that he could learn anything from the man who made boats.

That has passed and it is being increasingly accepted that the body of knowledge described as Management is equally applicable not only to any kind of business undertaking, but to voluntary and governmental and charitable institutions, indeed, to any form of organized human cooperation for a defined objective. There are, of course, difficulties in applying it to men of different cultural and racial backgrounds, because of differing traditions and ideals.

But they are difficulties which the Western countries will fail to overcome at their peril. As Sir Charles Snow has observed "In all non-industrialized countries, people are not eating better than at the subsistence level. . . . Whatever else in the world we know survives to the year 2000, that won't. . . . The West has got to help in this transformation. The trouble is, the West with its divided culture finds it hard to grasp just how big and, above all, just how fast, the transformation must be."[32] The U.S.A. has set the industrialized countries a noble example in the energy and generosity with which they have set to work to tackle this problem.

It is an unprofitable, indeed a dangerous, moment for professors of management in the United States to be deeply divided as to what they do know and have got to teach. All human institutions today are or should be crisis-oriented. All should have a sufficient substratum of agreed routine to enable them to go forward with the immense tasks which face them without expending too much effort on reconciling differences of theory. All should be knowledge-oriented because the world is living in the middle of the biggest technological revolution in human history, and the Army, the Business or the University which is not prepared to be adaptable is useless.

To the writer it seems strange that Professor Suojanen should be seeking for a new basis of classification when American democratic theory and practice have already offered the world an analysis of the processes of government which goes far to reconcile the divergent "schools," if they would once agree to a few common definitions and a system of classification. The well-established distinction between the "political or legislative, executive and judicial" aspects of government can go far to assimilate the views of different theorists if they will once accept it.

For decisions of a "political" character the writer would agree with Professor Suojanen that a committee form of organization is probably the most appropriate. But at whatever decisions a committee may arrive about policy it cannot, as a committee, communicate them. If the members present attempt to do so individually there will be as many different versions of what the committee has decided as there are members. If the attempt is made to reduce the decision to an agreed form of writing, usually described as a "minute," the probability is that the document, in trying to satisfy everyone, will end by being understandable only to those present at the discussion. Moreover, if the members of the committee are also the persons who carry out its decisions, the chances are that their action will be imperfectly coordinated because of differences in timing.

There is therefore an executive function of government, embodied in the United States in the Presidency, which deals with *action*. But because any individual who deals with action may be oppressive or mistaken in the treatment of individuals, there is also a judicial function of government to see that this does not happen.

Admittedly the judicial function has been very imperfectly developed in systems of business government, though some recent legislation is a step in that direction. And probably a great deal of the friction in business between managers and workers can be traced to the absence of machinery for this purpose.

But if theorists would once agree to say which of these aspects of management they were talking about, progress would follow. And the writer suggests that these are the right lines on which to seek a solution. In the meanwhile "the tactics of jungle warfare" have generated a great deal of "emotional heat," and have created adverse conditions for a "take-over bid" by any of the parties. Perhaps if they could agree that scientific method involves certain systematic steps—definition, analysis, measurement, hypothesis, experiment, proof—and come to a mutual decision to arrive at

---

32. C. P. Snow, *Op. Cit. N.* (6), pp. 39–40.

agreement on steps 1. and 2. before discussing each other's work under headings 3. and 4., they might find the outskirts of the jungle cleared and the possibility that some border skirmish would set it alight proportionately reduced.

A recent book by a member of the behavioural science group observed "Work groups which have high peer group loyalty and common goals appear to be effective in achieving their goals."[33] From the small sample of teachers of management in the United States known personally to the writer, it would seem to him unthinkable that *both* those conditions should not be achieved quite quickly.

3 — Notes on a General Theory of Administration

EDWARD H. LITCHFIELD

With the introduction of this *Quarterly* it is perhaps appropriate to review the state of our thinking about administration. In addition I hope that this essay will add several propositions which may bring us a little closer to a working theory of the nature of the administrative process. I do not believe we have such a theory today.

We would probably all agree that the years since World War II have seen an unprecedented increase in our knowledge of selected aspects of administration. There has been an acceleration of empirical investigation in the corporation, the government department, the hospital, the air wing, and other institutional settings. Likewise, there has been a tremendous growth in group dynamics and human relations research. Perhaps most important, the decade has seen either the introduction, or the first major unfolding, of operations research, game theory, cybernetics, and communication theory. Statistical theory and analysis and tremendous technological development in machine operation have provided new tools and new dimensions for decision-making activities. Spurred by the postwar growth of the behavioral sciences and assisted by a growing body of learning theory, both research worker and practitioner have given considerable attention to the individual's behavior in his role as an administrator.

These are contributions of far-reaching consequence, for they have not only added factual data which help in our understanding of administration, but they have also provided a conceptual depth which is urgently needed by a technically disposed profession supported by largely institutionally oriented academic disciplines. When fully absorbed and accepted in our thinking, the new materials will greatly assist administration's effort to achieve scientific stature. But beyond the substantive value of these individual contributions lie two further considerations of import both for practicing and academic members of the administrative profession.

First, it will be noted that most of the new thought has come from the fields of mathematics, engineering, anthropology, sociology, or some one of the emerging behavioral sciences. Relatively little has been contributed by academic students of administration, per se, by practicing members of the profession, or by the disciplines of economics and political science. Members of cultures in which law is the dominant discipline in administration will observe that none of the new thinking has come from the legal profession. Second, it is equally apparent that these additions to our knowledge have been concerned with selected parts of administration and not with the whole. Indeed, for the most part, their contribution to administration was incidental to another purpose. Thus, game theory enriches our view of policy formulation, knowledge of the dynamics of group relations provides new insights for the exercise of authority, and learning theory offers new perspective for decision making, but none of these is concerned with the larger problem of the total administrative process.

The last decade saw another development of parallel significance for the field of administration. As other disciplines were illuminating selected portions of the administrative process, Talcott Parsons and others were elaborating at least the beginnings of a comprehensive theory of social action which might provide an over-all framework within which to develop a more

33. Rensis Likert, *New Patterns of Management*, New York, McGraw-Hill Book Company, 1931, p. 30.

"Notes on a General Theory of Administration," *Administrative Science Quarterly*, 1 (June 1956), 3–29. Reprinted by permission of the author and the publisher. **Edward H. Litchfield**: Dean, Graduate School of Business and Public Administration, Cornell University; Chancellor of the University of Pittsburgh since July 1956.

specific theory of administration.[1] If Parsonian thought has not entirely satisfied administration's specialized needs, it must at least provoke us into the construction of a more acceptable framework.

Thus, it seems to me that we find ourselves at a critical juncture in our development. Associated disciplines are helping us to learn a great deal about portions of the subject of administration, while others are adumbrating concepts of the totality of action of which administration is a part. Flanked thus by singularly seminal movements, the question becomes, "What have we been doing to further our understanding as a whole?" For, until we know the process and its setting, we can neither effectively integrate new materials others give us nor orient our process in a larger concept of social action.

The answer to this question is not particularly encouraging. During the decade, public administration, after a half-century's diversion by Frank J. Goodnow, has readmitted policy formulation to its concept of administrative functions. This is helpful even if in their zeal some may have swung into the position of that school of academic business administration which is unable to discern anything but policy in administration. Business administration has made a considerable effort to digest such new knowledges as grew from operations research, from statistical theory in decision making, and from the several other subjects already discussed. Hospital administrators are coming to understand that administration in the context of the hospital is neither exclusively housekeeping on the one hand nor deciding substantive medical issues on the other. Military administration probably has been the most self-conscious and thorough in re-examining both its theory and practice. To its self-appraisal we owe a large part of the more fundamental work whose results have now begun to spill over into other applied fields. If much of theoretical or methodological importance has occurred in educational administration, it has escaped our attention.

These have been significant developments. I do not minimize them. On the other hand, they have not told us much about the whole administrative process, its essential characteristics, its relationship to its environment, the way in which it becomes behavior, or its function in modern society. They are of a lesser order of magnitude than either the generic thought of Parsons or the more specific insights which others have given us of selected aspects of administration. Throughout the decade Herbert Simon's work was the only constant exception to this general disregard of the whole process and its behavioral implications.[2] Despite his real contributions, and occasional important additions from Alexander Leighton and others outside the profession of administration, we closed the ten-year period with little more by way of a comprehensive theory of administration than we had been given by Chester Barnard almost twenty years before.

CRITICISM OF EXISTING THOUGHT AND THEORY

If we are lacking in comprehensive theory, we do at least have some thought which we may examine. It is scattered from field to field, seldom internally consistent and often unarticulate. Viewed in aggregate, it has a number of inadequacies which hamper the growth of administration as a science. Let us begin with the simplest and most generally recognized. Our confusion of terminology makes it difficult to speak accurately to one another within any one field, let alone across fields and across cultures. Administration has an elevated meaning in some societies and a clerical connotation in others. "Management" and "administration" are thought of as interchangeable in much of the business world in this country but as quite distinct in much of public administration and in the military services.[3] Constitutional lawyers have distinguished between "administration" and "execution." "Decision making" and "policy formulation" may be used by one as synonymous and by another as discrete subjects. "Coordination" may either include, or specifically exclude, "control," and it may be either a process or a state of being. "Organization" is now a pattern for the distribution of authority, and again it becomes a total set of behavioral and value relationships. The consequence is that we are unable to speak precisely excepting in our own immediate circles where we have developed ephemeral professional dialects.

The second and, from my point of view, the most serious indictment which must be made of present thought is that it has failed to achieve a level of generalization enabling it to systematize and explain administrative phenomena which occur in related fields. Indeed, so far are we from broad generalizations about administration that

1. Talcott Parsons and Edward A. Shils, eds., Toward a General Theory of Action (Cambridge, Mass., 1951).

2. Herbert A. Simon, Administrative Behavior (New York, 1947). Other articles by Simon include: "Staff and Management Controls, Annals of the American Academy of Political and Social Sciences, Vol. 292 (March 1954), and "A Comparison of Organization Theories," Review of Economic Studies, Vol. 20 (1), No. 51 (1952–1953).

3. During the thirties the term "administrative management" was introduced. It meant everything and nothing. After years of usage in public administration it found its way into business and educational organizations by way of consulting firms working in all of these fields.

we appear to maintain that there is not a generic administrative process but only a series of isolated types of administration. We seem to be saying that there is business administration and hospital administration and public administration; that there is military administration, hotel administration, and school administration. But there is no administration. We buttress this conclusion and make a general theory more difficult of attainment by developing separate schools in these fields in our universities. We organize ourselves into separate professional societies, and we have developed separate bodies of literature which speak to one another infrequently.

Let us examine this splintering in the context of a specific situation. The reader is visited by a medical friend who has just accepted his first administrative post as superintendent of a large hospital. His board is composed in part of businessmen who "want the institution run on a businesslike basis." Being municipally owned, the hospital must function in accordance with civil service regulations, central budget controls, and a variety of other public administration concepts and practices. The new superintendent is soon deluged with invitations to become a member of several specialized hospital administration societies and is urged to subscribe to specialized hospital administration literature. Hearing reference to "good management" and "sound administrative practice" on all sides, he turns to the reader, who is an administration expert, and asks for some reading material which will help him to understand what his severally oriented colleagues are talking about. What shall the reader tell him — that there is no such thing as administration, there is only business administration and public administration and hospital administration? Almost certainly each of us would support the view that the three had much in common and that he would find that eventually he could deal with all three in many of the same terms. But what shall we suggest that he read which will clearly describe this common ground in administration? Where will he find a statement of the content and the character of the administrative process? We will almost certainly be forced to give him materials in all three fields, along with some of the technical writings in specialized management fields such as finance and personnel, and then expect him to do his own synthesizing. If he is not satisfied, we will introduce him to Barnard, and if he still feels we haven't given him sufficient guidance, we will conclude with our ultimate bromide, "There is much of this that a man just has to learn for himself."

Actually our practice is years ahead of our thought. There is abundant evidence to demonstrate our unexpressed conviction that there is much that is common in administration. Here are a few illustrations of the point. The emerging concepts of human relations, communications, or operations research are as applicable to a hospital as they are to a bank. The constant movement of executive personnel from business to government, from the military forces into large business, from both government and business into education, is emphatic testimony supporting our conviction that knowledges and skills are transferable from field to field because of an essential universality in the administrative process itself. Again, it is a commonplace to observe that management consulting firms find their knowledges and skills applicable in the department store, on the one hand, and in the government bureau or the university, on the other. We are thus faced with the curious dichotomy of a practice which acknowledges common ground among applied fields of administration and of a body of thought which makes no effort to delineate areas of common interest. As theorists we have not yet established generalized concepts which keep pace with the facts of contemporary administration.

Third, if current thought fails to generalize the constants or universals in administration, it may also be criticized for its failure to accord a broad role to the variables in the administrative process. Thus, while we are prepared to insist that there are many applied types of administration, we seem to be saying that within any one field the process is relatively fixed. The often violent attack upon the "principles in administration" school of thought was a reaction against the view that in any single field administration must be regarded as a constant pattern of functions and activities. It is true that we have been influenced by social science research sufficiently to accommodate "the informal organization" and that under pressure of "good public relations" we have adapted administrative performance to some of the demands of the communities in which we find ourselves. It is also true that, in our unwillingness to seek broad generalizations about administration in all fields, we have admitted modifications in administration by insisting that the specialized situation of competition, or politics, or military necessity, and so on, made administration different in each of our fields. This admission is important in modifying our rigidity of thought in this particular connection even though we have found it stultifying in our attempts to develop conceptual generalization. In spite of all of these modifications in the type of absolutist administrative thought which reached its peak in the highly legalistic nineteenth-century public bureaucracies and in classical military management, we have not yet crossed an essential divide. That circumstances modify administrative activity we concede, but we must go further and affirm our view that administration is not only constant and universal in some respects but is also a variable in an equation of action; that one of its fundamental characteristics is its relationship to the other variables in that equation. Beyond this we must articulate those other variables so that we may understand their interrelationship. We must maintain that ultimate understanding of the administrative process comes only with an appreciation of the place of that process in a larger system of administrative action.

Fourth, I think it not unfair to say that our present thinking has a fractured quality about it. Communication theory may be good, budgetary concepts may be entirely sound, and it may be that we have a reasonably clear concept of how policies are formulated. These and the other parts of administration have concerned us more than the whole. We often regard these parts as discrete subjects. At best we regard them as sequential. POSDCORB,[4] like much earlier and later thought, was principally deficient in that it viewed administration more as a list of activities than as an organized arrangement of interdependent parts. I am not suggesting that we should know less about the constituent elements in the process. I am insisting that in addition to knowing the parts we must understand the attributes and characteristics of administration as a totality.

Finally, many of us have felt for a long time that such theory as we do have is set forth in terms which lend themselves neither to empirical verification nor to critical theoretical analysis. We urgently need our thought set forth in straightforward propositions which we may then establish, modify, or destroy as research or more careful analysis may dictate.[5] There is little prospect that the study of administration will ever approach scientific stature unless we are able to so articulate our thought.

NEED FOR A WORKING THEORY

This is not intended as an idle exercise in criticism. There are urgent reasons for the early development of at least a working theory of administration. Three are particularly compelling.

First, it is virtually impossible to codify our existing knowledge without some conceptual framework within which to do so. Theory is important for this purpose in any field of investigation, but it is crucially significant in an applied field which must ultimately draw together knowledges now scattered through all of the social and behavioral sciences and through the many applied areas of business, public, military, hospital, and educational administration. As a framework for the organization of materials, a working theory is equally needed by the management consultant, the teacher, the professionally conscious administrator, and the research worker.

Second, a comprehensive theory is needed as a guide to research. However tentative that theory may be, it should help to discern gaps in both existing knowledge and ongoing research and thus to further the design of other research efforts. It would also provide working hypotheses as guides to individual research efforts and as vehicles for the subsequent incorporation of research efforts into organized bodies of thought.

Finally, a tenable theory of administration could become an extremely useful guide to administrative behavior. The analytical and intellectually self-conscious practitioner will readily recognize the importance of a broad theoretical framework which he may use as a measure of his personal performance and which may provide a behavior check list in his day-to-day undertakings. Educators who do not subscribe to the "either you are born with it or you aren't" school will also find it of primary importance in shaping curricula and in guiding potential administrators.

However urgent a general theory of administration may be, it is unlikely that it can be set forth in the near future. In the first place, there appear to be few among us whose current range of thought would meet the criticisms set forth here. Second, our knowledge is still extremely fragmentary. Thus, while we have been learning about small group dynamics, as David Truman has pointed out,[6] we still know very little about the dynamics of the large institutions in which administration comes to full bloom. We have a new understanding of the functions of choice in decision making, but we know very little about the psychological mechanisms involved in its exercise. We have given little if any systematic attention to the impact of a total culture upon administrative values, practices, and behavior. Cross-cultural data are even fewer. Even Kurt Lewin's "elements of construction" are difficult to evolve in the ab-

4. Luther Gulick and L. Urwick, eds., *Papers on the Science of Administration* (New York, 1937).

5. Such propositions are well illustrated in Alexander H. Leighton's volume, *The Governing of Men* (Princeton, N.J., 1945).

6. David B. Truman, "The Impact on Political Science of the Revolution in the Behavioral Sciences," in *Research Frontiers in Politics and Government* (Washington, D.C., 1955).

sence of definitions which have achieved even minimal acceptance.[7]

Certainly this essay does not pretend to present a general theory of administration. It will attempt to set forth a series of working hypotheses or propositions which may provide at least the beginnings of a framework for a general theory of administrative action. They will serve their purpose best if they are used as targets for future effort. That they will provoke criticism one would expect. That they may prompt more constructive thought is what I earnestly hope. They are by no means complete, they are often less specific than they should be, and they are frequently less precise than I would wish. But whatever their imperfections, I suggest the following propositions.

FIRST MAJOR PROPOSITION

The administrative process is a cycle of action which includes the following specific activities:

A. Decision making
B. Programming
C. Communicating
D. Controlling
E. Reappraising

This pattern of actions is found in various forms in all phases of administration. It occurs in policy areas; it is essential to personnel, finance, and other types of resources management; and it is to be found in the executive function as well. The specific activities and the cycle as a whole provide the mechanism by means of which all of the separate functions of administration are carried on. It is at once a large cycle which constitutes the administrative process as a totality and a series of small cycles which provide the means for the performance of specific functions and sub-functions and even for individual technical activities.

In an idealized form it occurs as a logical sequence in which there is a progression from the making of a decision to the interpretation of the decision in the form of specific programs, to the communication of that programmed decision, to the establishment of controls for the realization of the decision, and finally to a reappraisal of the decision as programmed, communicated, and controlled. In fact, however, the cycle often occurs in abbreviated form. Thus the practicalities of programming a decision may lead to immediate reappraisal, eliminating the steps of communication and control. Again, total group participation in decision making may eliminate much of communication. If individual steps are abbreviated

or even eliminated, the cycle is nonetheless complete. In fact, the steps probably are there, even though in quite attenuated form.

Many such cycles are in action in the administrative process at any one time. One elaborate cycle may be. proceeding at board of directors' level regarding fundamental objectives, while smaller and still sequential cycles may be going forward in finance and sales, and at the same time very immediate, specific, and perhaps abbreviated cyclical actions occur in the office or in the mind of a district sales manager concerned with a particular problem devoid of any policy, methodological, financial, or human relations significance. There is thus a series of wheels within wheels, tangent now at one point, now at another. The totality is administrative action, and the wheels are similar not in size but in the articulate and inarticulate uniformity of their components.

The grouping of these activities is made cyclical by the presence of the activity of reappraisal, for this brings the sequence back to substantially the point at which it began. Yet while it completes a full cycle the sequence does not necessarily lead again to identical action. If the original decision is precisely reaffirmed, the sequence of the five activities is no more than a revolution around a constant axis. However, if the original decision is modified in the light of evidence presented in the reappraisal, the axis may move and the circle take on a cycloidal form. With the passage of time and subsequent revolutions in the cycle, an extensive cycloidal pattern may develop.

Minor Proposition: Decision making may be rational, deliberative, discretionary, purposive, or it may be irrational, habitual, obligatory, random, or any combination thereof. In its rational, deliberative, discretionary, and purposive form, it is performed by means of the following sub-activities:

a. Definition of the issue
b. Analysis of the existing situation
c. Calculation and delineation of alternatives
d. Deliberation
e. Choice[8]

The sequence of activity from definition of issue to choice is again idealized. It presumes rationality and the existence of discretion. It contemplates the opportunity for deliberation, the possibility of calculating alternatives, and the existence of knowledge with which to estimate the situation. It is seldom that all of these factors are in fact present. Yet only if we view the pattern in

---

7. Kurt Lewin, *Field Theory in Social Science* (New York, 1951).
8. For a parallel analysis, see Peter Drucker, *The Practice of Management* (New York, 1954), ch. xxviii.

its idealized form are we able to understand the nature of the parts as they occur individually or in combination.

Definition of the issue is the isolation both of problems (in the sense that a problem is a difficulty) and also of opportunities in which no difficulty is present. Thus it has both a corrective and creative aspect. A problem may require diagnosis, whereas an opportunity may be defined by research. In any event the function of issue definition is the clarification and description of the question at hand. Efficiency in subsequent steps in the cycle is obviously dependent upon the precision with which this first activity is undertaken.

Situation analysis involves a systematic effort to present facts regarding the existing situation where they may be known and estimates regarding that situation when facts are impossible to obtain. This must include a factual statement of prevalent values when those are part of the situation and relevant to subsequent choice. Many techniques assist the administrator in the performance of this activity. They include accounting, opinion surveys, market analyses, field testing of products, operations research, intelligence reports, and countless other similar analytical tools.

Alternative calculation involves two major steps: first, a systematic isolation and description of known alternative courses of action; and, second, a statement of the consequences of the alternatives where the latter are known. Where they are unknown, they must be estimated. These estimates will often themselves take the form of alternatives. In any event, this distinctive activity is concerned with known facts, assumed facts, and factual statement of values. Here we are assisted by such methods and techniques as economic forecasting, market projections, linear programming, and game theory.[9]

Deliberation is the next step. In it one is concerned with reviewing the issue in the light of what is known in the existing situation and with regard to the alternative courses of action which appear to be available. It involves an assessment of values, an appraisal of probabilities where chance alone is involved and strategy where knowledge is imperfect. Deliberation approaches rationality as the values become explicit, as probabilities are analyzed, and as risk calculation can be reduced to a mathematical operation.

Having defined the issues, assembled and stated the facts regarding the existing situation, calculated and delineated the alternative courses of action with their known and estimated consequences, and reviewed all in terms of an explicit statement of ordered values, one is then prepared

to choose. Choice under these circumstances is influenced by several considerations: first, free will or discretion and second, the presence of rationality. Thus, a "wise choice" is apt to be one which the administrator had the discretion to make, had the rationality to base upon the known and estimated data at hand, and had the critical faculty to appraise in terms of the relative significance of those data.

In making choices, the administrator must understand that there is not always one right answer. Truth is frequently plural, and therefore the objective in the exercise of choice is rationality and not a pursuit of a nonexistent absolute. Failure to recognize both the plurality and relativity of correctness in decision making may lead to a time-losing indecision and a precarious mental health for those who must choose.

Actually few decisions are made by means of this full sequence of actions. The issue may be so patent as to make definition unnecessary. Often little effort is made to ascertain or estimate facts. Built-in biases frequently result in only the most superficial calculation of alternatives, and deliberation may be short-circuited by unspecified values or an unwillingness or inability to think in strategic terms. The elimination of certain of the steps may mean poor decisions, or again it may mean that specialized circumstances make one or more steps self-evident or unnecessary.

We must also recognize the extent to which decision making is influenced by limitations upon rationality. Simon has developed this at some length.[10] The administrator must not only allow for his own irrationality, he must also calculate the actions of others as being both rational and irrational. Thus, our decisions may be partly rational and partly irrational. To the extent that they are rational they must anticipate opponents' decisions which are also both irrational as well as rational. The character of calculated irrationality may be analyzed both by probability theory and by strategic calculation.

We may say much the same thing about the purposive-involuntary variable in decision making. Again, discretion in the selection of values and actual choice is circumscribed by community and professional standards and by prior decisions which may be part of tradition or which are

9. For game theory, see J. von Neumann and Oskar Morgenstern, *Theory of Games and Economic Behavior* (Princeton, N.J., 1944); Martin Shubik, *Readings in Game Theory and Political Theory* (Garden City, N.Y., 1954); J. D. Williams, *The Compleat Strategyst* (New York, 1954); and J. C. C. McKinsey, *Introduction to the Theory of Games* (New York, 1952). Linear programming is well set out in A. Charnes, W. W. Cooper, and A. Henderson, *An Introduction to Linear Programming* (New York, 1953).

10. Simon, *Administrative Behavior*, ch. iv.

passed down through the organization from higher levels. Likewise, factors of time modify deliberation and the opportunity both to analyze an existing situation fully and to calculate possible alternatives. Yet with all of its variables and modifiers, the progression from definition to choice is constant. Only the internal relationships among steps will vary.

Minor Proposition: Decisions become guides to action after they have been interpreted in the form of specific programs.

Decisions must be interpreted by specific programs which provide the direction for detailed operation. These might be called plans, were "planning" not a confused term which is sometimes used with reference to an "outline of alternatives," and in this sense is a part of decision making. Again, the term is used as synonymous with "programming" as the latter term is used here. One may therefore more accurately speak of planning alternatives (in the decision-making process) and of program planning as an activity designed to implement decisions. Program planning rests on a wide range of specific methods and techniques. These include capital budgets, operating budgets, manning tables, organization charts, tables of equipment, and a variety of similar means of translating a decision into specific programs for the allocation of money, manpower, authority, physical resources, and so on. The completeness of the program is a determining consideration in the effectiveness of the original decision.

Minor Proposition: The effectiveness of a programmed decision will vary with the extent to which it is communicated to those of whom action is required.

Communication follows the programming of decisions in cases in which those who must act have not participated in the original decision. Communication is a method by which an individual or group transmits stimuli which modify the behavior of another individual or group. While it is an activity employed in administration, it is obviously broader than the administrative process, for there is communication among individuals who have no administrative relationship to one another. We may therefore say that we are concerned here with the use of the method of communication for the restricted purposes of the administrative process.

Carl Hovland has focused our attention upon three aspects of communication: the stimuli (which he calls "cues"), the responses to the stimuli, and finally the laws and principles relating these two classes of events.[11] This threefold focus

has applicability to communication as a method of administration. Let us examine each. We already give considerable attention to the stimuli in our analyses of the role of staff meetings, policy manuals, training sessions, annual reports, house organs, and similar communication media. We are learning to pay an increasing amount of attention to responses as a result of our increasing concern with employee motivations and morale. But most important is the relation of stimuli to response. Communication as a deliberate and purposive act of administration must determine whether it seeks a response which sets off patterns of behavior already well established or whether it seeks a response which is basically new. At this point administrative science must look to learning theory for assistance.

Communication in administration involves three primary responsibilities. First, the administrator must establish the channels, the methods, and the opportunities for communicating with all of those above, below, and around him whose actions he would influence. Second, he must establish channels and provide the opportunity for others to communicate with him. Third, he must assure the existence of channels of communication among all those in the organization who must influence one another if the organization is to achieve its total objectives. Each of these is a deliberate action which he must take. In two instances it is his responsibility to provide structure on the one hand and to utilize it on the other.

Minor Proposition: Action required by a programmed and communicated decision is more nearly assured if standards of performance are established and enforced.

Standard setting and enforcement may be more generally known as "control." Communication was concerned with stimuli which would call up desired responses, and control is concerned with a definition of the desired response and the methods of assuring its occurrence. In other words, control is an action which provides norms which will serve as a guide to the actors and against which to measure their actions. Both standard setting and enforcement are carried on by means of elaborate techniques of control. They may be techniques designed to control basic programs and operations, such as a budget, an organization chart, or a functional statement. Or they may be processive tools such as job standardization, wage and salary schedules, purchasing

11. Carl Hovland, "Psychology of the Communication Process," in Wilbur Schramm, ed., *Communications in Modern Society* (Urbana, Ill., 1948), p. 59.

specifications, or cost and quality controls. All play essentially the same role in the action cycle.

A notable characteristic of control action is its tendency to become an end in itself. Thus we have the familiar phenomenon of the controller who seems more concerned with his accounting mechanisms than with the management purpose which they presumably exist to further. This often results from the fact that there is an internal element of completeness within the control activity. Having set a standard, reviewed performance in terms of the standard, and then enforced the standard, the person performing the action has, in a sense, completed a full and satisfying cycle. Standard enforcement in fact becomes standard realization and, hence, achievement. It is the only action in the cycle outside of decision making which has this organic unity about it which encourages its use as end rather than means.

While the subactions of control are standard setting and enforcement, the primary working methods are determined by the properties of the thing which is controlled. Thus control of people is achieved by means of a skillful manipulation of various types of rewards and punishments designed to appeal to the several motives of the groups and individuals concerned. Control of money comes with skillful manipulation of that resource in terms of its own laws of behavior.

Minor Proposition: Decisions are based on facts, assumptions, and values which are subject to change. To retain their validity, decisions must therefore be reviewed and revised as rapidly as change occurs.

A decision which has been programmed, communicated, and controlled has validity only for the limited period in which the facts, assumptions, and values upon which it was based have retained their original character. Only for such a period can the first four steps in the action cycle be regarded as static. In fact, not only are the facts, assumptions, and values in a state of constant flux, but the fact of decision in itself often brings substantial alteration in the total pattern of circumstance on the basis of which the decision was made. Hence a fully articulated decision —that is, one which has been made, programmed, communicated, and controlled—in itself brings about sufficient change to necessitate its own reconsideration. This is the activity of reappraisal.

Reappraisal is necessitated not only by change but by the possible imperfection of the original decision which time and circumstance may make apparent. New insights may be gained which improve the administrator's understanding of a more nearly correct decision, even though the facts themselves have not been altered. Here we return to a recognition of the plurality of truth as noted in our discussion of the decision-making activity. Thus we reappraise decisions because of our acceptance of the concepts of "contingent universe" and "organic incompleteness" which are implicit in cybernetic thought.[12]

Reappraisal may be accomplished in several ways. In its simplest form it is no more than a review of the original issues in terms of new data, new assumptions, new strategies, and new values which have bearing on the decision but which arise from extraneous sources. Thus, new information about Soviet military production may require the reappraisal of a foreign policy decision which had been based upon different fact assumptions. This may be referred to as a "feed-in" activity. Quite different is the process of "feedback," which is the essence of cybernetic theory. Here we contemplate the reappraisal of an original decision upon the basis of facts and values which have been generated by and as a result of the original decision. Reappraisal therefore provides for self-generated change and growth.

Whether the reappraisal be "feed-in," "feedback," or a combination, its function is the same. It is needed to complete the action cycle in order to make it dynamic rather than static. This is the action which induces change and growth. It must be specifically provided for in the action pattern if growth is to be accepted as both constant and necessary. Only through reappraisal can administration adjust to the constancy of evolution; otherwise the administrator is apt to pursue a concept of the permanent and absolute. This is a vehicle for incorporating into administration an understanding of stability through change rather than through an artificial staticity.

SECOND MAJOR PROPOSITION

The administrative process functions in the areas of:

A. Policy
B. Resources
C. Execution

A "policy" is a definition of those objectives which guide the actions of a whole enterprise or a significant portion thereof. It is thus distinguished from the general term "decision", which may guide actions without reference to such objectives. The "resources" of administration are four: people, money, authority, and materials.

---

12. See Norbert Wiener, *The Human Use of Human Beings* (Boston, Mass., 1950).

"Execution" is a function of integration and synthesis which is intended to achieve a dynamic and total organism. All functional areas are requisite to the process. Execution divorced from policy is aimless. Similarly, the policy function tends to become remote and sterile unless associated with resources and execution.

Minor Proposition: Action in each functional area is accomplished by means of the action cycle previously described.

The policy function is conventionally referred to as "policy making" or "policy formulation." In fact it is far more. Policies are not only made, they are also programmed, communicated, controlled, and reappraised. It is only in this total sweep of the action cycle that the policy function has full meaning and is satisfactorily distinguished from the activity of decision making.

The action cycle is also the vehicle for the accomplishment of the resources function. In determining the need for money or people, the administrator defines his problem, estimates his situation, calculates his alternatives, makes a choice, and thus in fact makes a decision. In allocating personnel by manning tables, authority by functional statements or charts, or money by budgets, he is in fact programming his decision. Direction of personnel is communication. Organization charts and manuals, budgets and inventories, are forms of control of money, authority, and materials. The final step of reappraisal is provided for in budget analysis and revision and in a whole series of other resource function techniques.

The action cycle is repeated in the executive function. Setting the policies and resources in motion, synthesizing their conflicting values and tendencies, and integrating the resulting management are achieved by a constant series of cyclical movements from decision to reappraisal to new decision and further reappraisal. Maintaining them in dynamic equilibrium is realized in the same way.

Minor Proposition: Each function seeks a value which when realized is its contribution to the administrative process.

Policy seeks purposive direction for the enterprise. The resource function seeks economy both in the sense of productivity and of frugality. Execution seeks and is evaluated by the degree to which it achieves a state of dynamic coordination. These are the contributions of the three functional areas. Together they constitute an organism whose direction is purposive and whose resources are productively and frugally employed.

Minor Proposition: Each function has distinctive characteristics which govern the application of the cycle to it.

We have observed that policies involve questions of value and fact. Values are plural and facts are contingent. As a consequence the action cycle employed in the policy function is modified. The four resources have different characteristics. People are moved by varying combinations of rewards and punishments. Money is moved by factors of scarcity. Authority has properties which influence the way in which it may be allocated and exercised. The executive function achieves synthesis and maintains a dynamic organism by observing the laws of equilibrium and decay whether they be drawn from modern group dynamics or are as remote as Henri Bergson's "law of twofold frenzy."[13] In each case, the cycle is constant, but it is performed in the context of a function which responds to its specialized properties.

Minor Proposition: The functional areas of administration are integrally related to one another.

We have already observed that each of the functions is requisite to the total process. It is equally true that the areas are integrally related to one another. Obviously policy is the major determinant of the character of the resource and executive functions, but it is also true that resources are important determinants of policy and that execution may be either the realization or destruction of policy. Administrative behavior must be calculated to recognize that a new policy has immediate implications for authority, finance, and personnel. One follows the other automatically. No one can be isolated from the other, for they are in fact a continuum of reciprocating parts.

THIRD MAJOR PROPOSITION

The administrative process is carried on in the context of a larger action system, the dimensions of which are:[14]

A. The administrative process
B. The individual performing the administrative process
C. The total enterprise within which the individual performs the process
D. The ecology within which the individual and the enterprise function

---

13. Henri Bergson, *The Two Sources of Morality and Religion* (Garden City, N.Y., 1954).
14. Here the term "dimension" refers to a category of variables.

Each of these dimensions has both constant properties and variables. We have examined the constants of the administrative process and must now note its variables. Likewise, we must observe the way in which these dimensions are related. In fact, the process which we have examined in the abstract becomes a real thing only in the hands of the persons performing it and in the context of specific total organizations and, in particular, total environments. These three dimensions affect the administrative process by altering its variables. It in turn alters each of them in its impact upon their variables. We thus have a concept of a system containing four dimensions, each of which has a structure comprising a number of variables which interact upon one another.

Furthermore, the other dimensions have no constant impact on the administrative process. At one point the impact of the individual administrator may be decisive and at another time relatively inconsequential. Thus in a highly articulated bureaucracy, the variations among administrators will affect the way in which the process is performed to lesser extent than in a new organization which has been less rigidly structured. In other words, there are not only variables within each dimension but there is variation in the relative roles among the dimensions in this total action system.

There are significant parallels between this proposition and the broad aspects of Parsons' theory of action.[15] He postulates three systems of action — personality, social, and culture. He further maintains that these are "reciprocally interrelated" and suggests the existence of "roles" within systems. His personality system corresponds to the dimension of the individual as an administrator. His cultural system is quite similar to the concept of the total ecological setting. Our administrative process and the total enterprise dimensions probably assume the status of "roles" in his social system. Our thinking finds further parallels in his article in this issue of the *Administrative Science Quarterly*.

Minor Proposition: While constant in basic structure, the administrative process will vary in important aspects, depending upon the personality of the person performing it.

The cycle of administrative action and the functions of the administrative process are constants regardless of who performs them. The manner in which the actions are taken and the functions are accomplished, however, will vary with the characteristics of the individual. These variations in manner are as important as the individual. These variations in manner are as im-

portant as the constancy in structure. The self-contained administrator may deliberate alone, while the new and uncertain executive may take elaborate counsel. Deliberation is present in both cases, but the methods of its exercise are importantly different. Or, in estimating the existing situation, a Wilson may collect his own facts, whereas an Eisenhower will assemble information by means of an elaborate staff organization. Different individual administrators have radically different effects upon the whole organization. Authority as a resource may be delegated to many by a generalist, or to a few by a specialist. As a consequence the authority structure will be flat in one case and pyramided in the other. The consequences of these varying ways in which two types of personalities allocate authority are far reaching, but the resource function has nevertheless been satisfied.

Bureaucracy seeks to minimize the impact of these variables among personalities through the use of standardizing practices which will offset personality differences. For example, a military staff study requires concurrence among all units in the organization which may be affected by the proposal which the staff study contains. This assures a widespread participation in decision making and thus offsets the variation between officer X, who may realize the importance of participation, and officer Y, whose tendencies are to proceed unilaterally.

Minor Proposition: While constant in basic structure, the administrative process will vary in important respects, depending upon the character of the total enterprise within which it is performed.

The way in which the administrative process is performed will vary with the character of the organization. One-man decision making in an academic atmosphere is less likely than in a family-owned manufacturing organization, yet there is decision making in both cases. Reappraisal may be infrequent in a conservative British textile firm but constant in a young and aggressive corporation like General Dynamics.

The administrator communicates in a different way in an organization with a well-developed, informal structure than he does in an enterprise which has a high turnover rate and which is composed of persons whose backgrounds and associations are quite diverse. Yet the communication activity is there; only the ways of its exercise and the degree of its effectiveness will change. The impersonality of social relations which increases as an organization grows in size and complexity

---

15. Parsons and Shils, *op. cit.*

presents problems in communication unknown in simpler organizations. Standard setting (control) is one thing in an organization without internal social cohesion and quite another in Hawthorne's Bank Wiring room.[16]

In one sense the administration profession has overemphasized the impact of the total enterprise upon the administrative process. Here I am referring to the insistence that the fields of business, government, hospital, or the military administration are all discrete subjects. Yet the true meaning of difference escapes us unless we first isolate the constant properties or universal characteristics of administration. Our point here is that the study of difference occasioned by enterprise variations is necessary, but only following a prior understanding of the constants in this process.

Minor Proposition: While constant in basic structure, the administrative process will vary in important respects depending upon the environment in which the individual and total enterprise function.

The administrative process will also vary with the physical, cultural, and technological environment within which it is performed. Communication is obviously influenced by a changing technology which eliminates much of the significance of distance. It is similarly influenced by conversational practice resulting from social systems of rank and class. Effectiveness of the control activity may depend upon the financial and psychological resources which the community provides as alternatives to acceptance of a distasteful standard of working norms. Indonesian understanding of "the good neighbor" raises problems in limiting supervisory spans which are missing in societies where efficiency means more and neighborliness less. Controls which may be imposed and enforced in one atmosphere may be vitiated by the existence of community or professional standards or values which preclude the individual's accepting the control provided by administration. Part of the theory of the Nürnberg trials is closely related to this.

Minor Proposition: The types of relationships existing among the three dimensions other than the administrative have an effect upon the administrative process.

My colleague, James Thompson, has suggested that "there appear to be four major types of relationships which an enterprise may have with organized elements of environment."[17] He notes competition, bargaining, cooptation, and coalition as the primary types of relationships between the dimension of the whole enterprise and the dimension of the environment. He then points out that these relationships between two dimensions

have important bearing on the decision-making activity, for they alter the way in which it is carried on and vary the number of the participants therein. Thus the relationships between two dimensions have caused variation in the third, the administrative process.

It would appear probable that we may generalize beyond this and say that there are definable relationships among each of the three nonadministrative dimensions and that the variations among those relationships will have consequent bearing upon the administrative process itself.

In this major proposition we have thus been concerned with three different considerations. In the first place, we have noted the way in which variations in any one of the three dimensions directly affect the administrative process. Second, we have noted the way in which variations in the total combination of the three will affect the administrative process. Finally, it has been pointed out that varying relationships between any two (other than the administrative process dimension) will have corresponding variable effects upon the process per se.

FOURTH MAJOR PROPOSITION

Administration is the performance of the administrative process by an individual or a group in the context of an enterprise functioning in its environment.

The administrative process is a series of interdependent steps which may be isolated and described in the abstract. Administration, on the other hand, is the performance of the process in the specific contexts of enterprise and environment. As such it is primarily behavior, though in other times and cultures it may have been thought of as largely law.

We have already observed that the parts of the action cycle are reciprocally influential, that the functions performed by the administrative process are integrally related to one another. They suggest an interdependence which is increased once the interdimensional influences have been introduced.

This complex of interrelationships probably constitutes a whole, though it is not yet clear whether this entity can be referred to as a "system" with all of the "organic" implications of that term as it is used in the life sciences.[18] There

---

16. F. J. Roethlisberger and William J. Dickson, *Management and the Worker* (Cambridge, Mass., 1939).

17. Administrative Process Working Papers (unpublished Cornell manuscript, Dec. 31, 1955).

18. See Walter B. Cannon, *The Wisdom of the Body* (New York, 1932); Joseph Needham, *Order and Life* (New Haven, Conn., 1936); and Sir Charles Sherrington, *Man on His Nature* (Garden City, N.Y., 1953).

would, however, appear to be a totality in administration (not in the administrative process) which is significant.

Minor Proposition: Administration as a totality has definable attributes. They are:

a. *It seeks to perpetuate itself.* As a definable complex, administration has many of the characteristics of other total organizations. Like them, its first attribute is its tendency to perpetuate itself.

b. *It seeks to preserve its internal well-being.* It is sufficiently self-conscious to attempt to protect itself against disruption from within or destruction from without. It is therefore concerned with its own internal workings and the morale and welfare of its participants.

c. *It seeks to preserve itself vis-à-vis others.* Each individual behavior pattern composing a complete administrative process maintains a competitive relationship with other behavior patterns constituting other processes.

d. *It seeks growth.* Like all other organisms, it is aware of the fact that it cannot stand still for long but must go either forward or backward. In its dynamic phases, therefore, it normally seeks to grow. Much of the impetus for mergers, for "empire building," and for entrepreneurial effort in general is made not only on behalf of the corporation, or the bureau, or the institution, but also on behalf of a separate and identifiable administration.

Minor Proposition: The attributes of the totality of administration have significant effects upon administrative behavior.

These attributes of totality are really properties of organic compulsion and as such are compulsive as far as behavior is concerned. Thus, the successful administrator seeks internal cohesion among the members of the administrative group. He seeks to keep his group intact. He presses for individual identification with the total process. He stresses competition as a means of preserving his "administration's" relationship to others. In short, he performs in such a way as to attempt to perpetuate the process, maintain its internal well-being, preserve its position among competitors, and, indeed, to help it grow.

FIFTH MAJOR PROPOSITION

Administration and the administrative process occur in substantially the same generalized form in industrial, commercial, civil, educational, military, and hospital organizations.

The concept of the universality of administration and of the administrative process had been implicit in much which has been set forth above. It must now be made explicit as a separate proposition. This is particularly important both for the classification of existing knowledge and as a hypothesis for subsequent investigation.

The cyclical development of administrative action, beginning with decision making and moving through reappraisal, occurs in all types of organizations. Similarly, each of them is served by administration through the accomplishment of the same basic functions in the areas of policy, resources, and execution. Again, the process is no less organic in a hospital than it is in a manufacturing establishment. Finally, the process is but a portion of a larger action system, whether that system occurs in the Department of the Interior or in General Motors. The process becomes a whole as administration when performed by an individual within an enterprise functioning in its own ecological setting.

In every case, there is a constancy in fundamental properties. The differences which exist from one field of application to another are differences which result from the factors suggested in our discussion of the four dimensions constituting action. These are the fundamental differences; the variations in institutional application are derivative. When thus analyzed, however, these more fundamental differences are seen to be but variations in the way in which a constant process is performed or accomplished. They do not argue against a basic universality.

CONCLUSION

These propositions are far from complete, are seldom as precise as they should be, and doubtlessly are but partially correct. Whatever their inadequacies, my intention has been to frame the propositions in such a way as to meet the criticisms of existing administrative thought which were made earlier in this paper. Specifically, I have sought generalizations broad enough to encompass phenomena in several applied fields. The propositions have been calculated to view the whole administrative process and the whole of administration rather than any one or less-than-whole combination of its parts. I have attempted to relate the process of administration to larger concepts of action systems. Finally, the propositions themselves have been stated in terms which it is hoped will make it possible to test them both empirically and in subsequent analysis. At best they are notes looking in the direction of broad theory.

4 – A Preview to Administrative Science

MANECK S. WADIA

INTRODUCTION

Within the past decade there has been a strong emphasis toward the development of an administrative science. There is increasing research toward developing a distinct administrative science – an identifiable process which occurs in all organizations. This research hopes to bring together knowledge from a variety of fields, but especially the social sciences. Anthropologists, economists, mathematicians, management specialists, sociologists, political scientists and psychologists are for the first time formally banding together, at places like the Administrative Science Center at the University of Pittsburgh, to work toward the development of an administrative science. Other universities have established, or hope to establish, similar research foundations with emphasis on interdisciplinary research.[1]

Though there are many obstacles that still need to be surmounted, and much work still required, it is possible to make some generalizations as to what the emerging administrative science will be like. The objective of this paper is to present this broad preview.

A SOCIAL SCIENCE

Administrative science will be a social science. One of the many definitions of the word social is that pertaining to the activities of men. The minimum definition of science is a body of systematized knowledge. Hence a social science may be defined as a body of systematized knowledge pertaining to the activities of human beings. The behavioral sciences – anthropology, sociology, and psychology – may therefore be considered social sciences. Within this broad definition of social science other fields may also be included such as history, political science and business administration. However, what is included in the area of social sciences varies from person to person and from institution to institution. For example, the Indiana Academy of Sciences does not recognize sociology as a social science and there are many individuals who will not include history in the realm of the social sciences.

What a social science is will become clearer by comparing it to physical science. The social science's primary concern is with the human being and the total environment as it affects the human being, whereas the primary concern of a physical science is with the physical environment per se. Physical sciences deal primarily with those phenomena that can be duplicated whereas the subject matter of the social sciences does not lend itself readily to controlled experimentation since the measurement of the basic variables cannot be precise. The major difference is that the social scientist himself is a part of his subject matter and the way he develops his science will affect his subject matter. Thus, a social scientist tries to comprehend society's action often in terms of his own experiences, which differ from one social scientist to another. Again, the theories he develops may change his very subject matter which is not true in the case of a physical science. For example, a new "physical" theory of the world being flat will not change the shape of the earth even if everyone were to subscribe to such a theory, whereas a new "social" theory of "black supremacy," if acceptable to all concerned, would change human behavior.

The effects of constant change are so strong on the social scientist's subject matter, that it is well nigh impossible for him to come up with a "pure science," i.e., a science with laws rather than principles. A principle is a general proposition sufficiently applicable to a series of phenomena under consideration. A law is the relationship between cause and effect which will give, so far as existing experience goes, always the same result.[2] For example, the discovery of the atom bomb has considerably affected all social spheres whereas the discovery of motivation research will not change one iota the components of the atom. This does not mean that one should take a defeatist attitude towards eventual control of some of the many variables that confront a social scientist. However, this discussion does try to point out the problems that the emerging administrative science will face. Although all these problems cannot be solved, it is not an idle hope that man will develop greater control over most variables and complete control over some.

The main subject matter of the administrative science is people in a goal oriented organization,

"A Preview to Administrative Science," *International Review of Administrative Sciences*, XXVIII, No. 1 (1962), 39 – 42. Reprinted by permission of the International Institute of Administrative Sciences, Brussels. **Maneck S. Wadia**: Graduate School of Business, Stanford University.

1. For further discussion on the interdisciplinary approach see Edward H. Litchfield, "Organization in Large American Universities: The Faculties," *Journal of Higher Education*, 30:353 – 364 (7), October 1959.

2. For the best discussion of principles in the realm of business administration, see R. C. Davis, *The Fundamentals of Top Management*, Harper and Bros., 1951.

operating within a broader organization (society). This definitely implies that administrative science will be a social science. The explicit recognition of this fact will help accelerate the development of the social science of administration.

A UNIVERSAL SCIENCE

Administrative science will be a universal science.

The major objective of research toward the development of administrative science is to find the universals of the administrative process, to find administrative tools of universal significance and to develop models and methods of universal application. Administrative science will be applicable in a variety of organizational contexts such as hospitals, labor unions, research foundations, the armed forces, universities, government and business.

The emerging administrative science will also be applicable in cross-cultural frameworks. It will be of significance in industrial as well as agrarian societies, in communistic as well as free enterprise oriented societies.

The fact that administrative science will be of universal significance does not imply that environment will be of little or no significance. On the contrary, one of the major steps in the development of this science is to find out the inherent aspects of administrative science and distinguish them from the environmental aspects. The study of the environment within which an organization operates will become of great significance in administrative science. This in turn will lead to greater use and application of the behavioral sciences and greater research in the international area of administration.

A SYNTHESIZING RESEARCH ORIENTED SCIENCE

Administrative science hopes to bring together all knowledge pertaining to administration into one distinct discipline. By doing so, administrative science will bring together methods and research findings of various disciplines. This will lead not only to the advance of the field of administrative science, but also of the contributing disciplines through the interchange of knowledge within these disciplines and with administrative science.

Like the other social sciences, and especially the behavioral sciences, administrative science will be a strongly research oriented science. Three methods of research will be of special signifi-

cance—the field work method, the applied research method, and the comparative method.

The *field work method* of research is at present used most widely in the field of anthropology. Its most distinguishing characteristic is the researcher's identification with the subject matter of his study. The administrative science researcher will increasingly become an active participant in the organization he studies. Though this is a time consuming method, it is the best research method for studying total organizations.

The *applied research method* has been very successfully utilized by industrial sociologists.

The applied researcher ordinarily accepts certain criterion goals as objectives toward which all research is focused. These may include productivity, morale, organizational stability, low operating costs, and similar market or internal goals of the firm. If he works skillfully, he will solve some immediate problems for his business client, and he may also make some substantial additions to basic knowledge.[3]

The significance and use of this method in administrative science will provide ample opportunity for consulting work for those interested and expert in this field.

The *comparative method* has been widely utilized by social scientists for centuries. This method will be of the greatest significance in administrative science. The major objective of this method is to arrive at similarities and differences in the administrative process within various organizations in various cultural contexts.

Once these similarities and differences have been ascertained, they are analyzed. The reasons for, and the degree of, similarities are sought in order to arrive at universals. Once these universals in the administrative process are arrived at, they will be added to the existing and ever growing body of knowledge in administrative science. These universals may be theories, principles, processes, models, or other factors which hold true for all administrative activities.

The differences found through comparative studies cannot and will not be ignored in developing administrative science. The reasons for, and the degree of, these variations will also be sought in order to determine to what extent environment factors affect the administrative process. These variations will be of great importance in the application of administrative science.

The study of comparable phenomena—similar yet somehow different—is indispensable in the search for

3. Delbert C. Miller, "How Behavioral Scientists Can Help Business," *Business Horizons*, 3:33 (2), Summer 1960.

FIGURE 1
BASIC MANAGEMENT FACTORS

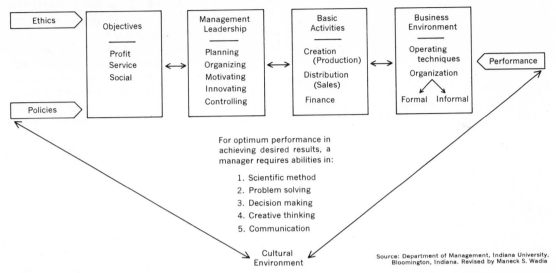

For optimum performance in achieving desired results, a manager requires abilities in:

1. Scientific method
2. Problem solving
3. Decision making
4. Creative thinking
5. Communication

Source: Department of Management, Indiana University, Bloomington, Indiana. Revised by Maneck S. Wadia

variables, their range of variation, and the consequences of those variations.

The dominant schools of administration have established curricula and research programs on the assumption that each field of administration rests on unique elements, on constants and variables which are not merely different in degree from one field to another, but are different in kind. The challenge to this position has come from those who assert that administration, in whatever context, is basically the same phenomenon. They have advanced a series of abstract models or theories of administration, management, organization, decision-making and communication. The comparative approach seems to be the most promising way of settling this issue. If in fact there are important similarities in the several types of administration, comparisons should reveal them. Yet to the extent that the more abstract formulations may conceal important variations, comparison should act as a correcting factor.[4]

The comparative method will serve as the most unique and the most important factor in the emerging field of administrative science and will gain in importance as the field develops further.

THE TAKE-OFF POINT

The greatest contribution to the knowledge of administration so far has come from the area of business management. It is therefore not surprising that for its overall framework, and as its take-off point, the emerging administrative science should borrow most heavily from the field of business management.

The framework presented in Figure I is a revision of that developed by the Department of Management at Indiana University. This framework is the take-off point. In most management circles, barring semantics, this framework, or something very similar to it, is considered the final word.

This framework is considered to be of universal application and on this, management and administrative science are not in complete agreement. The management school of thought has been preoccupied mainly with the business world, whereas the administrative science school of thought wants a science applicable to all varieties of administration. Hence, this framework, built specifically for the business sector, and for the United States, will eventually be further revised to apply to all administered organizations all over the world.

In the field of administrative science, this framework is considered the starting point. From here, a science of administration will be developed. It will be developed along the lines of a social science; it will be of universal application in terms of organizations as well as environments; it will bring together a variety of disciplines; it will be research oriented with strong reliance on the comparative method; and it will rely heavily on the cooperation of businessmen and management specialists.

4. Peter B. Hammond, Robert W. Hawkes, Buford H. Junker, James D. Thompson, and Arthur Tuden, *Comparative Studies in Administration* (Chapter I—"On the Study of Administration"), University of Pittsburgh Press, 1959, pp. 8–9.

SECTION *II*
OBJECTIVES
AND
STRATEGIES

Business objectives provide the goals toward which all the functions of management are directed. Not too long ago, profit was considered to be the sole objective of a business enterprise. Now, it is increasingly being recognized that to survive successfully in our society, a business enterprise has to achieve more than the profit objective. Drucker (#5) examines the survival needs of a business enterprise and their contributions toward better practice as well as toward the development of a general theory of business enterprise.

Schleh's article (#6) is concerned with the blending of individual and organizational goals—with the human element and organizational success.

In Anthony's article (#7), we return to the controversy over profit maximization as the most important, or even the sole, objective of business. This controversy has led to important changes in management philosophy, and Anthony answers some of the crucial questions concerning this subject.

Tilles (#8) shows how many business failures can be attributed to poor strategy or to the lack of any strategy. He cites examples of the importance of strategy and sets the criteria that must be met by goals and policies in order to permit the development of the right strategy.

5 — Business Objectives and Survival Needs

PETER F. DRUCKER

The literature of business management, confined to a few "how to do" books only fifty years ago, has grown beyond any one man's capacity even to catalogue it. Professional education for business has become the largest and most rapidly growing field of professional education in this country and is growing rapidly in all other countries in the free world. It also has created in the advanced postgraduate education for experienced, mature, and successful executives—perhaps first undertaken in systematic form at the University of Chicago—the only really new educational concept in a hundred and fifty years.

Yet so far we have little in the way of a "discipline" of business enterprise, little in the way of an organized, systematic body of knowledge, with its own theory, its own concepts, and its own methodology of hypothesis, analysis, and verification.

THE NEED FOR A THEORY OF BUSINESS BEHAVIOR

The absence of an adequate theory of business enterprise is not just an "academic" concern; on the contrary, it underlies four major problems central to business as well as to a free-enterprise society.

"Business Objectives and Survival Needs," *Journal of Business*, XXXI (April 1958), 81–90. Reprinted by permission of the author and The University of Chicago Press. Copyright 1958 by The University of Chicago Press. **Peter F. Drucker:** Department of Management, New York University.

1. One is the obvious inability of the layman to understand modern business enterprise and its behavior. What goes on and why, "at the top" or "on the fourteenth floor" of the large corporation—the central economic and one of the central social institutions of modern industrial society—is as much of a mystery to the "outsider" as the magician's sleight of hand is to the small boy in the audience. And the "outsiders" include not only those truly outside business enterprise. They include workers and shareholders; they include many professionally trained men in the business—the engineers or chemists, for instance—indeed, they include a good many management people themselves: supervisors, junior executives, functional managers. They may accept what "top management" does, but they accept on faith rather than by reason of knowledge and understanding. Yet such understanding is needed for the success of the individual business as well as for the survival of industrial society and of the free-enterprise system.

One of the real threats is the all-but-universal resistance to profit in such a system, the all-but-universal (but totally fallacious) belief that socialism—or any other ism—can operate an industrial economy without the "rake-off" of profit, and the all-but-universal concern lest profit be too high. That the danger in a dynamic, industrial economy is that profit may be too low to permit the risks of innovation, growth, and expansion—that, indeed, there may be no such thing as "profit" but only provision for the costs of the future—very few people understand.

This ignorance has resisted all attempt at education; this resistance to profits has proved impervious to all propaganda or appeals, even to the attempts at "profit-sharing."

The only thing capable of creating understanding of the essential and necessary function of profit in an expanding, risk-taking, industrial economy is an understanding of business enterprise. And that for all without personal, immediate experience in the general management of a business can come only through a general "model" of business enterprise, that is, through the general theory of a systematic discipline.

2. The second problem is the lack of any bridge of understanding between the "macro-economics" of an economy and the "micro-economics" of the most important actor in this economy, the business enterprise. The only "micro-economic" concept to be found in economic theory today is that of "profit maximization." To make it fit the actual, observable behavior of business enterprise, however, economists have had to bend, stretch, and qualify it until it has lost all meaning and all usefulness. It has become as complicated as the "epicycles" with which pre-Copernican astronomers tried to save the geocentric view of the universe: "profit maximization" may mean short-run, immediate revenue or long-range basic profitability of wealth-producing resources; it may have to be qualified by a host of unpredictables such as managerial power drives, union pressures, technology, etc.; and it completely fails even then to account for business behavior in a growing economy. It does not enable the economist to predict business reaction to public policy any more; to the governmental policy-maker business reaction is as "irrational" as government policy, by and large, seems to the businessman.

But in modern industrial society we must be able to "translate" easily from public policy to business behavior and back again. The policy-maker must be able to assess the impact of public policy on business behavior; and the businessman—especially in the large enterprise—must be able to assess the impact of his decisions and actions on the "macro-economy." "Profit-maximization" does not enable us to do either, as this paper intends to show, primarily because it fails to understand the role and function of profit.

3. The third area in which the absence of a genuine theory of business enterprise creates very real problems is that of the internal integration of the organization. The management literature is full of discussions of the "problem of the specialist" who sees only his own functional area or of the "problem of the scientist in business" who resents the demand that he subordinate his knowledge to business ends. Yet we will be getting ever more specialized; we will, of necessity, employ more and more highly trained "professionals." Each of those must be dedicated to his specialty; yet each must share a common vision and common goals and must voluntarily engage in a common effort. To bring this about is already the most time- and energy-consuming job of management, certainly in our big businesses, and no one I know claims to be able to do it successfully.

Twenty years ago it was still possible to see a business as a mechanical assemblage of "functions." Today we know that, when we talk of a "business," the "functions" simply do not exist. There is only business profit, business risk, business product, business investment, and business customer. The functions are irrelevant to any one of them. And yet it is equally obvious, if we look at the business, that the work has to be done by people who specialize, because nobody can know enough even to know all there is to be known about one of the major functions today—they are growing too fast. It is already asking a great deal of a good man to be a good functional man, and, in some areas, it is rapidly becoming almost too much to ask of a man. How, then, do we transmute functional knowledge and functional contribution into general direction and general results? The ability of big business—but even of many small ones—to survive depends on our ability to solve this problem.

4. The final problem—also a symptom both of the lack of discipline and of the need for it—is of course the businessman's own attitude toward "theory." When he says, "This is theoretical," he by and large still means: "This is irrelevant." Whether managing a business enterprise could or should be a "science" (and one's answer to this question depends primarily on how one defines the word "science"), we need to be able to consider theory the foundation for good practice. We would have no modern doctors, unless medicine (without itself being a "science" in any strict sense of the word) considered the life-sciences and their theories the foundation of good practice. Without such a foundation in a discipline of business enterprise we cannot make valid general statements, cannot therefore predict the outcome of actions or decisions, and can judge them only by hindsight and by their results—when it is too late to do anything. All we can have at the time of decision would be "hunches," "hopes," and "opinions," and, considering the dependence of modern society on business enterprise and the impact of managerial decisions, this is not good enough.

Without such a discipline we could also neither teach nor learn, let alone work systematically on the improvement of our knowledge and of our performance as managers of a business. Yet the need both for managers and for constant improvement of their knowledge and performance is so tremendous, quantitatively as well as qualitatively, that we simply cannot depend on the "natural selection" of a handful of "geniuses."

The need for a systematic discipline of business enterprise is particularly pressing in the under-developed growth countries of the world. Their ability to develop themselves will depend, above all, on their ability rapidly to develop men capable of managing business enterprise, that is, on the availability of a discipline that can be taught and can be learned. If all that is available to them is development through experience, they will almost inevitably be pushed toward some form of collectivism. For, however wasteful all collectivism is of economic resources, however destructive it is of freedom, dignity, and happiness, it economizes the managerial resource through its concentra-

tion of entrepreneurial and managerial decisions in the hands of a few "planners" at the top.

WHAT ARE THE SURVIVAL NEEDS OF BUSINESS ENTERPRISE?

We are still a long way from a genuine "discipline" of business enterprise. But there is emerging today a foundation of knowledge and understanding. It is being created in some of our large companies and in some of our universities. In some places the starting point is economics, in some marketing, in some the administrative process, in others such new methodologies as operations research and synthesis or long-range planning. But what all these approaches, regardless of starting point or terminology, have in common is that they start out with the question: What are the survival needs of business enterprise? What, in other words, does it have to be, to do, to achieve—to exist at all? For each of these "needs" there has, then, to be an "objective."

It may be said that this approach goes back to the pioneering work on business objectives that was done at the Bell Telephone System under the presidency of Theodore Vail a full forty years ago. Certainly, that was the first time the management of a large business enterprise refused to accept the old, glib statement, "The objective of a business is to make a profit," and asked instead, "On what will our survival as a privately owned business depend?" The practical effectiveness of the seemingly so obvious and simple approach is proved by the survival, unique in developed countries, of privately owned telecommunications in the United States and Canada. A main reason for this was certainly the "survival objective" Vail set for the Bell System: "Public satisfaction with our service." Yet, though proved in practice, this remained, until recently, an isolated example. And it probably had to remain such until, within the last generation, the biologists developed the approach to understanding of "systems" by means of defining "essential survival functions."

"Survival objectives" are general; they must be the same in general for each and every business. Yet they are also specific; different performance and different results would be needed in each objective area for any particular business. And every individual business will also need its own specific balance between them at any given time.

The concept of survival objectives thus fulfils the first requirement of a genuine "theory"—that it be both formal and yet concretely applicable, that is, "practical." Survival objectives are also "objective" both as to their nature and as to the specific requirements in a given situation. They do not depend on "opinion" or "hunch." Yet —and that is essential—they do not "determine" entrepreneurial or managerial decisions; they are not (as is so much of traditional economics or of contemporary behavioral science) an attempt to substitute formulas for risk-taking decision or responsible judgment. They attempt rather to establish the foundation for decision and judgment, to make what is the specific task of entrepreneur and manager possible, effective, and rational, and to make it understandable and understood.

We have reached the stage where we know the "functions" of a business enterprise, with "function" being used the way the biologist talks about "procreation" as a "function" essential for the perpetuation of a living species.

There are *five such "survival functions"* of business enterprise. Together they define the areas in which each business, to survive, has to reach a standard of performance and produce results above a minimum level. They are also the areas affected by every business decision and, in turn, affecting every business result. Together these five areas of "survival objectives" describe therefore (operationally) the "nature of business enterprise."

1. The enterprise needs, first, a *human organization designed for joint performance* and capable of perpetuating itself.

It is an assemblage not of brick and mortar but of people. These people must work as individuals; they cannot work any other way. Yet they must voluntarily work for a common result and must therefore be organized for joint performance. The first requirement of business is therefore that there be an effective human organization.

But business must also be capable of perpetuating itself as a human organization if only because all the things we decide every day—if, indeed, we are managers—take for their operation more time than the good Lord has allotted us. We are not making a single decision the end of which we are likely to see while still working. How many managerial decisions will be liquidated within twenty years, will have disappeared, unless they are totally foolish decisions? Most of the decisions we make take five years before they even begin to have an impact; this is the short range of a decision. And then they take ten or fifteen years before (at the very earliest) they are liquidated, have ceased to be effective, and, therefore, have ceased to have to be reasonably right.

This means that the enterprise as a human organization has to be able to perpetuate itself. It has to be able to survive the life-span of any one man.

2. The second survival objective arises from the fact that the enterprise exists in *society and economy*. In business schools and business thinking we often tend to assume that the business enterprise exists by itself in a vacuum. We look at it from the inside. But the business enterprise is a creature of society and economy. If there is one thing we do know, it is that society and/or economy can put any business out of existence overnight—nothing is simpler. The enterprise exists on sufferance and exists only as long as society and economy believe that it does a job and a necessary, a useful, and a productive one.

I am not talking here of "public relations"; they are only one means. I am not talking of something that concerns only the giants. And I am not talking of "socialism." Even if the free-enterprise system survives, individual businesses and industries within it may be—and of course often have been—restricted, penalized, or even put out of business very fast by social or political action such as taxes or zoning laws, municipal ordinances or federal regulation, and so forth. Anticipation of social climate and economic policy, on the one hand, and organized behavior to create what business needs to survive in respect to both are therefore genuine survival needs of each business at all times. They have to be considered in every action and have to be "factored" into every business decision.

Equally, the business is a creature of the economy and at the mercy of changes in it—in population and income, ways of life and spending patterns, expectations and values. Again here is need for objectives which anticipate so as to enable the business to adapt and which at the same time aim at creating the most favorable conditions.

3. Then, of course, there is the area of the specific purpose of business, of its contribution. The purpose is certainly to *supply an economic good and service*. This is the only reason why business exists. We would not suffer this complicated, difficult, and controversial institution except for the fact that we have not found any better way of supplying economic goods and services productively, economically, and efficiently. So, as far as we know, no better way exists. But that is its only justification, its only purpose.

4. There is another purpose characteristic which I would, so to speak, call the nature of the beast; namely, that this all happens in a *changing* economy and a *changing* technology. Indeed, in

the business enterprise we have the first institution which is designed to produce change. All human institutions since the dawn of prehistory or earlier had always been designed to prevent change—all of them: family, government, church, army. Change has always been a catastrophic threat to human security. But in the business enterprise we have an institution that is designed to create change. This is a very novel thing. Incidentally, it is one of the basic reasons for the complexity and difficulty of the institution.

This means not only that business must be able to adapt to change—that would be nothing very new. It means that every business, to survive, must strive to *innovate*. And innovation, that is, purposeful, organized action to bring about the new, is as important in the social field—the ways, methods, and organization of business, its marketing and market, its financial and personnel management, and so on—as it is in the technological areas of product and process.

In this country industrial research expenditures have risen from a scant one-tenth of 1 per cent of national income to 1½ or 2 per cent in less than thirty years. The bulk of this increase has come in the last ten years; this means that the impact in the form of major technological changes is still ahead of us. The speed of change in non-technological innovation, for instance, in distribution channels, has been equally great. Yet many businesses are still not even geared to adaptation to change; and only a mere handful are geared to innovation—and then primarily in the technological areas. Here lies therefore a great need for a valid theory of business enterprise but also a great opportunity for contribution.

5. Finally, there is an absolute requirement of survival, namely, that of *profitability,* for the very simple reason that everything I have said so far spells out *risk*. Everything I have said so far says that it is the purpose, the nature, and the necessity of this institution to take risks, to create risks. *And risks are genuine costs.* They are as genuine a cost as any the accountant can put his finger on. The only difference is that, until the future has become past, we do not know how big a cost; but they *are* costs. Unless we provide for costs, we are going to destroy capital. Unless we provide for loss, which is another way of saying for future cost, we are going to destroy wealth. Unless we provide for risk, we are going to destroy capacity to produce. And, therefore, a minimum profitability, adequate to the risks which we, by necessity, assume and create, is an absolute condition of survival not only for the enterprise but for society.

This says three things. First, the need for profitability is objective. It is of the nature of business

enterprise and as such is independent of the motives of the businessman or of the structure of the "system." If we had archangels running businesses (who, by definition, are deeply disinterested in the profit motive), they would have to make a profit and would have to watch profitability just as eagerly, just as assiduously, just as faithfully, just as responsibly, as the most greedy wheeler-dealer or as the most convincedly Marxist commissar in Russia.

Second, profit is not the "entrepreneur's share" and the "reward" to one "factor of production." It does not rank on a par with the other "shares," such as that of "labor," for instance, but above them. It is not a claim *against* the enterprise but the claim *of* the enterprise—without which it cannot survive. How the profits are distributed and to whom is of great political importance; but for the understanding of the needs and behavior of a business it is largely irrelevant.

Finally, "profit maximization" is the wrong concept, whether it be interpreted to mean short-range or long-range profits or a balance of the two. The relevant question is, "What minimum does the business need?" not "What maximum can it make?" This "survival minimum" will, incidentally, be found to exceed present "maxima" in many cases. This, at least, has been my experience in most companies where a conscious attempt to think through the risks of the business has been attempted.

Here are five dimensions; and each of these five is a genuine view of the whole business enterprise. It is a human organization, and we can look upon it only in that aspect, as does our human relations literature. We can look at it from its existence in society and economy, which is what the economist does. This is a perfectly valid, but it is a one-sided view.

We can, similarly, look at the enterprise only from the point of view of its goods and services. Innovation and change are yet another dimension, and profitability is yet another. These are all genuine true aspects of the same being. But only if we have all five of them in front of us do we have a theory of business enterprise on which practice can be built.

For managing a business enterprise means making decisions, every one of which both depends on needs and opportunities in each of these five areas and, in turn, affects performance and results in each.

THE WORK TO BE DONE

The first conclusion from this is that every business needs objectives—explicit or not—in each of these five areas, for malfunction in any one of these endangers the entire business. And failure in any one area destroys the entire business—no matter how well it does in the other four areas. Yet these are not interdependent but autonomous areas.

1. *Here, then, is the first task of a discipline of business enterprise:* to develop clear concepts and usable measurements to set objectives and to measure performance in each of these five areas.

The job is certainly a big one—and a long one. There is no area as yet where we can really define the objectives, let alone measure results. Even in respect to profitability we have, despite great recent advances in managerial economics, figures for the past rather than measurements that relate current or expected profitability to the specific future risks and needs. In the other areas we do not even have that, by and large. And in some—the effectiveness of the human organization, the public standing in economy and society, or the area of innovation—we may, for a long time to come, perhaps forever, have to be content with qualitative appraisal making possible judgment. Even this would be tremendous progress.

2. A second conclusion is hardly less important: *no one simple objective is "the" objective of a business; no one single yardstick "the" measure of performances, prospects, and results of a business; no one single area "the" most important area.*

Indeed, the most dangerous oversimplification of business enterprise may well be that of the "one yardstick," whether "return on investment," "market standing," "product leadership," or what have you. At their best these measure performance in one genuine survival area. But malfunction or failure in any one area is not counterbalanced by performance in any other area, just as a sturdy respiratory or circulatory system will not save an animal if its digestive or nervous system collapses. Success, like failure, in business enterprise is *multidimensional.*

3. This, however, brings out another important need: a rational and systematic approach to the *selection and balance among objectives* so as best to provide for survival and growth of the enterprise. These can be called the "ethics" of business enterprise, insofar as ethics is the discipline that deals with rational value choices among means to ends. It can also be the "strategy" of entrepreneurship. Neither "ethics" nor "strategy" is capable of being absolutely determined, yet neither can be absolutely arbitrary. We need a discipline here that encompasses both the "typical" decision which adapts to circumstances and "plays" the averages of statistical probability, and the innovating, "unique event" of entrepreneurial vision

and courage breaking with precedent and trends and creating new ones—and there are already some first beginnings of such a discipline of entrepreneurship. But such a discipline can never be more than theory of composition is to the musical composer or theory of strategy to the military leader: a safeguard against oversight, an appraisal of risks, and, above all, a stimulant to independence and innovation.

Almost by definition the demands of different survival objectives pull in different directions, at least for any one time period. And it is axiomatic that the resources even of the wealthiest business, or even of the richest country, never cover in full all demands in all areas; there is never so much that there has to be no allocation. Higher profitability can thus be achieved only by taking a risk in market standing, in product leadership, or in tomorrow's human organization, and vice versa. Which of these risks the enterprise can take, which it cannot take, and what it cannot afford not to take—these risk-taking, value-decisions between goals in one area versus goals in others, and between goals in one area today versus goals in others tomorrow, is a specific job of the entrepreneur. This decision itself will remain a "judgment," that is, a matter of human values, appraisal of the situation, weighing of alternatives, and balancing of risks. But an understanding of survival objectives and their requirements can supply both the rational foundation for the decision itself and the rational criteria for the analysis and appraisal of entrepreneurial performance.

AN OPERATIONAL VIEW OF THE BUDGETING PROCESS

The final conclusion is that we need a new approach to the process in which we make our value decisions between different objective areas—the budgeting process. And in particular do we need a real understanding of that part of the budget that deals with the expenses that express these decisions, that is, the "managed" and "capital" expenditures.

Commonly today, budgeting is conceived as a "financial" process. But it is only the notation that is financial; the decisions are entrepreneurial. Commonly today, "managed" expenditures and "capital" expenditures are considered quite separate. But the distinction is an accounting (and tax) fiction and misleading; both commit scarce resources to an uncertain future; both are, economically speaking, "capital" expenditures. And they, too, have to express the same basic decisions on survival objectives to be viable. Finally, today, most of our attention in the "operating budget" is given, as a rule, to other than the "managed" expenses, especially to the "variable" expenses, for that is where, historically, most money was spent. But, no matter how large or small the sums, it is in our decisions on the "managed" expenses that we decide on the future of the enterprise.

Indeed, we have little control over what the accountant calls "variable" expenses—the expenses which relate directly to units of production and are fixed by a certain way of doing things. We can change them, but not fast. We can change a relationship between units of production and labor costs (which we, with a certain irony, still consider "variable expenses" despite the fringe benefits). But within any time period these expenses can only be kept at a norm and cannot be changed. This is of course even more true for the expenses in respect to the decisions of the past, our "fixed" expenses. We cannot make them undone at all, whether these are capital expenses or taxes or what-have-you. They are beyond our control.

In the middle, however, are the expenses for the future which express our risk-taking value choices: the "capital expenses" and the "managed expenses." Here are the expenses on facilities and equipment, on research and merchandising, on product development and people development, on management and organization. This managed expense budget is the area in which we really make our decisions on our objectives. (That, incidentally, is why I dislike accounting ratios in that area so very much, because they try to substitute the history of the dead past for the making of the prosperous future.)

We make decisions in this process in two respects. First, what do we allocate people for? For the money in the budget is really people. What do we allocate people, and energy, and efforts to? To what objectives? We have to make choices, as we cannot do everything.

And, second, what is the time scale? How do we, in other words, *balance* expenditures for long-term permanent efforts against any decision with immediate impact? The one shows results only in the remote future, if at all. The development of people (a fifteen-year job), the effectiveness of which is untested and unmeasurable, is, for instance, a decision on faith over the long range. The other may show results immediately. To slight the one, however, might, in the long range, debilitate the business and weaken it. And, yet, there are certain real short-term needs that have to be met in the business—in the present as well as in the future.

Until we develop a clear understanding of basic survival objectives and some yardsticks for the decisions and choices in each area, budgeting will not become a rational exercise of responsible judgment; it will retain some of the "hunch" character that it now has. But our experience has shown that the concept of survival objectives alone can greatly improve both the quality and effectiveness of the process and the understanding of what is being decided. Indeed, it gives us, we are learning, an effective tool for the integration of functional work and specialized efforts and especially for creating a common understanding throughout the organization and common measurements of contribution and performance.

The approach to a discipline of business enterprise through an analysis of survival objectives is still a very new and a very crude one. Yet it is already proving itself a unifying concept, simply because it is the first *general* theory of the business enterprise we have had so far. It is not yet a very refined, a very elegant, let alone a very *precise,* theory. Any physicist or mathematician would say: This is not a theory; this is still only rhetoric. But at least, while maybe only in rhetoric, we are talking about something real. For the first time we are no longer in the situation in which theory is irrelevant, if not an impediment, and in which practice has to be untheoretical, which means cannot be taught, cannot be learned, and cannot be conveyed, as one can only convey the general.

This should thus be one of the "breakthrough" areas; and twenty years hence this might well have become the *central* concept around which we can organize the mixture of knowledge, ignorance, and experience, of prejudices, insights, and skills, which we call "management" today.

6 — How Management Can Establish Dynamic Objectives

EDWARD C. SCHLEH

If management is to obtain the best possible blending of the interests of the individual with those of the corporation, extreme care must be exercised in getting objectives down to the man concerned. Both the process of objective setting and the application of objectives to the individual must be realistic as they affect human beings, their individual motivations, their interests, their normal reactions.

Since the purpose is to stimulate the man, these human factors are all-important in obtaining the greatest value from objectives. Many companies err in this area because they accept too easily the authoritarian approach which assumes simply that delegations come from above and are referred downward. Organizationally speaking, this is sound. Delegations are determined by the superior.

If you want to make that delegation effective and most earnestly embraced by the subordinate, however, a whole series of principles of motivation must be observed.

First of all, *any objective must be set in light of all known existing conditions.* The determination of these conditions, includes an evaluation of past history, of competition, of the impact of other people in the enterprise on the man, and of any obstacles that may prevent his accomplishing results. When the conditions change, the objectives should change.

The superior should *set both basic and outstanding performance, objectives for each result.* He would do this by first asking himself, "In light of all the conditions as I know them, what would be reasonable job performance on this particular result?" Reasonable job performance usually means the answer to this question: If you had an experienced man who understood the job well, what might be considered reasonably good performance for him (not outstanding and not poor)? Ordinarily, anyone who would be kept on the payroll over a period of time should be expected to attain a performance of this level. Determine specifically what the objective should be and state this as the basic performance objective.

DEFINING GOOD PERFORMANCE

A superior should then ask himself further, "In the light of all these same conditions, what would

I consider to be an *outstanding* job?" In other words, define very good performance that could be achieved by a good man with high effort. A word of caution in this regard: "Outstanding" in this case would mean that the individual, by extra application or insight, would probably be able to reach this level. It should not be something almost unattainable. It should be attainable by a man doing a very good job under the conditions as envisioned for the coming year. This should then be set as the outstanding objective. You have determined the basic accomplishment expected of a man if he works well and in the right direction, and in addition, you have set what he should strive for in order to be recognized as outstanding. Do the same thing for each of the major results expected of him in the period (see example).

Many executives make the mistake of setting only one figure for an objective. Ordinarily they have only a loose idea as to whether it would represent normal or outstanding accomplishment. Should the man work hard and apparently accomplish the objective with ease (which happens frequently when men are set up against specific objectives), a subtle change develops in the mind of the superior. He tends to minimize the accomplishment of the subordinate. He feels that his objective was too loose in the first place. Much of the stimulus is taken away from the employee in that he feels that he has been tricked.

RECOGNIZING OBJECTIVES

Should the man, however, have some difficulty in accomplishing the objective, there is a tendency to view the objective then as something to be striven for but not necessarily attained. Both the man and the superior begin to look at the objective as something that the man is not accountable for. One of the common errors managers make in setting objectives is that they do not set both the basic and the outstanding accomplishment expected for each item.

Another common error made by managers is to assume that objectives apply to the job and not to the individual. This error can spoil a good man as he enters a job. It is worthwhile having a man work against objectives even when he is comparatively new on the job (after his initial training period). However, *objectives for a new man should be*

"How Management Can Establish Dynamic Objectives," *International Management*, XIX (May 1964), 71 – 73, 75 – 77. Based on material from *Management by Results* by Edward C. Schleh. Copyright © 1961 McGraw-Hill, Inc. Used by permission of McGraw-Hill Book Company. **Edward C. Schleh:** Schleh Associates, Minneapolis, Minnesota.

EXAMPLE

Result Area	Basic Performance Objective	Outstanding Performance Objective
1. Sales volume —	$100,000 (£35,71E)	$140,000 (£50,000)
2. Sales outlets —	10 new outlets	16 new outlets
3. Development of a product —	$150,000 (£53,571) profit in first two years after paying all development costs	$300,000 (£107,142) profit in first two years after paying all development costs
4. Cases completed —	8 per day	11 per day
5. Meet schedule —	90% of the time	98% of the time

set in light of his experience. In other words, one of the conditions affecting the setting of objectives is the lack of experience of the man (on this particular job).

On reflection it is perfectly logical that both the basic and the outstanding accomplishment expected of a beginner on a job would not be as high as that of an experienced man. Setting lower objectives for new men has important implications later on when determining their authority. Since authority should be set in light of objectives or accomplishment expected, the superior will then automatically consider authority for the beginner realistically.

Should you set the same objective for a beginner as you would for an experienced man, you may set the stage for failure. The man may do his best to achieve his objectives. In doing this he may step out of line and make errors, which will cast a reflection on him for years to come, a situation with serious implications for the future for a young manager, say, who is in one of his early management positions. On the other hand, he may simply give up, knowing full well that it will be almost impossible for him to achieve these objectives. His superior permits this, since the man is new. The man then develops an unsatisfactory lack of accountability for objectives. He will be weakened for the future.

CROSS-CHECKING OBJECTIVES

One of the most difficult phases of setting objectives is that of making each objective harmonious with others. A man who is working toward an objective may become impervious to the needs of other people in the firm. Objectives may accentuate "lone wolf" inclinations. Therefore, after all objectives have been set in a preliminary way, it is well to write them down and *cross-check to see that all objectives blend with each other.* The individ-

ual objectives for each man must be studied in their implication to see whether or not they will interfere with the objectives of other men. If so, adjustment should be made so that it is to the advantage of one man to help another.

Objectives should also be cross-checked upward so that the objectives of any man tie into those of his superior and eventually into the objectives of the enterprise. If this is done carefully, each echelon is allied with the echelons above. All are encouraged to work together toward an over-all company objective. They are all on the same team and heading in the same direction. If a subordinate fails, the superior shares his failure.

This cross check puts a great deal more strength behind any objective programme. It sets up a basis for realistic accountability, tying all levels of the organization together effectively. Better communications are encouraged. They become more realistic, as they are now part of a natural management flow. They are essential for the smooth working toward objectives.

A strong drive toward one particular result may lead to imbalance in the company. Very often there is an optimum level beyond which an achievement may actually be harmful to some other objective of the firm. In a plant, quality control carried too far may have detrimental effects on waste and on cost of production. In a procurement department, getting the material in on time may raise costs by not allowing time to get several bids.

DETERMINING OPTIMUM POINT

Each objective should be carefully scrutinized to determine the optimum point beyond which the objective might be detrimental to the achievement of other objectives. Setting the outstanding objective and giving no credit for accomplishment beyond it will minimize excessive pressure on any one result. To this extent such a limitation encourages further concentration on other objectives.

Another way to prevent imbalance is to set a counter-objective. For example, a purchasing agent may be held accountable for both a level of inventory and for down time due to lack of materials. Going too far on one generally affects the other. A built-in type of self-discipline is provided whereby the man can regulate himself. The need for constant checks by supervision is minimized, and the wise exercise of judgment by the purchasing agent is encouraged.

One loan company increased its volume of business (and profits) substantially by arbitrarily setting up a higher loss ratio. They were then able to accept much more of the business that came to the counter. They could do this profitably at a comparatively low cost, and as a consequence their net profits were more than enough to overcome the added credit losses they incurred.

IMPORTANCE OF PARTICIPATION

People trained in precise figure work, such as engineering and accounting people, are inclined to feel that once objectives are set the job is done. Nothing could be farther from the truth. The prime value of an objective is in the stimulation of a man. The emotional impact on the man must, therefore, be carefully considered when objectives are installed.

If objectives are to stimulate, *the man must feel* that the objectives are fair. It is not enough that they are actually fair; what is important is that the man feels that they are fair. What makes him feel that they are fair? A man is usually much more sold on objectives if he participates in setting them. He understands them better and is better sold on their fairness. Resentment, opposition, and alibis generally develop if objectives are set above and simply handed down for compliance.

MAINTAINING STATUS QUO

There is a difficulty, however. Essentially, objective setting is the job of the superior—it is the final expression of his delegation. How can you get the subordinate to set objectives and still avoid the violation of this superior-subordinate relationship? Ordinarily the following procedure works quite well: The superior should first discuss the general conditions under which the man will be working and in a broad way point out to the man the over-all expectation in company objectives. In a way he is pointing out the general track on which the total operation is running.

It is also helpful for the superior to point out some of the places in the man's job where he thinks objectives might be especially worthwhile that year. He should then ask the man to take this information, carefully review his own sphere of action, and come back later to suggest what he considers to be sound objectives for himself. Ask him how he will shoulder his share of the total responsibility. Most men do not wish to be considered laggards. The man will often suggest much more difficult objectives for himself than his superior might otherwise have set. And he will generally be more sold on their fairness than if someone else had forced him to accept these objectives.

CREATING OWN OBJECTIVES

An important additional benefit results from this method of setting objectives. Since a man has to go back and think through the objectives, he will think much more broadly than he would otherwise and plan ahead. He is usually careful to analyse his whole operation so that when he comes back with objectives he is fairly certain that he will be able to accomplish them. Before proposing objectives he will probably lay out a plan for reaching them. He becomes a broader man by the process, one who is able to plan ahead and think through problems without imposing them on his superior. Such a procedure places the planning function solidly on the subordinate.

What if the man returns with objectives that are much higher than those his superior had been considering? There is a temptation for the superior to accept these higher objectives since the man himself set them. In most cases this would be a grave mistake. If the superior is still convinced that these objectives are higher than they should be, he should reduce them. This would be true either for basic or for outstanding performance or for both. A good way to do this is to tell the man, "I appreciate your interest in setting such difficult objectives, but I would be well satisfied if the following (lower) objectives were met. If you meet them, I'll still consider that you have done the job."

PROVIDING STRONG STIMULUS

The impetus and drive that this approach gives to the man, and the confidence in the fairness of the superior, provides a strong stimulus. His general reaction is, "I can easily meet that." (Note the comment made earlier, that men are more stimulated by success than they are by failure.) Do not set tougher objectives for a man simply because he proposes them. If the subordinate shows in the discussion that the superior's first idea of sound objectives was really too loose, then it is perfectly all right to accept a higher objective. Since this is an easy rationalization for the superior, however, he should try to be very critical of this step before he takes it.

It is also helpful to ask the man to set percentage values for each of his objectives. The superior may then compare these with the percentages that he would have assigned and have a good basis for a discussion of the relative value of the different objectives. Both on the objectives and on the percentage values, however, the final decision still has to be made by the superior.

Many managers find this participation procedure difficult to accept; they feel they are giving away some of their prerogative. Nothing is given away, because the man is still finally accountable for the accomplishment which has been agreed to by the superior. If the man should return with objectives that are too low, these would not be accepted. They would be used as a basis for a discussion with the man to build him up to accepting higher objectives.

ADOPTING POSITIVE ATTITUDES

It is very important that the superior should adopt a positive attitude toward objective setting. In other words, once objectives have been set, it should be tacitly assumed that they will be met. Otherwise a subordinate may develop a negative approach. He just can't meet them. This points up all the more the importance of setting reasonable objectives that can be met. Setting objectives that you assume will not be met or that would be extremely difficult to meet may very well take much of the steam out of the programme. There is then a tendency for the man to grumble too much and for the superior to be too quick to relieve a man of accountability because of some unusual condition. A part of the conditions under which objectives have been set should be the "normal" unpredictable occurrences that affect the job.

Many executives ask whether or not they should adjust objectives in the middle of the year should conditions change. Ordinarily, the answer is no. Adjustments tend to weaken an objective programme. However, there are some circum-

stances that may require an adjustment. These get right back to fairness to the individual. It is assumed that the normal give-and-take of a job is covered earlier in establishing the conditions. Objectives may be revised, however, if there is a radical change in the conditions assumed when setting the objectives. A mid-period review may be advisable to consider whether the conditions are actually as anticipated.

For example, one of these conditions might be the fact that a plant from which all products were to be sold in a given territory was burned down. It is quite obvious that no salesman could possibly sell high volume if he has few products to sell. His objectives may therefore be adjusted in light of the potential now available to him. The fact that competition was a little tougher than anticipated or that the economy went up or down five or ten per cent should not change the objectives. Ordinarily, within these limits, objectives should hold for the year. The man is expected to carry the load for the company. Perhaps a 20 per cent drop in the potential may justify a change. If at the end of the year objectives prove to be wrong one way or the other, they may be adjusted or changed for the coming year. Any errors would be corrected then, because objectives would be reviewed for change anyway at the beginning of the year.

SLIDING OBJECTIVES

In some cases it may be perfectly sound to set sliding objectives in the beginning of the year and tie them to possible changes in key conditions. In a mail-order house a supervisor may have cost objectives tied to the number of orders sent in each week. If it is up, his cost objective is higher. If it is down, his cost objective is lower.

How should accomplishment on one objective be looked at versus accomplishment on another? Very frequently an employee on a job may feel that one objective is much more difficult or much more valuable and put a great deal of time into it. As a consequence, he may achieve accomplishments far beyond the outstanding objective for that particular item.

However, he may not even reach the basic performance on one of the other objectives. The objective that he focused on may actually prove to be worth more money in that particular period. Should the supervisor balance off the very superior accomplishment on one objective against the below-normal accomplishment on another? Let us examine what would happen if this were done.

If he permitted this, he would, in effect, be

allowing the man to determine his own delegation without the consent of the superior. In subsequent years the man would also pick and choose among the objectives irrespective of the percentage weights that had been agreed to for each. Severe imbalance in the operation could result.

FAILURE TO REACH TARGETS

Failure to accomplish a given objective may also seriously impinge on the work of other people in the operation so that serious losses may be incurred and bottlenecks develop. For example, concentration on the type of product in a plant department in order to get long runs may cause too many back orders. On the other hand, unbalanced sales volume may easily cause shutdowns of entire lines in a plant. The man concerned may not feel accountable for these losses. In order to maintain balance *the superior should require at least basic accomplishment on all objectives in each period.* If he does not, he will lose control of the operation. Unusual accomplishment on one objective should almost never be accepted as excusing lack of accomplishment on other objectives. Otherwise the superior will not be able to depend on the man for balanced accomplishment in the future. Lack of balance is one of the most costly errors in most operations.

PROGRAMMING OBJECTIVES

Frequently, the first reaction of managers considering a management-objective programme is that they do not have enough figures or data on which to set objectives. It seems impossible to determine accurately what objectives or measurements should be used. Fortunately it is not necessary to require perfection in your objective programme at the outset. Crude objectives or measurements that are not completely accurate are usable in getting the programme started. Experience will later prove where they are in error. You can make adjustments in the next period. They will still operate as a better stimulus.

At the start records may not seem particularly well adapted to the objective programme. Parts of a job may be hard to measure. There is therefore a tendency to retreat from objectives because the whole position cannot be covered. It does not have to be. In the beginning, concentrate on one or two of the major results such as cost reduction, sales increase, waste reduction, or better schedule performance.

Initially it is a good idea to select those items for which measurements are readily available even though they are somewhat crude. It is not essential that every facet of the job be covered in the first year. A perfectly workable plan might set objectives for only part of the job in the first year. Men develop a better understanding of objectives and will usually get improvements without forcing any major long-range imbalance. In subsequent periods all major parts of the job should be covered as soon as possible, however, or you will probably push toward an imbalanced operation.

When executives first approach an objective programme, they often become very enthusiastic about it and try to accomplish the ultimate in the first year. There is something about the analysis that precedes objective setting that opens up one's eyes to possible improvements. A new millennium of perfection seems quickly within reach. It is not that easy. *Do not demand the ultimate the first year.*

7 – The Trouble with Profit Maximization

ROBERT N. ANTHONY

"Why are college graduates who are trained in our mother science, economics, so ill equipped to handle real-life business problems?" This question, asked by a businessman some time ago, set me to wondering about a similar one: "Why do graduate students, by applying what they avow are sound analytical tools learned in college, often arrive at naive solutions to the problems in business cases?"

I have finally concluded that the trouble stems from the assumption in most college economics texts and college classrooms that the objective of a business is to maximize profits. Unhappily, this assumption is not confined to the campus. Countless writers of fiction and nonfiction have

"The Trouble with Profit Maximization," *Harvard Business Review*, XXXVIII (November–December 1960), 126–134. Reprinted by permission of the author and the publisher. **Robert N. Anthony:** Graduate School of Business Administration, Harvard University.

seemingly taken it for granted that management's purpose is to maximize profits. Lawyers, labor union spokesmen, and government officials often indicate that they share the same belief.

Moreover—as if to confirm that what all these other people think is true—businessmen themselves sometimes *say* they operate on this assumption. One observer, after a study of corporate annual reports, public relations, and other activities, has reported:

It is surprising and ironical, that, to judge by what businessmen often *say*, one would think that they, too, agree that the nature of business corporations is exactly and precisely what critics say it is; namely, that the corporation has no other purpose, and recognizes no other criterion of decision except profits, and that it pursues these profits just as single-mindedly and irresponsibly as it can.[1]

This article is therefore addressed not only to young men in, or preparing to enter, positions of management, but to their seniors as well. And my purpose is not only to help ease the transition from the classroom world of profit maximization to the realities of life, but also to remind business leaders of the importance of narrowing the gap between their world as often represented and their world as it actually is.

Before tackling this rather huge task, I should make one point to businessmen readers who may find it difficult to believe that today's students are in fact taught profit maximizing economics: they are. I have reviewed what I am told are the five largest selling economics texts, accounting for some 250,000 copies a year.[2] All of them base their analysis of business decisions on profit maximization. One has no qualification—no mention that this assumption may not be valid in practice. Another has a one-sentence qualification. The longest qualification is one of some three pages, but these pages are sandwiched almost exactly in the middle of 251 pages of analysis in which the profit maximization assumption is governing.[3]

Of course, who says what or exactly how much does not really matter. The net effect on students is the only fact that counts, and I can testify to that both from evidence by businessmen and from my own observations of graduate students in the business school classroom.

My argument can be set forth usefully in the form of a catechism.

REALISTIC GOALS

QUESTION: *Is profit maximization the dominant objective of American business?*

In general, no. Many companies formed to achieve some specific, short-run objective (e.g., a real estate syndicate, a stock promotion) undoubtedly fit the profit-maximization pattern. So do speculators in both securities and commodities. So do various types of fly-by-night operators and get-rich-quick artists. But I know of no study of general business practice that supports the profit maximization premise, and I shall mention later studies whose findings are inconsistent with it.

Although we find leaders of the business community stressing the importance of a *satisfactory* profit, we also find them discussing business responsibilities, the need for a fair division of income among the parties involved in a business, and other subjects that are incompatible with the profit maximization goal. Donald K. David, for example, has said:

Business leaders, who wish to preserve and strengthen the kind of society in which we believe, must run a business organization which, beyond being competitive, is a satisfactory social entity for those who work in it and a constructive entity in the national whole. To this basic purpose there must be added the study of the *responsibilities* of management.

The sense of obligation which management must undertake is at least twofold. On the one hand, it extends to the people who make up our thousands upon thousands of companies; it means providing for them not only the conditions essential to the effective performance of work but the realizing of their potentialities as persons so that freedom need not be futile or purposeless for any person. The community, which a company itself comprises, must be a *healthy* community, satisfying the noneconomic as well as the economic needs of the individuals who make it up and enabling them to consider their work a way of life as well as a livelihood.

But another responsibility, sometimes in apparent conflict with our human commitments inside our companies, extends to the businessman's public responsibilities to the community, to the nation and the world comprised of all such communities.[4]

1. J. D. Glover, *The Attack on Big Business* (Boston, Division of Research, Harvard Business School, 1954), p. 328.

2. George Leland Bach, *Economics: An Introduction to Analysis and Policy* (Englewood Cliffs, New Jersey, Prentice-Hall, Inc., 2nd edition, 1957); James H. Dodd and Carl W. Hasek, *Economics, Principles and Applications* (Cincinnati, South-Western Publishing Co., 3rd edition, 1957); Clement L. Harriss, *The American Economy; Principles, Practices, and Policies* (Homewood, Illinois, Richard D. Irwin, Inc., 3rd edition, 1959); Paul T. Homan, Albert G. Hart, and Arnold W. Sametz, *The Economic Order; an Introduction to Theory and Policy* (New York, Harcourt, Brace and Company, 1958); Paul A. Samuelson, *Economics, An Introductory Analysis* (New York, McGraw-Hill Book Company, Inc., 4th edition, 1958).

3. Samuelson, op. cit., pp. 181–183.

4. Address before the Transportation Association of America, January 20, 1954.

If profit maximization is the governing objective of business, such a statement is nonsense. And I am quite sure that it is not.

QUESTION: *Why, then, are economics courses constructed on this premise?*

Probably because its use permits a rigorous intellectual reasoning process. If one assumes profit maximization, a complete and completely consistent package of rules for operating a business can be devised, rules that can be expressed precisely in equations and illustrated by graphs, rules that provide correct answers to classroom problems, and rules which, when they do not work in practice, can always be explained by "other things being equal."

The usefulness of such an all-inclusive package for teaching purposes, for the exploration and extension of theories, and as a device for communicating to one's colleagues, should not be minimized. How can one grade an economics examination if there are a whole range of "correct" answers to the problem, or if the correct answer depends on what is "satisfactory" to the individual student? And what does it matter if the assumption underlying the package is not correct, so long as the application of the rules requires rigorous reasoning in solving classroom problems?

In the better economics courses, and especially in advanced courses, students are told that the structure they are studying is a theoretical one, to be explored for its own sake, and not because it conforms to reality.[5] There is a natural temptation, however, not to detract from the interest in the subject by stressing this point, and in the case of many students, this does not sink in.

The professor acts for reasons roughly like those that led tribal medicine men to assume the existence of evil spirits. Medicine men knew of remedies that were effective for certain ailments, but they also knew the great limitations of these simple remedies. By inventing evil spirits who were assumed to cause all illness, and by incorporating the known remedies into a system of potions, incantations, and rituals that were consistent with this assumption, they were able to gain much more influence in the community than if they had relied solely on prescribing the known remedies. Indeed, it is quite likely that the community gained from this, because without this additional influence the medicine men might not have been able to induce their clients to take those medicines that were in fact beneficial.

There is much merit in making apparently reasonable assumptions when the evidence is inconclusive. For instance, there was merit in the notions of the eighteenth century physicists about a substance called phlogiston, the assumed existence of which was thought to be necessary as an explanation of the process of combustion. The assumption turned out to be completely wrong, but many believe that its existence facilitated the development of correct principles of physics. Modern physicians, however, have discovered that they can retain the community's respect without the "evil spirit" principle, even though this requires an admission of their inability to cure, or even understand, a great many illnesses.

QUESTION: *What really is the dominant objective of American business, then?*

As a general statement, I suggest that the objective of a business is to use its resources as efficiently as possible in supplying goods and services to its customers and to compensate equitably those who supply these resources. As a way of making this general statement *operational*, I suggest that the objective be considered as earning a satisfactory return on capital employed (a "satisfactory" return being equitable compensation paid for the use of capital).

QUESTION: *What is the difference between satisfactory return and profit maximization?*

In the first place, there are a great many problems in economics to which the solution is the same under either assumption. These are problems that involve means of achieving goals, rather than the goals themselves. As Herbert A. Simon has pointed out,[6] there are wide differences in the goals of various organizations—businesses, governments, churches, and so forth—but any organization should try to achieve whatever its goal may be in as efficient a manner as it knows how. Marginal analysis, the favorite tool of the economist, is a valid technique for helping to decide which of the alternative solutions to certain problems is the most efficient; that is, which has the lowest cost.

---

5. A number of authors who criticize the validity of the profit maximization premise are referred to in the excellent article by Julius Margolis, "The Analysis of the Firm: Rationalism, Conventionalism, and Behaviorism," *Journal of Business*, July 1958, pp. 187–199. See also James G. March and Herbert A. Simon, *Organizations* (New York, John Wiley & Sons, Inc., 1958), pp. 140–141. Another exception is Edgar M. Hoover, "Some Institutional Factors in Business Investment Decisions," *American Economic Review*, May 1954, Suppl., pp. 201–213; but note how the conventional economists castigated him, pp. 228–235. See also Edward S. Mason, "The Apologetics of 'Managerialism,'" *The Journal of Business*, January 1958, p. 1.

6. *Administrative Behavior, A Study of Decision-Making Processes in Administrative Organization* (New York, The Macmillan Company, 1947), pp. 1–14.

EXHIBIT I EXAMPLE OF NECESSARY ESTIMATES OF DEMAND AND COSTS

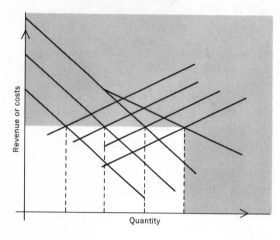

The alternative choice problems where marginal analysis is useful tend to be those where the possible alternatives can be fairly clearly specified, and where it is possible to make reasonably good estimates of the costs and revenue implications of each alternative. Such problems include the acceptance or rejection of certain investment opportunities (Shall we acquire this machine or not?), the choice among various ways of accomplishing a desired result (Shall we buy or lease this machine?), the best way of producing a given mix of products (production scheduling), the best inventory policy for a given sales pattern and set of production facilities, and so on.

Many of these problems are complex and difficult—and many of them involve large sums of money—but in a relative sense they are simple and unimportant; that is, they are simple and unimportant relative to such problems as pricing, choice of the product line, marketing strategy, the direction of research efforts, what size plant to build, and a long list of others. It is problems like these that are not in practice solved by rules based on profit maximization.

Incidentally, relating marginal analysis to the efficiency criterion answers the following question which is embarrassing to the profit maximizers: If marginal analysis depends on the profit maximization assumption, why is the technique so widely used in situations where profit maximization is known *not* to be the objective? The Russians, the nationalized industries in Britain and elsewhere, regulated public utilities, U.S. and other government agencies, and a wide range of nonprofit organizations, all make extensive use of marginal costs for analyzing certain types of problems. All these organizations have in com-

mon with each other, and with profit-seeking businesses, the task of reaching their objectives as efficiently as possible.

There is another type of situation in which marginal analysis is useful, namely, in times of crisis. In normal times, if a product does not earn a satisfactory return, the businessman is likely to drop it and seek a better replacement unless marketing considerations indicate otherwise. When the going gets rough, on the other hand, he is apt to keep the product so long as it makes a contribution. He is also more apt to shave prices in bad times—an action based on marginal analysis—although he does not raise prices in boom times to the level that the profit maximization principle would indicate. (The most dramatic example is the automobile companies' decision not to take full advantage of the postwar shortage.)

There are at least two important areas that do involve the objectives of a business, and in which the profit maximization assumption leads to theoretical conclusions that are inconsistent with practice: pricing and capital budgeting.

WHAT ABOUT PRICING?

If he is to maximize profits, the businessman must set a price such that the marginal revenue equals the marginal cost. This means that as a minimum he must estimate the demand at all prices and the marginal cost at all volumes, and he must further estimate the extent to which demand is interdependent with cost because of advertising and other order-getting expenditures. In short, he is supposed to estimate all the values for all the lines on Exhibit I.

This is a fantastically difficult task, so difficult that it is rarely attempted in practice. All studies of actual practice that I am aware of testify to its rarity.[7] Who can accurately estimate the demand for a product at even one price? Instead, the studies show that in most pricing problems the emphasis is on the construction of a "normal" price. Rather than attempting the ritual suggested by the economist's diagram in Exhibit I, the businessman goes through a much simpler process:

He builds up a cost—including direct costs, a fair share of indirect costs, and a satisfactory profit margin; he speculates whether he can probably obtain

---

7. One of the earliest of these studies was reported in "Price Theory and Business Behavior" by R. L. Hall and C. J. Hitch (Oxford, Clarendon Press, 1939, Oxford Economic Paper, No. 2); see also Robert F. Canzillotti, "Pricing Objectives in Large Companies," *American Economic Review*, December 1958, pp. 921–940.

an adequate volume at a price based on this cost; he considers competitive pressures and strategic matters; and thus he arrives at his price. He may vary the profit margin, depending on circumstances, and he may also vary the cost by changing the design of the product, but his starting point is a price based on total cost as derived from a conventional cost accounting system, not a price based on marginal cost. His reasoning is that if each product contributes a fair share toward overhead costs and profit, then he will make a satisfactory profit on the aggregate of all products.

The profit arrived at by this method will probably not be the maximum profit that could be earned from prices computed from economic analyses, but the businessman is much more comfortable about the likelihood of obtaining this profit than he would be if he relied on the host of guesses required under the marginal approach.

Furthermore, pricing is not the dominant focus of management attention that the economists suggest. Pricing is one element of the total marketing mix which includes also merchandising, branding, channels of distribution, personal selling, advertising, promotions, packaging, display, and servicing.

TIMES FOR RE-EXAMINATION

Having established his normal price, he will find that he must re-examine it in many situations. The profit maximizer's approach to these situations, too, is unrealistic. For example, Customer A tells the salesman of a manufacturing firm: "I'll give you an order for Product X if you'll cut 5¢ a pound off the regular price." To decide whether to accept this offer, a profits maximizer requires at least this information:

▶ The marginal revenue and marginal costs associated with this specific order, which require an analysis of each cost element that may be affected by it.

▶ The probable consequences of losing the customer's business, both on sales of Product X and on sales of other products, if the order is refused.

▶ The probable effect on other customers who buy Product X and on buyers of all other products, so as to determine whether idle capacity will exist.

▶ The probability that the customer means what he says.

Textbook analyses of such a problem usually suggest that the order should be accepted if marginal revenue exceeds marginal costs, if idle capacity is available, and if the impact on future

business with Customer A and on other customers is not serious. Some authors even favor a computation of the present value of the expected values of various chains of consequences on prices and costs that might ensue if the order were accepted, or if it were rejected. The only time in which these computations would not be made is when the cost of obtaining the information exceeds the value of the order.

To be sure, there *are* circumstances under which the businessman will undertake parts of such an analysis—when the company is hungry for business, for example. But he will not do this every day for every order. Instead, he will reason in some fashion like this:

Let's stick to our price. To deviate from it would touch off a lot of reactions, the consequences of which are too difficult to figure. Maybe we will lose some marginal profit, but maybe also we can pick up some unforeseen new business that will produce a profit from the same production facilities.

The profit maximizer tells the businessman to accept the order unless he knows of other orders that will use the same capacity. The businessman ordinarily takes the opposite approach: "I don't have any idea where the orders are coming from, or even if they are coming, but I'm sure going to try to get them." The fact that the sales force will work harder to get business when times are bad is another idea that is not consistent with profit maximization.

It is interesting to speculate what would happen if, when you take your automobile to the garage for servicing, you and the service manager negotiated a price according to the rules of the profit maximizers, with both of you attempting to estimate, among other things, the probability that other cars will use up today's service capacity and the utility of having your car available at a certain time!

If the only relevant costs are marginal costs, then cost accounting with its allocations of depreciation, overhead, and other joint costs to products is a useless ritual, or at most an unnecessarily complicated way of determining inventory values. Some economists indeed assert that cost accounting is useless for pricing. For example, take this quotation: "It is difficult to name an occasion when pure cost-plus pricing is in the seller's best interest."[8] Yet practical businessmen would find it very easy to name *many* such occasions, I believe. And hundreds of thousands of companies have

8. Alfred R. Oxenfeldt, *Pricing New Products*, p. 27 of AMA Management Report No. 8, 1958.

cost accounting systems that do allocate costs to products, they spend not insignificant amounts to operate such systems, and presumably they think these expenditures are worthwhile.

WHAT ABOUT CAPITAL BUDGETING?

To be consistent with the profit maximization premise, a firm should invest in new assets whenever the return from the investment is equal to or greater than the marginal cost of capital, provided that there is no other available investment opportunity which will permit an even greater return. In theory, therefore, the businessman is supposed always to know his marginal cost of capital, and he is supposed to know about and evaluate all other investment opportunities every time a project is presented for consideration.

In practice, this is too difficult. John R. Meyer and Edwin Kuh, for example, analyzed all the studies of investment behavior they could find, and in only one of them—a 1951 study of public utilities—was there any evidence supporting the validity of the profit maximization premises. They themselves analyzed published data on 750 firms over a five-year period, and found "nothing to justify any claim to unique superiority for any one theory above all other alternatives."[9]

Evidently, businessmen take a much less complicated approach; they set up criteria such as maximum payback or minimum acceptable return, which if things work out as anticipated will ensure a satisfactory profit. This leads to quite different working rules from those prescribed by the economists; indeed, the difference in the literature between articles by economists and articles by practical businessmen on this subject is so great that it is difficult to believe they are writing about the same problem.

CLARIFYING THE DIFFERENCES

Pricing and capital investment problems are not the only soft spots in the profit maximization concept. Let us proceed with our catechism.

QUESTION: *Are there other inconsistencies between practice and profit maximization?*

There are a number of them. The practice of corporate donations is one which, although not of great magnitude, is of special interest because the

contrast between profit maximization and practice is so clear-cut.

The profit maximizer attempts to explain away a corporate donation to the Community Fund by saying it is made to promote a favorable climate for the company in the community and hence is consistent with long-run profit maximization. But how, then, can he explain the fact that corporate contributions to charity decline in a recession? If the size of the contribution were derived from a maximization kind of reasoning, one would expect either that a recession would have no effect or, since the need is greater and many companies are quite liquid in a recession, that contributions actually would increase. The obvious explanation is that managements feel *less able* to give when times are bad, a phenomenon perfectly consistent with the idea that they seek to maintain a satisfactory profit.

Performance appraisal techniques are another illustration. When we are judging how well a manager has performed, the profit maximizer says we must be indifferent to the fact that the business made a profit, or even to the fact that its profit performance is better than that of competitors or better than the results of a year ago. Instead, we should give the management a pat on the back if, *and only if,* we are convinced that it has squeezed out the last possible dollar of profits. Actually, however, it is nonsense to assert that this is the way managements are in fact judged. They are judged, and their bonuses paid, on the basis of improvement or of comparisons against other managements; this is a comparative, not a maximization idea.

Looking around us at the real world of business, we might raise other questions about the consistency of profit maximization with management practice:

► Why give an employee a separation payment when he is discharged?

► Why don't executives spend all their waking hours at work?

► Why have a lawn around the plant, and why spend money to mow it?

► Why do research expenditures tend to vary directly, rather than inversely, with profits?

► Why are cost-cutting campaigns instituted in times of recession?

► What is the sense of a cost-cutting campaign anyway if costs are always supposed to be at a minimum?

► If prices are always as high as possible, how can a wage or material cost increase lead to a price increase?

9. *The Investment Decision, An Empirical Study* (Cambridge, Harvard University Press, 1957), p. 204.

QUESTION: *Are not the phenomena earlier described* approximately *the same as profit maximization?*

They most certainly are not. A pricing theory that starts with a marginal analysis is completely different from a pricing theory that starts with a full cost analysis. An investment theory built around the cost of capital is in important respects different from an investment theory built around a satisfactory return concept.

QUESTION: *Are not these phenomena consistent with long-run profit maximization?*

No. It is true that in the long run all costs are incremental, and a pricing calculation made in accordance with a long-run profit maximization premise would contain the same elements as a pricing calculation based on conventional full costs. The numbers in these two calculations would be quite different, however. The profit maximizer's long-run cost calculation must be an estimate of future replacement costs; the conventional cost calculation deals with current costs. The two would be the same only in an absolutely static economy.

QUESTION: *Are business policies and business practices consistent with other maximization concepts?*

No, they are not consistent with welfare maximization — nor satisfaction maximization, nor minimax, nor any of the other elaborate concepts that economists have conjured up in an attempt to find a maximizing theory that can be reconciled with real life. In short, the events we observe in business are not consistent with *any* version of maximization. They are instead related to such notions as "balance," "equity," or "adequacy." The calculus of maximization will not fit these notions any more than it will define what constitutes an excellent dinner, a beautiful woman, a healthy man, a sound tax policy, or an adequate military establishment.

IMPOSSIBLE IDEAL

QUESTION: *Should not businessmen maximize, even if they do not in practice?*

It is, of course, appropriate to make a distinction between a descriptive statement and a normative statement, between what businessmen actually do and what they should do. But if the normative statement differs from real life, then the theorist is obligated to explain the discrepancy. Profit maximizers can make this explanation on only two grounds: either businessmen are stupid or they are ignorant. The first is not worth discussing. Ignorance, in its literal sense of "not being aware of," is in fact a valid explanation of why sound new ideas are not immediately and universally adopted. It therefore at least qualifies as a possible explanation.

But the profit maximizer's techniques are not new. Most of them have been around for 50 years or more. Many responsible businessmen were exposed to them as college students. When we observe how such intricate concepts as statistical quality control, economic lot size, linear programing, information processing, and other techniques for improving efficiency gain fast and widespread acceptance, while the concepts of marginal income pricing and cost of capital cutoffs are not noticeably more prevalent than they were a generation ago — then clearly we have grounds for wondering if the economist's error is perhaps a better explanation than the businessman's ignorance.

There are two excellent reasons why businessmen do not attempt to maximize: it would be too difficult, and it would be immoral. The practical difficulties of applying a profit maximization concept have been discussed in the sections on pricing and capital budgeting. What about the moral aspects?

The ethical problem is that profit maximization requires that the business manager think only of the best interest of the shareholders, whereas any responsible manager knows that he must actually consider the interest of all parties who have a stake in the business, of which the shareholders are only one. Profit maximization requires the businessman to use every trick he can think of to keep wages and fringe benefits down, to extract the last possible dollar from the consumer, to sell as low quality merchandise as he can legally hoodwink the customer into buying, to use income solely for the benefits of the stockholder, to disclaim any responsibility to the community, to finagle the lowest possible price from his vendors regardless of its effect on them, and so on.

The profit maximizers admit that in doing these things, the businessman must have regard for the long-run consequences of his actions, but as they themselves point out, the "long run" is a long way off and its effect on current decisions is nebulous. They deny the existence of a businessman's conscience, and they exclude ethical considerations as being irrelevant to the subject.

A businessman is a human being, and it is completely unrealistic to assume that he should act in an ethical vacuum. As a human being, he is deeply concerned with how his actions jibe with his own conscience, the respect of his family, and the opinions of his associates. Moral standards change, and whereas 50 or 100 years ago the profit maximizing manager would perhaps have been tolerated in some circles of some communities, today society clearly expects the businessman to act responsibly. He cannot do this and at the same time seek to maximize the share of income going to just one of the several parties that have a stake in the business.

SOCIAL PRESSURES

Laws reflect a society's ethical standards, and by such laws as the Fair Labor Standards Act, Robinson — Patman Act, Sherman Act, Clayton Act, and the many state pricing and labor acts, society is telling business that it disapproves of profit maximization. When President Eisenhower asks the steel companies to hold the line on prices, he is not displaying the complete naiveté assumed by the economists; rather, he expresses the nation's conviction as to how steel companies should act. It is blindness to build a theory on the premise that businessmen completely disregard such beliefs. In fact, I doubt very much if an economist could imagine himself running a business with no ethical standard, as required by profit maximization.

In short, businessmen could not maximize if they wanted to, and they would not want to if they could.

In his normative statements, the economist assumes that the businessman should be an "economic man" — an omniscient, completely rational, unfeeling, amoral automaton. The social psychologists have long since given up theories based on the thesis that the individual worker is an "economic man," nor are theories of the market based on the assumption that the consumer is an "economic man" regarded as having any validity today. Why do the profit maximizers believe that Adam Smith was right about managers when they know that he was wrong about workers and consumers?

THE ALTERNATIVE

QUESTION: *Does not the satisfactory return idea lead to a loose set of concepts?*

The concepts of a satisfactory return model are indeed not as precise as those erected on a profit maximization base. However, to criticize

the satisfactory return assumption on this account is comparable to criticizing the physicists for their acceptance of Heisenberg's uncertainty principle. In both cases, the resulting body of theory is less precise, but it is also more realistic.

The satisfactory return assumption does not imply that decision rules are swept away and that management actions become entirely subjective. The satisfactory return for a particular business can be described — not precisely, but within reasonable limits. The lower limit is the company's expected cost of capital, and the upper limit is related to the profit opportunities inherent in the industry. Within these limits, the figure will vary with circumstances — chiefly the aggressiveness of the management and its attitude toward risk and growth.

Nor does it follow that the acceptance of this assumption means that income is distributed according to the dictates of management, as implied by Mason.[10] Labor unions, boards of directors, investors, bankers, and the government all exert pressure to ensure that the group each represents receives an equitable share of the revenue. Mason is quite right in pointing out that the share going to each group cannot be precisely determined by the satisfactory return theory, whereas the profit maximization theory does give a precise answer to this problem. The trouble is that this precise answer is wrong.

It is equally fallacious to argue that the satisfactory return concept implies that managers are lazy. Certainly, they will vigorously seek out opportunities to improve profits when they can do so ethically, and competition will force them to seek ways to improve efficiency even if no increase in profits results. In our vigorous, dynamic society, considerable effort is required merely to hold one's own.

Let me suggest that those who believe that satisfactory return is not an adequate stimulus to management ought to take a try at managing before they publicize such opinions.

IMPROVEMENTS NEEDED

Admittedly, the concepts based on the satisfactory return idea are far from adequately worked out at present. This is because economists have only recently begun to work on them. If, for example, economists interested in price theory turned their attention away from the fine points of marginal income analysis to the problems of constructing the most useful full cost, they could make important contributions. And, incidentally,

---

10. Mason, op. cit.

such a change in focus would have the happy consequence that economists would become less patronizing toward cost accountants. In the capital budgeting area, they could develop useful approaches to the many perplexing problems that arise in attempting to select the most attractive investment opportunities from those available. They might even make important contributions to accounting theory, which is now a curious mixture of concepts implying profit maximization and concepts implying satisfactory return.

The model of a business that results from all this work will be less exact than the model that the student now learns about. This inexactness should not be glossed over; it should instead be stressed in much the same way that models of weather systems or of community relationships are taught as being only rough approximations of reality. Much less attention should be given to the fine points implied in the over-all model and much more attention to an analysis of the realities of specific business situations. The latter is more valuable than drawing diagrams that require omniscience and clairvoyance to duplicate in practice.

CONCLUSION

I have tried to show that profit maximization is not a valid assumption to explain either how businessmen actually behave or how they should behave. I believe that this assumption is unrealis-

tic because (1) *profit maximization is too difficult* and (2) *it is immoral.*

The consequences of the profit maximizers' misinterpretation are not only that their concepts are not useful to businessmen, but also that they happen to be conveying a false impression of what our economy really is like. Consider this statement, which is part of Samuelson's summary of the essence of our economic system:

A rich man's dog may receive the milk that a poor child needs to avoid rickets. Why? Because supply and demand are working badly? No. Because they are doing what they are designed to do—putting goods in the hands of those who can pay the most, who have the money votes.[11]

This is a shocking statement. If it were true, no one should be proud of the American system; such a system would certainly not be welcomed in other countries. If it were true, we should prefer communism.

The plain fact is that this statement is not true. Our system does not condone, let alone encourage, fattening dogs by starving children. Our system *is* one of which we may be proud. It can be described accurately if the assumption of profit maximization is discarded for the idea of satisfactory return. Such a change will lead to more accurate reporting and to the development of more useful rules and concepts, concepts which focus on the businessman's responsibility to all the parties at interest, concepts which we can be proud of, and which will lead to improvements in our system of which we can be even more proud.

8—How to Evaluate Corporate Strategy

SEYMOUR TILLES

No good military officer would undertake even a small-scale attack on a limited objective without a clear concept of his strategy. No seasoned politician would undertake a campaign for a major office without an equally clear concept of his strategy. In the field of business management, however, we frequently find men deploying resources on a large scale without any clear notion of what their strategy is. And yet a company's strategy is a vital ingredient in determining its

future. A valid strategy will yield growth, profit, or whatever other objectives the managers have established. An inappropriate strategy not only will fail to yield benefits, but also may result in disaster.

In this article I will try to demonstrate the truth of these contentions by examining the experiences of a number of companies. I shall discuss what strategy is, how it can be evaluated, and how, by evaluating its strategy, a management can do much to assure the future of the enterprise.

11. Samuelson, op. cit., p. 42.

"How to Evaluate Corporate Strategy," *Harvard Business Review*, XLI (July–August 1963), 111–121. Reprinted by permission of the author and the publisher. **Seymour Tilles:** Graduate School of Business Administration, Harvard University.

DECISIVE IMPACT

The influence of strategy can be seen in every age and in every area of industry. Here are some examples:

►From the time it was started in 1911 as the Computing-Tabulating-Recording Co., International Business Machines Corporation has demonstrated the significance of a soundly conceived strategy. Seeing itself in the data-system business at a time when most manufacturers were still preoccupied with individual pieces of equipment, IBM developed a set of policies which resulted in its dominating the office equipment industry.

►By contrast, Packard in the 1930's was to the automobile industry everything that IBM is today to the office machine industry. In 1937, it sold over 109,000 cars, compared with about 11,000 for Cadillac. By 1954 it had disappeared as an independent producer.

Strategy is, of course, not the only factor determining a company's success or failure. The competence of its managerial leadership is significant as well. Luck can be a factor, too (although often what people call good luck is really the product of good strategy). But a valid strategy can gain extraordinary results for the company whose general level of competence is only average. And, conversely, the most inspiring leaders who are locked into an inappropriate strategy will have to exert their full competence and energy merely in order to keep from losing ground.

When Hannibal inflicted the humiliating defeat on the Roman army at Cannae in 216 B.C., he led a ragged band against soldiers who were in possession of superior arms, better training, and competent "noncoms." His strategy, however, was so superior that all of those advantages proved to be relatively insignificant. Similarly, when Jacob Borowsky made Lestoil the hottest-selling detergent in New England some years ago, he was performing a similar feat—relying on strategy to battle competition with superior resources.

Strategy is important not only for aspiring Davids who need an offensive device to combat corporate Goliaths. It is significant also for the large organization faced with a wide range of choice in domestic and international operations. For instance, the following corporations are all in the midst of strategic changes, the implications of which are worldwide in scope:

►Massey-Ferguson, Ltd., with 26 factories located around the world, and vying for leadership in the farm-equipment industry.

► General Electric Company and Westinghouse Electric Corporation, the giant producers of electrical equipment who are recasting their competitive policies.

► Singer Sewing Machine Company, trying to make its vast assets yield a greater return.

DYNAMIC CONCEPT

A strategy is a set of goals and major policies. The definition is as simple as that. But while the notion of a strategy is extremely easy to grasp, working out an agreed-upon statement for a given company can be a fundamental contribution to the organization's future success.

In order to develop such a statement, managers must be able to identify precisely what is meant by a goal and what is meant by a major policy. Otherwise, the process of strategy determination may degenerate into what it so often becomes—the solemn recording of platitudes, useless for either the clarification of direction or the achievement of consensus.

IDENTIFYING GOALS

Corporate goals are an indication of what the company as a whole is trying to *achieve* and to *become*. Both parts—the achieving and the becoming—are important for a full understanding of what a company hopes to attain. For example:

► Under the leadership of Alfred Sloan, General Motors achieved a considerable degree of external success; this was accomplished because Sloan worked out a pattern for the kind of company he wanted it to be internally.

► Similarly, the remarkable record of Du Pont in the twentieth century and the growth of Sears, Roebuck under Julius Rosenwald were as much a tribute to their modified structure as to their external strategy.[1]

Achieving. In order to state what a company expects to achieve, it is important to state what it hopes to do with respect to its environment. For instance:

Ernest Breech, chairman of the board of the Ford Motor Company, said that the strategy formulated by his company in 1946 was based on a desire "to hold our own in what we foresaw would be a rich but hotly competitive market."[2] The view of the environment

---

1. For an interesting discussion of this relationship, see A. D. Chandler, Jr., *Strategy and Structure* (Cambridge, Massachusetts Institute of Technology Press, 1962), pp. 1–17.
2. See Edward C. Bursk and Dan H. Fenn, Jr., *Planning the Future Strategy of Your Business* (New York, McGraw-Hill Book Company, Inc., 1956), p. 8.

implicit in this statement is unmistakable: an expanding over-all demand, increasing competition, and emphasis on market share as a measure of performance against competitors.

Clearly, a statement of what a company hopes to achieve may be much more varied and complex than can be contained in a single sentence. This will be especially true for those managers who are sophisticated enough to perceive that a company operates in more external "systems" than the market. The firm is part not only of a market but also of an industry, the community, the economy, and other systems. In each case there are unique relationships to observe (e.g., with competitors, municipal leaders, Congress, and so on). A more complete discussion of this point is contained in a previous HBR article.[3]

Becoming. If you ask young men what they want to accomplish by the time they are 40, the answers you get fall into two distinct categories. There are those—the great majority—who will respond in terms of what they want to *have*. This is especially true of graduate students of business administration. There are some men, however, who will answer in terms of the kind of men they hope to *be*. These are the only ones who have a clear idea of where they are going.

The same is true of companies. For far too many companies, what little thinking goes on about the future is done primarily in money terms. There is nothing wrong with financial planning. Most companies should do more of it. But there is a basic fallacy in confusing a financial plan with thinking about the kind of company you want yours to become. It is like saying, "When I'm 40, I'm going to be *rich*." It leaves too many basic questions unanswered. Rich in what way? Rich doing what?

The other major fallacy in stating what you want to become is to say it only in terms of a product. The number of companies who have got themselves into trouble by falling in love with a particular product is distressingly great.[4] Perhaps the saddest examples are those giants of American industry who defined their future in terms of continuing to be the major suppliers of steam locomotives to the nation's railroads. In fact, those companies were so wedded to this concept of their future that they formed a cartel in order to keep General Motors out of the steam locomotive business. When the diesel locomotive proved its superiority to steam, these companies all but disappeared.

The lesson of these experiences is that a key

element of setting goals is the ability to see them in terms of more than a single dimension. Both money and product policy are part of a statement of objectives; but it is essential that these be viewed as the concrete expressions of a more abstract set of goals—the satisfaction of the needs of significant groups which cooperate to ensure the company's continued existence.

Who are these groups? There are many—customers, managers, employees, stockholders, to mention just the major ones. The key to corporate success is the company's ability to identify the important needs of each of these groups, to establish some balance among them, and to work out a set of operating policies which permits their satisfaction. This set of policies, as a pattern, identifies what the company is trying to be.

THE GROWTH FAD

Many managers have a view of their company's future which is strikingly analogous to the child's view of himself. When asked what they want their companies to become over the next few years, they reply, "bigger."

There are a great many rationalizations for this preoccupation with growth. Probably the one most frequently voiced is that which says, "You have to grow or die." What must be appreciated, however, is that "bigger" for a company has enormous implications for management. It involves a different way of life, and one which many managers may not be suited for—either in terms of temperament or skills.

Moreover, whether for a large company or a small one, "bigger," by itself, may not make economic sense. Companies which are highly profitable at their present size may grow into bankruptcy very easily; witness the case of Grayson-Robinson Stores, Inc., a chain of retail stores. Starting out as a small but profitable chain, it grew rapidly into receivership. Conversely, a company which is not now profitable may more successfully seek its survival in cost reduction than in sales growth. Chrysler is a striking example of this approach.

There is, in the United States, a business philosophy which reflects the frontier heritage of the country. It is one which places a high value on growth, in physical terms. The manager whose corporate sales are not increasing, the number of whose subordinates is not growing, whose plants are not expanding, feels that he is not successful.

---

3. Seymour Tilles, "The Manager's Job—A Systems Approach," HBR January—February 1963, p. 73.
4. See Theodore Levitt, "Marketing Myopia," HBR July—August 1960, p. 45.

But there is a dangerous trap in this kind of thinking. More of the same is not necessarily progress. In addition, few managers are capable of running units several times larger than the ones they now head. The great danger of whole-hearted consumer acceptance or an astute program of corporate acquisition is that it frequently propels managers into situations that are beyond their present competence. Such cases — and they are legion — emphasize that in stating corporate objectives, bigger is not always better. A dramatic example is that of the Ampex Corporation:

> From 1950 to 1960, Ampex's annual sales went from less than $1,000,000 to more than $73,000,000. Its earnings went from $115,000 to nearly $4,000,000. The following year, the company reported a decline in sales to $70,000,000, and a net loss of $3,900,000. The *Wall Street Journal* reported: "As one source close to the company put it, Ampex's former management 'was intelligent and well-educated, but simply lacked the experience necessary to control' the company's rapid development."[5]

ROLE OF POLICY

A policy says something about *how* goals will be attained. It is what statisticians would call a "decision rule," and what systems engineers would call a "standing plan." It tells people what they should and should not do in order to contribute to achievement of corporate goals.

A policy should be more than just a platitude. It should be a helpful guide to making strategy explicit, and providing direction to subordinates. Consequently, the more definite it is, the more helpful it can be. "We will provide our stockholders with a fair return," is a policy no one could possibly disagree with — or be helped by. What *is* a fair return? This is the type of question that must be answered before the company's intentions become clear.

The job of management is not merely the preparation of valid policies for a standard set of activities; it is the much more challenging one of first deciding what activities are so strategically significant that explicit decision-rules in that area are mandatory. No standard set of policies can be considered major for all companies. Each company is a unique situation. It must decide for itself which aspects of corporate life are most relevant to its own aspirations and work out policy statements for them. For example, advertising may be insignificant to a company which provides research services to the Defense Department, but critical to a firm trying to mass-merchandise luxury goods.

It is difficult to generalize about which policies are major, even within a particular industry, because a number of extraordinarily successful companies appear to violate all the rules. To illustrate:

▶ In the candy industry it would seem safe to generalize that advertising should be a major policy area. However, the Hershey Company, which is so successful that its name is practically the generic term for the product, has persistently followed a policy of no advertising.

▶ Similarly, in the field of high-fidelity components, one would expect that dealer relations would be a critical policy area. But Acoustics Research, Inc., has built an enviable record of sales growth and of profitability by relying entirely on consumer pull.

NEED TO BE EXPLICIT

The first thing to be said about corporate strategy is that having one is a step forward. Any strategy, once made explicit, can quickly be evaluated and improved. But if no attempt is ever made to commit it to paper, there is always the danger that the strategy is either incomplete or misunderstood.

Many successful companies are not aware of the strategy that underlies their success. It is quite possible for a company to achieve initial success without real awareness of its causes. However, it is much more difficult to successfully *branch out into new ventures* without a precise appreciation of their strategic significance. This is why many established companies fail miserably when they attempt a program of corporate acquisition, product diversification, or market expansion. One illustration of this is cited by Myles L. Mace and George G. Montgomery in their recent study of corporate acquisitions:

> "A basic resin company . . . bought a plastic boat manufacturer because this seemed to present a controlled market for a portion of the resin it produced. It soon found that the boat business was considerably different from the manufacture and sale of basic chemicals. After a short but unpleasant experience in manufacturing and trying to market what was essentially a consumer's item, the management concluded that its experience and abilities lay essentially in industrial rather than consumer-type products."[6]

5. "R₂ for Ampex: Drastic Changes Help Solve Big Headache of Fast Corporate Growth," *Wall Street Journal*, September 17, 1962, p. 1.

6. *Management Problems of Corporate Acquisitions* (Boston, Division of Research, Harvard Business School, 1962), p. 60.

Another reason for making strategy explicit is the assistance it provides for delegation and for coordination. To an ever-increasing extent, management is a team activity, whereby groups of executives contribute to corporate success. Making strategy explicit makes it far easier for each executive to appreciate what the over-all goals are, and what his own contribution to them must be.

MAKING AN EVALUATION

Is your strategy right for you? There are six criteria on which to base an answer. These are:

1. Internal consistency.
2. Consistency with the environment.
3. Appropriateness in the light of available resources.
4. Satisfactory degree of risk.
5. Appropriate time horizon.
6. Workability.

If all of these criteria are met, you have a strategy that is right for you. This is as much as can be asked. There is no such thing as a good strategy in any absolute, objective sense. In the remainder of this article I shall discuss the criteria in some detail.

1. *Is the strategy internally consistent?* Internal consistency refers to the cumulative impact of individual policies on corporate goals. In a well-worked-out strategy, each policy fits into an integrated pattern. It should be judged not only in terms of itself, but also in terms of how it relates to other policies which the company has established and to the goals it is pursuing.

In a dynamic company consistency can never be taken for granted. For example:

Many family-owned organizations pursue a pair of policies which soon become inconsistent: rapid expansion and retention of exclusive family control of the firm. If they are successful in expanding, the need for additional financing soon raises major problems concerning the extent to which exclusive family control can be maintained.

While this pair of policies is especially prevalent among smaller firms, it is by no means limited to them. The Ford Motor Company after World War II and the New York Times today are examples of quite large, family-controlled organizations that have had to reconcile the two conflicting aims.

The criterion of internal consistency is an especially important one for evaluating strategies because it identifies those areas where strategic choices will eventually have to be made. An inconsistent strategy does *not* necessarily mean that the company is currently in difficulty. But it does mean that unless management keeps its eye on a particular area of operation, it may well find itself forced to make a choice without enough time either to search for or to prepare attractive alternatives.

2. *Is the strategy consistent with the environment?* A firm which has a certain product policy, price policy, or advertising policy is saying that it has chosen to relate itself to its customers — actual and potential — in a certain way. Similarly, its policies with respect to government contracts, collective bargaining, foreign investment, and so forth are expressions of relationship with other groups and forces. Hence an important test of strategy is whether the chosen policies are consistent with the environment — whether they really make sense with respect to what is going on outside.

Consistency with the environment has both a static and a dynamic aspect. In a static sense, it implies judging the efficacy of policies with respect to the environment as it exists *now*. In a dynamic sense, it means judging the efficacy of policies with respect to the environment *as it appears to be changing*. One purpose of a viable strategy is to ensure the long-run success of an organization. Since the environment of a company is constantly changing, ensuring success over the long run means that management must constantly be assessing the degree to which policies previously established are consistent with the environment as its exists now; and whether current policies take into account the environment as it will be in the future. In one sense, therefore, establishing a strategy is like aiming at a moving target: you have to be concerned not only with present position but also with the speed and direction of movement.

Failure to have a strategy consistent with the environment can be costly to the organization. Ford's sad experience with the Edsel is by now a textbook example of such failure. Certainly, had Ford pushed the Falcon at the time when it was pushing the Edsel, and with the same resources, it would have a far stronger position in the world automobile market today.

Illustrations of strategies that have not been consistent with the environment are easy to find by using hindsight. *But the reason that such examples are plentiful is not that foresight is difficult to apply.* It is because even today few companies are seriously engaged in analyzing environmental trends and using this intelligence as a basis for managing their own futures.

3. *Is the strategy appropriate in view of the available resources?* Resources are those things that a company *is* or *has* and that help it to achieve its corporate objectives. Included are money, competence, and facilities; but these by no means complete the list. In companies selling consumer goods, for example, the major resource may be the name of the product. In any case, there are two basic issues which management must decide in relating strategy and resources. These are:
► What are our critical resources?
► Is the proposed strategy appropriate for available resources?
Let us look now at what is meant by a "critical resource" and at how the criterion of resource utilization can be used as a basis for evaluating strategy.

CRITICAL RESOURCES

The essential strategic attribute of resources is that they represent action potential. Taken together, a company's resources represent its capacity to respond to threats and opportunities that may be perceived in the environment. In other words, resources are the bundle of chips that the company has to play with in the serious game of business.

From an action-potential point of view, a resource may be critical in two senses: (1) as the factor limiting the achievement of corporate goals; and (2) as that which the company will exploit as the basis for its strategy. Thus, critical resources are both what the company has most of and what it has least of.

The three resources most frequently identified as critical are money, competence, and physical facilities. Let us look at the strategic significance of each.

Money. Money is a particularly valuable resource because it provides the greatest flexibility of response to events as they arise. It may be considered the "safest" resource, in that safety may be equated with the freedom to choose from among the widest variety of future alternatives. Companies that wish to reduce their short-run risk will therefore attempt to accumulate the greatest reservoir of funds they can.

However, it is important to remember that while the accumulation of funds may offer short-run security, it may place the company at a serious competitive disadvantage with respect to

other companies which are following a higher-risk course.

The classical illustration of this kind of outcome is the strategy pursued by Montgomery Ward under the late Sewell Avery. As reported in *Fortune*:

"While Sears confidently bet on a new and expanding America, Avery developed an *idée fixe* that postwar inflation would end in a crash no less serious than that of 1929. Following this idea, he opened no new stores but rather piled up cash to the ceiling in preparation for an economic debacle that never came. In these years, Ward's balance sheet gave a somewhat misleading picture of its prospects. Net earnings remained respectably high, and were generally higher than those of Sears as a percentage of sales. In 1946, earnings after taxes were $52 million. They rose to $74 million in 1950, and then declined to $35 million in 1954. Meanwhile, however, sales remained static, and in Avery's administration profits and liquidity were maintained at the expense of growth. In 1954, Ward had $327 million in cash and securities, $147 million in receivables, and $216 million in inventory, giving it a total current-asset position of $690 million and net worth of $639 million. It was liquid, all right, but it was also the shell of a once great company."[7]

Competence. Organizations survive because they are good at doing those things which are necessary to keep them alive. However, the degree of competence of a given organization is by no means uniform across the broad range of skills necessary to stay in business. Some companies are particularly good at marketing, others especially good at engineering, still others depend primarily on their financial sophistication. Philip Selznick refers to that which a company is particularly good at as its "distinctive competence."[8]

In determining a strategy, management must carefully appraise its own skill profile in order to determine where its strengths and weaknesses lie. It must then adopt a strategy which makes the greatest use of its strengths. To illustrate:
► The competence of *The New York Times* lies primarily in giving extensive and insightful coverage of events—the ability to report "all the news that's fit to print." It is neither highly profitable (earning only 1.5% of revenues in 1960—far less than, say, the *Wall Street Journal*), nor aggressively sold. Its decision to publish a West Coast and an international edition is a gamble that the strength

7. "Montgomery Ward: Prosperity Is Still Around the Corner," *Fortune*, November 1960, p. 140.
8. *Leadership in Administration* (Evanston, Illinois, Row, Peterson & Company, 1957), p. 42.

of its "distinctive competence" will make it accepted even outside of New York.

► Because of a declining demand for soft coal, many producers of soft coal are diversifying into other fields. All of them, however, are remaining true to some central skill that they have developed over the years. For instance:

a. Consolidation Coal is moving from simply the mining of soft coal to the mining *and transportation* of soft coal. It is planning with Texas Eastern Transmission Corporation to build a $100-million pipeline that would carry a mixture of powdered coal and water from West Virginia to the East Coast.

b. North American Coal Company, on the other hand, is moving toward becoming a chemical company. It recently joined with Strategic Materials Corporation to perfect a process for extracting aluminum sulfate from the mine shale that North American produces in its coal-running operations.

James L. Hamilton, president of the Island Creek Coal Co., has summed up the concept of distinctive competence in a colorful way:

"We are a career company dedicated to coal, and we have some very definite ideas about growth and expansion within the industry. We're not thinking of buying a cotton mill and starting to make shirts."[9]

Physical Facilities. Physical facilities are the resource whose strategic influence is perhaps most frequently misunderstood. Managers seem to be divided among those, usually technical men, who are enamored of physical facilities as the tangible symbol of the corporate entity; and those, usually financial men, who view physical facilities as an undesirable but necessary freezing of part of the company's funds. The latter group is dominant. In many companies, return on investment has emerged as virtually the sole criterion for deciding whether or not a particular facility should be acquired.

Actually, this is putting the cart before the horse. Physical facilities have significance primarily in relationship to over-all corporate strategy. It is, therefore, only in relationship to *other* aspects of corporate strategy that the acquisition or disposition of physical facilities can be determined. The total investment required and the projected return on it have a place in this determination —but only as an indication of the financial implications of a particular strategic decision and not as an exclusive criterion for its own sake.

Any appraisal of a company's physical facilities as a strategic resource must consider the relationship of the company to its environment. Facilities have no intrinsic value for their own sake. Their value to the company is either in their location relative to markets, to sources of labor, or to materials; or in their efficiency relative to existing or impending competitive installations. Thus, the essential considerations in any decision regarding physical facilities are a projection of changes likely to occur in the environment and a prediction about what the company's responses to these are likely to be.

Here are two examples of the necessity for relating an evaluation of facilities to environmental changes:

► Following the end of World War II, all domestic producers of typewriters in the United States invested heavily in plant facilities in this country. They hypothesized a rapid increase of sales throughout the world. This indeed took place, but it was short-lived. The rise of vigorous overseas competitors, especially Olivetti and Olympia, went hand in hand with a booming overseas market. At home, IBM's electric typewriter took more and more of the domestic market. Squeezed between these two pressures, the rest of the U.S. typewriter industry found itself with a great deal of excess capacity following the Korean conflict. Excess capacity is today still a major problem in this field.

► The steady decline in the number of farms in the United States and the emergence of vigorous overseas competition have forced most domestic full-line manufacturers of farm equipment to sharply curtail total plant area. For example, in less than four years, International Harvester eliminated more than a third of its capacity (as measured in square feet of plant space) for the production of farm machinery.

The close relationship between physical facilities and environmental trends emphasizes one of the most significant attributes of fixed assets—their temporal utility. Accounting practice recognizes this in its treatment of depreciation allowances. But even when the tax laws permit generous write-offs, they should not be used as the sole basis for setting the time period over which the investment must be justified. Environmental considerations may reveal that a different time horizon is more relevant for strategy determination. To illustrate again:

► As Armstrong Cork Company moved away from natural cork to synthetic materials during the early 1950's, management considered buying facilities for the production of its raw materials—particularly polyvinyl chloride. However,

---

9. *Wall Street Journal,* September 11, 1962, p. 30.

before doing so, it surveyed the chemical industry and concluded that producers were overbuilding. It therefore decided not to invest in facilities for the manufacture of this material. The projections were valid; since 1956 polyvinyl chloride has dropped 50% in price.

A strategic approach to facilities may not only change the time horizon; it may also change the whole basis of asset valuation:

▶ Recently a substantial portion of Loew's theaters was acquired by the Tisch brothers, owners and operators of a number of successful hotels, including the Americana in Florida.[10] As long as the assets of Loew's theaters were viewed only as places for the projection of films, its theaters, however conservatively valued, seemed to be not much of a bargain. But to a keen appraiser of hotel properties the theater sites, on rather expensive real estate in downtown city areas, had considerable appeal. Whether this appraisal will be borne out is as yet unknown. At any rate, the stock, which was originally purchased at $14 (with a book value of $22), was selling at $23 in October 1962.

ACHIEVING THE RIGHT BALANCE

One of the most difficult issues in strategy determination is that of achieving a balance between strategic goals and available resources. This requires a set of necessarily empirical, but critical, estimates of the total resources required to achieve particular objectives, the rate at which they will have to be committed, and the likelihood that they will be available. The most common errors are either to fail to make these estimates at all or to be excessively optimistic about them.

One example of the unfortunate results of being wrong on these estimates is the case of Royal McBee and the computer market:

In January 1956 Royal McBee and the General Precision Equipment Corporation formed a jointly owned company—the Royal Precision Corporation—to enter the market for electronic data-processing equipment. This joint operation was a logical pooling of complementary talents. General Precision had a great deal of experience in developing and producing computers. Its Librascope Division had been selling them to the government for years. However, it lacked a commercial distribution system. Royal McBee, on the other hand, had a great deal of experience in marketing data-processing equipment, but lacked the technical competence to develop and produce a computer.

The joint venture was eminently successful, and within a short time the Royal Precision LPG-30 was the leader in the small-computer field. However, the very success of the computer venture caused Royal McBee some serious problems. The success of the Royal Precision subsidiary demanded that the partners put more and more money into it. This was no problem for General Precision, but it became an ever more serious problem for Royal McBee, which found itself in an increasingly critical cash bind. In March 1962 it sold its interest in Royal Precision to General Precision for $5 million—a price which represented a reported $6.9 million loss on the investment. Concluding that it simply did not have sufficient resources to stay with the new venture, it decided to return to its traditional strengths: typewriters and simple data-processing systems.

Another place where optimistic estimates of resources frequently cause problems is in small businesses. Surveys of the causes of small-business failure reveal that a most frequent cause of bankruptcy is inadequate resources to weather either the early period of establishment or unforeseen downturns in business conditions.

It is apparent from the preceding discussion that a critical strategic decision involves deciding: (1) how much of the company's resources to commit to opportunities currently perceived, and (2) how much to keep uncommitted as a reserve against the appearance of unanticipated demands. This decision is closely related to two other criteria for the evaluation of strategy: risk and timing. I shall now discuss these.

4. *Does the strategy involve an acceptable degree of risk?* Strategy and resources, taken together, determine the degree of risk which the company is undertaking. This is a critical managerial choice. For example, when the old Underwood Corporation decided to enter the computer field, it was making what might have been an extremely astute strategic choice. However, the fact that it ran out of money before it could accomplish anything in that field turned its pursuit of opportunity into the prelude to disaster. This is not to say that the strategy was "bad." However, the course of action pursued *was* a high-risk strategy. Had it been successful, the payoff would have been lush. The fact that it was a stupendous failure instead does not mean that it was senseless to take the gamble.

Each company must decide for itself how much risk it wants to live with. In attempting to assess the degree of risk associated with a particular strategy, management may use a variety of techniques. For example, mathematicians have developed an elegant set of techniques for choosing among a variety of strategies where you are willing to estimate the payoffs and the probabilities

10. See "The Tisches Eye Their Next $65 Million," *Fortune,* January 1960, p. 140.

associated with them. However, our concern here is not with these quantitative aspects but with the identification of some qualitative factors which may serve as a rough basis for evaluating the degree of risk inherent in a strategy. These factors are:

1. The amount of resources (on which the strategy is based) whose continued existence or value is not assured.

2. The length of the time periods to which resources are committed.

3. The proportion of resources committed to a single venture.

The greater these quantities, the greater the degree of risk that is involved.

UNCERTAIN TERM OF EXISTENCE

Since a strategy is based on resources, any resource which may disappear before the payoff has been obtained may constitute a danger to the organization. Resources may disappear for various reasons. For example, they may lose their value. This frequently happens to such resources as physical facilities and product features. Again, they may be accidentally destroyed. The most vulnerable resource here is competence. The possible crash of the company plane or the blip on the president's electrocardiogram are what make many organizations essentially speculative ventures. In fact, one of the critical attributes of highly centralized organizations is that the more centralized they are, the more speculative they are. The disappearance of the top executive, or the disruption of communication with him, may wreak havoc at subordinate levels.

However, for many companies, the possibility that critical resources may lose their value stems not so much from internal developments as from shifts in the environment. Take specialized production know-how, for example. It has value only because of demand for the product by customers—and customers may change their minds. This is cause for acute concern among the increasing number of companies whose futures depend so heavily on their ability to participate in defense contracts. A familiar case is the plight of the airframe industry following World War II. Some of the companies succeeded in making the shift from aircraft to missiles, but this has only resulted in their being faced with the same problem on a larger scale.

DURATION OF COMMITMENT

Financial analysts often look at the ratio of fixed assets to current assets in order to assess the extent to which resources are committed to long-term programs. This may or may not give a satisfactory answer. How important are the assets? When will they be paid for?

The reasons for the risk increasing as the time for payoff increases is, of course, the inherent uncertainty in any venture. Resources committed over long time spans make the company vulnerable to changes in the environment. Since the difficulty of predicting such changes increases as the time span increases, long-term projects are basically more risky than are short ones. This is especially true of companies whose environments are unstable. And today, either because of technological, political, or economic shifts, most companies are decidedly in the category of those that face major upheaval in their corporate environments. The company building its future around technological equipment, the company selling primarily to the government, the company investing in underdeveloped nations, the company selling to the Common Market, the company with a plant in the South—all these have this prospect in common.

The harsh dilemma of modern management is that the time span of decision is increasing at the same time as the corporate environment is becoming increasingly unstable. It is this dilemma which places such a premium on the manager's sensitivity to external trends today. Much has been written about his role as a commander and administrator. But it is no less important that he be a *strategist*.

SIZE OF THE STAKES

The more of its resources a company commits to a particular strategy, the more pronounced the consequences. If the strategy is successful, the payoff will be great—both to managers and investors. If the strategy fails, the consequences will be dire—both to managers and investors. Thus, a critical decision for the executive group is: What proportion of available resources should be committed to a particular course of action?

This decision may be handled in a variety of ways. For example, faced with a project that requires more of its resources than it is willing to commit, a company either may choose to refrain from undertaking the project or, alternatively, may seek to reduce the total resources required by undertaking a joint venture or by going the route of merger or acquisition in order to broaden the resource base.

The amount of resources management stands ready to commit is of particular significance where there is some likelihood that larger competitors, having greater resources, may choose to enter the company's field. Thus, those companies which entered the small-computer field in the past few years are now faced with the penetration into this area of the data-processing giants. (Both IBM and Remington Rand have recently introduced new small computers.)

I do not mean to imply that the "best" strategy is the one with the least risk. High payoffs are frequently associated with high-risk strategies. Moreover, it is a frequent but dangerous assumption to think that inaction, or lack of change, is a low-risk strategy. Failure to exploit its resources to the fullest may well be the riskiest strategy of all that an organization may pursue, as Montgomery Ward and other companies have amply demonstrated.

5. *Does the strategy have an appropriate time horizon?* A significant part of every strategy is the time horizon on which it is based. A viable strategy not only reveals what goals are to be accomplished; it says something about *when* the aims are to be achieved.

Goals, like resources, have time-based utility. A new product developed, a plant put on stream, a degree of market penetration, become significant strategic objectives only if accomplished by a certain time. Delay may deprive them of all strategic significance. A perfect example of this in the military sphere is the Sinai campaign of 1956. The strategic objective of the Israelis was not only to conquer the entire Sinai peninsula; it also was to do it in seven days. By contrast, the lethargic movement of the British troops made the operation a futile one for both England and France.

In choosing an appropriate time horizon, we must pay careful attention to the goals being pursued, and to the particular organization involved. Goals must be established far enough in advance to allow the organization to adjust to them. Organizations, like ships, cannot be "spun on a dime." Consequently, the larger the organization, the further its strategic time horizon must extend, since its adjustment time is longer. It is no mere managerial whim that the major contributions to long-range planning have emerged from the larger organizations—especially those large organizations such as Lockheed, North American Aviation, and RCA that traditionally have had to deal with highly unstable environments.

The observation that large corporations plan far ahead while small ones can get away without doing so has frequently been made. However, the significance of planning for the small but growing company has frequently been overlooked. As a company gets bigger, it must not only change the way it operates; it must also steadily push ahead its time horizon—and this is a difficult thing to do. The manager who has built a successful enterprise by his skill at "putting out fires" or the wheeler-dealer whose firm has grown by a quick succession of financial coups is seldom able to make the transition to the long look ahead.

In many cases, even if the executive were inclined to take a longer range view of events, the formal reward system seriously militates against doing so. In most companies the system of management rewards is closely related to currently reported profits. Where this is the case, executives may understandably be so preoccupied with reporting a profit year by year that they fail to spend as much time as they should in managing the company's long-term future. But if we seriously accept the thesis that the essence of managerial responsibility is the extended time lapse between decision and result, currently reported profits are hardly a reasonable basis on which to compensate top executives. Such a basis simply serves to shorten the time horizon with which the executive is concerned.

The importance of an extended time horizon derives not only from the fact that an organization changes slowly and needs time to work through basic modifications in its strategy; it derives also from the fact that there is a considerable advantage in a certain consistency of strategy maintained over long periods of time. The great danger to companies which do not carefully formulate strategies well in advance is that they are prone to fling themselves toward chaos by drastic changes in policy—and in personnel—at frequent intervals. A parade of presidents is a clear indication of a board that has not really decided what its strategy should be. It is a common harbinger of serious corporate difficulty as well.

The time horizon is also important because of its impact on the selection of policies. The greater the time horizon, the greater the range in choice of tactics. If, for instance, the goals desired must be achieved in a relatively short time, steps like acquisition and merger may become virtually mandatory. An interesting illustration is the decision of National Cash Register to enter the market for electronic data-processing equipment. As reported in *Forbes:*

"Once committed to EDP, NCR wasted no time. To buy talent and experience in 1953 it acquired Computer Research Corp. of Hawthorne, California. . . . For speed's sake, the manufacture of the 304's central units was turned over to GE. . . . NCR's research and development outlays also began curving steeply upwards."[11]

---

11. "NCR and the Computer Sweepstakes," *Forbes,* October 15, 1962, p. 21.

6. *Is the strategy workable?* At first glance, it would seem that the simplest way to evaluate a corporate strategy is the completely pragmatic one of asking: Does it work? However, further reflection should reveal that if we try to answer that question, we are immediately faced with a quest for criteria. What is the evidence of a strategy "working"?

Quantitative indices of performance are a good start, but they really measure the influence of two critical factors combined: the strategy selected and the skill with which it is being executed. Faced with the failure to achieve anticipated results, both of these influences must be critically examined. One interesting illustration of this is a recent survey of the Chrysler Corporation after it suffered a period of serious loss:

"In 1959, during one of the frequent reorganizations at Chrysler Corp., aimed at halting the company's slide, a management consultant concluded: 'The only thing wrong with Chrysler is people. The corporation needs some good top executives.' "[12]

By contrast, when Olivetti acquired the Underwood Corporation, it was able to reduce the cost of producing typewriters by one-third. And it did it without changing any of the top people in the production group. However, it did introduce a drastically revised set of policies.

If a strategy cannot be evaluated by results alone, there are some other indications that may be used to assess its contribution to corporate progress:

► The degree of consensus which exists among executives concerning corporate goals and policies.

► The extent to which major areas of managerial choice are identified in advance, while there is still time to explore a variety of alternatives.

► The extent to which resource requirements are discovered well before the last minute, necessitating neither crash programs of cost reduction nor the elimination of planned programs. The widespread popularity of the meat-axe approach to cost reduction is a clear indication of the frequent failure of corporate strategic planning.

CONCLUSION

The modern organization must deploy expensive and complex resources in the pursuit of transitory opportunities. The time required to develop resources is so extended, and the time-scale of opportunities is so brief and fleeting, that a company which has not carefully delineated and appraised its strategy is adrift in white water.

In short, while a set of goals and major policies that meets the criteria listed above does not guarantee success, it can be of considerable value in giving management both the time and the room to maneuver.

---

12. "How Chrysler Hopes to Rebound," *Business Week,* October 6, 1962, p. 45.

PART TWO

The Functions
of
Management

*They are ill discoverers that think there is no land when
they see nothing but sea.*

Francis Bacon

The concept of management functions was first identified by the French industrialist Henri Fayol in 1916. He referred to five functions: planning, organizing, commanding, coordinating, and controlling. In 1925, when Fayol's ideas were translated into English, the concept of management functions was transplanted to the United States, where it flourished and led to a variety of classifications. Mee has cited a list of examples that show how different authorities identify the various functions of management.[1]

Though there is disagreement over the grouping and classification of management functions, there is general agreement that certain management functions exist. As Simon has stated, scholars interested in managerial behavior are interested in management functions.[2] These functions, no matter what their variety and definitions, are concerned with the achievement of organizational purposes through human effort within the internal and external environment of the organization.

The various functions of management, considered as a whole, make up the management process. Hence, planning, organizing, motivating, innovating, and controlling, considered separately, are management functions; when looked upon in their total approach to achieving objectives, they form a management process. The management process is determined by the functions, and though "there are some slight differences of opinion among the authorities, the instructors,

and the practitioners on the breakdown of the subfunctions and their identifying terms, the nature of the process seems to have general agreement."[3]

The management process has often been misinterpreted by its advocates and its critics alike either as a sequence of functions that follow one another in a particular order or as a group of separate and unrelated functions. Some of the literature implies that the management process, whatever its functions, is concerned primarily with each function as a separate entity and concerned very little with its relationship to other functions or to the internal and external environment of the organization. These misinterpretations are due to the fact that the concept of functions has been borrowed from the social sciences without due regard for the theoretical complexities involved. Some scholars either fail to discuss what the concept involves or give an oversimplified definition such as "function is any distinct phase of work."[4]

Radcliffe-Brown, an eminent anthropologist,

1. John F. Mee, *Management Thought in a Dynamic Economy* (New York: New York University Press, 1963), pp. 56–57.
2. Herbert A. Simon, "Approaching the Theory of Management," in Harold Koontz, ed., *Toward a Unified Theory of Management* (New York: McGraw-Hill Book Co., 1964), p. 77.
3. Mee, *Management Thought in a Dynamic Economy*, p. 56.
4. Ralph Currier Davis, *Industrial Organization and Management* (New York: Harper & Brothers, 1957), p. 23.

has taken a complicated but more realistic view of this concept. To him, the concept of function

involves the notion of a structure consisting of a set of relations among unit entities, the continuity of the structure being maintained by a life-process made up of the activities of the constituent units. . . . By the definition here offered "function" is the contribution which a partial activity makes to the total activity of which it is a part. The function of a particular social usage is the contribution it makes to the total social life as the functioning of the total social system. Such a view implies that a social system (the total social structure of a society together with the totality of social usages, in which that structure appears and on which it depends for its continued existence) has a certain kind of unity, which we may speak of as a functional unity.[5]

A management function is thus not a separate entity but an integral part of a larger entity made up of various functions that are related to one another as well as to the larger entity. Hence, as Gestalt psychologists have pointed out, the total is different from the sum of its parts. Only when the concept of function is viewed in this light does the management process emerge as truly dynamic.

In this book, we consider the functions of management to be planning and decision-making, organizing, motivating, innovating, and controlling. Figure 1 shows one image of the management process created by an improper understanding of the concept of functions.

FIGURE 1

planning
↓
organizing
↓
motivating
↓
innovating
↓
controlling

Figure 2, on the other hand, shows the more realistic image of the management process created by the more dynamic approach to the concept of functions as expounded by Radcliffe-Brown and further elaborated by Leighton.[6] The history of social sciences teaches us not to look upon the sequence of activities as either completely random or rigidly predetermined. The process of management is a complex one, with varying degrees of interaction among the functions.

FIGURE 2

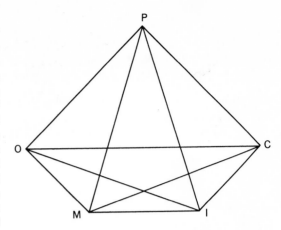

Mee has suggested that the concept of management process has lately come under strong criticism.[7] The management process, through its functions, is but the framework within which one may study the various aspects of management, however. What has come under stronger criticism is not the framework but the structure that has been built onto it and the principles that have been derived from it. One can criticize a rigorous step-by-step approach to planning without rejecting the function of planning; one can reject a nonempirical approach to organizing without rejecting the function of organizing; one can criticize close control of human effort without rejecting the function of control; and one can criticize different approaches to motivating and innovating without suggesting that these functions are unimportant in the management process.

The concepts of management function and management process have been most useful in developing an identifiable discipline for study and research. No scholar or practitioner has questioned that managers perform certain functions and that these functions are performed in a variety of organizations and at different managerial levels. The controversy arises when various approaches are used to explore, understand, and teach the art and science of management. Part Two provides a functional framework for study, with articles reflecting different approaches but having the common goal of advancing our knowledge of administration.

5. A. R. Radcliffe-Brown, "Concept of Function in Social Science," *American Anthropologist*, XXXVII (July–September 1935).
6. Alexander H. Leighton, *Human Relations in a Changing World* (New York: E. P. Dutton & Co., Inc., 1949), pp. 156–161.
7. Mee, *Management Thought in a Dynamic Economy*, pp. 87–92.

SECTION *III*
PLANNING AND DECISION-MAKING

Fayol's classical abstract (#9) provides what was perhaps the first description of the function of planning; though it was written more than fifty years ago, it still offers food for thought. The Friedman (#10) and Ansoff (#11) articles both examine what has been learned and what still needs to be learned about planning.

Although decision-making may be considered as a separate function — and a very crucial one — it is central to planning and is so examined here. Followers of Barnard's approach, in fact, often think of decision-making as the only major function of management. The abstract from Barnard (#12) shows the immense importance of this function and the ideas on which much of the present knowledge about decision-making is based. Dale (#13) examines the current status of the field, and March (#14) is concerned with how executives make decisions within business organizations.

9 — Planning

HENRI FAYOL

The maxim, "managing means looking ahead," gives some idea of the importance attached to planning in the business world, and it is true that if foresight is not the whole of management at least it is an essential part of it. To foresee, in this context, means both to assess the future and make provision for it; that is, foreseeing is itself action already. Planning is manifested on a variety of occasions and in a variety of ways, its chief manifestation, apparent sign and most effective instrument being the plan of action. The plan of action is, at one and the same time, the result envisaged, the line of action to be followed, the stages to go through, and methods to use. It is a kind of future picture wherein proximate events are outlined with some distinctness, whilst remote events appear progressively less distinct, and it entails the running of the business as foreseen and provided against over a definite period.

The plan of action rests: (1) On the firm's resources (buildings, tools, raw materials, personnel, productive capacity, sales outlets, public relations, etc.). (2) On the nature and importance of work in progress. (3) On future trends which depend partly on technical, commercial, financial and other conditions, all subject to change, whose importance and occurrence cannot be pre-determined. The preparation of the plan of action is one of the most difficult and most important matters of every business and brings into play all departments and all functions, especially the management function. It is, in effect, in order to carry out his managerial function that the manager takes the initiative for the plan of action, that he indicates its objective and scope, fixes the share of each department in the communal task, coordinates the parts and harmonizes the whole; that he decides, in fine, the line of conduct to be followed. In this line of conduct it is not only imperative that nothing should clash with principles and rules of good management, but also that the arrangement adopted should facilitate application of these principles and rules. Therefore, to the divers technical, commercial, financial and other abilities necessary on the part of a business head and his assistants, there must be added considerable managerial ability.

"Planning," *General and Industrial Management*, trans. Constance Storrs (London: Sir Isaac Pitman & Sons, Ltd., 1949), pp. 43–52. Reprinted by permission of the publisher. **Henri Fayol**: French industrialist, lecturer, and author.

GENERAL FEATURES
OF A GOOD PLAN OF ACTION

No one disputes the usefulness of a plan of action. Before taking action it is most necessary to know what is possible and what is wanted. It is known that absence of plan entails hesitation, false steps, untimely changes of direction, which are so many causes of weakness, if not of disaster, in business. The question of and necessity for a plan of action, then, does not arise and I think that I am voicing the general opinion in saying that a plan of action is indispensable. But there are plans and plans, there are simple ones, complex ones, concise ones, detailed ones, long- or short-term ones; there are those studied with meticulous attention, those treated lightly; there are good, bad, and indifferent ones. How are the good ones to be singled out from among the others? Experience is the only thing that finally determines the true value of a plan, i.e., on the services it can render to the firm, and even then the manner of its application must be taken into account. There is both instrument and player. Nevertheless, there are certain broad characteristics on which general agreement may be reached beforehand without waiting for the verdict of experience.

Unity of plan is an instance. Only one plan can be put into operation at a time; two different plans would mean duality, confusion, disorder. But a plan may be divided into several parts. In large concerns, there is found alongside the general plan a technical, commercial, and a financial one, or else an overall one with a specific one for each department. But all these plans are linked, welded, so as to make up one only, and every modification brought to bear on any one of them is given expression in the whole plan. The guiding action of the plan must be continuous. Now the limitations of human foresight necessarily set bounds to the duration of plans, so, in order to have no break in the guiding action, a second plan must follow immediately upon the first, a third upon the second, and so on. In large businesses the annual plan is more or less in current use. Other plans of shorter or longer term, always in close accord with the annual plan, operate simultaneously with this latter. The plan should be flexible enough to bend before such adjustments, as it is considered well to introduce, whether from pressure or circumstances or from any other reason. First as last, it is the law to which one bows. Another good point about a plan is to have as much accuracy as is compatible with the unknown factors bearing on the fate of the concern. Usually it is possible to mark out the line of proximate action fairly accurately, while a simple general indication does for remote activities, for before the moment for their execution has arrived sufficient enlightenment will have been forthcoming to settle the line of action more precisely. When the unknown factor occupies a relatively very large place there can be no preciseness in the plan, and then the concern takes on the name of venture.

Unity, continuity, flexibility, precision: such are the broad features of a good plan of action.

As for other specific points which it should have, and which turn on the nature, importance and condition of the business for which the plan is drawn up, there could be no possibility of settling them beforehand save by comparison with other plans already recognized as effective in similar businesses. In each case, then, comparable elements and models must be sought in business practice, after the fashion of the architect with a building to construct. But the architect, better served than the manager, can call upon books, courses in architecture, whereas there are no books on plans of action, no lessons in foresight, for management theory has yet to be formulated.

There is no lack of good plans, they can be guessed at from the externals of a business but not seen at sufficiently close quarters to be known and judged. Nevertheless, it would be most useful for those whose concern is management to know how experienced managers go about drawing up their plans. By way of information or sample, I am going to set out the method which has long been followed in a great mining and metallurgical concern with which I am well acquainted.

METHOD OF DRAWING UP THE PLAN OF ACTION IN A LARGE MINING AND METALLURGICAL FIRM

This company includes several separate establishments and employs about ten thousand personnel. The entire plan is made up of a series of separate plans called forecasts; and there are yearly forecasts, ten-yearly forecasts, monthly, weekly, daily forecasts, long-term forecasts, special forecasts, and all merge into a single programme which operates as a guide for the whole concern.

(i) *Yearly Forecasts.* Each year, two months after the end of the budgetary period, a general report is drawn up of the work and results of this period. The report deals especially with production, sales, technical, commercial, financial position, personnel, economic consequences, etc. The report is accompanied by forecasts dealing with those same matters, the forecasts being a kind of anticipatory summary of the activities and results of the new budgetary period. The two months of the new plan which have elapsed are not left without plan, because of provisional forecasts drawn up fifteen days before the end of the previous period. In a large mining and metallurgical firm not many activities are quite completed during the course of one year. Co-operative projects of a technical, commercial, and financial nature, which provide the business with its activities, need more time for their preparation and execution. From another aspect, account must be taken of the repercussions which proximate activities must have on ultimate ones and of the obligation to prepare far ahead sometimes for a requisite state of affairs.

Finally, thought must be given to constant

YEARLY AND TEN-YEARLY FORECASTS

CONTENTS

Technical Section

Mining rights. Premises. Plant.
Extraction. Manufacture. Output.
New workings. Improvements.
Maintenance of plant and buildings.
Production costs.

Commercial Section

Sales outlets.
Marketable goods.
Agencies. Contracts.
Customer importance. Credit standing.
Selling Price.

Financial Section

Capital. Loans. Deposits.

Circulating assets {
Supplies in hand.
Finished goods.
Debtors.
Liquid assets.

Available assets.
Reserves and sundry appropriations.

Creditors {
Wages.
Suppliers.
Sundry.

Sinking funds. Dividends. Bankers.

Accounting

Balance sheet. Profit and Loss account. Statistics.

Security

Accident precautions.
Works police. Claims. Health service.
Insurance.

Management

Plan of action.
Organization of personnel. Selection.
Command.
Co-ordination. Conferences.
Control.

---

modifications operating on the technical, commercial, financial and social condition of the industrial world in general and of the business in particular, to avoid being overtaken by circumstances. These various circumstances come outside the framework of yearly forecasts and lead on to longer-term ones.

(ii) Ten-yearly Forecasts. Ten-yearly forecasts deal with the same matters as yearly ones. At the outset these two types of forecast are identical, the yearly forecast merging into the first year of the ten-yearly one, but from the second year onwards notable divergences make their appearance. To maintain unity of plan each year the ten-yearly forecasts must be reconciled with annual ones so that at the end of some years the ten-yearly forecasts are generally so modified and transformed as to be no longer clear and need re-drafting. In effect the custom of re-drafting every five years has become established. It is the rule that ten-yearly forecasts always embrace a decade, and that they are revised every five years. Thus there is always a line of action marked out in advance for five years at least.

(iii) Special Forecasts. There are some activities whose full cycle exceeds one or even several ten-yearly periods, there are others which, occurring suddenly, must sensibly affect the conditions of the business. Both the one and the other are the object of special forecasts whose findings necessarily have a place in the yearly and ten-yearly forecasts. But it must never be lost sight of that there is one plan only.

These three sorts of forecasts, yearly, ten-yearly, and special, merged and harmonized, constitute the firm's general plan.

So, having been prepared with meticulous care by each regional management, with the help of departmental management, and then revised, modified, and completed by general management and then submitted for scrutiny and approval to the Board of Directors, these forecasts become the plan which, so long as no other has been put in its place, shall serve as guide, directive, and law for the whole staff.

Fifty years ago I began to use this system of forecasts, when I was engaged in managing a colliery, and it rendered me such good service that I had no hesitation in subsequently applying it to various industries whose running was entrusted to me. I look upon it as a precious managerial instrument and have no hesitation in recommending its use to those who have no better instrument available. It has necessarily some shortcomings, but its shortcomings are very slight compared with the advantages it offers. Let us glance at these advantages and shortcomings.

ADVANTAGES AND SHORTCOMINGS OF FORECASTS

(a) The study of resources, future possibilities, and means to be used for attaining the objective call for contributions from all departmental heads within the framework of their mandate, each one brings to this study the contribution of his experience together with recognition of the responsibility which will fall upon him in executing the plan.

Those are excellent conditions for ensuring that no resource shall be neglected and that future possibilities shall be prudently and courageously assessed and that means shall be appropriate to ends. Knowing what are its capabilities and its intentions, the concern goes boldly on, confidently tackles current problems and is prepared to align all its forces against accidents and surprises of all kinds which may occur.

(b) Compiling the annual plan is always a delicate operation and especially lengthy and laborious when done for the first time, but each repetition brings some simplification and when the plan has become a habit the toil and difficulties are largely reduced. Conversely, the interest it offers increases. The attention demanded for executing the plan, the indispensable comparison between predicted and actual facts, the recognition of mistakes made and successes attained, the search for means of repeating the one and avoiding the other—all go to make the new plan a work of increasing interest and increasing usefulness.

Also, by doing this work the personnel increases in usefulness from year to year, and at the end is considerably superior to what it was in the beginning. In truth, this result is not due solely to the use of planning but everything goes together; a well-thought-out plan is rarely found apart from sound organizational, command, co-ordination, and control practices. This management element exerts an influence on all the rest.

(c) Lack of sequence in activity and unwarranted changes of course are dangers constantly threatening businesses without a plan. The slightest contrary wind can turn from its course a boat which is unfitted to resist. When serious happenings occur, regrettable changes of course may be decided upon under the influence of pro-found but transitory disturbance. Only a programme carefully pondered at an undisturbed time permits of maintaining a clear view of the future and of concentrating maximum possible intellectual ability and material resources upon the danger.

It is in difficult moments above all that a plan is necessary. The best of plans cannot anticipate all unexpected occurrences which may arise, but it does include a place for these events and prepare the weapons which may be needed at the moment of being surprised. The plan protects the business not only against undesirable changes of course which may be produced by grave events, but also against those arising simply from changes on the part of higher authority. Also, it protects against deviations, imperceptible at first, which end by deflecting it from its objective.

CONDITIONS AND QUALITIES ESSENTIAL FOR DRAWING UP A GOOD PLAN OF ACTION

To sum up: the plan of action facilitates the utilization of the firm's resources and the choice of best methods to use for attaining the objective. It suppresses or reduces hesitancy, false steps, unwarranted changes of course, and helps to improve personnel. It is a precious managerial instrument.

The question may be asked as to why such an instrument is not in general use and everywhere developed to the farthest extent. The reason is that its compilation demands of managerial personnel a certain number of qualities and conditions rarely to be found in combination. The compilation of a good plan demands for the personnel in charge—

1. The art of handling men.
2. Considerable energy.
3. A measure of moral courage.
4. Some continuity of tenure.
5. A given degree of competence in the specialized requirements of the business.
6. A certain general business experience.

(i) *The Art of Handling Men.* In a large firm the majority of departmental managers take part in the compiling of the working arrangements. The execution of this task from time to time is in addition to ordinary everyday work and includes a certain responsibility and does not normally carry any special remuneration. So, to have in such conditions loyal and active co-operation from departmental heads an able manager of men is needed who fears neither trouble nor responsibility. The art of handling men is apparent from keenness of subordinates and confidence of superiors.

(ii) Energy. Yearly and ten-yearly forecasts and special forecasts demand constant vigilance on the part of management.

(iii) Moral Courage. It is well known that the best-thought-out plan is never exactly carried out. Forecasts are not prophecies, their function is to minimize the unknown factor. Nevertheless, the public generally, and even shareholders best informed about the running of a business, are not kindly disposed towards a manager who has raised unfulfilled hopes, or allowed them to be raised. Whence the need for a certain prudence which has to be reconciled with the obligation of making every preparation and seeking out optimum possible results.

The timid are tempted to suppress the plan or else whittle it down to nothing in order not to expose themselves to criticism, but it is a bad policy even from the point of view of self-interest. Lack of plan, which compromises smooth running, also exposes the manager to infinitely graver charges than that of having to explain away imperfectly executed forecasts.

(iv) Continuity of Tenure. Some time goes by before a new manager is able to take sufficient cognizance of the course of affairs, its general set-up and future possibilities, so as usefully to undertake the compiling of the plan. If, at such a moment, he feels that he will not have enough time to complete the work or only enough to start putting it into execution, or if, on the other hand, he is convinced that such work, condemned to bear no fruit, will only draw criticism upon him, is it to be thought that he will carry it out enthusiastically or even undertake it unless obliged? Human nature must be reckoned with. Without continuity of tenure on the part of management personnel there can be no good plan of action.

(v and vi) Professional Competence and General Business Knowledge. These are abilities just as necessary for drawing up a plan as for carrying it out.

Such are the conditions essential for compiling a good plan. They presuppose intelligent and experienced management. Lack of plan or a bad plan is a sign of managerial incompetence. To safeguard business against such incompetence—

1. A plan must be compulsory.
2. Good specimen plans must be made generally available. (Successful businesses could be asked to furnish such specimens. Experience and general discussion would single out the best.)
3. Planning (as a subject) must be introduced into education. Thus could general opinion be better informed and react upon management personnel, so that the latter's inefficiency would be less to be feared—a state of affairs which would in no wise detract from the importance of men of proven worth.

10 — Long-Range Planning and Cloudy Horizons

JACK R. FRIEDMAN

Whatever other doubts he may have had, the average executive of the late 1950s was confident of one point: business was moving into the era of the Soaring Sixties, when there would be growth markets aplenty and profits for everyone. But whatever happened to them? Dr. Herbert R. Brinberg, director of corporate commercial research at the American Can Co., feels that he knows at least part of the cause for the near disappearance of the Soaring Sixties. It was the same long-range planning that had first uncovered them for top managements on every side.

A surprising assertion? Not to Dr. Brinberg. "A few years ago," he points out, "everyone was trying to dope out the growth markets. As a result, everyone went into the same markets. The competition was intense, profits didn't turn out as expected—and that's one reason the economy has been under strain."

Certainly one need not search long for proof of Dr. Brinberg's assertion. Oil companies piled into petrochemicals in numbers that managed to sharply reduce the return on even that fabulous

"Long-Range Planning and Cloudy Horizons," *Dun's Review and Modern Industry,* LXXXI (January 1963), 42–43, 66. Reprinted by permission of the author and the publisher. Copyright 1965, Dun & Bradstreet Publications Corp. Jack R. Friedman: Executive Methods Editor, *Dun's Review and Modern Industry,* New York.

investment. The planemakers ran into heavy turbulence by overproducing jet transports. And so did the airlines, who are still waiting for customers to fill the vast number they bought.

All of which is not to say that *all* long-range planning has resulted in nothing but mishaps. Too many successful companies, too many newly developed markets, prove that long-range planning can be one of the most effective weapons in the corporate arsenal. Yet there are also the failures, where long-range planning led to what can only be called painful results. Somehow, it operated on a false assumption. Somewhere, it reached a fateful conclusion.

WHAT WENT WRONG?

That being so, thoughtful businessmen and not a few consultants these days are re-examining long-range planning, its concepts and its execution. For planning is too vital, too far-reaching in its consequences, to be left to the workings of mere chance. When it has gone wrong, they are asking, just what was the cause—and how can it be remedied?

From their findings come growing evidence that long-range planning is one corporate function that may well be more prone to error than perhaps any other. In view of its very nature—the task of trying to foretell the future—that is hardly surprising. What is surprising, however, is the lack of unanimity among corporations on long-range planning. Its basic aims sometimes are in doubt. Its execution is often based on misleading assumptions. And the question of just who should do the corporation's planning seems one that will bedevil top management for years to come.

Starting at the very beginning, it would appear that long-range planning often goes astray because management often tries to forecast the future with the approach of the past. For it will plan for the future by emphasizing that the corporation must adapt itself to change as it occurs, rather than anticipating or planning for it.

The need for a change in this approach is pointed up by no less an authority than Assistant Professor E. Kirby Warren of Columbia University, who spent a year studying the planning process of fifteen of the nation's largest companies. Says Warren: "With the growth of large corporations and the increased amount, speed and magnitude of change (economic, social, technological and competitive), adaptation alone has often proved inadequate to insure corporate survival and profitability."

Roughly a similar view is held by Michael J. Kami, director of long-range planning at International Business Machines and one of the most respected names in the field. Not only must the corporation prepare for change, Kami argues, it can expect those changes to come faster than ever.

Says Kami: "Major innovations used to occur in various fields every fifteen or twenty years. The intervals have now shortened to five or ten years—and may shrink even further in the period ahead. Since the allowable delay for decision making is becoming shorter, we must have at our disposal a background of information, facts, and 'prethinking' with which to render rapid and informed decisions. Planning should provide a new and faster trigger mechanism for top management."

The fact that it sometimes does not may well be the fault of top management itself. For it appears that the question of just who should do the long-range planning has never been really resolved. Indeed, it may well be one of the most haphazard processes in all of business. Should it be the president or chairman? Should it be an operating man or a trained, dedicated planner? Should it be done by divisions close to the markets, or by central headquarters despite the danger of an ivy tower approach?

Kirby Warren is particularly emphatic in his assertion that long-range planning no longer can be carried out by the one or two top corporate officers as it has been in so many companies for so many years. The harassed chief executive can guess the reason for that. As Warren phrases it: "The sheer magnitude of the work when added to the numerous other responsibilities of these top officers makes this impossible."

But in trying to solve that problem, top management often commits a grievous error. As Warren describes it: "Typically, the president appoints a taskforce to study the feasibility of planning. The taskforce's report invariably urges a go-ahead. The president then appoints a planning committee and asks his key operating people to cooperate with it."

So far, so good. But almost immediately, complications appear. "The committee points out that it is too small and its budget too skimpy to be effective," says Warren. "Consequently, no one will expect much and a shoddy job won't be condemned." Warren's solution: a simple statement that top management does expect better, skimpy budget and small committee notwithstanding.

Yet it can be argued that top management, a perennial scapegoat if there ever was one, may be to blame for only some of the planning failures.

For even the specialists appear to differ on many aspects of a long-range planning.

Canco's Brinberg, for example, tends to the professional planner approach. "If the planner is not removed from the mainstream of business activity and assigned solely to plan," he argues, "you are not going to get good results. The man who has to worry about meeting next week's production quota is carrying a big emotional load. If pressed to do planning, he'll probably delegate the job—with disastrous results."

THE OTHER SIDE

IBM's Kami, in contrast, favors operating managers, "the men who have the facts and can make the decisions." John O. Tomb, a director of McKinsey & Co., agrees. "Most planning and control systems," claims Tomb, "are not rooted in the realities of business. Executives are asked to put a number in a blank space on a form submitted to them by planning-staff personnel. They aren't even asked how the numbers are to be achieved."

Planning and control, Tomb goes on, should be integrated. Then if a sales manager has to produce a sales target, he will develop a marketing plan before setting his goal. Adds Tomb: "If poor distribution is holding back sales, he'll plan a program to obtain better outlets before predicting a sales increase."

Some specialists insist that such a system would submit the sales executive to excessive pressure. It should be noted, however, that this has not been the experience of so eminently successful a company as General Electric. The nation's fourth largest company claims that long-range planning is intimately woven into the job of every manager.

Planning at GE starts at the operating department level, where the department general manager and his section managers draw up a rolling ten-year forecast of budgets and plans for their own product range. At the next level, division general managers map the future course of their divisions five and ten years in the future by balancing the plans of all their department managers.

To avoid one of the pitfalls of many companies, it should be noted that GE planning at the division level is a personal responsibility and may not be delegated. This planning concept threads its way to the very top of the corporate structure. At GE's executive offices in New York, the company's over-all objectives, policies and plans are hammered out by the chairman, president and fifteen other top executives.

Does it make sense to submit planning to GE's elaborate decentralization policy? Cramer W. LaPierre, one of the company's two executive vice presidents, thinks so. "About the worst that can happen under our system," LaPierre points out, "is the simultaneous occurrence of small mistakes in different divisions. The impact, company-wide, would be small. But a single mistake at the top could be a disaster."

The proof: "In 1949," LaPierre goes on, "one of our most highly respected scientists insisted that the ICBM was a fantasy. Suppose he had headed a centralized planning process? I shudder to think where we would be now."

The inevitable result of decentralized planning, it should be added, is some overlap in projects by divisions. GE views this as part of the price. As a check, though, GE controls planning through budgetary control, to avoid letting the divisions plan themselves into projects that, in total, would be too much for the company to bear.

At the other end of the spectrum—and this may be one of the few clear trends in the whole area of long-range planning—some corporations are trying to hit the happy medium between headquarters and the field. The way is to appoint a high-level executive with long operating experience to specialize in long-range planning.

For all its decentralization, GE recently placed LaPierre in just that position, with orders to think only about the over-all corporate future, from new business lines for the company to the role of technology in GE's future. Similarly, the American Can Co. named William F. May vice president and general manager of its new corporate planning and development department.

The selection of such a man, however, must be done with extreme care. As McKinsey & Co.'s director E. Everett Smith points out, too many companies draft the "corporate achiever" to pilot their planning. "This simply doesn't work," says Smith. "The achiever is generally looking for short-term results. He's the man who made the big sale, swung the big deal or spun off a division painlessly. His personality seeks reward, applause and recognition. But no one applauds when a project takes fifteen years to bear fruit, even if it is a roaring success."

In contrast is the call to various departments to supply planners. Who appears? "Castoffs," snorts Herbert Brinberg. "Say the sales department has a man it wants to dump. Now it sees its chance. The result is a second-rate staff that guarantees planning will flop."

Aside from personnel, of course, the very nature of the long-range planning process itself can lead to error. In essence, and with all fancy verbiage stripped away, the job of the long-range planner is to foretell the future. True, he will use as many tools as possible to avoid error and the hit-or-miss approach. Nevertheless, he must make certain assumptions about the environment in which the company will function—the course of the economy, size of the market and so forth.

Very often, and perhaps quite understandably, that assumption can lead to trouble. A few years ago, by way of example, W.R. Grace & Co. realized that its basic shipping business was hardly a growth one. So Grace looked around for more fruitful endeavors. It could hardly be blamed for settling on chemicals; they were indeed a prime example of a growth industry. Yet no sooner had Grace built its massive chemical complexes than overcapacity settled around the entire industry. And only recently has Grace found the improved profits that it expected from the chemical industry.

One reason for miscalculations is that many companies confuse economic forecasting with long-range planning. The two are completely different. Economic forecasting is a basic tool in long-range planning, not the process. Says Columbia's Warren: "Too many companies mechanically extrapolate the figures on trends and call this planning." Adds GE's LaPierre: "Forecasts help to define the environment, but they don't dictate your decisions."

THE SAFE GROUND

All of which is not to say that a company cannot make assumptions about the future. It must. Yet it would appear that it will be on safest ground if it adheres to assumptions that are close to its own business, to the field it knows best.

Once they have made their assumptions, American companies tend to spread their planning out over a five-year range. Here, though, the nature of the industry again must be considered a factor, for cycles vary greatly in length. Twenty years is roughly a single cycle for oil tanker procurement, but half the cycle of tree maturity in the paper industry.

Again, if a five-year program is followed, variations within that cycle must not be overlooked. Consider the program worked out by American Machine & Foundry Co. "We plan ahead in five-year cycles," notes President Rodney C. Gott. "But while the first year's planning is very detailed, the second year's is less so, though it is fairly accurate. We find that the third and fourth years are almost meaningless, and so we have tended to skip them. The fifth year, of course, is the objective."

Will long-range planning ever reach the point where that objective is fairly well assured? The last word must remain with Kirby Warren. "Only time," he comments, "will tell whether long-range planning is any good. In the meantime, there is no sure way of knowing. The only thing one has to evaluate over the short term is the way people plan. Did they take into account all the significant data? Did they give adequate weight to the right factors? Did they overemphasize the importance of competition, markets, foreign trade?"

They are questions more and more corporations are asking these days.

11 — Planning as a Practical Management Tool

H. IGOR ANSOFF

For our purposes we need a quite simple, although fundamental, picture of the business firm. It can be viewed as a social organization composed of three basic resources: Physical in the form of plant, machinery, inventory; human in the form of managers, engineers, and workers; and a financial resource in money, securities, debtor obligations and borrowing power. The principal *function* of the firm is to convert these resources into goods and/or services.

Two important factors have to be recognized. All three resources are continually "used up" and need to be replenished, and the total amount of resources available to the firm at any given time is limited.

So far the social organization we have described is not particularly distinctive: There are other organizations which are also involved in resource conversion: Goodwill Industries, Army, Govern-

"Planning as a Practical Management Tool," *Financial Executive*, XXXII (June 1964), 34–37. Reprinted by permission of the author and the publisher. **H. Igor Ansoff**: Graduate School of Industrial Administration, Carnegie Institute of Technology.

ment, etc. A business firm is made distinctive by its motivation or what we normally call objectives. We generally recognize that a business firm's behavior is purposive and that a business firm characteristically seeks to obtain the best return on its resources whatever the properties of this return may be.

The conception of the firm as a resource conversion mechanism becomes useful because we can immediately see one way in which to gain this objective. This is to optimize the firm's resource conversion efficiency: To organize, to control costs, to produce, to develop the product line, to merchandise in such a way as to get the most performance possible out of the firm's investment in its *current markets*. We will refer to this as the *operating problem* of the firm.

However, this is addressing only half the problem. A relevant question is whether the present product-market structure is the most potentially profitable allocation of the firm's resources, or whether some different products and markets will produce better results.

To use a somewhat crude but descriptive analogy, in the operating problem we are seeking the best way to milk a cow, but if our basic interest is not the cow but in the most milk we can get for our investment, we must also make sure that we have the best cow money can buy.

Thus we have a second way in which the firm can solve its fundamental problem: Through allocating the firm's resources to product markets which offer the largest potential return. We will refer to this as the *strategic problem* of the firm.

SOLVING A TWO-LEVEL PROBLEM

The distinction between the operating and the strategic problem is useful for several reasons. First, is the fact that their solution is the responsibility of the two primary levels of management. Generally speaking, the operating line management, from general manager on down, is responsible for maximizing the profitability of the resources entrusted to it on assigned products and markets. The corporate management, the president, his staff, and the Board are responsible for seeing to it that these products and markets are well chosen and that the firm is making best possible use of the various investment opportunities available to it. Secondly, the decisions involved in the two areas are different. Strategic decisions are concerned with questions such as what kinds of new business should the firm enter, which of its present products should it discontinue, how

should resources of the firm be allocated between new and old business, whether to grow through external acquisition or internal development, what directions should the firm's basic and applied research take. The operating decisions deal with the questions of competition, pricing, product quality, product development, marketing effectiveness, manufacturing efficiency, inventory levels, and with the overall question of organizational efficiency.

A third reason why a distinction between the operating and the strategic problem is useful is because it highlights traditional management attitudes. Because the operating problem is a matter of day-to-day concern, because it involves all levels of management, and because managers, being human, feel more comfortable in dealing with known, tried, and familiar problems—for all these and some other reasons—top managements of a majority of firms have traditionally focussed their major attention on finding the best way of milking the cow: Of attaining the firm's objectives through maximizing the resource conversion efficiency in pursuit of traditional markets and product lines.

Recent economic, technological, political and business trends have been such as to make exclusive concentration on the operational problem progressively less profitable and sometimes even dangerous to survival of the firm. The mechanism which causes this is a kind of two-way squeeze on the firm: (a) On the one hand, many of the basic industries are witnessing a saturation of demand which is best recognized when the rate return on earnings reinvested in traditional business begins to decrease; and (b) on the other hand, the useful life-span of products is progressively being shortened through technological innovation. The resultant instability of product markets is a problem which has been of increasing concern to business during the post-WWII era. And this means, of course, increased concentration of management attention to the strategic problem of the firm.

THE MANAGEMENT DECISION PROCESS

With this background, let us study the relation of planning to the management decision process. According to one of the most commonly used definitions, management is "a process of getting things done through people." Two questions underlie this definition: *What* is to be done and *how* is it to be done. Or, as Peter Drucker put it, "The end product of a manager's work are decisions and actions."

While the individual styles of decision-making have an infinite variety, they can generally be categorized into two modes of behavior: What is commonly known as day-to-day or *current* decision-making and deliberate or *planned* decision-making. The difference between the two can be illustrated by first describing what is meant by a planned decision. Planned decisions have the following characteristics:

▶ An *anticipation* of decision needs;

▶ A clear recognition of the desired outcome of the decision;

▶ Construction of several alternative decisions which can be made;

▶ Evaluation of each alternative with respect to its ability to meet the purpose; and finally

▶ Selection of the preferred alternative. In brief, a planned decision involves a *systematic prior examination of the consequences* of the required decision.

The current decision, by definition, lacks the elements of anticipation—it is made when the need arises; and it lacks, in most cases, a comparison of alternatives through prediction of their outcomes. It is the type of decision which a businessman is continuously called upon to make. In making it in his daily work he relies on either judgment and past experience, or refers back to a precedent, or applies a standing rule or policy of the firm. No systematic prior analysis takes place.

There is no ironclad proof that planned decisions will necessarily lead to results superior to decisions based on outright judgments. Much depends on the complexity of the situation and the experience and ability of the decision-maker. However, if the decision situation is very complex such as, for example, the decision whether to develop a new product, or if the problem falls outside the decision-maker's experience, such as the decision whether to diversify, then both intuitively, as well as on the basis of a considerable amount of evidence, we would feel that planning pays off.

TIME-PHASED IMPLEMENTATION

Apart from its value in making decisions the planned approach has considerable value in *implementation*. Here the prediction of consequences takes the form of a time-phased schedule of accomplishments and resource commitments required to meet the end goal of the decision. Such a time-phased *program* provides a powerful management tool for coordination, monitoring, and control of performance as well as for periodic assessment of whether the decision was in fact a good one.

As a matter of fact it is exactly this type of program document which is usually identified as *the plan* by most companies which do planning. It may have different names: Business plan, profit plan, management forecast, management budget. It may vary with respect to time horizon. Two documents are frequently prepared, one for the forthcoming year and another for a longer term which varies from three to ten years. But essentially it is a time-phased spelling out of the accepted course of action for the firm. It will typically start with a sales forecast by product and customer and will translate this forecast into schedules of accomplishments by manufacturing, engineering, and marketing. It will contain associated schedules of expenditures usually classed by direct and indirect categories. The over-all picture is integrated into a P&L forecast, cash flow forecast and a capital budget.

Thus to the question "Is planning practical?" the answer could be "Of course it is, since it is a widely used management budgeting and control tool." However, a natural rejoinder would be to say, "If this is all there is to planning, then why all the fuss, why have a lot of planners around? To engage in this kind of budgeting all the firm needs are some competent market researchers, financial analysts, and a few good cost estimators." We would agree provided two facts were true: (a) If this kind of budgeting were *all* there is to planning and (b) if the present budgeting techniques and formats were satisfactory for the purposes for which they are used. In point of fact, neither condition exists: (a) There is much more to planning than just the management budget and (b) the techniques and the formats are creaking at the joints.

Limitations of space prevent us from a discussion of item (b). In passing it should be pointed out that the techniques and format problems arise out of their inadequacies as operational control documents. It is this kind of problem that has given rise, for example, to the PERT and PERT/COST techniques for project planning.

PLANNING FOR
THE ENTIRE ALLOCATION PATTERN

We now see that the planning document discussed above is only one of several needed by the firm. That document we can recognize as addressed to the operating problem of the firm. From the new vantage point we can see that before such an operations plan is constructed, it is highly desirable to examine the entire resource allocation pattern of the firm and to make two fundamental decisions: What should be the division of the firm's effort and resources between traditional and new business areas, and what specific new business areas should the firm seek to enter? The document which embodies these decisions is what we will call the *strategic plan*. The operations plan can then follow, based on the resource allocation for pursuit of traditional business and the guidance provided by the strategic plan.

The resources allocated to pursuit of new business must also be planned. The following decisions need to be made: (a) Selection of specific types of products and markets to be pursued in new business areas, (b) choice of the means for diversification: whether to acquire, to develop with the company's own resources, or to do both, (c) means of financing: through reinvestment of earnings, borrowing additional equity, or exchange of equity. All these decisions need to be elaborated in a time-phased development program listing milestone accomplishments and allocations of personnel, money and facilities. We will call the resulting document the *development plan*.

Yet another document is needed to complete the structure. The development plan will allocate resources between external acquisition and internal development. Some of the latter will be in support of the present product line and some for new business areas. Basic decisions need to be made: What should be allocated between basic research, applied research and product development; what directions and projects will research pursue; what product development projects will be undertaken; what will be the mix between brand new and improved products.

Product development without a parallel effort to analyze and develop appropriate markets would result in what has been called "solutions in search of a problem." R&D planning activity should include, therefore, parallel decisions with respect to markets: What areas of customer needs will the firm seek to fill, what market research projects will be undertaken, what steps will be taken to establish sales capabilities for the new products.

The document which embodies the entire complex of activities in internal product research and development we will call the *research and development plan*.

THE GENERATION OF SUBSIDIARY PLANS

Starting with an analysis of the problems of the firm we have thus generated a rather complicated structure of plans, each addressed to a specific problem of the firm and yet related to one another. The job of planning does not stop here. Each of the major plans generates subsidiary plans. The development plan needs to be supported by a plan for mergers and acquisitions as well as by a plan for such divestments of existing products and markets as may be necessary. The R&D plan must be backed up by functional plans for marketing, manufacturing, finance, and administration. Similar functional plans are needed in support of the operations plan.

The structure of plans we have discussed with related inputs and outputs is shown on the chart below.

It should be recalled that each of the boxes implies two types of planning activities. The first step is to analyze the alternatives and to *arrive at the appropriate decisions*. The second is to program the decisions: To specify results and costs over time in a way designed to expedite management action, control, and lower-level decision-making.

While these two steps are closely related they require different analytic approaches, different types of talent and different format. There is no generally accepted business terminology used to describe the respective documents. The military terminology refers to the first type of document as the "plan" and the second as the "program." Perhaps more appropriate to business would be to describe the respective steps as "plans and budgets." In this definition the standard business

STRUCTURE OF PLANS

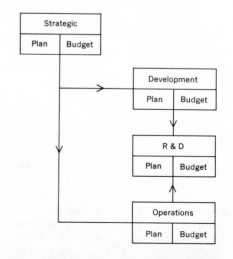

planning document which we discussed earlier would be referred to as an "operations budget."

Now let us return to the original question, "Is planning practical?" Since we have already agreed that the operations plan has been proved by experience, the question can be rephrased into: "What kinds of plans should the firm make and how far down the organizational level should it carry them?"

PLANNING MUST BE RESPONSIVE TO THE FIRM'S PROBLEMS

The answer to the first part is dictated by the relative management emphasis on the basic problems of the firm. If the firm is among the very few fortunate ones which can see a long path of growth in its traditional business, it can put a major emphasis on operations planning and R&D planning. The strategic plan and the development plans will be dictated largely by the evolutionary trends within the industry. While important, they will not require a major job of analysis. On the other hand, a firm in a dying industry will need to concentrate its major effort on strategic and development plans. To generalize, *the importance of strategic and development planning is directly related to the instability of the product-market demand in the firm's industry.*

The second part of the question—"How far down in organization should planning proceed?"—will vary from firm to firm depending on its size, diversification of the product line, complexity of its product and the nature of its product-market problems. However, some general rules can be suggested:

Generally, planning should be undertaken whenever the potential improvement of the operational unit (in terms of either increased output or reduced operating costs) can be shown to exceed the costs of the planning activity.

Somewhat more specifically, *planning of decisions* is appropriate at a particular level whenever it can be shown that the quality of decision-making can be improved through systematic analysis. This will generally occur when the decision problem is affected by many variables, when the outcomes of alternatives are not readily visualized, or when the decision area is new to the manager.

Planning of implementation is appropriate whenever the manager is in charge of a number of interdependent activities whose outcomes affect one another and whose relationship cannot be readily perceived.

Some qualifications are in order. The rules for deciding whether to plan are not precise formulas, but are rather intended as decision guidelines to be applied through intelligent judgment. There has been a steady growth of understanding of the meaning of social planning in general and business planning in particular, accompanied by continuous sharpening of planning tools and concepts. There is still work to be done before we have what can be called a discipline or theory of planning. However, enough tools are available now to enable planners to be of real assistance in increasing the profitability of business firms.

12 — The Environment of Decision

CHESTER I. BARNARD

The acts of individuals may be distinguished in principle as those which are the result of deliberation, calculation, thought, and those which are unconscious, automatic, responsive, the results of internal or external conditions present or past. In general, whatever processes precede the first class of acts culminate in what may be termed "decision." Involved in acts which are ascribed to decision are many subsidiary acts which are themselves automatic, the processes of which are usually unknown to the actor.

When decision is involved there are consciously present two terms—the end to be accomplished and the means to be used. The end itself may be the result of logical processes in which the end is in turn a means to some broader or more remote end; or the immediate end, and generally the ultimate end, may not be a result of logical processes, but "given"—that is, unconsciously impressed—by conditions, including social conditions past or present, including orders of organizations. But whenever the end has been determined, by

From "The Environment of Decision" and "The Theory of Opportunism," *The Functions of the Executive* (Cambridge, Mass.: Harvard University Press, 1938), Ch. XIII, pp. 185, 189–198, Ch. XIV, pp. 201–205. Reprinted by permission of the publisher. Copyright 1938 by the President and Fellows of Harvard College. **Chester I. Barnard:** President of New Jersey Bell Telephone Company.

whatever process, the decision as to means is itself a logical process of discrimination, analysis, choice—however defective either the factual basis for choice or the reasoning related to these facts. . . .

THE OCCASIONS OF DECISION

The making of decisions, as everyone knows from personal experience, is a burdensome task. Offsetting the exhilaration that may result from correct and successful decision and the relief that follows the terminating of a struggle to determine issues is the depression that comes from failure or error of decision and the frustration which ensues from uncertainty. Accordingly, it will be observed that men generally try to avoid making decisions, beyond a limited degree when they are rather uncritical responses to conditions. The capacity of most men to make decisions is quite narrow, although it is a capacity that may be considerably developed by training and especially by experience.

The executive is under the obligation of making decisions usually within approximately defined limits related to the position he has accepted; and is under the necessity of keeping within the limits of his capacity if he is continuously to discharge this obligation. He must, therefore, to be successful, distinguish between the occasions of decision in order to avoid the acceptance of more than he can undertake without neglecting the fields to which his position relates. For the natural reluctance of other men to decide, their persistent disposition to avoid responsibility, and their fear of criticism, will lead them to overwhelm the executive who does not protect himself from excessive burdens of decision if he is not already protected by a well regulated and habitual distribution of responsibilities.

It is for this reason necessary in the making of decisions to maintain a balance between the fields from which the occasions of them arise. I suppose this is rarely a matter of conscious selection, and is probably subject to no general rules. It involves in itself important decisions. For our purposes, however, it may be helpful to note that the occasions for decision originate in three distinct fields: (a) from authoritative communications from superiors; (b) from cases referred for decision by subordinates; (c) from cases originating in the initiative of the executive concerned.

(a) Occasions for decision are frequently furnished by instructions or by general requirements of superior authority. Such decisions relate to the interpretation, application, and distribution of instructions. These occasions cannot be avoided, though the burden may be reduced by delegation of responsibility to subordinates. They involve serious decisions when the instructions seem morally wrong, harmful to the organization, or impossible of execution.

(b) The cases referred for decision may be called appellate cases. They arise from incapacity of subordinates, uncertainty of instructions, novelty of conditions, conflict of jurisdiction or conflicts of orders, or failure of subjective authority. The control of the number of appellate cases lies in adequacy of executive organization, of personnel, of previous decision; and the development of the processes of informal organization. The test of executive action is to make these decisions when they are important, or when they cannot be delegated reasonably, and to decline the others.

(c) The occasions of decision on the initiative of the executive are the most important test of his capacity. Out of his understanding of the situation, which depends upon his ability and initiative, and on the character of the communication system of his organization, it is to be determined whether something needs to be done or corrected. To decide that question involves not merely the ordinary elements but the executive's specific justification for deciding. For when the occasions for decision arise from above or below the position of the executive, others have in advance granted him authority; but when made on his own initiative, this always may be (and generally is) questioned, at least tacitly (in the form whether decision was necessary, or related to scope of obligations, etc.). Moreover, failure to decide is usually not specifically subject to attack, except under extreme conditions. Hence there is much incentive to avoid decision. Pressure of other work is the usual self-justification. Yet it is clear that the most important obligation is to raise and decide those issues which no one else is in a position to raise effectively.

From the point of view of the *relative* importance of specific decisions, those of executives properly call for first attention. From the point of view of *aggregate* importance, it is not decisions of executives but of non-executive participants in organization which should enlist major interest. Indeed it is precisely for this reason that many executive decisions are necessary—they relate to the facilitation of correct action involving appropriate decisions among others. In large measure this is a process of providing for the clear presentment of the issues or choices. At any event, it is easily evident merely from the inspection of the action of the non-executive participants in organization that coördination of action requires repeated organization decisions "on the spot" where the effective action of organization takes place. It is here that the final and most concrete objectives of purposes are found, with the maximum of definiteness. There is no further stage of organization action. The final selection of means takes place at this point.

It should be noted, however, that the types of decisions as well as the conditions change in character as we descend from the major executive to the non-executive positions in organization. At the upper limit decisions relating to ends to be pursued generally require the major attention, those relating to means being secondary, rather general, and especially concerned with personnel, that is, the development and protection of organization itself. At intermediate levels the breaking of broad purposes into more specific ends and the technical and technological problems, including economic problems, of action become prominent. At the low levels decisions characteristically relate to technologically correct conduct, so far as the action is organization action. But it is at these low levels, where ultimate authority resides, that the *personal* decisions determining willingness to contribute become of relatively greatest aggregate importance.

THE EVIDENCES OF DECISION

Not the least of the difficulties of appraising the executive functions or the relative merits of executives lies in the fact that there is little direct opportunity to observe the essential operations of decision. It is a perplexing fact that most executive decisions produce no direct evidence of themselves and that knowledge of them can only be derived from the cumulation of indirect evidence. They must largely be inferred from general results in which they are merely one factor, and from symptomatic indications of roundabout character.

Those decisions which are most directly known result in the emission of authoritative communications, that is, orders. Something is or is not to be done. Even in such cases the basic decision may not be evident; for the decision to attempt to achieve a certain result or condition may require several communications to different persons which appear to be complete in themselves but in which the controlling general decision may not be disclosed.

Again, a firm decision may be taken that does not result in any communication whatever for the time being. A decision properly timed must be made in advance of communicating it, either because the action involved must wait anticipated developments or because it cannot be authorita-tive without educational or persuasive preparation.

Finally, the decision may be not to decide. This is a most frequent decision, and from some points of view probably the most important. For every alert executive continually raises in his own mind questions for determination. As a result of his consideration he may determine that the question is not pertinent. He may determine that it is not now pertinent. He may determine that it is pertinent now, but that there are lacking adequate data upon which to base a final decision. He may determine that it is pertinent for decision now, but that it should or must be decided by someone else on the latter's initiative. He may determine that the question is pertinent, can be decided, will not be decided except by himself and yet it would be better that it be not decided because his competence is insufficient.

The fine art of executive decision consists in not deciding questions that are not now pertinent, in not deciding prematurely, in not making decisions that cannot be made effective, and in not making decisions that others should make. Not to decide questions that are not pertinent at the time is uncommon good sense, though to raise them may be uncommon perspicacity. Not to decide questions prematurely is to refuse commitment of attitude or the development of prejudice. Not to make decisions that cannot be made effective is to refrain from destroying authority. Not to make decisions that others should make is to preserve morale, to develop competence, to fix responsibility, and to preserve authority.

From this it may be seen that decisions fall into two major classes, positive decisions—to do something, to direct action, to cease action, to prevent action; and negative decisions, which are decisions not to decide. Both are inescapable; but the negative decisions are often largely unconscious, relatively non-logical, "instinctive," "good sense." It is because of the rejections that the selection is good. The best of moves may be offset by a false move. This is why time is usually necessary to appraise the executive. There is no current evidence of the all-important negative decisions. The absence of effective moves indicates failure of initiative in decision, but error of action probably often means absence of good negative decisions. The success of action through a period of time denotes excellence of selection and of rejection of possible actions.

THE NATURE OF THE ENVIRONMENT

Whatever the occasions or the evidences of decision, it is clear that decisions are constantly being made. What is the nature of the environment of decisions, the materials with which they deal, the field to which they relate? It consists of two parts: (a) purpose; and (b) the physical world, the social world, the external things and forces and circumstances of the moment. All of these, including purpose, constitute the objective field of decision; but the two parts are of radically different nature and origin. The function of decision is to regulate the relations between these two parts. This regulation is accomplished either by changing the purpose or by changing the remainder of the environment.

(a) We may consider purpose first. It may seem strange perhaps that purpose should be included in the objective environment, since purpose of all things seems personal, subjective, internal, the expression of desire. This is true; but *at the moment of a new decision,* an existing purpose, the result of a previous decision under previous conditions, is an objective fact, and it is so treated at that moment in so far as it is a factor in new decision.

This is especially true because organization decisions do not relate to personal purposes, but to organization purposes. The purpose which concerns an organization decision may have been given as a fact to and accepted as such by the person who is responsible for making a new decision. But no matter how arrived at, when decision is in point, the purpose is fact already determined; its making is a matter of history; it may be as objective as another man's emotions may be to an observer.

We must next note, however, that purpose is essential to give any meaning to the rest of the environment.[1] The environment must be looked at from *some* point of view to be intelligible. A mere mass of things, atoms, movements, forces, noises, lights, could produce some response from a sensitive creature or certainly would have some effect on it, or on other things, but the reduction of this mass of everything to something significant requires a basis for discrimination, for picking out this and that as pertinent, relevant, interesting. This basis is that in *this* situation something is or is not to be done. The situation aids, obstructs, or is neutral from *this* point of view. The basis for this discrimination is a purpose, an end, an object to be accomplished.

Purpose itself has no meaning, however, except in an environment. It can only be defined in terms of an environment.[2] Even to want to go somewhere, anywhere, supposes some kind of environment. A very general purpose supposes a very general undifferentiated environment; and if the purpose is stated or thought of it must be in

terms of that general environment. But when formed, it immediately (if it is not in suspense or dormant, so to speak) serves for reducing that environment to more definite features; and the immediate result is to change purpose into a more specific purpose. Thus when I decide I want to go from A to B my idea of terrain is vague. But as soon as I have decided, the terrain becomes less vague; I immediately see paths, rocks, obstacles that are significant; and this finer discrimination results in detailed and smaller purposes. I not only want to go from A to B, but I want to go this way, that way, etc. This constant refinement of purpose is the effect of repeated decisions, in finer and finer detail, until eventually detailed purpose is contemporaneous accomplishment. But similarly with each new edition of purpose, a new discrimination of the environment is involved, until finally the last obstacle of progressive action represents a breaking up of a general purpose into many concrete purposes, each as it is made almost simultaneously associated with the action. The thing is done as soon as decided; it becomes a matter of history; it constitutes a single step in the process of experience.

Thus back and forth purpose and environment react in successive steps through successive decisions in greater and greater detail. A series of final decisions, each apparently trivial, is largely accomplished unconsciously and sums up into an effected general purpose and a route of experience.

(b) We may now consider the environment of decision exclusive of purpose. It consists of atoms and molecules, agglomerations of things in motion, alive; of men and emotions; of physical laws and social laws; social ideas, norms of action, of forces and resistances. Their number is infinite and they are all always present. They are also always changing. They are meaningless in their variety and changes except as discriminated in the light of purpose. They are viewed as static facts, if the change is not significant from the viewpoint of the purpose, or as both static and dynamic facts.

This discrimination divides the world into two parts; the facts that are immaterial, irrelevant, mere background; and the part that contains the

---

1. I am under the impression that in a general way both the form of expression and the concepts stated in the next several paragraphs were derived from or influenced by A. N. Whitehead's *Process and Reality.*
2. Care should be taken to keep in mind that environment throughout does not mean merely physical aspects of the environment, but explicitly includes social aspects, although physical rather than other aspects are used for illustration as simpler. In many organizations, however, the physical aspects are constant and it is the social aspects which are pertinent. This is the case especially when the purpose is a concrete expression of social ideas or attitudes, as, for example, in ritualistic types of action whether religious or political.

facts that apparently aid or prevent the accomplishment of purpose. As soon as that discrimination takes place, decision is in bud. It is in the state of selecting among alternatives. These alternatives are either to utilize favorable factors, to eliminate or circumvent unfavorable ones, or to change the purpose. Note that if the decision is to deal with the environment, this automatically introduces new but more detailed purposes, the progeny, as it were, of the parent purpose; but if the decision is to change the purpose rather than deal with the environment, the parent is sterile. It is abandoned, and a new purpose is selected, thereby creating a *new* environment in the light of *that* purpose.

This looks like metaphysical speculation if one thinks of it as individual and personal — undemonstrable assumptions, speculative reasoning. But it can be observed in an organization, at least sufficiently to corroborate it roughly. Thus if the president of a telephone company for good reasons orders[3] two poles carrying a cable removed from the north side of First Street between A and B Streets to the opposite side of First Street, it can, I think, be approximately demonstrated that carrying out that order involves perhaps 10,000 decisions of 100 men located at 15 points, requiring successive analyses of several environments, including social, moral, legal, economic, and physical facts of the environment, and requiring 9000 redefinitions and refinements of purpose, and 1000 changes of purpose. If inquiry be made of those responsible, probably not more than a half-a-dozen decisions will be recalled or deemed worthy of mention — those that seem at the moment difficult or momentous, or that were subject to question, or proved erroneous. The others will be "taken for granted," all a part of the business of knowing one's business. However, a large part of the decisions, purposes, and descriptions and analyses of the various environments will be a matter of record — short-cut, abbreviated, to be sure, but marking the routes of decisions with fair definiteness. Only in the case of individual workmen shall we be almost completely reduced to speculation as to the number and character of the decisions required, because many of them certainly will relate to physiological action. . . .

THE THEORY OF OPPORTUNISM

The opportunistic element refers to the objective field within which action must take place. The process of decision so far as it relates to this objective field is essentially one of analysis, even though in practice much of the process will be intuitive or not conscious. The analysis of present circumstances is in part the definition of purpose in immediate terms; but it is also the process of finding what present circumstances are significant with reference to that purpose. What events, what objects, what conditions aid, what prevent, the attainment of purpose?

This analysis will lead to the rejection from present interest or attention of most of the innumerable events, objects, details, circumstances of the situation, since under the conditions they are irrelevant to the purpose. This, of course, is sometimes an easy, sometimes a difficult task. It is easy if it has been done before for similar circumstances, if it yields to an established technique of analysis, if it is a solved scientific problem. It is difficult if it is novel, if there is no technique, or no science. For then the analysis is in effect partly unaided surmise, hypothesis, assumption. This fact, even when the decider is aware of it, does not permit escape from decision, though it may lead to negative decision, that is, to decision not to decide the question for the present. Hence, there is no escape from *some* decision once the process of setting up purpose against environment has begun.

The analysis required for decision is in effect a search for the "strategic factors." The notion of the "strategic factor," a term I borrow from Professor John R. Commons,[4] is related to the term "limiting factor" which is common in scientific work. Professor Commons' use of the word is restricted to certain aspects of managerial and bargaining operations in economic systems, but the restriction to this field is unnecessary; the principle involved is the same in whatever circumstances decision is required. The theory of the strategic factor is necessary to an appreciation of the process of decision, and therefore to the understanding of organization and the executive functions as well as, perhaps, individual purposive conduct. As generally as I can state it, this theory is as follows:

If we take any system, or set of conditions, or conglomeration of circumstances existing at a given time, we recognize that it consists of elements, or parts, or factors, which together make

3. Partly to illustrate several statements in this essay I may say that it is necessary to imagine extreme conditions to suppose he would issue such an order. Ordinarily what he would do would be to inquire whether it would be feasible to take the action suggested, or what would be involved in doing so, or he would state the problem and ask for its solution, etc. The executive art is nine-tenths inducing those who have authority to use it in taking pertinent action.

4. John R. Commons, *Institutional Economics* (New York: The Macmillan Co., 1934), *passim*, but especially chapter IX at pp. 627–633.

up the whole system, set of conditions, or circumstances. Now, if we approach this system or set of circumstances, with a view to the accomplishment of a purpose (and only when we so approach it), the elements or parts become distinguished into two classes: those which if absent or changed would accomplish the desired purpose, provided the others remain unchanged; and these others. The first kind are often called limiting factors, the second, complementary factors. Moreover, when we concentrate our attention upon a *restricted* or subsidiary system or set of circumstances, we often find, on the basis of previous experience or knowledge, that the circumstances fail to satisfy the requirements of purpose because they lack an additional element or elements, that is, elements which are known to exist in the *larger* environment. These are likewise limiting factors.

The limiting (strategic) factor is the one whose control, in the right form, at the right place and time, will establish a new system or set of conditions which meets the purpose. Thus, if we wish to increase the yield of grain in a certain field and on analysis it appears that the soil lacks potash, potash may be said to be the strategic (or limiting) factor. If a tank of water is to be used for cleaning purposes, and is found to contain sediment, the sediment is the strategic (limiting) factor in the use of the water for cleaning. If a machine is not operable because a screw is missing, the screw is the strategic (limiting) factor.[5]

Where the crucial element or part present or absent is a thing or physical element or compound or ingredient it is convenient to call it "limiting" factor; but when personal or organizational action is the crucial element, *as it ultimately is in all purposive effort,* the word "strategic" is preferable. This preference relates to a distinction in the use of the analysis. If its purpose is knowledge for its own sake, that is, if the purpose is immediately scientific, the term "limiting factor" conveys the relatively static situation of the analyst. If the purpose is not knowledge but decision as to action, "strategic factor" conveys the relatively changing position of the analyst, in which the subjective aspects of decision interact with the objective field in which it is developed.

The fact that a strategic factor is always involved is overlooked because the personal or organization action required often seems trivial; the necessary effort is less than that required to analyze the situation or system. For example, it may require great effort to determine that the land needs potash, but little effort to get the potash. Nevertheless, when the need has been determined, a new situation has arisen because of the fact of knowledge or the assumption that potash is the limiting factor; and instead of potash, the limiting factor *obtaining* potash then becomes the strategic factor; and this will change progressively into *obtaining* the money to *buy* potash, then *finding* John to *go* after potash, then *getting* machines and men to *spread* potash, etc., etc. Thus the determination of the strategic factor is itself the decision which at once reduces purpose to a new level, compelling search for a new strategic factor in the new situation. Says Commons:

> But the limiting and complementary factors are continually changing places. What was the limiting factor becomes complementary, when once it has come under control; then another factor is the limiting one. The limiting factor, in the operation of an automobile, at one time may be the electric spark; at another the gasoline, at another the man at the wheel. This is the meaning of efficiency—the control of the changeable limiting factors at the right time, right place, right amount, and right form in order to enlarge the total output by the expected operation of complementary factors.[6]

If we rephrase this last sentence to accord with our terminology and our broader subject, it will read: "This is the meaning of effective decision—the control of the changeable strategic factors, that is, the exercise of control at the right time, right place, right amount, and right form so that purpose is properly redefined and accomplished."

Professor Commons continues:

> But out of the complex happenings, man selects the limiting factors for his purposes. If he can control these, then the other factors work out the effects intended. The "cause" is volitional control of the limiting or strategic factors. . . . The "effects" are the operations of the complementary factors. . . .[7]

With the distinctions in phraseology which Commons makes for his purposes we are not concerned. I think it sound to say that the strategic factor always determines the *action* that is controlling, even in the case of what he calls the limiting factor. It is not the element that is missing but the action that could procure the missing element that is the controlling factor. To determine what element should be changed or is missing is the first step in defining the *action* required. Decision relates to *action,* whether it be in the field of business transactions, political transactions, me-

---

5. There may be more than one limiting factor, in which they may all be taken as a limiting set, or broken down to single factors for action in some order.

6. *Institutional Economics,* p. 629.

7. *Ibid.,* p. 632.

chanical operations, chemical combinations, scientific experimentation, or whatever relates to accomplishment of intention.

The strategic factor is, then, the center of the environment of decision. It is the point at which choice applies. To *do* or not to do *this*, that is the question. Often there are tentatively several strategic factors, any one of which meets the immediate situation or satisfies the necessity of immediate purpose. This expands the horizon into the less immediate future, increases the objective field. The final strategic selection will be made on the basis of the estimate of less immediate future consequences.

13 — New Perspectives in Managerial Decision-Making

ERNEST DALE

Studies in managerial decision-making have become increasingly popular in the last few years. This is due partly to the growing interest in applied economics and in training for practical business affairs. It also stems from a widespread concern about the concentration of economic and managerial power in the hands of a few individuals. Finally, it is realized that the studies of economists have frequently reached a point of rapidly diminishing returns, that they have carried their refinements beyond the point which the social metallurgist would consider profitable. As it has been well put: "In the alloy of human behavior the economic motive may be as significant as the carbon content of steel, but a more adequate understanding of human behavior requires some knowledge of iron as well as carbon."

For the purpose of better analysis and prediction of businessmen's decision, new sets of questions need to be devised and many more empirical studies of human behavior in industry and commerce undertaken. The result of such studies may be that the present structure of economic theory can provide at best only a partial explanation and sometimes gives quite an incorrect explanation, because it omits some factors altogether and weights others incorrectly. In this connection many of the studies of wage determination, labor mobility, and occupational choice have shown the importance of noneconomic factors.

While most economists pay lip service to the influence of those noneconomic factors, they usually ignore them in their writings or relegate them to the bag of "assuming other things being equal." Or they may establish some arbitrary rate of ex-

change between the economic and the non-economic influences. On the whole, the economist appears to assume far more certainty and rationality in decision-making than is actually the case.

TYPES OF DECISIONS

A major reason for the influence of noneconomic forces is the factor of uncertainty in businessmen's decisions. In order to study the impact of uncertainty more effectively, decisions might be divided into different classes, the various categories depending on the degree of uncertainty involved. There are, first of all, the routine decisions, such as the operation of a payroll procedure or a cafeteria; such decisions often affect only one department and can be handled by precedent and habit. Even though decisions may be difficult to make because of the uncertainty involved, if they are repeated frequently, such as similar price decisions, they can be routinized. The aim of companies is frequently to increase the area of routine decisions in order to reduce the high expenses of continually making new decisions (and mistakes). Next there is the decision which affects several departments, such as the choice between a hand-operated and a mechanical system of bookkeeping. The relevant factors can be estimated with a fair degree of accuracy. In the third area uncertainty may be considered to be one of the major factors involved, as, for example, in the hiring of a top executive or the decision to force a strike. The final area may be described as one in which uncertainty predominates, such as company action on a wage

"New Perspectives in Managerial Decision-Making," *Journal of Business*, XXVI (January 1953), 1–8. Reprinted by permission of the author and The University of Chicago Press. Copyright 1953 by The University of Chicago Press. **Ernest Dale:** Graduate School of Business, Columbia University. The author gratefully acknowledges the aid of a grant received from the Columbia University Social Science Research Council for work in this field.

demand which will be decided by a government board. We might conclude from this series of categories that the greater the knowledge of the future and the greater the influence of economic forces, the greater the degree of the company's control.

REASONS FOR UNCERTAINTY

INACCURACY OF THE DATA

The nature of most economic data is not precise in the sense that they can be defined, measured, and verified accurately. Hence judgment is involved in determining the data to be used and how to use them. At the level of the firm this is evident in the use of financial statements, because there is an arbitrary cutoff point before the actual value of many items is finally determined, such as, for example, the expiration of fixed assets. Important differences arise, depending on whether acquisition value or replacement value is used, especially during these last twelve years of continuous price increases. There are also important differences regarding the definition of accounting concepts, such as, for example, the profit-and-loss figure indicating a company's ability to pay. For instance, one writer has shown how for

a group of companies, over the eight-year period reviewed the most restrictive application of these [general accounting] principles with relation to profits would have produced an aggregate net profit for all the companies combined of about $125 million, while the most liberal application, if consistently followed, would have produced an aggregate profit of about $275 million. It is noteworthy that none of these differences results from the difficulties of the measurement of values (which play such a role in accounting and are a major reason for inaccurate data); they arise exclusively from differences of opinion as to what constitutes a profit.[1]

There are many other important areas of disagreement about economic and business data, such as, for example, the productivity of labor (and how to separate it from other factors of production), and, in the national field, the aggregate measures about the economy as a whole, such as the national income and its components.[2] This area of uncertainty is only gradually being reduced.

THE INFLUENCE OF THE PAST AND FUTURE

A second major factor which is not readily adaptable to rigorous economic theorizing is the hidden effect of past events and traditions and the uncertainty of the future. Custom, experience, background, folklore, and subconscious memories and drives may exercise an important influence on decisions, even though that influence may not be apparent on the surface. And, even if complete knowledge of all the essential economic, technical, and administrative factors within the company could be assumed, many decisions still would involve interpretation of the unknown requiring the use of intuition, the "hunch," speculation, and extrapolation.

For major policy decisions, the chief unknowns may well be the great underlying secular trends (to which one may merely be able to adapt one's self), the reactions of consumers and competitors, the actions of government (in turn influenced by the vagaries of foreign policy), the availability of outside technical and administrative ability, the provision of a steady labor supply, and the sources of financial funds. In comparison to these unknowns, the rate of wages which must be paid and the rate of interest on capital are in many cases probably of minor importance.

Thus the likelihood of error about the past and the future increases the weight of intuitive judgment. This second major noneconomic influence on decision-making can probably be best studied through a detailed examination and cross-checking of a number of major decisions.

PERSONALITY AND STATUS

Finally, there is the influence of personality and status. The major significance which this factor may assume in company decision-making is evident if one thinks of the dominating influence which the chief executive of the firm may exercise and how entirely different are the decisions that may be made in similar situations—for instance, Henry Ford, Sr., and Henry Ford II. The influence of the personality of the chief may be particularly strong in times of prosperity and in companies with a surplus revenue. Under conditions that do not demand economic rationality for the survival of the firm, the possibly irrational influence of personalities (irrational from the economic point of view) is not necessarily catastrophic for the firm. Costly decisions and mistakes

1. Howard C. Greer, "What Are Accepted Principles of Accounting?" *Accounting Review,* March, 1938.
2. Oskar Morgenstern, *On the Inaccuracy of Economic Observations* (Princeton, N.J.: Princeton University Press, 1950).

not only are possible but are also tolerated — if made by the right people. This is also one reason why experiences of one firm cannot be exactly copied by other firms.

This last noneconomic factor in decision-making — personality — is perhaps the most important and most inscrutable of all these factors in decision-making by one man or by a small group of executives. It may therefore be worth while to explore in some more detail the role of personality in business decision-making. We might investigate more specifically the locus of decision-making: Which executives make the major decisions? What decisions do they make? How do they make these decisions — from what point of view, with short- or long-run considerations in mind, with what degree of participation, and with what results?

THE LOCUS OF DECISION-MAKING

An attempt was made to find the locus of decision-making in twenty large companies, varying in size from 4,000 to 20,000 employees. Typical decisions were selected, and each level of management was asked for the nature of its authority on the particular subject, such as, for example, the level on which various salary changes could be initiated or the amount of capital expenditures which could be incurred at different levels. In this way the authority limitations were ascertained for the chairman of the board of directors, the president, the executive vice-president, the various vice-presidents, and so on down the line to the foreman. Inquiry at these different levels also served as a check. Emphasis was placed principally on decisions dealing with money expenditures, since these can be ascertained more accurately than, say, grievances.

The result of this limited inquiry was that there tends to be a high degree of centralization of major decision-making in most of the companies studied. This is particularly so in regard to decisions which are concerned with financial, legal, and industrial relations problems and to a lesser extent in manufacturing and marketing. Decisions are centralized at the top directly by requiring a check before a decision is made or indirectly by such devices as the use of manuals; detailed spelling-out of all executives' limitations; training and indoctrination in line with the wishes of the chief executive; a rather complete knowledge of what the chief would do and would like to have done if he were there; central controls and group approvals; sanctions to enforce centralization.

To illustrate from the special field of industrial relations, a high degree of centralization of final decision-making by the chief or the group around him was found in the following matters:

a) Determination of and Changes in Salaries above $4,000–$6,000 Per Annum and All Bonus, Pension, and Stock-Purchase Arrangements. A widely held view was that recognition of managerial merit and the equitable distribution of salaries are so vital to the maintenance and improvement of managerial efficiency that it needs to be left to the chief executive who may be most nearly in the position of an "impartial umpire" and who should be most concerned with managerial succession and development. Decision on salaries by the chief executive also seemed to be a device for keeping salaries within the company's ability to pay and in line with its other obligations, as well as to prevent unmerited increases. If it is merely known that the chief executive may examine any one request for a salary increase, it encourages care in presenting only those requests which can be justified if challenged.

b) Basic Provisions in the Union Contract. The wage-rate increase, fringe benefits, and the costs of job evaluation were considered major cost factors affecting future profits and hence requiring the chief's approval in many instances. This was especially true where labor costs formed a considerable proportion of total costs, where the profit margin was narrow, or where competitive factors were important. Basic changes regarding union or management security, job assignments, technological changes, output standards, and arbitration provisions are considered to be of such vital import in the business — for reasons of cost or power relationships — that they required approval by the chief executive.

c) Hiring, Development, and Promotion of Executives. Since sums involved in the hiring and training of executives are heavy and responsibility for succession is urgent, this function was often considered a basic responsibility of the chief.

d) Precedent-Setting Grievances. These grievances may have to be checked with the chief executive.

DIFFERENT TYPES OF CHIEF EXECUTIVES

From this analysis of the locus of decision-making, different types of control emerge — control by one man, control by a few, control by many.

ONE-MAN CONTROL

First, there is the "one-man business" which appears to be considerably more widespread than is believed by many writers and observers. In many firms there is one-man control not only of most major decisions but also of a host of minor ones.

Among the major reasons for the one-man business may be mentioned principally tradition and necessity.

Tradition. In many businesses that have grown up under one-man direction, it is frequently difficult for the founder to give up his responsibilities to someone else. He may have the personal problem of not being able or willing to relinquish one of his major activities. He may fear that others would be less competent than he in exercising them. He may be concerned with a possible loss of prestige or of power. To the chief executive delegation may threaten undue dependence on others, while centralized power may seem to suggest unlimited personal capacity. He also may fear that extended delegation of powers will lead to the establishment of a rival organization within his own empire.

The chief also faces the problem of personnel. Those who grew up with him in the business may not be able (or willing) to shoulder any additional responsibility, yet may expect to receive it. If he brings in outside personnel, capable of taking on additional responsibilities, the newcomers may be thwarted by uncooperative old-timers.

The chief finally faces the problem that the power of vested ideas may well be stronger than the power of vested economic interests. It is hard for the one man in control to jettison all his intellectual investments.

If the founder's successor is one of his sons, the new chief may be reluctant to give up powers of decision-making for reasons of pride, desire to carry on the family tradition, or lack of stature to acknowledge that others, too, can make a contribution. If the successor is not a member of the family, he may want to imitate his old chief, to compensate for his previous lack of power, or to defend his newly won power against all insiders and outsiders.

Necessity. Delegation of decision-making may be costly. There are the expense of training and the cost of mistakes by junior executives. Costly duplication of functions may result: for example, additional personnel men may have to be hired for the various divisions or branches, in addition to the central personnel department. The talents of these men may not be fully utilized. Moreover, there may be friction, jealousy, and lack of uniformity among semi-independent and divergent sections.

Closer personal supervision may seem to be required in hard times resulting from increased competition, a downturn of the business cycle, or long-run decline of the industry. Yet, as more decisions are centralized, often less time and thought can be given to problems lower down in the management hierarchy. Because at the top there is less familiarity with the circumstances, decisions may be delayed by the necessity for gathering information or may be made hastily without all relevant data, and the action decided upon may be less sound and the expense greater than if the responsibility had been delegated.

Continued failure of effective decision-making because of overcentralization may lead to even more centralization than before, with increasingly adverse results. This vicious circle may contribute to the deterioration of an already depressed business condition.

CONTROL BY THE FEW

Not so different from one-man control is what may be described as "control by the few" or "oligarchic" control. In this case the major decisions of the firm are made, more or less exclusively, by a group of persons ranging in number from two to more than half a dozen, most often three or four. Usually each of these men has an area of decision-making of his own in which he has the final say, such as finance, production, or marketing. However, on vital matters that go beyond his area of jurisdiction other members of the top group may participate in the decision. This appears to be the situation in an increasing number of firms.

The distinguishing characteristic of oligarchic control is that each member of the group has equality in making important decisions for the firm. Such an arrangement may lead to considerable delay in making decisions and even to a complete deadlock on important matters if the top executives cannot agree among themselves and none of them has the power of final decision-making.

In one large corporation three executives have had approximately equal powers of decision-making. Each is supreme in his own field — public relations, production, or finance. On several important labor questions there recently was a serious split, the production specialist urging agreement with the union, largely for the sake of continued operations, while the other two opposed an agreement, chiefly on the basis of the principles involved. The deadlock was resolved only when a competitive firm signed with the union, thus forcing the two dissenters to capitulate. Since this event the company has moved steadily toward one-man control by the production executive. The management feels that there must be one final, decisive vote if complete standstill and breakdown are to be avoided.

Another type of oligarchic control is that exercised by financial interests, sometimes operated from a distance and based largely on narrow financial considerations, with little regard for the local people. This situation may result in a bitter struggle between a human relations-conscious local management and the outside financial interests which lack this consideration.

Oligarchic control often is a passing phenomenon that may either regress to one-man control or progress toward greater participation by an increasing number of executives. The latter tendency develops as the members of the oligarchy attempt to arrive at genuine joint decisions, better than those that any one individual could reach alone and involving an increasing number of the persons affected by them. In formal or informal meetings these executives seeking this goal tend to confine themselves to contributions that will advance group thinking, without necessarily advancing the individuals making them, into channels and procedures that tend to produce integration rather than domination or conflict.

CONTROL BY MANY

The control-by-many type of decision-making may be called "integrative" or "participative" (these probably are better terms than "democratic," because the latter, taken from political science, assumes an equality of men that usually does not exist in this context, certainly not in terms of status and income and normally not in terms of the power to influence business decisions). Most frequently this participation takes the form of informal, friendly consultation among the leading executives and possibly their subordinates.

The criterion of real delegation or participation is the extent to which the individual can differ from the opinions of others, especially those of his superiors, and the extent to which he can really influence decisions. In many firms this participation exists to some extent for the staff specialists and staff assistants. Their power is conferred principally by technical competence and such necessities as those resulting from the superior's lack of time to consider the problems thoroughly, as, for example, capital expenditures. Thus in many companies the advisability of highly complex capital expenditures is passed to the engineering department to decide on the basis of the technical possibilities, the availability of capital and skilled labor, the potential market. The participation of the technical staff is likely to be greater, the more certain and tangible the considerations involved and the smaller the area of intuition and shadowy judgment.

Another use of staff participation is in cases where divergent personalities are involved at the top. Their subordinate staff members are required to resolve the problems among themselves, at a level where there is less possibility of "loss of face" and more chance for open discussion and differences of opinion. Sometimes the staffs can enforce a decision on the strength of their reputation for technical competence because the higher-ups are afraid to mix in technical matters.

The line more frequently is handled on a military basis, and, as a consequence, participation is less frequent. When participation does occur, it is ordinarily through consultation or conferences.

Sometimes participation is haphazard. The chief executive may be influenced by a chance event, such as an unforeseen conversation with an employee far down the line or a chance remark heard at a party or on a train ride to the office. For example, one railroad is said to have converted from steam to diesel engines because the chief executive on one of his trips happened to talk to the engineer of his train and the latter was enthusiastic about diesel engines.

Sometimes such a chance decision may be reached during an enforced period of rest. Charles E. Wilson, until recently president of the General Motors Corporation, says that the idea of the wage escalator clause and the linkage of wage rates to a national productivity index came to him when he was confined to his bed for several weeks after a skating accident.

At the top level of management, participation may occur through a series of stepup conferences, in which members of each level of management jointly formulate suggested solutions to company problems. More frequently real power to disagree rests with a top company committee consisting of the heads of all the major functions, deliberating on a basis of real equality. In this type of participation the chief executive has a vote merely as one member of the committee.

CONTROL BY "REBUTTAL POWER"

One-man control may be modified by participation above the chief executive. The board of directors has the power to remove the chief executive if he no longer adequately carries out the objectives of the corporation. However, the chief may be able to "pack" the board with his own friends or achieve the same effect through superior knowledge or persuasiveness.

An important "rebuttal" power may exist in one of the committees of the board of directors or on the board itself through the appointment of specialists or former company executives. They may serve as a check on unsound proposals, either because their presence and competence discourage presentation of such proposals or because they have the power to veto them. In addition, the power of the chief executive may be modified through the appointment of outside directors from other industries; public institutions; or consumer, supplier, or banking interests.

The power of the chief executive also may be limited by "monopsony," the counterbargaining power of other concerns, labor unions, and government officials. Some have suggested that the chief's term of office may be confined to a certain period of years, also as a means of avoiding the possible exhaustion of his ideas and the vitality of his leadership.

Finally, certain important control functions may be transferred from the chief executive to the board of directors. For instance, the chief financial official in a number of companies reports directly to the finance committee of the board, which in this way has an independent financial check. Many chief executives welcome such effective "rebuttal power" because they feel it helps them to a more effective performance of their duties.

CONCLUSIONS

From our brief survey of the current status of decision-making in American industry, it is clear that important changes have taken place since the traditional concepts of management were formulated. We have moved from the owner-manager to the professional manager in a large number of companies. This may have resulted in some important changes of businessmen's objectives, possibly a shift from the emphasis on profits to that of power, to the improvement of status and professional performance, to more rationalized and responsible policies. The essential nature of the decision-making of the owner-manager may not have been modified too radically by the professional manager. The great economist Alfred Marshall's conception of the employer as "himself exercising a general control over everything and preserving unity in the main plan of business" may still apply to the professional heads of many businesses today. To some extent, however, one-man control may still be buttressed by financial control (though this is relatively rare). Sometimes this leads to a return of one-man control, sometimes to an extension of participation, through formal or informal participation in major decisions by a number of top executives, by the board of directors, or by staff specialists. These groups may have some veto power, either through their legal position (as representatives of the shareholders) or through technical competence. It may be that the newer tendencies toward participation in decision-making may lead to an important modification of the concept of the chief executive: he may change from an absolute ruler to a constitutional monarch who merely listens or gives advice and makes the final decision only in exceptional circumstances. But the road of such a development is not likely to be smooth. For the ideals of participation may well be used by the tyrant-entrepreneur as a more effective means of keeping control: his subordinates are made to think that they are participating in his decisions, whereas, in fact, they merely conform to the goals of the chief without even realizing it. On the contrary, they may believe that they are genuinely participating, and when something irks them they may be unable to find the source of the trouble—as they could do with the old, outspoken entrepreneur. On the other hand, a number of companies appear to have pioneered rather successfully in increasing participation by their executives in a constructive effort. Such may be the powers for good or ill of the new studies and techniques of psychology and sociology.

14 – Business Decision Making

JAMES G. MARCH

Since World War II, a desire to understand and improve business decision making has stimulated a small but growing research effort directed toward both of those ends. On the one hand, we have the new fields of operations research and management science, which have substantially improved managerial decision making. Simultaneously, we have witnessed the birth of organization theory and behavioral theories of the firm.

This chapter is a preliminary progress report on recent developments in the latter areas. Specifically, it reports what we at Carnegie Tech's Graduate School of Industrial Administration think we are learning about how business organizations make decisions.

An executive existing in the complex environment of the business organization has a three-stage decision problem: 1. To which of his many problems should he direct his attention? 2. How much time, effort, and expense should he invest in resolving uncertainty about that problem? 3. What solution to the problem should he use?

Most classical theories of problem solving are theories of the last stage of this process. But recent research suggests the first two are more important.

WHICH PROBLEM TO SOLVE?

What determines the problems an executive will attempt to solve? Obviously, if he had few and simple enough problems, he could solve them all as completely as he wished. But at any one time he's likely to have a long-range budget to approve, a letter to a government agency to dictate, a speech before the Rotary to prepare, and a telephone to answer.

We have attempted to reproduce in the laboratory some of the critical characteristics of the executive's decision problem. In a preliminary experiment, subjects were asked to handle a relatively simple administrative job. The job involved three kinds of activities:

▶ Routine communication. *They were to communicate to relevant clerks information on the current inventory levels in various warehouses.*

▶ Intermediate planning. *They were to make any necessary reassignments of warehouses to groups of clerks so as to maintain an approximately equal work load in each group.*

▶ General planning. *They were to suggest any other changes in procedure that might be appropriate.*

The subjects were told that each of the three jobs was equally important and should be given equal attention. After a training period to allow the "executives" to become accustomed to the task, the work load (the rate at which information on warehouses was received) was varied systematically. As the work load varied, we observed the proportion of communications dealing with routine activities as opposed to planning activities by the subjects.

Two results of this experiment are significant here. First, despite instructions to spend only one-third of the time on routine matters, the subjects spent a good deal more than that even when the work load was relatively light. Second, consistently as the work load increased, subjects spent a smaller proportion of their total time on planning activities. At peak loads, virtually no planning was evidenced.

Nor are these results limited to experimental studies. In a series of case studies of business decision making, organizations frequently were found to have difficulty allocating time to planning. Day-to-day problems tend to dominate.

Planning does occur in large-scale organizations, of course, but that planning is a relatively vulnerable activity compared to other activities. A person with responsibility for both routine day-to-day activities and long-term planning is likely to find the routine taking the much greater share of his time. This proposition – the so-called "Gresham's Law" of planning – is of considerable importance to understanding the attention focus of business executives.

From these and other studies it has become clear that factors affecting the attention focus of business decision-makers are critical to an understanding of business decisions. When a school burns down in Chicago, the problem of the day is safety. When sales dip, the problem is marketing. When a competitor's bookkeeper absconds with $100,000, the problem is fidelity. And so on.

ACHIEVEMENT AFFECTS SEARCH

What happens once a problem is identified? The textbook answer is that the executive obtains all relevant information and chooses the alternative which maximizes profits (or other objective). Such a theory seems implausible.

"Business Decision Making," *Industrial Research*, I (Spring 1959), 65–70. Reprinted by permission of the author and Industrial Research Magazine, Beverly Shores, Indiana. **James G. March:** Graduate School of Industrial Administration, Carnegie Institute of Technology.

An alternative theory, proposed by H. A. Simon and others, draws heavily on the early work of a group of German psychologists, particularly Kurt Lewin. It rests on these very simple propositions:

► Individuals do not attempt to maximize utility, but seek to achieve alternatives that are "satisfactory." A satisfactory alternative is one that is better than the "level of aspiration."

► The level of aspiration changes over time, going up when achievement goes up, coming down when achievement comes down. It adjusts upward faster than downward.

► If the individual sees an alternative that is satisfactory, he will not search very vigorously for additional alternatives.

For the first two of these propositions there has been considerable evidence for at least 20 years. It is the combination of these two with the third, however, that makes the system an interesting and dynamic one. As a result, some of our recent work has been focussed particularly on testing the effect of achievement on search behavior.

One such study is an examination of behavior in a simulated trouble-shooting situation. The subjects were asked to identify which one of three components in a machine was bad. They could do this only by inspecting the components in turn until they found the trouble. The decision problem arose because the cost of inspecting the components varied, as did the probability that the trouble would be in any particular one. The subjects were paid the same amount for finding the trouble regardless of what it cost them.

As a result, the amount earned depended on a subject's ability to choose a good inspection strategy. After being given considerable experience with the machine, each subject was asked what he thought would be the best order in which to inspect the components.

The rate at which subjects were paid during the "training" period was varied. One group was paid at such a rate that it could not help but make money, no matter what it did. A second group was paid so it would lose money on the less-efficient inspection strategies and make money on the better ones. A third group was paid such that it could not help but lose money no matter what it did.

Results?

HIGH PAY YIELDS EASY SATISFACTION

The strategies recommended by the group paid at the very high rate averaged 23% more costly in terms of inspection costs than the strategies recommended by the other two groups. We infer that the high-pay subjects more easily achieved satisfactory solutions and were less likely than their low-pay associates to discover better ones — as predicted by the theory.

But the intensity with which individuals search for alternatives or information about alternatives is only one side of the problem. Some people engage in vigorous, yet strikingly unproductive, search. We need to know not only how hard employes and executives look, but also how and where they look. Particularly, we need to know how individuals organize and utilize their memories.

HUMAN-LIKE COMPUTERS

To study the phenomena associated with complex executive decision making, a group of Carnegie Tech and Rand Corp. psychologists — A. Newell, J. C. Shaw, H. A. Simon, and their associates — are programming a computer to play chess. The computer exhibits some human-like characteristics. For instance, it will not always make the same move in the same situation.

Neither the machine nor human chess players — even the most expert — examine all possible combinations of all possible future moves. The reason is simple. In anything but the most trivial problem, the number of future possibilities that would have to be examined is so enormous as to overload the computational capacities of our largest computers, let alone those of a human being. Instead, human beings (and properly programmed computers) use "insight" and "hunches." They ask questions like: *To what other problems is this one similar?*

Although much work remains to be done, this computer-human research has brought us substantially closer to theories of problem-solving that incorporate the concepts of "insight," "hunch," and "problem similarity."

THE ORGANIZATIONAL HUNCH

How are these individual concepts applied in the business organization complex? What features are there about a business organization that affect the decision made in the organization — particularly such critical decisions for the organization as pricing, capital expenditures, and resource allocation?

Research by R. M. Cyert, W. R. Dill, and other economists and behavioral scientists at Carnegie indicates that the organization affects decisions in these ways:

► It sets and enforces organizational objectives, criteria by which the success of the business operations are to be judged.

► It collects and communicates through the firm information about factors to be considered in a decision. By the time information reaches the responsible executive in a firm it is at least second-hand and often fourth, fifth, or sixth-hand information.

► It executes the decision. There often is, of course, a large difference between what top management "decides" and what the organization does.

In talking about business firms it is sometimes tempting to assume that the objective of the firm is well-defined, unambiguous, and unitary. An often-heard but naive theory is that the objective of the firm is to maximize profits. While it is extremely difficult to demonstrate conclusively that a particular decision does not maximize profits over the long run, the burden of the evidence shows that business firms rarely define their objectives in such a pristine way.

OBJECTIVES: CLEAR AND OBSCURE

Even more rarely do firms act as though profit maximization were their sole objective. Instead, our studies in business organizations indicate that the firm is likely to have a melange of objectives. Some of these objectives will be clear; some will be ambiguous. Some will be easy to achieve; some will be difficult. Some will be considered at one time; some will be considered at another. Some will be viewed as important by one part of the organization; some will be important to another part.

A firm's objectives change with experience and through the demands of individuals. After a few years of $1.2 million profits, $1 million profits no longer are viewed as satisfactory. After persistent failure to gain more than 10% of the market, a goal of 15% no longer is considered reasonable.

At the same time objectives change in response to demands made on the organization by individuals or groups whose services are necessary. When a firm hires a new research director it frequently makes some commitments about the allocation of resources to research. When it signs a consent decree as a result of some governmental action, it makes commitments. When it reacts to consumer complaints about product quality, it makes commitments. Over the years, these commitments accumulate, change, and are forgotten, usually with rather little attention to their internal consistency.

What are the implications of such a theory of organizational objectives? One implication is that different objectives will be attended to at different times.

THE 'WORLD' THE ORGANIZATION LIVES IN

A second implication of such a theory is more subtle. Whether one objective is consistent with a second partly depends on what those objectives are. But it also depends on what kind of a "world" the organization lives in. To take an extreme example, if the organization had unlimited resources, it could satisfy almost all of its commitments. Although no organization ever achieves such a utopian existence, some firms approximate it in good times.

What happens? So long as the world is good, old commitments and new demands of various parts of the organization are met quite freely without much questioning. New staff is taken on. New equipment is purchased.

The "successful" firm acts like the "successful" subject in our trouble-shooting experiment. It engages in little search for better alternatives because the existing ones are good enough.

As a result, "organizational slack" develops. Slack represents expenditures in time, money, manpower, and policy decisions that arise in a benign environment. It also represents a form of "fat" in the organization that can be cut back if economic conditions are less favorable. Thus, research expenditures in firms have increased steadily since the war *except* in two recession periods. Similarly, in 1957–58 a number of firms were reported to have cut back substantially on their secretarial and clerical staffs without noticeable decrease in secretarial and clerical output.

In an analysis of one industry we were able to predict, on the basis of the organizational slack concept, which firms would make an intensive effort to increase sales in a particular time period. These predictions are confirmed substantially.

BIAS BY DOUBLE FILTER

Traditionally the problem of organizational information has been treated much like the problem of organizational objectives—by simple fiat. Textbooks might proclaim that it is the responsibility of management to secure adequate and accurate information. Our theories of organizational decision making, however, need to be somewhat less hortatory. Specifically, we need to know what biases are introduced into the information that is processed through an organization.

Biases are introduced by selective perception, by uncertainty absorption, and by deliberate falsification. Executives do not see all the facts. Any particular individual is exposed to only a small portion of the relevant information and "sees" only a part of that to which he is exposed. The effects of this double filter of selective perception have long been recognized in psychological research.

Recently, attempts have been made to investigate the operation of selective perception in a business setting. In one study by D. Dearborn and H. A. Simon, a group of middle-management executives was asked to read a long, carefully factual description of a company and its current position. Each executive then was asked to indicate what problem in the company a new president should deal with first. Eighty-three per cent of the sales executives thought the main problem was sales. But only 29% of other-division executives saw it as sales. Virtually all executives saw the "facts" in a way closely related to their organizational positions.

STAFF INFORMATION—PLUS

Uncertainty absorption—the second way in which bias is introduced—is the transformation of raw information into inferences. For example, staff units in an organization do not communicate the detailed figures on which they base their predictions. They communicate the predictions with perhaps some supporting data.

This obvious but often ignored fact makes a substantial difference to decision making in an organization. It means, for example, that it is ordinarily impossible for other parts of the organization to check the conclusions of an estimating unit. Information that initially is highly ambiguous tends to become more and more precise as it passes through the organization.

What happens in this kind of information condensation? One aspect of this problem is the extent to which organization members will treat the same quantitative figures differently depending on what kinds of data they represent.

We gave two groups of graduate students in industrial administration the task of communicating to a superior a single estimate on the basis of a pair of estimates from subordinates. One group was told to condense and pass along estimates of probable costs of a new product; the other to communicate estimates of its probable sales. The subordinates' estimates in each case are identical. Yet a consistent difference exists between the communicated information of the two groups.

WHO 'MAKES' A DECISION?

Similarly, in a series of field studies we have found considerable condensation (and biasing) of information as it passes through the organization. By the time complex information is used for formal decision making, it frequently has been reduced to a few simple statements. As a result it is often very difficult to say with much meaning who "makes" a decision in an organization, or when it is made. Instead, there seems to be a process of gradual commitment to a course of action.

Contributing to this picture is a third form of organizational bias in information—conscious falsification. For the situation of uncertainty in which organization members operate, "falsification" may be too harsh a word. A buyer prefers a prediction of next year's sales that will not be too difficult to achieve. A staff member committed to the purchase of a piece of new equipment admits privately, "If anybody brings up a cost item not thought of, I can balance it elsewhere."

Finally, company decision making is affected strongly by the way top management "decisions" are carried out by the rest of the organization.

NEGOTIATIONS
FORMAL AND INFORMAL

In some theories of business decision making, simple assumptions are made about the employment contract. These assumptions add up to the proposition that in return for his wages an employe does what he is told to do. An employe who doesn't want to do what he is told can quit, refuse to do as instructed and be fired, or negotiate a higher salary in return for doing what is desired.

Our theory, however, suggests another major alternative. He can negotiate not only about salary, but also about duties. "Negotiate" is an inadequate term if it suggests the formal bargaining table. The bargaining table is only one type of negotiation; a much more important part of negotiating occurs in the day-to-day decisions of subordinates on how they comply with instructions, and the day-to-day decisions of superiors on what instructions they will issue and what sanctions they will impose.

COMMUNICATION CONSTRAINT

At Carnegie Tech, H. J. Leavitt is studying how groups implement methods for solving a collective problem under varying constraints on communication and information. Three subjects are asked to play a game. At each play of the game each player announces a number (by throwing a switch connected to the experimenter's control board) from zero to 10.

The objective of the group is to announce numbers so that their sum is a number stated at the start of the play by the experimenter. Since the subjects cannot communicate to each other, their problem is to develop and implement a system to deal with any number the experimenter might announce from zero to 30. There are a large number of possible systems involving a wide range of complexity.

One of the interesting implications of the preliminary results from this experiment is that the "efficiency" of a particular system for solving the problem depends not only on the intrinsic characteristics of the system, *but also on the ease with which it can be introduced into the group.*

For example, one very simple system is to have the first person give the target number if it is 10 or less, and otherwise give "10"; have the second subject announce "zero" if the target is 10 or less, or announce the second digit of the number if it is between 11 and 19, or otherwise state "10"; and have the third person announce "zero" if the target is 20 or less, announce the second digit of the number if it is between 21 and 29, or announce "10" if it is 30. This system handles all possible numbers in a way calculated to introduce few, if any, errors. However, in many groups such a system is quite hard to establish.

NEW DIRECTIONS

Along with the empirical studies described here is a trend toward the use of computer simulation of organizational problem solving. Many of our future efforts literally will be computer models. One such model we have developed predicts with some accuracy the share of market for two major firms in the American can industry over a 40-year period. This is true despite the fact that the model is by all odds too simple and incomplete.

In the next few years we can expect to see a substantial increase in both the numbers and quality of such computer-simulation models. There seems little doubt that simulation—by machine—will contribute to improvements in our theories of organizational decision making.

SECTION *IV*

ORGANIZING

As the title of Scott's article (#15) indicates, this section begins with an overview of the function of organizing. Scott traces the development of knowledge in this area and gives a critical analysis of the present state of that knowledge.

The major areas within the function are covered in the articles that follow. Once again, Barnard (#16) throws light on the formal organization. Selznick (#17) follows with an analysis of the informal organization and the paradox inherent in the activities of the formal and informal structures of an organization. Dale (#18) examines another paradox—centralization and decentralization in relation to authority—and the problem of establishing a proper balance of these two theoretical extremes within the organization. Dalton's study (#19) is a report of his research on the interaction between line and staff industrial managers. Thompson (#20) discusses the concept of span of control in terms of cost and effectiveness rather than rules of thumb; he also presents "span-of-control mathematics," which opens new avenues in the supervisory area of organizing.

15 – Organization Theory: An Overview and an Appraisal

WILLIAM G. SCOTT

Man is intent on drawing himself into a web of collectivized patterns. "Modern man has learned to accommodate himself to a world increasingly organized. The trend toward ever more explicit and consciously drawn relationships is profound and sweeping; it is marked by depth no less than by extension."[1] This comment by Seidenberg nicely summarizes the pervasive influence of organization in many forms of human activity.

Some of the reasons for intense organizational activity are found in the fundamental transitions which revolutionized our society, changing it from a rural culture, to a culture based on technology, industry, and the city. From these changes, a way of life emerged characterized by the *proximity* and *dependency* of people on each other. Proximity and dependency, as conditions of social life, harbor the threats of human conflict, capricious antisocial behavior, instability of human relationships, and uncertainty about the nature of the social structure with its concomitant roles.

Of course, these threats to social integrity are present to some degree in all societies, ranging from the primitive to the modern. But, these threats become dangerous when the harmonious functioning of a society rests on the maintenance of a highly intricate, delicately balanced form of human collaboration. The civilization we have created depends on the preservation of a precarious balance. Hence, disrupting forces impinging on this shaky form of collaboration must be eliminated or minimized.

Traditionally, organization is viewed as a vehicle for accomplishing goals and objectives. While this approach is useful, it tends to obscure the inner workings and internal purposes of organization itself. Another fruitful way of treating organization is as a mechanism having the ultimate purpose of offsetting those forces which undermine human collaboration. In this sense, organization tends to minimize conflict, and to lessen the significance of individual behavior which deviates from values that the organization has established as worthwhile. Further, organization increases stability in human relationships by reducing uncertainty regarding the nature of the system's structure and the human roles which are inherent to it. Corollary to this point, organization enhances the predictability of human action, because it limits the number of behavioral alternatives available to an individual. As Presthus points out:

> Organization is defined as a system of structural interpersonal relations . . . individuals are differentiated in terms of authority, status, and role with the result that personal interaction is prescribed. . . . Anticipated reactions tend to occur, while ambiguity and spontaneity are decreased.[2]

In addition to all of this, organization has built-in safeguards. Besides prescribing acceptable forms of behavior for those who elect to submit to it, organization is also able to counter-

"Organization Theory: An Overview and an Appraisal," *Academy of Management Journal,* IV (April 1961), 7–26. Reprinted by permission of the author and the publisher. **William G. Scott:** College of Commerce, DePaul University.

1. Roderick Seidenburg, *Post Historic Man* (Boston: Beacon Press, 1951), p. 1.
2. Robert V. Presthus, "Toward a Theory of Organizational Behavior," *Administrative Science Quarterly,* June, 1958, p. 50.

balance the influence of human action which transcends its established patterns.[3]

Few segments of society have engaged in organizing more intensively than business.[4] The reason is clear. Business depends on what organization offers. Business needs a system of relationships among functions; it needs stability, continuity, and predictability in its internal activities and external contacts. Business also appears to need harmonious relationships among the people and processes which make it up. Put another way, a business organization has to be free, relatively, from destructive tendencies which may be caused by divergent interests.

As a foundation for meeting these needs rests administrative science. A major element of this science is organization theory, which provides the grounds for management activities in a number of significant areas of business endeavor. Organization theory, however, is not a homogeneous science based on generally accepted principles. Various theories of organization have been, and are being evolved. For example, something called "modern organization theory" has recently emerged, raising the wrath of some traditionalists, but also capturing the imagination of a rather elite *avant-garde*.

The thesis of this paper is that modern organization theory, when stripped of its irrelevancies, redundancies, and "speech defects," is a logical and vital evolution in management thought. In order for this thesis to be supported, the reader must endure a review and appraisal of more traditional forms of organization theory which may seem elementary to him.

In any event, three theories of organization are having considerable influence on management thought and practice. They are arbitrarily labeled in this paper as the classical, the neo-classical, and the modern. Each of these is fairly distinct; but they are not unrelated. Also, these theories are on-going, being actively supported by several schools of management thought.

THE CLASSICAL DOCTRINE

For lack of a better method of identification, it will be said that the classical doctrine deals almost exclusively with the *anatomy of formal organization*. This doctrine can be traced back to Frederick W. Taylor's interest in functional foremanship and planning staffs. But most students of management thought would agree that in the United States, the first systematic approach to organization, and the first comprehensive attempt to find

organizational universals, is dated 1931 when Mooney and Reiley published *Onward Industry*.[5] Subsequently, numerous books, following the classical vein, have appeared. Two of the more recent are Brech's, *Organization*[6] and Allen's, *Management and Organization*.[7]

Classical organization theory is built around four key pillars. They are the division of labor, the scalar and functional processes, structure, and span of control. Given these major elements just about all of classical organization theory can be derived.

(1) The division of labor is without doubt the cornerstone among the four elements.[8] From it the other elements flow as corollaries. For example, *scalar* and *functional* growth requires specialization and departmentalization of functions. Organization *structure* is naturally dependent upon the direction which specialization of activities travels in company development. Finally, *span of control* problems result from the number of specialized functions under the jurisdiction of a manager.

(2) The scalar and functional processes deal with the vertical and horizontal growth of the organization, respectively.[9] The scalar process refers to the growth of the chain of command, the delegation of authority and responsibility, unity of command, and the obligation to report.

The division of the organization into specialized parts and the regrouping of the parts into compatible units are matters pertaining to the functional process. This process focuses on the horizontal evolution of the line and staff in a formal organization.

(3) Structure is the logical relationships of functions in an organization, arranged to accomplish

3. Regulation and predictability of human behavior are matters of degree varying with different organizations on something of a continuum. At one extreme are bureaucratic type organizations with tight bonds of regulation. At the other extreme are voluntary associations, and informal organizations with relatively loose bonds of regulation.

This point has an interesting sidelight. A bureaucracy with tight controls and a high degree of predictability of human action appears to be unable to distinguish between destructive and creative deviations from established values. Thus the only thing which is safeguarded is the *status quo*.

4. The monolithic institutions of the military and government are other cases of organizational preoccupation.

5. James D. Mooney and Alan C. Reiley, *Onward Industry* (New York: Harper and Brothers, 1931). Later published by James D. Mooney under the title *Principles of Organization*.

6. E. F. L. Brech, *Organization* (London: Longmans, Green and Company, 1957).

7. Louis A. Allen, *Management and Organization* (New York: McGraw-Hill Book Company, 1958).

8. Usually the division of labor is treated under a topical heading of departmentation, see for example: Harold Koontz and Cyril O'Donnell, *Principles of Management* (New York: McGraw-Hill Book Company, 1959), Chapter 7.

9. These processes are discussed at length in Ralph Currier Davis, *The Fundamentals of Top Management* (New York: Harper and Brothers, 1951), Chapter 7.

the objectives of the company efficiently. Structure implies system and pattern. Classical organization theory usually works with two basic structures, the line and the staff. However, such activities as committee and liaison functions fall quite readily into the purview of structural considerations. Again, structure is the vehicle for introducing logical and consistent relationships among the diverse functions which comprise the organization.[10]

(4) The span of control concept relates to the number of subordinates a manager can effectively supervise. Graicunas has been credited with first elaborating the point that there are numerical limitations to the subordinates one man can control.[11] In a recent statement on the subject, Brech points out, "span" refers to ". . . the number of persons, themselves carrying managerial and supervisory responsibilities, for whom the senior manager retains his over-embracing responsibility of direction and planning, co-ordination, motivation, and control."[12] Regardless of interpretation, span of control has significance, in part, for the shape of the organization which evolves through growth. Wide span yields a flat structure; short span results in a tall structure. Further, the span concept directs attention to the complexity of human and functional interrelationships in an organization.

It would not be fair to say that the classical school is unaware of the day-to-day administrative problems of the organization. Paramount among these problems are those stemming from human interactions. But the interplay of individual personality, informal groups, intraorganizational conflict, and the decision-making processes in the formal structure appears largely to be neglected by classical organization theory. Additionally, the classical theory overlooks the contributions of the behavioral sciences by failing to incorporate them in its doctrine in any systematic way. In summary, classical organization theory has relevant insights into the nature of organization, but the value of this theory is limited by its narrow concentration on the formal anatomy of organization.

NEOCLASSICAL THEORY OF ORGANIZATION

The neoclassical theory of organization embarked on the task of compensating for some of the deficiencies in classical doctrine. The neoclassical school is commonly identified with the human relations movement. Generally, the neoclassical approach takes the postulates of the classical

school, regarding the pillars of organization as givens. But these postulates are regarded as modified by people, acting independently or within the context of the informal organization.

One of the main contributions of the neoclassical school is the introduction of behavioral sciences in an integrated fashion into the theory of organization. Through the use of these sciences, the human relationists demonstrate how the pillars of the classical doctrine are affected by the impact of human actions. Further, the neoclassical approach includes a systematic treatment of the informal organization, showing its influence on the formal structure.

Thus, the neoclassical approach to organization theory gives evidence of accepting classical doctrine, but superimposing on it modifications resulting from individual behavior, and the influence of the informal group. The inspiration of the neoclassical school were the Hawthorne studies.[13] Current examples of the neoclassical approach are found in human relations book like Gardner and Moore, *Human Relations in Industry,*[14] and Davis, *Human Relations in Business.*[15] To a more limited extent, work in industrial sociology also reflects a neoclassical point of view.[16]

It would be useful to look briefly at some of the contributions made to organization theory by the neoclassicists. First to be considered are modifications of the pillars of classical doctrine; second is the informal organization.

EXAMPLES OF THE NEOCLASSICAL APPROACH TO THE PILLARS OF FORMAL ORGANIZATION THEORY

(1) The *division of labor* has been a long stading subject of comment in the field of human relations. Very early in the history of industrial psychology study was made of industrial fatigue and monotony caused by the specialization of the work.[17] Later, attention shifted to the isolation of

10. For a discussion of structure see: William H. Newman, *Administrative Action* (Englewood Cliffs: Prentice-Hall, Incorporated, 1951), Chapter 16.

11. V. A. Graicunas, "Relationships in Organization," *Papers on the Science of Administration* (New York: Columbia University, 1937).

12. Brech, *op. cit.,* p. 78.

13. See: F. J. Roethlisberger and William J. Dickson, *Management and the Worker* (Cambridge: Harvard University Press, 1939).

14. Burleigh B. Gardner and David G. Moore, *Human Relations in Industry* (Homewood: Richard D. Irwin, 1955).

15. Keith Davis, *Human Relations in Business* (New York: McGraw-Hill Book Company, 1957).

16. For example see: Delbert C. Miller and William H. Form, *Industrial Sociology* (New York: Harper and Brothers, 1951).

17. See: Hugo Munsterberg, *Psychology and Industrial Efficiency* (Boston: Houghton Mifflin Company, 1913).

the worker, and his feeling of anonymity resulting from insignificant jobs which contributed negligibly to the final product.[18]

Also, specialization influences the work of management. As an organization expands, the need concomitantly arises for managerial motivation and coordination of the activities of others. Both motivation and coordination in turn relate to executive leadership. Thus, in part, stemming from the growth of industrial specialization, the neoclassical school has developed a large body of theory relating to motivation, coordination, and leadership. Much of this theory is derived from the social sciences.

(2) Two aspects of the *scalar and functional* processes which have been treated with some degree of intensity by the neoclassical school are the delegation of authority and responsibility, and gaps in or overlapping of functional jurisdictions. The classical theory assumes something of perfection in the delegation and functionalization processes. The neoclassical school points out that human problems are caused by imperfections in the way these processes are handled.

For example, too much or insufficient delegation may render an executive incapable of action. The failure to delegate authority and responsibility equally may result in frustration for the delegatee. Overlapping of authorities often causes clashes in personality. Gaps in authority cause failures in getting jobs done, with one party blaming the other for shortcomings in performance.[19]

The neoclassical school says that the scalar and functional processes are theoretically valid, but tend to deteriorate in practice. The ways in which they break down are described, and some of the human causes are pointed out. In addition the neoclassicists make recommendations, suggesting various "human tools" which will facilitate the operation of these processes.

(3) *Structure* provides endless avenues of analysis for the neoclassical theory of organization. The theme is that human behavior disrupts the best laid organizational plans, and thwarts the cleanness of the logical relationships founded in the structure. The neoclassical critique of structure centers on frictions which appear internally among people performing different functions.

Line and staff relations is a problem area, much discussed, in this respect. Many companies seem to have difficulty keeping the line and staff working together harmoniously. Both Dalton[20] and Juran[21] have engaged in research to discover the causes of friction, and to suggest remedies.

Of course, line-staff relations represent only one of the many problems of structural frictions described by the neoclassicists. As often as not,

the neoclassicists will offer prescriptions for the elimination of conflict in structure. Among the more important harmony-rendering formulae are participation, junior boards, bottom-up management, joint committees, recognition of human dignity, and "better" communication.

(4) An executive's *span of control* is a function of human determinants, and the reduction of span to a precise, universally applicable ratio is silly, according to the neoclassicists. Some of the determinants of span are individual differences in managerial abilities, the type of people and functions supervised, and the extent of communication effectiveness.

Coupled with the span of control question are the human implications of the type of structure which emerges. That is, is a tall structure with a short span or a flat structure with a wide span more conducive to good human relations and high morale? The answer is situational. Short span results in tight supervision; wide span requires a good deal of delegation with looser controls. Because of individual and organizational differences, sometimes one is better than the other. There is a tendency to favor the looser form of organization, however, for the reason that tall structures breed autocratic leadership, which is often pointed out as a cause of low morale.[22]

THE NEOCLASSICAL VIEW OF THE INFORMAL ORGANIZATION

Nothing more than the barest mention of the informal organization is given even in the most recent classical treatises on organization theory.[23] Systematic discussion of this form of organization has been left to the neoclassicists. The informal organization refers to people in group associations at work, but these associations are not specified in the "blueprint" of the formal organization. The informal organization means natural groupings of people in the work situation.

In a general way, the informal organization appears in response to the social need—the need of people to associate with others. However, for

---

18. Probably the classic work is: Elton Mayo, *The Human Problems of an Industrial Civilization* (Cambridge: Harvard University, 1946, first printed 1933).

19. For further discussion of the human relations implications of the scalar and functional processes see: Keith Davis, *op. cit.,* pp. 60–66.

20. Melville Dalton, "Conflicts between Staff and Line Managerial Officers," *American Sociological Review,* June, 1950, pp. 342–351.

21. J. M. Juran, "Improving the Relationship between Staff and Line," *Personnel,* May, 1956, pp. 515–524.

22. Gardner and Moore, *op. cit.,* pp. 237–243.

23. For example: Brech, *op. cit.,* pp. 27–29; and Allen, *op. cit.,* pp. 61–62.

analytical purposes, this explanation is not particularly satisfying. Research has produced the following, more specific determinants underlying the appearance of informal organizations.

(1) The *location* determinant simply states that in order to form into groups of any lasting nature, people have to have frequent face-to-face contact. Thus, the geography of physical location in a plant or office is an important factor in predicting who will be in what group.[24]

(2) *Occupation* is key factor determining the rise and composition of informal groups. There is a tendency for people performing similar jobs to group together.[25]

(3) *Interests* are another determinant for informal group formation. Even though people might be in the same location, performing similar jobs, differences of interest among them explain why several small, instead of one large, informal organizations emerge.

(4) *Special issues* often result in the formation of informal groups, but this determinant is set apart from the three previously mentioned. In this case, people who do not necessarily have similar interests, occupations, or locations may join together for a common cause. Once the issue is resolved, then the tendency is to revert to the more "natural" group forms.[26] Thus, special issues give rise to a rather impermanent informal association; groups based on the other three determinants tend to be more lasting.

When informal organizations come into being they assume certain characteristics. Since understanding these characteristics is important for management practice, they are noted below:

(1) Informal organizations act as agencies of *social control*. They generate a culture based on certain norms of conduct which, in turn, demands conformity from group members. These standards may be at odds with the values set by the formal organization. So an individual may very well find himself in a situation of conflicting demands.

(2) The form of human interrelationships in the informal organization requires *techniques of analysis* different from those used to plot the relationships of people in a formal organization. The method used for determining the structure of the informal group is called sociometric analysis. Sociometry reveals the complex structure of interpersonal relations which is based on premises fundamentally unlike the logic of the formal organization.

(3) Informal organizations have *status and communication* systems peculiar to themselves, not necessarily derived from the formal systems. For example, the grapevine is the subject of much neoclassical study.

(4) Survival of the informal organization requires stable continuing relationships among the people in them. Thus, it has been observed that the informal organization *resists change*.[27] Considerable attention is given by the neoclassicists to overcoming informal resistance to change.

(5) The last aspect of analysis which appears to be central to the neoclassical view of the informal organization is the study of the *informal leader*. Discussion revolves around who the informal leader is, how he assumes this role, what characteristics are peculiar to him, and how he can help the manager accomplish his objectives in the formal organization.[28]

This brief sketch of some of the major facets of informal organization theory has neglected, so far, one important topic treated by the neoclassical school. It is the way in which the formal and informal organizations interact.

A conventional way of looking at the interaction of the two is the "live and let live" point of view. Management should recognize that the informal organization exists, nothing can destroy it, and so the executive might just as well work with it. Working with the informal organization involves not threatening its existence unnecessarily, listening to opinions expressed for the group by the leader, allowing group participation in decision-making situations, and controlling the grapevine by prompt release of accurate information.[29]

While this approach is management centered, it is not unreasonable to expect that informal group standards and norms could make themselves felt on formal organizational policy. An honestly conceived effort by managers to establish a working relationship with the informal organization could result in an association where both formal and informal views would be reciprocally modified. The danger which at all costs should be avoided is that "working with the informal organization" does not degenerate into a shallow disguise for human manipulation.

24. See: Leon Festinger, Stanley Schachter, and Kurt Back, *Social Pressures in Informal Groups* (New York: Harper and Brothers, 1950), pp. 153–163.

25. For example see: W. Fred Cottrell, *The Railroader* (Palo Alto: The Stanford University Press, 1940), Chapter 3.

26. Except in cases where the existence of an organization is necessary for the continued maintenance of employee interest. Under these conditions the previously informal association may emerge as a formal group, such as a union.

27. Probably the classic study of resistance to change is: Lester Coch and John R. P. French, Jr., "Overcoming Resistance to Change," in Schuyler Dean Hoslett (editor), *Human Factors in Management* (New York: Harper and Brothers, 1951), pp. 242–268.

28. For example see: Robert Saltonstall, *Human Relations in Administration* (New York: McGraw-Hill Book Company, 1959), pp. 330–331; and Keith Davis, op. cit., pp. 99–101.

29. For an example of this approach see: John T. Doutt, "Management Must Manage the Informal Group, Too," *Advanced Management*, May, 1959, pp. 26–28.

Some neoclassical writing in organization theory, especially that coming from the management-oriented segment of this school, gives the impression that the formal and informal organizations are distinct, and at times, quite irreconcilable factors in a company. The interaction which takes place between the two is something akin to the interaction between the company and a labor union, or a government agency, or another company.

The concept of the social system is another approach to the interactional climate. While this concept can be properly classified as neoclassical, it borders on the modern theories of organization. The phrase "social system" means that an organization is a complex of mutually interdependent, but variable, factors.

These factors include individuals and their attitudes and motives, jobs, the physical work setting, the formal organization, and the informal organizations. These factors, and many others, are woven into an overall pattern of interdependency. From this point of view, the formal and informal organizations lose their distinctiveness, but find real meaning, in terms of human behavior, in the operation of the system as a whole. Thus, the study of organization turns away from descriptions of its component parts, and is refocused on the system of interrelationships among the parts.

One of the major contributions of the Hawthorne studies was the integration of Pareto's idea of the social system into a meaningful method of analysis for the study of behavior in human organizations.[30] This concept is still vitally important. But unfortunately some work in the field of human relations undertaken by the neoclassicists has overlooked, or perhaps discounted, the significance of this consideration.[31]

The fundamental insight regarding the social system, developed and applied to the industrial scene by the Hawthorne researchers, did not find much extension in subsequent work in the neoclassical vein. Indeed, the neoclassical school after the Hawthorne studies generally seemed content to engage in descriptive generalizations, or particularized empirical research studies which did not have much meaning outside their own context.

The neoclassical school of organization theory has been called bankrupt. Criticisms range from, "human relations is a tool for cynical puppeteering of people," to "human relations is nothing more than a trifling body of empirical and descriptive information." There is a good deal of truth in both criticisms, but another appraisal of the neoclassical school of organization theory is offered here.

The neoclassical approach has provided valuable contributions to the lore of organization. But, like the classical theory, the neoclassical doctrine suffers from incompleteness, a shortsighted perspective, and lack of integration among the many facets of human behavior studied by it. Modern organization theory has made a move to cover the shortcomings of the current body of theoretical knowledge.

MODERN ORGANIZATION THEORY

The distinctive qualities of modern organization theory are its conceptual-analytical base, its reliance on empirical research data and, above all, its integrating nature. These qualities are framed in a philosophy which accepts the premise that the only meaningful way to study organization is to study it as a system. As Henderson put it, the study of a system must rely on a method of analysis, ". . . involving the simultaneous variations of mutually dependent variables."[32] Human systems, of course, contain a huge number of dependent variables which defy the most complex simultaneous equations to solve.

Nevertheless, system analysis has its own peculiar point of view which aims to study organization in the way Henderson suggests. It treats organization as a system of mutually dependent variables. As a result, modern organization theory, which accepts system analysis, shifts the conceptual level of organization study above the classical and neoclassical theories. Modern organization theory asks a range of interrelated questions which are not seriously considered by the two other theories.

Key among these questions are: (1) What are the strategic parts of the system? (2) What is the nature of their mutual dependency? (3) What are the main processes in the system which link the parts together, and facilitate their adjustment to each other? (4) What are the goals sought by systems?[33]

Modern organization theory is in no way a unified body of thought. Each writer and researcher has his special emphasis when he considers the

30. See: Roethlisberger and Dickson, *op. cit.*, Chapter 24.

31. A check of management human relations texts, the organization and human relations chapters of principles of management texts, and texts on conventional organization theory for management courses reveals little or no treatment of the concept of the social system.

32. Lawrence J. Henderson, *Pareto's General Sociology* (Cambridge: Harvard University Press, 1935), p. 13.

33. There is another question which cannot be treated in the scope of this paper. It asks, what research tools should be used for the study of the system?

system. Perhaps the most evident unifying thread in the study of systems is the effort to look at the organization in its totality. Representative books in this field are March and Simon, *Organizations*,[34] and Haire's anthology, *Modern Organization Theory*.[35]

Instead of attempting a review of different writers' contributions to modern organization theory, it will be more useful to discuss the various ingredients involved in system analysis. They are the parts, the interactions, the processes, and the goals of systems.

THE PARTS OF THE SYSTEM
AND THEIR INTERDEPENDENCY

The first basic part of the system is the *individual,* and the personality structure he brings to the organization. Elementary to an individual's personality are motives and attitudes which condition the range of expectancies he hopes to satisfy by participating in the system.

The second part of the system is the formal arrangement of functions, usually called the *formal organization*. The formal organization is the interrelated pattern of jobs which make up the structure of a system. Certain writers, like Argyris, see a fundamental conflict resulting from the demands made by the system, and the structure of the mature, normal personality. In any event, the individual has expectancies regarding the job he is to perform; and, conversely, the job makes demands on, or has expectancies relating to, the performance of the individual. Considerable attention has been given by writers in modern organization theory to incongruencies resulting from the interaction of organizational and individual demands.[36]

The third part in the organization system is the *informal organization*. Enough has been said already about the nature of this organization. But it must be noted that an interactional pattern exists between the individual and the informal group. This interactional arrangement can be conveniently discussed as the mutual modification of expectancies. The informal organization has demands which it makes on members in terms of anticipated forms of behavior, and the individual has expectancies of satisfaction he hopes to derive from association with people on the job. Both these sets of expectancies interact, resulting in the individual modifying his behavior to accord with the demands of the group, and the group, perhaps, modifying what it expects from an individual because of the impact of his personality on group norms.[37]

Much of what has been said about the various expectancy systems in an organization can also be treated using status and role concepts. Part of modern organization theory rests on research findings in social-psychology relative to reciprocal patterns of behavior stemming from role demands generated by both the formal and informal organizations, and role perceptions peculiar to the individual. Bakke's *fusion process* is largely concerned with the modification of role expectancies. The fusion process is a force, according to Bakke, which acts to weld divergent elements together for the preservation of organizational integrity.[38]

The fifth part of system analysis is the *physical setting* in which the job is performed. Although this element of the system may be implicit in what has been said already about the formal organization and its functions, it is well to separate it. In the physical surroundings of work, interactions are present in complex man-machine systems. The human "engineer" cannot approach the problems posed by such interrelationships in a purely technical, engineering fashion. As Haire says, these problems lie in the domain of the social theorist.[39] Attention must be centered on responses demanded from a logically ordered production function, often with the view of minimizing the error in the system. From this standpoint, work cannot be effectively organized unless the psychological, social, and physiological characteristics of people participating in the work environment are considered. Machines and processes should be designed to fit certain generally observed psychological and physiological properties of men, rather than hiring men to fit machines.

In summary, the parts of the system which appear to be of strategic importance are the individual, the formal structure, the informal organization, status and role patterns, and the physical environment of work. Again, these parts are woven into a configuration called the organizational system. The processes which link the parts are taken up next.

---

34. James G. March and Herbert A. Simon, *Organizations* (New York: John Wiley and Sons, 1958).
35. Mason Haire (editor), *Modern Organization Theory* (New York: John Wiley and Sons, 1959).
36. See Chris Argyris, *Personality and Organization* (New York: Harper and Brothers, 1957), esp. Chapters 2, 3, 7.
37. For a larger treatment of this subject see: George C. Homans, *The Human Group* (New York: Harcourt, Brace and Company, 1950), Chapter 5.
38. E. Wight Bakke, "Concept of the Social Organization," in *Modern Organization Theory*, Mason Haire (editor) (New York: John Wiley and Sons, 1959), pp. 60–61.
39. Mason Haire, "Psychology and the Study of Business: Joint Behavioral Sciences," in *Social Science Research on Business: Product and Potential* (New York: Columbia University Press, 1959), pp. 53–59.

THE LINKING PROCESSES

One can say, with a good deal of glibness, that all the parts mentioned above are interrelated. Although this observation is quite correct, it does not mean too much in terms of system theory unless some attempt is made to analyze the processes by which the interaction is achieved. Role theory is devoted to certain types of interactional processes. In addition, modern organization theorists point to three other linking activities which appear to be universal to human systems of organized behavior. These processes are communication, balance, and decision making.

(1) Communication is mentioned often in neoclassical theory, but the emphasis is on description of forms of communication activity, i.e., formal-informal, vertical-horizontal, line-staff. Communication, as a mechanism which links the segments of the system together, is overlooked by way of much considered analysis.

One aspect of modern organization theory is study of the communication network in the system. Communication is viewed as the method by which action is evoked from the parts of the system. Communication acts not only as stimuli resulting in action, but also as a control and coordination mechanism linking the decision centers in the system into a synchronized pattern. Deutsch points out that organizations are composed of parts which communicate with each other, receive messages from the outside world, and store information. Taken together, these communication functions of the parts comprise a configuration representing the total system.[40] More is to be said about communication later in the discussion of the cybernetic model.

(2) The concept of *balance* as a linking process involves a series of some rather complex ideas. Balance refers to an equilibrating mechanism whereby the various parts of the system are maintained in a harmoniously structured relationship to each other.

The necessity for the balance concept logically flows from the nature of systems themselves. It is impossible to conceive of an ordered relationship among the parts of a system without also introducing the idea of a stabilizing or an adapting mechanism.

Balance appears in two varieties—quasi-automatic and innovative. Both forms of balance act to insure system integrity in face of changing conditions, either internal or external to the system. The first form of balance, quasi-automatic, refers to what some think are "homeostatic" properties of systems. That is, systems seem to exhibit built-in propensities to maintain steady states.

If human organizations are open, self-maintaining systems, then control and regulatory processes are necessary. The issue hinges on the degree to which stabilizing processes in systems, when adapting to change, are automatic. March and Simon have an interesting answer to this problem, which in part is based on the type of change and the adjustment necessary to adapt to the change. Systems have programs of action which are put into effect when a change is perceived. If the change is relatively minor, and if the change comes within the purview of established programs of action, then it might be fairly confidently predicted that the adaptation made by the system will be quasi-automatic.[41]

The role of innovative, creative balancing efforts now needs to be examined. The need for innovation arises when adaptation to a change is outside the scope of existing programs designed for the purpose of keeping the system in balance. New programs have to be evolved in order for the system to maintain internal harmony.

New programs are created by trial and error search for feasible action alternatives to cope with a given change. But innovation is subject to the limitations and possibilities inherent in the quantity and variety of information present in a system at a particular time. New combinations of alternatives for innovative purposes depend on:

(a) the possible range of output of the system, or the capacity of the system to supply information.

(b) the range of available information in the memory of the system.

(c) the operating rules (program) governing the analysis and flow of information within the system.

(d) the ability of the system to "forget" previously learned solutions to change problems.[42] A system with too good a memory might narrow its behavioral choices to such an extent as to stifle innovation. In simpler language, old learned programs might be used to adapt to change, when newly innovated programs are necessary.[43]

Much of what has been said about communication and balance brings to mind a cybernetic model in which both these processes have vital roles. Cybernetics has to do with feedback and

40. Karl W. Deutsch, "On Communication Models in the Social Sciences," *Public Opinion Quarterly*, 16 (1952), pp. 356–380.

41. March and Simon, *op. cit.*, pp. 139–140.

42. Mervyn L. Cadwallader, "The Cybernetic Analysis of Change in Complex Social Organization," *The American Journal of Sociology*, September, 1959, p. 156.

43. It is conceivable for innovative behavior to be programmed into the system.

control in all kinds of systems. Its purpose is to maintain system stability in the face of change. Cybernetics cannot be studied without considering communication networks, information flow, and some kind of balancing process aimed at preserving the integrity of the system.

Cybernetics directs attention to key questions regarding the system. These questions are: How are communication centers connected, and how are they maintained? Corollary to this question: what is the structure of the feedback system? Next, what information is stored in the organization, and at what points? And as a corollary: how accessible is this information to decision-making centers? Third, how conscious is the organization of the operation of its own parts? That is, to what extent do the policy centers receive control information with sufficient frequency and relevancy to create a real awareness of the operation of the segments of the system? Finally, what are the learning (innovating) capabilities of the system?[44]

Answers to the questions posed by cybernetics are crucial to understanding both the balancing and communication processes in systems.[45] Although cybernetics has been applied largely to technical-engineering problems of automation, the model of feedback, control, and regulation in all systems has a good deal of generality. Cybernetics is a fruitful area which can be used to synthesize the processes of communication and balance.

(3) A wide spectrum of topics dealing with types of decisions in human systems makes up the core of analysis of another important process in organizations. Decision analysis is one of the major contributions of March and Simon in their book *Organizations*. The two major classes of decisions they discuss are decisions to produce and decisions to participate in the system.[46]

Decisions to produce are largely a result of an interaction between individual attitudes and the demands of organization. Motivation analysis becomes central to studying the nature and results of the interaction. Individual decisions to participate in the organization reflect on such issues as the relationship between organizational rewards versus the demands made by the organization. Participation decisions also focus attention on the reasons why individuals remain in or leave organizations.

March and Simon treat decisions as internal variables in an organization which depend on jobs, individual expectations and motivations, and organizational structure. Marschak[47] looks on the decision process as an independent variable upon which the survival of the organization is based. In this case, the organization is viewed as having,

inherent to its structure, the ability to maximize survival requisites through its established decision processes.

THE GOALS OF ORGANIZATION

Organization has three goals which may be either intermeshed or independent ends in themselves. They are growth, stability, and interaction. The last goal refers to organizations which exist primarily to provide a medium for association of its members with others. Interestingly enough these goals seem to apply to different forms of organization at varying levels of complexity, ranging from simple clockwork mechanisms to social systems.

These similarities in organizational purposes have been observed by a number of people, and a field of thought and research called general system theory has developed, dedicated to the task of discovering organizationed universals. The dream of general system theory is to create a science of organizational universals, or if you will, a universal science using common organizational elements found in all systems as a starting point.

Modern organization theory is on the periphery of general system theory. Both general system theory and modern organization theory studies:

(1) the parts (individuals) in aggregates, and the movement of individuals into and out of the system.

(2) the interaction of individuals with the environment found in the system.

(3) the interactions among individuals in the system.

(4) general growth and stability problems of systems.[48]

Modern organization theory and general system theory are similar in that they look at organization as an integrated whole. They differ, however, in terms of their generality. General system theory is concerned with every level of system, whereas modern organizational theory focuses primarily on human organization.

The question might be asked, what can the science of administration gain by the study of system levels other than human? Before attempt-

44. These are questions adapted from Deutsch, *op. cit.*, 368–370.

45. Answers to these questions would require a comprehensive volume. One of the best approaches currently available is Stafford Beer, *Cybernetics and Management* (New York: John Wiley and Sons, 1959).

46. March and Simon, *op. cit.*, Chapters 3 and 4.

47. Jacob Marschak, "Efficient and Viable Organizational Forms" in *Modern Organization Theory*, Mason Haire, editor (New York: John Wiley and Sons, 1959), pp. 307–320.

48. Kenneth E. Boulding, "General System Theory—The Skeleton of a Science," *Management Science*, April, 1956, pp. 200–202.

ing an answer, note should be made of what these other levels are. Boulding presents a convenient method of classification:

(1) The static structure—a level of framework, the anatomy of a system; for example, the structure of the universe.

(2) The simple dynamic system—the level of clockworks, predetermined necessary motions.

(3) The cybernetic system—the level of the thermostat, the system moves to maintain a given equilibrium through a process of self-regulation.

(4) The open system—level of self-maintaining systems, moves toward and includes living organisms.

(5) The genetic-societal system—level of cell society, characterized by a division of labor among cells.

(6) Animal systems—level of mobility, evidence of goal-directed behavior.

(7) Human systems—level of symbol interpretation and idea communication.

(8) Social system—level of human organization.

(9) Transcendental systems—level of ultimates and absolutes which exhibit systematic structure but are unknowable in essence.[49]

This approach to the study of systems by finding universals common at all levels of organization offers intriguing possibilities for administrative organization theory. A good deal of light could be thrown on social systems if structurally analogous elements could be found in the simpler types of systems. For example, cybernetic systems have characteristics which seem to be similar to feedback, regulation, and control phenomena in human organizations. Thus, certain facets of cybernetic models could be generalized to human organization. Considerable danger, however, lies in poorly founded analogies. Superficial similarities between simpler system forms and social systems are apparent everywhere. Instinctually based ant societies, for example, do not yield particularly instructive lessons for understanding rationally conceived human organizations. Thus, care should be taken that analogies used to bridge system levels are not mere devices for literary enrichment. For analogies to have usefulness and validity, they must exhibit inherent structural similarities or implicitly identical operational principles.[50]

Modern organization theory leads, as it has been shown, almost inevitably into a discussion of general system theory. A science of organization universals has some strong advocates, particularly among biologists.[51] Organization theorists in administrative science cannot afford to overlook the contributions of general system theory. Indeed, modern organization concepts could offer a great

deal to those working with general system theory. But the ideas dealt with in the general theory are exceedingly elusive.

Speaking of the concept of equilibrium as a unifying element in all systems, Easton says, "It (equilibrium) leaves the impression that we have a useful general theory when in fact, lacking measurability, it is a mere pretence for knowledge."[52] The inability to quantify and measure universal organization elements undermines the success of pragmatic tests to which general system theory might be put.

ORGANIZATION THEORY: QUO VADIS?

Most sciences have a vision of the universe to which they are applied, and administrative science is not an exception. This universe is composed of parts. One purpose of science is to synthesize the parts into an organized conception of its field of study. As a science matures, its theorems about the configuration of its universe change. The direction of change in three sciences, physics, economics, and sociology, are noted briefly for comparison with the development of an administrative view of human organization.

The first comprehensive and empirically verifiable outlook of the physical universe was presented by Newton in his *Principia*. Classical physics, founded on Newton's work, constitutes a grand scheme in which a wide range of physical phenomena could be organized and predicted. Newtonian physics may rightfully be regarded as "macro" in nature, because its system of organization was concerned largely with gross events of which the movement of celestial bodies, waves, energy forms, and strain are examples. For years classical physics was supreme, being applied continuously to smaller and smaller classes of phenomena in the physical universe. Physicists at one time adopted the view that everything in their realm could be discovered by simply subdividing

49. *Ibid.*, pp. 202–205.
50. Seidenberg, *op. cit.*, p. 136. The fruitful use of the type of analogies spoken of by Seidenberg is evident in the application of thermodynamic principles, particularly the entropy concept, to communication theory. See: Claude E. Shannon and Warren Weaver, *The Mathematical Theory of Communication*, (Urbana: The University of Illinois Press, 1949). Further, the existence of a complete analogy between the operational behavior of thermodynamic systems, electrical communication systems, and biological systems has been noted by: Y. S. Touloukian, *The Concept of Entropy in Communication, Living Organisms, and Thermodynamics*, Research Bulletin 130, Purdue Engineering Experiment Station.
51. For example see: Ludwig von Bertalanffy, *Problem of Life* (London: Watts and Company, 1952).
52. David Easton, "Limits of the Equilibrium Model in Social Research," in *Profits and Problems of Homeostatic Models in the Behavioral Sciences*, Publication 1, Chicago Behavioral Sciences, 1953, p. 39.

problems. Physics thus moved into the "micro" order.

But in the nineteenth century a revolution took place motivated largely because events were being noted which could not be explained adequately by the conceptual framework supplied by the classical school. The consequences of this revolution are brilliantly described by Eddington:

> From the point of view of philosophy of science the conception associated with entropy must I think be ranked as the great contribution of the nineteenth century to scientific thought. It marked a reaction from the view that everything to which science need pay attention is discovered by microscopic dissection of objects. It provided an alternative standpoint in which the centre of interest is shifted from the entities reached by the customary analysis (atoms, electric potentials, etc.) to qualities possessed by the system as a whole, which cannot be split up and located — a little bit here, and a little bit there. . . .
>
> We often think that when we have completed our study of *one* we know all about *two* because "two" is "one and one." We forget that we have still to make a study of "and." Secondary physics is the study of "and" — that is to say, of organization.[53]

Although modern physics often deals in minute quantities and oscillations, the conception of the physicist is on the "macro" scale. He is concerned with the "and," or the organization of the world in which the events occur. These developments did not invalidate classical physics as to its usefulness for explaining a certain range of phenomena. But classical physics is no longer the undisputed law of the universe. It is a special case.

Early economic theory, and Adam Smith's *Wealth of Nations* comes to mind, examined economic problems in the macro order. The *Wealth of Nations* is mainly concerned with matters of national income and welfare. Later, the economics of the firm, micro-economics, dominated the theoretical scene in this science. And, finally, with Keynes' *The General Theory of Employment Interest and Money*, a systematic approach to the economic universe was re-introduced on the macro level.

The first era of the developing science of sociology was occupied by the great social "system builders." Comte, the so-called father of sociology, had a macro view of society in that his chief works are devoted to social reorganization. Comte was concerned with the interrelationships among social, political, religious, and educational institutions. As sociology progressed, the science of society compressed. Emphasis shifted from the macro approach of the pioneers to detailed, empirical study of small social units. The compres-sion of sociological analysis was accompanied by study of social pathology or disorganization.

In general, physics, economics, and sociology appear to have two things in common. First, they offered a macro point of view as their initial systematic comprehension of their area of study. Second, as the science developed, attention fragmented into analysis of the parts of the organization, rather than attending to the system as a whole. This is the micro phase.

In physics and economics, discontent was evidenced by some scientists at the continual atomization of the universe. The reaction to the micro approach was a new theory or theories dealing with the total system, on the macro level again. This third phase of scientific development seems to be more evident in physics and economics than in sociology.

The reason for the "macro-micro-macro" order of scientific progress lies, perhaps, in the hypothesis that usually the things which strike man first are of great magnitude. The scientist attempts to discover order in the vastness. But after macro laws or models of systems are postulated, variations appear which demand analysis, not so much in terms of the entire system, but more in terms of the specific parts which make it up. Then, intense study of microcosm may result in new general laws, replacing the old models of organization. Or, the old and the new models may stand together, each explaining a different class of phenomenon. Or, the old and the new concepts of organization may be welded to produce a single creative synthesis.

Now, what does all this have to do with the problem of organization in administrative science? Organization concepts seem to have gone through the same order of development in this field as in the three just mentioned. It is evident that the classical theory of organization, particularly as in the work of Mooney and Reiley, is concerned with principles common to all organizations. It is a macro-organizational view. The classical approach to organization, however, dealt with the gross anatomical parts and processes of the formal organization. Like classical physics, the classical theory of organization is a special case. Neither are especially well equipped to account for variation from their established framework.

Many variations in the classical administrative model result from human behavior. The only way these variations could be understood was by a microscopic examination of particularized, situa-

53. Sir Arthur Eddington, *The Nature of the Physical World* (Ann Arbor: The University of Michigan Press, 1958), pp. 103–104.

tional aspects of human behavior. The mission of the neoclassical school thus is "micro-analysis."

It was observed earlier, that somewhere along the line the concept of the social system, which is the key to understanding the Hawthorne studies, faded into the background. Maybe the idea is so obvious that it was lost to the view of researchers and writers in human relations. In any event, the press of research in the microcosmic universes of the informal organization, morale and productivity, leadership, participation, and the like forced the notion of the social system into limbo. Now, with the advent of modern organization theory, the social system has been resurrected.

Modern organization theory appears to be concerned with Eddington's "and." This school claims that its operational hypothesis is based on a macro point of view; that is, the study of organization as a whole. This nobility of purpose should not obscure, however, certain difficulties faced by this field as it is presently constituted. Modern organization theory raises two questions which should be explored further. First, would it not be more accurate to speak of modern organization theor*ies*? Second, just how much of modern organization theory is modern?

The first question can be answered with a quick affirmative. Aside from the notion of the system, there are few, if any, other ideas of a unifying nature. Except for several important exceptions,[54] modern organization theorists tend to pursue their pet points of view,[55] suggesting they are part of system theory, but not troubling to show by what mystical means they arrive at this conclusion.

The irony of it all is that a field dealing with systems has, indeed, little system. Modern organization theory needs a framework, and it needs an integration of issues into a common conception of organization. Admittedly, this is a large order. But it is curious not to find serious analytical treatment of subjects like cybernetics or general system theory in Haire's, *Modern Organizational Theory* which claims to be a representative example of work in this field. Beer has ample evidence in his book *Cybernetics and Management* that cybernetics, if imaginatively approached, provides a valuable conceptual base for the study of systems.

The second question suggests an ambiguous answer. Modern organization theory is in part a product of the past; system analysis is not a new idea. Further, modern organization theory relies for supporting data on microcosmic research studies, generally drawn from the journals of the last ten years. The newness of modern organization theory, perhaps, is its effort to synthesize recent research contributions of many fields into

a system theory characterized by a reoriented conception of organization.

One might ask, but what is the modern theorist reorienting? A clue is found in the almost snobbish disdain assumed by some authors of the neoclassical human relations school, and particularly, the classical school. Re-evaluation of the classical school of organization is overdue. However, this does not mean that its contributions to organization theory are irrelevant and should be overlooked in the rush to get on the "behavioral science bandwagon."

Haire announces that the papers appearing in *Modern Organization Theory* constitute, "the ragged leading edge of a wave of theoretical development."[56] Ragged, yes; but leading, no! The papers appearing in this book do not represent a theoretical breakthrough in the concept of organization. Haire's collection is an interesting potpourri with several contributions of considerable significance. But readers should beware that they will not find vastly new insights into organizational behavior in this book, if they have kept up with the literature of the social sciences, and have dabbled to some extent in the esoteria of biological theories of growth, information theory, and mathematical model building. For those who have not maintained the pace, *Modern Organization Theory* serves the admirable purpose of bringing them up-to-date on a rather diversified number of subjects.

Some work in modern organization theory is pioneering, making its appraisal difficult and future uncertain. While the direction of this endeavor is unclear, one thing is patently true. Human behavior in organizations, and indeed, organization itself, cannot be adequately understood within the ground rules of classical and neoclassical doctrines. Appreciation of human organization requires a *creative* synthesis of massive amounts of empirical data, a high order of deductive reasoning, imaginative research studies, and a taste for individual and social values. Accomplishment of all these objectives, and the inclusion of them into a framework of the concept of the system, appears to be the goal of modern organization theory. The vitality of administrative science rests on the advances modern theorists make along this line.

Modern organization theory, 1960 style, is an amorphous aggregation of synthesizers and re-

---

54. For example: E. Wight Bakke, *op. cit.*, pp. 18–75.

55. There is a large selection including decision theory, individual-organization interaction, motivation, vitality, stability, growth, and graph theory, to mention a few.

56. Mason Haire, "General Issues," in Mason Haire (editor), *Modern Organization Theory* (New York: John Wiley and Sons, 1959), p. 2.

staters, with a few extending leadership on the frontier. For the sake of these few, it is well to admonish that pouring old wine into new bottles may make the spirits cloudy. Unfortunately, modern organization theory has almost succeeded in achieving the status of a fad. Popularization and exploitation contributed to the disrepute into which human relations has fallen. It would be a great waste if modern organization theory yields to the same fate, particularly since both modern organization theory and human relations draw from the same promising source of inspiration — system analysis.

Modern organization theory needs tools of analysis and a conceptual framework uniquely its own, but it must also allow for the incorporation of relevant contributions of many fields. It may be that the framework will come from general system theory. New areas of research such as decision theory, information theory, and cybernetics also offer reasonable expectations of analytical and conceptual tools. Modern organization theory represents a frontier of research which has great significance for management. The potential is great, because it offers the opportunity for uniting what is valuable in classical theory with the social and natural sciences into a systematic and integrated conception of human organization.

16 — The Theory of Formal Organization

CHESTER I. BARNARD

An organization comes into being when (1) there are persons able to communicate with each other (2) who are willing to contribute action (3) to accomplish a common purpose. The elements of an organization are therefore (1) communication; (2) willingness to serve; and (3) common purpose. These elements are necessary and sufficient conditions initially, and they are found in all such organizations. The third element, purpose, is implicit in the definition. Willingness to serve, and communication, and the interdependence of the three elements in general, and their mutual dependence in specific coöperative systems, are matters of experience and observation.

For the continued existence of an organization either *effectiveness* or *efficiency* is necessary; and the longer the life, the more necessary both are. The vitality of organizations lies in the willingness of individuals to contribute forces to the coöperative system. This willingness requires the belief that the purpose can be carried out, a faith that diminishes to the vanishing point as it appears that it is not in fact in process of being attained. Hence, when effectiveness ceases, willingness to contribute disappears. The continuance of willingness also depends upon the satisfactions that are secured by individual contributors in the process of carrying out the purpose. If the satisfactions do not exceed the sacrifices required,

willingness disappears, and the condition is one of organization inefficiency. If the satisfactions exceed the sacrifices, willingness persists, and the condition is one of efficiency of organization.

In summary, then, the initial existence of an organization depends upon a combination of these elements appropriate to the external conditions at the moment. Its survival depends upon the maintenance of an equilibrium of the system. This equilibrium is primarily internal, a matter of proportions between the elements, but it is ultimately and basically an equilibrium between the system and the total situation external to it. This external equilibrium has two terms in it: first, the effectiveness of the organization, which comprises the relevance of its purpose to the environmental situation; and, second, its efficiency, which comprises the interchange between the organization and individuals. Thus the elements stated will each vary with external factors, and they are at the same time interdependent; when one is varied compensating variations must occur in the other if the system of which they are components is to remain in equilibrium, that is, is to persist or survive.

We may now appropriately consider these elements and their interrelations in some detail, having in mind the system as a whole. [On pages 113-116] we shall consider each element in greater detail with reference to its variability in dependence upon external factors, and the inter-

From "The Theory of Formal Organization" and "The Structure of Complex Formal Organizations," *The Functions of the Executive* (Cambridge, Mass.: Harvard University Press, 1938), Ch. VII, pp. 82 – 95, Ch. VIII, pp. 104 – 113. Reprinted by permission of the publisher. Copyright 1938 by the President and Fellows of Harvard College. **Chester I. Barnard:** President of New Jersey Bell Telephone Company.

relations of the elements as determining the character of the executive functions.

WILLINGNESS TO COÖPERATE

By definition there can be no organization without persons. However, as we have urged that it is not persons, but the services or acts or action or influences of persons, which should be treated as constituting organizations, it is clear that *willingness* of persons to contribute efforts to the coöperative system is indispensable.

There are a number of words and phrases in common use with reference to organization that reach back to the factor of individual willingness. "Loyalty," "solidarity," "*esprit de corps*," "strength" of organization, are the chief. Although they are indefinite, they relate to intensity of attachment to the "cause," and are commonly understood to refer to something different from effectiveness, ability, or value of personal contributions. Thus "loyalty" is regarded as not necessarily related either to position, rank, fame, remuneration, or ability. It is vaguely recognized as an essential condition of organization.

Willingness, in the present connection, means self-abnegation, the surrender of control of personal conduct, the depersonalization of personal action. Its effect is cohesion of effort, a sticking together. Its immediate cause is the disposition necessary to "sticking together." Without this there can be no sustained personal effort as a contribution to coöperation. Activities cannot be coördinated unless there is first the disposition to make a personal act a contribution to an impersonal system of acts, one in which the individual gives up personal control of what he does.

The outstanding fact regarding willingness to contribute to a given specific formal organization is the indefinitely large range of variation in its intensity among individuals. If all those who may be considered potential contributors to an organization are arranged in order of willingness to serve it, the scale gradually descends from possibly intense willingness through neutral or zero willingness to intense unwillingness or opposition or hatred. The *preponderance of persons in a modern society always lies on the negative side* with reference to any particular existing or potential organization. Thus of the possible contributors only a small minority actually have a positive willingness. This is true of the largest and most comprehensive formal organizations, such as the large nations, the Catholic Church, etc. Most of the persons in existing society are either indifferent to or positively opposed to any single one of them; and if the smaller organizations subordinate to these major organizations are under consideration the minority becomes of course a much smaller proportion, and usually a nearly negligible proportion, of the conceivable total.

A second fact of almost equal importance is that the willingness of any individual cannot be constant in degree. It is necessarily intermittent and fluctuating. It can scarcely be said to exist during sleep, and is obviously diminished or exhausted by weariness, discomfort, etc., a conception that was well expressed by the saying "The spirit is willing, but the flesh is weak."

A corollary of the two propositions just stated is that for any given formal organization the number of persons of positive willingness to serve, but near the neutral or zero point, is always fluctuating. It follows that the aggregate willingness of potential contributors to any formal coöperative system is unstable—a fact that is evident from the history of all formal organizations.

Willingness to coöperate, positive or negative, is the expression of the net satisfactions or dissatisfactions experienced or anticipated by each individual in comparison with those experienced or anticipated through alternative opportunities. These alternative opportunities may be either personal and individualistic or those afforded by other organizations. That is, willingness to coöperate is the net effect, first, of the inducements to do so in conjunction with the sacrifices involved, and then in comparison with the practically available net satisfactions afforded by alternatives. The questions to be determined, if they were matters of logical reasoning, would be, first, whether the opportunity to coöperate grants any advantage to the individual as compared with independent action; and then, if so, whether that advantage is more or less than the advantage obtainable from some other coöperative opportunity. Thus, from the viewpoint of the individual, willingness is the joint effect of personal desires and reluctances; from the viewpoint of organization it is the joint effect of objective inducements offered and burdens imposed. The measure of this net result, however, is entirely individual, personal, and subjective. Hence, organizations depend upon the motives of individuals and the inducements that satisfy them.

PURPOSE

Willingness to coöperate, except as a vague feeling or desire for association with others, cannot develop without an objective of coöperation. Unless there is such an objective it cannot be known or anticipated what specific efforts will be required of individuals, nor in many cases what satisfactions to them can be in prospect. Such an objective we denominate the "purpose" of an organization. The necessity of having a purpose is axiomatic, implicit in the words "system," "co-ordination," "coöperation." It is something that is clearly evident in many observed systems of co-operation, although it is often not formulated in words, and sometimes cannot be so formulated. In such cases what is observed is the direction or effect of the activities, from which purpose may be inferred.

A purpose does not incite coöperative activity unless it is accepted by those whose efforts will constitute the organization. Hence there is initially something like simultaneity in the accept-ance of a purpose and willingness to coöperate.

It is important at this point to make clear that every coöperative purpose has in the view of each coöperating person two aspects which we call (*a*) the coöperative and (*b*) the subjective aspect, respectively.

(*a*) When the viewing of the purpose is an *act of coöperation*, it approximates that of detached ob-servers from a special position of observation; this position is that of the interests of the organiza-tion; it is largely determined by organization knowledge, but is personally interpreted. For example, if five men are coöperating to move a stone from A to B, the moving of the stone is a different thing in the organization view of each of the five men involved. Note, however, that what moving the stone means to each man personally is not here in question, but what he thinks it means to the organization *as a whole*. This includes the significance of his own effort as an element in coöperation, and that of all others, in his view; but it is not at all a matter of satisfying a personal motive.

When the purpose is a physical result of simple character, the difference between the purpose as objectively viewed by a detached observer and the purpose as viewed by each person coöperating *as an act of coöperation* is ordinarily not large or im-portant, and the different coöperative views of the persons coöperating are correspondingly sim-ilar. Even in such cases the attentive observer will detect differences that result in disputes, errors of action, etc., even though no *personal* interest is implicated. But when the purpose is less tangi-ble — for example, in religious coöperation — the difference between objective purpose and pur-pose as coöperatively viewed by each person is often seen ultimately to result in disruption.

We may say, then, that a purpose can serve as an element of a coöperative system only so long as the participants do not recognize that there are serious divergences of their understanding of that purpose as the object of coöperation. If in fact there is important difference between the aspects of the purpose as objectively and as coöperatively viewed, the divergencies become quickly evident when the purpose is concrete, tangible, physical; but when the purpose is general, intangible, and of sentimental character, the divergencies can be very wide yet not be recognized. Hence, an ob-jective purpose that can serve as the basis for a coöperative system is one that is *believed* by the contributors (or potential contributors) to it to be the determined purpose of the organization. The inculcation of belief in the real existence of a com-mon purpose is an essential executive function. It explains much educational and so-called morale work in political, industrial, and religious organi-zations that is so often otherwise inexplicable.

(*b*) Going back to the illustration of five men moving a stone, we have noted "that what moving the stone means to each man personally is not here in question, but what he thinks it means to the *organization as a whole*." The distinction em-phasized is of first importance. It suggests the fact that every participant in an organization may be regarded as having a dual personality — an organ-ization personality and an individual personality. Strictly speaking, an organization purpose has directly no meaning for the individual. What has meaning for him is the organization's relation to him — what burdens it imposes, what benefits it confers. In referring to the aspects of purpose as coöperatively viewed, we are alluding to the *or-ganization* personality of individuals. In many cases the two personalities are so clearly devel-oped that they are quite apparent. In military action individual conduct may be so dominated by organization personality that it is utterly contra-dictory of what personal motivation would re-quire. It has been observed of many men that their private conduct is entirely inconsistent with official conduct, although they seem completely unaware of the fact. Often it will be observed that participants in political, patriotic, or religious organizations will accept derogatory treatment of their personal conduct, including the assertion that it is inconsistent with their organization obli-gations, while they will become incensed at the slightest derogation of the tenets or doctrines of their organization, even though they profess not to understand them. There are innumerable other cases, however, in which almost no organi-zation personality may be said to exist. These are cases in which personal relationship with the coöperative system is momentary or at the margin of willingness to participate.

In other words we have clearly to distinguish between organization purpose and individual motive. It is frequently assumed in reasoning about organizations that common purpose and individual motive are or should be identical. With the exception noted below, this is never the case; and under modern conditions it rarely even appears to be the case. Individual motive is necessarily an internal, personal, subjective thing; common purpose is necessarily an external, impersonal objective thing even though the individual interpretation of it is subjective. The one exception to this general rule, an important one, is that the accomplishment of an organization purpose becomes itself a source of personal satisfaction and a motive for many individuals in many organizations. It is rare, however, if ever, and then I think only in connection with family, patriotic, and religious organizations under special conditions, that organization purpose becomes or can become the *only* or even the major individual motive.

Finally it should be noted that, once established, organizations change their unifying purposes. They tend to perpetuate themselves; and in the effort to survive may change the reasons for existence. . . . [I]n this lies an important aspect of executive functions.

aspect of communication.[1] I do not think it is generally so recognized. It is necessary because of the limitations of language and the differences in the linguistic capacities of those who use language. A very large element in special experience and training and in continuity of individual association is the ability to understand without words, not merely the situation or conditions, but the *intention*.

The techniques of communication are an important part of any organization and are the preeminent problems of many. The absence of a suitable technique of communication would eliminate the possibility of adopting some purposes as a basis for organization. Communication technique shapes the form and the internal economy of organization. This will be evident at once if one visualizes the attempt to do many things now accomplished by small organizations if each "member" spoke a different language. Similarly, many technical functions could hardly be carried on without special codes; for example, engineering or chemical work. In an exhaustive theory of organization, communication would occupy a central place, because the structure, extensiveness, and scope of organization are almost entirely determined by communication techniques. . . . Moreover, much specialization in organization originates and is maintained essentially because of communication requirements.

COMMUNICATION

The possibility of accomplishing a common purpose and the existence of persons whose desires might constitute motives for contributing toward such a common purpose are the opposite poles of the system of coöperative effort. The process by which these potentialities become dynamic is that of communication. Obviously a common purpose must be commonly known, and to be known must be in some way communicated. With some exceptions, verbal communication between men is the method by which this is accomplished. Similarly, though under crude and obvious conditions not to the same extent, inducements to persons depend upon communication to them.

The method of communication centers in language, oral and written. On its crudest side, motions or actions that are of obvious meaning when observed are sufficient for communication without deliberate attempt to communicate; and signaling by various methods is an important method in much coöperative activity. On the other side, both in primitive and in highly complex civilization "observational feeling" is likewise an important

EFFECTIVENESS OF COÖPERATION

The continuance of an organization depends upon its ability to carry out its purpose. This clearly depends jointly upon the appropriateness of its action and upon the conditions of its environment. In other words, effectiveness is primarily a matter of technological[2] processes. This

1. The phrase "observational feeling" is of my coining. The point is not sufficiently developed, and probably has not been adequately studied by anyone. I take it to be at least in part involved in group action not incited by any "overt" or verbal communication. The cases known to me from the primitive field are those reported by W. H. R. Rivers on pages 94–97 of his *Instinct and the Unconscious* (2nd edition Cambridge University Press, 1924), with reference to Polynesia and Melanesia. One case is summarized by F. C. Bartlett, in *Remembering* (Cambridge University Press, 1932), at p. 297. Rivers states in substance that in some of the relatively small groups decisions are often arrived at and acted upon without having ever been formulated by anybody.

I have observed on innumerable occasions apparent unanimity of decision of equals in conferences to quit discussion without a word to that effect being spoken. Often the action is initiated apparently by someone's rising; but as this frequently occurs in such groups *without* the termination of the meeting, more than mere rising is involved. "Observational feeling," I think, avoids the notion of anything "occult."

2. Using "technological" in the broad sense. . . .

is quite obvious in ordinary cases of purpose to accomplish a physical objective, such as building a bridge. When the objective is non-physical, as is the case with religious and social organizations, it is not so obvious.

It should be noted that a paradox is involved in this matter. An organization must disintegrate if it cannot accomplish its purpose. It also destroys itself by accomplishing its purpose. A very large number of successful organizations come into being and then disappear for this reason. Hence most continuous organizations require repeated adoption of new purposes. This is concealed from everyday recognition by the practice of generalizing a complex series of specific purposes under one term, stated to be "*the* purpose" of this organization. This is strikingly true in the case of governmental and public utility organizations when the purpose is stated to be a particular kind of service through a period of years. It is apparent that their real purposes are not abstractions called "service" but specific acts of service. A manufacturing organization is said to exist to make, say, shoes; this is its "purpose." But it is evident that not making shoes in general but making specific shoes from day to day is its series of purposes. This process of generalization, however, provides in advance for the approximate definition of new purposes automatically—so automatically that the generalization is normally substituted in our minds for the concrete performances that are the real purposes. Failure to be effective is, then, a real cause of disintegration; but failure to provide for the decisions resulting in the adoption of new purposes would have the same result. Hence the generalization of purpose which can only be defined concretely by day-to-day events is a vital aspect of permanent organization.

ORGANIZATION EFFICIENCY

It has already been stated that "efficiency" as conceived in this treatise is not used in the specialized and limited sense of ordinary industrial practice or in the restricted sense applicable to technological processes. So-called "practical" efficiency has little meaning, for example, as applied to many organizations such as religious organizations.

Efficiency of effort in the fundamental sense with which we are here concerned is efficiency relative to the securing of necessary personal contributions to the coöperative system. The life of an organization depends upon its ability to secure and maintain the personal contributions

of energy (including the transfer of control of materials or money equivalent) necessary to effect its purposes. This ability is a composite of perhaps many efficiencies and inefficiencies in the narrow senses of these words, and it is often the case that inefficiency in some respect can be treated as the cause of total failure, in the sense that if corrected success would then be possible. But certainly in most organization—social, political, national, religious—nothing but the absolute test of survival is significant objectively; there is no basis for comparison of the efficiencies of separate aspects.

A more extensive consideration of the inducements that result in personal willingness to coöperate will be had [in a subsequent chapter]. The emphasis now is on the view that efficiency of organization is its capacity to offer effective inducements in sufficient quantity to maintain the equilibrium of the system. It is efficiency in this sense and not the efficiency of material productiveness which maintains the vitality of organizations. There are many organizations of great power and permanency in which the idea of productive efficiency is utterly meaningless because there is no material production. Churches, patriotic societies, scientific societies, theatrical and musical organizations, are cases where the original flow of *material* inducements is toward the organization, not from it—a flow necessary to provide resources with which to supply material inducements to the small minority who require them in such organizations.

In those cases where the primary purpose of organization is the production of material things, insufficiency with respect to the non-material inducements leads to the attempt to substitute material inducements for the non-material. Under favorable circumstances, to a limited degree, and for a limited time, this substitution may be effective. But to me, at least, it appears utterly contrary to the nature of men to be sufficiently induced by material or monetary considerations to contribute enough effort to a coöperative system to enable it to be productively efficient to the degree necessary for persistence over an extended period.

If these things are true, then even in purely economic enterprises efficiency in the offering of non-economic inducements may be as vital as productive efficiency. Perhaps the word efficiency as applied to such non-economic inducements as I have given for illustration will seem strange and forced. This, I think, can only be because we are accustomed to use the word in a specialized sense.

The non-economic inducements are as difficult to offer as others under many circumstances. To establish conditions under which individual pride of craft and of accomplishment can be secured without destroying the material economy of standardized production in coöperative operation is a problem in real efficiency. To maintain a character of personnel that is an attractive condition of employment involves a delicate art and much insight in the selection (and rejection) of personal services offered, whether the standard quality be high or low. To have an organization that lends prestige and secures the loyalty of desirable persons is a complex and difficult task in efficiency—in all-round efficiency, not one-sided efficiency. It is for these reasons that good organizations—commercial, governmental, military, academic, and others—will be observed to devote great attention and sometimes great expense of money to the non-economic inducements, because they are indispensable to fundamental efficiency, as well as to effectiveness in many cases.

The theory of organization set forth in this chapter is derived from the study of organizations which are exceedingly complex, although it is stated in terms of ideal simple organizations. The temptation is to assume that, in the more complex organizations which we meet in our actual social life, the effect of complexity is to modify or qualify the theory. This appears not to be the case. Organization, simple or complex, is always *an impersonal system of coördinated human efforts;* always there is purpose as the coördinating and unifying principle; always there is the indispensable ability to communicate, always the necessity for personal willingness, and for effectiveness and efficiency in maintaining the integrity of purpose and the continuity of contributions. Complexity appears to modify the quality and form of these elements and of the balance between them; but fundamentally the same principles that govern simple organizations may be conceived as governing the structure of complex organizations, which are composite systems. . . .

THE GROWTH OF COMPLEX FORMAL ORGANIZATIONS

[I]t will be noted that when the origin of organization is spontaneous, or is the result of the initiative of one man, or is the deliberate creation of a parent organization, the beginning is small. The organization comes into being when two or more persons begin to coöperate to a common end. Where there is division by schism, rebellion, this is likewise true, but is usually not so recognized because attention is given to the final breakup of a large complex organization. What takes place

beforehand is the growth of a new counter organization or independent organization supported by the efforts of individuals who may in part still continue to support the older organization. So far as I have learned, this beginning is always small; that is, it results from the spontaneous acception of a new purpose, independent of and perhaps definitely conflicting with the older purpose, by a small group; or it is prompted by one individual who associates others with himself. Hence, all organizations of complex character grow out of small, simple organizations.[3] It is impossible for formal organizations to grow except by the process of combining unit organizations already existing, or the creation of new units of organization to be added to those in an existing complex.

It may, therefore, be said that all large formal organizations are constituted of numbers of small organizations.[4] It is impossible to create a large organization except by combining small organizations.[5]

The basic organization, if measured by the number of persons simultaneously contributing to it, is usually quite small—from two to fifteen or twenty persons, and probably not having an average of more than ten. Certain special types of simple

---

3. Perhaps this will be clearer if the process is visualized of trying to organize a group of one hundred or five hundred men. Under the most favorable circumstances, i.e., when they are willing to be organized because there has come about some consensus of opinion as to purpose or objective, the mass must be broken up into small groups with group leaders. Only when by this process unit organizations have been created is it possible to combine these units into a complex organization that can manage itself.

In this connection, I should regard a mob not as a formal organization, simple or complex, but a special type of informal organization, until it has formal leaders.

4. I exclude the very extreme and special case of large audiences as being of limited pertinence to a discussion of the functions of the executive.

5. The origins of the major organizations being historically so remote, and the processes of reorganization being apparently often directed from central points or by central authority, we are much under the delusion that large mass organizations are subdivided as a secondary process, the mass having first been created. This is the order in which intellectually we approach the understanding of most large complex organizations; it is the method of analysis, of breaking down a whole into parts. Thus, if we wish to study a government organization of a large telephone system, we may often effectively begin with the constitution, the major departments, the parent company, etc. But this procedure is as if we subdivided a trunk of a tree or a piece of flesh into fibres and membranes and finally into cells, being misled into thinking that these subdivisions developed after the existence of an undifferentiated protoplasm of the same mass.

Many theoretical and practical errors arise from employing this analytical approach except for immediate limited purposes. For it is, I think, as true of organization as it is of all living things that they grow by the multiplication of cells and begin with single cells. It is true that quite often a fusion of two existing simple or complex organizations into one complex organization takes place; but fundamentally the growth is from single-cell organizations.

organization, however, are very large, just as in biology some cells, such as birds' eggs, are very large. The largest of such organizations which I have observed are a full orchestra or orchestra and chorus; and a public speaker and his audience, which under radio technique reaches enormous size.[6]

The clue to the structural requirements of large complex organizations lies in the reason for the limitations of the size of simple organizations. The limitations are inherent in the necessities of intercommunication.[7] [On page 111] we discussed communication between persons as an essential element of coöperative systems; it is also the limiting factor in the size of simple organizations and, therefore, a dominant factor in the structure of complex organizations. We must now consider why this is true.

Under most ordinary conditions, even with simple purposes, not many men can see what each is doing or the whole situation; nor can many communicate essential information regarding or governing specific action without a central channel or leader. But a leader likewise is limited in time (and capacity) in communicating with many persons contemporaneously, especially if they are widely separated so that he must move about. In practice a limit of usually less than fifteen persons obtains, and for many types of coöperation five or six persons is the practicable limit.

These limits are widely exceeded in certain special cases, chiefly those where the action involved is that of extreme habitual practice within narrow limits, as in military drill and orchestral performance, where there are both individual and collective habituation and a precise special system of language or some other special means of communication; and those where the action is limited substantially to one person, the others being relatively passive, as in an audience. In this case the organization is practically limited (at least for the time being) to communication in one direction only.[8] Moreover, in the case of audiences and speakers, this communication is an end in itself.

Fundamentally, communication is necessary to translate purpose into terms of the concrete action required to effect it—what to do and when and where to do it. This necessitates knowledge of the conditions of the environment, and of the action under way. Under very simple and usually temporary conditions and with small numbers of persons the communication problem often appears simple, but under many conditions, even with small numbers, a special channel of communication is required. For if all talk at once there is

confusion; and there is indecision particularly as to timing of actions. This creates the necessity for a leader. The size of the unit, therefore, usually is determined by the limitations of effective leadership. These limitations depend upon (*a*) the complexity of purpose and technological conditions; (*b*) the difficulty of the communication process; (*c*) the extent to which communication is necessary; (*d*) the complexity of the personal relationships involved, that is, of the social conditions.

(*a*) It is clear that when the purpose is not simple—that is, when its requirements are complex and not obvious, or the conditions require precision of coördinated movements, or the nature of the individual action necessary is difficult to grasp by the actor (or by the leader)—much more communication is necessary than under the contrary conditions.

(*b*) It is also evident that the difficulty of the communication process has an important bearing on the size of the organization unit. There are many things that are difficult to communicate by words—in some matters it is impossible. When the difficulty is great it is evident that the time required may limit the number between whom communication may be effectively had; for example, communication perhaps must be accomplished by demonstration.

(*c*) It is apparent that if each actor can see what the other is doing and can see the situation as a whole, the amount of positive communication is reduced. Thus, if five men are working together on a simple task (say pulling a boat into the water) little communication is required; but if five men are coördinating efforts under conditions such that they cannot see each other and the whole situation, constant communication is often necessary. Moreover, if men know what to do from previous experience and can work on the basis of habit and acquired skill, a minimum of communication is required; or if they are accustomed to working together, a special language which they evolve cuts down the time of communication.

(*d*) The complexity of the relationships in any group increases with great rapidity as the number of persons in the group increases. If the simplest possible relationship between two persons is that

---

6. A descriptive catalogue and classification of organizations from the standpoint of unit size would be of interest in a more exhaustive treatment. For example, clubs furnish an illustration of rather large units which are partly structured by "working" units (staff, officers, committees and official meetings of members), and temporary "playing" or "social" units.

7. These limitations, therefore, arise out of the joint effect of physical, biological, and social factors. . . .

8. Where not limited to one direction, a leader—moderator, chairman, i.e., an executive—is required.

of "knowing" each other as accomplished by a mutual introduction, then the relational complexity at the very least increases as follows:

Number in Group	Number of Relationships	Increase in Relationships with Each Addition to Group
2	1	—
3	3	2
4	6	3
5	10	4
6	15	5
7	21	6
8	28	7
9	36	8
10	45	9
15	105	—
20	190	—
50	1225	—

The relationships between persons in a group will be "active" in a great variety of subgroupings which may constantly change. If A, B, C, D, and E constitute a group of five, then subgroups may be made as follows: ten pairs, ten triplets, five groups of four, one of five. If only one person be added to the group of five, the possible subgroups become: fifteen pairs, twenty triplets, fifteen groups of four, six groups of five, and one of six.

A person has relationships not only with others individually and with groups, but groups are related to groups. As the number of possible groups increases, the complexity of group relationship increases in greater ratio.[9]

The complexity of relationships within groups is important in two aspects: technologically and socially. Technologically, the burden of coördination, that is, the communication function of a leader, will increase in the proportion that the relationships increase; and the ability of individuals and groups without leadership to coördinate is also quickly outrun with increase in the size of groups. The same is true of the social or informal organization relationships. The capacity of persons to maintain social relationships is obviously limited. If the technological group is larger than is adapted to social limitations, the social organization groupings cannot correspond to the technological requirements. Since a large part of the communication of organizations is informal, the burden on formal channels is thereby increased.[10]

These factors, and probably others also, limit the size of the fundamental organization cell. I shall call the simple basic organization form a "unit" organization. It differs from the ideal organization . . . in that it is never found isolated from other organizations and is always subordinate to some other formal organization directly or indirectly, being ultimately subordinate to and dependent upon either a church or a state or both.

The size of a unit organization being usually restricted very narrowly by the necessities of communication, it follows that growth of organization beyond the limits so imposed can only be accomplished by the creation of new unit organizations, or by grouping together two or more unit organizations already existing. When an organization grows by the addition of the services of more persons it is compelled, if it reaches the limit of size, to establish a second unit; and henceforward it is a complex of two unit organizations. All organizations except unit organizations are a group of two or more unit organizations. Hence, a large organization of complex character consists not of the services of individuals directly but of those of subsidiary unit organizations. Nowhere in the world, I think, can there be found a large organization that is not composed of small units. We think of them as having descended from the mass, whereas the mass can only be created from the units.[11]

Usually when two and always when several unit organizations are combined in one complex organization, the necessities of communication impose a super-leader, who becomes, usually with assistants, an "overhead" unit of organization. Similarly, groups of groups are combined into larger wholes. The most obvious case of complex

9. A suggestive exposition of this subject in quantitative terms is given by V. A. Graicunas' "Relationship in Organization," reprinted in Papers on the Science of Administration, edited by Gulick and Urwick (New York: Institute of Public Administration, 1937).

10. . . . . I have strongly the opinion that there may be substantial variations in social satisfactions related to disparities between the size of organizations as determined technologically by organization purpose and the size of "natural" social groups. "Natural" would be affected by the personalities involved.

11. A group of two or more unit organizations may coöperate as a whole without a formal superior organization or leader. Under many conditions this is observed, especially where two small organizations (or a large and a small) work together under contract for specified purposes. The method of communication is primarily that of conference. Because of our habit of considering an organization as a group of persons rather than as systems of coöperative services of persons, the usually temporary combinations that are made as a result of contracts or agreements are not recognized as organizations, since they have no name or common officials. Most large building operations are so organized, however; and it will be readily seen that a very large part of the organized activities of today are carried only by temporary limited combinations under contracts without a general coördinating "authority." The state, through the law of contracts and the provisions of courts, is a general formal executive in these cases in limited degree; but the real general executive is custom, etc.

structure of this type is an army. The fact that these large organizations are built up of small unit organizations is neglected in the spectacular size that ensues, and we often pass from the whole or major divisions to "men." The resulting dismissal from the mind of the inescapable practice of unit organization often leads to utterly unrealistic attitudes regarding organization problems.

THE EXECUTIVE ORGANIZATION

In a unit organization there are executive functions to be performed, but not necessarily by a single individual continuously. They may be performed alternately by the several persons who contribute to the organization. In complex organizations, on the other hand, the necessities of communication result almost invariably in the localization of the executive functions of the subordinate unit organizations normally in one person. This is necessary for reasons of formal communication; but it is also necessary to establish executive organizations, that is, those units specializing in the executive functions. The executives of several unit organizations as a group, usually with at least one other person as a superior, form an executive organization. Accordingly, persons specializing in the executive functions in most cases are "members" of, or contributors to, two units of organization in one complex organization—first, the so-called "working" unit, and second, the executive unit. This is clearly seen in practice, it being customary to recognize a foreman, or a superintendent of a shop section, or a captain, at one time or from one point of view as a "member" of his gang, shop crew, or company, at another time or from another point of view as a member of a "district management group," or the "shop executives' group," or the "regimental organization." Under such condition a single concrete action or decision is an activity of two different unit organizations. This simultaneous contribution to two organizations by a single act appears to be the critical fact in all complex organization; that is, the complex is made an organic whole by it.

Here again, it will be noted that the definition of formal organization as an impersonal system of efforts and influences is supported by the facts more closely in accord with concrete phenomena than the "group membership" idea. One person often functions in or contributes services to several different units of the same complex organization, as well as to different external organizations. For payroll, and many other formal purposes, it is convenient to regard every person as being "in" only one unit organization; but this is merely a matter of convenience for certain purposes, and is misleading as to the actual operation of organizations even for many other practical purposes.

The size of executive units of organizations is limited generally by the same conditions that govern the size of unit organizations of other kinds. When there are many basic working units, therefore, there must be several primary executive unit organizations, from the heads of which will be secured the personnel of superior executive units. And so on, in extensive pyramids of executive units in very large complex organizations.[12]

In summary, we may say that historically and functionally all complex organizations are built up from units of organization, and consist of many units of "working" or "basic" organizations, overlaid with units of executive organizations; and that the essential structural characteristics of complex organizations are determined by the effect of the necessity for communication upon the size of a unit organization.

12. Professor Philip Cabot, in a published address, once quoted my opinion that organizations are best regarded as circular or spherical, with the chief executive positions in the center. This was based on discussions with him and an unpublished manuscript which he was kind enough to examine. I have, however, followed the conventional figures here, because they are well established, and because there appears to be no practicable way to diagram the system of authoritative communication that does not result in a "pyramid" (usually in two-dimensional perspectives, however) which put the chief executive positions at the top. They also are frequently located on top floors. Probably all spatial figures for organization are seriously misleading; but if they are used to cover the functioning of organizations as distinguished from its structural aspects, either the center of a circle or of a sphere better suggests the relationships. The nearest approach to this, I think, is the practice of regarding the location of G.H.Q. in field armies as *behind* the lines centrally.

17 — The Informal Organization

PHILIP SELZNICK

This analysis will consider bureaucracy as a special case of the general theory of purposive organization. Recent sociological research has made explicit several conceptions which must serve as essential background for any analysis such as that to follow. Based upon that research, three hypotheses may be introduced here:

1. Every organization creates an informal structure.

2. In every organization, the goals of the organization are modified (abandoned, deflected, or elaborated) by processes within it.

3. The process of modification is effected through the informal structure.

Three recent sociological studies have elucidated these hypotheses.

1. In an intensive examination of a shop department, Roethlisberger and Dickson found clear evidences of an informal structure. This structure consisted of a set of procedures (binging, sarcasm, ridicule) by means of which control over members of the group was exercised, the formation of cliques which functioned as instruments of control, and the establishment of informal leadership. "The men had elaborated, spontaneously and quite unconsciously, an intricate social organization around their collective beliefs and sentiments."[1]

The informal structure of the worker group grew up out of the day-to-day practices of the men as they groped for ways of taking care of their own felt needs. There was no series of conscious acts by which these procedures were instituted, but they were no less binding on that account. These needs largely arose from the way in which the men defined their situation within the organization. The informal organization served a triple *function:* (a) it served to control the behavior of the members of the worker group; (b) within the context of the larger organization (the plant), it was an attempt on the part of the particular group to control the conditions of its existence; (c) it acted as a mechanism for the expression of personal relationships for which the formal organization did not provide. Thus the informal structure provided those avenues of aggression, solidarity, and prestige-construction required by individual members.

The *consequence* of the activity of the men through the informal organization was a deleterious effect upon the professed goal of the organization as a whole: it resulted in the restriction of output. In asserting its control over the conditions of the job, the group wanted above all to protect itself from outside interference, exhibiting a strong resistance to change.

Thus the facts in this empirical investigation illustrate the hypotheses noted above: the creation of an informal organization, the modification of the professed goal (maximum output), and the effectuation of this modification through the informal structure. In addition, three important characteristics of the informal structure were observed in the study: (a) it arises spontaneously; (b) the bases of the relationships are personal, involving factors of prestige, acceptance within the group, friendship ties, etc.; and (c) the relationships are *power* relationships, oriented toward techniques of *control*. These characteristics are general, and they are important for conceiving of the theory of bureaucratic behavior as a special case of the general theory of organization.

2. C. I. Barnard, in his theoretical analysis of organizational structure, concerned mainly with the problems of the executive, discusses explicitly the character and function of informal structures which arise out of the attempts to solve those problems. By informal structures he means "the aggregate of the personal contacts and interactions and the associated groupings of people" which do not have common or joint purposes, and which are, in fact, "indefinite and rather structureless."[2] He says, further, that "though common or joint purposes are excluded by definition, common or joint results of an important character nevertheless come from such organization."[3]

Barnard lists three functions of informal structures as they operate in formal organizations: (a) as a means of communication, establishing norms of conduct between superordinates and subordinates; (b) "maintenance of cohesiveness in formal organizations through regulating the willingness to serve and the stability of objective authority"; (c) "the maintenance of the feeling of personal integrity, of self-respect, of independent choice."[4] The last mentioned function means simply that the individual's "integrity" is protected by the *appearance* of choice, at the same time that subtle

---

From "An Approach to a Theory of Bureaucracy," *American Sociological Review*, VIII (February 1943), 47 – 48. Reprinted by permission of the author and the American Sociological Association. **Philip Selznick:** Fellow, Social Science Research Council, New York.

1. F. J. Roethlisberger and W. J. Dickson, *Management and the Worker*, Cambridge: Harvard University Press, 1941, 524.

2. C. I. Barnard, *The Functions of the Executive*, Cambridge: Harvard University Press, 1940, p. 115.

3. *Ibid.*

4. *Loc. cit.*, pp. 122 – 123.

group pressures guarantee control of his actions. Barnard's view of the functions of the informal structure is primarily in terms of the needs of the executive (control through friendship ties, personal authority, a "grape-vine" system, etc.), but it is clear that his analysis agrees with the hypothesis that the informal organization is oriented essentially toward the techniques of control. In the Roethlisberger and Dickson study, it was the worker group which was attempting to control the conditions of its existence; in this case, it is the executive who is doing the same thing.

3. A discussion by Waller and Henderson[5] based on the study of institutions of segregative care, gives further evidence for the theses presented here. The general hypotheses about organizational processes are confirmed by the examination of such structures as private schools, transient camps, prisons, flop-houses, reformatories and military organizations. The authors set the problem in this way:

Each of our institutions has an idea or purpose — most of them have several purposes more or less compatible with one another — and this idea or purpose gives rise to an institutional structure. The institutional structure consists of a system of organized groups. The interaction of these elements is a principal clue to the understanding of institutions of segregative care. Without a structure, the purpose of an institution would be an empty form of words, and yet the process of translating the purpose into an institutional structure always somehow deflects and distorts it.

It is thus the iron necessity of an organizational structure for the achievement of group goals which creates the paradox to which we have referred. The ideals of those who construct the organization are one thing; the "facts of life" operating independently of and often against those ideals are something else again.

PROFESSED AND OPERATIONAL GOALS

Running an organization, as a specialized and essential activity, generates problems which have no necessary (and often an opposed) relationship to the professed or "original" goals of the organization. The day-to-day behavior of the group becomes centered around specific problems and proximate goals which have primarily an internal relevance. Then, since these activities come to consume an increasing proportion of the time and thoughts of the participants, they are — from the point of view of actual behavior — *substituted* for the professed goals.

The day-to-day activity of men is ordered by those specific problems which have a direct relevance to the materials with which they have to deal. "Ultimate" issues and highly abstract ideas which do not specify any concrete behavior have therefore little direct influence on the bulk of human activities. (The general ideas, of course, may influence action by setting its context and, often, defining its limits.) This is true not because men are evil or unintelligent, but because the "ultimate" formulations are not *helpful* in the constant effort to achieve that series of equilibria which represent behavioral solutions to the specific problems which day-to-day living poses. Besides those professed which do not specify any concrete behavior, which are analogous to nonprocedural formulations in science, there are other professed goals which require actions which conflict with what must be done in the daily business of running an organization. In that conflict the professed goals will tend to go down in defeat, usually through the process of being extensively ignored. This phenomenon may be introduced as a fourth hypothesis in the general theory of organization.

18 — Centralization Versus Decentralization

ERNEST DALE

"Decentralization" like "politeness" means different things to different people, but in no case should it be taken to imply a value judgment. The term itself means the delegation of business decisions by the owners to their immediate representatives (the board of directors and the chief executive), and then to others further down in the management hierarchy. This is done with the

5. W. Waller and W. Henderson, "Institutions of Segregative Care and the Organized Group" (unpublished manuscript), 1941.

"Centralization Versus Decentralization," *Advanced Management,* XX (June 1955), 11–16. Reprinted by permission of the author and the publisher. **Ernest Dale**: School of Business and Public Administration, Cornell University.

aim of furthering the objectives and values of the enterprise; hence decentralization is only a means to an end.

In addition, "decentralization" is not an absolute term. There are varying degrees of decentralized authority, and the extent to which any company is decentralized must be gauged by tests.

The *locus* or *place* of the decision-making authority in the management hierarchy is one criterion. The lower the rank of the executives who make given decisions, the greater the degree of decentralization. For example, decentralization is greater where larger amounts of money can be spent at lower levels for such things as capital equipment, administrative or operating purposes, or salary changes. The degree of authority for decisions that could result in a loss may also be a test. In a carpet factory, a mistake in the weave would not be serious; hence the function of quality control could be placed far down in the management hierarchy without any great degree of decentralization. In a pharmaceutical company, on the other hand, an error might cause a death, and quality decisions need to be made near the top level.

In addition, the *degree* of decision-making power at the lower levels will be a factor. This can be determined by studying the authority which can be exercised (1) without any check with higher authority at all (routinized decisions such as the billing procedure, safety enforcement, purchase of stock orders); (2) with a check or regular report after the decision is made and carried out (engagement of clerical personnel, purchases of equipment covered by budget); or (3) with a check before the decision is made or put into effect (decisions without precedent, special appropriation requests). Or there may be the simple requirement to check with a superior on all matters of policy changes, of financial appropriations, or potential and actual disagreements.

In determining the degree of decentralization, moreover, it must always be remembered that an enterprise has both *formal and informal decision-making* rules. Official policy statements may decree one type of decision-making, but actual practice may be quite different. Thus there may be a high degree of formal centralization, but if successful business conduct is not possible under such circumstances, decisions may be, in fact, made much lower down.

For instance, in one firm with about a billion dollars of sales, all purchases over $2,500 must be submitted to the president; and all changes in salaries above $4,000, all expense accounts and all public appearances of executives have to be approved by the chief. Obviously, this chief executive is unable to handle all these approvals himself. The large majority of the purchasing decisions are, in fact, made by executives lower down the line, because merchandise has to be bought and sold if the business is to continue. .

When objectives clash with the assignment of responsibility and authority, one or the other is likely to be disregarded. Thus, informal, centralized controls may make possible over-riding the effectiveness of formally decentralized responsibility and authority.

Again formal centralization may be offset to some extent by physical decentralization. For example, the production of certain products may be undertaken at a separate physical location; accounting records may be assembled and placed next to the immediate user. Thus in decentralization movements, headquarters are sometimes shifted away from the plant to prevent the close control that can come from propinquity.

CURRENT STATUS IN THE UNITED STATES

There is no statistical information on the extent of centralization and its reverse, the decentralization of decision-making, in U.S. industry. Business literature usually carries accounts of corporate decentralization, largely because such moves are considered "progressive" and hence newsworthy (one rarely reads today of a president boasting of centralization.) However, general reasoning will show that centralization is still quite widespread. Probably "one-man control" is found in more companies and affects more employees than "control by the few" or "control by the many."

One-man control stems partly from tradition and partly from human nature. Men in commanding positions like to believe that they are indispensable — secretly hope, perhaps, that they may always be there to carry on. They fear that delegation of authority may foster the creation of "empires within the empire," and make them more dependent on others. In addition, it is hard for the one man in control to jettison all his intellectual investments. He may be committed to a belief in benevolent dictatorship, and the power of vested ideas may be stronger than the power of economic interests.

And this may well be a long-run trend. For there may be a difference (and sometimes an appreciable one) between the maximum profit that a company *could* make and the actual profit it must make to keep the stockholders from complaining too loudly. To this extent the compulsion to maximum profits no longer exists to the same degree that it did 50 years ago when owner-management was much more common. Nor is the maximization of profits as advantageous for the individual executive as it used to be, since income taxes, the decline in the value of money, and the long-run decline in the rate of interest all make large accumulations of wealth difficult and often impossible. Andrew Carnegie made many millions of dollars, but the present heads of the Carnegie-Illinois Steel Corporation have no such prospects, even though the job is probably considerably more difficult and complex than in Carnegie's time. For this reason, it may not be worthwhile to risk public opprobrium by squeezing customers or employees, and the consequent trend to "awareness of social responsibilities" may be affecting even family-owned and operated businesses to some extent.

Hence, one may be justified in studying the shift from profit to power as a major business objective and its effect on decentralization. "Power" may be sought in volume of sales or percentage of market, in professional distinction (i.e., the emphasis on "management as a profession," as an "elite," etc.). The chief executive may demonstrate his power by setting the tone in the local community or the industry, by accepting important positions in government or the foreign service. Or he may simply hold on to all major and many minor decisions in the enterprise. Even in allegedly decentralized companies the delegation of powers may go no further than from the chief executive to his vice presidents, and subordinates cannot complain because the holders of power are their immediate superiors.

Factors making for centralization in an enterprise may be many. Most important, perhaps, is the example of the chief executive. To the extent to which he retains powers, his subordinates are likely to imitate him. To the extent that he welcomes "checking," "consultation" and dependence, his subordinates are likely to do the same. Of course, the chief does not actually have to make each decision himself. He merely needs to "spot-check." For example, if he insists on passing on all increases in salaries above $400 a month and 1,000 such applications reach him every month, he needs to pass on only one or a few of them. If he raises a question (or an eyebrow) everyone will be careful to propose only such increases as can be justified under questioning by the chief.

MEASUREMENT OF RESULTS NECESSARY BUT COMPLEX

Then all the devices used to coordinate an enterprise may be used to foster centralization. Such "tools" as organization and policy manuals, methods and procedures manuals, authority limitation manuals (dealing with authority for capital expenditures, salary and personnel changes, etc.) may actually take away more authority than they confer. Sometimes they enforce systems of communication along the lines of a pyramid. Or the chief executive may set up checks and sources of information that nullify the delegation of powers. Measurement of results is, of course, necessary; the chief must know how the delegated powers are exercised. But the controls may bring about so much checking, transmission of so much information so continuously, and so much correction that the "decentralized" operators may spend a considerable part of their time explaining and defending themselves. In some companies, the saying goes: "It takes two tons of paper to make one ton of product." There is also the possibility that the chief's general staff may deliberately force executives to refer many decisions to headquarters or influence decisions without adequate consultation. Or the special staff may exercise central command powers because of actual or assumed technical knowledge, direct operation of services, "concurrent authority," superior articulation, physical proximity to the chief, or simply in default of decision-making elsewhere. There are the possible abuses of group work, the enforcement of compatibility and conformity, the use of manipulative techniques to strengthen centralization.

Finally there are the modern means of communication—telephone, telegraph, teletype, radio, and now television—which make it physically possible for the chief executive to issue direct orders to distant subordinates. And it is even possible that future technical developments may eliminate one of the main reasons for decentralization. If enough information can be brought to a central point quickly enough, there may no longer be a need to have problems settled at a point close to their source. The development of electronic devices, calculators, punch card systems, etc., together with such tools as operations research and Cybernetics, may so greatly and so quickly increase the information available to central management that the basic desire of many chiefs—to continue to make as many decisions as possible or to widen the range of their decision-making—might be gratified.

FORCES BEHIND
GREATER DECENTRALIZATION

But even if these powerful factors making for "one-man control" did not exist, extensive delegation might still not be possible. For the personnel who can shoulder the additional responsibilities might not be available. Those who grew up with the chief in the business may not be able (or willing) to take more responsibility. Yet if the chief brings in outside personnel, the newcomers may be thwarted by uncooperative oldtimers.

Thus effective delegation of decision-making may be costly. Difficult personalities may be hard to replace, and both the training of new executives and their initial mistakes may be expensive. Additional functional personnel (accounting, research, industrial relations, etc.) may have to be hired in the now semi-autonomous divisions and branches and the difficult relationships to head-office worked out. Informal work groups and long-established relationships may be upset and destroyed. It is difficult and time-consuming to get executives to assume and exercise additional responsibility.

Finally, hard times and increased competition may foster centralization. When the chief executive feels that the company cannot afford mistakes, he is likely to want more power in his own hands.

So it is clear that the tendencies toward greater centralization or at least preservation of the *status quo* may be strong.

CONTROL BY THE FEW

When the founder or sole directing head of the enterprise passes away, or when there is a reorganization, the struggle for succession may be resolved through the assumption of control by a group whose members have more or less equal status. If the major decisions of the enterprise are made by a small number of men, we speak of "control by the few." Usually each of these men handles one or several management functions and makes the major decisions concerning them. Insofar as a decision affects more than one executive — that is, if it requires coordination or cuts across the business as a whole — several executives may have an important voice and the decision-making power of each may be practically equal. Control is often exercised by informal consultation, but there may be formal meetings held at regular intervals — of executive committees, management committees, etc.

Motives for establishing "control by the few" are varied. Sometimes it is believed that the company is too large to be managed successfully by one man. That is how Myron Tayor is said to have felt, after Judge Gary's death, about the management of the U.S. Steel Corporation. So he brought in Fairless to handle production, gave Olds charge of the legal and public relations functions, and Voorhees responsibility for finance. Each had more or less equal power on intracompany problems. In other cases, equality of decision-making is designed to train successors to the chief executive by inducing a number of senior vice presidents to compete for the top position. With the increasing emphasis on the social responsibility of business, new members of the board of directors or new top operating executives may be added to represent the point of view of some of the various "publics" affected by the enterprise. Finally, control by the few may be the end result of one of the plans of "group dynamics" or executive participation.

Genuine equal control by a group of individuals rarely attains long-run equilibrium, and usually only where there is long experience and training, careful selection, an established tradition and long personal acquaintance and respect, such as exists in the Management Committees of the Crown-Zellerbach Company or the Executive Committee of the du Pont Company. If it is to be successful, the group should be homogeneous in outlook, heterogeneous in ability. Objectives and authority must be fairly similar; otherwise disagreements are likely to upset the equilibrium sooner or later. Participants must have a degree of sensitivity toward situations and toward each other and be broadminded enough to disagree without quarrel, e.g., there must be both informality and careful appreciation of all the usual committee mechanics — definition of functions, agenda, assignment of responsibilities, etc.

The great drawback to control by the few is the potential paralysis of decision-making. It takes time to obtain unanimity, and it may sometimes be achieved only by a compromise that is less effective than the decision of one man; such as agreement on the lowest common denomination. Or the group may split and the majority dominate. The more heterogeneous the composition of the group, the greater the probability of such conflict. For example, the difference in viewpoint between financially minded and production minded executives may make it impossible to arrive at lasting solutions of labor and human problems.

Thus control by the few may be a passing phenomenon. When conditions change to an extent affecting the course of the business perceptibly, one-man control may be restored. Alternately, progress may be made toward "control by the many," that is, participation in important decisions by an increasing number of executives. This tends to develop as members of the "oligarchy" attempt to arrive at genuine joint decisions better than those any one individual or a few of them could reach alone.

CONTROL BY THE MANY

The control-by-many type of decision-making may be called "integrative" or "participative." (These are probably better terms than "democratic," because the latter, taken from political science, assumes an equality of men that usually does not exist in this context, certainly not in terms of status and income, and usually not in terms of power to influence business decisions.)

Most frequently this participation takes the form of informal, friendly consultation among leading executives and possibly their subordinates. This is, however, of a haphazard nature and could be quickly changed or destroyed by the whim of any important executive involved. Informal consultation may be useless as a starting point or as a means of continuing and stabilizing far-reaching control by the many. For this reason formal control by the many, often called "decentralization," may be adopted.

HISTORY OF DECENTRALIZATION IN AMERICA

The decentralization movement in American business was probably begun by Henry V. Poor in the 1850's through his proposals for the reorganization of American railroads, when he sought to help those first large-scale organizations overcome the drawbacks of diminishing returns from management. This remarkable man coined the phrase "the science of management." Poor's suggestions were first applied by Daniel McCallum, General Superintendent on the Erie Railroad 1854 to 1857 and later one of the chief organizers of the American transport system during the Civil War.

The first successful large-scale plan of decentralization in manufacturing industry was probably that presented in 1920 to W. C. Durant, President of General Motors by Alfred P. Sloan, Jr., then G.M. Vice President. This was a most remarkable and far-sighted document, largely formed the basis of the present General Motors organization and was put into effect by many other companies. This was adopted when General Motors was reorganized in 1921. Independently of this, A. W. Robertson, lately Chairman of the Board of the Westinghouse Electric Corporation; Ralph Kelly, Vice President and F. D. Newbury, Economist (now Assistant Secretary of Defense) developed and carried out such a decentralization program at Westinghouse from 1936 to 1939, and it proved to be extremely successful. Standard Oil of California was a pioneer in systematic organization planning under L. L. Purkey. Outstanding post-war examples of decentralization with a successful record of over seven years include the work of L. F. McCollum at the Continental Oil Co. and the decentralization of the Ford Motor Co. Among successfully decentralized smaller companies the "cooperative capitalism" of the C. J. Bath Company should be mentioned — in this firm all levels of management participate in major policy decisions. Essentially one or more of the following characteristics mark a program of decentralization in a large corporation.

(1) *The administrative unit that usually covers the company as a whole as well as all its plants is broken into smaller administrative units — often on either a geographical or product basis.* Each is headed by a manager who may be compared to the head of a smaller enterprise. Usually he has fairly complete control over basic line functions, such as manufacturing and marketing; if he also has staff services such as accounting, engineering, research and personnel, the unit may be largely self-contained.

(2) *Provision is made for the effective utilization of a centralized staff of specialists to aid the decentralized operations to increased profitability and better relationships in order to combine the advantages of a large unit of management with those of a small one.* Central staff specialists are said to "advise and assist" the chief executive and the line operators, and perhaps handle certain centralized functions for the company as a whole, such as public relations, law and taxation. In other cases, the centralized staff specialists maintain "functional supervision" over divisional operations in their fields of expertise such as industrial relations, finance, and possibly manufacturing and sales. Functional supervision may cover formulation of major company objectives, policies, plans and programs for line management's approval and seeing that decisions are carried out, furnishing administrative and technical advice, setting up standards, systems, procedures, controls and measurement of performance, concurring in selection of key personnel and in changes in their assignment.

DELEGATION OF AUTHORITY TO SPECIALISTS

The essential problem in this area of decentralization is the delineation of the authority of the staff specialists. The theoretical "indirect" authority of the central staff may vary in fact from advice to command. For example, the headquarters staff specialist in personnel administration may be an adviser on personality problems, a coordinator of union negotiations, a policy-maker in job and salary evaluation, a researcher on executive development, a statistical compiler of personnel data, an operator of cafeteria services (and of his own department) or he may "concur" on urgent problems of safety (e.g., prohibiting a worker from continuing on a dangerous machine), a controller of the observance of personnel policies. Clearly there are numerous opportunities for widespread participation by "staff" in the decision-making of the enterprise, through the actual use of authority of various kinds, including the "authority" of knowledge.

(3) *A series of general staffs may be provided for the chief executive* to handle the functions which he cannot delegate and which may become increasingly burdensome as the company increases in size. For example, growth of the enterprise requires more attention to the increasing number of people affected by it. When the chief represents the company personally in these contacts, an increasing proportion of his time is spent away from his subordinates. Or it may be difficult or impossible for the chief executive to handle the growing demands of coordination and communication. Hence he may acquire staff assistance in the person of an "assistant to," who has been called "an extension of the personality of his chief," and as such acts in his name.

APPLICATION OF MILITARY TO BUSINESS ORGANIZATION

The use of a general staff, widely and successfully employed in the armed forces of the world, has been urged by President Eisenhower to the author as "the major application of military to business organization." It is interesting to note that a number of business leaders and pioneers of scientific management started out as "assistants to." For example, Gantt, Barth and S. E. Thompson were assistants to Taylor. Alfred P. Sloan, Jr., and Walter P. Chrysler were assistants to W. C. Durant.

Other staff variants are the "Pentagon Staff" which handles long-range planning for the company as a whole (e.g., the Bell Telephone Laboratories) and the "personal staff" whose job is to make the business life of the chief smoother and more convenient.

(4) *Centralized Controls are designed to find out how well the delegated authority and responsibility are exercised.* Controls may include budgets, standards, reports, audits, visits, regular meetings and exchange of information. Instead of measuring results for the company as a whole, an attempt is made to break down profit or (controllable) cost responsibilities by operating units. This is merely a modernization of the practice of some of the great department store founders who let individual managers alone for a year or two, and then "looked at the record." Perhaps the "decentralization of measurement" partly explains the success of the Standard Oil Company of New Jersey's system of "wholly owned subsidiaries." Furthest in this direction went Orlando F. Webber, for some time the chief executive of Allied Chemical and Dye Company who ran the company on the basis of detailed monthly reports brought to him at the Waldorf Towers, his New York hotel. Not only may costs be effectively controlled by "decentralized measurement," but managerial analysis of results and remedial action are facilitated. A closer tie between effort and reward is made possible.

In a more formal sense there may be a "control office" attached to the chief executive to enable him to "manage on the exception principle." This may be supplemented by manpower controls (varying with the state of business), organization, executive development, planning departments. Essentially the task of the control office is to know the multitude of factors, weigh them and present them in an orderly fashion to someone far removed who makes basic decisions and still has the ultimate cost responsibility, yet can decide only by the rule of "exception."

DECIDING THE DEGREE OF DECENTRALIZATION

Decentralization is not an ideal. It is not a series of principles or prescriptions that a businessman ought necessarily to follow. Decentralization is not necessarily good, nor is centralization necessarily bad.

Centralization or decentralization may be, in part, merely the result of circumstances. Many labor problems are handled centrally because the laws of the country require it or the union insists on it. Many operating or sales decisions are decentralized because it would be physically impossible to operate successfully if they were centralized. Frequently, the centralization or decentralization of a decision is merely an accident. Finally, there is an immense variety of possible human behavior, a vast multiplicity of minute, undiscoverable causes and effects that cannot be encompassed in any principle or standard of evaluation. Thus there is a large area in which necessity, intuition, and luck decide the issue between centralization and decentralization.

DECENTRALIZATION BRINGS SPEEDIER DECISIONS

Where a conscious decision to decentralize is made, ideally it should be based on economic factors. The assignment of a management decision, or any part of it, higher or lower in the management hierarchy, should depend on *the additional revenue to be gained as compared to the additional cost.*

Under decentralization, decisions may be made more speedily because problems of communications are minimized. Often the decisions will be wiser also, because the men who make them will be closer to the problems. Other economies may be achieved through better utilization of lower and middle management, greater incentive, more and improved training opportunities, insurance that some products will not be pushed at the expense of others. In addition, when the administrative unit is smaller—absolutely or as a proportion of the employable population of the community—there are likely to be closer and better employee-management and community relations. And for the business as a whole, the decentralization of activities may mean a more widespread distribution of sales and purchases, which may reduce proportionately the unfavorable impact of sales decline.

Finally, decentralization may result in an increase in the marginal social net product—i.e., benefits to the community as distinct from benefits to the company. These general benefits may include more freedom of action for individuals, more widespread opportunity for constructive individual participation, less social stratification within the business.

The contributions of decentralization to profits must be weighed against the costs, both those that can be measured in dollars and cents and those that are more intangible. Easily measurable are the permanent extra costs that result from the larger staffs necessary, and some temporary expenses of introducing the change in management. More intangible costs are the disturbances caused by the change and their possible effects on morale. In addition, there may be "disguised unemployment" (high-priced men not fully utilized) and losses from watertight thinking or over-specialization. Finally, there are the costs (and gains) of destroying or delaying educational and promotional opportunities for some executives and creating them for others in the process of reorganization.

Basically the economic issue between centralization and decentralization is between lower total administrative costs and more effective performance. This is indicated by a quantitative comparison of centralized and decentralized personnel departments in a recent study by E. C. Weiss of the Department of Psychology, University of Maryland. In a small, but apparently not unrepresentative sample of 38 companies, decentralized organizations had a larger ratio of administrative employees to total employment than centralized firms, but lower rates of labor turnover, absenteeism, accident frequencies and severities.

THE STAGES OF DECENTRALIZATION

In reorganization the shift from centralization to decentralization can be compared to a capital investment. There is a heavy initial outlay which may be recovered after some years with a permanent net gain.[1]

In the development of every corporation there comes a point at which the gains of increasing size are such that the still increasing costs of coordination are likely to exceed them. Diminishing returns from the management factor begin to set in when the top executives are no longer intimately acquainted with the major problems of the company and are unable to coordinate them effectively or lose their health in attempting the task. (In this the "managerial optimum" differs from the "technical optimum." The latter merely relates to a minimum scale of operations below which the greatest efficiency cannot be achieved.) But if the managerial optimum is exceeded, costs, through declining managerial efficiency and the need for additional coordination, begin to rise. The managerial optimum sets, therefore, an upper limit to the scale of operations unless there is a reorganization and some decentralization.

Reorganization implies an analysis of basic com-

1. (F. W. Taylor once observed "the building of an efficient organization is necessarily slow and sometimes very expensive," *Shop Management*, p. 62.)

pany objectives to determine how well the existing structure meets them, the elimination of existing deficiencies and the introduction of new organizational techniques to overcome the diminishing returns from the factor management.

PROCESSES OF REORGANIZATION IN THREE STAGES

The immediate impact of delegation of decision-making tends to bring about economies. At the top management level the need for coordination of all major decisions is considerably reduced. Top management's time is freed to some extent for more important activities. In the smaller administrative (product) units responsibility for basic operating costs is more clearly fixed. There is likely to be an immediate reduction of "red tape and bureaucracy," and elimination of duplication. Better dissemination of more nearly correct information is obtained and faster action taken. Joint responsibility for costs is reduced. There is a new spirit about, and there are many other immediate savings.

Some immediate increase in cost also occurs, since there must be some increase in the number of executives and specialists. Headquarters requires a larger staff to provide more expert advice and control the results of delegated responsibility and authority; and the heads of the various administrative units each require staff assistance also. Flexible budgets, standard cost systems, and other means of analyzing results may be introduced.

In the second stage, the increase in controllers and staff specialists leads to a net increase in administrative expenses, part of which is permanent, and part of which is due to the necessity of gaining experience in the new system.

Eventually, however, the controls and the expert counsel from headquarters and field staff specialists are likely to make for greater profitability. In the long run, therefore, the corporation should not only recoup its initial outlay, but achieve gains that more than offset the continuing extra costs.

Thus decentralization is clearly a difficult process. This explains the necessity of considering it in balance with centralization. Even if the effort does not result in actual delegation of decision-making, it may still prevent an increase in centralization and afford prestige and opportunity to those receiving it.

19 — Conflicts Between Staff and Line Managerial Officers

MELVILLE DALTON

In its concentration on union-management relations, industrial sociology has tended to neglect the study of processes inside the ranks of industrial management. Obviously the doors to this research area are more closely guarded than the entry to industrial processes through the avenue of production workers, but an industrial sociology worthy of the name must sooner or later extend its inquiries to include the activities of all industrial personnel.

The present paper is the result of an attempt to study processes among industrial managers. It is specifically a report on the functioning interaction between the two major vertical groupings of industrial management: (1) the *staff* organization, the functions of which are research and advisory; and (2) the *line* organization, which has exclusive authority over production processes.

Industrial staff organizations are relatively new. Their appearance is a response to many complex interrelated forces, such as economic competition, scientific advance, industrial expansion, growth of the labor movement, and so on. During the last four or five decades these rapid changes and resulting unstable conditions have caused top industrial officials more and more to call in "specialists" to aid them toward the goal of greater production and efficiency. These specialists are of many kinds including chemists, statisticians, public and industrial relations officers, personnel officers, accountants, and a great variety of engineers, such as mechanical, draughting, electrical, chemical, fuel, lubricating, and industrial engineers. In industry these individuals are usually known as "staff people." Their functions, again, for the most part are to increase and apply their

"Conflicts Between Staff and Line Managerial Officers," *American Sociological Review*, XV (June 1950), 342–351. Reprinted by permission of the author and the American Sociological Association, Washington, D. C. **Melville Dalton:** Department of Anthropology and Sociology, Institute of Industrial Relations, University of California, Los Angeles.

specialized knowledge in problem areas, and to advise those officers who make up the "line" organization and have authority[1] over production processes.

This theoretically satisfying industrial structure of specialized experts advising busy administrators has in a number of significant cases failed to function as expected. The assumptions that (a) the staff specialists would be reasonably content to function without a measure of formal authority[2] over production, and that (b) their suggestions regarding improvement of processes and techniques for control over personnel and production would be welcomed by line officers and be applied, require closer examination. In practice there is often much conflict between industrial staff and line organizations and in varying degrees the members of these organizations oppose each other.[3]

The aim of this paper is, therefore, to present and analyze data dealing with staff-line tensions.

Data were drawn from three industrial plants[4] in which the writer had been either a participating member of one or both of the groups or was intimate with reliable informants among the officers who were.

Approached sociologically, relations among members of management in the plants could be viewed as a general conflict system caused and perpetuated chiefly by (1) power struggles in the organization stemming in the main from competition among departments to maintain low operating costs; (2) drives by numerous members to increase their status in the hierarchy; (3) conflict between union and management; and (4) the staff-line friction which is the subject of this paper.[5] This milieu of tensions was not only unaccounted for by the blue-print organizations of the plants, but was often contradictory to, and even destructive of, the organizations' formal aims. All members of management, especially in the middle and lower ranks,[6] were caught up in this conflict system. Even though they might wish to escape, the obligation of at least appearing to carry out formal functions compelled individuals to take sides in order to protect themselves against the aggressions of others. And the intensity of the conflict was aggravated by the fact that it was formally unacceptable and had to be hidden.

For analytical convenience, staff-line friction may be examined apart from the reciprocal effects of the general conflict system. Regarded in this way, the data indicated that three conditions were basic to staff-line struggles: (1) the conspicuous ambition and "individualistic" behavior among staff officers; (2) the complication arising from staff efforts to justify its existence and get

acceptance of its contributions; and, related to point two, (3) the fact that incumbency of the higher staff offices was dependent on line approval. The significance of these conditions will be discussed in order.

MOBILE BEHAVIOR OF STAFF PERSONNEL

As a group, staff personnel in the three plants were markedly ambitious, restless, and individu-

1. *Inside* their particular staff organization, staff officers also may have authority over their subordinates, but not over production personnel.

2. To the extent that staff officers influence line policy they do, of course, have a certain *informal* authority.

3. Some social scientists have noted the possibility of staff-line friction, and industrial executives themselves have expressed strong feelings on the matter. See Burleigh B. Gardner, *Human Relations in Industry* (Chicago: Richard D. Irwin, Inc., 1945) and H. E. Dimock, *The Executive in Action* (New York: Harper & Brothers, 1945). Dimock believes that we are too "staff-minded" and that we should become more "executive-minded" (p. 241). A high line officer in a large corporation denounced staff organizations to the writer on the ground of their "costing more than they're worth," and that "They stir up too much trouble and are too theoretical." He felt that their function (excepting that of accountants, chemists, and "a few mechanical engineers") could be better carried out by replacing them with "highly-select front-line foremen [the lowest placed line officers] who are really the backbone of management, and pay them ten or twelve thousand dollars a year."

4. These plants were in related industries and ranged in size from 4,500 to 20,000 employees, with the managerial groups numbering from 200 to nearly 1,000. Details concerning the plants and their location are confidential. Methodological details concerning an intensive study embracing staff-line relations and several other areas of behavior in one of the plants are given in the writer's unpublished doctoral thesis, "A Study of Informal Organization Among the Managers of an Industrial Plant," (Department of Sociology, University of Chicago, 1949).

5. Because these conflict areas were interrelated and continually shifting and reorganizing, discussion of any one of them separately—as in the case of staff-line relations—will, of course, be unrealistic to some extent.

6. From bottom to top, the line hierarchy consisted of the following strata of officers: (1) first-line foremen, who were directly in charge of production workmen; (2) general foremen; (3) departmental superintendents; (4) divisional superintendents; (5) assistant plant manager; (6) plant manager. In the preceding strata there were often "assistants," such as "assistant general foreman," "assistant superintendent," etc., in which case the total strata of the line hierarchy could be almost double that indicated here.

In the staff organizations the order from bottom to top was: (1) supervisor (equivalent to the first-line foreman); (2) general supervisor (equivalent to the general foreman); (3) staff head—sometimes "superintendent" (equivalent to departmental superintendent in the line organization). Occasionally there were strata of assistant supervisors and assistant staff heads.

The term "upper line" will refer to all strata above the departmental superintendent. "Middle line" will include the departmental superintendent and assistants. "Lower line" will refer to general and first-line foremen and their assistants.

"Lower," "middle," and "upper" staff will refer respectively to the supervisor, general supervisor and staff head.

"Top management" will refer to the upper line and the few staff heads with whom upper line officers were especially intimate on matters of policy.

alistic. There was much concern to win rapid promotion, to make the "right impressions," and to receive individual recognition. Data showed that the desire among staff members for personal distinctions often over-rode their sentiments of group consciousness and caused intra-staff tensions.[7]

The relatively high turnover of staff personnel[8] quite possibly reflected the dissatisfactions and frustrations of members over inability to achieve the distinction and status they hoped for. Several factors appeared to be of importance in this restlessness of staff personnel. Among these were age and social differences between line and staff officers, structural differences in the hierarchy of the two groups, and the staff group's lack of authority over production.

With respect to age, the staff officers were significantly younger than line officers.[9] This would account to some extent for their restlessness. Being presumably less well-established in life in terms of material accumulations, occupational status, and security, while having greater expectations (see below), and more energy, as well as more life ahead in which to make new starts elsewhere if necessary, the staff groups were understandably more dynamic and driving.[10]

Age-conflict[11] was also significant in staff-line antagonisms. The incident just noted of the young staff officer seeking to get direct acceptance by the line of his contribution failed in part—

judging from the strong sentiments later expressed by the line superintendent—because of an age antipathy. The older line officers disliked receiving what they regarded as instruction from men so much younger than themselves, and staff personnel clearly were conscious of this attitude among line officers.[12] In staff-line meetings staff officers frequently had their ideas slighted or even treated with amusement by line incumbents. Whether such treatment was warranted or not, the effects were disillusioning to the younger, less experienced staff officers. Often selected by the organization because of their outstanding academic records, they had entered industry with the belief that they had much to contribute, and that their efforts would win early recognition and rapid advancement. Certainly they had no thought that their contributions would be in any degree unwelcome. This naiveté[13] was apparently due to lack of earlier first-hand experience in industry (or acquaintance with those who had such experience), and to omission of realistic instruction in the social sciences from their academic training. The unsophisticated staff officer's initial contacts with the shifting, covert, expedient arrangements between members of staff and line usually gave him a severe shock. He had entered industry prepared to engage in logical, well-formulated relations with members of the managerial hierarchy, and to carry out precise, methodical functions for which his training had equipped

---

7. In a typical case in one of the plants, a young staff officer developed a plan for increasing the life of certain equipment in the plant. He carried the plan directly to the superintendent of the department in which he hoped to introduce it, but was rebuffed by the superintendent who privately acknowledged the merit of the scheme but resented the staff officer's "trying to lord it over" him. The staff organization condemned the behavior of its member and felt that he should have allowed the plan to appear as a contribution of the staff group rather than of one of its members. The officer himself declared that "By G— it's my idea and I want credit. There's not a damn one of you guys [the staff group] that wouldn't make the same squawk if you were in my place!"

8. During the period between 1944 and 1950 turnover of staff personnel in these plants was between two and four times as great as that of line personnel. This grouping included all the non-managerial members of staff and line and all the hourly-paid (non-salaried) members of management (about 60 assistant first-line foremen). Turnover was determined by dividing the average number of employees for a given year (in line or staff) into the accessions or separations, whichever was the smaller.

9. Complete age data were available in one of the larger plants. Here the 36 staff heads, staff specialists, and assistants had a mean age of 42.9 years. This value would have been less than 40 years, except for the inclusion of several older former line officers, but even a mean of 42.9 years was significantly less (C.R. 2.8) than that of the 35 line superintendents in the plant who had a mean age of 48.7 years. The age difference was even more significant when the staff heads were compared with the 61 general foremen who had a mean age of 50.0 years. And between the 93 salaried first-line foremen (mean age of 48.5 years) and the 270 sala-

ried nonsupervisory staff personnel (mean age of 31.0 years) the difference was still greater.

10. One might also hypothesize that the drive of staff officers was reflected in the fact that the staff heads and specialists gained their positions (those held when the data were collected) in less time than did members of the line groups. E.g., the 36 staff officers discussed above had spent a median of 10 years attaining their positions, as against a median of 11 years for the first-line foremen, 17 years for the general foremen, and 19 years for the superintendents. But one must consider also that some of the staff groups were relatively new (13—15 years old) and had grown rapidly, which probably accelerated their rate of promotions as compared with that of the older line organization.

11. E. A. Ross in *Principles of Sociology* (New York: D. Appleton-Century Co., 1938) pp. 238—48, has some pertinent comments on age conflict.

12. Explaining the relatively few cases in which his staff had succeeded in "selling ideas" to the line, an assistant staff head remarked: "We're always in hot water with these old guys on the line. You can't tell them a damn thing. They're bull-headed as hell! Most of the time we offer a suggestion it's either laughed at or not considered at all. The same idea in the mouth of some old codger on the line'd get a round of applause. They treat us like kids."

Line officers in these plants often referred to staff personnel (especially members of the auditing, production planning, industrial engineering, and industrial relations staffs) as "college punks," "sliderules," "crackpots," "pretty boys," and "chairwarmers."

13. John Mills, a research engineer retired from the telephone industry, has noted the worldly naiveté of research engineers in that field in his *The Engineer in Society* (New York: D. Van Nostrand Co., 1946).

him. Now he learned that (1) his freedom to function was snared in a web of informal commitments; (2) his academic specialty (on which he leaned for support in his new position) was often not relevant[14] for carrying out his formal assignments; and that (3) the important thing to do was to learn who the informally powerful line officers were and what ideas they would welcome which at the same time would be acceptable to his superiors.

Usually the staff officer's reaction to these conditions is to look elsewhere for a job or make an accommodation in the direction of protecting himself and finding a niche where he can make his existence in the plant tolerable and safe. If he chooses the latter course, he is likely to be less concerned with creative effort for his employer than with attempts to develop reliable social relations that will aid his personal advancement. The staff officer's recourse to this behavior and his use of other status-increasing devices will be discussed below in another connection.

The formal structure, or hierarchy of statuses, of the two larger plants from which data were drawn, offered a frustration to the ambitious staff officer. That is, in these plants the strata, or levels of authority, in the staff organizations ranged from three to five as against from five to ten in the line organization. Consequently there were fewer possible positions for exercise of authority into which staff personnel could move. This condition may have been an irritant to expansion

among the staff groups. Unable to move vertically to the degree possible in the line organization, the ambitious staff officer could enlarge his area of authority in a given position only by lateral expansion — by increasing his personnel. Whether or not aspiring staff incumbents revolted against the relatively low hierarchy through which they could move, the fact remains that (1) they appeared eager to increase the number of personnel under their authority,[15] (2) the personnel of staff groups *did* increase disproportionately to those of the line,[16] and (3) there was a trend of personnel movement from staff to line,[17] rather than the reverse, presumably (reflecting the drive and ambition of staff members) because there were more positions of authority, as well as more authority to be exercised, more prestige, and usually more income in the line.

Behavior in the plants indicated that line and staff personnel belonged to different social status groups and that line and staff antipathies were at least in part related to these social distinctions. For example, with respect to the item of formal education, the staff group stood on a higher level than members of the line. In the plant from which the age data were taken, the 36 staff officers had a mean of 14.6 years of schooling as compared with 13.1 years for 35 line superintendents, 11.2 years for 60 general foremen, and 10.5 years for 93 first-line foremen. The difference between the mean education of the staff

14. Among the staff heads and assistants referred to earlier, only 50 per cent of those with college training (32 of the 36 officers) were occupied with duties related to their specialized training. E.g., the head of the industrial relations staff had a B.S. degree in aeronautical engineering; his assistant had a similar degree in chemical engineering. Considering that staff officers are assumed to be specialists trained to aid and advise management in a particular function, the condition presented here raises a question as to what the criteria of selection were. (As will be shown in a separate paper, the answer appeared to be that personal — as well as impersonal — criteria were used.) Among the college-trained of 190 line officers in the same plant, the gap between training and function was still greater, with 61 per cent in positions not related to the specialized part of their college work.

15. This was suggested by unnecessary references among some staff officers to "the number of men under me," and by their somewhat fanciful excuses for increase of personnel. These excuses included statements of needing more personnel to (1) carry on research, (2) control new processes, (3) keep records and reports up-to-date. These statements often did not square with (1) the excessive concern among staff people about their "privileges" (such as arriving on the job late, leaving early, leaving the plant for long periods during working hours, having a radio in the office during the World Series, etc.); (2) the great amount of time (relative to that of line officers) spent by lower staff personnel in social activities on the job, and (3) the constantly recurring (but not always provoked) claims among staff personnel of their functional importance for production. The duties of middle and lower staff personnel allowed them sufficient time to argue a great deal over their respective functions (as well as many irrelevant topics) and to challenge the relative merit of one another's contributions or "ideas." In some of the staffs

these discussions could go on intermittently for hours and develop into highly theoretical jousts and wit battles. Where staff people regarded such behavior as a privilege of their status, line officers considered it as a threat to themselves. This lax control (in terms of line discipline) was in part a tacit reward from staff heads to their subordinates. The reward was expected because staff superiors (especially in the industrial relations, industrial engineering, and planning staffs) often overlooked and/or perverted the work of subordinates (which was resented) in response to pressures from the line. This behavior will be noted later.

16. In one of the larger plants, where exact data were available, the total staff personnel had by 1945 exceeded that of the line. At that time the staff included 400 members as against 317 line personnel composed of managerial officers and their clerical workers, but not production workers. By 1948 the staff had increased to 517 as compared with 387 for the line (during this period *total* plant personnel declined over 400). The staff had grown from 20.8 per cent larger than the line in 1945 to 33.6 per cent larger in 1948, and had itself increased by 29.3 per cent during the three years as against a growth in the line of 22.1 per cent. Assuming the conditions essential for use of probability theory, the increase in staff personnel could have resulted from chance about 1.5 times in a hundred. Possibly post-war and other factors of social change were also at work but, if so, their force was not readily assessable.

17. This movement from staff to line can disorganize the formal managerial structure, especially when (1) the transferring staff personnel have had little or no supervisory experience in the staff but have an academic background which causes them to regard human beings as mechanisms that will respond as expected; (2) older, experienced line officers have hoped — for years in some cases — to occupy the newly vacated (or created) positions.

group and that of the highest line group (14.6 – 13.1) was statistically significant at better than the one per cent level. The 270 nonsupervisory staff personnel had a mean of 13.1 years—the same as that of the line superintendents. Consciousness of this difference probably contributed to a feeling of superiority among staff members, while the sentiment of line officers toward staff personnel was reflected in the name-calling noted earlier.

Staff members were also much concerned about their dress, a daily shave, and a weekly hair-cut. On the other hand line officers, especially below the level of departmental superintendent, were relatively indifferent to such matters. Usually they were in such intimate contact with production processes that dirt and grime prevented the concern with meticulous dress shown by staff members. The latter also used better English in speaking and in writing reports, and were more suave and poised in social intercourse. These factors, and the recreational preferences of staff officers for night clubs and "hot parties," assisted in raising a barrier between them and most line officers.

The social antipathies of the two groups and the status concern of staff officers were indicated by the behavior of each toward the established practice of dining together in the cafeterias reserved for management in the two larger plants. Theoretically, all managerial officers upward from the level of general foremen in the line, and general supervisors in the staff, were eligible to eat in these cafeterias. However, in practice the mere taking of one of these offices did not automatically assure the incumbent the privilege of eating in the cafeteria. One had first to be invited to "join the association." Staff officers were very eager to "get in" and did considerable fantasying on the impressions, with respect to dress and behavior, that were believed essential for an invitation. One such staff officer, a cost supervisor, dropped the following remarks:

There seems to be a committee that passes on you. I've had my application in for three years, but no soap. Harry [his superior] had his in for over three years before he made it. You have to have something, because if a man who's in moves up to another position the man who replaces him doesn't get it because of the position—he might not get it at all. I think I'm about due.

Many line officers who were officially members of the association avoided the cafeteria, however, and had to be *ordered* by the assistant plant manager to attend. One of these officers made the following statement, which expressed more pointedly the many similar spontaneous utterances of resentment and dislike made by other line officers:

There's a lot of good discussion in the cafeteria. I'd like to get in on more of it but I don't like to go there —sometimes I have to go. Most of the white collar people [staff officers] that eat there are stuck-up. I've been introduced three times to Svendsen [engineer], yet when I meet him he pretends to not even know me. When he meets me on the street he always manages to be looking someplace else. G—d—such people as that! They don't go in the cafeteria to eat and relax while they talk over their problems. They go in there to look around and see how somebody is dressed or to talk over the hot party they had last night. Well, that kind of damn stuff don't go with me. I haven't any time to put on airs and make out I'm something that I'm not.

COMPLICATIONS OF STAFF NEED TO PROVE ITS WORTH

To the thinking of many line officers, the staff functioned as an agent on trial rather than as a managerial division that might be of equal importance with the line organization in achieving production goals. Staff members were very conscious of this sentiment toward them and of their need to prove themselves. They strained to develop new techniques and to get them accepted by the line. But in doing this they frequently became impatient, and gave already suspicious line officers the impression of reaching for authority over production.

Since the line officer regards his authority over production as something sacred, and resents the implication that after many years in the line he needs the guidance of a newcomer who lacks such experience, an obstacle to staff-line cooperation develops the moment this sore spot is touched. On the other hand, the staff officer's ideology of his function leads him to precipitate a power struggle with the line organization. By and large he considers himself as an agent of top management. He feels bound to contribute something significant in the form of research or ideas helpful to management. By virtue of his greater education and intimacy with the latest theories of production, he regards himself as a managerial consultant and an expert, and feels that he must be, or appear to be, almost infallible once he has committed himself to top management on some point. With this orientation, he is usually disposed to approach middle and lower line with an attitude of condescension that often reveals itself in the heat of discussion. Consequently, many staff officers involve themselves in trouble and report their failures as due to "ignorance" and "bull-headedness" among these line officers.

On this point, relations between staff and line in all three of the plants were further irritated by a rift inside the line organization. First-line foremen were inclined to feel that top management had brought in the production planning, industrial relations, and industrial engineering staffs as clubs with which to control the lower line. Hence they frequently regarded the projects of staff personnel as manipulative devices, and reacted by cooperating with production workers and/or general foremen (whichever course was the more expedient) in order to defeat insistent and uncompromising members of the staff. Also, on occasion (see below), the lower line could cooperate evasively with lower staff personnel who were in trouble with staff superiors.

EFFECT OF LINE AUTHORITY OVER STAFF PROMOTION

The fact that entry to the higher staff offices in the three plants was dependent on approval of top line officers had a profound effect on the behavior of staff personnel. Every member of the staff knew that if he aspired to higher office he must make a record for himself a good part of which would be a reputation among upper line officers of ability to "understand" their informal problems without being told. This knowledge worked in varying degrees to pervert the theory of staff-line relations. Ideally the two organizations cooperate to improve existing methods of output, to introduce new methods, to plan the work, and to solve problems of production and the scheduling of orders that might arise. But when the line offers resistance to the findings and recommendations of the staff, the latter is reduced to evasive practices of getting some degree of acceptance of its programs, and at the same time of convincing top management that "good relations" exist with officers down the line. This necessity becomes even more acute when the staff officer aspires (for some of the reasons given above) to move over to the line organization, for then he must convince powerful line officers that he is worthy. In building a convincing record, however, he may compromise with line demands and bring charges from his staff colleagues that he is "selling out," so that after moving into the line organization he will then have to live with

enemies he made in the staff. In any case, the need among staff incumbents of pleasing line officers in order to perfect their careers called for accommodation in three major areas:[18] (1) the observance of staff rules, (2) the introduction of new techniques, and (3) the use of appropriations for staff research and experiment.

With respect to point one, staff personnel, particularly in the middle and lower levels, carried on expedient relations with the line that daily evaded formal rules. Even those officers most devoted to rules found that, in order not to arouse enmity in the line on a scale sufficient to be communicated *up* the line, compromising devices were frequently helpful and sometimes almost unavoidable both for organizational and career aims. The usual practice was to tolerate minor breaking of staff rules by line personnel, or even to cooperate with the line in evading rules,[19] and in exchange lay a claim on the line for cooperation on critical issues. In some cases line aid was enlisted to conceal lower staff blunders from the upper staff and the upper line.[20]

Concerning point two, while the staff organizations gave much time to developing new techniques, they were simultaneously thinking about how their plans would be received by the line. They knew from experience that middle and lower line officers could always give a "black eye"

18. The relative importance of one or more of these areas would vary with the function of a given staff.

19. In a processing department in one of the plants the chemical solution in a series of vats was supposed to have a specific strength and temperature, and a fixed rate of inflow and outflow. Chemists (members of the chemical staff) twice daily checked these properties of the solution and submitted reports showing that all points met the laboratory ideal. Actually, the solution was usually nearly triple the standard strength, the temperature was about 10 degrees Centigrade higher than standard, and the rate of flow was in excess of double the standard. There are, of course, varying discrepancies between laboratory theory and plant practice, but the condition described here resulted from production pressures that forced line foremen into behavior upsetting the conditions expected by chemical theory. The chemists were sympathetic with the hard-pressed foremen, who compensated by (1) notifying the chemists (rather than their superior, the chief chemist) if anything "went wrong" for which the laboratory was responsible and thus sparing them criticism; and by (2) cooperating with the chemists to reduce the number of analyses which the chemists would ordinarily have to make.

20. Failure of middle and lower staff personnel to "cooperate" with line officers might cause the latter to "stand pat" in observance of line rules at a time when the pressures of a dynamic situation would make the former eager to welcome line cooperation in rule-breaking. For example, a staff officer was confronted with the combined effect of (1) a delay in production on the line that was due to an indefensible staff error; (2) pressure on the line superintendent—with whom he was working—to hurry a special order; and (3) the presence in his force of new inexperienced staff personnel who were (a) irritating to line officers, and (b) by their inexperience constituted an invitation to line aggression. Without aid from the line superintendent (which could have been withheld by observance of formal rules) in covering up the staff error and in controlling line personnel, the staff officer might have put himself in permanent disfavor with all his superiors.

to staff contributions by deliberate mal-practices. Repeatedly top management had approved, and incorporated, staff proposals that had been verbally accepted down the line. Often the latter officers had privately opposed the changes, but had feared that saying so would incur the resentment of powerful superiors who could informally hurt them. Later they would seek to discredit the change by deliberate mal-practice and hope to bring a return to the former arrangement. For this reason there was a tendency for staff members to withhold improved production schemes or other plans when they knew that an attempt to introduce them might fail or even bring personal disrepute.

Line officers fear staff innovations for a number of reasons. In view of their longer experience, presumably intimate knowledge of the work, and their greater remuneration, they fear[21] being "shown up" before their line superiors for not having thought of the processual refinements themselves. They fear that changes in methods may bring personnel changes which will threaten the break-up of cliques and existing informal arrangements and quite possibly reduce their area of authority. Finally, changes in techniques may expose forbidden practices and departmental inefficiency. In some cases these fears have stimulated line officers to compromise staff men to the point where the latter will agree to postpone the initiation of new practices for specific periods.

In one such case an assistant staff head agreed with a line superintendent to delay the application of a bonus plan for nearly three months so that the superintendent could live up to the expedient agreement he had made earlier with his grievance committeeman to avoid a "wildcat" strike by a group of production workmen.[22] The lower engineers who had devised the plan were suspicious of the formal reasons given to them for withholding it, so the assistant staff head prevented them (by means of "busy work") from attending staff-line meetings lest they inadvertently reveal to top management that the plan was ready.

The third area of staff-line accommodations growing out of authority relations revolved around staff use of funds granted it by top management. Middle and lower line charged that staff research and experimentation was little more than "money wasted on blunders," and that various departments of the line could have "accomplished much more with less money." According to staff officers, those of their plans that failed usually did so because line personnel "sabotaged" them and refused to "cooperate." Specific costs of "crack-pot experimentation" in certain staff groups were pointed to by line officers. Whatever the truth of the charges and counter-charges, evidence indicated (confidants in both groups supported this) that pressures from the line organization (below the top level) forced some of the staff groups to "kick over" parts of the funds appropriated for staff use[23] by top management. These compromises were of course hidden from top management, but the relations described were carried on to such an extent that by means of them—and line pressures for manipulation of accounts in the presumably impersonal auditing departments—certain line officers were able to show impressively low operating costs and thus win favor[24] with top management that would relieve pressures and be useful in personal advancement. In their turn the staff officers involved would receive more "cooperation" from the line and/or recommendation for transfer to the line. The data indicated that in a few such cases men from accounting and auditing staffs were given general foremanships (without previous line experience) as a reward for their understanding behavior.

SUMMARY

Research in three industrial plants showed conflict between the managerial staff and line groups that hindered the attainment of organizational goals. Privately expressed attitudes among some of the higher line executives revealed their hope that greater control of staff groups could be achieved, or that the groups might be eliminated and their functions taken over in great part by carefully selected and highly remunerated lower-line officers. On their side, staff members wanted more recognition and a greater voice in control of the plants.

All of the various functioning groups of the plants were caught up in a general conflict sys-

21. Though there was little evidence that top management expected line officers to refine production techniques, the fear of such an expectation existed nevertheless. As noted earlier, however, some of the top executives were thinking that development of a "higher type" of first-line foreman might enable most of the staff groups to be eliminated.
22. This case indicates the over-lapping of conflict areas referred to earlier. A later paper will deal with the area of informal union-management relations.
23. In two of the plants a somewhat similar relation rising from different causes, existed *inside* the line organization with the *operating* branch of the line successfully applying pressures for a share in funds assigned to the *maintenance* division of the line.
24. The reader must appreciate the fact that constant demands are made by top management to maintain low operating costs.

tem; but apart from the effects of involvement in this complex, the struggles between line and staff organizations were attributable mainly to (1) functional differences between the two groups; (2) differentials in the ages, formal education, potential occupational ceilings, and status group affiliations of members of the two groups (the staff officers being younger, having more education but lower occupational potential, and forming a prestige-oriented group with distinctive dress and recreational tastes); (3) need of the staff groups to justify their existence; (4) fear in the line that staff bodies by their expansion, and well-financed research activities,would undermine line authority; and (5) the fact that aspirants to higher staff offices could gain promotion only through approval of influential line executives.

If further research should prove that staff-line behavior of the character presented here is widespread in industry, and *if* top management should realize how such behavior affects its cost and production goals—and be concerned to improve the condition—then remedial measures could be considered. For example, a corrective approach might move in the direction of (1) creating a separate body[25] whose sole function would be the coordination of staff and line efforts; (2) increasing the gradations of awards and promotions in staff organizations (without increase of staff personnel); (3) granting of more nearly equal pay to staff officers, but with increased responsibility (without authority over line processes or personnel) for the practical working of their projects; (4) requiring that staff personnel have a minimum supervisory experience and have shared repeatedly in successful collaborative staff-line projects before transferring to the line; (5) steps by top management to remove the fear of veiled personal reprisal felt by officers in most levels of both staff and line hierarchies (This fear—rising from a disbelief in the possibility of bureaucratic impersonality—is probably the greatest obstacle to communication inside the ranks of management); (6) more emphasis in colleges and universities on realistic instruction in the social sciences for students preparing for industrial careers.

20 — Span of Control — Conceptions and Misconceptions

ROBERT E. THOMPSON

Span of control has long been a controversial subject. Unfortunately, discussion for the most part has been limited to consideration of Urwick's simple hypothesis: "No superior can supervise directly the work of more than five, or at most six, subordinates whose work interlocks."[1] The controversy, though bitter, has been limited to a few active participants. Among most managers the rule is widely quoted (without the final qualification) as one of the cardinal principles of management.

Rules of thumb are extremely handy, a quality that undoubtedly contributes to their popularity. But such important decisions as those involving organization structure should be guided by more than a simple rule, particularly when the basis for the rule is unknown to most. Only a full awareness of the basic issues involved will result in organization structures truly suited to the fundamental purposes of each enterprise.

Certain features of the span-of-control problem, though possibly more complex than the basis for Urwick's rule, seem closer to real management issues. I believe that broader average spans can and should be applied to today's organizations. However, this will not occur until managements in general have analyzed and discarded some of their favorite misconceptions on the subject, and until they have come to grips with the forces that militate against broader spans. These concepts and forces have been revealed repeatedly to me in personal interviews during organization analyses.

---

25. This body, or "Board of Coordination," would be empowered to enforce its decisions. Membership would consist of staff and line men who had had wide experience in the plant over a period of years. The Board would (a) serve as an arbiter between staff and line; (b) review, screen, and approve individual recommendations submitted; and (c) evaluate contributions after a trial period. Such a body would incidentally be another high status goal for seasoned, capable, and ambitious officers who too often are trapped by the converging walls of the pyramidal hierarchy.

"Span of Control—Conceptions and Misconceptions," *Business Horizons*, VII (Summer 1964), 49—58. Reprinted by permission of the author and Indiana University. **Robert E. Thompson:** Senior consultant, Haskins & Sells, New York.

1. See Lyndall F. Urwick, "The Manager's Span of Control," *Harvard Business Review*, XXXIV (May-June, 1956), 39.

CONVERSATION RAISES ISSUES

In span-of-control considerations, we are concerned essentially with a manager's work load. Span of control should therefore embrace the number of individuals who report directly to the manager and who require significant planning and control efforts on his part. This eliminates secretaries and "assistant to" positions, since these functions, if anything, tend to reduce the supervisory load imposed by the other subordinates.

A typical conversation between an organization analyst and a line manager regarding possible changes in the manager's organization structure will raise many issues related to this subject.

ORGANIZATION ANALYST: I asked for some of your time today to discuss the possibility of reorganizing your department to broaden the average span of control. As you know, the company feels that certain benefits will come from such changes. Perhaps you heard that the president has already taken steps to broaden his span from two to ten.

LINE MANAGER: Yes, I heard about that. If you ask me, the whole thing is a farce. You fellows in organization planning have been claiming that this will reduce costs. That's a good one!

ANALYST: But don't you think that costs were reduced by the change the president made?

MANAGER: Of course not. We used to have two vice-presidents; now we've got ten. That's what I call a top-heavy organization. Just watch our overhead climb.

ANALYST: I can't agree with you. The change in span from two to ten was made when the two former vice-presidents retired and the ten division directors were elevated to vice-presidencies. We now have two less executives in the organization, two less secretaries, and two available offices. How does this increase costs?

MANAGER: But what about the salary increases the ten got when they were made vice-presidents?

ANALYST: Actually their responsibilities have not changed significantly. They still direct the same functions and the same number of people. I don't know what they got, if anything, but obviously each would have to receive an increase equivalent to more than 10 per cent of the previous vice-presidents' *combined* salaries to offset the savings. Personally, I think that's rather doubtful.

MANAGER: Maybe, but the change still doesn't make any sense. Back when there were only two vice-presidents, all the operating divisions reported to one of them and the staff divisions reported to the other. Now that made a lot of sense. We in the manufacturing division had a man who could place our problems directly before the president. In other words, we were well represented at the top level. Also, since all the operating divisions reported to him, the efforts of these divisions were well coordinated.

ANALYST: You mean that because all the operating divisions reported to one man, he could coordinate your activities and represent your interests to the president?

MANAGER: Exactly.

ANALYST: But don't you still all report to one man—the president? And can't your interests be even better represented now that the manufacturing V.P.—previously the manufacturing director—talks directly to the president?

MANAGER: Yes, but—

ANALYST: Remember the difficulties you fellows used to have with the administration division? You felt they couldn't understand your problems and were encouraging unnecessary and unjust restrictions on your method of operating.

MANAGER: Do I! When the two vice-presidents stopped talking to each other, the whole company seemed to be going in two different directions.

ANALYST: I think that describes the situation very well. But, remember, the men in administration were having even greater difficulties with you. They were unable to get any information, cooperation, or understanding from the operating groups, simply because it was known that their boss and your boss were feuding. I know that the president was aware of the problem. Part of his wish to broaden his span stemmed from the need to pull the two parts together.

MANAGER: I don't see how it's going to help.

ANALYST: He feels that with all the operating and staff divisions reporting directly to him, he'll be able to coordinate the activities of *all* divisions and resolve some of these difficulties. You see, he doesn't fight with himself the way the two old V.P.'s used to fight with each other. If the operating divisions are correct in the things they do, and the staff divisions are all wrong—as you undoubtedly think—he'll now have a better chance of finding that out and rectifying the situation.

MANAGER: Amen to that! Maybe it isn't such a bad idea at the president's level, but that still doesn't prove it's good at lower levels. For example, everybody agrees that the company needs better-trained supervisors. If you eliminate supervisory positions by broadening average spans, you're providing less opportunity for that training.

ANALYST: I certainly agree that we need an improvement in the average quality of our supervisors. But we feel that increasing the average span will help bring about this improvement, even though the number of supervisory positions has been decreased. After all, there's no real need for a supervisor to be efficient when he has lots of time — as he normally has with a short span of control. He can define, redefine, and re-redefine assignments as he finds his previous definitions were not accurately or effectively communicated. He can also look constantly over the shoulders of his subordinates and work with them at every step to compensate for sloppy delegation. That isn't desirable from the subordinate's point of view.

MANAGER: On that last point, I certainly agree with you. I wish my boss would stop following me around. I never get an opportunity to make a decision on my own.

ANALYST: Exactly. You don't get an opportunity to build the kind of independence and reliance on your own judgment that is necessary for a future executive. Also, with the amount of backstopping you receive, it's very difficult to determine your potential for promotion.

MANAGER: Well, I can tell you my performance would be a lot better without my boss's interference.

ANALYST: It seems that we agree on a few things, at least. Now let's talk about your department.

MANAGER: As you know, my department is rather new, so my problems are different. I needed a lot of help in getting organized, crystallizing internal procedures, and so on. So I set up a group of subordinate supervisors that I could count on. They were a big help in shaping up the operation. Now things are pretty well organized, so I delegate everything to them and spend my time thinking of ways to improve the operation.

ANALYST: And what is your current structure?

MANAGER: I have a secretary and three subordinate supervisors; each of the supervisors has four men assigned to him.

ANALYST: Some of your comments are interesting. For example, didn't you know that assistance could have been obtained from administration in setting up your department, writing the procedures, and the like? They have some highly trained specialists for that kind of thing.

MANAGER: Back in those days, administration was the common enemy of all operating divisions. Even if I'd wanted to, my boss wouldn't have stood still for calling them in.

ANALYST: All right, but what about this idea of spending all your time thinking?

MANAGER: What's wrong with that? I thought that's what a manager was supposed to do. The company wants improvement, doesn't it?

ANALYST: Certainly. Have you asked the Systems Department for any studies?

MANAGER: Actually I haven't gotten to that point yet. Quite frankly, I've had some difficulty in determining where I should start improving things. My supervisors seem to have things well in hand; at least they tell me they're not having any problems.

ANALYST: Oh, I see. But once you get under way with your improvements, will they occupy you full time?

MANAGER: Yes, I believe they will. You see, when I'm not thinking, I usually spend my time coordinating things with my boss.

ANALYST: Wouldn't he be satisfied with a weekly meeting?

MANAGER: Maybe, but the other supervisor who reports to him spends a good deal of time in his office.

ANALYST: Then possibly I should talk to your colleague about a weekly meeting also.

MANAGER: That's a good idea. If you can convince him to settle for the weekly meeting, I'll be glad to, too.

ANALYST: So if your colleague would spend less time with the boss, you would too. Let's assume for a moment that this problem can be licked and consider what would happen if your three supervisors were moved to another area. This would mean then that the twelve nonsupervisors would report directly to you. The change would be advantageous to the three men who would undoubtedly be placed in the new division that's being set up. This would broaden their experience and probably provide an opportunity for a fairly rapid promotion.

MANAGER: Granted, it would be nice for them. But I'm concerned about the effectiveness of my department. The company won't thank you for reducing the control here.

ANALYST: I don't necessarily believe that control would be reduced, even though it would be necessary to change from the concentrated personal-contact type of control to more formal means. But even if it did cause some reduction in departmental effectiveness, this is not necessarily bad.

MANAGER: Now I know you're crazy. The company needs the best possible management in each department.

ANALYST: Look at it this way. The company needs the best possible management, the best possible facilities, the best possible research, the best possible advertising, and everything else. Unfortunately, there isn't enough money in the state, let alone the company, to provide the best of everything.

MANAGER: That may be, but I'm not concerned about facilities, research, and advertising. I'm just concerned about the management of this department.

ANALYST: That's true. I'm simply trying to explain why less than perfect supervision in your department may be to the company's advantage. It's quite possible, isn't it, that the $30,000 or so a year spent on your supervisors would do the company more ultimate good if spent on research or marketing—even with slightly reduced effectiveness in your department.

MANAGER: But that's no concern of mine.

ANALYST: No, but you must admit that from the company viewpoint it is an argument for broader span. Do you see any other disadvantages to you personally if we remove these supervisors from your department?

MANAGER: What happens to my labor grade if the supervisors are removed from the department? The twelve nonsupervisors are all in labor grade 4; the supervisors are in grade 6, and I'm in grade 8.

ANALYST: To answer your question, consider what your grade would now be had you never installed the supervisors between the men and yourself.

MANAGER: It would probably be less than an 8.

Obviously the conversation has not ended yet. But several significant issues have been raised.

SOME ISSUES EXAMINED

COST IMPLICATIONS

Most managers remain convinced that large spans increase organizational cost. How often have we heard a manager, with ten or fifteen supervisors reporting directly to him, called an empire builder? How many times have European organizations been credited with a competitive cost edge because they average only two or three vice-presidents? Unfortunately, the obvious has been missed.

Assume, for example, that a manager has fifteen supervisors reporting directly to him. What will be the effect on costs if he were to reduce the average span in this segment of the organization to three? To achieve this, he must add to his costs the salaries of six assistant managers and arrange them in some fashion between himself and the original fifteen. (Of course, this example is somewhat idealized. It is assumed that the fifteen original supervisors will receive substantially the same pay in either situation—a reasonable assumption if the same performance is required of them.)

The theoretical manpower costs or savings re-

SPAN-OF-CONTROL SAVINGS
(Average span increased from six to ten)

Total Organization	Savings Through Supervisory Cut	Savings Through Nonsupervisory Addition
(A)	(B)	(C)
100	74,000	132,000
500	370,000	660,000
1,000	740,000	1,320,000
5,000	3,700,000	6,600,000
10,000	7,400,000	13,200,000

sulting from changes in average spans are interesting to calculate. (The necessary formulae are explained in the section of the article entitled "Span-of-Control Mathematics.") To demonstrate their magnitude, the accompanying chart shows the annual savings in supervisory salaries and fringe benefits that might be expected for various sizes of organizations. Columns B and C both indicate the dollar savings resulting from an increase in the average span of control throughout the organization from six to ten. That is, the number of people reporting directly to each supervisor at all levels is presumed to increase from an average of six to ten. However, column B shows the savings if the increase in average span is achieved by removing supervisors and maintaining the original number of nonsupervisors. Column C shows the savings if the increase is achieved, as it would be during organizational expansion, by increasing nonsupervisors and maintaining the original number of supervisors. Average supervisory salary plus fringe is taken as $10,000 a year. The savings indicated are substantial from any point of view.

COORDINATION

Coordination is a classical function of management. In general, it refers to the job of ensuring that different organizational components mesh both in time and function—that is, the time at which one component performs must be appropriate to the requirements of other components, and the functions performed by that component must contribute to, rather than conflict with or overlap, other components. The ease with which coordination within the organization can be achieved by the managers is of paramount consideration.

Frequently, however, the grouping of organizational components needing *close* coordination is overemphasized. The result is disregard for another equally important problem: that of achieving adequate coordination among *all* components. As management science progresses, as centralized data processing and centralized service functions become a way of life, and as management decision-making techniques are refined, organizations take on more and more the characteristics of systems. Each component becomes more closely interrelated with other components. Managements are beginning to recognize that little can be done in one component without affecting others, and therefore that the need for over-all coordination of *all* components becomes increasingly important.

This awareness should lead logically to broader spans of control. Unfortunately, human tendencies seem to militate against their acceptance. The first solution to problems of conflict between components is to group them together under one head, who can then "coordinate" them.

An experience of some years ago bears this out. In providing instruction on organization theory to several groups of industrial supervisors, I used a case example involving a six-level structure with a history of poor over-all coordination. All groups were given detailed indoctrination in the company's policy favoring broad spans, and all agreed generally on the advisability of broad spans and few organizational levels. Following the indoctrination, each group was divided into teams to consider the case and develop an improved structure.

Typically, the teams immediately forgot the precepts and proceeded to regroup the functions in each component into smaller components, each with a new head, "for better coordination." Most of the proposed structures contained about eight levels. When confronted with the conflict between the company policy and their recommendations, the teams exhibited initial surprise, followed by chagrin. They had acted on an inner compulsion to combine without considering the effect of the combinations. Any purchase of closer coordination in one part of the organization must be paid for by a lessening of over-all coordination. It cannot be otherwise.

An interesting approach to structuring an organization starts with the structure that would provide, if managers were superhuman, the best possible coordination, and then backs off to the practical point where human managers can operate.

Assuming unlimited ability for one individual, the best possible coordination can be achieved if everyone in the organization reports directly to him. He would have unlimited visibility into the organization; he would know precisely what every individual was doing. With this knowledge, he could immediately detect duplication of effort, efforts directed to cross purposes, resource expenditures out of line with company goals, and

so on. In short, he could direct expenditures and efforts to a point of extreme optimization.

The introduction of one in-between level would reduce his visibility somewhat and so limit his ability to optimize, but it brings us closer to a structure that is humanly manageable. The process of introducing levels should stop, of course, at the first practical point.

SUPERVISORY TRAINING AND EXECUTIVES

In suggesting broader spans to managers, we invariably encounter concern over the lack of supervisory training that will result. It is argued that supervisory positions should be established, even where not needed, in order to provide slots in which future managers can try their wings—as if this were the only way to provide supervisory training.

The concern is based on the idea that any training is better than no training. But certainly this is not true. Experience is the best teacher, but experience frequently teaches the wrong thing. If the experience is undemanding, the student is apt to develop faulty, inefficient methods of reacting. It is well known, for example, that reading speed and comprehension are seldom very high when students are permitted to read at their own comfortable rate. However, if the reader is consistently challenged by a stop watch and comprehension test, he will develop habits that increase his performance well beyond the average.

On-the-job supervisory training should prepare a man to delegate effectively and efficiently. It should teach him to handle different personality types, to coordinate their functions, to reconcile their differences, to make decisions without a great deal of help, and to ensure required results with a minimum of personal attention. Setting up additional supervisory positions for training purposes (and shortening average spans in the process) inevitably results in decreased training effectiveness.

If this were the only method of training future managers, the situation would be almost hopeless. Fortunately, job rotation provides a means for the effective training of any reasonable number of men without establishing an artificial and unnecessary subcomponent.

The complementary task, that of executive selection, is also adversely affected by narrow spans, because one is never quite sure who is responsible for good or bad performance. Too much supervision clouds the significance of the performance figures of the supervised. The dependent-aggressive personality, so typical of rising young executives in American business culture, is successful in the strongly supportive atmosphere of short spans of control. However, these young men usually fail to achieve expected performance when thrown into a position requiring independent judgment or the unpopular decision.

USE OF STAFF SERVICES

A flower does not burst into full-blown maturity; it requires special nurturing as a seedling, and later must be pruned carefully to reach full productivity.

Organizations are analogous. New organizations require the nurturing that can be provided only by men competent at organization design, work method structuring, personnel training, procedure writing, goal definition, and so on. After full growth is attained, unnecessary functions and unproductive steps in work methods should be trimmed periodically. Necessary adjustments in direction should be made to accommodate changes in the other functions of the business or in the business itself.

The nurturing and pruning can be performed by men assigned permanently to the organization, but, since these functions are needed only intermittently, it would seem more efficient to provide them in the form of staff assistance from the outside. Several advantages are gained; important among these are the perspective and objectivity that good outside men can bring. Centralized service groups develop a detailed knowledge of over-all operations that is extremely useful in deciding the proper relationship of a new component to the others in the company—that is, for optimizing the balance of functions between them. When pruning time arrives, objectivity is an absolute necessity. The horticulturist, after all, does not ask the plant to trim itself.

Heads of new organizational components have a strong tendency to design the supervisory structure without regard for realistic requirements. Their anticipations of rapid expansion, resulting in heavy initial supervision, are usually unwarranted. Their desire for administrative control of the means of improvement is perfectly natural, but it is a luxury few organizations can afford. The short spans that result are an unnecessary burden to the company.

THE SUPERVISOR'S JOB

The philosophy of supervision that many managers seem to have been taught goes something like this: the manager's job is to set up a stable, smooth-running organization in which no problems occur. When this happy condition obtains,

the manager should then sit with his feet on the desk and think about improving the operation. On the surface, the concept seems plausible, but underneath it exhibits undesirable features.

There is no real trick to establishing an organization without problems. One needs only to let it be known that no problems will be tolerated, and none will occur—at least none that become evident. With the slightest encouragement, subordinate levels of supervision can act as effective insulators between the manager and the problems.

These hidden problems seethe and grow until efficient operation becomes impossible. Direction relinquished by the manager will be exercised by others, but it will not be unifying direction, nor will it normally be the direction which the manager would have chosen had he been involved in the problems. The personal involvement of the manager in his operation is extremely important. Ernest Dale, in an article devoted primarily to this need, writes, ". . . there must be less emphasis [in management training] on delegation to the point where the manager is isolated from all practical matters affecting his company. The manager must delegate, but he must not be too devoted to keeping his desk clean to read the reports, ponder them, and pull together the ever-disunifying tendencies of his business."[2]

With a short span the manager does more than delegate work to subordinate managers; he also delegates the task of coordinating the work and so insulates himself from coordination problems, those "ever-disunifying tendencies" of his organization.

The manager *should* think. And he should arrange time to think. But few really productive managers can afford the luxury of creative thinking during working hours. Such a time is not conducive to clear, unemotional thought processes. Rather, it is then that the manager, through active participation, can submerge himself in the details of the operation and provide food for creative thought during his leisure. Usually while playing golf, washing the supper dishes, or pursuing some other purely physical pastime, perspective clears and simple solutions to complex problems occur.

EXPANSION OF INDUSTRIAL POLITICS

Business that is all "strictly business" is not good business. To a degree, trivial interaction between a man, his boss, his subordinates, and his colleagues is essential to the smooth functioning of the organization. It is important that a man un-

2. Ernest Dale, "Executives Who Can't Manage," *The Atlantic Monthly* (July, 1962), p. 58.

derstand the people with whom he works, that he develop insight into their capabilities, their deficiencies, their psychological problems, and their fundamental motivations. The subtle personal adjustments necessary for a group of human beings to produce the day's output absolutely depend upon this insight. Prerequisite to this insight are trivial conversations ranging from a comparison of golf scores to boasts about one's children.

Unfortunately, it is difficult to determine where productive triviality with one's boss ends and favor currying begins. To understand one's boss and to be able to anticipate his reactions are bona fide goals. To ingratiate oneself beyond this requirement can cause considerable mischief throughout the organization. Make no mistake — where one man has sufficient time (and supervisors with narrow spans frequently have sufficient time) to cross the line from productive triviality to bootlicking, other men will be watching closely to determine the boss's reaction. If the individual receives favored job assignments, promotions, confidential communications, all beyond his apparent merit, the others will usually follow suit.

In order to be free to copy the favored associate, they must separate themselves from their own operations. The simplest way to do this is to appoint one or two assistant managers who can direct operations in the manager's absence. Such action is usually justified as being necessary in order to train a replacement, a sacred management principle which few will argue with.

And so the process continues, adding more unproductive activity and more organization costs.

BALANCED MARGINAL UTILITY

One of the basic principles of business is that over-all utility (that is, value as measured by the criterion of organizational objectives) is greatest when the marginal utilities of each separate expenditure are equal. In other words, when the last dollar budgeted for marketing provides the same contribution to the organization as the last dollar budgeted for research, production, and so on, the company receives the maximum total contribution from all of its parts. If a disparity exists, then dollars should be shifted between functions until balance is achieved. Each dollar shifted raises the total contribution. Despite the logic of the principle, it is often overlooked, possibly because no one other than the president is sufficiently disinterested to be interested in over-all balance.

The principle can be applied to two dimensions of an organization structure. The horizontal dimension has been indicated above — the determination of how resources should be balanced among the various functional parts of the organization (how much to marketing, how much to production, and so on). Application to the vertical dimension implies a balance between the "coordinating-directing" elements and the "doing" elements — that is, how much for supervision and how much for nonsupervisory workers.

Obviously, since we are concerned with total effectiveness versus total cost, the two dimensions must be considered together. If greater total effectiveness is produced by a transfer of budget funds from a supervisory team to the nonsupervisors in the group, to the nonsupervisors in another group, to another supervisory team, or even to capital or expense purchases, then the transfer is warranted.

Such a transfer means, theoretically at least, that the reduced supervisory team will be somewhat less effective than formerly. To many managers, such a possibility raises a red flag. Visions of idle nonsupervisory personnel and gross unproductiveness of effort can cause considerable anxiety, but the anxiety is usually unwarranted. Competent supervisors will quickly adapt their methods to the increased work load, and the effectiveness lost will be small if the transfer of expenditures is intelligently made.

Several articles have appeared recently on the subject of methods for determining optimum spans of control.[3] My objective has been to show that certain firmly held concepts and several organizational forces frequently cause managements to structure organizations with unjustifiably short spans of control. Analysis of the concepts reveals them to be misconceptions; identification of the forces can lead to appropriate control measures.

Much can be gained by broadening average spans within an organization. These gains include reduced cost, improved supervisory training and executive selection, better over-all coordination, more effective communication, and a higher average quality of supervision through greater utilization of the most competent supervisors available. These gains are available for the asking. No capital equipment need be purchased; no new technology need be learned; no additions to the labor force are required. Clear-headed thinking and hard-headed decisions are the sole requirements.

3. See particularly Harold Stieglitz, "Optimizing Span of Control," *Conference Board Management Record* (September, 1962), pp. 25–29, and C. W. Barkdull, "Span of Control—A Method of Evaluation." *Michigan Business Review*, XV (May, 1963), 25–32.

SPAN-OF-CONTROL MATHEMATICS

For those who may be interested in the mathematics of span-of-control cost reductions, the more important derivations are presented below. Throughout these derivations the following symbols are used:

s = the number of true supervisors in the organization (group leaders, task force managers, and the like are not included)

n = number of nonsupervisors in the organization who require significant planning and control efforts on the part of their supervisor (secretaries and "assistant-to" positions are normally excluded from this group)

a = average annual salary plus fringe benefits, cost of office space, and so on for all supervisors in the organization

m = average span of control throughout the organization (though we deal with an average for the sake of mathematical convenience, this is not meant to imply that all spans should equal the average)

Δm = increment of increase in the average span of control; for example, if average span is increased from six to ten, then $\Delta m = 4$

c = annual cost saving to the organization (a negative value for c indicates a cost increase)

First, the average span of control for the organization can be defined. Since all supervisors as well as nonsupervisors must be supervised—excluding, of course, the top supervisor—the average span is not simply the ratio of nonsupervisors to supervisors. Rather, it turns out to be:

$$(1) \qquad m = \frac{s + n - 1}{s}.$$

The validity of this basic formula can be seen if we think of an organization of, say, thirteen people in which three supervisors report to the manager and three nonsupervisors report to each supervisor; $s = 4$ and $n = 9$ so, by the formula, as by intuition, m = 3.

Increasing m in (1) by the increment, Δm, decreasing s by Δs, and maintaining the original value for n, gives:

$$(2) \qquad m + \Delta m = \frac{(s - \Delta s) + n - 1}{s - \Delta s}.$$

Substituting (1) for m and solving for Δs gives:

$$(3) \qquad \Delta s = \frac{\Delta m \times s^2}{(\Delta m \times s) + n - 1}$$

where Δs represents the reduction in supervisory requirement due to the increase in average span of control. To determine the annual saving due to this reduction, we need simply multiply both sides by the average annual cost per supervisor, a, to obtain:

$$(4) \qquad a \, \Delta s = c = \frac{\Delta m \times a \times s^2}{(\Delta m \times s) + n - 1}.$$

On the other hand, to determine the number of nonsupervisors who can be added without additional supervisors, assuming a given increase in span, an increment is added to n in (1):

$$(5) \qquad m + \Delta m = \frac{s + (n + \Delta n) - 1}{s}.$$

Again substituting (1) for m and solving for Δn gives:

$$(6) \qquad \Delta n = s \, \Delta m.$$

To calculate the saving from organizational expansion with fixed supervisory force, increments are added to both s and n in (1), maintaining m at its original level:

$$(7) \qquad m = \frac{(s + \Delta s) + (n + \Delta n) - 1}{(s + \Delta s)}$$

and Δs—that is, the number of supervisors who would normally have been added but were not because of the fixed supervisory requirement—is determined by:

$$(8) \qquad \Delta s = \frac{s \, \Delta n}{n - 1}.$$

Substituting (6) for Δn and multiplying both sides by a gives:

$$(9) \qquad a \, \Delta s = c_1 = \frac{\Delta m \times a \times s^2}{n - 1}.$$

To determine the increase in average span required to meet a predetermined annual cost saving, cross multiplying equation (4) and solving for Δm gives:

$$(10) \qquad \Delta m = \frac{c(1 - n)}{s(c - as)}.$$

SECTION **V**
MOTIVATING

The articles in this section first provide the reader with an overview and then cover in more detail those areas considered crucial to the function of motivating—leadership, communication, human relations, and training.

The overview is provided by Likert (#21), who summarizes the important research findings concerning motivation. Bavelas (#22) comments on the pros and cons of the trait approach to leadership and on the idea of leadership as an organizational function. Chase (#23) investigates semantic roadblocks to effective communication. McNair (#24) sounds a note of warning against overemphasis on human relations at the cost of administrative leadership, and Wikstrom (#25) describes and evaluates sensitivity training, one of the many training methods used to develop managerial competence.

21 — Motivation: The Core of Management

RENSIS LIKERT

It is widely recognized that there are large differences in the productive efficiency of different companies. Even within a company there are usually substantial differences in productivity among the different plants or departments. These differences in productivity are often due to differences in managerial policy and practice.

There is too little information on what a good management does that makes the difference between high and low productivity, between high and low employee morale. American business is spending millions of dollars every year applying the scientific method to product development and the improvement of production methods, but it is not similarly applying its resources to discover how the most effective managers and supervisors function and how their principles and practices can be applied more generally.

The Institute for Social Research of the University of Michigan is one of the few organizations conducting systematic research on this problem.[1] It is trying to find what makes an organization tick; trying to discover the principles of organizational structure and the principles and

practices of leadership that are responsible for high productivity and high job satisfaction.

The Institute program is designed to provide a mirror for business so that it can see in its own operations and experience what works best and why. Studies have been conducted or are under way in a wide variety of organizations. These include public utilities, an insurance company, an automotive company, a heavy machinery factory, a railroad, an electric appliance factory, and some government agencies. The work of the organizations studied has varied from highly routine clerical and assembly operations to complex scientific research.

One of the basic concepts underlying this research is that no matter how varied the task—whether in government, industry, or any part of the military organization—there are common fundamental principles applicable to the effective organization of human activity. In addition to these general principles, there may be specific principles that apply to particular types of work—such as selling, as opposed to office management. But the philosophy behind this whole

"Motivation: The Core of Management," *Personnel Series*, No. 155 (New York: American Management Association, 1953), pp. 3–21. Reprinted by permission of the author and the publisher. **Rensis Likert:** Departments of Psychology and Sociology and Director of the Institute for Social Research, University of Michigan.

1. This program was started by a contract with the Office of Naval Research. Since its initiation, business organization and governmental agencies, as well as ONR, have contributed to its support.

program of research is that scientifically valid data can be obtained which will enable us to state general principles. Once we know the general principles, we must learn how to transfer them from one situation to another. We are doing this research at all levels of organization—not only at the employee level and the small-unit level but at the plant level and the company level. We expect that some principles will carry right on through; others will be specific, perhaps, for the different levels or parts of an organization.

In carrying forward this program of research, two major criteria have been used to evaluate administrative effectiveness:

1. Productivity per man-hour or some similar measure of the organization's success in achieving its productivity goals.

2. The job satisfaction and other satisfactions derived by employees or members of the group.

The results being obtained show that a consistent pattern of motivational principles and their application is associated with high productivity and high job satisfaction, irrespective of the particular company or industry in which the study is conducted. I shall present some of these results and briefly summarize some of the generalizations that are emerging from this research.

FACTORS IN HIGH AND LOW PRODUCTIVITY

There are some factors which are commonly assumed to increase productivity but which, when actual results are examined, are found not to be related to productivity or else to have a negligible relationship. Thus we are finding very little relationship, *within a company*, between employees'

attitudes toward the company and their productivity. The more productive employees or sections do not have appreciably more favorable attitudes than do the less productive employees. Chart 1 illustrates the pattern of relationship that we are finding. The common assumption that developing a favorable attitude among employees toward the company will result in increased productivity does not seem to be warranted.

A favorable over-all attitude toward one's company and job does result in less absence from the job. I suspect also that it may result in less turnover and may attract a better labor force in a tight labor market, but we do not yet have any data on these points.

Illustrative, again, of the kind of variables that show no relationship to productivity or even a negative relationship is the material in Chart 2. We are finding, in some situations at least, that there is a negative relationship between the extent to which employees participate in a recreational program and their productivity. The less productive sections participate in recreational activities more often than do those sections that are more productive.

THE SUPERVISOR: EMPLOYEE-CENTERED OR PRODUCTION-CENTERED

In contrast to these patterns involving factors of a nonpersonal nature, we are consistently finding that there is a marked relationship between the kind of supervision an employee receives and both his productivity and the satisfactions which he derives from his work. When the worker (or a person at any level in a hierarchy) feels that his

CHART 1   RELATION OF ATTITUDE TOWARD COMPANY AND PRODUCTIVITY

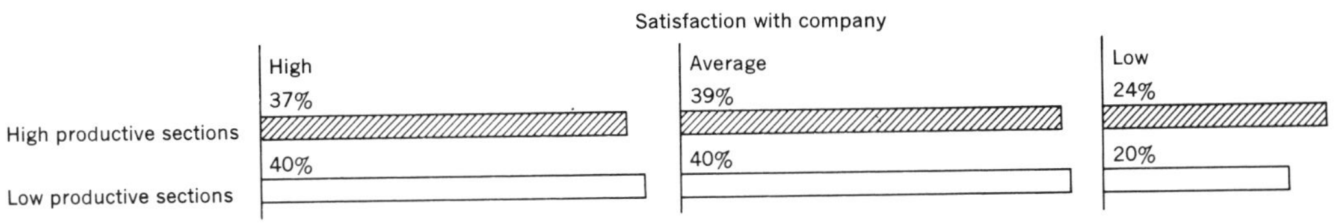

CHART 2   PARTICIPATION IN COMPANY RECREATIONAL ACTIVITIES

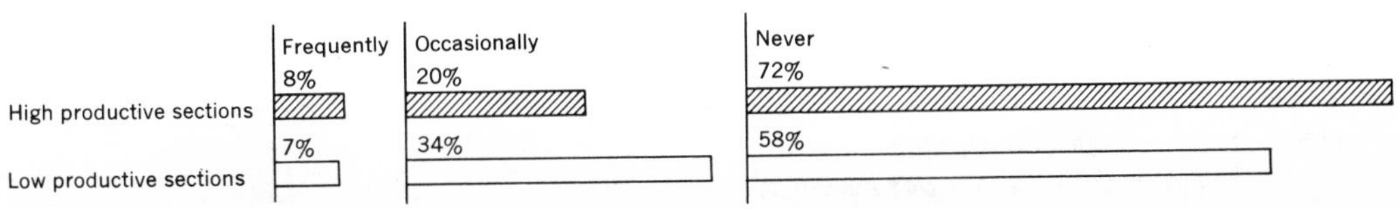

CHART 3 "EMPLOYEE-CENTERED" SUPERVISORS ARE HIGHER PRODUCERS THAN "PRODUCTION-CENTERED" SUPERVISORS

Number of first-line supervisors

	Production-centered	Employee-centered
High sections	1	6
Low sections	7	3
High divisions	3	7
Low divisions	7	4

boss sees him only as an instrument of production, as merely a cog in a machine, he is likely to be a poor producer. However, when he feels that his boss is genuinely interested in him, his problems, his future, and his well-being, he is more likely to be a high producer. Some typical results are shown in Chart 3.

The employee-centered supervisor not only trains people to do their present job well but tends to train them for the next higher job. He is interested in helping them with their problems on the job and off the job.

The following illustrations represent typical viewpoints of supervisors whom we have classified as employee-centered or production-centered:

Employee-centered supervisors are those who describe their work as did this one:

"I've tried to help my girls in getting better jobs and to get advanced, but there're so few positions for them to go to. That's why I teach them how to supervise. A lot of my girls are assistant section heads today."

In spite of the fact that this supervisor has promoted many of her ablest girls to better positions, she still has a high-production section. By giving her girls supervisory experience or letting one of them supervise two or three others in small groups, she builds effective teamwork and a friendly, cooperative atmosphere.

Another supervisor, also employee-centered, commented as follows:

"I study the girls' work, find out who works together and put them together. The main thing is to keep the girls happy. I talk with them and learn what their peculiarities are so that if a girl gets excited, I know whether it is important or not. Your girls have to feel that you are one of them, not the boss. Some girls get sort of cranky, and you can't just say, 'Do it.' It is much better to ask them to do the work in other ways; that's only human nature."

Another employee-centered section head commented as follows:

"I try to understand each girl. I remember I was one once and that I liked to be the kind that was known by
my supervisor. Knowing the girls helps with handling the work here. You also have to know what happens outside to help them inside here at their work."

In contrast, this comment is illustrative of the attitude of a production-centered supervisor in charge of a low-production section:

"I know we're doing what is supposed to be done in our section. Hit the work in and out—and hit it right—not slipshod."

Another production-oriented, low-producing section head commented as follows:

"It is my job to get the employee to stay on the job and produce. I have to work up efficiency charts. My efficiency chart is my argument if I have to make any complaint. My biggest headache is to get the employees to do their best."

Still another production-centered supervisor commented as follows:

"The girls sometimes stop work before the bell rings; I have been after them and I keep them overtime to do the work. You have to do something drastic and make examples of them."

PRODUCTIVITY AND CLOSENESS OF SUPERVISION

Related to pressing for production is the *closeness* of supervision that a person experiences. Close supervision tends to be associated with lower productivity and more general supervision with higher productivity. This relationship is shown in Chart 4.

Low productivity may at times lead to closer supervision, but it is clear that it may also cause low productivity. In one of the companies involved in this research program it has been found that switching managers of high- and low-production divisions results in the high-production managers raising the productivity of the low-production divisions faster than the former high-production divisions slip under the low-production managers. Supervisors, as they are shifted from

CHART 4 LOW-PRODUCTION SECTION HEADS ARE MORE CLOSELY SUPERVISED THAN ARE HIGH-PRODUCTION HEADS

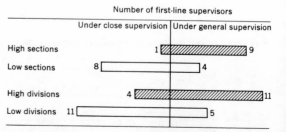

Number of first-line supervisors

	Under close supervision	Under general supervision
High sections	1	9
Low sections	8	4
High divisions	4	11
Low divisions	11	5

CHART 5 SUPERVISORY COMMUNICATIONS AND PRODUCTIVITY

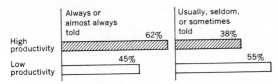

job to job, tend to carry with them and to maintain their habitual attitudes toward the supervisory process and toward their subordinates. This suggests that supervisory attitudes and habits tend to be the causal influence. For example, an assistant manager of a low-production department, in discussing his situation, said, "This interest-in-people approach is all right, but it is a luxury. I've got to keep pressure on for production, and when I get production up then I can afford to take time to show an interest in my employees and their problems." Being under pressure for increased production, and being primarily concerned with it, seem to cause supervisors to neglect important human dimensions of the supervisory process which in the long run determine the production of their groups.

Heads of low-producing sections seem to recognize that close supervision adversely affects their work. They show more dissatisfaction with the way their job is organized than do high-producing section heads and give as the reason for this dissatisfaction "too little delegation of authority."

In studying the results one gets the impression that persons who use general supervision tend more often to specify the goal or tasks to be accomplished and give subordinates some leeway in how it is accomplished. Persons using close supervision, however, are more likely to specify the precise activities of subordinates. Those using general supervision may, of course, make available to subordinates the resources of work simplification, etc., but do not specify in every detail precisely how they will be used.

When people are given general supervision, it is necessary to keep them well-informed. As shown in Chart 5, supervisors in charge of high-production groups report more often that they are kept informed about developments than do supervisors in charge of low-production groups.

We are finding conflicting patterns of relationship between morale and productivity. In some situations there is high morale and high productivity; in others we find high morale and low productivity or the converse. There are good reasons for these variations, and they are related to the kind of supervision that exists. But the significant finding for this discussion is that the kind of supervision which results in the highest productivity also results in the highest morale. Thus, for example, employee-centered supervision produces high levels of job satisfaction as well as high productivity.

Chart 6 illustrates the kind of findings being obtained. Where work groups with the highest and lowest morale were asked to describe what their supervisors did, the results were as shown in Chart 6. The workers in low-morale groups mentioned just as often as workers in high-morale groups that their supervisors performed such

CHART 6 PERCENTAGES OF HIGH AND LOW MORALE GROUPS DESCRIBING WHAT THEIR SUPERVISORS DO

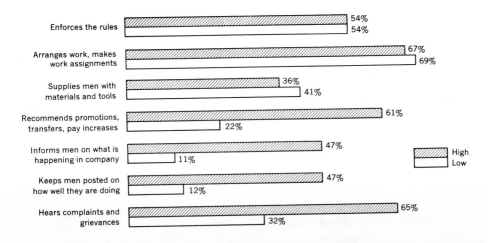

CHART 7 RELATIONS OF EMPLOYEE MORALE TO FEELING THAT COMPANY IS INTERESTED IN EMPLOYEES' IDEAS AND SUGGESTIONS

Percentage who feel that discussions with supervisor help

Level of morale	White collar	Blue collar
High	93%	87%
Medium	72%	57%
Low	42%	24%

production-centered tasks as "enforces the rules," "arranges work and makes work assignments," and "supplies men with materials and tools." But the high-morale groups mentioned much more frequently than the low such employee-centered functions as "recommends promotions and pay increases," "informs men on what is happening in the company," "keeps men posted on how well they are doing," and "hears complaints and grievances."[2]

IMPORTANCE OF
THE GROUP RELATIONSHIP

Books on management and administration tend to deal with the relationship between superior and subordinates, between supervisors and employees, as *individuals*. Research on management similarly has tended to focus on the relationship between the superior and the subordinates as individuals. We are encountering increasing evidence, however, that the superior's skill in supervising his subordinates *as a group* is an important variable affecting his success: the greater his skill in using group methods of supervision, the greater are the productivity and job satisfaction of the work group.

Chart 7 shows the relationship between the feeling that the "company is interested in employees' ideas and suggestions" and the level of employee morale. For both blue-collar and white-collar workers, there is a marked relationship between worker morale and how much employees feel that their boss is interested in discussing work problems with the work group.

Another important and striking relationship is shown in Chart 8. Foremen of high-production work groups report much more frequently than the foremen of low-production groups that their

work groups perform well when they, the foremen, are absent. High-production supervisors, through group methods of supervision, apparently develop within the work group the expectation and capacity to function effectively whether the foreman is present or not. This ability to function well in the absence of the supervisor is, no doubt, one of the reasons for the greater productivity of the high-production groups.

Chart 9 shows the relationship between group pride (or loyalty) and group productivity. The high-production groups show greater group loyalty and greater group pride than do the low production groups. We are finding that this relationship holds for many kinds of groups and many kinds of work. In Chart 9, for example, "Situation I" deals with clerical workers and "Situation II" deals with maintenance-of-way crews on a railroad.

In the study of the clerical operations, the workers and supervisors who displayed pride in their work group would make such comments as: "We have a good group," "We work together well," or "We help out each other." One supervisor said about her group:

"They all have definite assignments, and they're a nice cooperative crowd. They just jump in and do things and never bother me. They have a responsibility toward the group."

HOW GROUP PRIDE
AND GROUP LOYALTY OPERATE

There appear to be several reasons why work groups with high group pride and loyalty are the more productive. One reason is that the workers cooperate more and help one another in getting the work done. Work groups with high group loyalty show more teamwork and more willingness to help each other than do those with low group loyalty. In the high-loyalty groups there tends to be a flow of work back and forth between the workers depending upon the load. In groups with low group loyalty there tends to be more of a feeling that each worker is on his own and that how he gets along with his work is his own responsibility.

The effect upon productivity of workers helping one another is shown in Chart 10. When foremen were asked, "How does your section

2. In this discussion the term "morale" is used as meaning the total satisfactions the individual derives from his work situation. It is not being used as synonymous with the degree to which the individual is motivated to do his work.

CHART 8   HIGH-PRODUCTIVITY WORK GROUPS PERFORM WELL WHEN FOREMAN IS ABSENT

Sectional productivity	Men fool around, wander off job	Talk and joke but stay on job	Get stalled—no one to handle trouble	Men work as usual

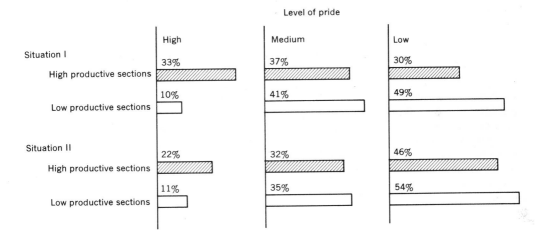

CHART 9   RELATION OF PRIDE IN WORK GROUP TO PRODUCTIVITY

Level of pride

	High	Medium	Low
Situation I			
High productive sections	33%	37%	30%
Low productive sections	10%	41%	49%
Situation II			
High productive sections	22%	32%	46%
Low productive sections	11%	35%	54%

CHART 10   GROUP SOLIDARITY AND PRODUCTIVITY

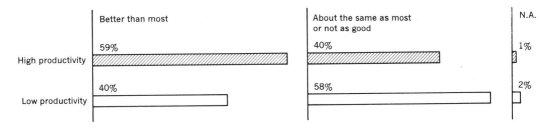

	Better than most	About the same as most or not as good	N.A.
High productivity	59%	40%	1%
Low productivity	40%	58%	2%

compare with other sections in the way the men help each other on the job?" the answers showed a marked relationship to group productivity. The foremen of high-production groups reported much more often than the foremen of low-production groups that their men helped one another in getting the work done.

The workers in the high-production work groups not only have greater group loyalty and help one another more but give this help on their own initiative. Workers in groups with low group loyalty at times help one another, but then it is more often upon the request of the foreman. The willingness to help one another displayed by the groups with high group loyalty seems to come

from a better team spirit and better interpersonal relationships that the foreman has developed in the group. This atmosphere seems to come from group methods of supervision and assigning work tasks as a whole to the group. Low group loyalty seems to occur where the foreman deals with workers individually and makes individual work assignments. One supervisor of a low productive clerical group described his pattern of supervision as follows:

"I apportion out the work to the people in my section and generally supervise the work handled. If a clerk is out, I have to make arrangements to have her work done. The work must go on even though there are

CHART 11 GROUP SOLIDARITY: WHITE-COLLAR MEN

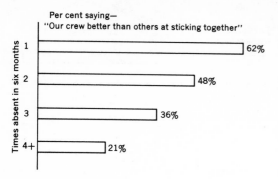

Per cent saying—
"Our crew better than others at sticking together"

Times absent in six months

1 — 62%
2 — 48%
3 — 36%
4+ — 21%

absences. This involves getting work redistributed to those who are there."

Another factor contributing to the higher productivity of groups with high group loyalty is their lower rate of absence from the job. As Chart 11 shows, persons in groups with high group loyalty are much less likely to be absent from work than persons in groups with lower group loyalty. This chart is based on data from white-collar workers. Similar results were obtained for blue-collar workers. Liking the work group clearly results, for all kinds of workers, in less absence from the job.

As might be expected, work groups with high group loyalty have more favorable attitudes toward production than do groups with low group loyalty. Thus we find that high-loyalty groups differ from groups of low group loyalty in having higher production goals. Their opinion as to what is reasonable production is higher and is more nearly the same as that of their foreman. Moreover, the high-loyalty groups have a more favorable attitude toward the high producer. This is shown in Chart 12.

We are finding that the high-loyalty groups

differ from the low in ways that form a consistent pattern. In addition to the differences already mentioned, the following characteristics have been found. The groups with greater group loyalty are more likely to

▶ Have greater identification with their group and a greater feeling of belonging to it.

▶ Have more friends in the group and in the company—rather than outside the company.

▶ Have better interpersonal relations among the members of the work group.

▶ Have a more favorable attitude toward their job and their company.

▶ Not only have higher production goals but produce more with less sense of strain or pressure.

There is evidence that whenever a supervisor (or manager) abdicates his leadership role and does not develop a good team spirit, other persons within the group will take over and develop some kind of group loyalty. Often the informal leadership which emerges establishes groups with goals counter to the goals of the over-all organization. Human nature is such that there seems to be no question as to whether or not groups will be formed. If constituted leadership lacks group skills and fails to establish group leadership, other leadership will emerge and take over.

DEVELOPING GROUP LOYALTY AND TEAM SPIRIT

Since high group loyalty and a good team spirit seem to result in greater production, greater job satisfaction, less absence, and, I suspect, less turnover, it is important to ask, "How can group loyalty be developed?" One factor which exercises an influence is shown in Chart 13. When a superior

CHART 12 THE RELATIONSHIP OF THE EMPLOYEE'S ATTITUDE TOWARD THE HIGHLY PRODUCTIVE WORKER AND SECTIONAL PRIDE IN WORK GROUP

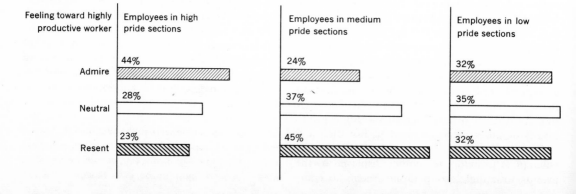

Feeling toward highly productive worker	Employees in high pride sections	Employees in medium pride sections	Employees in low pride sections
Admire	44%	24%	32%
Neutral	28%	37%	35%
Resent	23%	45%	32%

CHART 13 THE RELATIONSHIP OF THE SUPERVISOR'S ATTITUDE TOWARD HIS EMPLOYEES AND THE EMPLOYEES' DEGREE OF PRIDE IN WORK GROUP

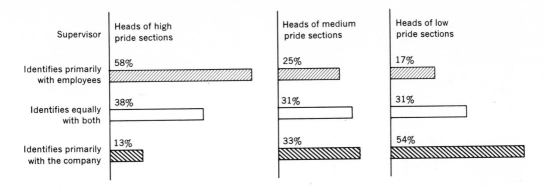

CHART 14 THE RELATIONSHIP OF THE SUPERVISOR'S ATTITUDE TOWARD HIS EMPLOYEES AND THE EMPLOYEES' DEGREE OF PRIDE IN WORK GROUP

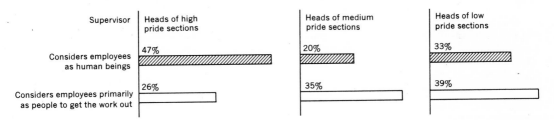

treats subordinates as human beings, it results in greater group loyalty and pride. Moreover, as Chart 14 shows, when supervisors stay sufficiently close psychologically to their workers to be able to see the problems of the workers through the eyes of the workers, the supervisors are better able to develop good group loyalty.

The good supervisor is able to identify with his employees and keep psychologically close to them. This seems to foster a good team spirit with open communicaton. It permits the supervisor to understand problems as employees see them and to interpret for top and middle management the employees' points of view. The supervisor who fails to identify with employees becomes psychologically far from them. This makes him incapable of seeing and dealing with problems as employees see them and hence unable to arrive at mutually satisfactory decisions. This supervisor is also unable to help middle and top management to see problems as employees see them and thereby to help management to arrive at policy decisions which will be mutually satisfactory.

Our research results indicate that it is important for supervisors to accept the goals of the over-all organization and to have a clear under-

standing of the role and function of their work group in achieving the over-all goals. When supervisors recognize and accept responsibility for performing the functions required of their work group and at the same time have the capacity to identify with their employees, effective results are obtained.

There are, of course, many other factors which are important in developing group loyalty and team spirit. Scattered research in industry and elsewhere indicates that commonly recognized methods of group leadership will yield good group loyalty when used. These methods and skills include those developed and taught by the National Training Laboratory in Group Development. Among the most important of these methods are those involving group participation in decisions affecting the group. There is evidence that group participation and involvement are beneficial at all levels in an organization. One of the best ways, for example, to have supervisors become aware of the job that needs to be done by their work group and to have them accept responsibility for it is to involve them in decisions where the functions and responsibilities of their work group are examined and reviewed.

CHART 15 THE EFFECT OF PARTICIPATION ON PRODUCTION

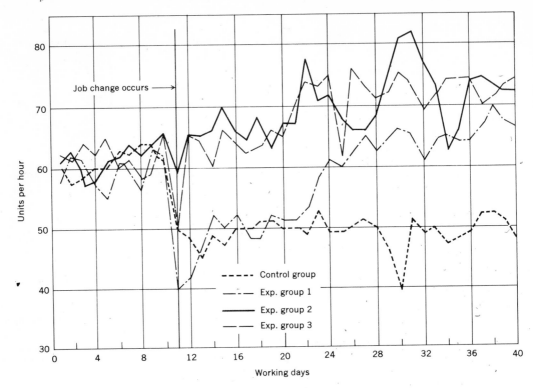

CONCLUSION: NATURE OF HUMAN MOTIVATION

Some general conclusions have been stated here as the different results were presented. Additional conclusions emerge, however, as the results are looked at in an over-all manner. Thus these results suggest an important conclusion as to the nature of human motivation. An examination of the results presented here and of results from other research shows that every human being earnestly seeks a secure, friendly, and supportive relationship and one that gives him a sense of personal worth in the face-to-face groups most important to him. The most important face-to-face groups are almost always his immediate family group and his work group. If his formal face-to-face work group is hostile, he develops new friendly informal groups. Human nature seems to motivate each of us to establish and maintain these friendly supportive relationships in those face-to-face groups in which we spend most of our lives. Either we successfully establish these friendly and supportive relationships or we crack up.

It is not surprising, therefore, that we see people generally striving for a sense of dignity and personal worth. We all seem to seek recognition and a sense of importance in terms of the values

and goals which we cherish and which our most important face-to-face groups also cherish.

To say that people seek friendly and supportive relationships does not mean that they seek to be coddled. Quite the contrary. People seek to achieve a sense of importance from doing difficult but important tasks which help to implement goals which they and their friends seek.

THE FINDINGS APPLIED

If there is anything of value in the results presented and the conclusions drawn, then when these findings are applied there should be an increase in productivity and in job satisfaction. We have been running several tests applying these results. These tests involve hundreds of employees in widely different kinds of industries. I shall report briefly the results obtained in one of these tests.

Chart 15 indicates the effect of participation upon productivity. This chart is based on the experiment by Coch and French[3] designed to employ three variations in participation procedure.

3. Lester Coch, and John R. P. French, Jr., "Overcoming Resistance to Change," *Human Relations*, vol. I, no. 4, 1948.

The first variation involved participation through representation of the workers in designing the changes to be made in the jobs. The second variation consisted of total participation by all members of the group in designing the changes. A third (control) group was also used. Two experimental groups received the total participation treatment. The (control) group went through the usual factory routine when they were changed. The production department modified the job, and a new piece rate was set. A group meeting was then held in which the control group was told that the change was necessary because of competitive conditions, and that a new piece rate had been set. The new piece rate was thoroughly explained by the time study man, questions were answered, and the meeting dismissed. Experimental group 1 was changed in a different manner. Before any changes took place, a group meeting was held with all the operators to be changed.

The need for the change was presented as dramatically as possible, showing two identical garments produced in the factory; one was produced in 1946 and had sold for 100 per cent more than its fellow in 1947. The group was asked to identify the cheaper one and could not do it. This demonstration effectively shared with the group the entire problem of the necessity of cost reduction. A general agreement was reached that a savings could be effected by removing the "frills" and "fancy" work from the garment without affecting the folders' opportunity to achieve a high efficiency rating. Management then presented a plan to set the new job and piece rate:

1. Make a check study of the job as it was being done.

2. Eliminate all unnecessary work.

3. Train several operators in the correct methods.

4. Set the piece rate by time studies on these specially trained operators.

5. Explain the new job and rate to all the operators.

6. Train all operators in the new method so they can reach a high rate of production within a short time.

The group approved this plan (though no formal group decision was reached) and chose the operators to be specially trained. A submeeting with the "special" operators was held immediately following the meeting with the entire group. They displayed a cooperative and interested attitude and immediately presented many good suggestions. This attitude carried over into the working out of the details of the new job; and when the new job and piece rates were set, the "special" operators referred to the resultants as "our job," "our rate," etc. The new job and piece rates were presented at a second group meeting to all the operators involved. The "special" operators served to train the other operators on the new job. Experimental groups 2 and 3 went through much the same kind of change meetings. The groups were smaller than experimental group 1, and a more intimate atmosphere was established. The need for a change was once again made dramatically clear; the same general

CHART 16 A COMPARISON OF THE EFFECT OF THE CONTROL PROCEDURE WITH THE TOTAL PARTICIPATION PROCEDURE ON THE SAME GROUP

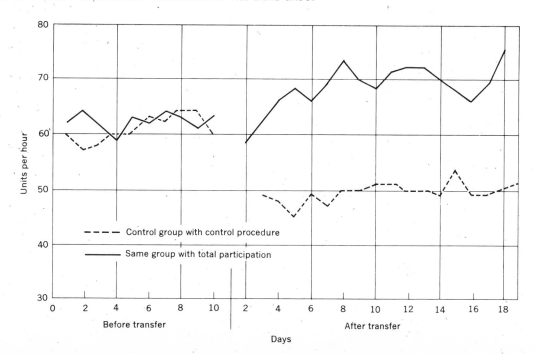

Group	Variability	
	Before Change	After Change
Experiment I:		
Control group	9.8	1.9
Experimental 1	9.7	3.8
Experimental 2	10.3	2.7
Experimental 3	9.9	2.4
Experiment II:		
Control group	12.7	2.9

plan was presented by management. However, since the groups were small, all operators were chosen as "special" operators; that is, all operators were to participate directly in the designing of the new jobs, and all operators would be studied by the time study man. It is interesting to note that in the meetings with these two groups, suggestions were immediately made in such quantity that the stenographer had great difficulty in recording them. The group approved of the plans, but again no formal group decision was reached.

The results shown in Chart 15 clearly demonstrate the effectiveness of participation upon production. It is significant that the control group, when treated like experimental groups 2 and 3 in another change that occurred some months later, showed a productivity record identical to that shown by experimental groups 2 and 3. Chart 16 shows these curves.

The following, also taken from Coch and French, presents evidence on the power of group standards:

Probably the most important force affecting the recovery under the control procedure was a group standard, set by the group, restricting the level of production to 50 units per hour. Evidently this explicit agreement to restrict production is related to the group's rejection of the change and of the new job as arbitrary and unreasonable. Perhaps they had faint hopes of demonstrating that standard production could not be attained and thereby obtain a more favorable piece rate. In any case there was a definite group phenomenon which affected all the members of the group. . . . An analysis was made for all groups of the individual differences within the group in levels of production. In Experiment I the 40 days before change were compared with the 30 days after change; in Experiment II the 10 days before change were compared to the 17 days after change. As a measure of variability, the standard deviation was calculated each day for each group. The average daily standard deviations before and after change are shown in the left-hand column. There is indeed a marked decrease in individual differences with the control group after their first transfer. In fact the restriction of production resulted in a lower variability than in any other group. Thus we may conclude that the group standard at 50 units per hour set up strong group-induced forces. . . . The table of variability also shows that the experimental treatments markedly reduced variability in the other four groups after transfer.

This experiment by Coch and French shows that the results from research can be applied in the shop and can yield substantial improvements in production. This experiment also yields improvement in attitudes toward the job.

Personnel departments have a very large and important task to perform in helping the line organization to apply the results of human relations research. This includes helping the line organization to appreciate that employee-centered supervision yields better production and better job satisfaction than production-centered supervision. Chart 17, which shows what the foremen in a very well-managed company say are the most important things they have to do, gives an indication of the magnitude of the job that personnel people face in helping the line organization to become employee-centered in its supervision. Over three-quarters of the foremen in that company state that pushing for production is the most important part of their job. The line organization, moreover, needs help in learning the skills required for using employee-centered supervision effectively. Research results pointing to effective ways to develop these skills are available, but that is a topic for other discussions.

CHART 17 WHAT FOREMEN SAY ARE THE MOST IMPORTANT THINGS THEY HAVE TO DO

Production	78%
Human relations	7%
Both	15%

22 — Leadership: Man and Function

ALEX BAVELAS

There is a useful distinction to be made between the idea of leadership as a personal quality and the idea of leadership as an organizational function. The first refers to a special combination of personal characteristics; the second refers to the distribution throughout an organization of decision-making powers. The first leads us to look at the qualities and abilities of individuals; the second leads us to look at the patterns of power and authority in organizations. Both of these ideas or definitions of leadership are useful, but it is important to know which one is being talked about, and to know under what conditions the two must be considered together in order to understand a specific organizational situation.

Early notions about leadership dealt with it almost entirely in terms of personal abilities. Leadership was explicitly associated with special powers. An outstanding leader was credited not only with extensions of the normal abilities possessed by most men but with extraordinary powers such as the ability to read men's minds, to tell the future, to compel obedience hypnotically. These powers were often thought of as gifts from a god, as conditional loans from a devil, or as the result of some accidental supernatural circumstance attending conception, birth, or early childhood. Today, claims of supernatural powers are made more rarely, but they are not entirely unknown. Of course, milder claims — tirelessness, infallibility of intuition, lightning quick powers of decision — are made in one form or another by many outstandingly successful men. And when they do not make them for themselves, such claims are made for them by others who, for their own reasons, prefer such explanations of success to other more homely ones.

Outright supernatural explanations of leadership have, in recent times, given way to more rational explanations. Leadership is still generally thought of in terms of personal abilities, but now the assumption is made that the abilities in question are the same as those possessed by all normal persons: individuals who become leaders are merely presumed to have them to a greater degree.

For many years, attempts to define these abilities and to measure them failed. This was not only because the early techniques of measurement were primitive and unreliable but for a more important reason. The traits that were defined as important for leadership were often nothing more than purely verbal expressions of what the researcher felt leaders *ought* to be like. Few of the many lists of traits that were developed had very much in common. Typical of the items that frequently appeared on such lists were piety, honesty, courage, perseverance, intelligence, reliability, imagination, industriousness. This way of thinking about leadership is still very common. It persists, not because it is helpful in analyzing and understanding the phenomenon of leadership, but because it expresses a deep and popular wish about what leaders *should* be like.

Modern trait research proceeds in a very different way. Leadership traits are no longer selected arbitrarily. They are, instead, largely derived from the results of tests that are carefully designed, administered, and interpreted. And the techniques of measurement and analysis which are applied to the data that are gathered have been extensively developed and refined. Numerous trait studies have been made of the physical, intellectual, and social characteristics of leaders. On various tests, persons who are leaders tend to be brighter, tend to be better adjusted psychologically, and tend to display better judgment. Studies that have concentrated on the social behavior of leaders show that they "interact" more than nonleaders. They tend to give more information, ask for more information, and to take the lead in summing up or interpreting a situation.

Despite these accomplishments, the trait approach has in recent years been subjected to increasing criticism. A common objection is that the results are obtained by a method that requires an initial separation of people into "leaders" and "nonleaders" or "good leaders" and "not-so-good leaders." The validity of the distinguishing traits that come out of such work, the argument goes, can only be as good as the validity of the preliminary grouping of the persons being studied. All of this leads to the question, "On what basis is the initial separation of subjects made, and how is it justified?"

At first glance, this may appear a trivial and carping question. In fact, however, it is one of the most serious obstacles in the way of all leadership research. It is obviously impossible to define "good leaders" without reference to a system of values. To say that a man is a "good leader" means that his behavior and its consequences are

"Leadership: Man and Function," *Administrative Science Quarterly*, IV (March, 1960), 491–498. Reprinted by permission of the author and the publisher. **Alex Bavelas:** Graduate School of Business and Department of Psychology, Stanford University.

held to be of greater worth than other behaviors and results.

What system of values shall the researcher adopt that is both scientifically acceptable and socially useful in distinguishing good or successful leaders from others? Many attempts have been made to find a suitable criterion, but the results have been generally unsatisfactory—not that it is difficult to find standards which are desirable and inspiring, but that such standards tend to be based, just as the early lists of traits were, on qualities that are difficult or impossible to measure. And often they just do not seem to "work." For example, there have been attempts to distinguish leaders from nonleaders in terms that rest essentially on moral and ethical considerations. It may be a significant commentary on our society that there appears to be no particular correlation between a man's ethics and morals and his power to attract followers.

It has been suggested that many of the philosophical difficulties that attend the definition of "good leader" can be avoided if one accepts the more limited task of defining "good executive." In business and industry, one would like to think, there should be practical, quantitative ways of making the distinction. Many attempts have been made in this direction. Reputation, financial success, hierarchical position, influence, and many other criteria have been tried without much satisfaction. The inadequacies of such standards are obvious to any experienced executive.

There is a second and more interesting objection that has been made to the trait approach. It is based not on the question of the accuracy or the validity of the assumptions that are made but upon the nature of the "traits" themselves. Traits are, after all, statements about personal characteristics. The objection to this is that the degree to which an individual exhibits leadership depends not only on *his characteristics*, but, also on the *characteristics of the situation* in which he finds himself. For example, a man who shows all the signs of leadership when he acts as the officer of a well-structured authoritarian organization may give no indication of leadership ability in a less-structured, democratic situation. A man may become influential in a situation requiring deliberation and planning but show little evidence of leadership if the situation demands immediate action with no opportunity for weighing alternatives or thinking things out. Or, to take still another instance, a man may function effectively and comfortably in a group whose climate is friendly and co-operative but retreat and become ineffective if he perceives the atmosphere as hostile.

The case for the situational approach to leadership derives its strength from this fact: while organizations in general may exhibit broad similarities of structure and function, they also, in particular, show strong elements of uniqueness.

It is a matter of common observation that within any normal industrial organization, providing there has been a sufficient past, there will be found patterns of relationships and interaction that are highly predictable and highly repetitive. Some of these reoccurring situations will be unique to that organization. It is this uniqueness that is referred to when one speaks of the "personality" of a company. This is what a management has in mind when it selects a new member with an eye to how he will "fit in." The argument of the researcher who stresses the situational aspects of leadership is that these unique characteristics of an organization are often crucial in determining which of two equally competent and gifted men will become a "leader," and further that in the very same organization these unique patterns may change significantly at different levels of the hierarchy. The very same "leadership abilities" that helped a man rise to the top may, once he is there, prove a positive detriment.

The status of trait and situational leadership research can be summed up in this way: (1) the broad similarities which hold for a greater number of organizations make it possible to say useful things about the kind of person who is likely to become a leader in any of those organizations, and (2) the unique characteristics of a particular organization make it necessary to analyze the situational factors that determine who is likely to become a leader *in one particular organization*. To put it another way, when specific situational patterns are different from organization to organization, one cannot say what personal traits will lead to acknowledged leadership. Instead, one must try to define the leadership functions that must be performed in those situations and regard as leadership those acts which perform them. This point of view suggests that almost any member of a group may become its leader under circumstances that enable him to perform the required functions of leadership and that different persons may contribute in different ways to the leadership of the group.

In these terms we come close to the notion of leadership, not as a personal quality, but as an *organizational function*. Under this concept it is not sensible to ask of an organization "who is the leader?" Rather we ask "how are the leadership functions distributed in this organization?" The distribution may be wide or narrow. It may be so narrow—so many of the leadership functions may be vested in a single person—that he is the leader in the popular sense. But in modern organizations this is becoming more and more rare.

What are these "leadership functions"? Many have been proposed: planning, giving information, evaluating, arbitrating, controlling, rewarding, punishing, and the like. All of these stem from the underlying idea that leadership acts are those which help the group achieve its objectives, or, as it is also put, to satisfy its "needs." In most face-to-face groups, the emergence of a leader can well be accounted for on this basis. That person who can assist or facilitate the group most in reaching a satisfactory state is most likely to be regarded as the leader. If one looks closely at what constitutes assistance or facilitation in this sense, it turns out to be the making of choices or the helping of the group to make choices—"better" choices, of course.

But can the function of leadership be reduced simply to decision making or the facilitation of decision making? The objection can be raised that such a definition is much too wide to be useful. Every action, even every physical movement one makes, is after all "chosen" out of a number of possible alternatives. If when I am at my workbench I pick up a screwdriver in preference to a hammer, I am clearly making a choice; am I, by virtue of that choice, displaying leadership? Something is obviously wrong with a definition of leadership which imputes it to any act that can be shown to have involved a choice. Common sense would argue that customary, habitual, and "unconscious" actions, although they may logically contain elements of choice, should be separated from actions that are subjectively viewed by the person taking them as requiring a decision. Common sense would also argue that questions of choice that can be settled on the basis of complete information should be considered differently from questions of choice in which decisions must be taken in the face of uncertainty. And common sense would argue that some distinction should be made between decisions that, although made on equally uncertain grounds, involve very different orders of risk.

This is, of course, the implicit view of the practicing manager, and although it may contain very knotty problems of logic it is the view that will be taken here. Stated in general terms, the position that will be taken is that organizational leadership consists of *uncertainty reduction*. The actual behavior through which this reduction is accomplished is the making of choices.

We saw above that not all choices are equally difficult or equally important. Some choices are considered unimportant or irrelevant and are ignored, and of course whole areas may be seen as so peripheral to the interests of the organization that they are not perceived as areas of choice at all. Other choices that *must* be made are so well understood that they become habitual and automatic. Some of these are grouped into more or less coherent bundles and given a job name. The employee learns to make them correctly as he becomes skilled in the job. In most job evaluation plans, additional credit is given if the job requires judgment. This is a way of saying that there are choices remaining in the job that cannot be completely taken care of by instructions but must be made by the employee as they come along.

There are other choices which, although they are equally clear and habitual, are of a more general nature and do not apply just to a specific job but apply to all. These are customarily embodied in rules and procedures. Rules and procedures are, in this sense, decisions made in advance of the events to which they are to be applied. Obviously, this is possible and practical only to the extent that the events to which the rules and procedures apply can be foreseen, and the practical limit of their completeness and specificity depends on how these future events can be predicted.

Following this line of analysis, it is theoretically possible to arrange all the logically inherent choices that must be made in operating an industrial organization along scales of increasing uncertainty and importance. At some level in this hierarchy of choices, it is customary for management to draw a line, reserving for itself from that point on the duty and the privilege of making the required decisions.

Precisely where a management draws this line defines its scope. The way in which a management distributes the responsibility for making the set of choices it has thus claimed to itself defines its structure. What organizational leadership *is* and what kinds of acts constitute it are questions that can be answered only within this framework of scope and structure. In these terms leadership consists of the continuous choice-making process that permits the organization as a whole to proceed toward its objectives despite all sorts of internal and external perturbations.

But as every practicing manager knows, problems occasionally arise that are not amenable to the available and customary methods of analysis and solution. Although uncertain about which choice to make, a management may nevertheless have to make a decision. It is in situations of this kind that many of the popular traits attributed to leaders find their justification: quickness of decision, the courage to take risks, coolness under stress, intuition, and, even, luck. There is no doubt that quick, effective, and daring decisions are a highly prized commodity in a crisis, but just as precious a commodity is the art of planning and organizing so that such crises do not occur. The trend of management has been to remove as many of its decisions as possible from the area of hunch and intuition to that of rational calculation. More and more, organizations are choosing to depend less on the peculiar abilities of rare individuals and to depend instead on the orderly processes of research and analysis. The occasions and opportunities for personal leadership in the old sense still exist, but they are becoming increasingly rare and circumscribed.

This new emphasis has not eliminated the role of personal leadership, but it has significantly redefined it. Under normal conditions of operation, leadership in the modern organization consists not so much in the making of decisions personally as it does of maintaining the operational effectiveness of the decision-making systems which comprise the management of the organization. The picture of the leader who keeps his own counsel and in the nick of time pulls the rabbit out of the hat is out of date. The popular stereotype now is the thoughtful executive discussing in committee the information supplied by a staff of experts. In fact it may be that the brilliant innovator, in the role of manager, is rapidly becoming as much an organizational embarrassment as he is an asset.

This trend, reasonable though it may appear on the surface, conceals two serious dangers. First, we may be systematically giving up the opportunity of utilizing the highest expressions of personal leadership in favor of managerial arrangements which, although safer and more reliable, can yield at best only a high level of mediocrity. And second, having committed ourselves to a system that thrives on the ordinary, we may, in the interests of maintaining and improving its efficiency, tend to shun the extraordinary.

It is no accident that daring and innovation wane as an organization grows large and successful. On different levels this appears to have been the history of men, of industries, of nations, and even of societies and cultures. Success leads to "obligations" — not the least of which is the obligation to hold what has been won. Therefore, the energies of a man or administration may be absorbed in simply maintaining vested interests. Similarly, great size requires "system," and system, once established, may easily become an end in itself.

This is a gloomy picture, because it is a picture of decay. It has been claimed, usually with appeals to biological analogies, that this is an inevitable cycle, but this view is, very probably, incorrect. Human organizations are not biological organisms; they are social inventions.

23 — Executive Communications: Breaking the Semantic Barrier

STUART CHASE

The modern executive lives in an increasingly complicated network of communication, with lines leading up, down, and sideways from his desk. He has to keep lines clear, not only to those below in the business hierarchy, but to whatever levels may be above. Some years ago, a New Jersey company called in a consultant to set up a so-called "vertical round table" — a discussion group designed to keep lines open between *seven* levels of management, from top drawer to assistant supervisor. (The experiment introduced them to each other for the first time, and worked out most helpfully.)

Important communication lines run outside the company, too, of course, to dealers, suppliers, consumers, government officials, and the general public — whose good will is so essential today.

Many excellent studies on the problems of communication have already been published. But there is a close relationship between communication and the lively young science of semantics, and executives interested in improving communication can take advantage of this new tool.

Semantics has been defined as "the systematic study of meaning." It deals mostly with words, but may include other methods of signaling, such as gestures, facial expressions, signs, and symbols.

"Executive Communications: Breaking the Semantic Barrier," *Management Review*, XLVI (April, 1957), 58 – 66. Reprinted by permission of the author and the American Management Association, New York. **Stuart Chase**: Social scientist, commentator, and author.

UNESCO has been working on a system of high-way symbols (curves, side roads, danger, etc.) which can be understood in any part of the world, irrespective of the language spoken.

Semantics goes far beyond dictionary defini-tions. It attempts to evaluate what a speaker really means, as contrasted with what he says. To call a man a "horse-thief," in literal dictionary terms, is to accuse him of a serious crime. But when Jones greets Robinson with "Hullo, you old horse-thief!" his intention may be nothing but affection.

The goal of semantics is a better understanding inside our heads of what goes on *outside* them, and consequently a better adjustment to our en-vironment. It can help us to clarify meanings in much the same way as a good pair of glasses can clarify a landscape to one suffering from astigma-tism.

From the outside world come signals and mes-sages in the form of light waves, sound waves, shock waves, pressures. They follow nerve cur-rents from eye, ear, fingertips, to the brain. What do they mean? If we interpret them incorrectly, we are in trouble. The sight of an oncoming car crossing into our lane can, in a sense, become a problem in semantics. So can the task of unscram-bling such terms as "fair price," "reasonable profit," and "security risk." Insurance men, I un-derstand, are having as much trouble defining "explosion" as the United Nations is having with "aggression."

The present author tried to bring the whole subject of semantics to a wider audience in 1938 with his book, *The Tyranny of Words*. Since then, there have been many books, monographs, lec-tures, and seminars devoted to semantics, and more than 100 colleges now give courses in the subject.[1]

Semantics takes its place beside a dozen other disciplines concerned with communication, rang-ing from the rigorous mathematical theory of Claude Shannon of the Bell Laboratories to stud-ies in how to listen. Automation is the child of cybernetics, and cybernetics, developed by Dr. Norbert Wiener of M.I.T., is a branch of commu-nication theory.

When I investigated the excellent communica-tion system at Pitney-Bowes, Inc.,[2] I was doing a little semantic research to determine how the rank and file got their suggestions, grievances, and stories up to top management and how man-agement got its stories down. There were at least five upward channels, and more than that down-ward.

One particularly interesting channel at Pit-ney-Bowes is the annual "Jobholders Meeting," which follows the stockholders meeting and takes

a similar form. (The semanticist is shy of the word "same," since no two events are ever *precisely* the same.) Workers hear the president, treasurer, and other officers give an account of what has hap-pened in the past fiscal year and predict the for-tunes of the company for the new year. Questions are in order from the floor, and plenty come. "I see here on the balance sheet that all our patents are only worth one dollar. That doesn't seem right," says a machinist. This one gives the treas-urer some minutes of acute mental activity!

ROADBLOCKS TO COMMUNICATION

Perhaps the major principle of semantics is to stop, look, and listen when a message comes in to be decoded by the brain and not let it trigger off an emotional response. If there is time, consider what this particular message means coming from this particular source.

Equally important is the proper sending of messages. Will your words correspond well enough to the past experience of the hearer so that he can understand what you say? To use the terminology of Claude Shannon, will he decode what you encode? Without common experience stored in the memories of both speaker and hearer, the communication line is dead. "For-eigners" are not ignorant, they've just had differ-ent experiences. "Workers" (or "bosses") are not necessarily stupid; they, too, have had different experiences. If an Indian from the Amazon has never seen or felt snow, it is useless to talk to him about skiing.

How does one identify roadblocks on the com-munication line? Out of more than a dozen which have been classified, here are the six most com-mon:

1. THE CONFUSION OF WORDS WITH THINGS

Words are so cardinal in human affairs that we tend to assume that behind every word must stand a physical thing to which the word refers.

1. Semantics was introduced into the language by Lady Viola Welby in a book called *What Is Meaning?* published in 1903. In 1921, Ogden and Richards brought out their devas-tating *Meaning of Meaning*, which, among other things, turned the great philosophers from Aristotle to Hegel upside down, and shook them vigorously for verbal content. Alfred Korzybski, a Polish-American mathematician, published *Science and Sanity* in 1933, introducing what he called "General Semantics"—a discipline which emphasized psy-chological aspects of meaning.

2. See "Communication Up, Down, and Sideways," *Reader's Digest*, September, 1952.

Take the term "unemployment." It sounds pretty specific, but to the student of semantics, it is exceedingly indefinite. He might make a list of various kinds of unemployment, using an index notation like this:

Unemployment₁ is where a man has lost his job and is looking hard for another one.

Unemployment₂ is where a man has lost his job but is not looking for another one. His wife can balance the budget.

Unemployment₃ is where a man needs a job, is looking for a job, but is physically incapable of doing a job (unemployable).

Unemployment₄ is where a man is laid off for a month while the model is changed to the biggest, longest, most beautiful number the world has ever seen!

Unemployment₅ is where a man is working part time and is looking for another part-time job to pay the grocer.

No wonder honest statisticians, trying to figure the exact number of "unemployed" on a given day, are driven to distraction!

The executive with a little semantic training never forgets that *words are not things.* "Unemployment" is a word in our heads, with no precise *referent* out there in the world of space and time. It can be applied to a whole spectrum of referents.

The Empire State Building, on the other hand, is more manageable. We can point to it, see the clouds form around the TV mast, go up and kick its solid cornerstone, and agree on a physical thing to which the term "Empire State Building" refers. When we discuss the "architectural beauty" of the building, however, agreement may vanish and a hassle develop. Why? Because "architectural beauty" is a term in our heads, for which everyone has a somewhat different meaning.

2. THE CARELESS USE OF ABSTRACT WORDS

This roadblock is close to the one above. An abstract term should not be used carelessly. Everyone interested in international affairs today is talking about "aggression." The British committed "aggression" in Egypt, the Russians committed "aggression" in Hungary, the Chinese committed "aggression" in Korea. A committee of the United Nations, however, after two years' intensive study, has been unable to define the term. The committee is in despair, but no semanticist is surprised. "Aggression" is an abstraction of a high order with severely limited usefulness. It has many meanings, on various levels. In international politics it has a "bad" meaning, but aggressive-

ness in business is quite different. We think well of an aggressive salesman, and we say a good executive should be alert and aggressive. But we don't like it when an executive displays "aggression" towards his associates.

Also up in the stratosphere are two formidable abstractions glowering at each other—"capital" and "labor." As all cartoonists know, one wears a plug hat, the other a kind of square cap popular with stone masons in the 1840's. These high abstractions can never come to terms; their combat is supposed to be eternal, and is formalized in the "class struggle" of Karl Marx. But the semanticist goes down the abstraction ladder to the real world. There he finds Company X in constant hot water with the unions, and Company Y not only living at peace with them, but using union shop discipline to produce better dividends. He also finds that "capital" is an increasingly muzzy term, now that the legal owners of most large corporations leave control to self-perpetuating managers who may own very little stock. This semantic exercise, incidentally, again demolishes the class struggle concept of Marx, which assumed a monolithic, unchanging "capitalism."

Abstract terms are necessary—indeed, we could not think without them—but we should be aware of their limitations, aware of the level they are on. When a politician sounds off about "liberty"—just liberty—the semanticist remembers the saying, "Your liberty to swing your arms ends where my nose begins." "Liberty" means little until we bring it down and ask: *liberty to do what?* Has a businessman, for example, unlimited "liberty" to cut prices, or to enter into agreements in restraint of trade?

3. THE CONFUSION OF FACTS WITH PERSONAL OPINIONS

We meet this roadblock on every mental highway. Children should be warned about it at the age of ten, but seldom are. In Madison, Wisconsin, reporters for the *Capital Times* took a sidewalk poll, asking some 300 citizens: "What is a Communist?" A farmer in from the country gave a typical reply: "They're no good in my opinion. I don't know what they are." Observe that he had no facts, could draw no inferences, but did not hesitate to jump to the opinion level and deliver a moral judgment!

The correct way to get at the truth of an event is precisely the reverse. First gather the relevant facts, then draw logical deductions from them. Finally, if the occasion warrants, deliver your personal *opinions.*

When two men from the Department of Justice

arrived one day at Pitney-Bowes, rumors might well have gone racing through the plant: "They're going to close us up!" Management, anticipating such rumors, immediately posted this notice on every bulletin board:

All employees should assist the bureau's representatives in every way . . . such investigations by the Department of Justice have become almost routine throughout American industry. They represent a necessary policing of our economic system.

Thus management substituted a true meaning for a wild one. Rumors, which may be as dangerous to a business firm as fire and go even faster, are often dizzy leaps to the opinion level. They can usually be extinguished by a flood of plain facts. The alert executive will get his facts on the notice board *before* the event, if he knows it is coming.

4. JUDGING PEOPLE AND EVENTS IN TERMS OF BLACK OR WHITE

Sometimes this roadblock is called "either-or thinking," sometimes "two-valued thinking." Many situations are indeed black or white, without shades of gray. A man is alive or he is dead, for example. But the vast majority of our big social, political, and economic problems are many-sided, not just two-sided.

The either-or thinker says, "Those who are not with us are against us," and consigns India to the Communist camp. The semanticist recoils at such a conclusion. It is bad enough, he thinks, to cope with Russia and Red China without taking on the half-billion inhabitants of the "neutral" nations.

If an employer takes the position that *unions are bad,* period, he is inviting unnecessary trouble in the world of today. If, however, he takes the position that *some unions are badly led,* or *some union members are bad actors,* he will find life easier, for he is coming closer to the actual situation.

The bell-shaped frequency distribution curve is a useful offset to rigid two-valued thinking. If all the men in a given society are measured for height, and the figures charted, the curve will show a few seven-footers at one end, a few five-footers at the other end, and most of us in the middle. The case is similar for union members (or for employers) — the saints at one end, the so-and-so's at the other, and most of us in the middle. The curve represents the semantic multi-valued view, as against the two-valued view.

5. FALSE IDENTITY BASED ON WORDS

This roadblock was the cause of great confusion in the days of Senator McCarthy. Any-

one who disagreed with him risked being labeled a Communist, on the syllogism:

Communists are against McCarthy.
Spifkins is against McCarthy.
Therefore, Spifkins is a Communist.

"Things equal to the same thing are equal to each other" may be true of the *words* in a syllogism, but not necessarily of the actual situation. False identity can also be established by the old saying, "The enemy of my enemy is my friend." Similar reasoning would put the U.S. in the predicament of being Russia's friend when both censured the British for the invasion of Egypt.

Guilt by verbal association can also be shown in the classic case of the late Senator Taft. When he introduced his bill for public housing in 1947, he was attacked by certain real estate interests whose arguments boiled down to this syllogism:

Communists favor public housing.
Senator Taft has sponsored a bill for public housing.
Therefore, Senator Taft is following the Moscow line.

Following the same type of reasoning, a student of semantics could prepare another syllogism:

Communists favor apple pie.
Senator Taft favors apple pie.
Therefore . . . etc.

The trick is to find one characteristic, just one, shared by your victim and a common enemy, and then leap to the conclusion that *all* their characteristics are identical. Since all of us have literally thousands of characteristics — sex, weight, height, eye color, race, religion, occupation, aptitudes, attitudes, beliefs — it is child's play to find one shared by any two persons, or by a person and an organization. With this common bond established, guilt (or innocence) can be "proved," at least well enough to make the headlines. Indeed, with this monstrous logic it is possible to prove anybody guilty of anything.

6. GOBBLEDEGOOK

The last semantic roadblock we shall investigate is the clouding of meaning by fancy words. On the campus it is known as "pedageese" — the pedageese of the pedagogues, a variety of protective coloration. The term "gobbledegook" was invented by the late Maury Maverick, Congressman from Texas, to describe the language of paperwork in big government offices. Any big office is likely to come down with a severe attack.

A member of Parliament, A. P. Herbert, exasperated with bureaucratic jargon, once translated Nelson's immortal phrase, "England expects every man to do his duty," into standard big-office prose:

England anticipates that, as regards the current emergency, personnel will face up to the issues and exercise appropriately the functions allocated to their respective occupational groups.

An American office manager sent this memo to his chief:

Verbal contact with Mr. Blank regarding the attached notification of promotion has elicited the attached representation intimating that he prefers to decline the assignment.

Translation: Mr. Blank doesn't want the job.

On reaching the top of the Finsteraarhorn in 1845, M. Dolfuss-Ausset, when he got his breath, exclaimed: "The soul communes with the infinite in those icy peaks which seem to have their roots in the bowels of eternity."

Translation: He likes the view.

A Washington department announced:

Voucherable expenditures necessary to provide adequate dental treatment required as adjunct to medical treatment being rendered a pay patient on in-patient status may be incurred as required at the expense of the Public Health Service.

Translation: You can charge your dentist bill to the Public Health Service. Or can you?

To be fair to Washington, I should point out that the Federal Security Agency in 1950 made an intensive study of interoffice gobbledegook and issued an excellent report thereon, a report which every executive in business as well as government might well have on his desk.[3] It is not only instructive, but funny. For example:

The problem of extending coverage to all employees, regardless of size, is not as simple as surface appearances indicate. . . .
Though the proportions of all males and females in ages 16 – 45 are essentially the same . . .
Dairy cattle, usually and commonly embraced in dairying . . .

These solemn statements, and many others found in the paperwork, enlivened the investigation.

SEMANTICS FOR THE EXECUTIVE

Semantics is no "monopoly" of heavy thinkers. It is for anyone to use who needs to keep his communication lines clear—and what businessman does not? It is common sense combined with a systematic study of how words behave at various levels and how meanings can be better sent and received.

Beardsley Ruml has observed: "Reasonable men always agree if they understand what they are talking about." "Always" may be a little strong, but we can safely settle for 95 per cent.

24 – Thinking Ahead: What Price Human Relations?

MALCOLM P. McNAIR

In 1956 the Inland Steel Company appointed a vice president of human relations. The Inland Steel Company, of course, is big business; but little business is not being neglected, for I note that the McGraw-Hill Book Company, Inc., is publishing a book on *Human Relations in Small Industry.* The Harvard Business School has had a chair of Human Relations since 1950; by now the number of courses in Human Relations in schools and colleges throughout the country has multi-

3. Hall and Grady, *Getting Your Ideas Across Through Writing*, Training Manual No. 7, 44 pages.

"Thinking Ahead: What Price Human Relations?" *Harvard Business Review*, XXXV (March – April 1957), 15 – 23. Reprinted by permission of the author and the publisher. **Malcolm P. McNair**: Graduate School of Business Administration, Harvard University.

plied substantially. Even more marked is the rapid growth of executive development programs, some in schools, some in industry, but almost all of them placing emphasis on human relations.

Doctoral theses increasingly carry such titles as "A Case Study of the Human Aspects of Introducing a New Product into Production," "An Intensive Study of Supervisory Training in Human Relations and Foreman Behavior at Work," "A Case Study of the Administration of Change in the Large Modern Office," and "Emergence of Leadership in Manufacturing Work Groups." And recently the *Harvard Business Review* has reprinted a dozen articles on human relations, under the title "How Successful Executives Handle People, 12 Studies on Communications and Management Skills," which include such intriguing subjects as "Making Human Relations Work," "Barriers and Gateways to Communication," and "The Fateful Process of Mr. A Talking to Mr. B."

It is obvious that human relations is very much the fashion in business thinking today. And fashions in business thinking are not a novelty; there have been many others. I can well recall that when I first joined the Harvard Business School faculty, the reigning vogue in business thinking was scientific management. Only a few years later, however, the grandiose claims of scientific management were sharply debunked. What was of solid worth remained—but a considerable amount of froth had been blown off the top.

Must we go through the same process—with all its waste and possible damage along the way—to get to what is worthwhile in human relations?

My quarrel is not with the solid substance of much that is comprehended by the phrase "human relations," but rather with the "cult" or "fad" aspects of human relations, which are assuming so much prominence.

There can be no doubt that people are of absorbing interest to other people. To verify this fact you have only to look at what makes headlines in the newspapers. There is a fascination for most of us in speculating about people and their behavior. So it is not surprising that human relations has assumed so much prominence as a fashionable mode of thinking. But, as with any kind of fashion, it can be carried to the point where people accept it without questioning—and certainly this can be dangerous when we are dealing with such an important segment of man's activity.

Therefore, just because the tide has gone so far, I must make my points in the most emphatic manner possible. Though I feel I have not distorted the picture, I do not care whether businessmen accept my interpretation in full, or even

in large part, *so long as they get stirred up to do some critical thinking of their own.*

Before going any further let me try to indicate the things in this area of human relations which are really basic and with which there is no conceivable quarrel. In the first place, there can be no dispute with research in the social sciences, including the behavioral sciences. Ovbiously such research is highly important to business management and to business education. Business management and education must seek to understand the behavior of people as workers, the behavior of people as members of organizations, and, of course, the behavior of people as consumers. In all these areas we need more and better understanding of human behavior.

Neither is there any dispute in regard to the things that are important for a man's conduct in relation to his fellow men. The foundation is good Christian ethics, respect for the dignity of the individual human being, and integrity of character. On these we should stand fast. Personally I have always liked this paraphrase of what Theodore Roosevelt once said in a commencement address: "On the Ten Commandments and the Sermon on the Mount, uncompromising rigidity; on all else, the widest tolerance."[1] But between acceptance of high moral principles and the exigencies of day-to-day conduct of affairs there can be, with the best intentions, a very wide gap. This is the gap which by better understanding of human motivation we should try to fill.

Also there can be little dispute about the observations on the behavior of people at work which Professor Fritz J. Roethlisberger, the leader of the human relations group at Harvard, summed up half a dozen years ago:

People at work are not so different from people in other aspects of life. They are not entirely creatures of logic. They have feelings. They like to feel important and to have their work recognized as important. Although they are interested in the size of their pay envelopes, this is not a matter of their first concern. Sometimes they are more interested in having their pay reflect accurately the relative social importance to them of the different jobs they do. Sometimes even still more important to them than maintenance of socially accepted wage differentials is the way their superiors treat them.

They like to work in an atmosphere of approval. They like to be praised rather than blamed. They do not like to have to admit their mistakes—at least, not publicly. They like to know what is expected of them

---

1. From the Introduction to *Theodore Roosevelt's America*, edited by Farida Wiley (New York, Devin-Adair Company, 1955), p. xxi.

and where they stand in relation to their boss's expectations. They like to have some warning of the changes that may affect them.

They like to feel independent in their relations to their supervisors. They like to be able to express their feelings to them without being misunderstood. They like to be listened to and have their feelings and points of view taken into account. They like to be consulted about and participate in the actions that will personally affect them. In short, employees, like most people, want to be treated as belonging to and being an integral part of some group.[2]

In other words, "People behave like people." They have feelings. They don't always behave logically. The concept of the economic man can be a dangerous abstraction. Every individual wants to feel important, to have self-esteem, to have "face." Everybody likes to feel that he is "wanted." He likes to have a "sense of belonging." Group influences and group loyalties are important. The desire for psychological "security" is strong. People don't always reveal their feelings in words.

That all these human attitudes have important consequences for management is likewise not open to dispute. It is well accepted in management thinking today that leadership has to be earned, it cannot be conferred; that authority comes from below, not from above; that in any business unit there will be "social" groups which will cut across organization lines; that good communication involves both the willingness to listen and the ability to "get through" but not by shouting.

Dean Stanley F. Teele of the Harvard Business School recently made the statement, "As we have learned more and more about a business organization as a social unit, we have become increasingly certain that the executive's skill with people—or the lack of it—is the determining element in his long-range success or failure."[3] Here we are down to the nub of the matter. What is this skill? Can it be taught? Are there dangers in the teaching of it? Is skill an appropriate concept?

Perhaps I can give a clue to the line of thought which I am developing when I say that I am essentially disturbed at the combination of *skill* with *human relations*. For me, "human relations skill" has a cold-blooded connotation of proficiency, technical expertness, calculated effect.

There is no gainsaying the fact that a need long existed in many businesses for a much greater awareness of human relations and that, in some, perhaps in a considerable number, the need still exists. The very avidity with which people prone to fashionable thinking in business have seized on the fad of human relations itself suggests the presence of a considerable guilt complex in the minds of businessmen in regard to their dealings with people. So it is not my intent to argue that there is no need for spreading greater awareness of the human relations point of view among many businessmen. Nevertheless it is my opinion that some very real dangers threaten.

The world's work has to be done, and people have to take responsibility for their own work and their own lives. Too much emphasis on human relations encourages people to feel sorry for themselves, makes it easier for them to slough off responsibility, to find excuses for failure, to act like children. When somebody falls down on a job, or does not behave in accordance with accepted codes, we look into his psychological background for factors that may be used as excuses. In these respects the cult of human relations is but part and parcel of the sloppy sentimentalism characterizing the world today.

Undue preoccupation with human relations saps individual responsibility, leads us not to think about the job any more and about getting it done but only about people and their relations. I contend that discipline has its uses in any organization for accomplishing tasks. And this is especially true of self-discipline. Will power, self-control, and personal responsibility are more than ever important in a world that is in danger of wallowing in self-pity and infantilism.

Most great advances are made by individuals. Devoting too much effort in business to trying to keep everybody happy results in conformity, in failure to build individuals. It has become the fashion to decry friction, but friction has it uses; without friction there are no sparks, without friction it is possible to go too far in the direction of sweetness and light, harmony, and the avoidance of all irritation. The present-day emphasis on "bringing everybody along" can easily lead to a deadly level of mediocrity.

We can accept the first part of a statement by Peter Drucker: "The success and ultimately the survival of every business, large or small, depends in the last analysis on its ability to develop people. . . . This ability . . . is not measured by any of our conventional yardsticks of economic success; yet it is the final measurement." Drucker, however, goes on to add a further thought, which opens more opportunity for debate. He says, "In-

---

2. From a speech entitled "The Human Equation in Employee Productivity" before the Personnel Group of the National Retail Dry Goods Association, 1950.

3. From a speech entitled "The Harvard Business School and the Search for Ultimate Values" at the presentation to the *Harvard Business Review* of a citation from The Laymen's Movement for a Christian World, New York, October 25, 1955.

creasingly from here on this ability to develop people will have to be systematized by management as a major conscious activity and responsibility." In this concept there is the familiar danger of turning over to a program or a course or an educational director a responsibility that is a peculiarly personal one.

The responsibility for developing people belongs to every executive as an individual. No man is a good executive who is not a good teacher; and if Drucker's recommendation that executive development be "systematized by management as a major conscious activity" is interpreted as meaning that someone trained in the new mode of thinking should be appointed as director of executive development, then the probable outcome will be simply another company program in human relations. While this may be good for some of the executives, no long-run contribution to the development of good people will be made unless the good individuals personally take the responsibility for developing other individuals.

Please do not misunderstand me. I am not talking about old-fashioned rugged individualism or the law of the jungle, and I am not holding up as ideals the robber barons of the nineteenth century, or even some of the vigorous industrialists of the early twentieth century. But I ask you to consider whether some of today's business leaders, well known to all of us—Clarence Randall, Gardiner Symonds, Neil McElroy, Tex Colbert, Earl Puckett, Fred Lazarus, and so on—are not primarily products of a school of friction and competitive striving. We need more men like them, not fewer. It may be appropriate here to cite the recent observations of Dean Teele on "inner serenity" and "divine discontent":

Any realistic approach to the nature of top business management, and therefore to the problems of selection and development for top business management, makes abundantly clear that the balance between these two [attributes] is perhaps the most important determinant of success in top business management. Let me elaborate.

Psychiatrists, psychologists, and religious advisers join with ordinary lay observers in noting how often human efficiency is greatly reduced by sharp inner conflicts—conflicts which usually center around value judgments. That is to say, conflicts as to basic personal purposes and objectives, as to the values to be sought in life, are far more often the barriers to effective performance than intellectual incapacity or lack of necessary knowledge. The goal then from this point of view is the development of that inner serenity which comes from having struggled with and then resolved the basic questions of purpose and values.

On the other hand, in business as in the world generally, discontent is an element of the greatest importance. Dissatisfaction with oneself, with one's performance, is an essential for improvement. So important to the progress of the world is discontent on the part of the relatively few who feel it, that we have come to characterize it as divine discontent. Here . . . the need is for both inner serenity and divine discontent —a need for both in a balance between the two appropriate for the particular individuals.[4]

To keep that important balance of inner serenity and divine discontent in our future business leaders, we need to focus educational and training programs more sharply on the development of individuals than is the fashion today. What is important for the development of the individual? Obviously, many things; but one prime essential is the ability to think, and the nurturing of this ability must be a principal objective of all our educational effort.

In the field of business education this ability to think, to deal with situations, to go to the heart of things, to formulate problems and issues, is not an innate quality. It has to be cultivated, and it requires long and rigorous and often tedious practice in digging out significant facts in weighing evidence, foreseeing contingencies, developing alternatives, finding the right questions to ask. In all business education, whether at the college or graduate level or at the stage of so-called executive development, we must not omit the insistence on close analysis, on careful reasoning and deduction, on cultivation of the power to differentiate and discriminate.

There is a very real danger that undue preoccupation with human relations can easily give a wrong slant to the whole process of education for business leadership. For one thing, it tends to give a false concept of the executive job. Dealing with people is eminently important in the day's work of the business executive, but so are the processes of analysis, judgment, and decision making. It takes skill and persistence to dig out facts; it takes judgment and understanding to get at the real issues; it takes perspective and imagination to see the feasible alternatives; it takes logic and intuition to arrive at conclusions; it takes the habit of decision and a sense of timing to develop a plan of action.

On the letterhead of the general policy letters that are sent periodically to the managing directors of all 80-odd stores in the Allied Stores Corporation there is this slogan:

4. "The Fourth Dimension in Management," an address to the American Management Association, New York, May 25, 1956.

To LOOK is one thing.

To SEE what you look at is another.

To UNDERSTAND what you see is a third.

To LEARN from what you understand is still something else.

But to ACT on what you learn is all that really matters, isn't it?

An executive's ability to see, to understand, to learn, and to act comprises much more than skill in human relations.

Awareness of human relations as one aspect of the executive's job is of course essential. But, in my view, *awareness of human relations* and the *conscious effort to practice human relations on other people* are two different things, and I think this is crucial.

As soon as a man consciously undertakes to practice human relations, one of several bad consequences is almost inevitable. Consciously trying to practice human relations is like consciously trying to be a gentleman. If you have to think about it, insincerity creeps in and personal integrity moves out. With some this leads by a short step to the somewhat cynical point of view which students in Administrative Practices courses have described by coining the verb "ad prac," meaning "to manipulate people for one's own ends."

A less deliberate but perhaps even more dangerous consequence may be the development of a yen for managing other people's lives, always, of course, with the most excellent intentions. In the same direction the conscious practice of human relations leads to amateur psychiatry and to the unwarranted invasions of the privacy of individuals.

Hence I am disturbed about the consequences to business management of human relations blown up into pseudoscience — with a special vocabulary and with special practitioners and experts. In fact, to my mind there is something almost sinister about the very term "human relations practitioner," though I am sure that all sincere devotees of human relations would vigorously disclaim any such imputation.

For me much of the freshness and the insight which characterized a great deal of the earlier work in this field — exemplified by the quotation from Professor Roethlisberger which I cited in my introductory statement — has been lost as the effort has progressed to blow human relations up into a science-something to be explored and practiced for its own sake.

I realize that many people in the human relations field — Professor Roethlisberger in particular — are also disturbed about this trend, and about its unintended repercussions. But it was almost inevitable that other people would run

away with such a fruitful concept, and set it up as an idol with appropriate rituals of worship (usually called "techniques"). Once you throw yourself into trying to "listen," to "gain intuitive familiarity," to "think in terms of mutually independent relationship," and so on, you can easily forget that there is more to business — and life — than running around plying human relations "skill" to plumb the hidden thoughts of everybody with whom you come in contact, including yourself.

This is the same mistake that some consumer motivation researchers make, as Alfred Politz has pointed out — trying to find out the attitudes, opinions, and preferences in the consumer's mind *without regard* to whether these factors are what determine how he will act in a given buying situation.[5] In his words, the "truth" that such researchers seek — and he always puts the word in quotes — is not only of a lower order than the scientifically established facts of how consumers react in real life, but it is also of less use to managers in making marketing decisions.

The whole thing gets a little ridiculous when . . . foremen are assumed to have progressed when they have gained in "consideration" at the expense of something called "initiating structure" — yet such was the apparent objective of one company's training program.[6]

From the standpoint of developing really good human relations in a business context, to say nothing of the job of getting the world's work done, the kind of training just described seems to me in grave danger of bogging down in semantics and trivialities and dubious introspection. I am totally unable to associate the *conscious practice of human relations skill* (in the sense of making people happy in spite of themselves or getting them to do something they don't think they want to do) with the *dignity of an individual person created in God's image*.

Apparently this "skill" of the "human relations practitioner" consists to a considerable degree of what is called "listening." The basic importance of the ability to listen is not to be gainsaid; neither is it to be denied that people do not always reveal their inward feelings in words. But in the effort to blow human relations up into a science and develop a technique of communication, some of the enthusiasts have worked up such standard conversational gambits as "This is what I think I hear you saying," or "As I listen, this is what I think you mean."

---

5. "Science and Truth in Marketing Research," HBR January-February 1957, p. 117.

6. Kenneth R. Andrews, "Is Management Training Effective? II. Measurement, Objectives, and Policy," HBR, March-April 1957, p. 63.

No doubt there are times when a silent reaction of this kind is appropriate, but if the human relations practitioner makes such phrases part of his conversational repertoire, there are times when these cute remarks may gain him a punch in the nose. Sometimes people damn well mean what they are saying and will rightly regard anything less than a man-to-man recognition of that fact as derogatory to their dignity.

That a group of foremen who were given a course emphasizing human relations and thereafter turned out to be distinctly poorer practitioners than they had been before taking the course, as in the above case, would not, to my mind, be simply an accident. I think it a result that might well be expected nine times out of ten. In other words, the overemphasis on human relations, with all its apparatus of courses, special vocabulary, and so on, tends to create the very problems that human relations deals with. It is a vicious circle. You encourage people to pick at the scabs of their psychic wounds.

In evaluating the place of human relations in business, a recent incident is in point:

At a luncheon gathering Miss Else Herzberg, the highly successful educational director of a large chain of stores in Great Britain, Marks and Spencer, Ltd., described at some length the personnel management policies of that concern and the high state of employee morale that existed. Throughout her description I was listening for some reference to human relations. I did not hear it, and when she had finished I said, "But, Miss Herzberg, you haven't said anything about human relations." Immediately she flashed back, "We live it; we don't have to talk about it."

In point also is a recent remark of Earl Puckett, chairman of the board of Allied Stores Corporation, when in discussing a particular management problem he said, "Of course you treat people like people."

And so, although I concede that there is still too little awareness of human relations problems in many business organizations, I think that the present vogue for human relations and for executive development programs which strongly emphasize human relations holds some real dangers because it weakens the sense of responsibility, because it promotes conformity, because it too greatly subordinates the development of individuals, and because it conveys a one-sided concept of the executive job.

I turn now more specifically to the dangers to business education at the college level which seem to me inherent in the present overemphasis upon human relations. Business executives should have as much concern with this part of the subject as teachers—perhaps more, because they must use the young men we turn out; furthermore, they represent the demand of the market and so can have a real influence on what the educators do.

The dangers to the education of young men, in my opinion, are even more serious than the dangers to business executive development programs for mature men. After all, we are well aware that businessmen follow fads, and so fairly soon the human relations cult in business will begin to wane and operations research or something else will become the fashion. Also, as remarked earlier, there is still a substantial need in business for greater awareness of human relations, and more businessmen are sufficiently adult to separate the wheat from the chaff. Thus in advanced management training programs for experienced executives there is no doubt greater justification for courses in Human Relations than there is in collegiate and immediate graduate programs.

From the general educational standpoint perhaps the first question is whether human relations can be taught at all. I do not deny that something can be learned about human relations, but I do maintain that direct emphasis on human relations as subject matter defeats the purpose. When things must come from the heart, the Emily Post approach won't do; and if behavior does not come from the heart, it is phony. Clarence Budington Kelland, that popular writer of light fiction, in a recent *Saturday Evening Post* serial entitled "Counterfeit Cavalier," makes one of his characters say:

"A very nice person has to start by being nice inside and have an aptitude for it. . . . They don't have to learn. It comes natural. No trimmings, but spontaneous. . . . If you have to think about it, it is no good."[7]

Good human relations do not lend themselves to anatomical dissection with a scalpel. How do people normally acquire good human relations? Some of course never do. In the case of those who do enjoy success in human relations and at the same time retain their sincerity, the result, I am convinced, is a composite product of breeding, home, church, education, and experience generally, not of formal Human Relations courses.

Hence in my view it is a mistake in formal education to seek to do more than develop an awareness of human relations, preferably as an integral part of other problems. This does not mean, of course, that the results of research in human be-

---

7. May 26, 1956, p. 24.

havior should not be utilized in the teaching of business administration. Certainly such results should be utilized (with due circumspection to avoid going overboard on theories that are still mostly in the realm of speculation). To take account of human relations in marketing problems and in personnel management problems and in labor relations problems and industrial management problems, and so on, of course makes sense. What I am decrying is the effort to teach human relations as such. Thus, I applaud the training of personnel managers, but I am exceedingly skeptical of training human relations practitioners.

I should like also to venture the personal opinion that human relations in its fairly heavy dependence on Freudian psychology is headed the wrong way. In the long history of mankind, the few centuries, dating perhaps from the Sumerian civilization, during which we have sought to apply an intellectual and moral veneer to man the animal are a very short period indeed as compared with the time that has elapsed since our ancestors first began to walk erect; and it seems to me that a large part of the job of education still must be to toughen and thicken this veneer, not to encourage people to crack it and peel it off, as seems to have been the fashion for much of the last half century. I suspect that modern psychiatry is in a vicious circle, that some of the principal causes of increased mental disease lie in morbid introspection, lack of strong moral convictions, and leisure that we have not yet learned how to use.

I believe that one of these days a newer school of thought in these matters will re-emphasize the importance of will power, self-control, and personal responsibility. I can well recall hearing Charles William Eliot, on the occasion of his ninetieth birthday, repeat his famous prescription for a happy life: "Look up, and not down, look forward and not backward, look out and not in."

Our present preoccupation with the emotional and nonlogical aspects of life seems to me in many ways responsible for the prevalent wishful thinking of the American people. As a higher and higher proportion of American youth goes to college, it might be supposed that intelligently realistic ways of looking at things would be on the increase, but the contrary seems to be true. As people we are more prone than ever to let our desires color our thinking. More and more the few people who have the courage to present realistic viewpoints on national and world affairs find that the public will not listen to what it does not wish to hear. Why isn't education bringing us a more intelligent outlook on life?

Can it be that one of the reasons is that education itself has surrendered so far to the ideas that are concerned primarily with the current fashionable interest in the emotional and nonlogical aspects of living? In reviewing Joan Dunn's book, *Why Teachers Can't Teach—A Case History*, E. Victor Milione remarks, "Our educational system has substituted training in life adjustment for education."[8] Obviously there are many analogies between the doctrines of the progressives in education and the overemphasis on human relations. Personally I prefer a more rigorous educational philosophy. I can well recall a remark of A. Lawrence Lowell that "the business of education is making people uncomfortable."

In any event, I think it is the job of education to push for more and not less emphasis on logics and morals in dealing with social problems. The following quotation from C. C. Furnas, chancellor of the University of Buffalo, makes much sense to me:

We must recognize, of course, that it takes much more than pure intellect to answer social questions. Great problems involving many people are usually handled in an atmosphere of high emotion and the participants often show but little evidence of being rational human beings. But, even though it acts slowly, it is certainly true that intelligence can and does have some influence in shaping mass emotions. It is in this slow modification of mass emotional patterns that the average intelligent person can and should play a continuing role within his own sphere of influence.[9]

How can we do this if we encourage immature minds to regard the nonlogical aspects as the most important? Not that teachers necessarily intend it this way—though I am sure some have been carried so far—but simply that putting so much explicit emphasis on the emotional and irrational makes the student feel it is all-important. No protestation to the contrary can undo that impression—that perhaps *nonlogical* impression—which is exactly what an understanding of human behavior ought to lead us to expect in the first place.

But perhaps my principal quarrel with the teaching of human relations has to do with timing. Discussion of such problems as what men should learn, and how they should learn it, is probably as old as education itself, but much less attention has been given to the question, "When should men learn?"

The whole modern development of adult education has brought into disrepute the old adage that you can't teach an old dog new tricks. In fact, in the area of business administration it is quite

8. *The Freeman,* March 1956, p. 59.
9. *Ibid.,* p. 24.

plausible that teaching of certain managerial skills is best accomplished in later years, after men have gained considerable experience in business activities. William H. Whyte, Jr., the author of *Is Anybody Listening?* and *The Organization Man*, in discussing the Alfred P. Sloan Fellowship Program at the Massachusetts Institute of Technology, has this to say:

> But on one point there is considerable agreement: to be valuable, such a course should be taken only when a man has had at least five years' business experience. The broad view can be a very illusory thing. Until a man has known the necessity — the zest — of mastering a specific skill, he may fall prey to the idea that the manager is a sort of neutralist expediter who concerns himself only with abstractions such as human relations and motivation. Those who study these subjects after ten years or so of job experience have already learned the basic importance of doing a piece of work; in the undergraduate business schools, however, the abstractions are instilled in impressionable minds before they are ready to read between the lines and to spot the vast amount of hot air and wishful thinking that is contained in the average business curriculum.[10]

Among those managerial skills the specific teaching of which had better be left to later years is the handling of human relations. Thus I should not only rewrite the old adage in the form, "There are some tricks you can teach only to an old dog," but I should go on to the important corollary, "There are some tricks that you had better not try to teach to young dogs." The dangers in trying to teach human relations as such at the collegiate or immediate graduate level are substantial. Indeed, by developing courses in human relations for college graduates in their early twenties without previous business experience we are essentially opening Pandora's box.

Such courses lead to a false concept of the executive's job. There is a de-emphasis of analysis, judgment, and decision making. Someone has said that the job of the modern executive is to be intelligently superficial. This statement is true in the sense that when a man reaches an important executive post, he does not have time to go to the bottom of every problem that is presented to him, and he certainly should not undertake himself to do the work of his subordinates. If he does these things, he is a poor executive. But if an executive has not learned at some stage to go to the bottom of problems in one or more particular areas, he will not in the long run be a successful manager.

Human relations expertise is not a substitute

for administrative leadership, and there is danger in getting young men to think that business administration consists primarily of a battery of experts in operations research, mathematics, theory of games, and so on, equipped with a Univac and presided over by a smart human relations man. Undoubtedly many of the new techniques are substantial aids to *judgment*, but they do not fully replace that vital quality. One of the great dangers in teaching human relations as such at the collegiate or immediate graduate level is that the student is led to think that he can short-cut the process of becoming an executive.

The study of human relations as such also opens up a wonderful "escape" for the student in many of his other courses. Let's admit it: none of us is too much enamored of hard thinking, and when a student in class is asked to present an analysis of some such problem as buying a piece of equipment, or making a needed part instead of buying it, he frequently is prone to dodge hard thinking about facts in favor of speculation on the probable attitudes of workers toward the introduction of a new machine or new process.

For some students, as for some businessmen, the discussion of human relations aspects of business management problems can even lead to the development of the cynical "ad prac" point of view, which assumes that the chief end of studying human relations is to develop skill in manipulating people; this perhaps is the present-day version of high-pressure selling.

A different but equally dangerous result occurs in the case of the student who becomes so much interested in human relations that he turns himself into an amateur psychiatrist, appraises every problem he encounters in terms of human relations, and either reaches an unhealthy state of introspection or else develops a zeal for making converts to human relations and winds up with a passion for running other people's lives.

The sum of the matter is this. It is not that the human relations concept is wrong; it is simply that we have blown it up too big and have placed too much emphasis on teaching human relations as such at the collegiate and early graduate level. A sound program in business education, in my opinion, will of course envisage research in human behavior; it may, with some possible good results, venture on offering specific courses in Human Relations for mature executives; but for students in their twenties who have not yet become seasoned in practical business activities we should keep away from specific courses in Administrative Practices and Human Relations,

---

10. *Fortune*, June 1956, p. 248.

while at the same time inculcating an awareness of human relations problems wherever they appropriately appear in other management courses. In other words, let us look closely enough at what we are doing so we can be sure that the gains we make in this area turn out to be *net* gains.

Finally, to express a personal conviction on a somewhat deeper note, I should like to refer again to Dean Teele's comments, cited earlier, on "inner serenity." The attainment of that all-important goal, in my opinion, is not to be sought through the present vogue of interest in human relations. Inner serenity is an individual matter, not a group product. As Cameron Hawley puts it, "A man finds happiness only by walking his own path across the earth."[11]

Let's treat people like people, but let's not make a big production of it.

25 – Sensitivity Training

WALTER S. WIKSTROM

One of the newer training methods that has attracted attention in recent years is something called "sensitivity training." As the name suggests, the goal is to make men more sensitive to themselves and others, to make them aware of how, consciously and unconsciously, they affect others and others influence them. Its role in management development is based on the assumption that a manager will do a better job of achieving results through the efforts of others if he has this heightened sensitivity to others.

Many popular articles have suggested that it is an experience in which executives vent their hostility upon one another; other reports have suggested that it is training in being kind and helpful. Both of these extreme views are correct—but only partially so.

The professional practitioners of sensitivity training concede that it is extremely difficult to give an accurate description of this type of training. But their writings, couched as they are in the technical jargon of educational and clinical psychology, have not made it easier for most laymen to understand what sensitivity training is all about.[1]

Under the circumstances, it is not surprising that the method has not become widespread. In the Board's survey, only slightly over one third of the cooperators reported using sensitivity training. Significantly, however, of those firms that have experience with it, over 80% intend to continue its use; indeed, a third of them plan to give it an even more prominent place in their management development programs.

THE RATIONALE FOR SENSITIVITY TRAINING

The format and procedures used with sensitivity training are unlike anything that is normally thought of as "training." These unconventional procedures can be understood only in terms of the rationale that is the basis for the goals of this technique.

This rationale begins with the belief that all men are the product of their cultures. From the culture, men absorb concepts and values concerning themselves and their relationships with others. Most men are not aware of and do not question the assumptions upon which these concepts and values are based. This is as true of the business world as it is of any other part of the culture.

Among the widely accepted values and concepts with which sensitivity training is concerned are the following:

► An effective man controls his emotions and does not ordinarily express his feelings, especially his negative feelings, toward others.

► A "boss" is needed if a group is to accomplish anything.

► Authority in an organization always flows down from above.

---

11. "Walk Your Own Path!" *This Week Magazine*, December 11, 1955.

From "Developing Managerial Competence: Changing Concepts, Emerging Practices," *Studies in Personnel Policy*, No. 189 (New York: National Industrial Conference Board, 1964), pp. 90–94. Reprinted by permission of the author and the publisher. **Walter S. Wikstrom**: Division of Personnel Administration, National Industrial Conference Board, New York.

1. The practitioners also differ considerably among themselves. This section presents a general view of the training method rather than giving a detailed account of the beliefs and techniques of any of the "schools" of sensitivity training. The description given by Dr. Chris Argyris in *Interpersonal Competence and Organizational Effectiveness* (The Dorsey Press, Inc., & Richard D. Irwin, Inc., 1962) was a valuable guide in preparing this section.

▶ Purely rational processes are the most effective for reaching decisions.

One of the reasons these beliefs are widely accepted is that they work fairly well—most of the time. However, there may be occasions when these beliefs, and actions based upon them, do *not* work for an individual or a group.

For example, a manager may have difficulty with a subordinate because of unexpressed feelings that both men harbor. The boss may fear that the subordinate is trying to show him up; the subordinate may resent what he considers too tight supervision. Neither feels free to discuss their relationship. Their work suffers.

Another example: A boss may be confused by his employees' "unreasonable" resistance to changes that he has ordered. The employees may be less concerned with the changes than with the way they were introduced. They think: "He can't make me do this," and their attitude may destroy the effect of authority formally delegated to him. The change is finally carried out, but it does not produce the results that were anticipated.

When failures such as these occur, there is a tendency to find out whose "fault" it is. Sensitivity training contends that no one person may be at fault. All the people involved may have been hiding from one another (perhaps even from themselves) the feelings and reactions that could explain just what was going on in their relationships.

The purpose of sensitivity training, then, is to help men achieve a greater awareness of how human beings relate to one another. It accomplishes this by bringing to the surface, for conscious examination, the normally unquestioned assumptions about human relations.

REQUIREMENTS FOR SENSITIVITY TRAINING

Since the values and assumptions tend to be unquestioned in normal social and business situations, it follows that a normal training situation cannot be used to bring them to the surface. In fact, trainers contend that a normal training situation may have the effect of reinforcing existing values and assumptions. Formal training procedures involve a "boss" (in the person of the instructor) with greater knowledge or formal authority. There are "subordinates" (in the form of students) who accept his authority. Participants expect the instructor to "give them the word." They expect to learn about and to talk about their

understanding of a subject, rather than their own insightful response to a situation.

In sensitivity training the boss-subordinate atmosphere is avoided. The instructor uses his position and knowledge to create a situation where the assumptions cannot go unrecognized and unquestioned. The training session becomes, in effect, a laboratory in human relationships.[2]

Some of the characteristics of this "laboratory" are the following:

▶ No one has formal authority over the group and the participants are robbed of their status. No titles are used and the participants are usually strangers to one another.

▶ There is no established agenda for the training sessions.

▶ There is no established goal for the group to work toward—other than the goal of learning more about how individuals and groups function.

▶ There is no prescribed way for the group to reach decisions.

▶ The instructor (often called the "trainer") does not instruct the participants.

Groups set up in this fashion are called "T-groups"; the "T" stands for training. The T-group is the core of sensitivity training, although other training experiences are incorporated in most programs.

Three to four dozen men participate in the typical program of sensitivity training. They are assigned to three or four T-groups that meet concurrently, each with one or two trainers. Most programs last two weeks. The men live together at some spot remote from their families and business associates; communication with home is permitted only in emergencies. During the two weeks, the participants assemble for lectures, illustrative motion pictures, or for experiments in group behavior. But once or twice a day for several hours at a time, they meet in their assigned T-groups.

WHAT HAPPENS IN A T-GROUP?

Participating in the first session of a T-group is an extremely frustrating experience for all concerned. It is hard for the strangers in the group to get started when they have no agenda or goals, when the trainers refuse to provide leadership, and when their only introduction to the experience has been the warning that the training will probably be different from what they anticipate.

The announced agenda for a T-group session is "whatever you want to talk about." And, typi-

2. In fact, some sensitivity programs are called "management training laboratories" or "group dynamics laboratories."

cally, participants have trouble deciding what to talk about. They may have trouble deciding how to decide. Usually they also have trouble providing themselves with leadership. One or more members of the group may try to assume a leadership role; this seldom succeeds in the early sessions. All of this is quite frustrating to the successful business executives who participate in these training programs. After all, their success is based upon "getting things done." And now, nothing seems to be happening—let alone getting done. Most experienced trainers consider this initial frustration a necessary, though unpleasant, part of sensitivity training. Through this experience, the participants soon realize that their effectiveness in the past has depended in large measure upon their established relationships and upon their formal authority to command. Stripped of these, many of the participants have difficulty creating and maintaining working relationships with other men. Only as they become aware of this are they ready to question their assumptions about human relationships. They learn emotionally (not just intellectually) that there may be something more they need to know if they are to be effective when normal relationships break down.

However, the participants not only learn that old ways may not always work, they also try new ways of relating to one another. This usually begins quite tentatively. It may be one man's blurted admission that he doesn't yet trust the other men in the group. A man may say that he has always found it good practice to keep somewhat aloof from associates in order to gain their respect. Someone else may question whether these attitudes are helping this group accomplish anything. Gradually the participants begin to be more open and honest about their feelings and reactions to one another.

IS IT A "BLOOD BATH"?

Participants may express their reactions to one another quite bluntly. This has led some writers to call sensitivity training an emotional "blood bath." But the majority of participants say that this is not true, although they admit that the going can get rough. A man who has prided himself on his dignified manner and impressive utterances may hear that one of the other men considers him pompous. A man who has considered himself a forceful leader may learn that others resent the way he tries to railroad his own point of view. At the moment of hearing this, it can be a distinct shock, no matter how helpful the insight may seem later.

On the other hand, men learn that their fellows appreciate the constructive things they do that help to move the group along. A good question, an honest admission of feelings, even a joke that is timed to relieve tension, may gain the approval of the men.

The fact that the participants are strangers makes giving and receiving this feedback somewhat easier. It has often been noted that a man may tell an understanding stranger things that he would not reveal to even his closest friends. But the feeling that "we're all in this together" probably helps the most. Initially, the men accept one another as fellow participants in an unusual experience; gradually, they begin to accept one another as individuals. A man learns that others may not value him for what he has considered his good points but that they do not dislike him in spite of having seen his bad points. And, as a man learns that others can accept him as he is, he begins to accept himself. Ever since the Greeks coined the motto: "Know thyself," this has been acknowledged as the beginning of wisdom.

IS IT PSYCHOTHERAPY?

The techniques and procedures of the T-group resemble closely those that are used in group psychotherapy. Almost all trainers stress that there is a difference although they disagree on how closely sensitivity training must approach psychotherapy in order to be effective.

The difference lies primarily in the purposes of the two experiences. The goal of psychotherapy is greater insight into one's own personality, greater understanding of the self and its inner motivations. The goal of sensitivity training, on the other hand, is greater understanding of how groups operate and how individuals (including oneself) function in them.

Indeed, almost all experienced trainers agree that sensitivity training is intended for the healthy, not the sick. They say that a man should be emotionally stable enough to take the jolts that he will probably get if he participates. The neurotic manager needs other types of help.

Preventing the T-group from becoming group psychotherapy is one of the chief responsibilities of the trainers, many of whom are experienced therapists. They do this principally by controlling the depth of the probing that goes on. The trainers try to keep the group's focus on observable behavior rather than on inferences about motives.

For instance, in a T-group, the trainer would not interfere if one man said to another: "I get mad as hell when you try to steamroller the rest of us." He might well interject himself if, instead, someone said: "You try to steamroller us to cover up your own feelings of insecurity." He would probably point out that the speaker has no way of really knowing why the other man behaves as he does. The speaker can know, however, how he reacts to the other man's behavior.

Thus, sensitivity training remains near the surface of the personality. Its purpose is to help healthy men function more effectively with others, not to help sick men function more effectively within themselves.

THE T-GROUP BECOMES EFFECTIVE

If the T-group remained rambling and ineffective, the participants would not learn much that would be useful to them on their jobs. Obviously, this isn't the case. The men learn to trust one another and become more open and communicative. The men decide more easily what they want to do and how to do it. They are better able to achieve a consensus that recognizes both majority and minority viewpoints. They learn to seek the leadership they need and to accept it from one another as it is offered. They develop effective ways to control the members who need to be restrained and to invite into the discussion the members who may be holding back.

It is not unusual for a participant to say, near the end of the two weeks, "If we only had a bunch of guys like this back home, we'd set the world on fire."

The value of the T-group comes from the fact that the unusual structure of the experience makes almost anything the group does stand out clearly. Therefore, the members can see what procedures work under different sets of circumstances. In effect, they increase their understanding of what *does* happen in groups and they broaden their repertoire of skills for dealing with group situations.

IS THE T-GROUP ALL THERE IS?

While the T-group experience is the heart of sensitivity training, other training methods are also employed. The trainers usually lecture to the participants assembled as a total group. The topics of the lectures are usually closely geared to what is taking place in the T-groups. For instance, during the first few days when the participants are still strangers, there might be a lecture on "The Problem of the Stranger in a New Group." These lectures are intended to provide insights that can help the members to articulate what they are experiencing in their groups.

Motion pictures are sometimes used. For example, "Twelve Angry Men," a film about a jury trying to decide upon a verdict in a murder case, has been used to show how groups can struggle with problems. Other films may be used to pose questions about the use of power, the legitimacy of formal authority, or the difficulties of communicating.

In some cases, sensitivity training incorporates experiments in group behavior. For instance, T-groups may be pitted against one another to show the effects of competition upon group morale. Another experiment may be set up to demonstrate the difficulties involved when a representative for a group has to negotiate with representatives of other groups. Such experiments are considered additional ways to provide insight into the roles of individuals in groups.

SENSITIVITY TRAINING EVALUATED

One of the few concrete indicators of the value of this training method is the experience of companies that have used it: While few have used it, almost all (80%) that have, plan to continue with it.

There are some former participants who vociferously denounce this training as a complete waste of time. The majority consider the experience very valuable. And quite a number of former participants have become enthusiastic advocates of sensitivity training. Almost no one, however, is able to say precisely how the experience has helped his work as a manager.

Former participants tend to use rather vague generalizations to explain how they have benefited: "I seem to get more cooperation from others now." "Since my T-group, I really search for the other fellow's viewpoint; usually I'm able to get him to see mine, too. This seldom happened before." "I no longer get annoyed when meetings don't seem to be getting anywhere. Now I try to figure out what is getting in our way and often I can get us back on the track again." "I'm not sure exactly how I was helped but I know I'm a better manager; my boss says so too."

Sensitivity training is an unusual training experience, time-consuming and somewhat unpleasant in its early stages. But for the emotionally healthy manager, apparently it is an extremely effective means for deepening his understanding of how individuals work together to accomplish their purposes.

SECTION *VI*

INNOVATING

Innovating is not usually considered as a separate function of management. It is believed, however, that because of our rapidly changing environment and because of increased knowledge in this field, managers must develop competence as innovators. The emergence of innovation as a function of management is examined in Wadia's article (#26). McNulty (#27) presents a report and discussion of a research project concerning change in thirty companies, covering both its theoretical and its practical implications. Jasinski (#28) examines the organizational implications of innovations in technology and suggests ways in which management can remove or reduce the major points of variance between the organization and its technology. Sayles (#29) takes a systems approach to the change process in organizations and views change as an integral part of the administrator's task. McIsaac (#30) expounds the view that resistance to change is not inevitable; he cites examples to support this view and states that management can and should establish an environment that facilitates change, especially through application of the participative approach.

26 — The Administrative Function of Innovation

MANECK S. WADIA

OBJECTIVE

In a field where there is an acute shortage of a working theory[1] it is the objective of this paper to provide, from the social science point of view, the theoretical background and the essential tools for the administrative function of innovation. This is based on the belief that one of the major func-

tions of the administrator is to find ways and means of introducing changes in the most efficient and economical manner, in the shortest time possible, and with the least amount of disruption.

DEFINITION

Innovation is here defined as "the act or process of introducing any behavior or thing that is new."[2] In a strict sense innovation is an idea or a group of ideas, some of which can be expressed overtly. The field of administration emphasizes the production of new ideas and places a premium on *creative thinking*. However, just producing new ideas is not enough in the administrative world. What is essential is the ability to introduce these ideas successfully. "Innovation — the introduction of new or added activities — is the life-blood of any enterprise."[3] In other words,

"The Administrative Function of Innovation," *International Review of Administrative Sciences*, XXVII, No. 1 (1961), 324–328. Reprinted by permission of the International Institute of Administrative Sciences, Brussels. **Maneck S. Wadia:** Ford Foundation Faculty Fellow, Administrative Science Center, University of Pittsburgh.

1. Edward H. Litchfield, "Notes on a General Theory of

Administration," *Administrative Science Quarterly*, June 1956, page 10.

2. The basis for this definition and for certain aspects of this paper have been derived from H. G. Barnett, *Innovation: The Basis of Cultural Change.* New York, McGraw-Hill, 1953.

3. Louis A. Allen, "8 Skills Make a Manager," *Nation's Business*, Washington, D.C., February 1958, page 5.

the administrator must have the ability to innovate just as he must have the skill to plan, organize, motivate, and control.

THEORETICAL BACKGROUND

The present approach to innovation is neither statistical nor historical. The aim is to investigate processes and *universals*, rather than substance and singularities, so as to find some common *conditions* and consistent *mechanisms* in the hope of providing *tools* for a better understanding and use of innovation in administration.

PROCESS

Innovation begins the moment a new idea is originated, accepted or put into effect. *Without a new idea there can be no innovation.* Hence "innovation depends in a large measure upon releasing and encouraging the creative energies of people. The professional manager helps to create the necessary environment by stimulating and encouraging his subordinates to differ with accepted ways of doing things and to come up with constructive ideas for improvement. Only when a premium is placed on originality and initiative can true innovation exist."[4]

One must also bear in mind from the outset that innovation leads to the introduction of a change. This is essential to note because a change will affect, in varying degrees, all individuals and activities connected with the organization, both directly and indirectly. In a country like the United States, with its vast market facilities, excellent transportation and mass communications systems, the change in an organization has the potential force to have a more widespread effect than in countries which lack these facilities. How far-reaching these effects are will depend to a large measure upon the type of change and the time element involved.

UNIVERSALS

One may distinguish between two major types of change—the *routine* change and the *dynamic* change. This dichotomy will become more apparent if we exemplify. Suppose an individual has never worn a bow tie, receives one as a Christmas gift and wears it—this is routine change. Again, suppose an orthodox Hindu, who reveres the cow, has to eat beef in the United States—this is a dynamic change. The wearing of a bow tie will

have few, if any, after-effects on the individual though there has been a change. The change to eating beef by the orthodox Hindu will have more far reaching after-effects—he may not consider himself a Hindu anymore, his family may disown him, he may get sick, etc. Hence, a dynamic change suggests that the after-effects will be more far reaching, involve a wider relationship, create an internal as well as an external "crisis" and will therefore be more difficult to introduce successfully. The difference between routine change and dynamic change is quantitative as well as qualitative. Innovation deals mainly with the dynamic type of change.

The *environment* in which a change takes place is also of major importance in determining whether that change is routine or dynamic. Professional executives and administrators "have given little if any systematic attention to the impact of a total culture upon administrative values, practices, and behavior. Cross-cultural data are even fewer."[5] To exemplify the importance of environment let us take one of the above examples and set it in two different cultures. Suppose a missionary in the United States gives a bow-tie to an American who has never worn one. When the receiver wears the bow-tie in place of a neck-tie, a routine change has occurred. Now let us suppose a missionary gives a bow-tie to a pygmy in Equatorial Africa, where the function of the bow-tie is unknown. Suppose the pygmy wears it around his forehead and his people consider him to be possessed of mana (impersonal supernatural power) because of the bow-tie, then a dynamic change has occurred.

One may well ask at this stage what *relevance* these examples and remarks have for the administrator. The answer is not hard to find. The routine operations of any enterprise require continuous solution of problems. Whether consciously or subconsciously, the organization undergoes many routine changes which are adequately met by the existing structure and the efficient working of the planning, organizing, controlling and motivating functions. Thus it is that we often think of organizations performing automatically. It is true that if the fundamental objectives and policies are firmly established, the organization will propel itself smoothly through what has been described as routine changes. It is not my intention to belittle the routine functioning of the organization and its economic and efficient performance certainly has a place in administrative activities.

However, *the administrator must reach above and beyond the realm of routine change to the realm of dy-*

4. *Ibid.,* page 11.
5. Litchfield, *op. cit.,* page 11.

namic change, for in all organizations "it is plainly necessary to focus attention on dynamics, to study less routine kinds of adaptation. There is a vital sector of organizational experience that cannot be understood as simple problem-solving in which the organization remains essentially intact. Rather, in this sector, we find such adaptations of leadership to the interplay of internal and external forces as result in basic institutional changes. This is the area of 'character defining' commitments which affect the organization's capacity to control its own future behavior."[6] It is chiefly in the areas where dynamic changes occur that skills in planning, organizing, motivating and controlling could not be used to their best advantage without skill in innovating.

CONDITIONS

In the administrative sphere, as in the examples quoted above, innovations have different effects depending upon the *environment*. Certain environments are also more propitious than others for the origination and introduction of new ideas. The environment is influenced by two major types of variables—the social and the personal (individual).

The study of business falls within the scope of the social sciences. It is therefore only proper and profitable that we look upon the administered organizations in approximately the same light as anthropologists and sociologists look upon *social organizations* such as a village. This involves tracing the formal as well as the informal relationships within the organization, knowing who has what responsibility and commands what authority, what is the relationship of this social organization (e.g., the business firm) to other social organizations (e.g., the government, other business firms and the community), what is the ethos of this social organization, etc.

There may have been a time when it was excusable to think of an individual organization such as a hospital or a business firm, as *sui generis* and to take the position that the administrator must operate solely within those relationships of the organization that affect him directly. Though this attitude has atrophied in the United States, it is far from withered in the medium-sized owner-manager type of business organizations of other countries such as India. This is one of the reasons why innovation is so difficult and slow in those countries.

The innovator must think of his organization as being akin to the first ringlet formed when a pebble is thrown in a placid body of water. He must remember that a dynamic change within his organization will have a spreading effect over a number of rings depending upon the type of change, just as the number of rings formed in the water will depend upon the velocity and size of the stone. Of course, the primary concern of the administrator should be with the area encompassed by his own organization, but it should not be his only concern. If that is his only concern, he will find greater difficulty not only in finding new ideas, but also in introducing them.

Why should this be so? *Cultural background* has a significant effect upon the innovative potential as well as the acceptance or rejection of an innovation. All organizations function within the cultural inventory handed down from generation to generation. The end result of innovation is a change in this inventory; the end result of the innovation is equally, if not more important, than its conception. It is something akin to the birth of a baby. Brilliant ideas can be stillborn! Innovations are often miscarried in their embryonic stage. One of the major *characteristics of leadership* should be the ability to recognize a good idea and the persistency to leave no stone unturned to make it overtly acceptable. A perfect illustration of this faculty of leadership is the idea of non-violence as manipulated by Mahatma Gandhi to fit perfectly into the cultural background.

The second major variable which influences the environment is *the individual*. All individuals are creative, though the degree of creativeness may vary from one individual to another. Therefore, the administrator must provide for proper stimulus within his organization for the conception of new ideas, because external conditions have a definite effect upon an individual's innovation potential.

What has been implied above in the discussion of the environment and its social and individual determinants must be made explicit at this stage. The *interrelationship* among the three is a circular one, i.e., each of them influences the others and is in turn influenced by them. An innovation is conditioned by, and conditions in turn, the social and individual determinants, which also condition each other. This interplay of forces contributes markedly toward the acceptance or rejection of an innovation.

MECHANISMS

The word is defined here as "the agency by which a purpose is accomplished." In relation to

---

6. Philip Selznick, *Leadership in Administration.* White Plains, N. Y.; Row, Peterson and Company, 1957, page 35.

the topic under consideration we will deal with some of those agencies which lead to the acceptance of an innovation, which in the opinion of the administrator would be beneficial to the organization.

It is not possible to predict precisely how an innovation will be received. Yet its reception is not as unpredictable as one might be led to believe through a superficial analysis. Innovation involves qualitative variables and at this stage does not lend itself to variables that could be dealt with quantitatively. Yet, there are certain characteristics connected with innovation that lend themselves to *reasonable certainty of prediction,* within the framework of the environment and its social and individual determinants.

How an innovation will be received depends upon certain mechanisms. The following are some of *the major mechanisms which lead to the acceptance* of an innovation in any organization.

► The new idea must be entirely satisfactory to the innovator; if he himself has doubts about the new idea, he will find difficulty in making it acceptable. He must not innovate it until he is certain of its value. The greater the confidence that the innovator has in the new idea, the greater the chances of the innovation being accepted by the organization he leads.

► The prestige of the innovator has a bearing on the acceptance of the innovation. The innovator's prestige depends upon his past record; what he has already accomplished lends to his prestige. Though the prestige of the innovator may not be spread equally throughout the organization, the more widespread it is, the greater the chances of his innovation being successfully accepted.

► The personality of the innovator also plays an important role toward the acceptance of his innovation. The innovator has to "sell" his idea and he will not be able to do so if his personality creates antagonism. Personality is dynamic and if the innovator adjusts it to the circumstances he can make the difference between the acceptance or rejection of his innovation.

► The values embodied in a new idea are also influential toward the acceptance of an innovation. The nature of the change that the innovation will bring about is of importance to the potential acceptors and the *intrinsic* values must fit the acceptor's background. The extrinsic values, i.e., the feasibility of the innovation, are also important and they often involve both human and material cost. By analyzing the *compatibility* of the values embodied in the innovation with those of the potential acceptors, one can reasonably predict what reception the innovation will receive.

► Innovations should not be haphazard. *Ad-*

ministrative policy is one of the mechanisms through which innovation should be guided. When adequate policies for dynamic changes have been formulated, the acceptance within their framework will be comparatively rapid, economical and efficient.

► If the innovation is made acceptable to the *informal* and the *formal* leaders, through them it will receive the support of the majority. This means that the administrator must think of his organization as a social organization, as discussed earlier, and understand the relationships involved.

► The advantages of the innovation must be made readily ascertainable to the potential acceptors. By studying how well these advantages have been *communicated* to all concerned, one can predict how the innovation will be received.

► Finally, one must remember that each of the above mechanisms *complements* the others. By improving upon these mechanisms, the innovator will become successful in making his innovations acceptable.

TOOLS

An understanding of the full thesis presented in this article provides the main tools of innovations. To these one can add certain principles to aid the professional executive in the performance of the innovating function.

The *principle of innovation* states that innovation is necessary and inevitable if the organization is to continuously prosper and therefore it must be properly understood and guided. The *principle of acceptance* states that the innovation that clearly shows the relationship between the innovation and its advantageous results will be accepted more readily and with greater economy and efficiency. Conversely, the *principle of rejection* states that "people resist changes that appear to threaten basic securities; they resist being forced to change; they resist proposed changes they do not understand."[7] Many other principles of administration, already formulated, such as the principle of the objective, the principle of the situation, etc., can also prove useful in the function of innovating.

In dealing with the innovating function, it is necessary to find answers to these *questions:* How can the innovative potential be increased? Will the innovation be acceptable? If not, how can it be made acceptable? Only after these questions are answered can the professional executive go ahead

7. Edward H. Spicer, *Human Problems in Technological Change.* New York, Russell Sage Foundation, 1952, page 18.

with that process for the planning function which involves finding an answer to the six questions enumerated by Professor Mee.[8]

CONCLUSION

All reputable organizations have the objective of *continuous existence*. This can be achieved by progress through innovation. At General Electric the motto reads "Progress is Our Most Important Product." Most organizations are continuously searching for new and better methods for achieving their objectives. Throughout the world, the emphasis in all walks of life is being shifted toward the "new." This atmosphere, combined with the many ramifications involved in innovating, makes *innovation an important administrative function,* for both study and practice.

27 – Organizational Change in Growing Enterprises

JAMES E. McNULTY

A suitably comprehensive theory of organizational dynamics for the business enterprise, one must concede, is still an aspiration rather than a reality. We can deduce from existing static theory that there should be adaptation of the organization and communication structure when changes occur in basic environmental, technological, and human parameters. For example, if the demand for the products of an enterprise were to increase permanently (and therefore probably with geographical or product diversity), we expect from the "span of control" principle either an increase in the number of managers and/or "staff" and appropriate changes in the assignment of authority and responsibility. But this gross notion of long-run behavior is clearly of limited usefulness, even with respect to helping us with the most elementary kinds of questions about the transitional, or dynamical, behavior of the systems involved. We cannot talk with any degree of precision about the time required for organizational profile changes such as mentioned above, despite the relevance of the topic to such things as overall business planning.

THE PROBLEM AND THE RESEARCH PROCEDURE

When we try to speculate on more esoteric matters, there is almost nothing in the way of theory to help us. The case of the theory of "satisficing" behavior constitutes one example here. This theory, which has been advanced by Herbert Simon, is intended to be descriptive of business decision making in general.[1] However, it has the greatest relevance to the matter of organizational transition because of the complexity of the system problem involved – we know that as a practical matter changing an organization must entail new detailed assignments of nominal authority and responsibility, a reordering of the communication lines which carry vital information to decision makers, and appropriately compensatory motivational systems.

Like Keynes' theory of equilibrium at less than full employment, the theory of satisficing behavior makes a statement about the behavior of a system in transition, even though the theory is so stated as to fall into the realm of statics. Obviously we have to have a model representation of the dynamic processes to which the new theory may apply if we are fully to comprehend and evaluate it, whether we be academicians or administrators. Unfortunately such a presentation is lacking to a very substantial degree in the field of business organization theory, so that at present we cannot really do very much toward either using or testing the idea.

Another instance of our problems in this field – and a very important one from even the most prosaic administrative standpoint – arises in connection with a recent trend in results of work done in organization and communication "labo-

---

8. John F. Mee, "Management Philosophy for Professional Executives." *Business Horizons,* Indiana University, 1956.

"Organizational Change in Growing Enterprises," *Administrative Science Quarterly,* VII (June 1962), 1–21. Reprinted by permission of the author and the publisher. **James E. McNulty:** Wharton School of Finance and Commerce, University of Pennsylvania.

1. See Herbert A. Simon, A Behavioral Model of Rational Choice, *Quarterly Journal of Economics,* 69 (1955), 99–118.

ratories."[2] Simplified though some of this work may be in its experimental conception, there is the clear suggestion that some organizations change themselves in a satisfactory way, either because of built-in "switching" rules, or because of the induced loyalties and heuristic talents of the members.[3] March and Simon point out in their book *Organizations* that the received dogma in the field of organization theory on this matter is to the effect that satisfactory outcomes occur only with explicit reorganization.[4] Obviously again we need to know more about organization change, what favors it, and what hinders it, before we can evaluate these two conflicting viewpoints.

Much attention has of course been paid to the question of institutional (including organizational) development, stability, and change in studies other than the administrative literature, especially in the work stemming from the speculations of Marx and Max Weber. By and large, however, there is little translation into the field of organizational theory proper. The major exception would seem most likely to be the work of March and Simon cited above wherein an attempt is made to develop a theory of business innovation and to include in this a representation of organizational change.

As it turns out, March and Simon rather quickly turn off into a discussion of the relative efficacy of administrative centralization and decentralization, rather than remain with the problem of organizational change for its own sake. This indeed has been the course taken by other excellent, though more fragmentary, dynamic or quasi-dynamic treatments of the impact of changing environment on organization.[5]

One suspects that, despite the popularity of the centralization-decentralization question, an important reason for this turning away from a fuller treatment of the subject of organizational dynamics is that there has not been enough of even the most naïve kind of empirical investigation, nor even the promise of future empirical investigation, of some of the hypotheses which have been posed thus far and discussed above. Empirical investigation, while it tends to feed itself, has also proved to be a major stimulus to important theoretical work in many fields of study by virtue of the upsetting effect that it often has. The fact that we have had so little empirical work of any kind on questions of organizational change may thus well account for the lack of a substantial theoretical structure.

Out of such considerations the writer undertook to assess the effects of one kind of environmental change, that involving substantial growth

in markets, on administrative organization, with a view to finding out something about the dynamical propositions discussed above, notably the extent of adaptation — whether it appeared to have the Simon satisficing flavor — and the broad methods used for changing organization — whether they were especially developed for the occasion or whether they were built into existing organization systems. By means of questionnaire and interview techniques used on a cross section of thirty southern-California-based companies which participated in the growth of that area during the period 1947–1955, information was sought on two broad topics.[6]

The first of these was the character of administrative change which accompanied growth of sales during the period. Our interest here was not confined to change merely at the level of organization charts, which presumably might show additional management echelons, new committees, redepartmentation, and the like. We also inquired into change at the decision-making level — that is to say, into the question of whether or not paper changes in organization were accompanied by actual reformulation of managerial assignments, and additionally into the communication and morale aspects of the situation. The second broad topic concerned the nature and extent of purposeful administrative adaptation to growth. Was the administrative structure planned? Was there an explicit introduction of a new administrative system? What mechanisms if any for dealing with change were built into administrative systems? The intention here, as with the first topic, was not so much to be able to pronounce on particular details of organizing as to find out something about the nature and peculiarities of administrative change in growing companies.

The investigation was intended to be a preliminary one in view of the state of this branch of the field of organization analysis. Hence a procedure was used which has the strength of being insightful because of its open-endedness, but which also

2. See H. Guetzkow and A. Bowes, The Development of Organization in a Laboratory, *Management Science*, 3 (1957), 380–402. See also Lee Christie, "Task Types and Requirements for Organization," in J. F. McCloskey and J. M. Coppinger, eds., *Operations Research for Management II* (Baltimore, 1956).

3. Guetzkow and Bowes, *op. cit.* See also James G. March and Herbert A. Simon, *Organizations* (New York, 1958), p. 175.

4. *Ibid.*, p. 187.

5. See, for example, Thomas Marschak, Centralization and Decentralization in Economic Organizations, *Econometrica*, 27 (1959), 399–431.

6. This part of the research was financed by the Bureau of Business and Economic Research, Southern Section, of the University of California. The writer is indebted to Professor Ralph Cassady, Jr., for his many kindnesses in connection with expediting the work of the survey.

by the same token has various characteristics of imprecision. The sampling of firms was on a "judgment" basis,[7] but a bias was probably introduced, for a substantial proportion of the firms initially contacted did not choose to participate in the study.[8] Also, despite pretesting of the interview and written questionnaire forms, organization surveys entail considerable dealing in abstract and nonoperational concepts such that different shades of meaning are almost inherent in the answers obtained. Finally the practically unavoidable use of the formal interview technique in this cross-section analysis for purposes of interpretation of "factual data" on organization and for inquiring into a company's organization-planning processes brings with it a number of problems, including especially errors of memory, both on the part of the interviewer and interviewee, as well as the problem of purposeful bias in the answers to the questions raised.[9]

Despite these problems, it seemed wisest to attempt to study organizational changes using the type of procedure chosen. As was noted earlier some progress has been made in the development of laboratory procedures for the study of organizational phenomena. However, these methods of investigation, when they are at all comprehensive, appear to be extremely expensive at the present time.[10] They tend also to have difficulty in being both comprehensive and conclusive at the same time.[11] The other alternative, that of using an econometric-type model, has similar problems, which are the result in particular of difficulties in getting sufficient data, even though there has apparently been some recent progress on this score.[12]

In the section immediately following we shall report on the changes observed in the administrative structures and techniques of the companies in the survey, giving particular attention to the extent of adaptation indicated in the organizational changes effected by the thirty companies. Subsequently we shall turn to the question of whether or not the changes observed involved explicit, purposeful reorganization and whether the results of organizational planning for growth were in fact realized.

CHANGES IN ADMINISTRATIVE ASSIGNMENT

ORGANIZATION CHARTS

In terms of organization chart data there were marked increases in the size and complexity of administrative structures in the group of companies studied. Summary figures for the terminal years of 1947 and 1955 are shown by broad industry classification in Table 1. These statistics, which are based on company records, show (1) an increase in the relative importance of product departmentation relative to other modes of basic departmentation, (2) a lengthening of "chains of command," as measured by maximum number of management echelons in the two terminal years, (3) a rather pronounced increase in the use of separate staff and service units by the thirty companies, and (4) an increase in the use of committees of both the advisory and "line," or plural executive, type.[13] In general the changes seem to be most marked for the manufacturing companies in the sample and least pronounced for the five banking and financial companies which reported.

To get an idea of the relation of firm growth to these organization chart changes, various kinds of sales data were also obtained from the thirty companies and compared with the organization data. These supplemental figures are summarized in Appendix A.

In general there was some semblance of relationship in the several comparisons which were made (these are not reproduced here), the best being percentage sales volume change against change in the length of the administrative chain

7. The initial group of firms was selected from *Walker's Pacific Coast Securities*. Later a group of privately held companies was contacted. To be selected firms had to (a) have headquarters in southern California, (b) have over 100 employees in 1955, (c) show a sales increase for the 1947–1955 period, and (d) have at least 50 per cent nondefense business and not be a utility. Firms which were primarily defense contractors or public utilities were excluded on the grounds that their respective organization arrangements might be biased as the result of their operating under market conditions which are quite different from the "free-market" institution implicit in discussions of business organization.

8. In all 61 companies were contacted: 19 did not reply to the initial letter to the president; 9 refused, giving lack of time as the reason; 2 companies gave very incomplete data; one turned out to have a static sales record. The 30 firms which remained included 16 manufacturers, 9 in trade and service, and 5 in banking and finance; 24 were publicly held, and 6 were privately held. For other descriptive data see the Appendix Table.

9. To deal with part of the interviewee memory problem it was stipulated that the interviewee be either the president or someone designated by him as knowledgeable in matters of company organization and organization history.

10. See, for example, S. Enke, On the Economic Management of Large Organizations: A Laboratory Study, *Journal of Business*, 31 (1958), 280–293.

11. See C. Thomas and W. Deemer, The Role of Operational Gaming in Operations Research, *Operations Research*, 5 (1957), 1–28.

12. See M. A. Geisler, "Integration of Modelling and Simulation in Organization Studies" (Rand Corp. paper, P–1634, March 11, 1959).

13. It was not feasible to get from the companies data on the number of staff and service employees.

TABLE 1 CHARACTERISTICS OF STATED ADMINISTRATIVE ORGANIZATION STRUCTURES OF SELECTED SOUTHERN CALIFORNIA COMPANIES, 1947 AND 1955.

	Banks & Finance		Trade & Service		Manu-facturing		All	
	1947	1955	1947	1955	1947	1955	1947	1955
Departmentalizations								
Functional	1	1	2	2	12	10	15	13
Product	3	4	3	3	2	5	8	12
Geographic	1	0	2	2	1	0	4	2
Mixed, other	0	0	2	2	1	1	3	3
Total	5	5	9	9	16	16	30	30
Echelons								
9 and over	0	0	0	0	0	1	0	1
7 – 8	0	0	0	0	1	3	1	3
5 – 6	1	2	4	6	4	5	9	13
3 – 4	2	3	3	3	10	7	15	13
1 – 2	2	0	2	0	0	0	4	0
Data n.a.	—	—	—	—	1	—	1	—
Total	5	5	9	9	16	16	30	30
Staff and service units								
16 – 18	0	0	0	0	0	1	0	1
13 – 15	0	1	0	0	0	0	0	1
10 – 12	0	0	0	1	0	1	0	2
7 – 9	1	0	1	4	0	1	2	5
4 – 6	1	1	3	1	7	9	11	11
0 – 3	2	2	5	3	9	4	16	9
Data n.a.	1	1	—	—	—	—	1	1
Total	5	5	9	9	16	16	30	30
Advisory committees								
10 – 11	1	1	0	0	0	0	1	1
8 – 9	0	0	0	0	0	0	0	0
6 – 7	0	0	0	0	0	0	0	0
4 – 5	0	0	0	2	1	3	1	5
2 – 3	1	1	0	1	1	6	2	8
0 – 1	2	2	9	6	14	7	25	15
Data n.a.	1	1	—	—	—	—	1	1
Total	5	5	9	9	16	16	30	30
Line committees								
8 – 9	0	0	0	0	0	1	0	1
6 – 7	0	0	0	0	0	0	0	0
4 – 5	1	1	0	0	0	0	1	1
2 – 3	2	3	1	3	2	4	5	10
0 – 1	2	1	8	6	14	11	24	18
Total	5	5	9	9	16	16	30	30

of command. However, the associations were far from conclusive, as might be expected.

There were extreme items attributable to the indiscriminate giving out (and withholding) of titles. In other cases organizational adjustments to growth had clearly been made in advance or delayed, as will be discussed more fully later in this paper. In addition the age of a company, measured from date of founding, seemed to have something to do with organizational growth — older companies appeared to expand their organizations less than newer ones. Finally, some companies manifestly tried and to some extent succeeded in preserving a "flat" organization structure by resort to the "line-staff" device, while still others did the opposite out of a fear of "splintered authority."

TOP MANAGEMENT ACTIVITIES

From management theory, as well as from empirical studies of the large corporation, we have learned to expect substantial delegation of authority in operating matters with the growth of an enterprise. The administrative assignments of "top management" are supposed to become in-

TABLE 2   REPORTED TOP MANAGEMENT ACTIVITIES OF THIRTY SOUTHERN CALIFORNIA
COMPANIES IN 1955 AS COMPARED WITH EARLY POST-WORLD WAR II PERIOD.

Activities	Number of companies			
	Manu-facturing	Trade & Service	Banking & Finance	Totals
A. Same problems; same detail	1	1	1	3
B. Same problems; less detail	1	2	0	3
C. Same problems; more detail	4	2	3	9
D. Different problems; less detail	5	2	0	7
E. Different problems; same detail	2	0	0	2
F. Different problems; more detail	3	2	1	6
Total	16	9	5	30
A + C + E + F	10	5	5	20
A + C	5	3	4	12

creasingly concerned with matters of broad policy and less with detail, the latter being delegated to lower echelons.[14]

In recognition of the deficiencies of organization-chart comparisons an attempt was made in the survey of the thirty companies to get at the heart of this aspect of the impact of growth on organization by asking the following question:

In general would you say that you (president's office) attend to roughly the same type of management problem, and in the same detail, today as compared with the early post-World War II period? Please give examples.

A classification of the answers to this question by broad industry groupings is given in Table 2.

While the test here is in one sense not quite to the point in that it does not ask for a "time study" of the presidents' activities in the earlier and more recent periods, the responses quite probably reflect rough time weights. The most striking thing about the responses as a whole is that over two-thirds of the respondents were of the opinion that the "detail work" in the president's job was as great or greater than it had been at the beginning of the growth period studied. The companies which fell into the "trade and service" and, especially, the "banking and finance" classifications have a strong influence on these results, and may be involved in activities which are not as often delegated. However, almost two-thirds of the sixteen manufacturing companies studied reported the same or more detail work for the president.

As can be seen from the table, eight companies reported the same or more detail work for the president but suggested that the problem areas involved were different. Examples in general were not given. In two cases, however, the point was made that larger companies are more "visible" to federal and state regulatory agencies and that the company presidents involved felt that they could not or should not, in view of the penalties involved, delegate much of the substantial detail involved in compliance. It is perhaps of some significance to note here that both the companies giving this response had recently acquired smaller companies and that conceivably a difference in compliance traditions still remained to be worked out.

The responses to this direct question on the extent of delegation by top management nevertheless do not give us the picture of organization adaptation to growth which we expect from our look at the organization charts and from organization theory. All but two of the twenty-eight companies which reported employee numbers had more than five hundred employees in 1954, as can be seen from Appendix Table A, and more than two-thirds of the whole group of thirty had market expansions exceeding 200 per cent during the period studied. On this basis the rationalization which might be offered to the effect that presidential capabilities were not being strained by company growth does not seem reasonable.[15] It seems necessary to conclude, therefore, that either an insufficient number of new executives and staff assistants were added by the companies as a whole, or that the organizational adaptation

14. See Robert A. Gordon, *Business Leadership in the Large Corporation* (Washington, 1945), chs. iii, iv.

15. See also Sune Carlson, *Executive Behavior* (Stockholm, 1951).

suggested by the organization chart changes in most of the companies was somewhat fictitious.

COMMUNICATION AND LOWER-ECHELON PARTICIPATION

Another way of discovering the extent of organizational adaptation to change is to study the development of communication structures in business enterprises. This method is more indirect. As is well known, however, the direction and extent of information flow within the firm is or should be closely related to organization structure. Decision centers are located, *inter alia*, in light of communication considerations, and, conversely, given the pattern of administrative assignment, communication must be organized so that decision makers receive the information which has significance for the profitability of their decisions. In the event that a company decentralizes its administrative assignments, top management communication with the lowest management echelons should become more infrequent and impersonal. Also there should ordinarily be a growth of direct lateral communication amongst the middle- and lower-echelon decision units if effective co-ordination is to be achieved.

In order to run this test the following two questions were asked the thirty companies studied:

1) What is company policy concerning interdepartmental communications? Have any special attempts been made to implement this policy as the company has expanded?

2) What is the extent and substance of your (top management) contacts with executives and supervisors at the lower echelons of the company? Has the relationship changed with company growth?

The first question is a very general one. However, the intent was merely to get an indication of whether or not interdepartmental information transfer was being increased, rather than to get the precise pattern, as would be necessary in a study of the wisdom of particular organizational and communication arrangements. The second half of the second question was purposely left "open-ended" in order to draw out, if possible, any problems the company was having.

The responses to the two questions will be found in the top half of the right-hand column of Table 3. In the matter of lateral communication it can be seen that all but five of the respondents indicated that they looked favorably upon the idea. This certainly suggests some decentralization. On the other hand, ten companies, or one-third of the whole group, indicated that no particular attention had been given to the matter of interdepartmental communication as the company expanded. Three inferences are possible here. One is that the ten companies did not decentralize during the period. The second is that decentralization was being practiced using centralized communication, as might be the case if the firms had emphasized integrated data-processing systems. Third, the ten companies had decentralized but had not solved, at least formally, their communication problem. We shall re-

TABLE 3 COMPARISON OF RESPONSES ON SELECTED QUESTIONS BY COMPANIES PLANNING AND NOT PLANNING ORGANIZATION CHANGES.

Responses	Number of companies		
	Planned Organization Change N = 18	Unplanned Organization Change N = 12	Totals
Lateral communications policy?			
No	3	2	5
Yes (encouraged)	15	10	25
Implemented?			
No	6	4	10
Yes	12	8	20
Extent of vertical communications?			
Much	1	2	3
Some	16	9	25
Little	1	1	2
Changed (with growth)			
No	6	5	11
Yes (decreased)	11	6	17
No answer	1	1	2
Top management detail?			
Same or more	12	8	20
Less	6	4	10

serve judgment for the moment on which of these inferences is the most probable.

As can be seen from Table 3, all but five top management respondents reported having a medium amount of contact with executives and supervisors at the lower echelons of their respective companies. Of the five, three reported extensive contact and two little or no contact. Unfortunately very little was drawn in the questioning as to the precise substance of these contacts. Hence it was not really possible on this basis to assess the extent of adaptation in communication systems by inquiring into the nature of vertical communication in 1955.

It is to be noted that eleven of the thirty companies indicated that no change had taken place in the extent and substance of contacts between top management and lower echelons during the period. This stability in pattern for the eleven companies probably means that the effective degree of decentralization did not change, although it is possible that in the case of companies desiring "flat" organizational structures decentralization took place via "horizontal growth," that is to say, by means of the appointment of additional executives at given organizational levels. As can be seen from Table 4, which is discussed below, a substantial number of the respondents regarded "horizontal growth" as the most important effect of increases in sales volume on their companies' respective organization structures during the period studied.

The seventeen companies which did report a decline in the frequency of contact between top management and the lowest management echelons may well have done so because of decentralization going along with the lengthening of chains of command discussed earlier. Some respondents noted that current contacts were quite different (e.g., were now mainly concerned with other matters than everyday operations) than earlier contacts. This of course suggests increased authority for intermediate management echelons. On the other hand, the larger proportion of the group of seventeen companies reporting less contact seemed to see no particular change in the substance of the general relationship between top and lower management. (This breakdown is not shown in Table 3.)

In a few cases it was volunteered without much explanation that all seemed not well with the company's communication system. However, there was generally no adverse evaluation of this system. This lack of adverse criticism is quite remarkable, even taking into consideration the fact that the persons interviewed were at the top of their respective organizations, rather than in a position

to experience first-hand the facts and attitudes toward management and communication techniques. One would think that either more difficulties with both lateral and vertical communication would have come up, assuming decentralization as the general trend and taking note of the fact that at least one-third of the companies had not done much to change their communication systems. Or else, if decentralization was not an important development, the decline of contact between top and lower echelons should have, according to the human relations viewpoint, brought an adverse human relations feedback. The evidence, in sum, suggests incomplete administrative adaptation in a substantial number of cases with nevertheless no great dissatisfaction being manifested at the top management level. This of course is the essence of "satisficing" behavior.

THE ORGANIZATION PLANNING PROCESS

EXTENT OF PLANNED CHANGES

At this point one might easily hypothesize that the evidence on imperfect administrative adaptation to growth is to be attributed to a lack of explicit organizational planning for growth on the part of the companies studied. Such an allegation has to be denied, since eighteen of the group of thirty companies replied in the affirmative to a question as to whether they had consciously planned their respective organizations to deal with expected growth. Most of the companies who replied thus gave, moreover, a particular date for the initiation of new organizational arrangements. Also in a number of instances it was pointed out that a well-known management consulting firm had been retained and had come up (always) with the recommendation that a "line-staff" organization and a management development program be installed.

There is indeed a question as to the comprehensiveness of the planning done, both in terms of topics covered and results obtained. In response to a direct question only five of the eighteen companies who reported organizational planning (and only two of the twelve companies who did not) indicated that any policy had been explicitly promulgated with respect to lengthening of the management chain of command and therefore with respect to a leading problem of the larger firm.[16]

Perhaps a more important indicator of the comprehensiveness of the organizational planning

---

16. All seven companies with a policy had decided in favor of keeping chains of command as short as possible.

process is the extreme discontinuity that appeared to characterize the efforts of most companies which made explicit attempts at administrative change. This is underscored by the dating of reorganizations mentioned above. There was also very little evidence of continuing or periodic audit of organization and administrative procedures. This apparent lack of procedural provision for revision of organization and the consequent lack of controls was quite probably a major contributing factor to the inconsistencies and difficulties with administrative adaptation considered in the preceding section.

REALIZATIONS

Another and perhaps more fruitful way of looking at the effectiveness of organization planning is to compare the firms which reported planning with those which did not as regards some of the crucial matters of organization adaptation already discussed. Presumably we should expect to find some marked differences as between the two subgroups, with the planners showing more evidence of complete adaptation.

From Table 3 it is evident that these differences did not show up very strongly. The exception is the tabulation of answers to the question concerning changes in the extent of vertical communication which took place during the period of growth. Here the proportion of firms reporting no change in the nonplanning group is very clearly higher than that in the planning group. Otherwise, however, the proportions reporting implementation of lateral communications policies, high detail top management, and the like are about the same for the firms which planned and the firms which did not.

The question here is why the firms which did not report having planned their organizations for growth appear to have adapted themselves just about as well as those that did. Was it because the planning subgroup was so superficial in its approach as to negate completely the value of a systematic approach? This is possible. There is also a possibility, however, that the wording of the question on planning, "Has your company's management organization been in any sense constructed with the thought in mind of providing for possible further expansion of company operations?" was such as to overemphasize the incident of expansion and obscure the fact that some companies might have developed procedures and personnel which were automatically dealing with problems of organization and communications. As was suggested in our introduction, either automatic or "heuristic" organizational adaptation is indicated to be a reasonable expectation in some

of the laboratory-type analyses of organizational and communications change.

The top managements of the nonplanning firms of the present study which appear to have adapted themselves to growth thus could have deliberately abstained from attempts to impose *ad hoc* organizational solutions to their developing market situations. There was some suggestion of such an approach in some of the interviews, where it was stated that lower echelons had been given considerable autonomy and were encouraged to establish such communication channels as seemed appropriate with other units of their firm. It would appear that for an arrangement of this sort to work out there would have to be some guarantees that lower echelons would take up their expanded responsibilities and not succumb to bureaucratic indolence such as has been charged by at least one student of the larger business enterprise.[17] In any case things seem to have worked out for the nonplanners.

COMPANY OPINIONS ON SIGNIFICANT CHANGES

As a final means of getting at the extent of planned organization change in the thirty companies studied, we have the opinions of the top management respondents concerning the organizational changes occurring in major degree as the result of sales expansion in its several aspects. These opinions are summarized in Table 4. Comparing this table with the factual Table 1, we see that there is a general correspondence. While data were not collected on changes in the number of executives at given levels of organization, so that there is no direct factual test of the importance of horizontal growth in the management organizations of the thirty companies, we do have an indirect test from the data on changes in number of staff and service units, which are usually associated with broadened executive spans of control. The number of companies reporting larger numbers of staff and service units in 1955 as compared with 1947 increased markedly, it can be seen from Table 1.

The point of least correspondence between Tables 1 and 4 is the matter of vertical growth, which was not regarded as a very important effect of sales expansion by the respondents but which shows up very clearly in Table 1 under echelons. It may be that this is a semantic divergence and that a portion of the respondents who noted decentralization as being a result of prime importance really meant to say an increase in the number of echelons.

17. Gordon, op. cit., xiv, especially pp. 322 ff.

As a matter of fact the relative importance given to decentralization in opinions reported in Table 4 seems somewhat high in consideration of the facts given on top management activities and reported in Table 2. It has been suggested earlier that the continued attention of two-thirds of the top managements to substantial operating detail could imply either insufficient new echelons or too little authority for newer echelons. On the basis of the comparative character of Tables 1, 2, and 4 the latter of the two hypotheses would now appear to be the more reasonable. That is to say, it would seem that many companies in the group studied actually decentralized authority to a lesser degree than was appropriate, given the fact of growth, and also to a lesser degree than they intended.

CONCLUSION

To sum up the indications of the study reviewed here, two observations seem reasonable. The first of these is that organizational adaptations to the growth of markets of the thirty southern California companies studied was often incomplete, especially as concerns changes in assignment of authority and responsibility and appropriate changes in communication structures. However, very little suggestion of dissatisfaction on the part of the top managements with this incompleteness of adaptation was in evidence.

The second point is that in the cases where explicit, purposeful reorganization was instituted to deal with growth in markets the results in terms of adaptation do not seem to have been clearly better than when less formal methods were used, whether because of incomplete planning or poor implementation and control. Here again we have in mind especially the matters of new organizational assignments of authority and

responsibility and also implementation of communications policies.

Purely from an administrative standpoint, to the extent that the observations just made are accurate, their immediate implication for the businesses to which they pertain is lower profits (although from the data obtained in the present investigation we cannot say how much lower). Decision making in some firms was seemingly based on something less than all of the valuable information potentially available in cases where decentralization was really effected. Lack of attention to broad policy making, less than attainable efficiency in operation arising from *insufficient* attention to detail (despite the concern of top management with detail), and poor lower-echelon morale probably hurt profits in cases where decentralization was not carried out. The indication that most of the companies and their stockholders regarded profits as satisfactory and therefore that everything was satisfactory during the period studied does not refute this profit implication. It is well known that profit standards are frequently not sharp enough instruments to set off the "search mechanism" in organization and many other policy matters.

A longer-run implication of the findings for the organizations concerned is a good deal more serious. To the extent that decentralization was not carried out, as appeared to be the fact in many cases, both "middle management" and lower echelons were being deprived of what is widely regarded as essential training for top management responsibilities. Continued centralization of authority in top management quite probably resulted in the middle managers of many of the companies getting excellent training in essentially clerical tasks but not much training in making decisions and in seeing that these decisions were carried out. While no information was gathered on company promotion policies, the likelihood in a reasonably competitive situation is one of inter-

---

TABLE 4 RESPONDENT OPINIONS ON ORGANIZATIONAL EFFECTS OF SALES EXPANSION AND DIVERSIFICATION.*

Organizational Effects	Nature of Sales Change			
	Expansion Per Se	Product Diversification	Geographic Diversification	Total
Horizontal growth	9	3	6	18
Vertical growth (new echelons)	3	2	1	6
Redepartmentalization	6	8	—	14
"Decentralization"	8	4	3	15
Centralization	1	1	—	2
None or little	6	15	21	—
No opinion, not clear, etc.	3	—	—	—

*By number of responses; some respondents cited several effects.

nal conflict occurring at some point in the future for many of the companies studied, over the question of whether to fill top management jobs by promoting up from the middle management or by bringing in better-trained executives from the outside.

Finally, a broader question of administrative policy involves the efficacy of *ad hoc* adaptations to environmental change as opposed to providing, through programs and motivational techniques, for flexibility in organizations which permits automatic adjustments to take place. The findings certainly suggest exploration of the latter alternative in view of the failure of the former as a vehicle of completely satisfactory adaptation to change.

Academicians and professionals in the field of organization also have something to think about if their purposes include prediction and recommendation and aiding organizational adaptation through these. We have seemingly an affirmative answer to one of the theoretical propositions mentioned in the discussion of organizational dynamics at the outset of this paper, namely that adaptive organizational behavior is "satisficing" rather than optimal. It is therefore a pity that we do not as yet have the means to help us discuss orders of magnitude in departures from optimality.

The fact that the other theoretical fragment,

namely, the value of explicit reorganization as a means for dealing with a changed environment, does not seem to be clearly confirmed by the present investigation obviously does not make a case for academic smugness either. Perhaps now the possibilities for automatic and heuristic adaptation will be given more precise evaluation by students of organization.

Our results certainly cannot be regarded as conclusive, but they deserve attention. Hopefully they will stimulate more and better empirical research on problems of dynamic adjustment in organizations. In addition to the research ideas and procedures used or referred to in the present discussion, Philip Selznick's recommendation, as a sociologist interested in problems of organizational change, that we "draw on what we know about natural communities" seems very well taken.[18] Like the introductory remarks of the present paper, this recommendation essentially suggests that there is a shortage of hypotheses concerning organizational change in enterprise. Hence we must also hope for additional theoretical work on the subject of organizational change if we are to use fully our empirical procedures and thereby construct a comprehensive and accurate representation of the change process.

---

18. Philip Selznick, *Leadership in Administration* (Evanston, 1957), p. 13.

APPENDIX

TABLE A. CHARACTERISTICS OF SELECTED SOUTHERN CALIFORNIA FIRMS.

Number of employees in 1954		Stated age of firms in years in 1955	
Intervals	Frequency	Intervals	Frequency
2,500 or more	6	60 or higher	10
2,000 – 2,499	0	50 – 59	1
1,500 – 1,999	7	40 – 49	5
1,000 – 1,499	6	30 – 39	6
500 – 999	7	20 – 29	4
499 or less	2	10 – 19	4
Data n.a.	2		
Total	30	Total	30

Stated number of sales and production locations			Stated number of products and services				
Intervals	1947 Frequency	1955 Frequency	Intervals	1947 Frequency	1955 Frequency	1955 sales as percentage of 1947 sales*	
31 or more	4	7	21 or more	5	6	600 or more	2
26 – 30	1	2	16 – 20	0	1	400 – 599	3
21 – 25	1	1	11 – 15	3	2	200 – 399	16
16 – 20	3	0	6 – 10	6	6	199 or less	9
11 – 15	1	3	5 or less	15	14	Total	30
6 – 10	6	7	Data n.a.	1	1		
5 or less	12	8	Total	30	30		
Data n.a.	2	2					
Total	30	30					

*Loans for banking firms; calculations in current dollars.

28 — Adapting Organization To New Technology

FRANK J. JASINSKI

Getting a new machine or production process to live up to advance expectations is often a hard job. Few are the companies that have not had frustrating experiences at one time or another in achieving the improvements that were *supposed* to come from a new line of automatic presses, or a more modern extrusion process, or a promising change in the conveyer system.

Invariably the question comes up: What went wrong? Sometimes, of course, the trouble is simply that the estimates in cost savings or productivity increases were too optimistic. Sometimes the engineering is faulty. Sometimes the loss of a key supervisor, a strike, or a change in some other part of the plant is to blame. And sometimes the new technology is too hard on workers and supervisors, or threatens them in some way so that they resist it.

We are all familiar with such troubles. They are cited again and again. But there is another common type of difficulty — one that is rarely cited. It is a peculiarly *management* problem in that it both begins and ends with management, and no group *but* management can deal with it effectively.

Let me state this problem first in an abstract way; later we can go into detail and illustration. The idea is this: *a change in production or technology affects organizational relationships.* For example, a supervisor may find himself working with other supervisors and groups with whom he has had little contact before, or he may find himself reporting to different people, or different people reporting to him. *When management overlooks these social changes, it generally fails to realize the full potential of a change in technology,* however well thought out the innovation was from an engineering standpoint. The potential may then be achieved only after a difficult and costly period of readjustment. The duration of the readjustment period and the degree of technological potential finally attained depend, for the most part, upon management's awareness of the relationship between technology and organization and upon its ability to keep one in harmony with the other through changing times.

Management has established and maintains staffs of engineers who devote considerable time and effort to evaluating new plant sites, designing processes, and making meticulous plant layouts. In contrast, it makes only a nominal, if any, corresponding study of the organizational requirements of a new technological process. Rather, it usually tries to extend the existing organizational structure to the new process. And here is where much of the difficulty lies.

THE OUTMODED VERTICAL

Traditional business organization runs on a vertical line, relying almost solely on superior-subordinate relationships. Orders and instructions go down the line; reports and requests go up the line. But technology, including both integrated data processing and integrated machine production has developed on what might be called a horizontal plane; that is, the machine cuts across superior-subordinate relationships, affecting the jobs of people in different areas, departments, and work groups. Superimposing a strictly vertical organization structure on a technology which emphasizes horizontal and diagonal relationships can and does cause obvious difficulties.

Typical of the kinds of relationships required by modern technology is the progressive fabricating and assembly line. Here the need to make the right decision or take the necessary action at the right time at the right place is immediate. Managers, in order to solve an immediate problem, have to deal horizontally with their peers and diagonally with people at different levels who are neither superiors nor subordinates. To follow established, formal routes would be too time-consuming, too costly, and too disruptive.

Necessary as these horizontal and diagonal relations may be to smooth functioning of the technology, or work flow, they are seldom defined or charted formally. Nonetheless, wherever or whenever modern technology does operate effectively, these relations exist, if only on a non-formal basis. In other words, certain individuals have developed their own techniques to work satisfactorily outside of (or in place of) the formal framework. They have usually done so after a period of trial and error and emerge as outstanding performers because they can deal effectively with equals, nonsubordinates, and nonsupe-

"Adapting Organization to New Technology," *Harvard Business Review*, XXXVII (January–February 1959), 79–86. Reprinted by permission of the publisher. Frank J. Jasinski: Technology Project, Institute of Human Relations, Yale University.

riors—undefined relationships which nevertheless are essential to the technology.

Certainly it is management's job not only to recognize these new kinds of relationships but also to take steps to enable them to function definitely and smoothly. A few managers have recognized the discrepancy between organization and technology and have taken steps to integrate the two. They have achieved such integration in a variety of ways, which essentially may be classified as:

1. Changing the technology to conform with the existing organizational structure.

2. Changing the organization so as to define and formalize the relationships required by the technology.

3. Maintaining both the existing organization and the existing technology but introducing mechanisms to reduce or minimize the discrepancies between the two.

In appraising these steps we will want to look at the kinds of problems which arise when technology and organization are not integrated, and at specific examples of what can be and has been done to recognize and alleviate the basic causes of these problems.

HORIZONTAL RELATIONS

Let us start out by considering a technology which dramatizes the horizontal nature of the work flow—the automobile assembly line. I shall present the kinds of problems which can arise and the nonformal adjustments some members of management have made, as revealed by the Technology Project at Yale University.[1]

PRESSURE FOR SHORT CUTS

The automobile assembly line winds it way, almost uninterruptedly, for several miles through the plant. The conveyer carries each automobile "without a stop" through five departments, past the areas of 10 general foremen, through the sections of 50 or 60 foremen, and past the work stations of thousands of workers.

When the "body" starts out, it is a flat sheet of metal comprising the car floor; at the end of the conveyer the car, now complete, is driven off into the test area. In between there are innumerable feeder lines or tributaries which bring parts to the main conveyer to be attached to the gradually evolving body. The entire plant and the efforts of all the employees are geared to the task of getting the right part to the right place at the right time.

There is, therefore, considerable interdependence both among production workers and between the production and nonproduction groups. The holes for a particular bit of chromium trim are drilled before the body is prepared for painting; the trim is attached a mile or so down the line. The piece of trim has to be on hand, brought there by a materials handler. And the tools of both driller and "attacher" have to operate at top efficiency—the responsibility of the maintenance man.

In other words, the foreman, to be effective, has to synchronize and coordinate the efforts of many individuals to achieve his production goals. He has to supervise the work of his direct subordinates; he has to make sure that parts are readily and continuously available; he has to ensure peak performance of all equipment in his area; he has to keep "tabs" on quality; and he has to track down and attempt to correct defective work done in previous sections which may be hampering his operators' work.

Yet, despite the importance of all these relations to smooth work flow, the organization does not define them formally. In fact, the formal relations are such that additional difficulties are introduced. For example:

Although the workers report to the foreman and he, in turn, to the general foreman, others who are essential to the work flow do not. The materials handler reports up a separate and distinct vertical plane. So do the maintenance man and the inspector.

Again, although production defects are within the line production organization, they may be caused by a foreman who reports to a different general foreman and sometimes even to a different superintendent.

Theoretically, the foreman can report any deficiency in services from supporting groups to his general foreman. This procedure is formally and clearly defined. Time on the assembly line, however, is crucial; cars pass a given work station at the rate of one every 1.5 minutes. Unless an error is corrected immediately, the consequences can be far-reaching. The foreman cannot afford to spend time hunting down the general foreman; he has to attend to the matters immediately and directly. To do so he has to deal with other foremen (on the horizontal plane) and also with ma-

1. For previous findings, see Charles R. Walker and Robert H. Guest, *The Man on the Assembly Line* (Cambridge, Harvard University Press, 1952); Charles R. Walker, Robert H. Guest, and Arthur N. Turner, *The Foreman on the Assembly Line* (Cambridge, Harvard University Press, 1956); also Walker and Guest, "The Man on the Assembly Line," *Harvard Business Review*, May–June 1952, p. 71; and Arthur N. Turner, "Management and the Assembly Line," *Harvard Business Review*, September–October 1955, p. 40.

terials handlers, maintenance men, inspectors, and other foremen's workers (on the diagonal plane).

READJUSTMENTS REQUIRED

In view of the importance of horizontal and diagonal relations to assembly-line technology, the whole concept of superior-subordinate relations is out of place—at least, in much of the plant during much of the time. The formal boxes and directional arrows on the organization chart cannot set the tone for everyday activities. Unless this is recognized, problems can arise.[2] As one perceptive foreman commented: "When you deal with someone from another department, you have to show a smile."

Unfortunately, the Technology Project has revealed that many supervisors, accustomed to behaving according to the usual vertical channels, have not learned to relate effectively on a horizontal plane:

In case I get stuff coming into my department that is wrong I usually let my general foreman know . . . and he goes over and gets it straightened out. I couldn't do that myself because, after all, I'm just another foreman.

Actually, the job I'm doing now is that of a general foreman because I'm checking on these six foremen all the time. I've got the responsibility of letting them know that they're slipping up in one job or another, but I haven't got the authority to *tell* them to button up. Lots of times I have to go to my general foreman.

This lack of patterning and clarity in horizontal relationships frequently creates clashes between foremen. One worker provided this dramatic illustration:

The foremen go around sticking files into one another's heads in front of the men. Just today we thought we were going to see a fist fight between our foreman and another one. They were screaming like washerwomen at one another. Fine example—they hate one another.

Hardly the way to get a job done! Yet these difficulties do not derive from personality clashes. Repeated reports of similar incidents throughout this particular plant strongly indicate a basic shortcoming on the part of the organization to adjust to the incoming technology.

Interestingly enough, there are a number of foremen who *have* been able to establish and maintain satisfactory nonformal relations with other foremen and with staff and service groups.

This means spending much time with persons other than their immediate subordinates. Indeed, contrary to the traditional emphasis on the importance of the vertical foreman-worker relationships, the demands of technology are such that good foremen actually have to interact *most* of the time in horizontal and diagonal relations. As a matter of fact, the foremen judged most effective by their superiors are the very ones who spend the least amount of time with their own workers.

At the time of our study, management was not aware of the relations required by the work flow—or, at least, it had not done much to formalize those relations. In fact, the individual foremen making the necessary adjustments sometimes had to do so in violation of official policy.

KEY TO SUCCESS

Horizontal and diagonal relationships, such as those described, exist in virtually all business and industrial organizations.[3] A classic example involves a group of drill line operators in a factory who, even in the face of vigorous management disapproval, resisted the formal logics of an incentive system and continued to devise nonformal methods and relations for getting the work done.

There is no dearth of evidence to indicate that, whether or not the firm operates under the pressing immediacy of an automobile assembly line, the degree of production success depends in good measure upon the mutual adjustment or harmonious integration of the organizational structure and the technology. Where this integration is faulty, those individuals who are able to utilize satisfactorily the nonformal relations required are the successful ones. Where management has recognized the need for integration and has taken steps to achieve it, the efforts of individuals are made that much easier and more effective.

Having considered the kinds of conflict which can arise between the technology and the organization, let us now turn to examples of how some managers have effected a more satisfactory integration. As stated earlier, these methods are: changing the technology, changing the organization, and (less radically) introducing mechanisms to reduce discrepancies between organization and technology.

2. Frank J. Jasinski, "Foreman Relationships Outside the Work Group," *Personnel*, September 1956, pp. 130–136.

3. See William F. Whyte, *Money and Motivation* (New York, Harper & Brothers, 1955), pp. 53–66, and "Economic Incentives and Human Relations," *Harvard Business Review*, March–April 1952, p. 73.

CHANGING THE TECHNOLOGY

Ordinarily, managers consider technology to be inviolate. And frequently it is. After all, in making steel, for example, the metal has certain physical properties which require a certain timing and sequence of operations whether it is made in an American, Russian, or Indian mill. As a result, there are not many dramatic examples available of managers' making changes in the technology to adapt it to the existing organizational structure. The illustrations that are available, however, should serve to make the point. For instance, though it is not generally thought of in these terms, the shift from process to product layout in industry is a fairly widespread technique for effecting just such a change. Most of the integrated machine-processing units would fall into this category.

ONE-MAN SUPERVISION

Formerly, under the process layout, the manufactured item would go from the rough turning or lathe department to the mill and drill department, to the heat treat department, back to the grinding department, and so on until it finally went to the assembly department — with a different foreman in charge of each department. That is why there are so many meetings in such industrial organizations trying to pin down responsibility for schedule delays and errors in manufacturing.

It is true that, where volume warrants such a change, reorganizing the technology into a product layout brings about considerable savings in materials handling. This is usually the reason given for such a change. The product is no longer shunted between departments but goes uninterruptedly down a single line.

Yet the product layout conforms to the traditional organizational structure, and a number of managers have utilized it for that reason. With the product layout, one man, whether a foreman or superintendent, is responsible for the entire product. He has control over rough turning, mill and drill, heat treat, grinding, and even assembly. The operators who perform these diverse operations all report to him — in an established, clearly defined superior-subordinate relationship. Integration between organization and technology is thus achieved.

This kind of integration is possible only when the product can be made by the number of employees reporting to a specific foreman. When more workers are required, and two, three, or even more foremen are involved, closely knit integration becomes difficult.

As automatic equipment takes over more and more operations and as the actual number of employees is reduced, the number of products which can be manufactured in a product layout supervised by one foreman will increase. However, most industrial products, for one reason or another, still do not lend themselves to "one-foreman product layout" integration. In such instances, managers need to rely on one of the other methods to be discussed here.

CHANGING THE ORGANIZATION

The impact of recent technological innovations has forced many managers to take a second look at their organization, particularly with the advent of modern data-processing equipment. This equipment requires information in a certain form. Where managers have used it as more than simply a change in "hardware," the equipment has triggered sweeping revisions of data-processing departments. To prepare information efficiently for the processing equipment, managers have completely reorganized traditional departments. In this connection there are the telling, though perhaps exaggerated, stories of companies that revised their organizations in anticipation of delivery of data-processing equipment only to realize such great savings through the reorganization process itself that they canceled their orders for the equipment.

SUCCESSFUL SOLUTIONS

Charles R. Walker in his book, *Toward the Automatic Factory*,[4] describes one instance of conflict between the new technology and the existing formal organization and how that conflict was finally resolved:

A $40 million installation of a semiautomatic seamless tube mill failed to meet engineers' production estimates for nearly three years. There were a number of variables that were responsible for this delay, and most of them could be termed human factors.

Among these variables was the fact that the amount of production was pretty much regulated by the automatic machinery. An important variable in the level of production was "downtime" — the length of time it took to make a repair or a mill changeover for a different size of product. As with most industrial organizations, those interruptions of production involved "nonpro-

4. New Haven, Yale University Press, 1957, pp. 126–142; see also Walker's "Life in the Automatic Factory," *Harvard Business Review*, January–February 1958, p. 111.

duction" personnel: crane operators, maintenance men, and repairmen. Most of these nonproduction men did not report to line management directly; they reported vertically along separate lines of authority. Further, while the men on the mill crew were paid for what they produced by an incentive plan, the crane operators and maintenance men were paid on day rates.

In other words, though the technology required the mill crew, the crane operators, and the maintenance men to work as a cohesive unit, management through its formal organization and its incentive plan treated them as separate entities, even to the extent of paying them differently. Productivity suffered as a result.

It was not until the workers convinced management (and the union, as a matter of fact) that the incentive plan should be extended to cover the entire work group — as required by the technology of the semi-automatic steel mill — that productivity increased. Following this and other changes, production not only met the engineers' original estimates of capacity but far exceeded them.

Had management recognized the new organizational structure required and made the necessary adjustments at the outset, then much of the three-year period of costly adjustment might have been avoided.

Undoubtedly, other managers have had similar experiences as one of the consequences of rapid technological innovation. Some may have recognized the nature of the problem and acted to alleviate it. Others may have simply let it ride. It is quite possible for a plant to function for quite some time with a conflict between its organization and the technology — but at less than optimal efficiency. It is also possible for such a plant to benefit from integration even after a lengthy period of such conflict.

A case in point is A. K. Rice's now famous Indian weaving-shed study:

Organization and technology had been firmly established for a long time. As in the steel mill, the weaving technology required a high degree of coordination between the weavers and a variety of service people — especially during a change of cloth, a break in the yarn, and the loading and unloading of the loom. But the representatives from the servicing units who worked with a particular weaver varied considerably from one group activity to the next. The groups lacked uniformity and continuity over time. There was confusion as to who reported to whom and who had authority over whom. This, and the lack of group continuity, resulted in inefficiencies as well as high damage in production.

Then changes in the organization were introduced so that it would conform more closely with the techno-

logical requirements. For example, small work groups were created, with internal leadership, which existed as a unit over time and so were better able to cope with technological requirements satisfactorily. As a result, efficiency jumped 10% and damage dropped 7%.[5]

TEMPORARY MEASURES

Obviously, the dramatic and thorough revisions described above are not always feasible or practical in modern business and industry. But managers frequently have made smaller organizational changes that border on being mechanisms. They can be of a temporary or quasi-official nature, or permanently incorporated.

Such temporary measures include coordinators or project heads who provide an organizational short circuit for the duration of a crash program. Best known, perhaps, are the temporary realignments during World War II in invasion task forces. Just prior to and during the invasion one man headed all participating service units. Following the successful completion of the invasion, the task force regrouped into separate and independent units reporting along individual service lines.

In industry, similar groups or teams are temporarily formed to carry out a specified purpose. Many engineering research departments function on a project team basis permanently. Another kind of quasi-official organizational change is the use of an expediter, who, unlike the coordinator or project head, has no direct authority over the individuals with whom he relates.

Still another kind of organizational measure, widely used to cope with horizontal relations, is the meeting. This form enables representatives from the several departments to raise, discuss, and resolve problems requiring the joint efforts of two or more department heads attending the meeting. Here again, the traditional and time-consuming formal channel is bypassed. Usually interdepartmental or interdivisional meetings are held at a top-management level; their usefulness or necessity at lower levels has yet to be fully explored by many organizations.

Other managers have found it expedient to include functions which have been traditionally staff responsibilities under production personnel control. For instance, in an aircraft engine company on the East coast, management transferred its "tool trouble" groups from the master me-

5. "Productivity and Social Organization in an Indian Weaving Shed," *Human Relations*, November 1953, p. 297; see also a subsequent report, "The Experimental Reorganization of Non-Automatic Weaving in an Indian Mill," *Human Relations*, August 1955, p. 199.

chanic's department to production and created a new job classification (with quality control functions) under each production foreman.

In fact, considerable attention is currently being given by several large corporations to the question of how many of the service functions can be handed over to the foreman. This is an attempt, it would seem, to fall back on the well-established vertical, superior-subordinate relationships and thus avoid the nebulous and consequently difficult line-staff relationships. The limitations described previously in discussing the product-layout plan, however, would apply equally in this instance. The product must be one that requires no more individuals—machine operators and the transferred service personnel—than a foreman can adequately supervise or manage.

INTRODUCING MECHANISMS

Still other managers faced with a discrepancy between technology and organizational structure have attempted to solve the dilemma by changing neither technology nor organization but by introducing new mechanisms. In this case, we are not concerned with minor organizational moves such as have been described in the preceding section, but with procedures or routines.

A dramatic example taken from the restaurant industry of the introduction of a mechanism is provided by William F. Whyte.[6] The problem confronting him was a simple but vexing one:

Viewing the situation *in formal organizational terms*, the waitresses reported vertically to the hostess; the counterman reported along another vertical line of "command" to the kitchen supervisor. Although not explicit, there was some indication that the countermen considered themselves at a higher organizational level than the waitresses. But *technologically* the work flow was from the customer to the waitress to the counterman. This ran against the formal organization. Not only was the relationship between waitress and counterman formally undefined; it also went diagonally, from a lower to a higher level.

In the cases cited by Whyte, a few individuals were able to adjust to this nonformal relationship, but they emerged as exceptions to the usual conflict pattern. Unfortunately, management did not recognize and take advantage of this adjustment and formalize these effective nonformal relationships in order to extend them to others in the organization.

Recognizing the conflict, Whyte introduced a mechanism to reduce it:

As an experiment, one waitress wrote out her orders and placed them on a spindle. Her orders were always ready before those of other waitresses who had called theirs in at the same time. If she was not ready for a hot food order, the counterman would voluntarily place it in the warmer for her. Furthermore, he took a liking to her and made a bet with the bartender that she, like himself, was of Polish extraction—which she was not.[7]

Thus, an uncomplicated mechanism reduced the conflict between the technological work flow and the organizational setup without changing either.

OTHER ILLUSTRATIONS

The use of paper work as a mechanism to reduce possible conflict in formally undefined relationships is a commonplace in industry. Requests from production foremen, for example, go regularly to personnel, engineering, accounting, and other staff and service groups. Such requests cut across the formal organization both horizontally and diagonally. Conversely, reports may also cut across the organization through the "copy to . . ." technique while going up the line vertically.

Very often, the amount and type of paper work (copies of requests and reports) do not correspond to actual need. Many are destined to end up in the "circular file" simply because the paper work routes do not follow the lines required by the technology. (Machine accountants, aware of this discrepancy and pressed for tabulating time, occasionally run a check on the use made of various reports; they purposely delay circulation of a report for a few days or a week to see how many people will actually call for it. Thus they have been able, unofficially, to eliminate a number of outdated reports.)

The automobile assembly line provides additional illustrations of mechanisms employed by management to meet technologically required horizontal and diagonal relations:

An operator who hangs doors is in direct contact with the operator who puts them in proper sequence on the overhead conveyer. In the event of a misscheduled door, the line operator has a "squawk" box

6. *Human Relations in the Restaurant Industry* (New York, McGraw-Hill Book Company, Inc., 1948), Chapter 6.

7. *Human Relations in the Restaurant Industry* (New York, McGraw-Hill Book Company, Inc., 1948), p. 69.

through which he can call for a substitute door. Here we have a horizontal relationship between two hourly operators, one in production and one in material control.

The worker who loads the overhead conveyer is guided in turn in his door scheduling by the "telautograph," which transmits information from an earlier point on the line from another hourly operator in the material control department. This operator notes the sequence of models and body types of cars passing his station on the line. The information is transmitted simultaneously to various schedulers in the plant who have to synchronize their operations with this sequence.

In the event of a mechanical or tool breakdown, time is especially important. When a line worker cannot perform his operation because of such a breakdown, he immediately signals for help through a whistle system: he uses one signal for a mechanical breakdown, another for an electrical one. The appropriate repairman (who is stationed nearby) comes over to repair the defect with a minimum of delay. For a worker to stop the line until he finds his foreman to report the breakdown in the traditional vertical plane would be absurd.

Several managements have adopted programs to facilitate nonformal relations. These range from company-wide social affairs, such as picnics, banquets, or sports teams, to a systematic rotation program whereby individuals at supervisory and middle-management levels transfer periodically from one department to another. Ostensibly, the purpose of such a program is to "broaden" the experience of the individual; actually the more important by-product is that it establishes friendships horizontally and diagonally, and thus encourages and facilitates nonformal relations required by the work flow.

Although many of these and other mechanisms can be effective and may, indeed, be the only means to reduce a discrepancy between technology and organization, it still is worth-while to make broader and more basic changes in either the technology or the organization.

CONCLUSION

Frequently, the traditional, formally defined vertical relations in business and industrial organization prove inadequate to cope with modern technology. New technologies require new organizational setups, and it is being found increasingly that industrial processes require horizontal and diagonal relations which are not patterned or clearly defined.

Such lack of clarity can impair the production process. The work flow can create difficulty where the vertical lines are strongly emphasized and where the flow violates those lines—as was the case in the restaurant example cited. But when the formal organization is permissive, nonformal relations in the horizontal and diagonal planes arise to cope with the technological process. We saw that the more successful assembly-line foremen learned to relate with other foremen and their workers. But these relationships were not usually recognized formally; they existed on an individual and nonformal basis.

Management can work toward an integration between technology and organization in several ways: (1) by changing the technology, (2) by changing the organization, and (3) by introducing mechanisms. All these methods have been used effectively to some degree, but the difficulty occurs in that management's attempts toward integration generally lack a systematic and purposeful approach. They may just happen over time, arise as temporary expedients, or emerge as a solution to a crisis situation. Many managers have yet to explore the deeper relation between technology and the organization.

The advent of electronic data processing and integrated machine processing has forced some managers to reorganize departments to meet technological needs. Many such revisions, however, are limited to a small portion of the organization, to the areas of greatest immediate pressure. Cannot more be done? The case studies cited, as well as the successful partial steps taken by businessmen and industrialists thus far, indicate a need for a systematic analysis of technology and organization. This analysis might include the following steps:

1. Examine the work flow of the technology to determine what relations are required.

2. Identify the points where the formal organization meets these requirements and where it does not.

3. Discover what nonformal relationships exist at present to meet the technologically required relations which are not encompassed by the formal organization.

4. Determine what formalization does exist to cope with relations falling beyond the traditional vertical planes.

5. Decide which of the nonformal relations might be profitably formalized.

6. Provide measures to facilitate the nonformal relations which are still required but which may best remain nonformal.

It will not be possible to formalize through new mechanisms or through technology and organization changes all of the nonformal relations required by the work flow. It should be possible, however, to remove or reduce the *major* points of variance between the technology and the organization. It makes sense for a company that has been far-sighted enough to bring in a new technology to be equally far-sighted in recognizing

that established organizational patterns will not usually serve with the same effectiveness as they once did. If the new technology is to live up to production expectations, then management must see to it that organization relationships are carefully restudied and wisely redirected.

29 — The Change Process in Organizations: An Applied Anthropology Analysis

LEONARD R. SAYLES

Unfortunately, the subject of change in organizations (or of community or culture) is typically dealt with as a distinct, separate process, apart from the normal functioning of the system. Change is apparently viewed as something that is imposed on an unwilling, unresponsive audience or consumer. The problem of change, therefore, is usually one of gaining consent or acceptance through cajoling, force, participation, spotting the most likely sources of resistance and, occasionally, identifying gatekeepers or possible allies.

In other words, it is the difficulty of *introducing change* into a resistant system which has captured the attention of most students of the subject. However, if one observes the behavior of managers or leaders it will be noted that this aspect of the problem does not account for a significant amount of the total amount of time and energy expended on administration. Our purpose here, then, is to broaden the analysis to include the total process of change. This means viewing change as an intimate, integral part of the administrator's task of managing — really *stabilizing* — a system of human relations. Change, then, is not a special, for holidays only, activity. It is part and parcel of the normal administrative process of assessing how the system is operating, determining where *significant* deviations are occurring, identifying the source of the disturbances, taking administrative actions to eliminate the source of the instability (what we will call short-run change) and, finally, where the disturbance or deviation is

recurring — the introduction of "long-run" change and its implementation and control.

What follows is an exposition of the stages in this process and their interrelationship. This analysis also represents our view of the job of the administrator in operational or interactional terms. It is an effort to depart from subjective, unquantifiable variables that have usually been associated with the analysis of all management processes (not just change) often quasi-psychological variables like the degree of personal security or sensitivity of the leader, the degree of "consideration" he generates and his ability to give assignments which equate authority and responsibility (parenthetically, a most unrealistic and unlikely possibility).

One last point to the introduction and approach. It is naive to assume that the administrator-leader suddenly commits himself to the accomplishment of change and then devotes all his efforts to this objective. Change must be accomplished simultaneously with the continued operations of an organization or system of work relationships. There is no "breathing spell," typically, where the organization can go all-out in the effort to pull itself up by its boot straps. This, of course, is another reason for considering change as part of the total organizational process.

THE PARADOX: CHANGE AND STABILITY

Paradoxically, the manager's job is to accomplish both stability and change. In order to maximize both the productivity of the processes under his jurisdiction *and* maintain high motivation

"The Change Process in Organizations: An Applied Anthropology Analysis," *Human Organization*, XXI (Summer 1962), 62–67. Reprinted by permission of the author and the publisher. The material in this article is incorporated in Chapters 10 and 11 of *Managerial Behavior* by Leonard R. Sayles. Copyright © 1964 by McGraw-Hill, Inc. Used by permission of McGraw-Hill Book Company. **Leonard R. Sayles:** Graduate School of Business, Columbia University.

among subordinates (which in turn facilitates productive efforts), he must endeavor to minimize the frequency with which the patterns of work flow and coordination are disturbed. In fact, the frequency with which such actual or potential interruptions to the work patterns occur, as we have described in a recent book,[1] are the prime determinants of the work load of the manager. It is the development and maintenance of work flow routines which is his major objective, and these "predictable and repeated patterns of interaction" are the source of morale or the absence of debilitating stress and its concomitant: destructive emotional reaction (what we have called compensatory behavior).[2]

In a situation requiring cooperative endeavors, whether it is a work group, employees and managers, or staff and line officials, each tries to develop a stable pattern of work, of interaction. When these stable patterns are disturbed, individuals experience stress or an uncomfortable feeling of pressure and dissatisfaction. A breakdown in the flow creates opposition as the individuals struggle to restore it. The expected responses from the individuals in the sequence prove inadequate, and new coordination problems arise.

The regularities of actions and interactions disappear when this stress occurs, and erratic variation takes over. The difference is obvious between a smoothly running operation and one with a problem. Under stress, people react emotionally, and, because more than one individual is involved, the reactions usually conflict with each other.

Thus, a vicious circle is established. Something happens in the work situation that causes the relationship of individuals to change or to depart from the normal pattern. This creates a stress, either of opposition or nonresponse, that is further complicated by higher levels of supervision and staff specialists whose unexpected interactions, i. e., outside the usual organization pattern, irritate the disturbed work-flow relations. People get upset; they become angry with each other and, depending on their individual characteristics, react temperamentally. These personality conflicts have direct ramifications in the work process because the emotional reactions change the pattern of contact and interaction. Joe is angry with Bill, so he does not check with him before starting a new experimental run. Consequently, a special test that should have been included in the run is left out, and the whole thing has to be done over. To complete the circle, these emotional disturbances damage the work-flow sequence, which causes additional personality stresses.[3]

But, of course, as we "sophisticated" observers know, the achievement of this stability—which is the manager's objective—is a never-to-be-attained ideal. He is like a symphony orchestra conductor—endeavoring to maintain a melodious performance in which the contributions of the various instruments are coordinated and sequenced, patterned and paced—while the orchestra members are having various personal difficulties, stage hands are moving music stands, alternating excessive heat and cold is creating audience and instrument problems, and the sponsor of the concert is insisting on irregular changes in the music to be played.

In other words, the manager faces constant internal and external interruptions. As we shall see, some of these require mere palliatives—readjustments—in order to bring the system of relationships back to stability, for example, a disciplinary action (which is one type of change). Other disturbances require more drastic action if the system is to be stabilized, for example, the introduction of new methods or personnel as a result of a change in market conditions or the demands of some other part of the organization.

Presumably we might call this a moving equilibrium. External pressures and internal problems require constant "change," but the manager endeavors to accomplish this as he returns the system to equilibrium.

DETECTING DISTURBANCES OR DEVIATIONS

Thus, an important element in the manager's job is the detection of disturbances or deviations in the system of human relationships which comprise his work flows. This is the control function of the manager: developing methods of detection whereby he can assess and appraise how and where he should devote his managerial efforts, perhaps supplemented by the assistance of other specialists.

We need to be aware that a manager's scarcest resource is (or ought to be) his own time and energy, and that of other members of management. Therefore, he needs to devote his attention to what are indeed problems and avoid spending time in areas which are functioning well.

How does the manager "check" or control? He looks at statistical reports of quality, quantity, turnover, and what have you. He "inquires around" as to how people are doing and he endeavors to "sense" when people are acting dif-

1. Eliot D. Chapple and Leonard R. Sayles, *The Measure of Management*, Macmillan, New York, 1961, pp. 46–68.
2. *Ibid.*, pp. 114–141.
3. *Ibid.*, pp. 37–38.

ferently. Unfortunately, some of this is usually done intuitively and there is little systematic attention to an integrated control system.[4] In a well-developed theory of organization change, we would expect to set forth the actual pattern of control: how frequently and with whom or what the manager checks. We would also expect to see an integrated series of controls involving technical measures of performance (e.g. quality, quantity, etc.) embodied in relatively automatic data processing systems combined with measures of organizational relationships.

Among others, F. L. W. Richardson, Jr., has shown that one can interrelate variations in the technical performance of a system with variations in the human relations dimensions.[5] In other words, there are correlations between such things as output and changes in internal work group interactions, manager-subordinate interactions and subordinate-outside group interactions. These provide the new materials of an effective and objective monitoring system. The manager need not be able to "smell trouble."

ASSESSING THE SIGNIFICANCE OF THE DEVIATION

The next step in the process is the manager's assessment of the significance of the deviations he is observing. It is likely that Parkinson's Law could be stated more realistically in terms of managers making work for themselves and others by going into action to deal with a problem that is not a problem—in other words, to introduce a change in a system which is operating within *expected limits of variation*.

The mathematical statisticians have begun to work on just this problem—noting that management can introduce serious instabilities into inventory maintenance systems, that is, can really amplify variations—by endeavoring to overcorrect for variation. We see the same thing in human relations terms—where the supervisor contacts his own subordinates and others to discuss "mutual problems," where the contact itself creates the problem, and none existed before. The foolishness is never detected, of course, because the endeavor to overcorrect the system *does create a problem* which in turn justifies the supervisor's attention and energy expenditure.

Of course, the opposite is the more traditionally identified difficulty: the failure to detect quickly enough or to move quickly enough to quench a real fire. Thus the manager requires as part of his control apparatus a theory of significant differ-

ences which will enable him to place certain "limits" on the occurrence or amplitude of the phenomenon he is observing. This requires a knowledge of the limits on normal or expected variation, given the nature of the system. He then hoards his managerial actions for the significant deviations in the system—and avoids becoming himself a source of upset where none existed before.

It may be well to repeat here that this theory of change encompasses deviations or disturbances in the system that are imposed by superior fiat or environmental change as well as internal malfunctioning. We would expect that instabilities from the "outside" would be transmitted through his contacts with his own superior and other managers as well as through the flows of relationship in which his subordinates participate with "outsiders" in their job activities.

From the point of view of organization design and the specification of managerial actions, it thus becomes possible to set forth explicitly (and thus control and check the performance of) managerial surveillance actions. These would include operationally definable patterns for what to check, how and how often, as well as techniques of data analysis to ascertain significant differences. This becomes another step in the process of making managerial actions less art and intuition and more science, but within the realm of human relationships. For example, we can distinguish those checks that require the manager to initiate, those initiated to him, and, those that come from reports. All, however, require organizational analyses, that is, a knowledge of the time dimensions of the work-flow system which are to be controlled, prior to the elaboration of the "checking" and "evaluation" procedures.

CORRECTIVE OR STABILIZING ACTION

In moving toward a science of administration we would view the next task of the manager in the control-change sequence as taking corrective actions where significant deviations have been revealed. Here, too, we can be explicit about the interaction pattern required. These are the "short-run" changes. This area is the one usually encompassed by the human relations literature

---

4. There has been inadequate attention paid to the development of a theory of systems control outside of some of the recent efforts of the mathematical statisticians. Eliot Chapple is also concerned with this problem, and his remarks may concentrate on this area.

5. F. L. W. Richardson, *Talk, Work, and Action*, Monograph No. 3, Society for Applied Anthropology, 1961.

when it deals with getting a behavior change. This means the traditional techniques of order-giving, criticism, discipline, training, communication and persuasion (of course, we would insist that these can all be described in operational, interaction terms[6]).

We can, in fact, write sequences of remedial action which the supervisor takes (or should take) in endeavoring to bring the work flow system back to a stable state. Some of these patterns involve outside contacts as well which may serve to bring the system back to normal. For example, the unsatisfactory pacing of the activities of a service department may be creating internal problems. The manager may move through his superior or other channels in seeking to bring the tempo of these activities more in alignment with his needs. Or additional personnel may have to be secured through recruitment channels or permission to work overtime secured from higher management in order to adjust to pressures for increased output. From the point of view of the organization as a whole, the manager operating these controls also must be required to alert his manager and others who may be affected by the departures from equilibrium of his system. This enables them to take complementary actions to avoid having the disturbance spread from the jurisdiction of this manager through the entire organization. All of these actions can be prescribed and quantified interactionally.

ANALYZING RECURRING OR CONTINUING SOURCES OF DEVIATION AND STRESS

Some of the problems with which the supervisor must cope will not be solved by the administrative actions to which we have referred. These are the ones we distinguish as recurring problems. They are the cause of comments like this:

I am always having to go down to engineering and have a battle over specifications — hardly a week goes by in which there isn't an argument here and probably a big meeting as well.

Some are not recurring, they are just never solved. We have referred to these in our recent book as "spiralling" or cumulating deviations.[7] Figuratively an initial source of infection in the organizational system "spreads" to other flows and these, in turn, may react back on the original source, thus adding to the disturbance at that point. These are the so-called major crises or explosions. In either case the detection by the

supervisor that such a problem exists should bring into action additional remedial measures.

The first of these may well be an investigatory pattern. After all, these are the problems which consume inordinate amounts of supervisory time and create major losses to the organization. Their occurrence suggests that some more significant and far reaching change is required than an adjustment in the attention or the immediate activity pattern of the supervisor. So-called staff groups, or consultant-specialists, unfortunately even task force committees, may be used to assess the situation. They come into action, or should be mobilized *only* when the controls maintained by the manager identify this type of problem or when the auditing mechanisms of the staff group themselves so indicate. It is well to note at this point that large, complex organizations frequently assign to staff groups the responsibility for accumulating some of the data that the manager uses for control purposes.[8]

As part of the investigatory process, the manager needs to be intellectually aware of the likely structural sources of stubborn instability. At some future time control mechanisms may be developed which will identify the source as well as the problem. The applied anthropologist has contributed a great number of "classic cases" for such an analysis:

a) Heavily "unbalanced" interaction patterns such as some of the jobs in Whyte's restaurants,[9] and as exhibited by poor supervisors and conflict-laden union-management relations.[10]

b) Unstable or irregular patterns (e.g. Whyte's time-study-man analysis[11]), also other staff positions.

c) Contacts where there is an inadequate frequency of contact (e.g. see Sayles discussion of "Erratic Groups"[12] and Tavistock studies of the

6. Cf. Chapple and Sayles, *op. cit.*, pp. 48–64.

7. *Ibid.*, p. 161.

8. The so-called staff-line problem is usually the result of a failure to organize on this basis. Staff groups go into action and initiate to the supervisor in areas and at times when the supervisor has not agreed there is a significant deviation. Then his dealing with the staff itself becomes a stressful relationship and a time-consuming one. In turn, this is partially the result of the failures of traditional administrative management theory in conceptualizing the staff "role." Apart from its audit functions the staff ought to be measured on its success in bringing deviating systems back to equilibrium — which, in turn, would minimize their conflicts with line managers. For a fuller discussion of this problem see G. Strauss and L. Sayles, *Personnel*, Prentice-Hall, New York, 1960, pp. 399–417.

9. William F. Whyte, *Human Relations in the Restaurant Industry*, McGraw-Hill, New York, 1948.

10. William F. Whyte, *Pattern for Industrial Peace*, Harper & Bros., New York, 1955.

11. William F. Whyte, *Money and Motivation*, Harper & Bros., New York, 1955.

12. Leonard R. Sayles, *Behavior of Industrial Work Groups*, Wiley, New York, 1958, pp. 78–79.

Longwall coal-getting method[13] and the Indian Weaving Shed.[14])

The applied anthropologist has identified these as typical sources:

1) Locations where the manager's jurisdiction have been poorly conceived such that "unit work flows" are broken by the organization. These are interrelated work positions between which a constant "rhythm" needs to be maintained, that is, the parameters of the flow are identical.

2) Service groups outside of these flows which become "scarce resources."

3) Work positions where the requirements of the job are incompatible with personality of the incumbent.

4) Employees in positions which have undergone transformations to which they have not yet adjusted (e.g. the "succession" problem, the change in "status" and power of the nurse or the first line supervisor, and see also the many examples in H. O. Ronken and P. R. Lawrence, *Administering Changes*).[15]

5) "Men in the middle."

6) The impact of organizational innovations such as staff groups or incentives.

This then is an interim requirement for the change process—technical diagnoses of potential organizational trouble spots which can drain managerial time and energy. Beyond the diagnosis the manager has a great deal of work to do. This is the implementation process.

Usually we find that the manager must spend a great deal of time convincing superiors in the organization that a structural or "long-run" change is necessary, even before he gets an opportunity to engage in the difficult job of establishing the change in the organization. Many managers—or leaders—are kept so busy "putting out fires" that they never take on the job of seeking to find the source of recurring blazes. In a sense a rather great capital investment, in terms of time and energy, is necessary to provide a more permanent solution. The manager must take time away from his regular activities to undertake lengthy "selling" contacts with superiors and others plus the major problems of coping with affected subordinates. Many lack the energy and the ability to do this, and this is the major reason why "change" is not introduced at an appropriate rate in the organization, *not* the recalcitrance of subordinates, unions and habits!

IMPLEMENTING THE CHANGE

The traditional human relations literature has also concentrated on the problem of gaining acceptance for structural changes. Here is where one reads about participation and timing, the use of informal leaders, etc. Arensberg, however, again from the point of view of the applied anthropologist, has provided the only clearly operational description of the implementing process.[16]

a) First an increase in managerial initiative to subordinates.

b) Opportunity for increased inter-worker contacts (presumably informal group activity).

c) Followed by an increase in redressive contacts or initiations to the manager (and in turn the manager must be prepared time-wise to accept these).

d) Rewarding managerial responses to these subordinate initiations (often the change period is such a hectic one that time is not available for this step).

In our terminology both (b) and (c) represent compensatory behavior—reactions of the individuals to the stress of changed jobs, managerial contact patterns, etc.

Again these are time consuming patterns of administration and detract from the other commitments of the supervisor. In addition, the organization typically may neglect the more formalized accommodation patterns identified by the anthropologist as easing major dislocations in human patterns of interaction. We have in mind the *rites de passage* and symbolic ceremonies which the community has evolved for such crises.

VALIDATING THE CHANGE

The manager cannot afford to assume that a change he has introduced has actually become part of the operating system. We know that human relations systems tend to return to previous equilibria when pressures are removed which have shifted them away from that position. However, it would be a mistake to assume that all changes are imposed on "comfortable" equilibria, although these are the ones which are grist for the case writers. There are many situations in which people are under substantial stress and

13. E. L. Trist and E. W. Bamforth, "Social and Psychological Consequences of the Longwall Method of Coal-getting", *Human Relations*, IV (1951), 8.

14. A. K. Rice, "Productivity and Social Organization in an Indian Weaving Shed," *Human Relations*, VI (1953), 297–329.

15. Harvard University, Division of Research, Graduate School of Business Administration, Boston, 1952.

16. Cf. Conrad Arensberg and Geoffrey Tootell, "Plant Sociology: Real Discoveries and New Problems," in Mirra Komarovsky (ed.), *Common Frontier of the Social Sciences*, The Free Press, Glencoe, Illinois, 1957.

tension; the organization is not providing them with personal satisfactions, and they welcome change. Whether initially welcomed or not, the manager must utilize methods of appraisal to validate that the change has become stabilized. Essentially this means checking to see that the flow, sequence and coordinating patterns are as planned.

ORGANIZATION CHANGE VS. CONVERSION

It should now be evident that the applied anthropologist's theory of change and administration encompasses both traditional methods of persuasion and influence, usually emphasized in social psychological terms but operationally definable in behavioral, interaction terms, and more long-run or permanent alterations in the organizational constraints. In another work we have chosen to call the former "conversion" by which we meant simply that the manager seeks to convince or persuade a subordinate to shift his behavior in some way and thus eliminate a source of disturbance.[17]

Obviously, this type of administrative activity is important and constantly used. It is involved in the giving of brief orders and lengthy disciplinarian sessions. But the administrator who relies solely on this type of change is ignoring one of the most important parts of his job: seeking out and remedying the persisting and compounding problems. These require, as we have endeavored to illustrate, the introduction of changes in the organizational constraints: the flow of work, the components of jobs, the incumbents on jobs, the structure of authority, the incentives and even the controls themselves that are used.

CONCLUSION

We have endeavored to write an operational description of the change process as an integral part of the manager-leader's day-to-day administrative activities. This analysis lends itself to behavioral quantification and objective validation so that the organization can provide for change within its structure and appraise the success of its members in carrying forth these patterns. Rather than a "last straw", when all else has failed, change, in the applied anthropologist's view, can precede serious crises. Further, administrators can be trained in terms of unambiguous behavioral skills to carry forth such programs.

In our view, the process of change has consisted of these interrelated sequences of managerial action:

1) Specific organizational and technical checks (of prescribed characteristics and frequency) on the stability of the system under the jurisdiction of the manager.

2) Established criteria for evaluating significant deviations from the desired stable state.

3) Prescribed administrative patterns of corrective action to bring the system back to equilibrium. (Short-run change)

4) Appraisals of recurring or continuing instabilities in the system with provision for staff (or specialist) assistance in investigating potential structural sources of organization stress and remedial measures.

5) Administrative patterns for implementing "long-run" organizational structural change.

6) Administrative action to validate the change.

We have purposely ignored the usual shibboleths about starting at the top of the organization and getting "grass roots" support, etc., etc. In our view of change as part of every manager's operational job requirement, this pattern is repeated at each level with adjustments in controls to view the processes below. There is no starting or ending point as such—change is an integral and essential part of all organizational behavior.

What is the implication for this description of the change process in organizations for the growing social concern with the impact of large hierarchical structures on initiative and creativity? It would seem to me that this type of analysis presents a far different prognosis for the role of the individual than the usual political science view of delegated and strictly delimited authority or the psychologists' emphasis on palliatives to reduce the sting of hierarchical power.

In our recent research we have viewed the actual behavior of managers in a very large organization and we find that their organizational positions give them much "leeway" in utilizing their personality skills and energies in meeting the challenges of constant restabilization requirements and the need to initiate to introduce change. The notion that the lower level manager deals passively as a transmitter of orders from higher ups and a feedback mechanism, reporting what is going on below, is just not reality, except where the manager's personality is inadequate to taking the initiative. We would not want, however, to minimize the number in the latter category.

When the organization is viewed as a complex

---

17. Chapple and Sayles, *op. cit.*

series of interlocking patterns of human relationships, work flow patterns and control patterns, the opportunity for the individual to innovate and shape his own environment becomes apparent. Creativity and innovation are a product of the individual's ability to extract the time and energy from the "fire fighting" preoccupations of the moment, in order to modify the pressures and stresses which are being showered on himself and on his subordinates. The hierarchy is no barrier to this—it is, as it has been in every culture—the challenge to the able.

30—How To Practice What We Preach in Making Business Changes

GEORGE S. McISAAC

Corporate files are littered with practical, profitable ideas that never quite materialized. The failure of these ideas had nothing to do with their validity. Instead, it resulted from the fact that some individuals or groups within the corporation withheld their needed support. Their lack of support, which may have ranged from simple apathy to subtle sabotage, effectively undercut these opportunities to effect profitable changes in their companies' businesses.

Is this resistance to change a fact of life that must be accepted as an inevitable barrier to effective adaptation to the changing economic environment? A wide range of experience in helping companies to introduce change suggests that it is not. Management can take some specific steps to facilitate the acceptance and implementation of productive change. In taking these steps, the following considerations appear to be critical:

1. Resistance to change is a normal part of the process of change. Dealing with this resistance, therefore, must be a necessary component of the planning involved in any successful innovation.

2. The ablest practitioners of the art of management have long recognized the nature of this resistance. Indeed, the most successful managers and companies are those who—largely on an intuitive and personal basis—have known how to mobilize support effectively for changes that were vital for success.

3. Recent work in the behavioral sciences on the problems of change has reaffirmed and refined these intuitions and is providing a better understanding of the nature of resistance to change and various approaches to coping with it.[1]

The fact that resistance to change is still a major problem largely results from our failure to make full use of sound management experience and social science discoveries. For example, we have not used the growing body of information that has identified middle management as the locus of much of the problem of resistance. Nor are we using as widely as we might the proven techniques for dealing with the problem at the approximate levels and at the proper time.

As a nation we have an enviable reputation as innovators; our ability to move from theoretical physical science to technical development and production is unsurpassed. However, our skill in building on the intuition-inspired accomplishments of outstanding managers and in applying

"How To Practice What We Preach in Making Business Changes," *Business Horizons*, VI (Summer 1963), 29–36. Reprinted by permission of the author and Indiana University. **George S. McIsaac:** Management consultant, McKinsey & Company, Inc., New York.

1. Research related to these problems continues to progress at many centers both here and abroad. Among them are the Institute for Social Research, the University of Michigan; the Labor and Management Center, Yale University; the Tavistock Institute of Human Relations, London; and the New York School of Industrial and Labor Relations, Cornell University.
A bibliography of the research that has been conducted includes Curt Lewin, "Frontiers in Group Dynamics," *Human Relations*, 1, 5–41; Chris Argyris, *Personality and Organization* (New York: Harper & Brothers, 1957); Rensis Likert, *New Patterns of Management* (New York: McGraw-Hill Book Co., Inc., 1961); Ewing Reilley and Eli Ginzberg, *Effecting Change in Large Organizations* (New York: Columbia University Press, 1957); Peter Drucker, *The Practice of Management* (New York: Harper & Brothers, 1954); Douglas McGregor, *The Human Side of Enterprise* (New York: McGraw-Hill Book Co., Inc., 1960); Norman R. F. Maier, *Principles of Human Relations* (New York: John Wiley & Sons, Inc., 1952); Ronald Lippitt, Jeanne Watson, and Bruce Westley, *The Dynamics of Planned Change* (New York: Harcourt, Brace & Co., 1958); and A. H. Maslow, *Motivation and Personality* (New York: Harper & Brothers, 1954).
The University of Michigan Foundation for Research on Human Behavior has published a study of the general problems of corporate change entitled *Managing Major Change in Organizations*. Surveys specifically directed to EDP changes include American Management Association, *Gaining Acceptance for Major Methods Change*; U. S. Department of Labor, *Adjustments to the Introduction of Office Automation*; Peter McNerney, *Installing and Using an Automatic Data Processing System*; Philip Thurston, *Systems and Procedures Responsibility*; and James D. Gallagher, *Management Information Systems and the Computer*.

the knowledge developed by the social scientists is less developed. Despite our writings and preachings, our record in this area is dismal. As a result, potential major contributions to the problem of effective corporate change lie fallow.

Admittedly, theoreticians are still engaged in vigorous controversy over the present and future directions of this aspect of management practice. On the one hand are the proponents of decentralization and participation; on the other are those who lean toward increased authoritarianism and rigidity. Nevertheless, much can be derived and applied from their discussions, and the need for this application is critical both for the corporation and for the economy.

What needs to be done is a threefold process.

1. Top management needs to go beyond the intuitive approaches to resistance to change and to build upon the recent work of behavioral scientists on the nature of resistance and the means to overcome it.

2. A new insight must be developed at top management levels into programs of action that reach down to the levels of the company where resistance is decisive and the acceptance of change is most critical.

3. The approach to change has to be tailormade to suit the specific personality of the company and the kind of change involved.

AN ENVIRONMENT FOR CHANGE

The kind of change we are talking about ranges across the business spectrum from the introduction of a new piece of equipment to the launching of a new product, from the restructuring of the corporate organization to a methods change on an assembly line. To focus on the nature, cost, and size of the gap between social research and corporate applications of it, however, no better example exists than the recent experience of companies that have installed electronic data processing. All the problems typical of major change are to be found in the conversion to EDP. Introduction of the computer involves shifting organizational responsibilities and changing operating philosophy. The individual's sphere of influence is frequently modified. Work groups are restructured, and new procedures and relationships are required. The effects of EDP are felt at all corporate levels and in the relations between levels.

Furthermore, EDP experience is worth examining because it is based on a large and growing body of knowledge, which is relatively well defined and unequivocal. The process itself is generally understood, and its effects are measurable. The people associated with it—analysts, engineers, programmers, and accountants—are trained in a logical approach. Its use and applications are uniform, permitting exchange and comparison of experience.

And finally, the introduction of EDP will induce great stress in an organization. It places tough demands on the strength of the enterprise and on the skills of its people. In such situations, weaknesses in business structure, policy, and operating philosophy will be clearly exposed.

In short, EDP provides a ready-made opportunity to test the effectiveness with which management is using what we know about the process of change. Significantly, many major industrial users of EDP have failed to recover their investment, and some of these companies have little hope of doing so in the near future. More often than not, the reason is a failure to recognize the introduction of the computer as a typical problem in change. Let us consider two illustrative cases, each a lightly disguised version of actual experience.

In Company X, a multi-plant manufacturer of materials for a process industry, the EDP effort was centralized in a strong corporate systems group staffed by highly competent people. This group was given sole responsibility for identifying areas appropriate for the use of computers and, ultimately, for the EDP operations in all plants.

The systems analysts gathered their own data, including whatever interviews they thought necessary. On the basis of their own analyses, they selected areas for computer applications and decided on methods of development. Then they made their recommendations to corporate management and to division managers. These steps were taken with only nominal help from line personnel.

The line managers felt that the recommendations jeopardized their control, failed to provide for specific sets of circumstances, and were generally unsound. Ignored by the staff specialists, they felt bypassed and degraded. Inevitably, they strongly resisted the program. In the face of this situation, corporate management became reluctant to enforce systems decisions.

What developed was something more serious than the usual staff-line conflict. Communications between line personnel and the systems group deteriorated, and the latter obtained information that was incomplete or simply inaccurate. As a result, the use of computers has been restricted in this company to routine accounting and payroll applications—work that had been done on tabulating equipment for some time. After five years, during which time return on the computer investment has been minimal, the company has had to reorganize its entire EDP effort and start again from scratch.

Company Y, a financial institution, took a much firmer stand in backing its systems group, with results nearly as unfortunate. Here a major methods change from manual and tabulating systems to EDP was conducted in such a way as to discourage all participation below the level of top management. Management in this case took the position that soliciting ideas from people who had been doing the clerical work was a waste of time. Rather, they relied completely on the systems planners. Predictably, considerable ill will arose between the systems group and the operations supervisors. The end results were employee animosity, thinly veiled sabotage of the new system, and continuing high costs. The initial effort at EDP installation was a complete failure. A second attempt, bolstered by a management edict, got the system working but at a high cost and with a residue of resentment against top management and the computer systems group.

In the case of both companies, management knew what it wanted, and the systems analysts and programmers had the technical skill to give it to them. Where they failed was in not eliciting support from those directly affected. And this brings us back to the behavioral scientists' findings on the subject of change.

PARTICIPATION

For years, effective managers have intuitively recognized the basic principles of motivation and used them to achieve change throughout their organizations.

Social psychology has contributed the notion that the best way to create motivation in favor of change is not through discipline or the threat of punishment. Instead they recommend motivational rewards derived from participation in the change process. Management theorists such as Likert, Argyris, McGregor, Drucker, and others have compounded evidence that such participation leads to the most effective change.

In both of the cases cited above, these findings were ignored. Experience with a number of EDP installations indicates that participation techniques are fully and deliberately used in less than one case in five. And yet a trip to the nearest library will yield all that management and the systems analysts need to know about the conceptual basis of participation.

In a carefully controlled analysis of the effects of participation on productivity following a methods change at the Harwood Manufacturing Company in Marion, Va., Lester Coch and John R. P. French demonstrated dramatically the practical value of participation.[2] They isolated four groups of workers who were to undertake a difficult methods change. A control group (1) followed the normal pattern: they were told when and how their work methods would be changed, were trained in the new method, and then made the switch from old to new. Group 2 was told to select representatives to study the problems posed by the need for a methods change. These representatives played a major role in designing new production methods that would meet these problems. In Groups 3 and 4, all participated very actively in the problem-solving process without intermediary representatives.

After the change, the control (nonparticipating) group averaged barely 75 per cent of its previous production rate. Members of the group showed hostility and signs of conflict, and some quit the company. Discipline alone was not enough to make the change successful. Group 2, served by representatives, achieved 115 per cent of previous productivity. Groups 3 and 4, with full participation, reached 125 per cent. Subsequently, remaining members of the control group were retrained under the full participation method, and increased their productivity.

In designing their test, Coch and French had their eyes on some earlier work on the theory of group dynamics done by Curt Lewin and his associates. Lewin, also interested in the relation of participation to change, set out to compare the effects of participation with those of simple instruction. Specifically, he and his associates tried to see what it would take to get midwestern housewives to change their families' eating habits.

To one group of housewives, they gave a lecture, buttressed with facts and figures, explaining that certain changes in their diet would be beneficial. The resulting changes were unimpressive. To the second group they presented a problem: would certain changes in diet help them and their children? Following free discussion, the second group arrived at a consensus that certain changes would be beneficial. The resulting changes in diet were substantial. From his findings Lewin concluded that (1) involvement in the processes leading to a change sets in motion forces that can overcome the inertia of habit and tradition; and (2) participation is a highly effective tool in coping with the problems of change.

2. Lester Coch and John R. P. French, Jr., "Overcoming Resistance to Change," *Human Relations*, I (August, 1948), 512–32.

WHY PARTICIPATION WORKS

Once we have granted the efficacy of participation in securing change, the inquiry naturally turns to how and why it works. Here again any library has a great deal to offer. Maslow, Argyris, and others have approached the subject through their studies on the development and goals of a healthy personality, in which they have related the individual's personality needs to his working life. They have noted that rewards are to be found in the satisfaction of psychological needs, and that the search for these rewards constitutes motivation.

Participation rewards and motivates the individual in three ways:

1. It fulfills the developmental needs of a healthy personality.

2. It promotes security through knowledge of the environment and a sense of control over it.

3. It removes the barriers to change that are based on fear of the unknown.

In the opinion of most behavioral scientists, of the three, the most important is the first, fulfillment of the personality. The normal individual wants to use his skills in thinking and planning, to expand the scope of his awareness and his influence on his environment. He derives satisfaction from the chance to contribute to the solutions of problems, and he welcomes the recognition of his superiors and his peers.

DEVELOPING PARTICIPATION

The problem lies in developing the basic structures and techniques that will give employees this type of recognition.

A parenthetic conclusion to be drawn from the cases described above concerns the normal management practice of securing cooperation through edict. An implied threat often applies enough pressure through fear of punishment to overcome opposition. While this tactic may be effective to a degree in securing change, it seldom produces real involvement. The building of "pro" forces instead of the reduction of "contra" forces engenders increased conflict, and the results are bound to be less than satisfactory.

These tactics fail to recognize sufficiently the importance of an individual within any social structure. This may also be the flaw in the line of thinking developed by Harold Leavitt, who argues that participation techniques are outmoded by new technical developments within the management information field that allow us to bypass the individual and downgrade a segment of lower middle management. Theoretically appealing though this logic may be, it does not appear to be working out in practice. It is in the gap between theory and practical application that the behavioral scientists could be more helpful than they have been. There is little in the literature on specific practical techniques for achieving the kind of participation advocated or the recognition the theoreticians say is essential. Nor have the scientists dealt with such problems as the critical relationship between operative management and the technical staff groups, and the critical role of the supervisory group in corporate change. The importance of these levels of management has been suggested by Paul Lawrence[3] and others, but there has been no definite work on practical approaches to the problems involved.

Management can derive some guidelines, however, from the experience of companies that have successfully applied participative approaches.

PARTICIPATION AT WORK

Let us examine this approach at work in a real-life situation.

Company Z, a major manufacturer of nondurable consumer goods, installed its first computer in 1955. Before the arrival of the computer, a strong systems staff formed. This staff initiated a program designed to familiarize all functional and operating managers with data processing. Most division managers attended a two-day EDP training session. After a few commercial applications were placed on the computer, they were asked to consider whether EDP was desirable in their operations, and, if so, how it should be installed. Concurrently, statistics on clerical costs were circulated, and top management talked up the growing complexity of administrative processes within the corporation. Much of this groundwork was laid informally in the course of normal business and social contacts.

Following preliminary exploration, the problem of how to make a searching yet unbiased study of computer potential was posed by top management to the major manufacturing departments. A study group was created composed of twelve top-caliber (and therefore indispensable) men representing the major units involved. The group had a line to staff ratio of three to one. Detached from their routine responsibilities, they spent four months together and came up not only with recommendations but with a comprehensive, detailed plan on how to move from manual record keeping to an integrated computer control sys-

---

3. Paul R. Lawrence, "How to Deal with Resistance to Change," *Harvard Business Review*, XXXII (May–June, 1954), 49.

tem. In this way, the final recommendations truly involved the line group.

Following delivery of the recommendations, members of the line organization were detached in order to develop the applications of EDP in their areas. Before final plans jelled, successive levels of supervision down to and including foremen and group leaders were educated in the impact of data processing and were asked to contribute to the plans. The opinions of key people in sensitive jobs were solicited and respected. As a result, employees at all levels developed a well-grounded appreciation of the meaning of EDP.

In the experience of one key department, the complex of interests and attitudes thus evoked in the operating personnel produced some remarkably sophisticated solutions to systems problems. The systems designers received unusually good information. Operations people were quick to point out where the design might go astray and frequently suggested major elements of the system. They initiated radical changes in operating techniques to accommodate the computer. Even hourly paid production workers offered suggestions. The operating departments' identification with the change to EDP, and the release from their tension and fear that came with understanding, led to a proprietary desire for success.

The company is now profitably using EDP in distribution, order entry, billing, inventory, process, and production control. Savings from the transfer of routine clerical work are paying for the computer's operating costs, and improvements in customer service, inventory balance, distribution, scheduling, and information feedback are yielding additional return on the company's investment in EDP.

A COMPARISON

A tabular contrast between the methods pursued in Companies X and Y and Company Z underscores the significant characteristics of the participative approach (see Table 1).

Company Z went through four steps before it arrived at the first one taken by Companies X and Y. In this company, top management instinctively knew the value of participation and unobtrusively developed the mechanics on a top-down basis. In order to secure participation, they arranged for early involvement. Many companies engaged in EDP installation look on this practice as extravagant and inordinately time-consuming. These companies—and one has the impression that they are typical—feel that involvement campaigns are

Table 1 METHODS USED IN EDP CHANGE
Companies X and Y
1. Define problem.
2. Gather data.
3. Analyze data.
4. Develop alternatives.
5. Choose best alternative.
6. Recommend.
7. Get management acceptance.
8. Inform those affected by change.
9. Make change.
Company Z
1. Stimulate thinking regarding change possibility.
2. Define area of investigation. Explore need for change.
3. Educate personnel in concepts needed to investigate anatomy of change.
4. Develop mechanics of participation.
5. Define problem in specific terms.
6. Gather data.
7. Analyze data.
8. Develop alternatives.
9. Choose best alternative.
10. Recommend.
11. Make change.

wasted effort. They believe the problem should be tackled by a small group of experts and then presented full blown for acceptance and use. But as we have noted, this approach must rely on the ability of management to enforce change through discipline, which implies authoritarianism and social degradation. The price of such a method ranges from hard feelings to outright failure.

These observations contradict the theory that computers and information technology concepts will recentralize management control, lessen the importance of middle management, and make obsolete the participative approach to management. In practice, the opposite seems to be occurring. Successful computer use seems highly related to the effective involvement of middle management in the application of the computer.

This was illustrated by the example of Company Z, which planned the social aspects of change first and only considered the technical aspects when these plans were in hand. This procedure was more costly and time-consuming during the early stages. It also raised complaints about the time required of the participants. But as the process continued, it became apparent that success was virtually guaranteed and that it required less and less time from top management.

PROBLEMS OF PARTICIPATION

The participative approach, of course, is not free from problems. One of the most important of these is getting the lower echelon manager, foreman, department head, or employee to participate. It is often difficult to arouse interest in a major change before it has taken definite shape, or to create interest without arousing a corresponding bias against the change.

The success of existing techniques for securing involvement depends upon the corporate climate: freedom to explore and criticize is essential, and the effective participant must feel secure. Successful use of participation techniques presupposes certain corporate characteristics. No employee will be inclined to take part in any change unless he is sure it will not turn out to his detriment. This is especially true of changes that may result in transfers or diminution of responsibility. When severe disruption occurs, the people involved must be convinced that the company will make every reasonable effort to protect their interests.

These considerations lead directly to another: the problem of displacement. At the outset of a change, the management must establish, publicize, and adhere to a policy for dealing with severance and reductions in status. In the companies that have been most successful with EDP, this policy has been previously established as part of the corporate human relations package. Specific provisions might include retraining, transfer without loss of income, displacement through attrition, and an attractive severance program.

Two or three decades ago, a current saying had it that management was like a three-legged stool, depending on top-level leadership, staff support, and line involvement. Current change problems could well be treated in the light of some of this thinking—particularly now that the social psychologists have added so much to our store of knowledge regarding the process.

Although some may consider participation a cumbersome concept, Likert calls attention to the undeniable cultural trend in America toward developing more individual freedom and initiative. It will be impossible in our industrial life to buck the cultural process taking place in our schools, homes, and communities toward less use of authority, fewer direct and unexplained orders, and more participation in decision making.

SECTION VIII
CONTROLLING

The concept of control, states Sherwin (#31), is one of the most misunderstood concepts in management. He therefore examines the meaning of this function and provides a basis for understanding it. Anthony (#32) clarifies the process of control and its significance to management.

The evaluation of overall management performance and that of executives in particular is an important facet of control. Martindell (#33) presents a systematic procedure for such evaluation, developed by the American Institute of Management. McGregor (#34) examines the strategy of measuring executive performance and indicates how it can, and often does, lead to serious motivational problems. Tannenbaum (#35) describes a series of studies in order to determine specific supervisor-subordinate relationships and to discover the uniquely organizational dimensions of control.

31 — The Meaning of Control

DOUGLAS S. SHERWIN

"What exactly do you mean by management control?" When this question was asked of a number of managers, in both Government and industry, the answers showed a surprising lack of agreement — surprising, since in a field for which theory has been developed to the extent it has in business management, terms should be precise, specific, and unambiguous. The literature, as one might expect, reflects about the same variety of views as entertained by management men themselves, and so does little to clarify the situation.

Is it important that managers have a clear understanding of this concept? The question almost answers itself. A manager who does not understand management control cannot be expected to exercise it in the most efficient and effective manner. Nor can staff men whose duty it is to design systems and procedures for their organizations design efficient systems unless they possess a clear understanding of management control. And certainly (though the truth of this is seldom sufficiently appreciated) anyone who is subject to control by others has to understand clearly what that means if he is to be contented in that relationship.

Indeed, when management control is not understood, good management is a very improbable result. This is especially true when — as frequently it is — control is identified with management, or is confused with certain devices of management, such as objectives, plans, organization charts, policy statements, delegations of authority, procedures, and the like. The manager who believes managing and controlling are the same thing has wasted one word and needs a second to be invented. And one who believes he has provided for control when he has established objectives, plans, policies, organization charts, and so forth, has made himself vulnerable to really serious consequences. A clear understanding of control is therefore indispensable in an effective manager.

Understanding control really means understanding three principal things about it: What is control? What is controlled? And who controls? By proposing answers to these questions, I will try to frame a concept of control that will be useful to practitioners of the managerial art.

The conception of control which I advocate can be simply and briefly stated as follows:

The essence of control is action which adjusts operations to predetermined standards, and its basis is information in the hands of managers.

We have a ready-made model for this concept of control in the automatic systems which are widely used for process control in the chemical and petroleum industries. A process control system works this way. Suppose, for example, it is desired to maintain a constant rate of flow of oil through a pipe at a predetermined, or set-point value. A signal, whose strength represents the rate of flow, can be produced in a measuring device and transmitted to a control mechanism. The control mechanism, when it detects any deviation of the actual from the set-point signal, will reposition the valve regulating flow rate.

BASIS FOR CONTROL

A process control mechanism thus acts to adjust operations to predetermined standards and does so on the basis of information it receives. In a parallel way, information reaching a manager gives him the opportunity for corrective action and is his basis for control. He cannot exercise control without such information. And he cannot do a complete job of managing without controlling.

As mentioned earlier, some students of management have defined control as what results from having objectives, plans, policies, organization charts, procedures, and so forth; and they refer to these elements of the management system, consequently, as controls or means of control. It is not difficult to understand why these devices of managing are so described by proponents of this point of view. Without objectives, for example, we all know results are likely to be other than desired, so it is assumed they function to control the results. And so it is with the other elements of the system.

Nevertheless, these elements are neither controls nor means of control. They do have, however, as we shall see later, an important role to play in a control *system*, and we can therefore examine them now in a little detail.

Certainly, to accomplish a task except through accident, people must know what they are trying to do. Objectives fulfill this need. Without them, people may work quite industriously yet, working aimlessly, accomplish little. Plans and programs complement objectives, since they propose how and according to what time schedule, the objectives are to be reached.

"The Meaning of Control," *Dun's Review and Modern Industry*, LXVII (January 1956), 45–46, 83–84. Reprinted by permission of the author and the publisher. Copyright 1965, Dun & Bradstreet Publications Corp. **Douglas S. Sherwin:** Assistant Coordinator, Rubber Chemicals Division, Phillips Chemical Company, New York.

But though objectives, and plans and programs are indispensable to the efficient management of a business (or, for that matter, to the management of almost any human endeavor) they are not means of control. Control is checking to determine whether plans are being observed and suitable progress toward the objectives is being made, and acting, if necessary, to correct any deviations.

Policy is simply a statement of an organization's intention to act in certain ways when specified types of circumstances arise. It represents a general decision, predetermined and expressed as a principle or rule, establishing a normal pattern of conduct for dealing with given types of business events—usually recurrent. A statement of policy is therefore useful in economizing the time of managers and in assisting them to discharge their responsibilities equitably and consistently.

POLICY VERIFICATION

Nothing in these advantages, however, makes policy a means of control. Indeed, by their very nature, policies generate the need for control; they do not fulfill that need. Adherence to policies is not guaranteed, nor can it be taken on faith. It has to be verified. Without verification, there is no basis for control, no control, and incomplete managing.

Organization is often cited as a means of control. This detracts both from its own significance and from the concept of control.

Organization is part of the giving of an assignment. The organization chart, for example, is a first crude step in the defining of assignments. It gives to each individual, in his title, a first approximation to the nature of his assignment, and it orients him as accountable to a certain individual. But it is not in a fruitful sense a means of control. Control is checking to ascertain whether the assignment is being executed as intended—and acting on the basis of that information.

The relation between "internal check" and "internal control" is likewise not well understood. The two terms refer to quite different aspects of the managerial system. "Internal check" provides in practise for the principle that the same person should not have responsibility for all phases of a transaction. This makes it clearly an aspect of organization, rather than of control. For how do we provide for internal check? We provide for it through segregating the duties of recording and those of custodianship and assigning them to different employees or groups of employees.

Assigning duties is, of course, the very essence of organizing, and thus internal check is simply organizing in a special way in order to realize special objectives. Internal control, on the other hand, observes the actual performance of duties as against the assigned duties and acts, where necessary, to correct deviations of the actual from the assigned.

Internal check and internal control are obviously both very necessary in an enterprise. But they operate differently. The objective of internal check is to reduce the opportunity for fraud or error to occur. The objective of internal control is to restore operations to predetermined standards. Internal check is thus static or built-in; it is provided before-the-fact; and its operation is preventive in its effect. Internal control, in contrast, is active and continual; it is exercised after-the-fact; and its operation is corrective in its effect.

Assignments are far from defined, however, by the preparation of an organization chart. Among the ways we have for supplementing the titles and lines of authority of an organization chart are delegations of authority. Delegations of authority clarify the extent of authority of individuals and in that way serve to define assignments. That they are not means of control is apparent from the very fact that wherever there has been a delegation of authority the need for control increases, and this could hardly be expected to happen if delegations of authority were themselves means of control.

MANAGER'S RESPONSIBILITY

Control becomes necessary whenever a manager delegates authority to a subordinate, because he cannot delegate, then simply sit back and forget all about it. A manager's accountability to his own superior has not diminished one whit as a result of delegating part of his authority to a subordinate. It is therefore incumbent upon managers who delegate authority to exercise control over actions taken under the authority so delegated. That means checking results as a basis for possible corrective action.

The question whether budgets are a means of control does not yield a straightforward answer because budgets perform more than one function. They perform three: they present the objectives, plans, and programs of the organization and express them in financial terms; they report the progress of actual performance against these predetermined objectives, plans, and programs; and, like organization charts, delegations of authority, procedures, and job descriptions, they define the assignments which have flowed down from the chief executive.

In expressing the objectives and plans of the organization, budgets are of course not means of control, for reasons examined earlier when objectives and plans were considered. Nor do budgets qualify as means of control in their function of defining assignments. Though this service of budgets is frequently overlooked, defining an assignment is neither a means of control nor the exercise of control.

Budgets are a means of control only in the respect that they report progress of actual performance against the program—information which enables managers to take action directed toward bringing actual results into conformity with the program.

In the previous paragraphs I have tried to show that objectives, plans and programs, organization charts, and other elements of the managerial system are not fruitfully regarded as either "controls" or "means of control." They nevertheless do bear a very important relationship to the control function. They are the pre-established standards to which operations are adjusted by the exercise of management control.

It may seem unfamiliar to some to view these devices of management in that light. Perhaps "standards" is not the very best word. Yet these elements of the system are standards in a very real sense, for they have been laid down by competent authority as models or standards of desired performance.

These standards are, of course, dynamic in character, for they are constantly altered, modified, or revised. But for a moment let us give our attention to their static quality.

An objective is static until revised; a plan or program is static until it is abandoned. They possess a kind of temporary durability or limited permanence. They are in force until superseded. This same static quality inheres also in the other elements of the managerial system we spoke of. Policies, organizational set-up, procedures, delegations, job descriptions, and so forth, are, of course, constantly altered and added to. But, like objectives and plans, they retain their force until they are either abandoned or revised.

Suppose, for convenience, we use the phrase "framework of management" to mean all the elements of the managerial system taken together—objectives, plans and programs, policies, organization, and the like. Doubtless, a more descriptive phrase could be invented, but this one at least suggests the notion that there is something of a semipermanent nature in the managerial

system. Now we can in a new way identify what is controlled. Managers control adherence to the objectives, plans, policies, organizational structure, procedures, and so forth, which have been laid down. In brief, managers control adherence to a predetermined "framework of management."

Now we can turn to the very important question that must be answered: "Who should act?"

It has become almost axiomatic as a management principle (which is unfortunately not always given effect in practice) that that person should act who is responsible for the results. "Results" has to be interpreted here in a broad sense. For results include not only profits and costs—obvious items—but the conformity of all operations with all standards. Hence, whoever had responsibility for specifying and establishing a particular standard has to be ultimately responsible for controlling adherence to it and responsible, therefore, for such corrective action as is necessary. Of course, those below him in the chain of command may help him, but they cannot relieve him of final responsibility for control. Therefore, authority for managers to establish standards should be delegated as far down in the organization as practical wisdom permits. It then becomes their responsibility to control adherence of operations to the system they establish.

It is not only a responsibility, but a right; and it is asking for trouble to place in anyone else's hands the responsibility for controlling results in the operating manager's sphere of responsibility.

If the basis of control is information in the hands of managers, "reporting" is elevated to a level of very considerable importance. Used here in a broad sense, "reporting" includes special reports and routine reports; written, oral, and graphic reports; staff meetings, conferences, television screens, and any other means whereby information is transmitted to a manager as a basis for control action. Even the non-receipt of information, as where management is by exception, can be informational and imply the existence of control.

We are often told that reports should be timely and designed to meet the needs of managers. We are in a better position to appreciate this when we realize the important role that reporting plays in the control function. Certainly if it is to be the basis for control, information should be assembled with that objective in view. It should exclude material extraneous to the problem of control and must be placed at the disposal of managers quickly so that operations do not deviate any further from the desired norm—or for a longer period—than can be avoided.

That control occurs after the fact is a point that

sometimes troubles managers. It should not— since this is simply part of the nature of the concept. The situation is entirely comparable in the process control system described earlier. In that system the detecting device continuously evaluates results and transmits them back to the control mechanism, which, sensing the difference between the actual and the desired results, acts to restore results to the desired value. The results, just as in management control, precede the exercise of control. Control systems, human or mechanical, deal with transfers of energy and a transfer of energy takes time. We learn from this—and it underscores the importance of speed in reporting—that all we can do for the management problem is to minimize the time lag between results and action.

CONTROL SPECTRUM

There is another sometimes troublesome aspect of control, namely, that control over some things must be relinquished as successively higher echelons of management are reached. This again we must simply face. Managers in the first echelon require certain information as their basis for controlling. But in the next higher echelon, the character of required information changes; some information is dropped, some is added. There is thus a kind of "control spectrum." For the process of fading out and shading in of information is continued as you move up the pyramid until, just as in the visible spectrum the colors at one end are wholly unlike those at the other, the information reported to the top is wholly different from the information reported to first line managers.

This would hardly be worth pointing out except that some managers are burdened with a persistent sense of insecurity which undermines their self-confidence and ability to do the job, because they are unable to keep track of all the details under their management. Of course, they should not be able to keep track of all the results, or more accurately, should not allow themselves to do so. Relinquishing control over some operations is a calculated risk, taken so that managers can assume more important tasks.

It will bear mentioning that information serves other purposes than as the basis for control. The notion of a "framework of management," which we suggested earlier, is helpful in describing one of these purposes. This "framework," we said, is constantly undergoing change in one or another of its aspects. Such change takes place, not accidentally, but following conscious decisions for change by those responsible for such decisions. And decisions for changes in the framework are based on information that is conceptually different from information used for controlling adherence to the framework.

WHERE FORECASTS FIT

Forecasts and projections, for example, have no place in the problem of control (since control is after-the-fact while forecasts are before) but they are very important for setting objectives and formulating plans. Of course, information for aiming and for planning does not have to be before-the-fact. It may be an after-the-fact analysis proving that a certain policy has been impolitic in its effect on the relations of the company with customer, employee, or stockholder; or that a certain plan is no longer practical; or that a certain procedure is unworkable. The prescription here certainly would not be "control" (since in these cases control would simply bring operations into conformity with obsolete standards), but the establishment of new standards—a new policy, a new plan, and a new procedure—to be controlled to.

Besides furnishing evidence of a need for reconstructing the managerial framework, information is, of course, the basis of all communication. But since that subject is one of the most discussed in the management field today, there is no need to discuss it further here.

Control, we have seen, means something quite specific in the managerial art. This is certainly as it should be in an area of thought as well developed as business management. For in any field for which theory has been developed to an appreciable extent, terms should be precise and unambiguous. Control, when used in a management context, should mean one thing and one thing only. I have suggested that it means action directed toward bringing operations into conformity with predetermined standards and goals; that it is exercised by managers; and that its basis is information in their hands after-the-fact.

In addition to being a specific part of managing, control is also, quite evidently, an extremely important part of managing. In organizations, therefore, where the responsibility for control is not placed in the hands of managers, or not accepted by them, difficulties are certain to arise. Managers must control. Staff members of the organization may, by furnishing information, help a manager discharge this responsibility, but may not share in it. Where this philosophy is adopted by top management as the policy of the organization, the probability is enhanced that the energies of the organization will be channeled in fruitful directions.

TERMINOLOGY

Control is admittedly a term with emotional connotations. The denotation of the term, however, suffers from no such objection. Control is not supervision. Experienced managers perceive that as their authority is broadened, their superiors must place increased reliance on control as a means of safeguarding their own accountability. But at the same time, supervision of their activities by superiors become less close. There seems every reason to believe, therefore, that as the real nature of control becomes better understood, managers will come to recognize that their being subject to it in increasing measure is as sure a sign as any of their progress in the organization and in the fulfillment of their position.

32 — Effective Control for Better Management

EDWARD L. ANTHONY

The term "control" means something affording a standard of comparison, a means of verification, or a check. In small business management, control can be illustrated by these three situations:

A sales manager dictates a letter acknowledging receipt of an order and promising shipment before a certain date. He then asks his secretary to send a copy of that letter to the shipping room with a note: "Please date and return to me when order goes out." That's a control system.

A plant superintendent knows that to meet production requirements, he needs a reserve supply of about 100 small castings which go into his product. He buys in lots of 500 whenever his stock drops to 100. To relieve himself of this detail he has the storage bin divided into a small section which holds just 100 units, and a big section which will take up to 500. Then he assigns the job of keeping tabs on the castings to a stock clerk. The clerk is told to put through a reorder requisition for 500 castings as soon as the last one is removed from the big section of the bin. Production workers are told to hand in a parts-withdrawal chit for each unit they need to take out. Along with the requisition, the clerk is to send to the purchasing agent all the parts-withdrawal chits he has collected. When the new stock comes in, he is to see that the small section of the storage bin is completely filled. Periodically the superintendent inspects the 100-part section to see that there are no empty spaces. That's a control system, too.

A new president takes charge of a small company which produces four separate product lines. The president divides the company into semi-autonomous divisions, each one charged with a specific share of the total invested capital. Each division is also held accountable for earning a 10-percent return on that investment. A system of internal records and reports is set up by which the president can see regularly how each division is making out in terms of earnings as a percentage of sales and turnover — the factors which produce the return. That's also a control system.

TWO BASIC PROBLEMS

In devising effective controls in your small business, you must cope with two basic problems. First, to be of practical value, your system cannot be very costly because a small company cannot afford to be burdened with excessive personnel and overhead charges. This means that your control system should be simple and sparing of manpower.

Second, you must face the fact that almost everybody not only resents the idea of being controlled, but also objects to being judged. More often than not, the targets of a control system are regarded as personal report cards. According to studies made by the Controllers Institute, standards and budgets can be highly unpopular. Many supervisors hate them. They feel, for example, that standards put more and more pressure on

"Effective Control for Better Management," *Management Aids for Small Manufacturers*, No. 79 (Washington, D.C.: Small Business Administration, 1957), pp. 1–4. Reprinted by permission of the author and the publisher. **Edward L. Anthony**: Managerial Assistance Division, Small Business Administration, Washington, D.C.

employees, and more and more emphasis on past performance. Furthermore, these supervisors add, while standards don't show why the goal wasn't reached, they do strengthen the idea that supervisors have to be constantly goaded into greater efficiency. Those points are clear evidence that your control system should be installed with patience and tact so as to be accepted by those who will operate under it. Otherwise, it may not have much success.

The foregoing remarks will, of course, not surprise readers who have been plant supervisors. They will remember well that production men normally think in *unit* figures rather than in *dollars* or *percentages*. Many will also recall how they kept their own brand of back-of-an-envelope data — sufficient to show whether they were making out well enough to satisfy "the front office." Some will even be reminded of the suspicion with which they regarded the findings of statistical experts who depended upon "tabular views and colored charts for analyzing operations they'd never done."

This lack of a genuine meeting of the minds can be a significant road-block to control — particularly in a small plant where single individuals have a big influence on overall performance. In getting rid of this obstacle, plant owners are finding it is the figure man, not the operating man, who must shift his approach.

PRACTICAL BENEFITS

Despite its difficulties, there are practical benefits from control. There *are* ways to make it work better. For example, control often works best where the accounting man works directly with, and reports directly to the production boss. In this way "control" gets the feel of actual "operations" in the shop and reports them with a production viewpoint.

To be sure, many a control person resists this concept because he thinks that its effect is to demote him. On the one hand, the control man may have to turn over much of his authority to the production chief. On the other hand, he may be expected by the top manager to change from a figure specialist to a kind of consultant who knows the score on the whole business. This, of course, is precisely the objective. It may be a trying matter while the changes are being made, but moving from narrow statistical reporting to broad, company-wide figure interpretations can make for effective control and better management.

The payoff may come slowly, but the experience of successful companies proves that it *will* come. To be sure, control by itself will not produce profit; other elements, even good or bad luck, always influence earnings records. But control can help materially to reduce losses where they are occurring and to obtain profits where they are being missed.

TIME NEEDED TO DEVELOP CONTROL

At this point you may well say: "All right, that makes sense as far as it goes. We could use a better control setup. But you say the payoff may be slow. How much time do you really need to get an adequate system working?"

The answer depends on how much control you already have. If your company can build on an existing foundation of good basic records plus some experience with various kinds of budgets, you don't have so far to go. In that case, you can usually expect useful results in a matter of months. If, however, your company must have practice in recordkeeping and reporting, must build up a backlog of historical information, and must gain experience in forecasting, some authorities say you shouldn't expect the new system to be very effective until the third year.

This shouldn't be considered an insurmountable handicap. Every day you work at it you're a little better off than the day before. The key to the problem is to start at once by making some attempt, somewhere. Plan to make adjustments as you go along, and watch developments very closely during the first year.

Whether you set your sights on a 6-month or a 3-year shakedown period, don't attempt too ambitious a program at the start. Undoubtedly, control of individual activities does not have the same benefits as company-wide control. Nevertheless, the best approach is to insist that some progress be made constantly, but that innovations be adopted at a rate which lets your organization absorb each new technique.

You should recognize, too, that the picture brought into focus during the first few weeks by the control system may be disconcerting. There is something merciless about the way a control system shows up failures to reach planned goals. The shock is usually sufficient to produce immediate action on the part of those whose operations fell short. When that happens, watch out for two things: ill-considered, desperate action, and personal resentment. You're bound to get some of both.

Moreover, when goals are not met—especially when a control system is new—review carefully your company's available resources in money, personnel, and so on. If they are not adequate for the goal you set (and cannot be made so) each individual target should be re-analyzed, and your entire plan should be recast.

When you start with a definite idea of what you want to control and what results you want to get, you don't have to wait until all the groundwork is done before seeing evidence of progress. You can set tentative goals and check movement toward them within 60 days after the basic decisions are made.

THE CONTROL PROCESS

One of your main jobs as a manager is to give responsibility and authority to assistants who are capable of using it, but still to retain for yourself the means of assuring that performance is satisfactory. If you are to function effectively as the top man you should spend most of your time on planning, directing, and coordinating. Therefore, you need to be freed as much as possible from routine and detail work.

When they think about it carefully, many managers realize that they often get bogged down in too many authorizations, reviews, and approvals. Much of this sort of thing could be delegated to various subordinates if they were allowed to make final decisions on certain assignments. But much of it *isn't* delegated. Why? Typically, because the top man doesn't dare. He frequently feels that if he wants something done right he must do it himself. Or he frequently believes that he can't safely delegate authority because if a mistake were made things might get out of hand. This reasoning indicates inadequate control.

What is needed is a simple system of rules and limits for action so that things don't get out of hand. The starting point could be any recurring and bothersome task; for example, making out purchase requisitions such as might develop in the parts-reordering situation cited earlier.

Control always involves three ingredients:

The goal, which states what is to be done.

The procedure, which specifies (1) how and when something is to be done, (2) who is to do it, and (3) what makes up satisfactory performance.

The checkup, which indicates how well the job was carried out.

In the parts reordering situation, the goal was to have a reserve inventory of about 100 castings on hand. The procedure comprised setting up a method for recognizing when there were only 100 castings left, putting a clerk in charge of the stock, and telling him to reorder as soon as the last casting was removed from the big section in the storage bin. The checkup was made through typing in the parts-withdrawal chits, the purchase requisition, and the superintendent's inspection. This is a simple case, of course, but even so, all of the essential elements are present.

To set up effective control, you have to decide, first, what you want to accomplish in the long run. Second, you have to figure out how to obtain that result. In this connection, techniques are available which can be adapted to conditions in your individual plant.

For example, to control *wages*, the technique combines sound job evaluation, pay ranges for each classification established in proper relation to outside wage rates, careful review of any proposed exceptions or changes, and regular appraisals of actual performance.

To control *costs*, the technique involves comparing the results of actual operations with standard costs based on optimum conditions in the plant. This, in turn, presupposes some kind of cost accounting to reveal what the actual costs are, and to provide some basis for determining what they should be.

To control *methods and manpower*, the first step is to find out what is now being done, how it is being done, and by whom. Once those facts are established they can be studied to determine the activities that are necessary, the best methods for performing them, the number and type of people required, the proper pattern of organization, and the expected cost.

To control *overall profitability*, the return-on-investment concept is often used. This involves deciding—partly on the basis of past company experience, and partly on estimates of the future—what return the enterprise should make on the capital invested in it.

Here's how that works. Say you have a business worth $1,200,000 and you want to net a return on that capital of 10 percent. This goal means that you must earn profits at the rate of $10,000 each month in order to end the year with your budgeted $120,000. But profits as such are often hard to judge accurately as you go along. Sales figures are much easier to watch. Therefore, you might decide to figure your profits as a percentage of sales for a first step, and then as a second step to relate this figure to return on investment. By that procedure you might find that to earn your budgeted $10,000 profit each month, you needed a monthly sales volume of $200,000—because your net profit on sales consistently ran around 5 percent.

Thus, sales figures of less than $200,000 in any one month would be a signal to look into the causes of the shortage and to intensify efforts to make up for it in future months.

CONTROL BY EXCEPTION

Following out this line of reasoning, you might next break down your goal, say, in terms of individual products. Say you make five items, each of which accounts for about 20 percent of your total revenue. Each then would have to develop a sales volume of $40,000 in every month. You could then ask your bookkeeper to call to your attention *only* those situations where the monthly sales were, say, below $38,000 or above $42,000. In the first case, you would want to find out what the trouble was as soon as possible so that you could take corrective action; in the second case, you would want to see if something could be learned from that success to apply to the other products. This approach is called managing by exception.

TOO MUCH CONTROL?

Much has been said about the evils of insufficient control. A related point also should be raised: Is there a danger of having too much control? The answer is yes.

Not long ago a zealous and methodical manager got interested in controlling the replacement parts his company made and sold for the servicing of equipment which it manufactured. A system was devised and duly inaugurated. To test its merit, only a few large items were included at the beginning. Soon opportunities for savings were revealed. Fired by early success, the manager then insisted that every part be subject to the system. He reasoned that if control was good on a few parts it would be better on all of them.

But trouble was not long in developing. Delays in getting parts (caused by the extra recordkeeping) began to occur much to the annoyance of customers. In addition, such an intensive system was very expensive; in fact, the control cost more than many of the parts being controlled. Ulti-

mately the manager realized that he had built up too much of a good thing and that many small parts should be provided to customers without charge on a service and public-relations basis.

Control can also generate too many reports and records. One good example is the case of the unwanted overhead figures. The boss had decided that "full information" about job costs, including figures on both direct labor and overhead, should be circulated to all his executives. But the overhead figures produced by the control system often involved the use of different rates for estimating, for pricing, and for bidding on various jobs. These differences soon caused confusion and disputes in the engineering section. Furthermore, the cost sheets were seen by some in the shop who could not understand why the final figures on some jobs showed up in red ink, even though the production people had met the estimates on direct labor and materials.

After a period of such misunderstanding, the boss decided that the overhead figures should be eliminated from the cost sheets distributed to the engineering, production, and purchasing sections. The staff members in those sections who formerly saw the overhead figures seemed entirely satisfied not to be bothered with such information.

One production man, for example, said, "The new system is better because we have a straight target to hit. You can't explain overhead control to most shopmen, and they shouldn't be burdened with those figures. They just don't have the background to understand them."

These situations add up to a noteworthy conclusion for small business operators: Keep your control system appropriate and keep it simple.

THE PAYOFF

Effective control will pay off, profitably. In the first place, by showing the owner-manager where his company is heading profit-wise, control can forewarn of danger while there is still time to do something about it. In the second place, control can provide a means to larger, steadier returns on investment. In the third place, a control system which works, is a real asset when new money —either borrowed funds or equity capital—is sought. As Abraham Lincoln put it: "If we could first know where we are and whither we are tending, we could better judge what to do and how to do it."

33 — The Management Audit

JACKSON MARTINDELL

The Management Audit as developed by the American Institute of Management may be defined as a procedure for systematically examining, analyzing, and appraising a management's overall performance. To determine this overall performance, the Management Audit combines the evaluation of ten categories of appraisal, each a determination of the worth of the subject management in one category of the analysis, viewed historically and in comparison with other organizations.

The Management Audit concepts were originally developed as a tool for investment appraisal. Within the past fifteen years, however, their use has been expanded to cover virtually all kinds and sizes of business organizations, as well as nonprofit enterprises ranging from individual hospitals and colleges to the world-wide operations of the Roman Catholic Church.

As applied to a business organization, the Management Audit presents the qualities of the subject management relative to those of other managements in its particular industry, as well as in relation to the finest managements in other industries.

The ten categories of the Management Audit of business organizations are these:

Economic Function
Corporate Structure
Health of Earnings
Service to Stockholders
Research and Development
Directorate Analysis
Fiscal Policies
Production Efficiency
Sales Vigor
Executive Evaluation

These categories do not represent single functions of management, or pure variables.

In actual practice, preparation of a Management Audit of an organization consists of two distinct parts. The first is the compilation of data for analysis and evaluation. To insure completeness as well as comparability with data collected on other organizations, the American Institute of Management uses detailed prepared questionnaires covering management's performance in each appraisal category over a number of years. The information obtained through the Management Audit Questionnaire (questionnaires have been developed for a wide range of industries and types of business) is supplemented by interviews with members of management, directors, and a wide range of others associated with the company as employees, suppliers, competitors, customers, or investing owners. At the same time, material is assembled on the subject company's industry, to provide the comparative basis.

The second actually significant portion of the Management Audit is the analysis of all information obtained. This results in the appraisal of individual categories and, from these, of the overall performance of management. It must be stressed that management appraisal, even with the systematic approach of the Management Audit, cannot be considered a science in the full sense of that word, since subjective judgment ultimately enters the appraisal. One of the values of the Management Audit, however, is the extent to which it permits judgment to rest on the widest possible base of substantive information, and on a uniform and general conceptual foundation. The most basic concept underlying the system is that management, wherever it is found, is *the art of purposeful action.*

ECONOMIC FUNCTION

The category Economic Function in the Management Audit is a unique contribution of the American Institute of Management, assigning to management the continuing responsibility for the company's importance to our economy. In effect, Economic Function determines the *public value* of the company. This value is based on what the company has chosen to do — what products or services it produces — and how it does these things in the moral and ethical sense. It comprises such intangibles as the company's reputation and management's view and enlargement of the purpose of the enterprise. The *public* as referred to in Economic Function includes not merely the consumers of the company's products or its shareowners, but a number of distinct groups, all with varying interests, which the business organization must seek to satisfy (among them, its employees, suppliers, distributors, and the communities in which it operates.)

The fulfillment of Economic Function is cumulative, in the sense that time alone can test a company's public value. A new corporation may

"The Management Audit," *The Corporate Director*, IX (December 1962), 1–4, a paper presented before the Academy of Management at Pittsburgh, Pennsylvania, December 28, 1962. Reprinted by permission of the author and the publisher. **Jackson Martindell:** Chairman of the Board, American Institute of Management, New York.

quickly become an important element in our national life, but until it has endured trade cycles, met competition over the years, developed and replaced its management teams, and earned its reputation among its various publics, it cannot have achieved maximum Economic Function. It is by such outstanding companies as Procter & Gamble and Minnesota Mining and Manufacturing that the public value of new companies must be measured.

CORPORATE STRUCTURE

The category Corporate Structure in the Management Audit appraises the effectiveness of the structure through which management seeks to fulfill its aims. The organization structure of any company must expedite making and executing corporate decisions, must permit control of the enterprise, and must establish the areas of responsibility and authority of its executives. These are requirements that must be met regardless of the specific form of organization a company adopts; the American Institute of Management is not wedded to any particular organizational form in its appraisals.

In actual practice, the real form of organization of a company under study is seldom that of the nominal organization set out on the company's own organization charts. Published organization charts are, in fact, often so inaccurate in depicting the actual relationships and relative authorities within the company that they are of little use to the management analyst.

Companies that have developed product-division or other forms of decentralized organization have maximized the delegation of responsibility and authority, but they have not reduced the need for clear understanding of them throughout the organization. For the most part, corporations decentralize after the lines of authority have been well established; but at times, even large corporations have suffered as the result of a breakdown in the acceptance of exercise of authority. The classic example of this is still that of General Motors Corporation in the early 1920's, when that company suffered an $85 million inventory loss because division executives failed to accept the authority of the principal executives.

HEALTH OF EARNINGS

The evaluation of earnings is concerned with the historical and comparative aspects of corporate income formation, not merely with the income itself. Health of Earnings must determine whether the profit potential of the corporation's assets has been realized in full. (By assets are meant not merely company-owned net equity but, in addition, the assets represented by whatever debt is included in capitalization — the net capital invested. These capital factors are represented in the production process by fixed assets in the form of land, plant, and equipment, or by more liquid assets including actual cash or, more remotely liquid, inventories. No matter what form they take, the paramount question is whether they have been employed at the optimum for the full realization of their potential.)

For both manufacturing and non-manufacturing companies the fruitfulness of capital can be determined by a study of the risk assumed in the employment of resources, in the profit returns upon their employment, and in the nature and distribution of the assets among various categories. Industrial enterprises are particularly suited to this analysis. Although the actual value of their assets (in particular, of their patents and processes) cannot always be determined exactly, one can at least trace the cost of their acquisition, the rates at which they have been depreciated, and the extent to which they have been employed profitably or unprofitably. While prepared information is seldom available for other categories of the Management Audit, the information required in Health of Earnings is usually on public record in a company's annual reports and in digests of its financial structure.

SERVICE TO STOCKHOLDERS

Appraisal of a company's service to stockowners rests chiefly on a three-part mandate that stockholders give the board of directors of corporations: first, that their principal not be dissipated or exposed to unnecessary risks; second, that the principal be enhanced as much as possible through the sound use of undistributed profits, and third, that they receive a reasonable return on the principal in the form of dividends, while their ownership interest is protected through preemptive rights. How well a company satisfies these three requirements determines its *fairness* to stockowners.

In addition, the appraisal covers the obligation that every company has today to provide *service* to its shareowners — primarily, to keep them well enough *informed* so that they can evaluate the progress of their investment in the company and participate in decisions that are likely to affect that investment. Even the financially inexperienced shareholder can review his own relationship with the company to determine whether or not the essentials of stockholder service are present. And while stockholder relations are less vital than sound dividend policies, they indicate a management conscious of its responsibilities—a fundamental of excellent management in any company.

For the specifics of analyzing fairness to stockowners, companies and industries differ too widely in what earnings they can pay out as dividends to set optimum ratios of dividends to net income or other absolutes. Rather, the ultimate return and capital appreciation are the important determinants of fairness to stockowners, not any particular or current percentage.

RESEARCH AND DEVELOPMENT

Because adequate research efforts over a period of years can assure company growth and improvement of its industry position, evaluation of company research policies is crucial to a Management Audit.

Our giant corporations, almost without exception, know the importance of research as a continuing activity, regardless of how well they pursue it. Too many smaller corporations, however, still look upon it with fear, and often do not undertake meaningful research at all. They could benefit immeasurably by greater boldness—if that boldness were based on a clear concept of what research is and can do and a realistic approach to budgeting and evaluating it.

Evaluating research results can show how well the research dollar has been employed, but it does not show whether or not management has realized the maximum from its research potential. For this reason, research must be examined comparatively and historically—in dollars expended, in the number of research workers employed, in the ratio of research costs and staff total expenses and personnel, in new ideas, information, and products turned out. These expenditures, examined with past research results, provide an estimate of management's willingness to employ research for *future* growth and health.

Some companies establish an arbitrary pay-out period to evaluate their own research results. This arbitrary system focuses attention on the need for research profitability, but it may actually discourage future research. The Institute's analysis of research success depends on no formula; it attempts, rather, to determine what part of the company's past progress can properly be credited to research and how well research policies are preparing the company for future progress.

DIRECTORATE ANALYSIS

The company directorate selects and guides operating management in the interest of the business owners and the public. In appraising its effectiveness, the American Institute of Management considers three principal elements:

1. The quality of each director and the contribution he makes to the board.

2. How well the directors work together as a team—whether they complement and stimulate each other. This, of course, is a principal test, since it is the board's actions as a group that affect the company.

3. Whether the directors truly act as trustees for the enterprise.

The trusteeship responsibility of the directorate can best be examined in those areas in which a partial conflict of interest exists between a company's executives and the business owners and public. One of the clearest of these is the area of executive incentives, and how well the directorate resolves compensation and other incentive problems provides an excellent key to its quality.

FISCAL POLICIES

While the fiscal history of a company—the result of all management activity expressed in measurable money terms—is appraised in the category Health of Earnings, past and present financial policies are appraised directly in Fiscal Policies. This category includes three areas of study: the company's capital structure; its organizations for developing fiscal policies and controls; and the application of these policies and controls in different areas of corporate activity. The key problems are providing, controlling, and husbanding funds.

PRODUCTION EFFICIENCY

Evaluating production efficiency has obvious importance in appraising a manufacturing company. What is not so widely understood is that production efficiency or its equivalent, *operating efficiency*, is equally vital to non-manufacturing companies, whether they are in banking, insurance, transportation, communications, electric or other power, or any other field in which the end product is not a tangible good. Virtually all companies which are not merely agents for other companies must obtain and process some good or service before marketing it. This is the field of a company's overall operation evaluated in the category Production Efficiency.

The analysis of present-day production management must be divided into two parts. The first of these may be termed the appraisal of "machinery and material management," since it evaluates the mechanical production or processing of the company's products. This one part is often overemphasized, so that management's mastery of its machinery appears the major factor in production efficiency. However, a second aspect of production evaluation, that of "manpower management," is equally important. This facet of operations properly includes all personnel policies and practices for non-sales and non-executive employees developed by management. Only when both aspects are analyzed can overall production in operating efficiency be appraised.

SALES VIGOR

Within single industries and even within single companies sales practices can vary broadly enough to represent different marketing principles. Between different industries the variations are often still greater. Yet the comparative appraisal of sales vigor must encompass all the forms that marketing can take — must, for example, enable the management analyst to compare the vigor of Procter & Gamble's consumer sales program, with its multimillion dollar advertising budget and scores of millions of customers, with the effectiveness of North American Aviation's sales essentially to one customer, the United States government.

Sales Vigor can, of course, be appraised despite these variations, but only after the marketing goals of each subject company have been determined and assessed. These goals, in turn, must be appraised in terms of the overall goals of the entire organization. Then, as with other categories of the Management Audit, historical and comparative evaluation become possible, and how well past sales potential has been realized and how well present company sales policies prepare it to realize the future potential can be appraised. The treatment of sales personnel usually belongs in this category.

EXECUTIVE EVALUATION

Executive Evaluation is the most important single appraisal category of the ten that comprise the Management Audit. To a degree, of course, the other categories in this system of management appraisal also evaluate the organization's executives, since they appraise the results of executive thinking and action in each management function. But the quality of the executives themselves, their management philosophy, and the appropriateness of both to the purposes of the organization must still be appraised directly.

The American Institute of Management has found three personal qualities — ability, industry, and integrity — to be the essential elements for the business leader. These provide a framework for his evaluation in the Management Audit and should also be the criteria of the organization's leaders in selecting and advancing executives. Excellent management requires that executives work together in harmony, each with specific tasks contributing to the total effort, conscious that he is participating in this effort with men who command his respect. As a group, the executives must regard the continuity of the corporation as an important goal, assuring it by sound policies of executive selection, development, advancement, and replacement. A key problem is to assure sound succession in depth.

UNIVERSALITY OF EVALUATION

The principles of the Management Audit remain valid regardless of the nature of the enterprise. All human activity is confronted with the same management problems. When two or more individuals get together in any common endeavor, wanting the best possible result, they must ask, "What shall we do, and how shall we do it?" In order to get good results, whether they are aware of it or not, they must follow fundamental tenets of management, which can be appraised.

SOCIAL FUNCTION

Whatever the undertaking, its impact upon the public welfare must be helpful rather than harmful. In the affairs of a church society, this value may be termed Social Function. In an educational institution, it is Academic Function. The principles of evaluation remain the same.

ORGANIZATION

The activities of two or more individuals — members of a management team once they unite in a common venture—create lines of authority and responsibility. They may be adjusted as the organization grows in size and consequence and progresses with its undertakings, but the extent to which authority and responsibility are made clear provides a basis for evaluation.

GROWTH

The enterprise must exhibit growth of facilities, whether these come from gifts or profits derived from merchandising goods or services. The health of that growth can be appraised.

MEMBERSHIP

Members, shareowners, or proprietors of an enterprise are encouraged to cooperate and contribute, whether through dividends or less material rewards. How this is done is a matter of techniques peculiar to the kind of enterprise and varying with circumstances and time. But that it shall be done activates fundamental management principles and permits evaluation of its effectiveness.

RESEARCH

Management of whatever kind seeks the most reliable, comprehensive, accurate, and up-to-date information available. Research and development includes study of any phase of group activity with a view to betterment of either principles or techniques.

FISCAL POLICIES

The financial and other resources of any group effort are the life blood of its activity. Where they are obtained—and obtained in proper quantity—the enterprise can continue to exist and grow. How well resources are found and used can be appraised. Fitting financial policies and practices to the immediate and long-term needs that experience indicates and then altering them as the result of study or alertness is a management principle closely related to survival.

TRUSTEESHIP

Whether called trustees, directors, or guardians, those overseeing an undertaking have the responsibility of determining its leadership. In this way they exercise the power of the organization. Appraisal can be made of how well they recognize that their authority needs the sanction of morality and creates obligations to assume responsibility for the welfare of the total enterprise, including the public and all individuals concerned.

OPERATIONS

The operation of an undertaking has a degree of effectiveness no matter what the product, service, or purpose. This is true even within the areas of charitable, social, political, and spiritual endeavors. Every organization, then, has production or operating problems, just as it has a research need; it must understand and solve these problems to be well managed.

SALES

Everyone is concerned with persuading others to accept him, his services, his products, or his ideas, whether doctor, lawyer, merchant or priest. Every group activity must be sold or merchandized if the enterprise is to grow and prosper. The techniques to accomplish this vary with the enterprise, the occasion, and the purpose, but they can be assessed in terms of how well they persuade prospective purchasers, joiners, or whatever.

LEADERSHIP QUALITY

The quality of the leadership in any enterprise is the most important single aspect of the activity. The success of the executive group and the activity may depend on their integrity, ability, and industry, their devotion to the enterprise, their acceptance of responsibility, and their foresight in providing continued leadership after themselves. These qualities, all of which can be appraised, are not limited to the profit making corporation—they are fundamental wherever men join together for a common purpose, whatever the inspiration and the motive—commercial, divine or other.

In conclusion, administrative evaluation must recognize that for an organization to be well managed, it must have sound purposes and use good techniques. To be excellently managed, it must fit these techniques and practices within the framework of true administrative principles.

34 — Can You Measure Executive Performance?

DOUGLAS McGREGOR

Performance appraisal is often perceived simply as a technique of personnel administration. But where it is used for administrative purposes, it becomes part of a managerial strategy, the implicit logic of which is that in order to get people to direct their efforts toward organizational objectives, management must tell them what to do, judge how well they have done, and reward or punish them accordingly.

This strategy varies in detail from company to company, but in general it includes the following steps:

1. A formal position description, usually prepared by staff groups, which spells out the responsibilities of the job, determines the limits of authority, and thus provides each individual with a clear picture of what he is supposed to do.

2. Day-by-day direction and control by the superior within the limits of the formal position description. The superior assigns tasks, supervises their performance and, of course, is expected to give recognition for good performance and criticize poor performance, correct mistakes, and resolve difficulties in the day-to-day operation.

3. A periodic, formal summary of the subordinate's performance by the superior, using some kind of a standardized rating form. Typically, the rating will include judgments concerning the quantity and quality of the subordinate's work; his attitudes toward his work and toward the company (loyalty, cooperativeness, etc.); such personality characteristics as his ability to get along with others, his judgment, and his reactions under stress; and overall judgments of his "potential" and of his readiness for promotion.

4. A session in which the superior communicates his judgments to the subordinate, discusses the reason for them, and advises the subordinate on ways in which he needs to improve.

5. The subsequent use of the formal appraisal by others in the administration of salaries, promotions and management development programmes.

METHODS OF JUDGMENT

Variations of these procedures are utilized to improve the objectivity of the superior's judgments, to increase comparability of judgment among different superiors, and to improve the fineness of discrimination. For example, some plans utilize multiple judgments obtained independently from several superiors or developed in a group setting; some utilize the "forced choice" method in which a series of quite specific judgments are translated into general scores (the superior does not know the weighting of individual items and presumably does not know how he has evaluated the subordinate until the results are calculated). Many companies conduct programmes for training superiors in rating procedures and in counselling techniques.

Appraisal programmes are designed not only to provide more systematic control of the behaviour of subordinates, but also to control the behaviour of superiors. For example, it is believed that an appraisal programme will force the superior to face up to problems of poor performance and deal with them, and that it will force him to communicate to his subordinates his judgments of their performances.

A considerable amount of experience has accumulated with respect to the way in which this general strategy tends to work out in practice. How well does it achieve its purposes?

First, formal position descriptions provide management with an orderly picture of the organization and the comfortable conviction that people know what they are supposed to do. They establish formal chains of command and they delimit authority so that people will not interfere with each other. Position descriptions are a basis for an equitable salary classification scheme, provided it is recognized that at best they yield only a rough picture of reality.

CHANGING SKILLS

However, they are not a particularly realistic device for telling people what to do. Within the managerial hierarchy it is doubtful that any job is performed the same by two successive incumbents, or by the same incumbent over any long period of time. Not only do conditions change, but so do skills and relative abilities, and perceptions of priorities. Companies would utilize less of their human resources than they now do if man-

"Can You Measure Executive Performance?" *International Management*, XX (June 1964), 59 – 61, 63. Reprinted by permission of the author and the publisher. This article is based on material taken from *The Human Side of Enterprise* by Douglas McGregor. Copyright © 1960 McGraw-Hill, Inc. Used by permission of McGraw-Hill Book Company. **Douglas McGregor:** School of Industrial Management, Massachusetts Institute of Technology.

agers were to adjust to their position descriptions rather than the other way around.

Management at middle and lower levels makes little actual use of position descriptions. Typically, they are glanced over when they are received in order to determine whether they coincide with common-sense preconceptions, and then they are filed away and forgotten. Many research studies show up substantial differences in the perceptions of subordinates and superiors concerning the requirements and priorities of the positions of the former. Position descriptions do not often produce the clarity of understanding they are designed to provide.

Organizations which really attempt to use position descriptions for control purposes (government agencies, for example) stimulate a substantial amount of managerial behaviour the primary purpose of which is to defeat the system. The juggling of position descriptions by managers to enable them to do what they want to do—hire a particular person who does not fit a classification—make a salary adjustment, legitimize a promotion—is a common phenomenon in such organizations. The neat systems are often rendered ineffective by these countermeasures.

PARTICIPATIVE APPROACH

Organization planning groups sometimes attempt to eliminate these difficulties by a participative approach in which individual incumbents of jobs are encouraged to help the staff by contributing their own knowledge to the writing of the job description. While this process undoubtedly reduces the resistance to the whole idea, it is doubtful whether it results in greater use of the position descriptions themselves for direction and control of behaviour.

The dimensions of a managerial position can be precisely defined only for a particular incumbent in a particular set of circumstances at a given point in time. Among the variables which affect the "shape" of the position are the following:

1. The way in which superiors, subordinates and colleagues are performing their jobs. The position of a sales vice president, for example, will be vastly different if the president of the organization has had his major experience in sales than it will if the president's experience has been in research or in manufacturing.

2. The individual's qualifications. These include his experience and competence which change over time and thus lead him to perceive the requirements of his position differently and to perform differently.

3. The individual's personal interests. These are related to, but not identical with, his qualifications.

4. The individual's assumptions about his role as a manager. His position will be different depending upon the degree to which he delegates responsibility, for example.

5. The constantly changing requirements of the external situation. Economic conditions, peculiarities of the market, political circumstances, competitive conditions, and a host of other variables require changes in performance which affect the nature of the job.

Apart from providing guides for salary administration and some help in hiring and placement, the chief values of position descriptions are (1) to satisfy the needs of organization planners for order and systematization, and (2) to provide reassurance to top management that everyone has a piece of paper which tells him what to do. The danger is that both these groups will make the mistake of assuming that the descriptions represent reality.

PROCESS SUCCESS

Let us consider now how well the appraisal process itself achieves its purposes. One of these purposes is administrative: the results of appraisal are used for salary administration, promotion, transfer, demotion and termination. There are difficulties here, too.

In the first place, the problem of variation in the standards of different judges has never been completely solved, nor have we succeeded in eliminating the effects of bias and prejudice in making appraisal judgments. These variations among judges will be greater or smaller depending upon the particular method of appraisal used (whether it involves multiple judgments, for example) and the amount of training given in its use, but they remain substantial nevertheless. The answer given by an appraisal form to the question: "How has A done?" is as much a function of the superior's psychological make-up as of the subordinate's performance.

If we then take these somewhat questionable data and attempt to use them to make fine discriminations between people for purposes of salary administration and promotion, we can create a pretty picture, but one which has little relation to reality. Using fairly simple procedures, and some safeguards against extreme bias and prejudice, it is probably fair to say that we can discriminate between the outstandingly good, the satisfactory and the unsatisfactory performers.

When, however, we attempt to use the results of appraisal to make discriminations much finer than this, we are quite probably deluding ourselves. The fact is that many salary administration and promotion plans use appraisal results to make discriminations considerably smaller than the margin of error of the original judgments.

JUDGING PERFORMANCE

The problem of judging performance for administrative purposes is further complicated by the fact that any individual's performance is, to a considerable extent, a function of how he is managed. For example, the individual who operates best when he is given quite a bit of freedom may find himself under a superior who provides close and detailed supervision. Under these conditions, even the most objective measures of his performance will provide a better basis for judging his boss than him!

Finally, it is relatively easy to find evidence that the judgments which managers make of their subordinates' performances differ depending upon whether they are used for administrative purposes.

It would seem to be a fair generalization that performance appraisals are something less than a perfect tool for administering salaries, promotions, transfers and terminations. What about their value in achieving their informative purpose? Are they an adequate means for letting the subordinate know where he stands?

It is characteristic of human beings that they find it difficult to hear and accept criticism. Judgments which are positive can perhaps be communicated effectively, but it is rather difficult to communicate critical judgments without generating defensiveness.

This difficulty with the appraisal interview is well illustrated by a common dilemma. If the superior attempts to communicate his criticism in the form of abstractions and generalities, he is likely to be asked to be more specific, to give illustrations.

The subordinate feels that the generalizations do not give him a sufficient basis for correcting his behaviour. If, on the other hand, the superior attempts to communicate in terms of concrete illustrations, he is likely to find himself on the defensive as the subordinate attempts to show that there were extenuating circumstances surrounding any illustration which he brings up.

In attempting to communicate criticisms to a subordinate the superior usually finds that the effectiveness of the communication is inversely related to the subordinate's need to hear it. The more serious the criticism, the less likely is the subordinate to accept it. If the superior is insistent enough, he may be able to convey his negative judgments to a subordinate, but when this happens he often finds that he has done serious damage to the relationship between them.

Since the appraisal interview is an important occasion during which the attempt is made to give the subordinate a rather complete evaluation, it carries substantial overtones for him. It accentuates his dependence and thus readily arouses latent anxieties and hostilities. Critical judgments in this setting mean far more than when they are made with respect to specific incidents in the day-to-day relationship. Criticism of the latter type does not threaten the person himself as do the more general evaluative judgments communicated in connection with a formal appraisal, and they are easier to hear and respond to.

AN OPEN QUESTION

It is an open question whether subordinates in general really want to know where they stand. It is true that when asked, the great majority will insist that they do want to know. However, it is possible to interpret this expressed desire in several ways.

It may mean, for example, "I don't know whether my boss feels I am doing an adequate job because he says so little about my performance in our day-to-day relationship. I feel I am doing well, and I would certainly like to know whether he feels the same way."

This is not necessarily the desire for a cold-blooded, objective evaluation. It may be an expression of anxiety and a need for reassurance. If, in fact, the individual is doing well, and the evaluation involves only minor criticisms, the appraisal interview may fill the need. If the individual is not doing well, the interview will intensify the anxiety and make it extremely difficult for him to react realistically.

There is still another aspect of the appraisal interview as a communications device. Since most appraisals involve the superior's evaluation of attitudes and personality traits, in addition to objective performance, there is an invitation inherent in the situation to invade the personality of the subordinate. Recognizing the delicacy of this situation, many managements encourage the superior to use the interview for "counselling" purposes.

It can be stated categorically that few managers are competent to practise psychotherapy. Moreover, the situation of the appraisal interview, in which the superior is in the role of a judge, is the poorest possible one for counselling. The effective counselling relationship is one in which the counsellor is a neutral party who neither criticizes nor praises, and whose concern is solely for the health and well-being of the client.

To attempt to counsel in a formal appraisal interview is as much a travesty as to attempt bribery of a victim during a holdup. The manager, in making judgments about a subordinate, is in effect implying that the person needs to change his behaviour in certain ways, and clearly in the minds of both is the recognition that the superior is in a position to punish him if he does not change.

Surely this is not a situation for effective counselling, even if the superior is skilled in psychotherapy. The role of judge and the role of counsellor are incompatible.

EFFECTIVE MOTIVATION

Finally, consider the motivational purpose of appraisal. The common-sense assumption is that telling an individual where he is falling down will provide effective motivation to get him to change. Clearly it will not do so unless the person in question accepts the negative judgment and agrees with it. We have already seen that this is not too likely a possibility. Contrast the situation in which a subordinate is evaluating his own performance relative to specific targets which he set a few months ago with the situation in which he is listening to his superior evaluate his performance against the superior's standards and objectives. In the latter case, the stage is set for rationalization, defensiveness, inability to understand, reactions that the superior is being unfair or arbitrary. Most certainly, these are not conditions conducive to effective motivation.

35 — The Concept of Organization Control

ARNOLD S. TANNENBAUM

One of the advantages of programmatic research is the ability to pursue important problems through a series of related projects. The results of one study, and particularly the questions which it raises, contribute to the formulation of further research through which greater refinement and understanding can be achieved. This process has been applied by the Human Relations Program to a number of problems. We shall be concerned with the programmatic exploration of the concept of organizational control.

The importance of the control function stems both from its universality and its many implications for the way in which organizations behave. The widespread interest in "authoritarian-democratic" leadership, "centralization-decentralization," "flat" and "tall" organizational structures, "close" versus "general" supervision, and "joint management" reflects an interest in the effects of variation in patterns of control.

Several assumptions underlie our interest in control. The orderliness and predictability of organizational functioning is predicated on the regulation of individual behavior in conformance with organizational purposes. Control also has a number of psychological bases and implications. For example, numerous assumptions are made about the motivation toward power in organizations and many examples have been cited in support of the view that the lust for power is a primary and implacable drive.[1] While there may be some validity to this view, we cannot ignore the essentially pragmatic implications of control. Control for many is basically an instrumentality toward the achievement of rewards dispensed by the organization. These rewards fall into two categories: (a) rewards which accrue to, or simply parallel positions of control (for example, in many organizations positions of increased control are accompanied by increased prestige and remuneration); and (b) rewards which result through the exercise of control as a means toward some other end (for example, persons in control are able to influence the organization in a direction favorable to themselves or to some broader cause which they avow). The former is a fixed attribute of the role, likely to be more prominent in

"The Concept of Organization Control," *The Journal of Social Issues*, XII, No. 2 (1956), 50–60. Reprinted by permission of the author and the Society for the Psychological Study of Social Issues. **Arnold S. Tannenbaum:** Human Relations Program, Survey Research Center, University of Michigan.

1. See, for example, Bertrand Russell, *Power: A New Social Analysis*, London: George Allen and Unwin Ltd., 1946.

bureaucratic types of organizations. The latter is a variable function of the role, depending to a great degree on how the actor plays it. It is illustrated in some labor unions and political associations.

Finally, our interest in control reflects the assumption that in many formal organizations an individual's role in the control structure is a pervasive aspect of his larger role within the organization: a significant segment of his activities is subject to control or is concerned with the exercise of control. In so far as this is true, the nature of the control structure should have important implications for the adjustment of individuals to their work and for other aspects of the functioning of the organization.

Research on the question of organizational control within the Human Relations Program has addressed itself to two related questions: "How can we best describe and conceptualize the structure of control in organizations?" and "What are the implications of varying patterns of control?" It is primarily with the former that we shall be concerned in the present paper.

Approaches to the study of control in this program have developed through a number of stages. The first, which derived out of an interest in supervisory practices, suggested some implications for subordinate behaviors of the control exercised by the supervisor. The second went beyond the dyadic, supervisor-subordinate relationship in recognizing some of the uniquely organizational qualities of the control function. It proposed as one important index of organizational control the relative influence which the rank and file exercise as compared to that exercised by supervisors and upper hierarchical levels. The third extended this conceptualization to account explicitly for two aspects of organizational control: its hierarchical distribution and its total amount in the organization. The fourth added the notion of the hierarchical sociometry of control: which hierarchical levels exercise how much control over which. '

EARLY STUDIES[2]

Early programmatic treatment of the control variable was largely in terms of the interpersonal relationship of the supervisor and his subordinate. A number of relevant aspects of the supervisor's role were examined, including the amount of time he spent directing and planning the work as contrasted to the time spent simply working along with the men, the pressure which he applied to his subordinates, the extent to which his direction of the men was close and specific rather than general, and his satisfaction with his authority. Analysis of these qualities for supervisors of high as compared to low producing work groups produced a number of interesting differences. As the previous article has pointed out, the "effective" supervisor was found to differentiate his role as a leader from his role as a work group member; he spent his time regulating, planning, and coordinating the activities of his men rather than participating in the operation of the work group. He was found, in other words, to perform a distinct control function. Furthermore, the effective supervisor was found to be more satisfied with the amount of authority he had in his job — apparently because he had more.

In addition to these facts, the effective supervisor was found *in some cases* to exercise his control in a different manner than the ineffective supervisor. He did not pressure his men; he was not punitive; and his control was general rather than "close" or specific.

These early studies were largely an attempt to apply psychological conceptions to an organizational setting. Since the focus was primarily on supervisory practices, they did not attempt initially to define the control process in organizational terms nor to integrate this process with the larger pattern of events within the organization. Furthermore, they emphasized one side of the supervisor-subordinate relationship: the way in which the supervisor exercised control over the subordinate. It soon became apparent, however, that the supervisory role ought to be viewed in the context of its larger organizational setting. For example, whether or not the supervisor pressures his subordinates seems to be affected by whether or not the supervisor himself is subjected to pressure from his own superiors. Further analyses also demonstrated the importance of the supervisor's power in his department. The supervisor's influence over higher management, as well as his autonomy in running his work group, act to condition the effects of supervisory practices on subordinate reactions. For example, an expression of praise from a low-influence supervisor may be ignored or even resented by his subordinates, whereas the same expression from a high-influence supervisor would produce a highly favorable response.[3]

These early studies led to the general conclu-

2. Daniel Katz, Nathan Maccoby, and Nancy C. Morse, *Productivity, Supervision and Morale in an Office Situation*, Part 1. Survey Research Center, University of Michigan, 1950. Daniel Katz, Nathan Maccoby, Gerald Gurin, and Lucretia G. Floor, *Productivity, Supervision and Morale Among Railroad Workers*. Survey Research Center, University of Michigan, 1951.

3. Donald C. Pelz, "Leadership within a Hierarchical Organization." *Journal of Social Issues*, 1951, 7, No. 3, 49–55.

sion that an understanding of the control exercised by supervisors requires a broad view of the supervisory role, a role which is embedded in the larger context of the organizational control system. The supervisor has authority only to the degree that authority is delegated to him from above. The pattern of control exercised by the supervisor, or any hierarchical group, is part of a larger system of delegations, and it is this larger system of control which was considered the essential variable in the clerical experiment.

THE CLERICAL EXPERIMENT[4]

Three aspects of the control process were considered in defining the control variable in this experiment: the legislative phase, which is concerned with basic decision making; the administrative phase, which is concerned with the day to day expediting of legislative decisions; and the sanctions phase, which involves the punishment of non-conformity. Furthermore, these phases of control were conceived as being exercised relative to a number of "systems" or functional units (such as the work assignment system, work measurement system, the vacation system, the promotion system, etc.) which comprise the structure of the organization. Thus the independent variable was concerned with control (legislative, administrative, and sanctions) of the various company systems. It was measured through judgments of employees in terms of both *degree* and *location*: how much control resided with the rank and file, and how much resided with company personnel above the rank and file level. The ratio of control exercised by upper levels relative to that exercised by the rank and file group was chosen as the operational index of the independent variable. The experimental design involved the creation of two large work programs (in a clerical department) which differed on this independent variable.

The definition of the independent variable was such as to require changes not only at the rank and file level, but through an extended segment of the company hierarchy. In one program, the lower level employees were given a greater degree of control over many of the things which affected them. This was achieved through a series of delegations of control from the department head through the division managers, section heads, first line supervisors to the employees as a group. In the other program there was a greater concentration of control at upper hierarchical levels. The programs were thus made to differ in their ratios of "hierarchical" to rank and file control.

This experiment affected the study of control in a number of ways: Control was defined as an organizational rather than a purely interpersonal process. Groups rather than individuals were defined as the possible control agents. Control was conceived as being oriented not simply over individual action but over broad company systems. Furthermore, any specific act of control was seen as part of a larger pattern of control within the organizations. The control exercised by one group was to be understood in relation to that exercised by others, and the ratio of rank and file control relative to control exercised by all other hierarchical levels was considered an important organizational index.

The experiment also raised a number of questions regarding the conceptualization of control. While the importance of the hierarchical distribution of control was recognized and measures of the control exercised by the various hierarchical levels were obtained, an adequate representation of this hierarchical pattern was not provided. The ratio of employee to officer control which served as the operational index of the independent variable considers only two elements in the hierarchy: the rank and file as a group and all those above the rank and file as a group, thus obscuring the distribution of control within the hierarchy. Furthermore, the ratio gives no indication of variations in absolute amount of control. It is not affected by proportional changes in the amount of both the rank and file and officer control.

The development of the control concept employed in a study of four local unions benefited directly from the notions provided in the clerical experiment. It represents an attempt to reconcile some of the operational advantages suggested by the experiment with some of the more common characterizations of control in unions.

THE UNION STUDY[5]

The terms "democratic" and "autocratic" have probably been applied more frequently to unions than to any other type of social organization. Such concepts, of course, have many weak-

4. Nancy C. Morse, Everett Riemer, and Arnold S. Tannenbaum, "Regulation and Control in Hierarchical Organizations." *Journal of Social Issues*, 1951, 7, No. 3, 41–48. Nancy C. Morse and Everett Riemer, "The Experimental Change of a Major Organizational Variable." *Journal of Abnormal and Social Psychology*, 1956, 52, 120–129.

5. Arnold S. Tannenbaum and Robert L. Kahn, "Organizational Control Structure: A General Descriptive Technique As Applied to Four Local Unions." *Human Relations* (in press). Arnold S. Tannenbaum, "Control Structure and Union Functions," *American Journal of Sociology*, 61, 536–545.

nesses: they form a typology (class theoretical), they are often valuational, and they rarely have operational referents. Their wide use, however, does have at least two important implications. It recognizes the general importance of the control process, and it represents an attempt to characterize the *total* organization. The union study extended some of the notions of the clerical experiment in an attempt to encompass what appear to be the essential elements of these commonly used concepts, and to provide a more holistic description of organizational control.

In the union study, organizational control structure was described in terms of two axes of a graph. The horizontal axis of this graph represents the various hierarchical levels in the organization, from low to high. In the local unions, for example, the rank and file were placed at the low end of this axis and the president was placed at the high end. Other officer groups (the executive board and the bargaining committee) were placed at intermediate levels. The vertical axis represents the amount of control which is exercised by each of these hierarchical levels. Thus each level can be represented in terms of the amount of control it exercises over the affairs of the local. Various shapes of curve might be generated from these axes depending on the amount of control which each level has.

In the locals under study such curves were drawn on the basis of ratings which a representative sample of members gave in response to questions dealing with the amount of control which each hierarchical group exercised over the affairs of the local. Application of the control graph notion in the four local unions, and subsequently in a large industrial service organization has revealed a variety of curve shapes, including curves which rise with hierarchical ascent (said to describe the "oligarchic" or "autocratic" model), curves which decline with hierarchical ascent (said to describe the "democratic" model), and those which remain fairly flat.[6] Furthermore, the decentralization which characterizes the specific industrial plants studied was represented by a rise in the curve until the top of the hierarchy (located in the central office) was reached, at which point the curve declined.

Two aspects of organizational control structure are evident from the control curves: (a) the hierarchical distribution of control, represented by the shape of the curve, and (b) the total amount of control instituted in the organization, represented by the general height of the curve. The fact that these dimensions may vary independently emphasizes the importance of distinguishing them. Organizations, for example, might have the same general distribution of control, while the amount of control exercised within them differs sharply. On the other hand, organizations might be equal in the amount of control exercised over members, but might differ markedly in the way the control is distributed. Such variations have been found among the organizations to which the control graph has been applied.

THE INDUSTRIAL SERVICE ORGANIZATION STUDY[7]

A further innovation in the control graph technique which has been applied in the study of industrial plants illustrates one of the versatilities of this approach. In addition to obtaining a picture of the control structure as perceived by the employees, measures were designed to ascertain the control structure as the employees would like it to be. The super-imposition of curves representing the "actual" and the "desired" distributions of control provides an interesting comparison.

Figure 1 represents two plants in which employee perceptions of things as they are yield very similar control curves. When these curves are interpreted in the context of the control structure which the employees *desire*, some important differences emerge. While employees of both plants desire a less negatively sloped curve, the employees in Plant X would achieve this by lowering the power which each supervisory level exercises in the plant. They would increase only their own control. In Plant Y, however, while the rank and file are desirous of increasing their own influence in the running of the plant, they would not do so at the expense of the first line supervisor or the station managers—quite the contrary. Another indication of these differences is the fact that in Plant X the "desired" curve intersects the "actual" at a point between the men and first line supervisor; in Plant Y the point of intersection occurs between the station and plant managers. We have called this point of intersection the "crossover" point and hypothesize it to be an important index of organizational control.[8]

6. The flat curve might be relatively low or high on the vertical axis. The former, indicating relatively little control by any hierarchical level, is said to describe the "laissez faire" or "anarchic" model. The latter, indicating a high level of control by *all* hierarchical levels, is said to refer to the "polyarchic" model. See Tannenbaum, *op. cit.*

7. Arnold S. Tannenbaum and Basil S. Georgopoulos, "The Distribution of Control in Formal Organizations." Survey Research Center, 1956. (mimeo)

8. It is of further interest to note that Plant Y is functioning at a higher level of efficiency and worker satisfaction than X, although we cannot assert on the basis of this comparison that such differences are casually related to the differences in the actual and desired control patterns.

FIGURE 1   ACTUAL AND DESIRED CONTROL*

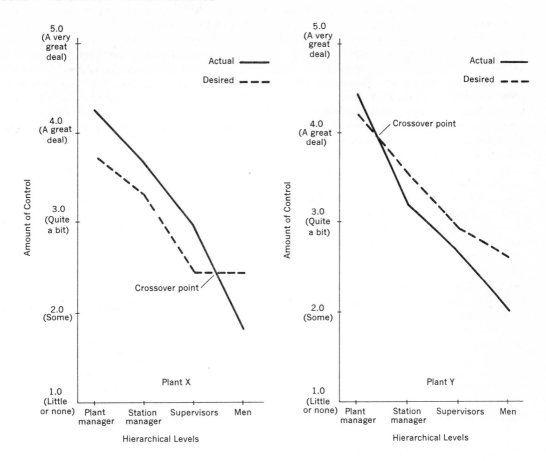

*Judged by the rank and file employees

While the control graphs provide a uniquely organizational description of the broad pattern of control, the curves depicted above ignore an important aspect of the control process—its directionality. Control has a point of origin, and an orientation or direction. Control involves the regulation or manipulation of something. Any act of control thus has both an active and passive phase; someone (or some group) *controls*, and something (or someone) *is controlled*. This distinction becomes particularly important when the immediate object of control is human action. The study of a large industrial service organization extended the application of the control graph notion to include this aspect of the control process in organizations.

The vertical axis of the control graph, representing the amount of control exercised by the various hierarchical levels, can be adapted to represent control in the passive sense—the extent to which each of the hierarchical groups is subject to

control within the organization. A curve describing the distribution of "passive" control can then be drawn and superimposed on the active control curve. Together, these curves provide a significant index of organizational control, the extent to which each hierarchical level exercises control as compared to the extent to which it is controlled. Such curves were obtained for the industrial plants by asking the first and second line supervisors to rate the degree of control which each hierarchical level exercises over each, including its own. While the active control curves in these plants were found to be negatively sloped, indicating greater influence by upper levels, the passive control curves were found to be positively sloped, indicating that lower levels are subject to more control than upper levels. This pattern of active-passive control is no doubt typical of industrial organizations, but one can conceive of variations from this pattern. For example, in the voluntary organization one is likely to find increases in passive control corresponding to increases in active control.

The industrial study attempted to answer a number of additional questions concerning the hierarchical sociometry of control: Over whom does any given level orient the control which it exercises? For example, how much control does the first line supervisor exercise over the rank and file employees, over the station manager, over the plant manager? Who exercises the control to which a specific level is subject? How much of the control, to which the rank and file is subject, comes from first line supervision, from the station manager, and from the plant manager? Such questions refer to what we have called the *orientation* and *sources* of control. The former indicates the direction or target toward which given levels orient their control; the latter indicates the sources from which control over any given level emanates. Figure 2 illustrates the way in which these patterns of control are described through the control graph. It represents the orientations of control for three hierarchical levels: higher management (which is physically distant from the plant), the plant man-

ager, and the first line supervisors. In all cases the data are based on the judgments of first and second line supervisors.

These curves convey information concerning the patterns of control exercised by higher management, the plant manager, and the first line supervisor. For example, the plant manager exercises a great deal of control over a fairly broad array of hierarchical groups, including the station managers, the first line supervisors, as well as himself. He also exercises quite a bit of control over the rank and file men and some control over higher management. Higher management exercises a great deal of control over its own actions and correspondingly less control over lower hierarchical groups within this plant. In contrast, the first line supervisors exercise more control over lower than over higher levels.

SUMMARY AND CONCLUSIONS

The series of studies described above has been concerned in part with the development of a more adequate conceptualization of organizational control. This series has moved from the study of specific supervisor-subordinate relationships to the development of a general schema describing the broader pattern of control in the organization. An attempt has been made in these studies to discover the uniquely organizational dimensions of control. The control graph elucidates a number of such dimensions:

1. The *distribution of control*, which is seen from the shape of curve. A number of indices are evident from the shape of curve, including the *general slope* and the *acceleration* of the curve. The general slope indicates which levels ordinarily have the greatest power. Curve accelerations reflect the relative increments of control which occur from one hierarchical level to the next. For example, positive acceleration (in a negatively sloped curve) means that major control increments occur at upper hierarchical levels, while negative acceleration means that major increments occur at lower levels. The curves, of course, may be more complicated, having accelerations which change signs at varying points.

2. The *total amount of control*, which is seen from the average height of the curve.

3. *Discrepancies between the "active" and "passive" control*, which indicate the extent to which the various hierarchical levels exercise control as compared to the extent to which they are subject to control within the organization. The point where

FIGURE 2   ORIENTATIONS OF CONTROL FOR HIGHER MANAGEMENT, PLANT MANAGER AND SUPERVISORS*

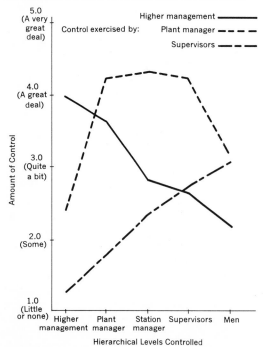

*Adapted partly from Tannenbaum, Georgopoulos, *op. cit.* For simplicity, the curves for station managers and the rank and file are not shown. These data are based on judgments of supervisors and station managers.

the active and passive curves intersect (assuming one intersection) represents the place in the hierarchy where these functions reverse.

4. The *orientation span of control*, which indicates whether a given hierarchical level exercises control over a wide or narrow array of hierarchical groups.

5. The *sources span of control*, which indicates whether a given hierarchical level is controlled by a wide or narrow array of hierarchical groups.

PART THREE

Recent Trends
and
New Developments

There are two kinds of fools. One says, "This is old, therefore it is good." The other says, "This is new, therefore it is better."

Dean Inge

A few years from now it may not be uncommon for schools of business to develop curricula around the fields of administration, the behavioral sciences, international business, and quantitative analysis. This development could be carried forward to the point where, instead of teaching business administration, public administration, educational administration, hospital administration, and other areas of administration, there would be a department or school of administration that would teach a unified art and science of administration. Similarly, there might be separate but interrelated departments or schools of behavioral science, international business, and quantitative analysis.[1]

These academic trends are interrelated not only with one another but also with other new developments such as the use of computers, research data from the behavioral sciences, and techniques like PERT. They all have supplemented one another in building the road to the business future, which may well have as its objective the theme of the Thirteenth International Management Congress (CIOS), "Human Progress Through Better Management." It is important to bear in mind, however, that this road is beset by many challenges. In his keynote address at the CIOS conference, David Rockefeller emphasized this point.

The more we learn about management, however, the more we realize how little we actually know about this generative force that gives order to men's ideas and direction to their aspirations. This much, though, is certain: in the quarter century ahead, the challenges to the competence, creativity and resourcefulness of managers — and the corresponding opportunities for contributing to human progress — will be greater than ever before.[2]

According to Rockefeller, businessmen will face three major challenges stemming from changing technology, the increasing complexity of a company's internal operations, and a greater need to understand man's environment including the impact of the world marketplace. In the academic

---

1. This trend is already evident to some extent in the Administrative Science Center at the University of Pittsburgh, in the Graduate School of Administration at the new University of California campus at Irvine, in the behavioral sciences curriculum at the University of Chicago, in the increasing recognition and use of behavioral scientists in the better schools of business, in the rapid international growth of United States business, which is being reflected in the academic world, and in the requirement of an increasing degree of quantitative background for admission into graduate schools of business.

2. David Rockefeller, "Managerial Work and Human Progress," *Proceedings, CIOS XIII International Management Congress, September 16 – 29, 1963, New York City* (New York: The Council for International Progress in Management, 1964), p. 2.

world, these challenges will require an eclectic approach to the study of management, for managers of the future will have to know administration not only as we know it today but also with a greater understanding of human behavior, of the internal and external environment of business organizations throughout the world, and of new and better techniques of management.

Three fields have made major contributions to the understanding of human behavior—anthropology, sociology, and psychology, referred to collectively as the behavioral sciences. Berelson and Steiner have clarified the behavioral sciences by stating that they "do not equate the behavioral sciences with the social sciences. The latter term is usually understood to cover six disciplines: anthropology, economics, history, political science, psychology, and sociology. By the behavioral sciences we mean the disciplines of anthropology, psychology, and sociology—minus and plus: *Minus* such specialized sectors as physiological psychology, archaeology, technical linguistics, and most of physical anthropology; *Plus* social geography, some psychiatry, and the behavioral parts of economics, political science, and law."[3] Other scholars also consider the study of business a behavioral science. "There is, of course, a close logical relationship between the study of business and the behavioral sciences. Indeed, the study of business is a behavioral science, studying a sample of behavior in a particular context."[4]

At this stage in the development of the behavioral sciences and of management, it may be premature to classify the study of business as a behavioral science. One could consider the behavioral sciences to be those aspects of various fields (especially anthropology, psychology, and sociology) that are concerned with human behavior. Then, in the sense that many aspects of business are behaviorally oriented, the study of business may be considered a behavioral science. However, the behavioral sciences are important to the administrator not merely because business has behavioral aspects but because the human element is crucial to success in the art and science of management. "Of all the subjects which he might undertake to study formally, none is more important to the businessman-to-be than human behavior."[5]

There is a reciprocal relationship between human behavior and environment—each strongly affects the other. While an understanding of human behavior is essential to administrative success, an understanding of the environment in which it takes place is also important. With the increasing importance of world markets, shrinking distances, and political necessities, knowledge

of differing environments and the ability to adjust to them constitute a major challenge. American businessmen and scholars who have ventured into the field of international management are fast recognizing the fact that one cannot consider the rest of the world, or any part of it, as merely a fifty-first state.

International business offers not only the usual rewards of domestic business but also an opportunity to present to the world the system of enterprise upon which our society is largely based. This system, and with it our whole society, is strongly challenged by the communist ideology; and the successful introduction of our system abroad can be a powerful weapon for democracy, especially in the developing nations of the world. Although the obstacles to be encountered in the international field are indeed formidable, the rewards, in terms of both profit and prestige, make accepting this challenge a very worthwhile venture.

Another important challenge to management stems from new technology.

The new technology does not yet have a single established name. We shall call it *information technology*. It is composed of several related parts. One includes techniques for processing large amounts of information rapidly, and it is epitomized by the high-speed computer. A second part centers around the application of statistical and mathematical methods to decision-making problems; it is represented by techniques like mathematical programming, and by methodologies like operations research. A third part is in the offing, though its applications have not yet emerged very clearly; it consists of the simulation of higher-order thinking through computer programs.[6]

Leavitt and Whisler believe that information technology will lead to major changes in management.[7] Their predictions include revision of the organization structure into corps of supervisors, program men, creators, and commitors; emphasis upon management training in universities; ap-

3. Bernard Berelson and Gary A. Steiner, *Human Behavior, An Inventory of Scientific Findings* (New York: Harcourt, Brace & World, Inc., 1964), p. 11.

4. Robert A. Dahl, Mason Haire, and Paul F. Lazarsfeld, *Social Science Research on Business: Product and Potential* (New York: Columbia University Press, 1959), p. 47.

5. Robert Aaron Gordon and James Edwin Howell, *Higher Education for Business* (New York: Columbia University Press, 1959), p. 166.

6. Harold J. Leavitt and Thomas L. Whisler, "Management in the 1980's," *Harvard Business Review*, XXXVI (November-December 1958), 41.

7. Leavitt and Whisler, "Management in the 1980's," pp. 47–48.

praisal by peers; team bonuses; compensation influenced by market forces; and routinization and mechanization of the middle management level, thereby reducing its forces. They believe that these changes will require readjustments in the organization, the most important one being the manager's own psychological adjustment to this new environment. The computer has been the most important technological development to affect management.

The unique achievement of the computer is that it is enabling the executive to clear away some of the uncertainty that surrounds him, to subtract some of the variables from the circumstances that fret him, to convert many ill-structured and inherently insoluble problems into well-structured and partly soluble ones, to rely less on hunches and intuition and more on analysis, to behave less as an artist and more as a scientist in disposing of routine matters, and to save his creativity and imagination for more important work.[8]

The technological and theoretical innovations that have affected every aspect of management to some degree have been rapid and far-reaching. They have resulted in changes in organization structure and behavior, in greater automation, in the use of business simulation exercises for management education, and in the use of models for education and research. The recent trends and new developments have been a major breakthrough in man's continuous search for better knowledge and tools to achieve his objectives. The challenges, opportunities, and rewards that these trends and developments offer to mankind point to the ever increasing importance of the art and science of management for the achievement of human progress.

---

8. Gilbert Burk, "Management Will Never Be the Same Again—The Boundless Age of the Computer," *Fortune*, LXX (August 1964), 126.

SECTION *VIII*
THE
BEHAVIORAL
SCIENCES

The development of new areas of knowledge within a given field requires a clear understanding of the definition and scope of that field. The first article in this section (#36) is an attempt by Wadia to provide such clarification and to demonstrate the value of the behavioral sciences for the development of an administrative science. Bernthal (#37) examines the contributions made by the behavioral sciences to various aspects of management by providing new insights into existing knowledge and by pointing out areas in which that knowledge can be applied to improve the practice of management.

Foremost among these areas are the interactions of individuals, groups, and the social systems in which they operate, and the effect of behavioral science on the administrative process. Argyris (#38) writes on how the development of individuals in our culture can lead to conflicts when these individuals join organizations managed under certain conditions. Cartwright and Lippitt (#39) examine the relationship between individuals and groups. Their article throws important light on problems of organizational behavior, as does Homan's article (#40), which suggests that we view social interaction as an exchange of material and nonmaterial goods to maintain a practical equilibrium. Finally, Leavitt (#41) gives us an appraisal of some of the major developments in the behavioral sciences and the effects they will have on the study and practice of management.

36 — Management Education and the Behavioral Sciences

MANECK S. WADIA

In the academic world of management, the area that has generated the greatest interest and controversy in the past few years has been the one on the role of the behavioral sciences in the study and practice of management. Most educators in the field of business agree that the behavioral sciences are important to any business curriculum and of even greater significance to the management curriculum. This view has been strongly seconded by the Carnegie Foundation and the Ford Foundation reports, as evidenced by the following quotes:

All workers in the field agree that there is a big job ahead in cooperation between business schools and behavioral science faculty members to reforge many of the tools of the behavioral sciences and to build new ones in order to develop this stem from the modest level at which it must now operate to the crucial position it will surely have as the years go by.[1]

Of all the subjects which he might undertake to study formally, none is more appropriate for the businessman-to-be than human behavior. . . . By human behavior we mean most of the subject matter of the fields of psychology, sociology, and (cultural) anthropology.[2]

This paper is, first, an attempt to provide the initial step in this emerging realm of knowledge, by providing the definition and scope of the behavioral sciences in the hopes that it will lead to more concrete studies and less confusion.[3] Sec-

ondly, this paper examines the major reason for the need and value of behavioral sciences in management education. Finally, this paper examines some of the means whereby the behavioral sciences may be integrated into a business or management curriculum.

DEFINITION AND SCOPE OF THE BEHAVIORAL SCIENCES

The term behavioral sciences has usually been utilized in conjunction with the social sciences. The Ford Foundation has perhaps been the most influential factor in making this term popular by covertly distinguishing it from the social sciences. Thus, Mr. Thomas H. Carroll, Vice President of Ford Foundation, makes the following statement: "In all likelihood the social and behavioral sciences will be applied increasingly to problems of business administration. The relevance of economics has always been apparent, but the application of other social sciences, particularly psychology, sociology, and social anthropology, are still in the pioneering stage."[4]

Usually *psychology*, *sociology* and *cultural anthro-*

"Management Education and the Behavioral Sciences," *Advanced Management*, XXVI (September 1961), 7–10. Reprinted by permission of the publisher. **Maneck S. Wadia:** Ford Foundation Fellow, Administrative Science Center, University of Pittsburgh.

1. Pierson, Frank C. and others. *The Education of American Businessmen*, McGraw-Hill, New York, 1959, p. 327.
2. Gordon, Robert Aaron, and Howell, James Edwin. *Higher Education for Business*, Columbia University Press, New York, 1959, pp. 166–167.
3. This area has been examined by the author in the Reader's and Editor's section of *Business Horizon*, Winter, 1960.
4. Carroll, Thomas H. "A Foundation Expresses Its Interests in Higher Education for Business Management," *Journal of the Academy of Management*, December, 1959, p. 163.

pology are considered the three main behavioral sciences. The study of human behavior is the common bond of these three disciplines. The main distinguishing characteristics among these three disciplines are that psychology emphasizes individual behavior, sociology deals mainly with group behavior in modern society and cultural anthropology devotes most of its efforts to the study of behavior among primitive groups. These sciences have the eventual objective of answering the question "why" of human behavior. *A behavioral science is a body of systematized knowledge pertaining to how people behave, what is the relationship between human behavior and the total environment, and why people behave as they do.*

There are at least three distinct areas of inquiry: (1) How people behave; (2) The relationship between human behavior and the total environment; and (3) Why people behave as they do. Acquiring knowledge of why people behave as they do is the most distinguishable characteristic of a behavioral science and the most difficult area of inquiry. It has to be based on the successful study of how people behave and the relationship between the total environment and human behavior. A large portion of the psychologist's, the sociologist's and the cultural anthropologist's time is devoted to the first two areas. It is absolutely necessary that one have knowledge of how people behave and the polaristic relationship between human behavior and the total environment, before one can even attempt to find out why people behave as they do.

By and large, the sociologists have been most successful in the first area, the anthropologists in the second and the psychologists in the third. Attempts to coordinate and combine these fields for mutual benefit have already been made, as in the area of social psychology, organization theory, leadership studies, and culture and personality studies, but the efforts in the synthesizing direction are not as strenuous as one would hope for.

All behavioral sciences are social sciences but the converse is not necessarily true. The common ground is that they both have human beings as their central theme. The minimal definition of a social science is a body of systematized knowledge pertaining to the activities of human beings. Thus, history, a social science, may be defined as a systematic written account of past events. The study of human activity in the past has a great bearing on history; but history does not attempt to answer the question "why" of human behavior. Again, management, another social science, is the process of achieving a desired result through the intelligent use of human effort, without necessarily attempting to delve into the areas of inquiry of the behavioral sciences. Whenever the questions of human behavior become important, the behavioral sciences usually step in; or, if another science attempts to delve into the areas of inquiry of the behavioral sciences within its own discipline, that discipline comes closer to becoming a behavioral science.

The areas of inquiry of a behavioral science are not, and should not become, the monopoly of the anthropologist, the sociologist or the psychologist. Some managers may be in a much better position to study their workers from a behavioral science point of view than would a sociologist, a psychologist or an anthropologist. Similarly, many historians have successfully entered the fold of the behavioral sciences by covering the major areas of inquiry of the behavioral scientists in their historical studies. However, the anthropologists, the sociologists and the psychologists still remain the "professionals" in the realm of the behavioral sciences.

THE NEED AND VALUE OF THE BEHAVIORAL SCIENCES

The most important single factor that has led to the interest in the behavioral and the social sciences is *the strong need felt for the development of a management (or administrative) science.* Due to the inherent nature of the discipline, management science has to be a social science. As a science it has to be of universal significance. Management science hopes to find the universals of the management process, to find managerial tools of universal significance and to develop models and methods of universal application. This science hopes to bring together all knowledge pertaining to management into one distinct discipline. This, it is hoped, will make management science a universally applicable science.

Hence, the emerging management science will be an applied science, standing approximately in relation to the behavioral sciences and certain social sciences, as medicine stands with respect to the biological and certain physical sciences.[5] Though at the risk of oversimplification, this concept can be better explained with a diagram [*see* page 231].

One of the major reasons why management has not further developed as a science is because so

5. I am grateful to Dr. James D. Thompson, Director, Administrative Science Center, the University of Pittsburgh, for this concept and for the diagram that follows. For further discussion of this concept see: Thompson, James D., "On Building an Administrative Science," *Administrative Science Quarterly*, June, 1956.

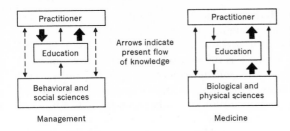

Arrows indicate present flow of knowledge

Management

Medicine

far we have relied mainly on *deductive* logic. We have adopted generalizations developed by educators and practitioners, then disseminated them to students of management as universal truths, without taking the variables into consideration. What we are seeking in management education is, in the words of Bross: "The successor to Reason-Science. The new techniques introduced by the scientists closed the gap between reason and the real world by means of an inductive logic.[6] In terms of our diagram, the biological and physical sciences, by emphasizing inductive logic, have provided the educator and the practitioner with a science of medicine. It is hoped that the behavioral sciences can do the same for management.

For better management education, and for an accelerated pace in the development of management science, we must look to the behavioral and other social sciences for scientific generalizations and empirical data, as well as for research techniques, which are applicable to our field and need to be translated into the already existing body of knowledge in management.

INTEGRATION OF THE BEHAVIORAL SCIENCES IN MANAGEMENT EDUCATION

This brings us to the third and the final major aspect of this paper, namely the means whereby the behavioral sciences may be integrated into a business or management curriculum.

Four separate, though not mutually exclusive, methods are envisaged. They are, in an increasing order of importance to integration: (1) The Traditional Method; (2) The Research Method; (3) The Multi-Specialist Method; and (4) The Cluster Organization Method.

The *Traditional Method* is the one which is presently used by most Schools of Business. According to this philosophy of integration, a student majoring in management takes some compulsory basic courses in one or more of the behavioral sciences, usually in the sophomore or junior year. It is presupposed by the proponents

of this philosophy, that these courses, usually offered by the departments of psychology, sociology and anthropology, will give the students the necessary background for the application of these fields to management.

This method is of little value unless there is a sufficient flow of information and understanding between the management faculty and the behavioral science faculties as well as among the faculty members encompassed by the behavioral sciences. Usually, where this method of integration is used exclusively, little effort is made in this direction. The result is that there is a wide chasm between what is taught in the behavioral science courses and its application to management. These courses offer the fundamentals of the behavioral sciences and leave the integrating up to the students.

The *Research Method* is useful for integrating the behavioral sciences in management education, especially at the faculty and graduate student levels. Faculty members from the department of management can and do undertake joint research projects with faculty members of the departments encompassed by the behavioral sciences. The research methods and tools of the behavioral sciences are more sophisticated than those in the realm of management, and are readily applicable to management research. Also, graduate students in management, interested in data collection and empirical analysis, can and do work under guidance of faculty members in the behavioral sciences.

The obvious shortcoming of the Research Method is difficulty in communication. However, research is an important basis of education and for the accumulation of knowledge. Students must be instilled with a desire to pursue truth objectively, no matter where it is found or where it will lead. The spirit of research, coupled with the presentation and analysis of current research findings, is an important method for the effective integration of the behavioral sciences in management education.[7]

The third method of integration is the one in which the departments of management retain the services of a person who possesses capabilities in the area of management as well as in one or more disciplines encompassed by the behavioral sciences. The *Multi-Specialists Method* is the ideal way of combining the Traditional as well as the Research Method.

6. Bross, Irwin D. J. *Design for Decision*, The Macmillan Company, New York, 1953, p. 17.

7. The first two methods were discussed at the Indiana University D.B.A. Conference, Spring Semester, 1959–1960, by Professor William G. Scott, College of Commerce, DePaul University. I am grateful to Professor Scott for some of the concepts discussed under these two methods.

If just a specialist in the behavioral sciences is retained by the management department or the school of business, it would incorporate the disadvantages of both the Traditional Method as well as the Research Method.

However, a multi-specialist is the best position to overcome the integrating problem posed by the Traditional Method and the communication problem posed by the Research Method. Perhaps, the greatest advantage of this method is that the multi-specialist is under the jurisdiction of the department of management and is therefore primarily concerned with management education, and his efforts are directed towards the objectives of the management department.

The major problem in utilizing the Multi-Specialist Method is the lack of sufficient number of multi-specialists to fill the ever increasing demand for their services. There is an increasing recognition of the value of interdisciplinary approach not only to management but also in other academic areas. Chancellor Litchfield has suggested some practices to correct some of the rigidities of over-compartmentalization in university organizations. Among Litchfield's suggestions is the one that "we must modify the thought that there can be only one organizational pattern existing at any one time. In fact, there are many intersecting organizational relationships of a formal character which new problems and opportunities will bring into being. To traditional departmental, school and college structures, we must add the clusters of crossing interests which also require formal structuring."[8]

The *Cluster Method* for the integration of behavioral sciences in management education would involve the establishment of a separate department.[9] Ideally this department would include a faculty composed of members from the three behavioral sciences, from management and from the other social sciences. Their primary objective would be furthering management education, and such a department could combine the Traditional, the Research and the Multi-Specialist Methods without incorporating any of their disadvantages.

The greatest advantage of the Cluster Method is that it is the best suited for the development of a management science. As pointed out earlier, this is the most important need for and value of the integration of the behavioral sciences in management education. The greatest disadvantage of the Cluster Method is the expenses involved in establishing such a department or center on a continuing basis. However, funds for the establishment of such clusters will be more readily available once the value of this method of integration is more widely accepted.

The behavioral sciences are still in a state of infancy when it comes to providing immediately useful analytical concepts and empirical knowledge for management education. They will not provide any immediate or easy solutions to any particular management problems. What the behavioral sciences will provide is theories, methods and research findings and a strong potential for more empirical knowledge, analytical concepts and models, which can be of value to the further development of management both as a science and as an art.

The behavioral scientists will not voluntarily make their contributions applicable and available. It is our responsibility as educators and practitioners in management, to investigate into these fields, separate the valuable from the useless, adopt the necessary ideas, promote research within the areas which are of special significance to us, and integrate the knowledge from the behavioral sciences into the study and practice management.

---

8. Litchfield, Edward H. "Organization in Large American Universities: The Faculties," *Journal of Higher Education*, October, 1959, p. 357.

9. The term "center" has come into greater usage where the Cluster Method has been employed. Two cases in point are: The Administrative Science Center, University of Pittsburgh, Pittsburgh, Pennsylvania; and the International Center for the Advancement of Management Education, Stanford University, Palo Alto, California.

37 — Contributions of the Behavioral Science Approach

WILMAR F. BERNTHAL

INTRODUCTION

Although our panel chairman has asked us to simulate the blind men describing the elephant, it should be clear that we only temporarily put our blindfolds on, to describe that part of our "elephant" which for the moment is of most intimate concern to us. As each of us focuses on one set of "contributions" to improved management practices, we do *not* mean to imply:

a. that these are the only or the most significant contributions

b. That these contributions are necessarily in conflict with contributions made by the other approaches

c. that these contributions have invalidated other, and particularly earlier, contributions to management practice.

Rather, what we imply is that the total subject cannot be viewed objectively without considering the contributions of each part and how these parts are inter-related in the whole. This may be the clue to the apparent difficulty managers experience in trying to apply certain management concepts, theory, and research findings to management practice. A single-track approach to management study or practice often fails to answer the complex problems of the entire system, or causes side-effects in other parts of the system which override the wholesome effects achieved in the subsystem. Placing too great a reliance (or faith) on one approach, to the exclusion of other equally valid approaches, may lead to disillusionment, and often to violent reaction against that approach.

With these reservations in mind, I will dutifully blind myself for the moment to the other relevant approaches, and will review the contributions that the behavioral science approach has made, or can make, to management practice.

BEHAVIORAL SCIENCE KNOWLEDGE AND MANAGEMENT PRACTICE

The question of behavioral science contribution to management practice is really twofold. The first part, "What are the behavioral science insights, concepts, research findings, and theories that are available for *improved understanding* of management?" can be answered by merely pointing out the fantastic development of this field within the last quarter century, and cataloguing the literature and research evolving from it.

The second part of the question, "What contribution has all this made to *improved management practices*?" is more difficult, if not impossible, to answer. One sometimes gets the impression that the behavioral science researcher lives in a world separated from the practicing manager by a wide gulf of interests, goals, values, and personality traits. The amount of idea-transfusion between these two worlds, via consultation, literature, and education, and the extent of actual application to business practice of known ideas, is largely a matter of conjecture which could well become a research subject for members of the Academy of Management.

In this paper, I would like to review the contributions of behavioral science theory and research to management knowledge and then add a few comments on the problem of translating knowledge into management practice.

CONTRIBUTION OF BEHAVIORAL SCIENCE TO MANAGEMENT KNOWLEDGE

On this panel, we are already segmenting rather artificially four "basic approaches" to improved management practice. Yet each of these approaches, for research purposes, may stem out of further specialized disciplines. Social science specialization has led to separate study of man in his various roles and environments. This segmented study of human behavior sometimes seems to assume that human behavior takes place in a series of watertight compartments, so that the economist can study "economic man," the sociologist "social man," the political scientist "political man," etc. The behavioral science approach to management draws upon all the social sciences, directly or indirectly, and attempts to integrate their insights into a way of thinking about organizational behavior.

The most significant *social science* contributions to management practice undoubtedly have come

"Contributions of the Behavioral Science Approach," *Academy of Management, Proceedings of the Annual Meeting, 1962* (Pittsburgh: Academy of Management, 1963), pp. 21–28. Reprinted by permission of the author and the publisher. **Wilmar F. Bernthal**: School of Business, University of Colorado.

from economics—the study of man as a consumer, and the development of organizations through which economic needs can be effectively satisfied. The behavioral science approach, however, is usually defined more narrowly to explain man's behavior as a member of producing organizations—individual behavior in a social system designed to achieve productive goals through cooperative effort. The study of history, economics, political sciences, and anthropology provides insights into the setting in which organizational behavior takes place, while psychology, sociology, social psychology, and applied anthropology provide the more immediate clues to the behavior itself. It is the contributions to management of these last-named areas of social science that I wish to summarize here.

The behavioral science approach to management knowledge also differs from some of the social sciences in terms of its research methodology. While some social scientists, and particularly economists, may analyze human behavior in society by developing logical abstract models incorporating given assumptions about human behavior, behavioral science stresses empirical (real-life) data resulting from controlled observation. Thus, the behavioral sciences can be a rich source of experience which may have immediate relevance to improvement of management practice.

A strict definition of behavioral science would limit our inquiry to research findings. Much of the so-called behavioral science literature for management, however, is interpretive, in that it attempts to translate behavioral science research findings into meaningful concepts for the practicing manager. For purposes of this paper, I will use the term "behavioral science" loosely to incorporate both the basic research and the interpretation.

THE PSYCHOLOGY OF INDIVIDUAL DIFFERENCES

The early traditional approach to management was based on a sort of "intuitive psychology" which led to emphasis on specialization of work and to economic incentive systems. It said little about man as a social being, although undoubtedly there was some awareness of man's social needs and behavior. However, in an economic context in which man's major purpose in work was to satisfy survival needs, the neglect of the social dimension was not critical. The history of output restriction, even under individual incentive systems, indicates, however, that this intuitive psychology proved inadequate in explaining or-

ganizational behavior in a developing economic and social environment.

The psychology of individual differences provides guidelines for matching men and jobs by selecting, testing, developing, and placing personnel so that their potential can best be utilized in organizations. At the same time, it also provides insights into designing machines and jobs to fit the capacities and limitations of the human mind and body. For example, the space age need for design of cockpits and capsules gives "human engineering" new importance as a means for solving problems stemming from the industrial revolution—that of relating man and technology.

Despite individual psychology's continuing contributions to management through selection and placement on the one hand, and through human engineering on the other hand, the emphasis in the behavioral sciences has been in another direction. The behavioral science approach to management has focused not so much on finding abilities as on determining motivations—willingness—of man to work productively. And the emphasis has not been upon man in isolation, but in a social setting. The major contribution of behavioral science is its view of business as a social system. This recognition that organizations are to be viewed as social systems, even if the purpose of the organization is economic, and its technology rational, provides new insights into problems that had been a frustration to managers oriented in a more limited management outlook.

BUSINESS AS A SOCIAL SYSTEM

The way of thinking about business as a social system received its major impetus from Chester Barnard in his *The Functions of the Executive*[1] in 1938. At the same time, Elton Mayo and his research group at Harvard came up with notions about informal organizations that reinforced the idea that a manager must think about organizations as systems of human relations, rather than purely as related functions or jobs.[2] Business organizations were viewed as cooperative systems having their own culture and subcultures. The approach was that of the anthropologist—to observe objectively the actual behavior of people at work, and to note and analyze these data without introducing assumptions that did not arise from the data.

1. Cambridge, Mass: Harvard University Press, 1938.
2. F. J. Roethlisberger and W. J. Dickson, *Management and the Worker* (Cambridge, Mass.: Harvard University Press, 1939). The Hawthorne researchers, in turn, were influenced by the concepts of a social system formulated by Vilfredo Pareto, *The Mind and Society* (New York: Harcourt, Brace and Company, 1935).

The conceptual scheme for analyzing organizational behavior in terms of a social system was formalized by George Homans in *The Human Group*,[3] drawing in part upon the earlier work of Eliot Chapple and other anthropologists. In this scheme, the relevant variables are the *activities, interactions*, and *sentiments* that result when technology, economic factors, management and leadership practices, and personal factors are combined in organizations. In this setting, the activities, interactions and sentiments ultimately produce the real (or emergent) behavior which determines the organization's productivity, the growth and development of the participants, and their satisfactions or morale.

This conceptual scheme provides a systematic way in which complex behavior patterns in organizations can be analyzed, and through which, hopefully, behavioral consequences of management action can be predicted. Although this scheme is often identified as the Harvard approach, it appears in different variations in many of the behavioral science researches.[4]

VARIATIONS ON A BASIC THEME

Within the broad analytical framework of business as a social system, behavioral scientists have staked out various subthemes for investigation. These differ primarily in the aspect of organizational behavior selected for study, and in the methodology of investigation.

The Small Group Approach. One such variation on the basic theme is the study of leadership, interpersonal relations, communication, and cooperation by controlled studies of small group behavior. This orientation has its roots in the group dynamics of Kurt Lewin, and is illustrated by the work of the Research Center for Group Dynamics at the University of Michigan, and the controlled laboratory studies of small group behavior by Alex Bavelas at Stanford and Robert Bales at Harvard. The case for use of democratic leadership in small groups is developed by Norman R. F. Maier in his *Principles of Human Relations*.[5] Attempts to apply group dynamics concepts to management practice by developing the manager's self-awareness and interpersonal competence are illustrated in the laboratory training (T-Group) of the National Training Laboratories and the sensitivity training of Robert Tannenbaum and his colleagues at the Human Relations Research Group, Institute of Industrial Relations, University of California, Los Angeles.[6]

The Survey Research Center Approach. The recent book by Rensis Likert, *New Patterns of Management*,[7] summarizes the conclusions of 15 years of research on the relationship of productivity, supervision, and morale by the Survey Research Center of the Institute for Social Research, University of Michigan. The contribution to management practice here is both in terms of the survey research method used to study organizational behavior, and the conclusions drawn from the research. As with other behavioral science research, the publications of the Institute for Social Research, and Likert's book, are loaded with implications for improving managers' leadership attitudes and practices.

The Worker and Technology Approach. One other approach that behavioral science has taken to improve management practice is to study the relationship of the worker and technology. The studies in the Yale Technology Project concerning the worker and the foreman on the assembly line illustrate research that can help determine the limits of job specialization and standardization in view of the realities of human needs and the social system.[8]

The Conflict of Individual and Organization. A variation on the basic theme which has caused considerable flurry among managers is the McGregor and Argyris thesis of the potential conflict between a healthy human personality and formal organizations administered strictly according to rational principles of organization.[9] Influenced by Freudian psychology, these authors suggest that the dependency relations created by hierarchical authoritarian organizations and enforced through

3. New York: Harcourt, Brace and Co., 1950.

4. A recent illustration of the Harvard approach is found in Paul Lawrence, *et al.*, *Organizational Behavior and Administration* (Homewood: R. D. Irwin, Inc., 1961). The interactionist approach to analyzing organizational behavior is identified with William F. Whyte in his *Money and Motivation* (New York: Harper and Brothers, 1955) and *Men at Work* (Homewood: R. D. Irwin, Inc., 1962). A recent attempt to translate it into management practice is found in Eliot Chapple and Leonard Sayles, *The Measure of Management* (New York: Macmillan Co., 1961).

5. New York: John Wiley and Sons, 1952.

6. The work of this latter group is reported in Robert Tannenbaum, Irving R. Weschler, and Fred Massarik, *Leadership and Organization* (New York: McGraw-Hill Book Co., Inc., 1961). For a study of the effects of sensitivity training upon managerial performance, see Chris Argyris, *Interpersonal Competence and Organizational Effectiveness* (Homewood: R. D. Irwin, Inc., 1962).

7. New York: McGraw-Hill Book Company, Inc., 1962.

8. Charles R. Walker and Robert Guest, *The Man on the Assembly Line* (Cambridge: Harvard University Press, 1952), and Charles R. Walker, Robert H. Guest, and A. N. Turner, *The Foreman on the Assembly Line* (Cambridge: Harvard University Press, 1956).

9. Douglas McGregor, *The Human Side of Enterprise* (New York: McGraw-Hill Book Company, Inc., 1960 and Chris Argyris, *Personality and Organizations* (New York: Harper and Brothers, 1957).

management direction and control conflict with basic human needs for reasonable independence and self-direction. Insensitive managers may force their employees into immature behavior patterns which will prevent the kind of human performance the managers are trying to achieve. McGregor and Argyris thus plead with the manager to check his assumptions about human behavior, and to use with discretion the authority vested in his formal position.

Modern Organization Theory — The Integrative Discipline? As new insights are developed into different aspects of human relations within the firm, it is only natural that researchers should try to fit these micro-contributions into a macro-framework. Conceivably, this could become the behavioral theory of the firm. Organization theory uses the rigorous methods of economic analysis, but incorporates findings of behavioral science research rather than working with models that assume rational maximizing behavior. In this sense, Chester Barnard laid the foundations for modern organization theory by conceiving of organizations as complex social systems. More recently, the application of research methods from different disciplines to the study of organizations promises to produce new insights for the manager into the relevant variables and their relationships in organizations.[10]

THE STEP FROM MANAGEMENT KNOWLEDGE TO MANAGEMENT PRACTICE

Knowledge is not the only precondition necessary for effective practice or action. Since behavioral science concerns itself with human behavior in its total complexity, the convenient *ceteris paribus* assumption of rationality is hardly applicable. Management is also a form of human behavior, motivated by a complex set of human needs, many of which are nonlogical.

One may hypothesize that the academic researcher in behavioral science has been interested largely in developing knowledge rather than changing management practice. Business and other organizations, on the other hand, have an immediate concern about management practice, and are concerned only secondarily with knowledge. Rather than going through the lengthy and tedious educational process, they tend to look for a short run payoff on training investments. Consequently, they often emphasize skill training, and may become susceptible to shortcuts, fads, gim-

micks, or self-defeating devices for changing management behavior.

The missing link in the behavioral science approach, then, seems to be the bridge between knowledge and practice. The barriers to bridging this gap are complex, consisting of rather mysterious psychological and sociological factors that tend to be roadblocks on the "pure rationality route" to organizational effectiveness.

The growing literature on the authoritarian personality is a good illustration of forces within the manager which may constitute impenetrable barriers to improved management action, even though he has full knowledge of alternative approaches to management practices.[11]

Some recent studies of the effectiveness of human relations training also have had a sobering effect on the optimistic assumption that equates knowledge and practice. Both individual personality factors and organizational demands (including the top management values and assumptions) may be real deterrents to translating behavioral science knowledge into practice.[12] This frontier of behavioral science will undoubtedly come in for increased attention in the near future.

Assuming that behavior change depends upon more than knowledge, professors of management and management trainers in industry face an interesting dilemma. It has been demonstrated that training the mind does not necessarily influence practice. Yet to tamper with the personality of the student or manager raises ethical issues about the limits to which one may legit-

10. See, for example, J. G. March and H. A. Simon, *Organizations* (New York: John Wiley and Sons, 1958); Mason Haire (editor), *Modern Organization Theory* (New York: John Wiley and Sons, 1959); Albert H. Rubenstein and Chadwick J. Haberstroh (editors), *Some Theories of Organization* (Homewood: The Dorsey Press, Inc., and Richard D. Irwin, Inc., 1960); Amitai Etzioni, *Complex Organizations* (New York: Holt, Rinehart and Winston, Inc., 1961); and Chris Argyris, *Understanding Organizational Behavior* (Homewood: The Dorsey Press, Inc., 1960).

11. See, for example, Milton Rokeach, *The Open and Closed Mind* (New York: Basic Books, Inc., 1960); T. W. Adorno, et al., *The Authoritarian Personality* (New York: Harper and Brothers, 1951); Chris Argyris, *Personality and Organization* (New York: Harper and Brothers, 1957), pp. 216–218; and, in a more popular vein, Eugene Jennings, "The Authoritarian Cultural Lag in Business," *Journal of the Academy of Management,* August, 1959, and Robert McMurry, "The Case for Benevolent Autocracy," *Harvard Business Review,* January–February, 1958.

12. Effectiveness of human relations training at the supervisory level was explored in F. J. Roethlisberger, "Training Supervisors in Human Relations," *Harvard Business Review,* September, 1951, and further studied and reported in E. A. Fleishman, E. F. Harris, and H. E. Burtt, *Leadership and Supervision in Industry* (Columbus: Personnel Research Board, The Ohio State University, 1955). For a recent study of the possibility of affecting top management behavior through laboratory training, see Chris Argyris, *Interpersonal Competence and Organizational Effectiveness* (Homewood: R. D. Irwin, Inc., 1962).

imately invade the privacy of an individual in the interests of organizational effectiveness.

One may visualize a continuum of management training, the goals of which range from simple intellectual experience to complete behavior transformation. On the left extreme of this continuum would be traditional methods of imparting knowledge, with little concern for behavior beyond an *intellectual experience*. These include lecture, guided discussion, and conferences designed to widen the manager's conceptual horizons. Moving toward greater ego-involvement are various training methods designed to give a *vicarious experience*, such as case study, incident method, role playing, and simulation. Beyond such intellectual and vicarious experiences are attempts to improve management behavior directly by developing greater *self-awareness and social sensitivity* in the manager. These methods are directed at the roots of interpersonal competence, and may even aim at personality transformation. It is this area of the management training continuum that forms the battleground on which the limits of the behavioral science approach to improved management practice will be determined.

Current attempts at using laboratory training (T-Group or sensitivity training) among select groups of actual or potential managers already indicate a cautious movement by industry toward influencing management behavior directly. The next logical step in this progression toward internationalizing management training and education could involve limited psychotherapy. Assuming such training is economically feasible, the manager faces difficult ethical questions of whether an organization can legitimately require its managers to submit to sensitivity training or psychotherapy, presumably in the interests of the organization's effectiveness. These questions become even more sticky when one realizes that this progression could lead to psychoanalysis (and perhaps even religious conversion) as means by which managers' personality transformations could be effected. Neither the business firm nor the business school has yet ventured this far in training its personnel for improved management practice.

Both the practical and ethical limits of using behavioral science to transform managers' personalities in the interests of organizational performance need to be explored. The criteria by which these limits are determined need to be made explicit if behavioral science is to assume its legitimate role in the improvement of management practice.

BEHAVIORAL SCIENCE CONTRIBUTIONS TO MANAGEMENT, IN SUMMARY

The contribution of behavioral science to management practice consists primarily of producing new insights rather than new techniques. It has developed or expanded a way of thinking about the role of the manager, the nature of organizations, and the behavior of individuals within organizations. In this sense, the behavioral sciences have contributed significantly to that part of the body of management knowledge concerned with *the manager's leadership role*.

a. The behavioral sciences have given special attention to a dimension of management that classical management theory assumed or took for granted, namely, the factors in addition to pay that determine the level of motivation and human performance in organizations. They questioned the assumptions about organizational behavior that were implied in early management theory.

b. The behavioral sciences developed the point of view of organizations as complex social systems. In this respect they expanded the conceptual sights of managers from focusing on formal organization as the only relevant perspective of organizational life to dealing with organizational realities in their total complexity.

c. More recently, the behavioral sciences have focused upon the forces in the manager himself, his inadequacies and limitations in developing and maintaining a managerial climate conducive to high human performance. This concern about self-awareness and social sensitivity as a criterion for success may have important repercussions in the selection and development of managers for leadership positions in organizations.

d. Indirectly, the behavioral sciences have confronted management with some difficult questions about the ethical constraints, or limits, the manager faces in using insights into human behavior in the interests of advancing the economic objectives of organizations.

38 – The Individual and Organization: Some Problems of Mutual Adjustment[1]

CHRIS ARGYRIS

It is a fact that most industrial organizations have some sort of formal structure within which individuals must work to achieve the organization's objectives.[2] Each of these basic components of organization (the formal structure and the individuals) has been and continues to be the subject of much research, discussion, and writing. An extensive search of the literature leads us to conclude, however, that most of these inquiries are conducted by persons typically interested in one or the other of the basic components. Few focus on both the individual and the organization.

Since in real life the formal structure and the individuals are continuously interacting and transacting, it seems useful to consider a study of their simultaneous impact upon each other. It is the purpose of this paper to outline the beginnings of a systematic framework by which to analyze the nature of the relationship between formal organization and individuals and from which to derive specific hypotheses regarding their mutual impact. Although a much more detailed definition of formal organization will be given later, it is important to emphasize that this analysis is limited to those organizations whose original formal structure is defined by such traditional principles of organization as "chain of command," "task specialization," "span of control," and so forth. Another limitation is that since the nature of individuals varies from culture to culture, the conclusions of this paper are also limited to those cultures wherein the proposed model of personality applies (primarily American and some Western European cultures).

The method used is a simple one designed to take advantage of the existing research on each component. The first objective is to ascertain the basic properties of each component. Exactly what is known and agreed upon by the experts about each of the components? Once this information has been collected, the second objective follows logically. When the basic properties of each of these components are known, what predictions can be made regarding their impact upon one another once they are brought together?

SOME PROPERTIES OF HUMAN PERSONALITY

The research on the human personality is so great and voluminous that it is indeed difficult to find agreement regarding its basic properties.[3] It is even more difficult to summarize the agreements once they are inferred from the existing literature. Because of space limitations it is only possible to discuss in detail one of several agreements which seems to the writer to be the most relevant to the problem at hand. The others may be summarized briefly as follows. Personality is conceptualized as (1) being an organization of parts where the parts maintain the whole and the whole maintains the parts; (2) seeking internal balance (usually called adjustment) and external balance (usually called adaptation); (3) being propelled by psychological (as well as physical) energy; (4) located in the need systems; and (5) expressed through the abilities. (6) The personality organization may be called "the self" which (7) acts to color all the individual's experiences, thereby causing him to live in "private worlds," and which (8) is capable of defending (maintaining) itself against threats of all types.

The self, in this culture, tends to develop along specific trends which are operationally definable and empirically observable. The basic developmental trends may be described as follows. The human being, in our culture:

(1) tends to develop from a state of being passive as an infant to a state of increasing activity as an adult. (This is what E. H. Erikson has called

"The Individual and Organization: Some Problems of Mutual Adjustment," *Administrative Science Quarterly*, II (June 1957), 1–24. Reprinted by permission of the author and the publisher. Chris Argyris: Department of Industrial Administration, Yale University.

1. This analysis is part of a larger project whose objectives are to integrate by the use of a systematic framework much of the existing behavioral-science research related to organization. The total report will be published by Harper & Brothers as a book, tentatively entitled *The Behavioral Sciences and Organization.* The project has been supported by a grant from the Foundation for Research on Human Behavior, Ann Arbor, Michigan, for whose generous support the writer is extremely grateful.

2. Temporarily, "formal structure" is defined as that which may be found on the organization charts and in the standard operating procedures of an organization.

3. The relevant literature in clinical, abnormal, child, and social psychology, and in personality theory, sociology, and anthropology was investigated. The basic agreements inferred regarding the properties of personality are assumed to be valid for most contemporary points of view. Allport's "trait theory," Cattell's factor analytic approach, and Kretschmer's somatotype framework are not included. For lay description see the author's *Personality Fundamentals for Administrators,* rev. ed. (New Haven, 1954).

self-initiative and Urie Bronfenbrenner has called self-determination.[4]

(2) tends to develop from a state of dependence upon others as an infant to a state of relative independence as an adult. Relative independence is the ability to "stand on one's own two feet" and simultaneously to acknowledge healthy dependencies.[5] It is characterized by the individual's freeing himself from his childhood determiners of behavior (e.g., the family) and developing his own set of behavioral determiners. The individual does not tend to react to others (e.g., the boss) in terms of patterns learned during childhood.[6]

(3) tends to develop from being capable of behaving in only a few ways as an infant to being capable of behaving in many different ways as an adult.[7]

(4) tends to develop from having erratic, casual, shallow, quickly dropped interests as an infant to possessing a deepening of interests as an adult. The mature state is characterized by an endless series of challenges where the reward comes from doing something for its own sake. The tendency is to analyze and study phenomena in their full-blown wholeness, complexity, and depth.[8]

(5) tends to develop from having a short-time perspective (i.e., the present largely determines behavior) as an infant to having a much longer time perspective as an adult (i.e., the individual's behavior is more affected by the past and the future.[9]

(6) tends to develop from being in a subordinate position in the family and society as an infant to aspiring to occupy at least an equal and/or superordinate position relative to his peers.

(7) tends to develop from having a lack of awareness of the self as an infant to having an awareness of and control over the self as an adult. The adult who experiences adequate and successful control over his own behavior develops a sense of integrity (Erikson) and feelings of self-worth (Carl R. Rogers).[10]

These characteristics are postulated as being descriptive of a basic multidimensional developmental process along which the growth of individuals in our culture may be measured. Presumably every individual, at any given moment in time, could have his degree of development plotted along these dimensions. The exact location on each dimension will probably vary with each individual and even with the same individual at different times. Self-actualization may now be defined more precisely as the individual's plotted scores (or profile) along the above dimensions.[11]

A few words of explanation may be given concerning these dimensions of personality development:

(1) They are only one aspect of the total personality. All the properties of personality mentioned above must be used in trying to understand the behavior of a particular individual. For example, much depends upon the individual's self-concept, his degree of adaptation and adjustment, and the way he perceives his private world.

(2) The dimensions are continua, where the growth to be measured is assumed to be continuously changing in degree. An individual is presumed to develop continuously in degree from infancy to adulthood.

(3) The only characteristic assumed to hold for all individuals is that, barring unhealthy personality development, they will move from the infant toward the adult end of each continuum. This description is a model outlining the basic growth trends. As such, it does not make any predictions about any specific individual. It does, however, presume to supply the researcher with basic developmental continua along which the growth of any individual in our culture may be described and measured.

(4) It is postulated that no individual will ever obtain maximum expression of all these developmental trends. Clearly all individuals cannot be maximally independent, active, and so forth all the time and still maintain an organized society. It is the function of culture (e.g., norms, mores, and so forth) to inhibit maximum expression and to help an individual adjust and adapt by finding his optimum expression.

A second factor that prevents maximum

4. E. H. Erikson, *Childhood and Society* (New York, 1950); Urie Bronfenbrenner, "Toward an Integrated Theory of Personality," in Robert R. Blake and Glenn V. Ramsey, *Perception* (New York, 1951), pp. 206–257. See also R. Kotinsky, *Personality in the Making* (New York, 1952), pp. 8–25.

5. This is similar to Erikson's sense of autonomy and Bronfenbrenner's state of creative interdependence.

6. Robert W. White, *Lives in Progress* (New York, 1952), pp. 339 ff.

7. Lewin and Kounin believe that as the individual develops needs and abilities the boundaries between them become more rigid. This explains why an adult is better able than a child to be frustrated in one activity and behave constructively in another. See Kurt Lewin, *A Dynamic Theory of Personality* (New York, 1935) and Jacob S. Kounin, "Intellectual Development and Rigidity," in R. Barker, J. Kounin, and H. R. Wright, eds., *Child Behavior and Development* (New York, 1943), pp. 179–198.

8. Robert White, *op. cit.*, pp. 347 ff.

9. Lewin reminds those who may believe that a long-time perspective is not characteristic of the majority of individuals of the billions of dollars that are invested in insurance policies. Kurt Lewin, *Resolving Social Conflicts* (New York, 1948), p. 105.

10. Carl R. Rogers, *Client-Centered Therapy* (New York, 1951).

11. Another related but discrete set of developmental dimensions may be constructed to measure the protective (defense) mechanisms individuals tend to create as they develop from infancy to adulthood. Exactly how these would be related to the above model is not clear.

expression and fosters optimum expression are the limits set by the individual's own personality. For example, some people fear the same amount of independence and activity that others desire, and some people do not have the necessary abilities to perform certain tasks. No given individual is known to have developed all known abilities to their full maturity.

(5) The dimensions described above are constructed in terms of latent or genotypical characteristics. If one states that an individual needs to be dependent, this need may be ascertained by clinical inference, because it is one that individuals are not usually aware of. Thus one may observe an employee acting as if he were independent, but it is possible that if one goes below the behavioral surface the individual may be quite dependent. The obvious example is the employee who always seems to behave in a manner contrary to that desired by management. Although this behavior may look as if he is independent, his contrariness may be due to his great need to be dependent upon management which he dislikes to admit to himself and to others.

One might say that an independent person is one whose behavior is not caused by the influence others have over him. Of course, no individual is completely independent. All of us have our healthy dependencies (i.e., those which help us to be creative and to develop). One operational criterion to ascertain whether an individual's desire to be, let us say, independent and active is truly a mature manifestation is to ascertain the extent to which he permits others to express the same needs. Thus an autocratic leader may say that he needs to be active and independent; he may also say that he wants subordinates who are the same. There is ample research to suggest, however, that his leadership pattern only makes him and his subordinates more dependence-ridden.

SOME BASIC PROPERTIES OF FORMAL ORGANIZATION

The next step is to focus the analytic spotlight on the formal organization. What are its properties? What are its basic "givens"? What probable impact will they have upon the human personality? How will the human personality tend to react to this impact? What sorts of chain reactions are probable when these two basic components are brought together?

FORMAL ORGANIZATIONS AS RATIONAL ORGANIZATIONS

Probably the most basic property of formal organization is its logical foundation or, as it has been called by students of administration, its essential rationality. It is the planners' conception of how the intended consequences of the organization may best be achieved. The underlying assumption made by the creators of formal organization is that within respectable tolerances man will behave rationally, that is, as the formal plan requires him to behave. Organizations are formed with particular objectives in mind, and their structures mirror these objectives. Although man may not follow the prescribed paths, and consequently the objectives may never be achieved, Herbert A. Simon suggests that by and large man does follow these prescribed paths:

> Organizations are formed with the intention and design of accomplishing goals; and the people who work in organizations believe, at least part of the time, that they are striving toward these same goals. We must not lose sight of the fact that however far organizations may depart from the traditional description . . . nevertheless most behavior in organizations is intendedly rational behavior. By "intended rationality" I mean the kind of adjustment of behavior to goals of which humans are capable—a very incomplete and imperfect adjustment, to be sure, but one which nevertheless does accomplish purposes and does carry out programs.[12]

In an illuminating book, L. Urwick eloquently describes this underlying characteristic.[13] He insists that the creation of a formal organization requires a logical "drawing-office" approach. Although he admits that "nine times out of ten it is impossible to start with a clean sheet," the organizer should sit down and in a "cold-blooded, detached spirit . . . draw an ideal structure." The section from which I quote begins with Urwick's description of how the formal structure should be planned. He then continues:

> Manifestly that is a drawing-office job. It is a designing process. And it may be objected with a great deal of experience to support the contention that organization is never done that way . . . human organization. Nine times out of ten it is impossible to start with a clean sheet. The organizer has to make the best possible use of the human material that is already available. And in 89 out of those 90 per cent of cases he has to adjust jobs around to fit the man; he can't change the man to fit the job. He can't sit down in a cold-blooded, detached spirit and draw an ideal structure, an optimum distribution of duties and responsibilities and relationships, and then expect the infinite variety of human nature to fit into it.

12. Herbert A. Simon, *Research Frontiers in Politics and Government* (Washington, D.C., 1955), ch. ii, p. 30.

13. L. Urwick, *The Elements of Administration* (New York, 1944).

To which the reply is that he can and he should. If he has not got a clean sheet, that is no earthly reason why he should not make the slight effort of imagination required to assume that he has a clean sheet. It is not impossible to forget provisionally the personal facts—that old Brown is admirably methodical but wanting in initiative, that young Smith got into a mess with Robinson's wife and that the two men must be kept at opposite ends of the building, that Jones is one of those creatures who can think like a Wrangler about other people's duties but is given to periodic amnesia about certain aspects of his own.[14]

The task of the organizer, therefore, is to create a logically ordered world where, as Fayol suggests, there is a "proper order" and in which there is a "place for everything (everyone)."[15]

The possibility that the formal organization can be altered by personalities, as found by Conrad M. Arensberg and Douglas McGregor[16] and Ralph M. Stogdill and Katheleen Koehler,[17] is not denied by formal organizational experts. Urwick, for example, states in the passage below that the planner must take into account the human element. But it is interesting to note that he perceives these adjustments as "temporary deviations from the pattern in order to deal with idiosyncrasy of personality." If possible, these deviations should be minimized by careful preplanning.

He [the planner] should never for a moment pretend that these (human) difficulties don't exist. They do exist; they are realities. Nor, when he has drawn up an ideal plan of organization, is it likely that he will be able to fit in all the existing human material perfectly. There will be small adjustments of the job to the man in all kinds of directions. But those adjustments are deliberate and temporary deviations from the pattern in order to deal with idiosyncrasy. There is a world of difference between such modification and drifting into an unworkable organization because Green has a fancy for combining bits of two incompatible functions, or White is "empire-building" . . . or Black has always looked after the canteen, so when he is promoted to Sales Manager, he might as well continue to sell buns internally, though the main product of business happens to be battleships.

What is suggested is that problems of organization should be handled in the right order. Personal adjustments must be made, insofar as they are necessary. But fewer of them will be necessary and they will present fewer deviations from what is logical and simple, if the organizer first makes a plan, a design—to which he would work if he had the ideal human material. He should expect to be driven from it here and there. But he will be driven from it far less and his machine will work much more smoothly if he starts with a plan. If he starts with a motley collection of human oddities and tries to organize to fit them all in, thinking first of their various shapes and sizes and colors, he may have a patchwork quilt; he will not have an organization.[18]

The majority of experts on formal organization agree with Urwick. Most of them emphasize that no organizational structure will be ideal. None will exemplify the maximum expression of the principles of formal organization. A satisfactory aspiration is for optimum expression, which means modifying the ideal structure to take into account the individual (and any environmental) conditions. Moreover, they urge that the people must be loyal to the formal structure if it is to work effectively. Thus Taylor emphasizes that scientific management would never succeed without a "mental revolution."[19] Fayol has the same problem in mind when he emphasizes the importance of esprit de corps.

It is also true, however, that these experts have provided little insight into why they believe that people should undergo a "mental revolution," or why an esprit de corps is necessary if the principles are to succeed. The only hints found in the literature are that resistance to scientific management occurs because human beings "are what they are" or "because it's human nature." But why does "human nature" resist formal organizational principles? Perhaps there is something inherent in the principles which cause human resistance. Unfortunately too little research specifically assesses the impact of formal organizational principles upon human beings.

Another argument for planning offered by the formal organizational experts is that the organization created by logical, rational design, in the long run, is more human than one created haphazardly. They argue that it is illogical, cruel, wasteful, and inefficient not to have a logical design. It is illogical because design must come first. It does not make sense to pay a large salary to an individual without clearly defining his position and its relationship to the whole. It is cruel be-

14. Ibid., pp. 36–39; quoted by permission of Harper & Brothers.

15. Cited in Harold Koontz and Cyril O'Donnell, Principles of Management (New York, 1955), p. 24.

16. Conrad M. Arensberg and Douglas McGregor, Determination of Morale in an Industrial Company, Applied Anthropology, 1 (Jan.-March 1942), 12–34.

17. Ralph M. Stogdill and Kathleen Koehler, Measures of Leadership Structure and Organization Change (Columbus, O., 1952).

18. Ibid., pp. 36–39; quoted by permission of Harper & Brothers.

19. For a provocative discussion of Taylor's philosophy, see Reinhard Bendix, Work and Authority in Industry (New York, 1956), pp. 274–319.

cause, in the long run, the participants suffer when no clear organizational structure exists. It is wasteful because, unless jobs are clearly predefined, it is impossible to plan logical training, promotion, resigning, and retiring policies. It is inefficient because the organization becomes dependent upon personalities. The personal touch leads to playing politics, which Mary Follett has described as a "deplorable form of coercion."[20]

Unfortunately, the validity of these arguments tends to be obscured in the eyes of the behavioral scientist because they imply that the only choice left, if the formal, rational, predesigned structure is not accepted, is to have no organizational structure at all, with the organizational structure left to the whims, pushes, and pulls of human beings. Some human-relations researchers, on the other hand, have unfortunately given the impression that formal structures are "bad" and that the needs of the individual participants should be paramount in creating and administering an organization. A recent analysis of the existing research, however, points up quite clearly that the importance of the organization is being recognized by those who in the past have focused largely upon the individual.[21]

In the past, and for the most part in the present, the traditional organizational experts based their "human architectural creation" upon certain basic principles or assumptions about the nature of organization. These principles have been described by such people as Urwick,[22] Mooney, Holden *et al.*, Fayol, Dennison, Brown, Gulick, White, Gaus, Stene, Hopf, and Taylor. Although these principles have been attacked by behavioral scientists, the assumption is made in this paper that to date no one has defined a more useful set of formal organization principles. Therefore the principles are accepted as givens. This frees us to inquire about their probable impact upon people, *if they are used as defined.*

TASK (WORK) SPECIALIZATION

As James J. Gillespie suggests, the roots of these principles of organization may be traced back to certain principles of industrial economics, the most important of which is the basic economic assumption held by builders of the industrial revolution that "the concentration of effort on a limited field of endeavor increases quality and quantity of output."[23] It follows from the above that the necessity for specialization should increase as the quantity of similar things to be done increases.

If concentrating effort on a limited field of endeavor increases the quality and quantity of output, it follows that organizational and administrative efficiency is increased by the specialization of tasks assigned to the participants of the organization.[24] Inherent in this assumption are three others. The first is that the human personality will behave more efficiently as the task that it is to perform becomes specialized. Second is the assumption that there can be found a one best way to define the job so that it is performed at greater speed.[25] Third is the assumption that any individual differences in the human personality may be ignored by transferring more skill and thought to machines.[26]

A number of difficulties arise concerning these assumptions when the properties of the human personality are recalled. First, the human personality we have seen is always attempting to actualize its unique organization of parts resulting from a continuous, emotionally laden, ego-involving process of growth. It is difficult, if not impossible, to assume that this process can be choked off and the resultant unique differences of individuals ignored. This is tantamount to saying that self-actualization can be ignored. The second difficulty is that task specialization requires the individual to use only a few of his abilities. Moreover, as specialization increases, the less complex motor abilities are used more frequently. These, research suggests, tend to be of lesser psychological importance to the individual. Thus the principle violates two basic givens of the healthy adult human personality. It inhibits self-actualization and provides expression for few, shallow, superficial abilities that do not provide the "endless challenge" desired by the healthy personality.

Harold L. Wilensky and Charles N. Lebeaux correctly point out that task specialization causes what little skill is left in a job to become very important.[27] Now small differences in ability may make enormous differences in output. Thus two machine-shovel operators or two drill-press operators of different degrees of skill can produce dramatically different outputs. Ironically, the increasing importance of this type of skill for the

---

20. Quoted in *ibid.*, pp. 36–39.

21. Chris Argyris, *The Present State of Research in Human Relations* (New Haven, 1954), ch. i.

22. Urwick, *op. cit.*

23. James J. Gillespie, *Free Expression in Industry* (London, 1948), pp. 34–37.

24. Herbert A. Simon, *Administrative Behavior* (New York, 1947), pp. 80–81.

25. For an interesting discussion see Georges Friedman, *Industrial Society* (Glencoe, Ill., 1955), pp. 54 ff.

26. *Ibid.*, p. 20. Friedman reports that 79 per cent of Ford employees had jobs for which they could be trained in one week.

27. Harold L. Wilensky and Charles N. Lebeaux, *Industrialization and Social Welfare* (New York, 1955), p. 43.

healthy, mature worker means that he should feel he is performing self-satisfying work while using a small number of psychologically unchallenging abilities, when in actuality he may be predisposed to feel otherwise. Task specialization, therefore, requires a healthy adult to behave in a less mature manner, but it also requires that he feel good about it!

Not only is the individual affected, but the social structure as well is modified as a result of the situation described above. Wilensky and Lebeaux, in the same analysis, point out that placing a great emphasis on ability makes "Who you are" become less important than "What you can do." Thus the culture begins to reward relatively superficial, materialistic characteristics.

CHAIN OF COMMAND

The principle of task specialization creates an aggregate of parts, each performing a highly specialized task. An aggregate of parts, each busily performing its particular objective, does not form an organization, however. A pattern of parts must be formed so that the interrelationships among the parts create the organization. Following the logic of specialization, the planners create a new function (leadership) the primary responsibility of which is to control, direct, and coordinate the interrelationships of the parts and to make certain that each part performs its objective adequately. Thus the planner makes the assumption that administrative and organizational efficiency is increased by arranging the parts in a determinate hierarchy of authority in which the part on top can direct and control the part on the bottom.

If the parts being considered are individuals, then they must be motivated to accept direction, control, and coordination of their behavior. The leader, therefore, is assigned formal power to hire, discharge, reward, and penalize the individuals in order to mold their behavior in the pattern of the organization's objectives.

The impact of such a state of affairs is to make the individuals dependent upon, passive, and subordinate to the leader. As a result, the individuals have little control over their working environment. At the same time their time perspective is shortened because they do not control the information necessary to predict their futures. These requirements of formal organization act to inhibit four of the growth trends of the personality, because to be passive, subordinate, and to have little control and a short time perspective exemplify in adults the dimensions of immaturity, not adulthood.

The planners of formal organization suggest three basic ways to minimize this admittedly difficult position. First, ample rewards should be given to those who perform well and who do not permit their dependence, subordination, passivity, and so forth to influence them in a negative manner. The rewards should be material and psychological. Because of the specialized nature of the worker's job, however, few psychological rewards are possible. It becomes important, therefore, that adequate material rewards are made available to the productive employee. This practice can lead to new difficulties, since the solution is, by its nature, not to do anything about the on-the-job situation (which is what is causing the difficulties) but to pay the individual for the dissatisfactions he experiences. The result is that the employee is paid for his dissatisfaction while at work and his wages are given to him to gain satisfactions outside his work environment.

Thus the management helps to create a psychological set which leads the employees to feel that basic causes of dissatisfaction are built into industrial life, that the rewards they receive are wages for dissatisfaction, and that if satisfaction is to be gained the employee must seek it outside the organization.

To make matters more difficult, there are three assumptions inherent in the above solution that also violate the basic givens of human personality. First, the solution assumes that a whole human being can split his personality so that he will feel satisfied in knowing that the wages for his dissatisfaction will buy him satisfaction outside the plant. Second, it assumes that the employee is primarily interested in maximizing his economic gains. Third, it assume that the employee is best rewarded as an individual producer. The work group in which he belongs is not viewed as a relevant factor. If he produces well, he should be rewarded. If he does not, he should be penalized even though he may be restricting production because of informal group sanctions.

The second solution suggested by the planners of formal organization is to have technically competent, objective, rational, loyal leaders. The assumption is made that if the leaders are technically competent presumably they cannot have "the wool pulled over their eyes" and that therefore the employees will have a high respect for them. The leaders should be objective and rational and personify the rationality inherent in the formal structure. Being rational means that they must avoid becoming emotionally involved. As one executive states, "We try to keep our personality out of the job." The leader must also be impartial; he must not permit his feelings to operate when he is evaluating others. Finally, the leader must be loyal to the organization so that he can inculcate the loyalty in the employees that Taylor, Fayol, and others believe is so important.

Admirable as this solution may be, it also violates several of the basic properties of personality. If the employees are to respect an individual for what he does rather than for who he is, the sense of integrity based upon evaluation of the total self which is developed in people is lost. Moreover, to ask the leader to keep his personality out of his job is to ask him to stop actualizing himself. This is not possible as long as he is alive. Of course, the executive may want to feel that he is not involved, but it is a basic given that the human personality is an organism always actualizing itself. The same problem arises with impartiality. No one can be completely impartial. As has been shown, the self concept always operates when we are making judgments. In fact, as Rollo May has pointed out, the best way to be impartial is to be as partial as one's needs predispose one to be but to be aware of this partiality in order to correct for it at the moment of decision.[28] Finally, if a leader can be loyal to an organization under these conditions, there may be adequate grounds for questioning the health of his personality make-up.

The third solution suggested by many adherents to formal organizational principles is to motivate the subordinates to have more initiative and to be more creative by placing them in competition with one another for the positions of power that lie above them in the organizational ladder. This solution is traditionally called "the rabble hypothesis." Acting under the assumption that employees will be motivated to advance upward, the adherents of formal organizations further assume that competition for the increasingly (as one goes up the ladder) scarcer positions will increase the effectiveness of the participants. D. C. S. Williams, conducting some controlled experiments, shows that the latter assumption is not necessarily valid. People placed in competitive situations are not necessarily better learners than those placed in noncompetitive situations.[29] M. Deutsch, as a result of extensive controlled experimental research, supports Williams' results and goes much further to suggest that competitive situations tend to lead to an increase in tension and conflict and a decrease in human effectiveness.[30]

UNITY OF DIRECTION

If the tasks of everyone in a unit are specialized, then it follows that the objective or purpose of the unit must be specialized. The principle of unity of direction states that organizational efficiency increases if each unit has a single activity (or homogeneous set of activities) that are planned and directed by the leader.[31]

This means that the goal toward which the employees are working, the path toward the goal, and the strength of the barriers they must overcome to achieve the goal are defined and controlled by the leader. Assuming that the work goals do not involve the egos of the employees, (i.e., they are related to peripheral, superficial needs), then ideal conditions for psychological failure have been created. The reader may recall that a basic given of a healthy personality is the aspiration for psychological success. Psychological success is achieved when each individual is able to define his own goals, in relation to his inner needs and the strength of the barriers to be overcome in order to reach these goals. Repetitive as it may sound, it is nevertheless true that the principle of unity of direction also violates a basic given of personality.

SPAN OF CONTROL

The principle of span of control[32] states that administrative efficiency is increased by limiting the span of control of a leader to no more than five or six subordinates whose work interlocks.[33]

It is interesting to note that Ernest Dale, in an extensive study of organizational principles and

28. Rollo May, "Historical and Philosophical Presuppositions for Understanding Therapy," in O. H. Mowrer, *Psychotherapy Theory and Research* (New York, 1953), pp. 38–39.

29. D. C. S. Williams, Effects of Competition between Groups in a Training Situation, *Occupational Psychology*, 30 (April 1956), 85–93.

30. M. Deutsch, An Experimental Study of the Effects of Cooperation and Competition upon Group Process, *Human Relations*, 2 (1949), 199–231.

31. The sacredness of these principles is questioned by a recent study. Gunnar Heckscher concludes that the principles of unity of command and unity of direction are formally violated in Sweden: "A fundamental principle of public administration in Sweden is the duty of all public agencies to cooperate directly without necessarily passing through a common superior. This principle is even embodied in the constitution itself, and in actual fact it is being employed daily. It is traditionally one of the most important characteristics of Swedish administration that especially central agencies, but also central and local agencies of different levels, cooperate freely and that this is being regarded as a perfectly normal procedure" (*Swedish Public Administration at Work* [Stockholm, 1955], p. 12).

32. First defined by V. A. Graicunas in an article entitled "Relationship in Organization," in L. Gulick and L. Urwick, eds., *Papers on the Science of Administration*, 2d ed. (New York, 1947), pp. 183–187.

33. L. Urwick, *Scientific Principles and Organization* (New York, 1938), p. 8.

practices in one hundred large organizations, concludes that the actual limits of the executive span of control are more often violated than not,[34] while in a recent study James H. Healey arrives at the opposite conclusion.[35] James C. Worthy reports that it is formal policy in his organization to extend the span of control of the top management much further than is theoretically suggested.[36] Finally, W. W. Suojanen, in a review of the current literature on the concept of span of control, concludes that it is no longer valid, particularly as applied to the larger government agencies and business corporations.[37]

In a recent article, however, Urwick criticizes the critics of the span-of-control principle.[38] For example, he notes that in the case described by Worthy, the superior has a large span of control over subordinates whose jobs do not interlock. The buyers in Worthy's organization purchase a clearly defined range of articles; therefore they find no reason to interlock with others.

Simon criticizes the span-of-control principle on the grounds that it increases the "administrative distance" between individuals. An increase in administrative distance violates, in turn, another formal organizational principle that administrative efficiency is enhanced by keeping at a minimum the number of organizational levels through which a matter must pass before it is acted on.[39] Span of control, continues Simon, inevitably increases red tape, since each contact between agents must be carried upward until a common superior is found. Needless waste of time and energy result. Also, since the solution of the problem depends upon the superior, the subordinate is in a position of having less control over his own work situation. This places the subordinate in a work situation in which he is less mature.

Although the distance between individuals in different units increases (because they have to find a common superior), the administrative distance between superior and subordinate within a given unit decreases. As Whyte correctly points out, the principle of span of control, by keeping the number of subordinates at a minimum, places great emphasis on close supervision.[40] Close supervision leads the subordinates to become dependent upon, passive toward, and subordinate to, the leader. Close supervision also tends to place the control in the superior. Thus we must conclude that span of control, if used correctly, will tend to increase the subordinate's feelings of dependence, submissiveness, passivity, and so on. In short, it will tend to create a work situation which requires immature, rather than mature, participants.

AN INCONGRUENCY BETWEEN THE NEEDS OF A MATURE PERSONALITY AND OF FORMAL ORGANIZATION

Bringing together the evidence regarding the impact of formal organizational principles upon the individual, we must conclude that there are some basic incongruencies between the growth trends of a healthy personality in our culture and the requirements of formal organization. If the principles of formal organization are used as ideally defined, then the employees will tend to work in an environment where (1) they are provided minimal control over their work-a-day world, (2) they are expected to be passive, dependent, subordinate, (3) they are expected to have a short-time perspective, (4) they are induced to perfect and value the frequent use of a few superficial abilities, and (5) they are expected to produce under conditions leading to psychological failure.

All of these characteristics are incongruent to the ones healthy human beings are postulated to desire. They are much more congruent with the needs of infants in our culture. In effect, therefore, formal organizations are willing to pay high wages and provide adequate seniority if mature adults will, for eight hours a day, behave in a less mature manner. If this analysis is correct, this inevitable incongruency increases (1) as the employees are of increasing maturity, (2) as the formal structure (based upon the above principles) is made more clear-cut and logically tight for maximum formal organizational effectiveness, (3) as one goes down the line of command, and (4) as the jobs become more and more mechanized (i.e., take on assembly-line characteristics).

As in the case of the personality developmental trends, this picture of formal organization is also a model. Clearly, no company actually uses the formal principles of organization exactly as stated by their creators. There is ample evidence to suggest that they are being modified constantly in actual situations. Those who expound these principles, however, probably would be willing to defend their position that this is the reason that human-

34. Ernest Dale, *Planning and Developing the Company Organization Structure* (New York, 1952), ch. xx.

35. James H. Healey, Coordination and Control of Executive Functions, *Personnel*, 33 (Sept. 1956), 106–117.

36. James C. Worthy, Organizational Structure and Employee Morale, *American Sociological Review*, 15 (April 1950), 169–179.

37. W. W. Suojanen, The Span of Control—Fact or Fable?, *Advanced Management*, 20 (1955), 5–13.

38. L. Urwick, The Manager's Span of Control, *Harvard Business Review*, 34 (May–June 1956), 39–47.

39. Simon, *op. cit.*, pp. 26–28.

40. William Whyte, "On the Evolution of Industrial Sociology" (mimeographed paper presented at the 1956 meeting of the American Sociological Society).

relations problems exist; the principles are not followed as they should be.

In the model of the personality and the formal organization, we are assuming the extreme of each in order that the analysis and its results can be highlighted. Speaking in terms of extremes helps us to make the position sharper. In doing this, we make no assumption that all situations in real life are extreme (i.e., that the individuals will always want to be more mature and that the formal organization will always tend to make people more dependent, passive, and so forth, all the time).[41] The model ought to be useful, however, to plot the degree to which each component tends toward extremes and then to predict the problems that will tend to arise.

Returning to the analysis, it is not difficult to see why some students of organization suggest that immature and even mentally retarded individuals probably would make excellent employees in certain jobs. There is very little documented experience to support such a hypothesis. One reason for this lack of information is probably the delicacy of the subject. Examples of what might be obtained if a systematic study were made may be found in a recent work by Mal Brennan.[42] He cites the Utica Knitting Mill, which made arrangements during 1917 with the Rome Institution for Mentally Defective Girls to employ twenty-four girls whose mental age ranged from six to ten years of age. The girls were such excellent workers that they were employed after the war emergency ended. In fact, the company added forty more in another of their plants. It is interesting to note that the managers praised the subnormal girls highly. According to Brennan, in several important reports they said that

when business conditions required a reduction of the working staff, the hostel girls were never "laid off" in disproportion to the normal girls; that they were more punctual, more regular in their habits, and did not indulge in as much "gossip and levity." They received the same rate of pay, and they had been employed successfully at almost every process carried out in the workshops.

In another experiment reported by Brennan, the Works Manager of the Radio Corporation, Ltd., reported that of five young morons employed, "the three girls compared very favourably with the normal class of employee in that age group. The boy employed in the store performed his work with satisfaction. . . . Although there was some doubt about the fifth child, it was felt that getting the most out of him was just a matter of right placement." In each of the five cases, the morons were reported to be quiet, respectful, well behaved, and very obedient. The Works Manager was especially impressed by their truthfulness. A year later the same Works Manager was still able to advise that "in every case, the girls proved to be exceptionally well-behaved, particularly obedient, and strictly honest and trustworthy. They carried out work required of them to such a degree of efficiency that *we were surprised they were classed as subnormals for their age.*"[43]

SUMMARY OF FINDINGS

If one were to put these basic findings in terms of propositions, one could state:

PROPOSITION I. *There is a Lack of Congruency between the Needs of Healthy Individuals and the Demands of the Formal Organization.*

If one uses the traditional formal principles of organization (i.e., chain of command, task specialization, and so on) to create a social organization, and

if one uses as an input agents who tend toward mature psychological development (i.e., who are predisposed toward relative independence, activeness, use of important abilities, and so on),

then one creates a disturbance, because the needs of healthy individuals listed above are not congruent with the requirements of formal organization, which tends to require the agents to work in situations where they are dependent, passive, use few and unimportant abilities, and so forth.

Corollary. 1. The disturbance will vary in proportion to the degree of incongruency between the needs of the individuals and the requirements of the formal organization.[44]

An administrator, therefore, is always faced with a tendency toward continual disturbance inherent in the work situation of the individuals over whom he is in charge.

Drawing on the existing knowledge of the human personality, a second proposition can be stated.

---

41. In fact, much evidence is presented in the book from which this article is drawn to support contrary tendencies.

42. Mal Brennan, *The Making of a Moron* (New York, 1953), pp. 13–18.

43. Mr. Brennan's emphasis.

44. This proposition does not hold under certain conditions.

PROPOSITION II. *The Results of This Disturbance Are Frustration, Failure, Short-Time Perspective, and Conflict.*[45]

If the agents are predisposed to a healthy, mature self-actualization, the following results will occur:

(1) They will tend to experience frustration because their self-actualization will be blocked.

(2) They will tend to experience failure because they will not be permitted to define their own goals in relation to their central needs, the paths to these goals, and so on.

(3) They will tend to experience short-time perspective, because they have no control over the clarity and stability of their future.

(4) They will tend to experience conflict, because, as healthy agents, they will dislike the frustration, failure, and short-time perspective which is characteristic of their present jobs. If they leave, however, they may not find new jobs easily, and even if new jobs are found, they may not be much different.[46]

Based upon the analysis of the nature of formal organization, one may state a third proposition.

PROPOSITION III. *The Nature of the Formal Principles of Organization Cause the Subordinate, at Any Given Level, to Experience Competition, Rivalry, Intersubordinate Hostility, and to Develop a Focus toward the Parts Rather than the Whole.*

(1) Because of the degree of dependence, subordination, and so on of the subordinates upon the leader, and because the number of positions above any given level always tends to decrease, the subordinates aspiring to perform effectively and to advance will tend to find themselves in competition with, and receiving hostility from, each other.[47]

(2) Because, according to the formal principles, the subordinate is directed toward and rewarded for performing his own task well, the subordinate tends to develop an orientation toward his own particular part rather than toward the whole.

(3) This part-orientation increases the need for the leader to coordinate the activity among the parts in order to maintain the whole. This need for the leader, in turn, increases the subordinates' degree of dependence, subordination, and so forth. This is a circular process whose impact is to maintain and/or increase the degree of dependence, subordination, and so on, as well as to stimulate rivalry and competition for the leader's favor.

A BIRD'S-EYE, CURSORY PICTURE OF SOME OTHER RELATED FINDINGS

It is impossible in the short space available to present all of the results obtained from the analysis of the literature. For example, it can be shown that employees tend to adapt to the frustration, failure, short-time perspective, and conflict involved in their work situations by any one or a combination of the following acts:

(1) Leaving the organization.

(2) Climbing the organizational ladder.

(3) Manifesting defense reactions such as daydreaming, aggression, ambivalence, regression, projection, and so forth.

(4) Becoming apathetic and disinterested toward the organization, its make-up, and its goals. This leads to such phenomena as: (a) employees reducing the number and potency of the needs they expect to fulfill while at work; (b) employees goldbricking, setting rates, restricting quotas, making errors, cheating, slowing down, and so on.

(5) Creating informal groups to sanction the defense reactions and the apathy, disinterest, and lack of self-involvement.

(6) Formalizing the informal group.

(7) Evolving group norms that perpetuate the behavior outlined in (3), (4), (5), and (6) above.

(8) Evolving a psychological set in which human or nonmaterial factors become increasingly unimportant while material factors become increasingly important.

(9) Acculturating youth to accept the norms outlined in (7) and (8).

Furthermore, it can also be shown that many managements tend to respond to the employees' behavior by:

(1) Increasing the degree of their pressure-oriented leadership.

(2) Increasing the degree of their use of management controls.

(3) Increasing the number of "pseudo"-participation and communication programs.

---

45. In the full analysis, specific conditions are derived under which the basic incongruency increases or decreases.

46. These points are taken, in order, from: Roger G. Barker, T. Dembo, and K. Lewin, "Frustration and Regression: An Experiment with Young Children," *Studies in Child Welfare*, vol. XVIII, No. 2 (Iowa City, Ia., 1941); John Dollard *et al.*, *Frustration and Aggression* (New Haven, 1939); Kurt Lewin *et al.*, "Level of Aspiration," in J. McV. Hunt, ed., *Personality and the Behavior Disorders* (New York, 1944), pp. 333–378; Ronald Lippitt and Leland Bradford, Employee Success in Work Groups, *Personnel Administration*, 8 (Dec. 1945), 6–10; Kurt Lewin, "Time Perspective and Morale," in Gertrude Weiss Lewin, ed., *Resolving Social Conflicts* (New York, 1948), pp. 103–124; and Theodore M. Newcomb, *Social Psychology* (New York, 1950), pp. 361–373.

47. These problems may not arise for the subordinate who becomes apathetic, disinterested, and so on.

These three reactions by management actually compound the dependence, subordination, and so on that the employees experience, which in turn cause the employees to increase their adaptive behavior, the very behavior management desired to curtail in the first place.

Is there a way out of this circular process? The basic problem is the reduction in the degree of dependency, subordination, submissiveness, and so on experienced by the employee in his work situation. It can be shown that job enlargement and employee-centered (or democratic or participative) leadership are elements which, if used correctly, can go a long way toward ameliorating the situation. These are limited, however, because their success depends upon having employees who are ego-involved and highly interested in the organization. This dilemma between individual needs and organization demands is a basic, continual problem posing an eternal challenge to the leader. How is it possible to create an organization in which the individuals may obtain optimum expression and, simultaneously, in which the organization itself may obtain optimum satisfaction of its demands? Here lies a fertile field for future research in organizational behavior.

39 – Group Dynamics and the Individual

DORWIN CARTWRIGHT
and RONALD LIPPITT

How should we think of the relation between individuals and groups? Few questions have stirred up so many issues of metaphysics, epistemology, and ethics. Do groups have the same reality as individuals? If so, what are the properties of groups? Can groups learn, have goals, be frustrated, develop, regress, begin and end? Or are these characteristics strictly attributable only to individuals? If groups exist, are they good or bad? How *should* an individual behave with respect to groups? How *should* groups treat their individual members? Such questions have puzzled man from the earliest days of recorded history.

In our present era of "behavioral science" we like to think that we can be "scientific" and proceed to study human behavior without having to take sides on these problems of speculative philosophy. Invariably, however, we are guided by certain assumptions, stated explicitly or not, about the reality or irreality of groups, about their observability, and about their good or bad value.

Usually these preconceptions are integral parts of one's personal and scientific philosophy, and it is often hard to tell how much they derive from emotionally toned personal experiences with other people and how much from coldly rational and "scientific" considerations. In view of the fervor with which they are usually defended, one might suspect that most have a small basis at least in personally significant experiences. These preconceptions, moreover, have a tendency to assume a homogeneous polarization—either positive or negative.

Consider first the completely negative view. It consists of two major assertions: first, groups don't really exist. They are a product of distorted thought processes (often called "abstractions"). In fact, social prejudice consists precisely in acting as if groups, rather than individuals, were real. Second, groups are bad. They demand blind loyalty, they make individuals regress, they reduce man to the lowest common denominator, and they produce what *Fortune* magazine has immortalized as "group-think."

In contrast to this completely negative conception of groups, there is the completely positive one. This syndrome, too, consists of two major assertions: first, groups really do exist. Their reality is demonstrated by the difference it makes to an individual whether he is accepted or rejected by a group and whether he is part of a healthy or sick group. Second, groups are good. They satisfy deep-seated needs of individuals for affiliation, affection, recognition, and self-esteem; they stimulate individuals to moral heights of altruism, loyalty, and self-sacrifice; they provide a means, through cooperative interaction, by which man can accomplish things unattainable through individual enterprise.

This completely positive preconception is the one attributed most commonly, it seems, to the so-called "group dynamics movement." Group dynamicists, it is said, have not only *reified* the

"Group Dynamics and the Individual," *International Journal of Group Psychotherapy,* VII (January 1957), 86 – 102. Reprinted by permission of the authors and the American Group Psychotherapy Association, Inc. **Dorwin Cartwright** and **Ronald Lippitt**: Research Center for Group Dynamics, University of Michigan.

group but also *idealized* it. They believe that everything should be done by and in groups — individual responsibility is bad, man-to-man supervision is bad, individual problem-solving is bad, and even individual therapy is bad. The only good things are committee meetings, group decisions, group problem-solving, and group therapy. "If you don't hold the group in such high affection," we were once asked, "why do you call your research organization the Research Center FOR Group Dynamics? And, if you are *for* groups and group dynamics, mustn't you therefore be *against* individuality, individual responsibility, and self-determination?"

FIVE PROPOSITIONS ABOUT GROUPS

This assumption that individuals and groups must necessarily have incompatible interests is made so frequently in one guise or another that it requires closer examination. Toward this end we propose five related assertions about individuals, groups, and group dynamics, which are intended to challenge the belief that individuals and groups must necessarily have incompatible, or for that matter, compatible interests.

1. Groups do exist; they must be dealt with by any man of practical affairs, or indeed by any child, and they must enter into any adequate account of human behavior. Most infants are born into a specific group. Little Johnny may be a welcome or unwelcome addition to the group. His presence may produce profound changes in the structure of the group and consequently in the feelings, attitudes, and behavior of various group members. He may create a triangle where none existed before or he may break up one which has existed. His development and adjustment for years to come may be deeply influenced by the nature of the group he enters and by his particular position in it — whether, for example, he is a first or second child (a personal property which has no meaning apart from its reference to a specific group).

There is a wealth of research whose findings can be satisfactorily interpreted only by assuming the reality of groups. Recall the experiment of Lewin, Lippitt, and White (15) in which the level of aggression of an individual was shown to depend upon the social atmosphere and structure of the group he is in and not merely upon such personal traits as aggressiveness. By now there can be little question about the kinds of results reported from the Western Electric study (18) which make it clear that groups develop norms for the behav-

ior of their members with the result that "good" group members adopt these norms as their *personal* values. Nor can one ignore the dramatic evidence of Lewin, Bavelas, and others (14) which shows that group decisions may produce changes in individual behavior much larger than those customarily found to result from attempts to modify the behavior of individuals *as* isolated individuals.

2. Groups are inevitable and ubiquitous. The biological nature of man, his capacity to use language, and the nature of his environment which has been built into its present form over thousands of years require that man exist in groups. This is not to say that groups must maintain the properties they now display, but we cannot conceive of a collection of human beings living in geographical proximity under conditions where it would be correct to assert that no groups exist and that there is no such thing as group membership.

3. Groups mobilize powerful forces which produce effects of the utmost importance to individuals. Consider two examples from rather different research settings. Seashore (22) has recently published an analysis of data from 5,871 employees of a large manufacturing company. An index of group cohesiveness, developed for each of 228 work groups, permitted a comparison of members working in high and in low cohesive groups. Here is one of his major findings: "Members of high cohesive groups exhibit less anxiety than members of low cohesive groups, using as measures of anxiety: (a) feeling 'jumpy' or 'nervous,' (b) feeling under pressure to achieve higher productivity (with actual productivity held constant), and (c) feeling a lack of support from the company" (p. 98). Seashore suggests two reasons for the relation between group cohesiveness and individual anxiety: "(1) that the cohesive group provides effective support for the individual in his encounters with anxiety-provoking aspects of his environment, thus allaying anxiety, and (2) that group membership offers direct satisfaction, and this satisfaction in membership has a generalized effect of anxiety-reduction" (p. 13).

Perhaps a more dramatic account of the powerful forces generated in groups can be derived from the publication by Stanton and Schwartz (24) of their studies of a mental hospital. They report, for example, how a patient may be thrown into an extreme state of excitement by disagreements between two staff members over the patient's care. Thus, two doctors may disagree about whether a female patient should be moved to another ward. As the disagreement progresses, the doctors may stop communicating relevant information to one another and start lining up allies in the medical and nursing staff. The patient, meanwhile, becomes increasingly restless until, at the height of the doctors' disagreement, she is in an acute state of excitement and must be secluded, put under sedation, and given special supervision. Presumably, successful efforts to improve the interpersonal relations and communications among members of the staff would improve the mental condition of such a patient.

In general, it is clear that events occurring in a group may have repercussions on members who are not directly involved in these events. A person's position in a group, moreover, may affect the way others behave toward him and such personal qualities as his levels of aspiration and self-esteem. Group membership itself may be a prized possession or an oppressive burden; tragedies of major proportions have resulted from the exclusion of individuals from groups, and equally profound consequences have stemmed from enforced membership in groups.

4. Groups may produce both good and bad consequences. The view that groups are completely good and the view that they are completely bad are both based on convincing evidence. *The only fault with either is its one-sidedness.* Research motivated by one or the other is likely to focus on different phenomena. As an antidote to such one-sidedness it is a good practice to ask research questions in pairs, one stressing positive aspects and one negative: What are the factors producing conformity? *and* what are the factors producing nonconformity? What brings about a breakdown in communication? *and* what stimulates or maintains effective communication? An exclusive focus on pathologies or upon positive criteria leads to a seriously incomplete picture.

5. A correct understanding of group dynamics permits the possibility that desirable consequences from groups can be deliberately enhanced. Through a knowledge of group dynamics, groups can be made to serve better ends, for knowledge gives power to modify human beings and human behavior. At the same time, recognition of this fact produces some of the deepest conflicts within the behavioral scientist, for it raises the whole problem of social manipulation. Society must not close its eyes to Orwell's horrible picture of life in 1984, but it cannot accept the alternative that in ignorance there is safety.

To recapitulate our argument: groups exist; they are inevitable and ubiquitous; they mobilize powerful forces having profound effects upon individuals; these effects may be good or bad; and through a knowledge of group dynamics there lies the possibility of maximizing their good value.

Many thoughtful people today are alarmed over one feature of groups: the pressure toward conformity experienced by group members. Indeed, this single "bad" aspect is often taken as evidence that groups are bad in general. Let us examine the specific problem of conformity, then, in order to attain a better understanding of the general issue. Although contemporary concern is great, it is not new. More than one hundred years ago Alexis de Tocqueville wrote: "I know of no country in which there is so little independence of mind and real freedom of discussion as in America. . . . In America the majority raises formidable barriers around the liberty of opinion. . . . The master (majority) no longer says: 'You shall think as I do or you shall die'; but he says: 'You are free to think differently from me and to retain your life, your property, and all that you possess, but they will be useless to you, for you will never be chosen by your fellow citizens if you solicit their votes; and they will affect to scorn you if you ask for their esteem. You will remain among men, but you will be deprived of the rights of mankind. Your fellow creatures will shun you like an impure being; and even those who believe in your innocence will abandon you, lest they should be shunned in their turn'" (25, pp. 273–275).

Before too readily accepting such a view of groups as the whole story, let us invoke our dictum that research questions should be asked in pairs. Nearly everyone is convinced that individuals should not be blind conformers to group norms, that each group member should not be a carbon copy of every other member, but what is the other side of the coin? In considering why members of groups conform, perhaps we should also think of the consequences of the removal of individuals from group membership or the plight of the person who really does not belong to any group with clear-cut norms and values. The state of anomie, described by Durkheim, is also common today. It seems as if people who have no effective participation in groups with clear and strong value systems either crack up (as in alcoholism or suicide) or they seek out groups which will demand conformity. In discussing this process, Talcott Parsons writes: "In such a situation it is not surprising that large numbers of people should . . . be attracted to movements which can offer them membership in a group with a vigorous esprit de corps with submission to some strong authority and rigid system of belief, the individual thus finding a measure of escape from painful perplexities or from a situation of anomie" (17, pp. 128–129).

The British anthropologist, Adam Curle, has stressed the same problem when he suggested that in our society we need not four, but five freedoms, the fifth being freedom from that neurotic anxiety which springs from a man's isolation from his fellows, and which, in turn, isolates him still further from them.

We seem, then, to face a dilemma: the individual needs social support for his values and social beliefs; he needs to be accepted as a valued member of some group which *he* values; failure to maintain such group membership produces anxiety and personal disorganization. But, on the other hand, group membership and group participation tend to cost the individual his individuality. If he is to receive support from others and, in turn, give support to others, he and they must hold in common some values and beliefs. Deviation from these undermines any possibility of group support and acceptance.

Is there an avenue of escape from this dilemma? Certainly, the issue is not as simple as we have described it. The need for social support for some values does not require conformity with respect to all values, beliefs, and behavior. Any individual is a member of several groups, and he may be a successful deviate in one while conforming to another (think of the visitor in a foreign country or of the psychologist at a convention of psychiatrists). Nor should the time dimension be ignored; a person may sustain his deviancy through a conviction that his fate is only temporary. These refinements of the issue are important and should be examined in great detail, but before we turn our attention to them, we must assert that we do *not* believe that the basic dilemma can be escaped. To avoid complete personal disorganization man must conform to at least a minimal set of values required for participation in the groups to which he belongs.

PRESSURES TO UNIFORMITY

Some better light may be cast on this problem if we refer to the findings of research on conformity. What do we know about the way it operates?

Cognitive Processes. Modern psychological research on conformity reflects the many different currents of contemporary psychology, but the major direction has been largely determined by the classic experiment of Sherif (23) on the development of social norms in perceiving auto-

kinetic movement and by the more recent study of Asch (1) of pressures to conformity in perceiving unambiguous visual stimuli.

What does this line of investigation tell us about conformity? What has it revealed, for instance, about the conditions that set up pressures to conformity? Answers to this question have taken several forms, but nearly all point out that social interaction would be impossible if some beliefs and perceptions were not commonly shared by the participants. Speaking of the origin of such cognitive pressures to uniformity among group members, Asch says: "The individual comes to experience a world that he shares with others. He perceives that the surroundings include him, as well as others, and that he is in the same relation to the surroundings as others. He notes that he, as well as others, is converging upon the same object and responding to its identical properties. Joint action and mutual understanding require this relation of intelligibility and structural simplicity. In these terms the 'pull' toward the group becomes understandable" (1, p. 484).

Consistent with this interpretation of the origin of pressures to uniformity in a perceptual or judgmental situation are the findings that the major variables influencing tendencies to uniformity are (a) the quality of the social evidence (particularly the degree of unanimity of announced perceptions and the subject's evaluation of the trustworthiness of the other's judgments), (b) the quality of the direct perceptual evidence (particularly the clarity or ambiguity of the stimuli), (c) the magnitude of the discrepancy between the social and the perceptual evidence, and (d) the individual's self-confidence in the situation (as indicated either by experimental manipulations designed to affect self-confidence or by personality measurements).

The research in this tradition has been productive, but it has emphasized the individual and his cognitive problems and has considered the individual apart from any concrete and meaningful group membership. Presumably any trustworthy people adequately equipped with eyes and ears could serve to generate pressures to conformity in the subject, regardless of his specific relations to them. The result of this emphasis has been to ignore certain essential aspects of the conformity problem. Let us document this assertion with two examples.

First, the origin of pressures to uniformity has been made to reside in the person whose conformity is being studied. Through eliminating experimentally any possibility that pressures might be exerted by others, it has been possible to study the conformity of people as if they existed in a world where they can see or hear others but not be reacted to by others. It is significant, indeed, that conformity does arise in the absence of direct attempts to bring it about. But this approach does not raise certain questions about the conditions which lead to *social* pressures to conformity. What makes some people try to get others to conform? What conditions lead to what forms of pressure on others to get them to conform? The concentration of attention on the conformer has diverted attention away from the others in the situation who may insist on conformity and make vigorous efforts to bring it about or who may not exert any pressures at all on deviates.

A second consequence of this emphasis has been to ignore the broader social meaning of conformity. Is the individual's personal need for a social validation of his beliefs the only reason for conforming? What does deviation do to a person's acceptance by others? What does it do to his ability to influence others? Or, from the group's point of view, are there reasons to insist on certain common values, beliefs, and behavior? These questions are not asked nor answered by an approach which limits itself to the cognitive problems of the individual.

Group Processes. The group dynamics orientation toward conformity emphasizes a broader range of determinants. Not denying the importance of the cognitive situation, we want to look more closely at the nature of the individual's relation to particular groups with particular properties. In formulating hypotheses about the origin of pressures to uniformity, two basic sources have been stressed. These have been stated most clearly by Festinger and his co-workers (5), who propose that when differences of opinion arise within a group, pressures to uniformity will arise (a) if the validity or "reality" of the opinion depends upon agreement with the group (essentially the same point as Asch's), or (b) if locomotion toward a group goal will be facilitated by uniformity within the group.

This emphasis upon the group, rather than simply upon the individual, leads one to expect a broader set of consequences from pressures to uniformity. Pressures to uniformity are seen as establishing: (a) a tendency on the part of each group member to change his own opinion to conform to that of the other group members, (b) a tendency to try to change the opinions of others, and (c) a tendency to redefine the boundaries of the group so as to exclude those holding deviate opinions. The relative magnitudes of these tendencies will depend on other conditions which need to be specified.

This general conception of the nature of the processes that produce conformity emerged from two early field studies conducted at the Research Center for Group Dynamics. It was also influenced to a considerable extent by the previous work of Newcomb (16) in which he studied the formation and change of social attitudes in a college community. The first field study, reported by Festinger, Schachter, and Back (7), traced the formation of social groups in a new student housing project. As each group developed, it displayed its own standards for its members. The extent of conformity to the standards of a particular group was found to be related directly to the degree of cohesiveness of that group as measured by sociometric choices. Moreover, those individuals who deviated from their own group's norms received fewer sociometric choices than those who conformed. A process of rejection for nonconformity had apparently set in. The second field study, reported by Coch and French (3), observed similar processes. This study was conducted in a textile factory and was concerned with conformity to production standards set by groups of workers. Here an individual worker's reaction to new work methods was found to depend upon the standards of his group and, here too, rejection for deviation was observed.

The next phase of this research consisted of a series of experiments with groups created in the laboratory. It was hoped thereby to be able to disentangle the complexity of variables that might exist in any field setting in order to understand better the operation of each. These experiments have been reported in various publications by Festinger, Back, Gerard, Hymovitch, Kelley, Raven, Schachter, and Thibaut (2, 6, 8, 9, 11, 20). We shall not attempt to describe these studies in detail, but draw upon them and other research in an effort to summarize the major conclusions.

First, a great deal of evidence has been accumulated to support the hypothesis that pressures to uniformity will be greater the more members want to remain in the group. In more attractive or cohesive groups, members attempt more to influence others and are more willing to accept influence from others. Note that here pressures to conformity are high in the very conditions where satisfaction from group membership is also high.

Second, there is a close relation between attempts to change the deviate and tendencies to reject him. If persistent attempts to change the deviate fail to produce conformity, then communication appears to cease between the majority and the deviate, and rejection of the deviate sets in. These two processes, moreover, are more intense the more cohesive the group. One of the early studies which documented the process of rejection was conducted by Schachter (20) on college students. It has recently been replicated by Emerson (4) on high school students, who found essentially the same process at work, but he discovered that among his high school students efforts to influence others continued longer, there was a greater readiness on the part of the majority to change, and there was a lower level of rejection within a limited period of time. Yet another study, conducted in Holland, Sweden, France, Norway, Belgium, Germany, and England, found the same tendency to reject deviates in all of these countries. This study, reported by Schachter, et al. (21), is a landmark in cross-cultural research.

Third, there is the question of what determines whether or not pressures to uniformity will arise with respect to any particular opinion, attitude, and behavior. In most groups there are no pressures to uniformity concerning the color of necktie worn by the members. Differences of opinion about the age of the earth probably would not lead to rejection in a poker club, but they might do so in certain fundamentalist church groups. The concept of *relevance* seems to be required to account for such variations in pressures to uniformity. And, if we ask, "relevance for what?" we are forced again to look at the group and especially at the goals of the group.

Schachter (20) has demonstrated, for example, that deviation on a given issue will result much more readily in rejection when that issue is relevant to the group's goals than when it is irrelevant. And the principle of relevance seems to be necessary to account for the findings of a field study reported by Ross (19). Here attitudes of fraternity men toward restrictive admission policies were studied. Despite the fact that there was a consistent policy of exclusion in these fraternities, there was, surprisingly, little evidence for the existence of pressures toward uniformity of attitudes. When, however, a field experiment was conducted in which the distribution of actual opinions for each fraternity house was reported to a meeting of house members together with a discussion of the relevance of these opinions for fraternity policy, attitudes then tended to change to conform to the particular modal position of each house. Presumably the experimental treatment made uniformity of attitude instrumental to group locomotion where it had not been so before.

SOURCES OF HETEROGENEITY

We have seen that pressures to uniformity are stronger the more cohesive the group. Shall we conclude from this that strong, need-satisfying, cohesive groups must always produce uniformity on matters that are important to the group? We believe not. We cannot, however, cite much convincing evidence since research has focused to date primarily upon the sources of pressures to uniformity and has ignored the conditions which produce heterogeneity. Without suggesting, then, that we can give final answers, let us indicate some of the possible sources of heterogeneity.

Group Standards about Uniformity. It is important, first, to make a distinction between conformity and uniformity. A group might have a value that everyone should be as different from everyone else as possible. Conformity to this value, then, would result not in uniformity of behavior but in nonuniformity. Such a situation often arises in therapy groups or training groups where it is possible to establish norms which place a high value upon "being different" and upon tolerating deviant behavior. Conformity to this value is presumably greater the more cohesive the group and the more it is seen as relevant to the group's objectives. Unfortunately, very little is known about the origin and operation of group standards about conformity itself. We doubt that the pressure to uniformity which arises from the need for "social reality" and for group locomotion can simply be obliterated by invoking a group standard of tolerance, but a closer look at such processes as those of group decision-making will be required before a deep understanding of this problem can be achieved.

Freedom to Deviate. A rather different source of heterogeneity has been suggested by Kelley and Shapiro (12). They reason that the more an individual feels accepted by the other members of the group, the more ready he should be to deviate from the beliefs of the majority under conditions where objectively correct deviation would be in the group's best interest. They designed an experiment to test this hypothesis. The results, while not entirely clear because acceptance led to greater cohesiveness, tend to support this line of reasoning.

It has been suggested by some that those in positions of leadership are freer to deviate from group standards than are those of lesser status. Just the opposite conclusion has been drawn by others. Clearly, further research into group properties which generate freedom to deviate from majority pressures is needed.

Subgroup Formation. Festinger and Thibaut (8) have shown that lower group-wide pressures to uniformity of opinion result when members of a group perceive that the group is composed of persons differing in interest and knowledge. Under these conditions subgroups may easily develop with a resulting heterogeneity within the group as a whole though with uniformity within each subgroup. This conclusion is consistent with Asch's (1) finding that the presence of a partner for a deviate greatly strengthens his tendency to be independent. One might suspect that such processes, though achieving temporarily a greater heterogeneity, would result in a schismatic subgroup conflict.

Positions and Roles. A more integrative achievement of heterogeneity seems to arise through the process of role differentiation. Established groups are usually differentiated according to "positions" with special functions attached to each. The occupant of the position has certain behaviors prescribed for him by the others in the group. These role prescriptions differ, moreover, from one position to another, with the result that conformity to them produces heterogeneity within the group. A group function, which might otherwise be suppressed by pressures to uniformity, may be preserved by the establishment of a position whose responsibility is to perform the function.

Hall (10) has recently shown that social roles can be profitably conceived in the context of conformity to group pressures. He reasoned that pressures to uniformity of prescriptions concerning the behavior of the occupant of a position and pressures on the occupant to conform to these prescriptions should be greater the more cohesive the group. A study of the role of aircraft commander in bomber crews lends strong support to this conception.

In summary, it should be noted that in all but one of these suggested sources of heterogeneity we have assumed the process of conformity—to the norms of a subgroup, to a role, or to a group standard favoring heterogeneity. Even if the price of membership in a strong group be conformity, it need not follow that strong groups will suppress differences.

MORE THAN ONE GROUP

Thus far our analysis has proceeded as though the individual were a member of only one group. Actually we recognize that he is, and has been, a member of many groups. In one of our current research projects we are finding that older adolescents can name from twenty to forty "important groups and persons that influence my opin-

ions and behavior in decision situations." Indeed, some personality theorists hold that personality should be viewed as an "internal society" made up of representations of the diverse group relationships which the individual now has and has had. According to this view, each individual has a unique internal society and makes his own personal synthesis of the values and behavior preferences generated by these affiliations.

The various memberships of an individual may relate to one another in various ways and produce various consequences for the individual. A past group may exert internal pressures toward conformity which are in conflict with a present group. Two contemporaneous groups may have expectations for the person which are incompatible. Or an individual may hold a temporary membership (the situation of a foreign student, for example) and be faced with current conformity pressures which if accepted will make it difficult to readjust when returning to his more permanent memberships.

This constant source of influence from other memberships toward deviancy of every member of every group requires that each group take measures to preserve its integrity. It should be noted, however, that particular deviancy pressures associated with a given member may be creative or destructive when evaluated in terms of the integrity and productivity of the group, and conformity pressures from the group may be supportive or disruptive of the integrity of the individual.

Unfortunately there has been little systematic research on these aspects of multiple group membership. We can only indicate two sets of observations concerning (a) the intrapersonal processes resulting from multiple membership demands, and (b) the effects on group processes of the deviancy pressures which arise from the multiple membership status of individual members.

Marginal Membership. Lewin (13), in his discussion of adolescence and of minority group membership, has analyzed some of the psychological effects on the person of being "between two groups" without a firm anchorage in either one. He says: "The transition from childhood to adulthood may be a rather sudden shift (for instance, in some of the primitive societies), or it may occur gradually in a setting where children and adults are not sharply separated groups. In the case of the so-called 'adolescent difficulties,' however, a third state of affairs is often prevalent: children and adults constitute two clearly defined groups; the adolescent does not wish any longer to belong to the children's group and, at the same time, knows that he is not really accepted in the adult group. He has a position similar to what is called in sociology the 'marginal man' . . . a person who stands on the boundary between two groups. He does not belong to either of them, or at least he is not sure of his belongingness in either of them" (p. 143). Lewin goes on to point out that there are characteristic maladjustive behavior patterns resulting from this unstable membership situation: high tension, shifts between extremes of behavior, high sensitivity, and rejection of low status members of both groups. This situation, rather than fostering strong individuality, makes belonging to closely knit, loyalty-demanding groups very attractive. Dependency and acceptance are a welcome relief. Probably most therapy groups have a number of members who are seeking relief from marginality.

Overlapping Membership. There is quite a different type of situation where the person does have a firm anchorage in two or more groups but where the group standards are not fully compatible. Usually the actual conflict arises when the person is physically present in one group but realizes that he also belongs to other groups to which he will return in the near or distant future. In this sense, the child moves between his family group and his school group every day. The member of a therapy group has some sort of time perspective of "going back" to a variety of other groups between each meeting of the therapy group.

In their study of the adjustment of foreign students both in this country and after returning home, Watson and Lippitt (26) observed four different ways in which individuals cope with this problem of overlapping membership.

1. Some students solved the problem by "living in the present" at all times. When they were in the American culture all of their energy and attention was directed to being an acceptable member of this group. They avoided conflict within themselves by minimizing thought about and contact with the other group "back home." When they returned to the other group they used the same type of solution, quickly shifting behavior and ideas to fit back into the new present group. Their behavior appeared quite inconsistent, but it was a consistent approach to solving their problem of multiple membership.

2. Other individuals chose to keep their other membership the dominant one while in this country. They were defensive and rejective every time the present group seemed to promote values and to expect behavior which they felt might not be acceptable to the other group "back home."

The strain of maintaining this orientation was relieved by turning every situation into a "black and white" comparison and adopting a consistently rejective posture toward the present, inferior group. This way of adjusting required a considerable amount of distorting of present and past realities, but the return to the other group was relatively easy.

3. Others reacted in a sharply contrasting way by identifying wholeheartedly with the present group and by rejecting the standards of the other group as incorrect or inferior at the points of conflict. They were, of course, accepted by the present group, but when they returned home they met rejection or felt alienated from the standards of the group (even when they felt accepted).

4. Some few individuals seemed to achieve a more difficult but also more creative solution. They attempted to regard membership in both groups as desirable. In order to succeed in this effort, they had to be more realistic about perceiving the inconsistencies between the group expectations and to struggle to make balanced judgments about the strong and weak points of each group. Besides taking this more objective approach to evaluation, these persons worked on problems of how the strengths of one group might be interpreted and utilized by the other group. They were taking roles of creative deviancy in both groups, but attempting to make their contributions in such a way as to be accepted as loyal and productive members. They found ways of using each group membership as a resource for contributing to the welfare of the other group. Some members of each group were of course threatened by this readiness and ability to question the present modal ways of doing things in the group.

Thus it seems that the existence of multiple group memberships creates difficult problems both for the person and for the group. But there are also potentialities and supports for the development of creative individuality in this situation, and there are potentialities for group growth and achievement in the fact that the members of any group are also members of other groups with different standards.

SOME CONCLUSIONS

Let us return now to the question raised at the beginning of this paper. How should we think of the relation between individuals and groups? If we accept the assumption that individuals and groups are both important social realities, we can then ask a pair of important questions. What kinds of effects do groups have on the emotional security and creative productivity of the individual? What kinds of effects do individuals have on the morale and creative productivity of the group? In answering these questions it is important to be alerted to both good and bad effects. Although the systematic evidence from research does not begin to provide full answers to these questions, we have found evidence which tends to support the following general statements.

Strong groups do exert strong influences on members toward conformity. These conformity pressures, however, may be directed toward uniformity of thinking and behavior, or they may foster heterogeneity.

Acceptance of these conformity pressures, toward uniformity or heterogeneity, may satisfy the emotional needs of some members and frustrate others. Similarly, it may support the potential creativity of some members and inhibit that of others.

From their experiences of multiple membership and their personal synthesis of these experiences, individuals do have opportunities to achieve significant bases of individuality.

Because each group is made up of members who are loyal members of other groups and who have unique individual interests, each group must continuously cope with deviancy tendencies of the members. These tendencies may represent a source of creative improvement in the life of the group or a source of destructive disruption.

The resolution of these conflicting interests does not seem to be the strengthening of individuals and the weakening of groups, or the strengthening of groups and the weakening of individuals, but rather a strengthening of both by qualitative improvements in the nature of interdependence between integrated individuals and cohesive groups.

BIBLIOGRAPHY

1. Asch, S. E.: *Social Psychology.* New York: Prentice Hall, 1952.

2. Back, K. W.: Influence Through Social Communication. *J. Abn. & Soc. Psychol., 46:*9–23, 1951.

3. Coch, L. and French, J. R. P.: Overcoming Resistance to Change. *Hum. Relat., 1:*512–32, 1948.

4. Emerson, R. M.: Deviation and Rejection: An Experimental Replication. *Am. Sociol. Rev., 19:*688–93, 1954.

5. Festinger, L.: Informal Social Communication. *Psychol. Rev., 57:*271–292, 1950.

6. Festinger, L., Gerard, H. B., Hymovitch, B., Kelly, H. H., and Raven, B.: The Influence Process in the Presence of Extreme Deviates. *Hum. Relat., 5:*327–346, 1952.

7. Festinger, L., Schachter, S., and Back, K.: *Social Pressures in Informal Groups.* New York: Harper, 1950.

8. Festinger, L. and Thibaut, J.: Interpersonal Communication in Small Groups. *J. Abn. & Soc. Psychol., 46:*92–99, 1951.

9. Gerard, H. B.: The Effect of Different Dimensions of Disagreement on the Communication Process in Small Groups. *Hum. Relat., 6:*249–271, 1953.

10. Hall, R. L.: Social Influence on the Aircraft Commander's Role. *Am. Sociol. Rev., 20:*292–99, 1955.

11. Kelley, H. H.: Communication in Experimentally Created Hierarchies. *Hum. Relat., 4:*39–56, 1951.

12. Kelley, H. H. and Shapiro, M. M.: An Experiment on Conformity to Group Norms Where Conformity Is Detrimental to Group Achievement. *Am. Sociol. Rev., 19:*667–677, 1954.

13. Lewin, K.: *Field Theory in Social Science.* New York: Harper, 1951.

14. Lewin, K.: Studies in Group Decision. In: *Group Dynamics: Research and Theory,* ed. D. Cartwright and A. Zander. Evanston: Row, Peterson, 1953.

15. Lewin, K., Lippitt, R., and White, R.: Patterns of Aggressive Behavior in Experimentally Created "Social Climates." *J. Soc. Psychol., 10:*271–99, 1939.

16. Newcomb, T. M.: *Personality and Social Change.* New York: Dryden, 1943.

17. Parsons, T.: *Essays in Sociological Theory.* (Rev. ed.) Glencoe: Free Press, 1954.

18. Roethlisberger, F. J. and Dickson, W. J.: *Management and the Worker.* Cambridge: Harvard University Press, 1939.

19. Ross, I.: Group Standards Concerning the Admission of Jews. *Soc. Prob., 2:*133–140, 1955.

20. Schachter, S.: Deviation, Rejection, and Communication. *J. Abn. & Soc. Psychol., 46:*190–207, 1951.

21. Schachter, S., *et al.*: Cross-cultural Experiments on Threat and Rejection. *Hum. Relat., 7:*403–39, 1954.

22. Seashore, S. E.: *Group Cohesiveness in the In-*

dustrial Group. Ann Arbor: Institute for Social Research, 1954.

23. SHERIF, M.: *The Psychology of Social Norms.* New York: Harper, 1936.

24. STANTON, A. H. and SCHWARTZ, M. S.: *The Mental Hospital.* New York: Basic Books, 1954.

25. TOCQUEVILLE, A.: *Democracy in America*, Vol. 1. New York: Alfred A. Knopf, 1945 (original publication, 1835).

26. WATSON, J. and LIPPITT, R.: *Learning Across Cultures.* Ann Arbor: Institute for Social Research, 1955.

40 – Social Behavior as Exchange

GEORGE C. HOMANS

THE PROBLEMS OF SMALL-GROUP RESEARCH

This essay will hope to honor the memory of Georg Simmel in two different ways. So far as it pretends to be suggestive rather than conclusive, its tone will be Simmel's; and its subject, too, will be one of his. Because Simmel, in essays such as those on sociability, games, coquetry, and conversation, was an analyst of elementary social behavior, we call him an ancestor of what is known today as small-group research. For what we are really studying in small groups is elementary social behavior: what happens when two or three persons are in a position to influence one another, the sort of thing of which those massive structures called "classes," "firms," "communities," and "societies" must ultimately be composed.

As I survey small-group research today, I feel that, apart from just keeping on with it, three sorts of things need to be done. The first is to show the relation between the results of experimental work done under laboratory conditions and the results of *quasi*-anthropological field research on what those of us who do it are pleased to call "real-life" groups in industry and elsewhere. If the experimental work has anything to do with real life — and I am persuaded that it has everything to do — its propositions cannot be inconsistent with those discovered through the field work. But the consistency has not yet been demonstrated in any systematic way.

The second job is to pull together in some set of general propositions the actual results, from the laboratory and from the field, of work on small groups — propositions that at least sum up, to an approximation, what happens in elementary social behavior, even though we may not be able to explain why the propositions should take the form they do. A great amount of work has been done, and more appears every day, but what it all amounts to in the shape of a set of propositions from which, under specified conditions, many of the observational results might be derived, is not at all clear — and yet to state such a set is the first aim of science.

The third job is to begin to show how the propositions that empirically hold good in small groups may be derived from some set of still more general propositions. "Still more general" means only that empirical propositions other than ours may also be derived from the set. This derivation would constitute the explanatory stage in the science of elementary social behavior, for explanation *is* derivation.[1] (I myself suspect that the more general set will turn out to contain the propositions of behavioral psychology. I hold myself to be an "ultimate psychological reductionist," but I cannot know that I am right so long as the reduction has not been carried out.)

I have come to think that all three of these jobs would be furthered by our adopting the view that interaction between persons is an exchange of goods, material and non-material. This is one of the oldest theories of social behavior, and one that we still use every day to interpret our own behavior, as when we say, "I found so-and-so rewarding"; or "I got a great deal out of him"; or, even, "Talking with him took a great deal out of me." But, perhaps just because it is so obvious, this view has been much neglected by social scientists. So far as I know, the only theoretical work that makes explicit use of it is Marcel Mauss's *Essai sur le don*, published in 1925, which is ancient as social science goes.[2] It may be that the tradition of neglect is now changing and that, for instance, the psychologists who interpret behavior in terms of transactions may be coming back to something of the sort I have in mind.[3]

"Social Behavior as Exchange," American Journal of Sociology, LXIII (May 1958), 597–606. Reprinted by permission of the author and The University of Chicago Press. Copyright 1958 by The University of Chicago Press. **George C. Homans:** Department of Sociology, Harvard University.

1. See R. B. Braithwaite, *Scientific Explanation* (Cambridge: Cambridge University Press, 1953).

2. Translated by I. Cunnison as *The Gift* (Glencoe, Ill.: Free Press, 1954).

3. In social anthropology D. L. Oliver is working along these lines, and I owe much to him. See also T. M. Newcomb, "The Prediction of Interpersonal Attraction," *American Psychologist*, XI (1956), 575–86.

An incidental advantage of an exchange theory is that it might bring sociology closer to economics—that science of man most advanced, most capable of application, and, intellectually, most isolated. Economics studies exchange carried out under special circumstances and with a most useful built-in numerical measure of value. What are the laws of the general phenomenon of which economic behavior is one class?

In what follows I shall suggest some reasons for the usefulness of a theory of social behavior as exchange and suggest the nature of the propositions such a theory might contain.

AN EXCHANGE PARADIGM

I start with the link to behavioral psychology and the kind of statement it makes about the behavior of an experimental animal such as the pigeon.[4] As a pigeon explores its cage in the laboratory, it happens to peck a target, whereupon the psychologist feeds it corn. The evidence is that it will peck the target again; it has learned the behavior, or, as my friend Skinner says, the behavior has been reinforced, and the pigeon has undergone *operant conditioning*. This kind of psychologist is not interested in how the behavior was learned: "learning theory" is a poor name for his field. Instead, he is interested in what determines changes in the rate of emission of learned behavior, whether pecks at a target or something else.

The more hungry the pigeon, the less corn or other food it has gotten in the recent past, the more often it will peck. By the same token, if the behavior is often reinforced, if the pigeon is given much corn every time it pecks, the rate of emission will fall off as the pigeon gets *satiated*. If, on the other hand, the behavior is not reinforced at all, then, too, its rate of emission will tend to fall off, though a long time may pass before it stops altogether, before it is *extinguished*. In the emission of many kinds of behavior the pigeon incurs *aversive stimulation*, or what I shall call "cost" for short, and this, too, will lead in time to a decrease in the emission rate. Fatigue is an example of a "cost." Extinction, satiation, and cost, by decreasing the rate of emission of a particular kind of behavior, render more probable the emission of some other kind of behavior, including doing nothing. I shall only add that even a hard-boiled psychologist puts "emotional" behavior, as well as such things as pecking, among the unconditioned responses that may be reinforced in operant conditioning. As a statement of the propositions of behavioral psychology, the foregoing is, of course,

inadequate for any purpose except my present one.

We may look on the pigeon as engaged in an exchange—pecks for corn—with the psychologist, but let us not dwell upon that, for the behavior of the pigeon hardly determines the behavior of the psychologist at all. Let us turn to a situation where the exchange is real, that is, where the determination is mutual. Suppose we are dealing with two men. Each is emitting behavior reinforced to some degree by the behavior of the other. How it was in the past that each learned the behavior he emits and how he learned to find the other's behavior reinforcing we are not concerned with. It is enough that each does find the other's behavior reinforcing, and I shall call the reinforcers—the equivalent of the pigeon's corn—*values*, for this, I think, is what we mean by this term. As he emits behavior, each man may incur costs, and each man has more than one course of behavior open to him.

This seems to me the paradigm of elementary social behavior, and the problem of the elementary sociologist is to state propositions relating the variations in the values and costs of each man to his frequency distribution of behavior among alternatives, where the values (in the mathematical sense) taken by these variables for one man determine in part their values for the other.[5]

I see no reason to believe that the propositions of behavioral psychology do not apply to this situation, though the complexity of their implications in the concrete case may be great indeed. In particular, we must suppose that, with men as with pigeons, an increase in extinction, satiation, or aversive stimulation of any one kind of behavior will increase the probability of emission of some other kind. The problem is not, as it is often stated, merely, what a man's values are, what he has learned in the past to find reinforcing, but how much of any one value his behavior is getting him now. The more he gets, the less valuable any further unit of that value is to him, and the less often he will emit behavior reinforced by it.

THE INFLUENCE PROCESS

We do not, I think, possess the kind of studies of two-person interaction that would either bear

4. B. F. Skinner, *Science and Human Behavior* (New York: Macmillan Co., 1953).

5. *Ibid.*, pp. 297–329. The discussion of "double contingency" by T. Parsons and E. A. Shils could easily lead to a similar paradigm (see *Toward a General Theory of Action* [Cambridge, Mass.: Harvard University Press, 1951], pp. 14–16).

out these propositions or fail to do so. But we do have studies of larger numbers of persons that suggest that they may apply, notably the studies by Festinger, Schachter, Back and their associates on the dynamics of influence. One of the variables they work with they call *cohesiveness*, defined as anything that attracts people to take part in a group. Cohesiveness is a value variable; it refers to the degree of reinforcement people find in the activities of the group. Festinger and his colleagues consider two kinds of reinforcing activity: the symbolic behavior we call "social approval" (sentiment) and activity valuable in other ways, such as doing something interesting.

The other variable they work with they call *communication* and others call *interaction*. This is a frequency variable; it is a measure of the frequency of emission of valuable and costly verbal behavior. We must bear in mind that, in general, the one kind of variable is a function of the other.

Festinger and his co-workers show that the more cohesive a group is, that is, the more valuable the sentiment or activity the members exchange with one another, the greater the average frequency of interaction of the members.[6] With men, as with pigeons, the greater the reinforcement, the more often is the reinforced behavior emitted. The more cohesive a group, too, the greater the change that members can produce in the behavior of other members in the direction of rendering these activities more valuable.[7] That is, the more valuable the activities that members get, the more valuable those that they must give. For if a person is emitting behavior of a certain kind, and other people do not find it particularly rewarding, these others will suffer their own production of sentiment and activity, in time, to fall off. But perhaps the first person has found their sentiment and activity rewarding, and, if he is to keep on getting them, he must make his own behavior more valuable to the others. In short, the propositions of behavioral psychology imply a tendency toward a certain proportionality between the value to others of the behavior a man gives them and the value to him of the behavior they give him.[8]

Schachter also studied the behavior of members of a group toward two kinds of other members, "conformers" and "deviates."[9] I assume that conformers are people whose activity the other members find valuable. For conformity is behavior that coincides to a degree with some group standard or norm, and the only meaning I can assign to *norm* is "a verbal description of behavior that many members find valuable for the actual behavior of themselves and others to conform to." By the same token, a deviate is a member whose behavior is not particularly valuable. Now Schachter shows that, as the members of a group come to see another member as a deviate, their interaction with him—communication addressed to getting him to change his behavior—goes up, the faster the more cohesive the group. The members need not talk to the other conformers so much; they are relatively satiated by the conformers' behavior: they have gotten what they want out of them. But if the deviate, by failing to change his behavior, fails to reinforce the members, they start to withhold social approval from him: the deviate gets low sociometric choice at the end of the experiment. And in the most cohesive groups—those Schachter calls "high cohesive-relevant"—interaction with the deviate also falls off in the end and is lowest among those members that rejected him most strongly, as if they had given him up as a bad job. But how plonking can we get? These findings are utterly in line with everyday experience.

PRACTICAL EQUILIBRIUM

At the beginning of this paper I suggested that one of the tasks of small-group research was to show the relation between the results of experimental work done under laboratory conditions and the results of field research on real-life small groups. Now the latter often appear to be in practical equilibrium, and by this I mean nothing fancy. I do not mean that all real-life groups are in equilibrium. I certainly do not mean that all groups must tend to equilibrium. I do not mean that groups have built-in antidotes to change: there is no homeostasis here. I do not mean that we assume equilibrium. I mean only that we sometimes *observe* it, that for the time we are with a group—and it is often short—there is no great change in the values of the variables we choose to measure. If, for instance, person A is interacting with B more than with C both at the beginning and at the end of the study, then at least by this crude measure the group is in equilibrium.

Many of the Festinger-Schachter studies are

6. K. W. Back, "The Exertion of Influence through Social Communication," in L. Festinger, K. Back, S. Schachter, H. H. Kelley, and J. Thibaut (eds.), *Theory and Experiment in Social Communication* (Ann Arbor: Research Center for Dynamics, University of Michigan, 1950), pp. 21–36.

7. S. Schachter, N. Ellertson, D. McBride, and D. Gregory, "An Experimental Study of Cohesiveness and Productivity," *Human Relations*, IV (1951), 229–38.

8. Skinner, *op. cit.*, p. 100.

9. S. Schachter, "Deviation, Rejection, and Communication," *Journal of Abnormal and Social Psychology*, XLVI (1951), 190–207.

experimental, and their propositions about the process of influence seem to me to imply the kind of proposition that empirically holds good of real-life groups in practical equilibrium. For instance, Festinger *et al.* find that, the more cohesive a group is, the greater the change that members can produce in the behavior of other members. If the influence is exerted in the direction of conformity to group norms, then, when the process of influence has accomplished all the change of which it is capable, the proposition should hold good that, the more cohesive a group is, the larger the number of members that conform to its norms. And it does hold good.[10]

Again, Schachter found, in the experiment I summarized above, that in the most cohesive groups and at the end, when the effort to influence the deviate had failed, members interacted little with the deviate and gave him little in the way of sociometric choice. Now two of the propositions that hold good most often of real-life groups in practical equilibrium are precisely that the more closely a member's activity conforms to the norms the more interaction he receives from other members and the more liking choices he gets from them too. From these main propositions a number of others may be derived that also hold good.[11]

Yet we must ever remember that the truth of the proposition linking conformity to liking may on occasion be masked by the truth of other propositions. If, for instance, the man that conforms to the norms most closely also exerts some authority over the group, this may render liking for him somewhat less than it might otherwise have been.[12]

Be that as it may, I suggest that the laboratory experiments on influence imply propositions about the behavior of members of small groups, when the process of influence has worked itself out, that are identical with propositions that hold good of real-life groups in equilibrium. This is hardly surprising if all we mean by equilibrium is that all the change of which the system is, under present conditions, capable has been effected, so that no further change occurs. Nor would this be the first time that statics has turned out to be a special case of dynamics.

PROFIT AND SOCIAL CONTROL

Though I have treated equilibrium as an observed fact, it is a fact that cries for explanation. I shall not, as structural-functional sociologists do, use an assumed equilibrium as a means of explaining, or trying to explain, why the other features of a social system should be what they are. Rather, I shall take practical equilibrium as something that is itself to be explained by the other features of the system.

If every member of a group emits at the end of, and during, a period of time much the same kinds of behavior and in much the same frequencies as he did at the beginning, the group is for that period in equilibrium. Let us then ask why any one member's behavior should persist. Suppose he is emitting behavior of value A_1. Why does he not let his behavior get worse (less valuable or reinforcing to the others) until it stands at $A_1 - \Delta A$? True, the sentiments expressed by others toward him are apt to decline in value (become less reinforcing to him), so that what he gets from them may be $S_1 - \Delta S$. But it is conceivable that, since most activity carries cost, a decline in the value of what he emits will mean a reduction in cost to him that more than offsets his losses in sentiment. Where, then, does he stabilize his behavior? This is the problem of social control.[13]

Mankind has always assumed that a person stabilizes his behavior, at least in the short run, at the point where he is doing the best he can for himself under the circumstances, though his best may not be a "rational" best, and what he can do may not be at all easy to specify, except that he is not apt to think like one of the theoretical antagonists in the *Theory of Games*. Before a sociologist rejects this answer out of hand for its horrid profit-seeking implications, he will do well to ask himself if he can offer any other answer to the question posed. I think he will find that he cannot. Yet experiments designed to test the truth of the answer are extraordinarily rare.

I shall review one that seems to me to provide a little support for the theory, though it was not meant to do so. The experiment is reported by H. B. Gerard, a member of the Festinger-Schachter team, under the title "The Anchorage of Opinions in Face-to-Face Groups."[14] The experimenter formed artificial groups whose members met to discuss a case in industrial relations and to ex-

10. L. Festinger, S. Schachter, and K. Back, *Social Pressures in Informal Groups* (New York: Harper & Bros., 1950), pp. 72–100.

11. For propositions holding good of groups in practical equilibrium see G. C. Homans, *The Human Group* (New York: Harcourt, Brace & Co., 1950), and H. W. Riecken and G. C. Homans, "Psychological Aspects of Social Structure," in G. Lindzey (ed.), *Handbook of Social Psychology* (Cambridge, Mass.: Addison-Wesley Publishing Co., 1954), II, 786–832.

12. See Homans, *op. cit.*, pp. 244–48, and R. F. Bales, "The Equilibrium Problem in Small Groups," in A. P. Hare, E. F. Borgatta, and R. F. Bales (eds.), *Small Groups* (New York: A. A. Knopf, 1953), pp. 450–56.

13. Homans, *op. cit.*, pp. 281–301.

14. *Human Relations*, VII (1954), 313–25.

press their opinions about its probable outcome. The groups were of two kinds: high-attraction groups, whose members were told that they would like one another very much, and low-attraction groups, whose members were told that they would not find one another particularly likable.

At a later time the experimenter called the members in separately, asked them again to express their opinions on the outcome of the case, and counted the number that had changed their opinions to bring them into accord with those of other members of their groups. At the same time, a paid participant entered into a further discussion of the case with each member, always taking, on the probable outcome of the case, a position opposed to that taken by the bulk of the other members of the group to which the person belonged. The experimenter counted the number of persons shifting toward the opinion of the paid participant.

The experiment had many interesting results, from which I choose only those summed up in Tables 1 and 2. The three different agreement classes are made up of people who, at the original sessions, expressed different degrees of agreement with the opinions of other members of their groups. And the figure 44, for instance, means that, of all members of high-attraction groups whose initial opinions were strongly in disagreement with those of other members, 44 per cent shifted their opinion later toward that of others.

In these results the experimenter seems to have been interested only in the differences in the sums of the rows, which show that there is more shifting toward the group, and less shifting toward the paid participant, in the high-attraction

than in the low-attraction condition. This is in line with a proposition suggested earlier. If you think that the members of a group can give you much—in this case, liking—you are apt to give them much—in this case, a change to an opinion in accordance with their views—or you will not get the liking. And, by the same token, if the group can give you little of value, you will not be ready to give it much of value. Indeed, you may change your opinion so as to depart from agreement even further, to move, that is, toward the view held by the paid participant.

So far so good, but, when I first scanned these tables, I was less struck by the difference between them than by their similarity. The same classes of people in both tables showed much the same relative propensities to change their opinions, no matter whether the change was toward the group or toward the paid participant. We see, for instance, that those who change least are the high-attraction, agreement people and the low-attraction, strong-disagreement ones. And those who change most are the high-attraction, strong-disagreement people and the low-attraction, mild-disagreement ones.

How am I to interpret these particular results? Since the experimenter did not discuss them, I am free to offer my own explanation. The behavior emitted by the subjects is opinion and changes in opinion. For this behavior they have learned to expect two possible kinds of reinforcement. Agreement with the group gets the subject favorable sentiment (acceptance) from it, and the experiment was designed to give this reinforcement a higher value in the high-attraction condition than in the low-attraction one. The second kind of possible reinforcement is what I shall call the "maintenance of one's personal integrity," which a subject gets by sticking to his own opinion in the face of disagreement with the group. The experimenter does not mention this reward, but I cannot make sense of the results without something much like it. In different degrees for different subjects, depending on their initial positions, these rewards are in competition with one another: they are alternatives. They are not absolutely scarce goods, but some persons cannot get both at once.

Since the rewards are alternatives, let me introduce a familiar assumption from economics—that the cost of a particular course of action is the equivalent of the foregone value of an alternative[15]—and then add the definition: Profit = Reward — Cost.

TABLE 1 PERCENTAGE OF SUBJECTS CHANGING TOWARD SOMEONE IN THE GROUP

	Agreement	Mild Disagreement	Strong Disagreement
High attraction	0	12	44
Low attraction	0	15	9

TABLE 2 PERCENTAGE OF SUBJECTS CHANGING TOWARD THE PAID PARTICIPANT

	Agreement	Mild Disagreement	Strong Disagreement
High attraction	7	13	25
Low attraction	20	38	8

15. G. J. Stigler, *The Theory of Price* (rev. ed.; New York: Macmillan Co., 1952), p. 99.

Now consider the persons in the corresponding cells of the two tables. The behavior of the high-attraction, agreement people gets them much in the way of acceptance by the group, and for it they must give up little in the way of personal integrity, for their views are from the start in accord with those of the group. Their profit is high, and they are not prone to change their behavior. The low-attraction, strong-disagreement people are getting much in integrity, and they are not giving up for it much in valuable acceptance, for they are members of low-attraction groups. Reward less cost is high for them, too, and they change little. The high-attraction, strong-disagreement people are getting much in the way of integrity, but their costs in doing so are high, too, for they are in high-attraction groups and thus foregoing much valuable acceptance by the group. Their profit is low, and they are very apt to change, either toward the group or toward the paid participant, from whom they think, perhaps, they will get some acceptance while maintaining some integrity. The low-attraction, mild-disagreement people do not get much in the way of integrity, for they are only in mild disagreement with the group, but neither are they giving up much in acceptance, for they are members of low-attraction groups. Their rewards are low; their costs are low too, and their profit—the difference between the two—is also low. In their low profit they resemble the high-attraction, strong-disagreement people, and, like them, they are prone to change their opinions, in this case, more toward the paid participant. The subjects in the other two cells, who have medium profits, display medium propensities to change.

If we define profit as reward less cost, and if cost is value foregone, I suggest that we have here some evidence for the proposition that change in behavior is greatest when perceived profit is least. This constitutes no direct demonstration that change in behavior is least when profit is greatest, but if, whenever a man's behavior brought him a balance of reward and cost, he changed his behavior away from what got him, under the circumstances, the less profit, there might well come a time when his behavior would not change further. That is, his behavior would be stabilized, at least for the time being. And, so far as this were true for every member of a group, the group would have a social organization in equilibrium.

I do not say that a member would stabilize his behavior at the point of greatest conceivable profit to himself, because his profit is partly at the mercy of the behavior of others. It is a commonplace that the short-run pursuit of profit by several persons often lands them in positions where

all are worse off than they might conceivably be. I do not say that the paths of behavioral change in which a member pursues his profit under the condition that others are pursuing theirs too are easy to describe or predict; and we can readily conceive that in jockeying for position they might never arrive at any equilibrium at all.

DISTRIBUTIVE JUSTICE

Yet practical equilibrium is often observed, and thus some further condition may make its attainment, under some circumstance, more probable than would the individual pursuit of profit left to itself. I can offer evidence for this further condition only in the behavior of subgroups and not in that of individuals. Suppose that there are two subgroups, working close together in a factory, the job of one being somewhat different from that of the other. And suppose that the members of the first complain and say: "We are getting the same pay as they are. We ought to get just a couple of dollars a week more to show that our work is more responsible." When you ask them what they mean by "more responsible," they say that, if they do their work wrong, more damage can result, and so they are under more pressure to take care.[16] Something like this is a common feature of industrial behavior. It is at the heart of disputes not over absolute wages but over wage differentials—indeed, at the heart of disputes over rewards other than wages.

In what kind of proposition may we express observations like these? We may say that wages and responsibility give status in the group, in the sense that a man who takes high responsibility and gets high wages is admired, other things equal. Then, if the members of one group score higher on responsibility than do the members of another, there is a felt need on the part of the first to score higher on pay too. There is a pressure, which shows itself in complaints, to bring the *status factors*, as I have called them, into line with one another. If they are in line, a condition of *status congruence* is said to exist. In this condition the workers may find their jobs dull or irksome, but they will not complain about the relative position of groups.

But there may be a more illuminating way of looking at the matter. In my example I have considered only responsibility and pay, but these may be enough, for they represent the two kinds of thing that come into the problem. Pay is clearly a

16. G. C. Homans, "Status among Clerical Workers," *Human Organization*, XII (1953), 5–10.

reward; responsibility may be looked on, less clearly, as a cost. It means constraint and worry—or peace of mind foregone. Then the proposition about status congruence becomes this: If the costs of the members of one group are higher than those of another, distributive justice requires that their rewards should be higher too. But the thing works both ways: If the rewards are higher, the costs should be higher too. This last is the theory of *noblesse oblige,* which we all subscribe to, though we all laugh at it, perhaps because the *noblesse* often fails to *oblige.* To put the matter in terms of profit: though the rewards and costs of two persons or the members of two groups may be different, yet the profits of the two—the excess of reward over cost—should tend to equality. And more than "should." The less-advantaged group will at least try to attain greater equality, as, in the example I have used, the first group tried to increase its profit by increasing its pay.

I have talked of distributive justice. Clearly, this is not the only condition determining the actual distribution of rewards and costs. At the same time, never tell me that notions of justice are not a strong influence on behavior, though we sociologists often neglect them. Distributive justice may be one of the conditions of group equilibrium.

EXCHANGE AND SOCIAL STRUCTURE

I shall end by reviewing almost the only study I am aware of that begins to show in detail how a stable and differentiated social structure in a real-life group might arise out of a process of exchange between members. This is Peter Blau's description of the behavior of sixteen agents in a federal law-enforcement agency.[17]

The agents had the duty of investigating firms and preparing reports on the firms' compliance with the law. Since the reports might lead to legal action against the firms, the agents had to prepare them carefully, in the proper form, and take strict account of the many regulations that might apply. The agents were often in doubt what they should do, and then they were supposed to take the question to their supervisor. This they were reluctant to do, for they naturally believed that thus confessing to him their inability to solve a problem would reflect on their competence, affect the official ratings he made of their work, and so hurt their chances for promotion. So agents often asked other agents for help and advice, and, though this was nominally forbidden, the supervisor usually let it pass.

Blau ascertained the ratings the supervisor made of the agents, and he also asked the agents to rate one another. The two opinions agreed closely. Fewer agents were regarded as highly competent than were regarded as of middle or low competence; competence, or the ability to solve technical problems, was a fairly scarce good. One or two of the more competent agents would not give help and advice when asked, and so received few interactions and little liking. A man that will not exchange, that will not give you what he has when you need it, will not get from you the only thing you are, in this case, able to give him in return, your regard.

But most of the more competent agents were willing to give help, and of them Blau says:

> A consultation can be considered an exchange of values: both participants gain something, and both have to pay a price. The questioning agent is enabled to perform better than he could otherwise have done, without exposing his difficulties to his supervisor. By asking for advice, he implicitly pays his respect to the superior proficiency of his colleague. This acknowledgment of inferiority is the cost of receiving assistance. The consultant gains prestige, in return for which he is willing to devote some time to the consultation and permit it to disrupt his own work. The following remark of an agent illustrates this: "I like giving advice. It's flattering, I suppose, if you feel that others come to you for advice.[18]

Blau goes on to say: "All agents liked being consulted, but the value of any one of very many consultations became deflated for experts, and the price they paid in frequent interruptions became inflated."[19] This implies that, the more prestige an agent received, the less was the increment of value of that prestige; the more advice an agent gave, the greater was the increment of cost of that advice, the cost lying precisely in the foregone value of time to do his own work. Blau suggests that something of the same sort was true of an agent who went to a more competent colleague for advice: the more often he went, the more costly to him, in feelings of inferiority, became any further request. "The repeated admission of his inability to solve his own problems . . . undermined the self-confidence of the worker and his standing in the group."[20]

The result was that the less competent agents went to the more competent ones for help less

17. Peter M. Blau, *The Dynamics of Bureaucracy* (Chicago: University of Chicago Press, 1955), 99–116.
18. *Ibid.,* p. 108.
19. *Ibid.,* p. 108.
20. *Ibid.,* p. 109.

often than they might have done if the costs of repeated admissions of inferiority had been less high and that, while many agents sought out the few highly competent ones, no single agent sought out the latter much. Had they done so (to look at the exchange from the other side), the costs to the highly competent in interruptions to their own work would have become exorbitant. Yet the need of the less competent for help was still not fully satisfied. Under these circumstances they tended to turn for help to agents more nearly like themselves in competence. Though the help they got was not the most valuable, it was of a kind they could themselves return on occasion. With such agents they could exchange help and liking, without the exchange becoming on either side too great a confession of inferiority.

The highly competent agents tended to enter into exchanges, that is, to interact with many others. But, in the more equal exchanges I have just spoken of, less competent agents tended to pair off as partners. That is, they interacted with a smaller number of people, but interacted often with these few. I think I could show why pair relations in these more equal exchanges would be more economical for an agent than a wider distribution of favors. But perhaps I have gone far enough. The final pattern of this social structure was one in which a small number of highly competent agents exchanged advice for prestige with a large number of others less competent and in which the less competent agents exchanged, in pairs and in trios, both help and liking on more nearly equal terms.

Blau shows, then, that a social structure in equilibrium might be the result of a process of exchanging behavior rewarding and costly in different degrees, in which the increment of reward and cost varied with the frequency of the behavior, that is, with the frequency of interaction. Note that the behavior of the agents seems also to have satisfied my second condition of equilibrium: the more competent agents took more responsibility for the work, either their own or others', than did the less competent ones, but they also got more for it in the way of prestige. I suspect that the same kind of explanation could be given for the structure of many "informal" groups.

SUMMARY

The current job of theory in small-group research is to make the connection between experimental and real-life studies, to consolidate the propositions that empirically hold good in the two fields, and to show how these propositions might be derived from a still more general set. One way of doing this job would be to revive and make more rigorous the oldest of theories of social behavior — social behavior as exchange.

Some of the statements of such a theory might be the following. Social behavior is an exchange of goods, material goods but also non-material ones, such as the symbols of approval or prestige. Persons that give much to others try to get much from them, and persons that get much from others are under pressure to give much to them. This process of influence tends to work out at equilibrium to a balance in the exchanges. For a person engaged in exchange, what he gives may be a cost to him, just as what he gets may be a reward, and his behavior changes less as profit, that is, reward less cost, tends to a maximum. Not only does he seek a maximum for himself, but he tries to see to it that no one in his group makes more profit than he does. The cost and the value of what he gives and of what he gets vary with the quantity of what he gives and gets. It is surprising how familiar these propositions are; it is surprising, too, how propositions about the dynamics of exchange can begin to generate the static thing we call "group structure" and, in so doing, generate also some of the propositions about group structure that students of real-life groups have stated.

In our unguarded moments we sociologists find words like "reward" and "cost" slipping into what we say. Human nature will break in upon even our most elaborate theories. But we seldom let it have its way with us and follow up systematically what these words imply.[21] Of all our many "approaches" to social behavior, the one that sees it as an economy is the most neglected, and yet it is the one we use every moment of our lives — except when we write sociology.

---

21. *The White-Collar Job* (Ann Arbor: Survey Research Center, University of Michigan, 1953), pp. 115–27.

41 – Recent Concepts in Administration

HAROLD J. LEAVITT

My purpose here, which I can not possibly achieve, is to try to organize and summarize recent theoretical developments in administration and organization.

Let me start by saying that I shall use the terms "administration" and "organization" more or less interchangeably; assuming simply that we are all concerned with understanding and perhaps directing the behavior of ongoing groups of people.

We have enough perspective now on the rash of new developments in these areas so that it is feasible to set up some gross categories, and then to describe some examples of novel and stimulating activity within these categories.

My categories are four: The first is the jumping-off place in organizational thinking; i.e., the state of classical organizational theory. This category contains nothing notably new, but it is worth a quick look because it will help us spotlight what *is* new in the "new."

Second, we can look quickly at new descriptive approaches to organization. This category specifically includes the new Marsh and Simon (1959) book; Mason Haire's (1959) use of biological analogies to organizational growth; a series of sociologically-based models like those of Whyte, Sayles, Selznick and others (which I shall not try to run through here); and the clinically-based work of Argyris (1957). Many of the sociological models and those of Argyris are not entirely descriptive; they have strong normative elements. These are not so much normative in an analytic sense, however, as in a value sense.

The next category covers analytic-normative studies. For the most part these have their origins in economics and mathematics, with close connection to game theory, and other quantitative and rigorous attacks on decision processes. I shall cite only one example of these, the work of Jacob Marschak (1959).

The fourth and final category is the action-influence category. The question here is not about theoretical developments that show promise of future influence but on currently influential ideas. Names cannot easily be attached to ideas in this realm, but I shall argue that the sophisticated practice of "human relations training" and the impact of "information technology" are the two currently vital and partially conflicting forces on the changing organizational scene.

THE JUMPING-OFF PLACE

Until relatively recently organization theory meant Taylor and Urwick and ideas like "span of control" and the "exception principle." It seems clear that the impact of these kinds of ideas on the thinking of managers and business school academicians (and they provide a pretty good cue about trends) has lessened. As Simon has pointed out, these early formalizations about administration suffered considerably from—among other things—their hortatory qualities. In retrospect we can isolate at least three other major limitations:

a. They tended to treat only the physiological attributes of persons, ignoring the complexities of motivation and perception.

b. They began, usually, with the assumption of a known and fixed organizational task, which can then be differentiated into subparts. They thereby carry a static quality with no provision for organizational search for new tasks, or redefinition of present ones under pressure from a changing environment.

c. Traditional theory has focused almost exclusively on the individual as the unit of the enterprise, working implicitly toward a goal of functional specialization down to pieces the size of one man. Perhaps one reason these early theories missed the major phenomena of individual behavior is precisely because they failed to consider interaction among subparts of organizations.

RECENT DESCRIPTIVE MODELS

The freshest ideas about organization and administration belong in this category. There are many of them, semi-independent of one another. They have in common a concern about understanding organizational phenomena and about developing a more adequate underpinning for eventual applications in the real world.

The most important aspect of these descriptive models is that they are descriptive; i.e., impersonal efforts to comprehend, analyze, and predict organizational behavior. They either draw on empirical evidence or permit empirical tests of their propositions and hypotheses.

The March and Simon book is a good example. It is an effort to state a set of interrelated propositions that will account for variation in such di-

From "Psychologists in Administration (A Symposium)," *Personnel Psychology*, XIII (Autumn 1960), 287–294. Reprinted by permission of the author and Personnel Psychology, Inc. **Harold J. Leavitt**: Graduate School of Industrial Administration, Carnegie Institute of Technology.

verse intra-organizational phenomena as, for example, intergroup conflict, innovative activities, and compensation.

It draws very heavily upon a dynamic model of individual motivation that includes variables like satisfaction level, search behavior, expected value of reward, and level of aspiration. It offers up some stimulating new concepts, too, differentiating "satisficing" from "optimizing" behavior and points out that the behavior of individuals and organizations is probably more accurately described by the first word than the second. Satisficing means searching for a satisfactory solution to a problem, rather than the optimal one—a process which is far more parsimonious of energy and other costs than optimizing, and a class of behavior which is also far more "sympatico" with dynamic personality theory than with classical economic theorizing.

Perhaps this is enough to give you a flavor of this view of organizational phenomena. It is descriptive-predictive; it is rigorous in that its propositions appear to be empirically testable; and it makes good use of what is known about individual and group behavior.

Let me turn now to another fresh look at organizations. Mason Haire has recently introduced some D'Arcy Thompson-type biological notions into organizational thinking. He cites the square-cube law; i.e., that as the mass of an object is cubed, its surface is only squared; then goes on to show how this surface-volume relationship becomes critical in relation to the biological size of organisms. The giant, in Jack the Giant Killer, were he proportioned like Jack but ten times as big, would include a mass so great as to break his own bones.

Haire's point is that as organisms grow they must change shape, and even create new organs to perform functions not required by another size and shape. He carries the analogy to organizations and then offers data to show similar, and predictable, change phenomena during organizational growth. Using historical data from small companies, he shows consistent relationships between, for example, numbers of people on the "surface" in the organization; i.e., who deal chiefly with the outside environment—receptionists, purchasing agents, salesmen, etc.—and numbers in the inside mass. The work is intriguing, suggestive, and a little worrisome.

Now to consider briefly the most clinically oriented of recent models of organization—the one offered up by Chris Argyris. Argyris' thesis, based largely on observational studies of worker-management relationships, is essentially that organizations are restrictive of individual psychological growth. Argyris argues that people grow from dependence toward independence, from an undifferentiated state to a differentiated one, etc., while some characteristics of large organizations press people back toward dependency, toward nondifferentiation, and toward other "unhealthy," "immature" conditions. Argyris offers prescriptions for cure, but not perfectly precise ones. He seems to offer at least a palliation in the form of organizational changes that will make for greater individual health; e.g., more freedom of decision-making for individual employees, etc.

Argyris' model does not belong entirely in the descriptive category. It lies rather in the limbo between description and prescription. It is concerned with individual mental "health" and the improvement thereof, and, whether intentionally or not, it has a hortatory quality—urging administrators to show greater concern for the mental health of their people.

In one sense Argyris' work seems to me an almost necessary outcome of the last decade's studies of human relations. It draws heavily upon human relations research, and measures almost entirely against criteria of individual and group "maturity." Very little emphasis is placed on other economic or social criteria of organizational effectiveness.

A NORMATIVE-ANALYTIC MODEL

The Marschak view, which is probably unfamiliar to most of you, is based less in psychology than the others I have described, and more in the mathematical economics from which he hails. But it is not psychological nonsense (as some ideas from economics seem to be); it is a good example of the way recent mathematico-economic developments can be focused on administrative processes.

Marschak makes an effort to construct a model of organizational behavior that does not contradict empirical data, and then to show an analytic method for deciding whether one organizational form is better than another.

Let me try to give you just a flavor of the Marschak model. Marschak treats an organization simply as "several persons" who "agree to follow a certain set of *rules* that are supposed to further certain *goals*." This set of rules (Marschak equates them with the sociologists' "roles") *is* the organizational form. Such rules are all concerned with communication: *action* rules about communication outside the organization; *internal communication* rules, which are rules about sending and receiving of messages between members (and which include communication with one's own memory); and *observation* rules which refer to the receipt of messages from outside the organization.

Marschak then specifies a simplified problem in which the issue is centralization vs. decentralization; which is to say, whether we build in a rule for intercommunication between subunits or do not. By considering three functions—a payoff function, a probability function, and a factor of the cost of communication—he demonstrates that one can analytically determine (in his little example) the efficiencies of the two alternatives. He argues that such cognitive, analytic methods can be refined for use in real organizations. I would argue further that I see no *fundamental* reason why such methods cannot be integrated into real organizations, made up of real and complicated people.

ACTION-INFLUENCE IDEAS

We can turn now from these efforts to describe or improve upon the behavior of complex organizations. The models we have sketched thus far exist mostly in universities, traveling in circles among academicians via academicians.

But it is appropriate also in this quick review to examine those ideas which are in fact currently having an impact on organizational practice—on the structure of organizations, on the relationships among members of organizations, and on the practices of administrators.

It might be said, first, that classical organization theories are having almost no noticeable *new* impact. Their old impact hangs on, of course; managers still talk about an authority-responsibility balance, about span of control, *et al.* But I have been unable to detect any recent changes in organizational behavior that appear to be consequent to extensions of old organization theory.

However, organizational practice is, I believe, changing under the serious and current influence of two kinds of phenomena, both of which are related to ideas we mentioned earlier. The two are "human relations" and "information technology."

By "human relations" I mean several fairly specific things: first, the techniques of human relations training, out of Lewis and Mayo, and graduated from Bethel; second, the related, business school-taught, business journal-promulgated, and consulting firm-carried-out techniques of "participative" management—techniques which include the use of committees, the encouragement of easy expression of feelings across status levels, etc.

These ideas are having effects, I believe, because they have been converted into technical mechanisms, and it is the technique that makes operational change possible.

These techniques are being adopted partially because they are novel, and we value the novel, but mostly because they offer promise for solving problems of social and self-esteem needs, and problems of interpersonal communication. These kinds of problems seem to have come necessarily to the fore in modern, complex organizations. They have come to the fore, I believe, mostly because some lower order problems have been resolved, and hence are less prominent; because, using Haire's analogy, the enlarged internal mass of most organizations has radically increased for better internal mechanisms for processing information.

Whatever the reasons, however, there is abundant evidence (numbers of consulting firms doing such work; the spread of Bethel-like activities into industry; the increasingly "human" views of executives about how to manage) that these ideas are changing industrial organizations, *especially at the middle levels* of the hierarchy.

Dr. Thomas Whisler and I (Leavitt & Whisler, 1958) have elsewhere pointed out the practical conflict between this trend toward human relating middle management and the other major current trend in the technics of management—the intrusion of information technology. Information technology is a label for the amalgam of new mathematical techniques applicable to managerial problems, plus those that are growing up around the computer.

In any case, information technology is moving in on organizations. It is beginning in a very small way to cause quite agonizing reassessments of ideas about decentralization, about where creativity is needed, about what constitutes an executive job, and about the relative merits of human and organizational values. It seems to be leading in many cases to solutions to those same problems of efficient information processing that are very different, perhaps polar, to those offered by human relations techniques.

These two, the techniques of human relations and the techniques of information processing, are the sets of ideas currently finding most widespread application to the practice of management. Right now they seem to me to be causing a mild schizophrenia in organizations. It is my own opinion that the potential, short run power of information technology is, by far, the greater of the two powers; at least as long as the two technologies remain separate from one another. But it is already becoming clear, back at the theoretical level of describing organizations and building organizational models, that the two are inseparably intertwined. The computer is already a tool for psychological and organizational research. Human relaters are already going cognitive, studying with new vigor the processes of conscious thinking and problem solving; studies which will, I am confident, yield a general descriptive theory of organization and administration; a theory which will, in turn, bear practical fruit.

REFERENCES

ARGYRIS, CHRIS. *Personality and Organizations.* Harper & Brothers, 1957.

HAIRE, M. "Biological Models and Empirical Histories of the Growth of Organizations." In M. Haire (Ed.), *Modern Organization Theory.* New York: John Wiley & Sons, 1959.

LEAVITT, H. J. AND WHISLER, T. L. "Management in the 1980's." *Harvard Business Review,* XXXVI (1958), 41–48.

MARCH, J. G. AND SIMON, H. A. *Organizations.* New York: John Wiley & Sons, 1959.

MARSCHAK, J. "Efficient and Viable Organizational Forms." In M. Haire (Ed.), *Modern Organization Theory.* New York: John Wiley & Sons, 1959.

SECTION *IX*

INTERNATIONAL MANAGEMENT

Though the process of management in its broadest sense may have universal application, variations in environments make the application of the process unique from culture to culture. This section examines some of these variations. The article by Clee and Di Scipio (#42), though it also covers other areas, describes the unique facets of organizational transition from a national to a world-wide enterprise. Fayerweather's article (#43) indicates the need for long-range planning in anticipation of future international operations. Oberg's article (#44) indicates the significance of cultural differences in applying management principles developed in the United States to business in other countries, and Hall (#45) cites various examples of cultural differences in human behavior. The fact that cultural characteristics affect administrative practices is readily evident from all these articles, and they clearly indicate that the science of management has not yet developed to the point where environment can be neglected.

42 – Creating a World Enterprise

GILBERT H. CLEE
and ALFRED DI SCIPIO

As American business accelerates its emergence into world-wide economic activity, the chief executives of many American corporations will face and accept the challenge of managing world-wide enterprises. And when they do, they will find superimposed upon the still thorny problems of managing large-scale domestic businesses the different and infinitely more complex problems of managing large-scale international enterprises.

One does not have to be much of a prophet to see that the trends of our time point to an increase in the scope of international activities by the American firms, large and small, that already have overseas operations. And these operations are not insignificant today. Specifically:

▶ Direct and indirect United States investments abroad have already passed the $40 billion mark.

▶ Combined sales from exports and from overseas operations of United States companies are at an annual rate of nearly $50 billion today and are expected to double during the next decade.

▶ There are also billions of dollars of United States capital in the form of minority interests or the extensive know-how, patent, and technical-assistance arrangements that are in effect.

Furthermore, the many American companies which are already doing business abroad in a major way (perhaps 3,000 or more) will undoubtedly be joined by many others that have not in the past been interested in international business to any appreciable degree.

STIMULATING FORCES

What forces stimulate the interest of American chief executives in world-wide business?

DOMESTIC SQUEEZE

During most of the past century, the dynamic American market has provided "green pastures," and has naturally been the area where most United States businessmen have concentrated their efforts. During the past decade, however, returns on investment for some companies have become less lush at home. Especially in the case of our more mature industries, high market penetration, high saturation points, and more than adequate productive capacity give promise of a further competitive profit squeeze. Even when there have been major volume increases, as is true for many industries, costs have often risen faster than prices, creating declining returns on sales and investment.

As a nation, we look ahead to a high level of economic activity in the 1960's stimulated by technological changes which should improve our economic well-being. Even so, many companies may face a profit squeeze and a lower, though still significant, rate of volume growth.

OVERSEAS COMPETITION

This past year has brought forth increasing evidence in many industries of more intense competition from overseas producers. Many companies that lack production sources abroad are encountering fiercer competition – not only in their export markets but in the United States market – both from foreign corporations and from American competitors that have established production sources abroad.

The increasing velocity of international trade winds has already been felt in many corners of American industry. In recent years:

▶ Foreign competition has made serious inroads on the domestic and foreign sales and/or profits of many U.S.-based companies, including those that produce automobiles, heavy electrical equipment, aluminum, and those that mill brass. (Within the last ten years, for example, the United States has been converted from an exporter to an importer of brass mill products.)

▶ Imports have accounted for over 25% of the U.S. market for bicycles, typewriters, steel flatware, nails, and fishing tackle.

▶ Foreign producers have captured more than 50% of the U.S. market for barbed wire, transistor radios, sewing machines, jeweled watches, and hardwood plywood.

No longer able to measure their competitive position by studying their domestic competitors, a significant number of American companies must today make their plans for capital expenditures and for market penetration with a full knowledge

"Creating a World Enterprise," Harvard Business Review, XXXVII (November – December 1959), 77 – 89. Reprinted by permission of the authors and the publisher. Gilbert H. Clee: McKinsey and Company, International Management Consultants, New York. Alfred di Scipio: Vice-President for Marketing, Singer Manufacturing Company, New York.

of what both their domestic *and* their overseas competitors are likely to do.

PROFITS ABROAD

Coupled with market growth, the industrial power of many foreign nations is expanding rapidly. In a number of countries, the gross national product is growing faster than that of the United States; for some products gross margins are higher; and the degree of saturation and market penetration in many countries is much lower than in the United States. Increased economic and financial stability further enhances the attractiveness of market opportunities in many areas abroad, as does the development of the European Common Market with its promise of further mass markets.

A recent survey by McKinsey & Company, Inc., of the international operations of some 40 representative companies revealed that the return on foreign investments by these businesses equaled or exceeded the rate of return on domestic investments. Over 30% reported that their foreign operations yielded a return more than double the return on investments within the United States! Almost without exception, executives interviewed were hastening to step up their ratio of foreign to domestic investment of corporate funds.

One firm that took early advantage of growth opportunities abroad is Colgate-Palmolive Company. Truly a pioneer among U.S. corporations in adopting a world-wide approach to market planning and development, this giant company's foresight has been applauded by Elizabeth M. Fowler in *The New York Times*:

"Just ten years ago, sales of [Colgate-Palmolive's] foreign subsidiaries accounted for $86,963,000, compared with $203,996,000 of domestic sales. Each year since, foreign sales have increased at a faster rate. In 1958 sales of the overseas companies reached a record of $262,725,000 and domestic sales . . . $271,322,000.

"More spectacular is the earnings record. Ten years ago foreign operations accounted for 16.6 per cent of total earnings. Last year the foreign subsidiaries paid a record of $8,131,000 to Colgate after taxes, compared with $7,180,000 from domestic operations. That did not include $5,855,000 of foreign earnings retained by the subsidiaries."[1]

Colgate's impressive record of growth in overseas sales and profits demonstrates dramatically the gains which can be enjoyed by companies quick to search out business opportunities, regardless of national boundaries.

WORLD MANAGEMENT

Against the kaleidoscope of these ever changing pressures, the American chief executive is faced with deciding: Where shall I put my company's time, effort, and money in the best long-term interests of my stockholders? Because of the forces just described, this problem increasingly requires that these three questions be answered:

▶ Where in the world can we market our products to assure ourselves of the most rapid and profitable sales growth?

▶ Where in the world should we do research and development to capitalize, at optimum cost, on the technical capabilities that exist in the world?

▶ Where in the world should we make our products so that we will be competitive in all major markets, including the United States?

Once the chief executive asks these questions, he is no longer operating a U.S. corporation with interests abroad; he has taken the position that his company is a "world enterprise" and that many major, fundamental decisions must be made on a global basis.

The implications of this "global thinking" are substantial, for they bring with them the need to develop concepts, business principles, organizational patterns, and management techniques that are significantly different from those that he has been using. Let us explore some of the factors which make managing a true world enterprise different from managing a purely domestic enterprise, or even a domestic enterprise with international subsidiaries, affiliates, or a so-called "international division."

MANAGEMENT'S PERSPECTIVE

Fundamental to the success of any international operation is a chief executive whose world-wide perspective serves as a model for his key line and staff executives. This perspective enables him to review such management questions as investing the corporation's assets, utilizing research and production facilities, deploying key personnel, and developing short- and long-range marketing strategies, all *in the light of alternative opportunities available to the company in any part of the world.*

Consider, for example, the question of plant location. How often (within a United States-based corporation) does a chief executive ask, *Where in the United States should the new plant be built?* as compared with, *Where in the entire world will it be most advantageous to locate a new production facility?* Phrasing the question in the latter sense in no way precludes the necessity of considering all factors

1. June 7, 1959, p. F–13.

within the United States in deciding on plant location. It merely means that such factors as our national interests and welfare, domestic labor relations, and effects on the U.S. portion of the company are put into perspective with the company's business opportunities and interests in other countries.

Or take the process of reviewing performance of domestic operations. The chief executive with a world-wide perspective will ascertain that the executive responsible for managing all or any part of the company's business in the United States is continually taking such steps as these:

▶ Evaluating the vulnerability of the United States market to foreign competition; that is, determining the degree of market penetration that has been, and is likely to be, achieved by products made overseas, as well as analyzing the effects that such infiltration is likely to have on the economics of the business.

▶ Considering the profit and ancillary implications of serving some portion of the U.S. market through importing products, either from company facilities abroad or from a "third-party" source.

▶ Exploring opportunities to program more efficiently supportive or advanced research and development projects in laboratories outside the United States.

ORGANIZATION STRUCTURE

The chief executive with such a broad view will realize that the concepts and principles employed in organization planning for a world enterprise differ markedly from those employed in a corporation that is domestically oriented, even though the latter may have substantial sales or investments overseas.

For a number of reasons (e.g., local legal requirements, tax advantages, or need for financial control), a company creating a world enterprise often sets up a statutory corporate structure that differs from the more fluid and informal (though very real) lines of communication followed in the day-to-day operations of the business. The *statutory organization* is designed to put the pieces of a company together into a legal structure that optimizes cash flow for the over-all corporation. The manner in which the company is actually coordinated and run involves a set of working relationships that are constructed to fit the managerial requirements of the company. For example, regardless of the form of its statutory structure, it must have a "working" structure by which to coordinate world research and development, to maintain technical competence in all plants, and to ensure that goods are shipped from producing points to markets so as to maximize total corporate profits.

Recognizing the distinction between the formal statutory organization and the manner in which the total business is coordinated and managed dispels much of the fog that often surrounds all foreign operations. Companies such as the Royal Dutch Shell Group and Philips' Lamps, as well as a few American firms, have learned by experience how to make a world enterprise work most effectively and still live within the framework of a rigid legal structure.

HEADQUARTERS ORGANIZATION

Truly international companies organize their corporate headquarters so that the entire upper-management echelon will (a) be exposed to and become skilled in international management problems, and (b) retain in its hands full responsibility for strategic planning and decision making, regardless of national or other geographic boundaries. The need for this kind of headquarters organization can be seen in the case of one leading manufacturer of consumer durable goods:

Some years ago this company established a production base in Europe to serve all world markets outside North America. The European subsidiary flourished and began to develop some products of its own. Soon it was deriving more than half of its volume from its own products not manufactured or sold in the United States.

The head of the overseas operation reported directly, and infrequently, to the chief executive officer of the parent corporation. No organizational provision whatever was made for world-wide coordination of such things as product-line planning, product development, manufacturing, or marketing. In effect, the American company continued to operate entirely as a domestic enterprise and to treat its substantial commitments abroad as if they were solely an investment. Thus, it failed to take advantage of the opportunity to add to the U.S. product line (either through importing or domestic production) some of the products developed by the subsidiary for overseas markets.

Further light is thrown on the headquarters organization problem when the conventional form of U.S. organization is viewed from these related points of view: (a) the varying ratios of domestic to foreign investments, and (b) the distribution of management responsibility for United States operations.

Among leading American corporations, investment of company assets outside the United States varies from an infinitesimal sum to an amount substantially in excess of the domestic investment. Nevertheless, whether a company has 8% or 80%

of its investment overseas, it is common practice to wrap the total offshore responsibility (i.e., all investments and interests, in all businesses and markets, in all countries other than the United States) in a package and hand it to a single executive.

The organization structure thus can be looked on as unbalanced to the extent that the company's foreign-to-domestic investment ratio differs from the ratio of international to domestic executives reporting to the chief executive. But an imbalance of this nature is merely a symptom of the problem, and cannot be corrected by adjusting the number of "players" on each side. Instead, it is necessary to field a team of key line and staff executives, each of whom views and exercises his management responsibility as world-wide in scope.

AREA MANAGEMENT

Below the world headquarters level, many successful international companies are using the "area management" concept. This concept calls for a division of the world into logical and manageable geographical areas, each of which is assigned to an area manager reporting directly to headquarters. Such a division must, of course, be tailored to the company's needs, just as the United States is often divided into regions or territories for sales-coverage purposes on the basis of such factors as compatibility of product lines, present and near potential sales volume, numbers of accounts, distances and travel times involved, and natural topographical barriers.

For a company seeking to operate effectively on an international basis, the area management concept or something similar to it deserves serious consideration. Designating a specific and distinct authority for all parts of the world is an effective means of preventing conflicts such as detrimental competition between several operating units for business in an "open" area of the world (that is, an area where the company does not have a subsidiary or its own production facilities).

A VALUABLE PRINCIPLE

If there is any underlying secret of success in managing an international business (or any similarly complex activity), it can be discovered in this deceptively simple maxim: *centralize responsibility for strategic planning and control; decentralize responsibility for "local" planning and operations.*

In many large American companies that have decentralized their operations, the planning and decision-making process is allowed to begin in the

divisions. Each of the latter formulates its own plans for submittal to headquarters, which then seeks to combine all the divisional plans to produce a master corporate plan. The end result of this process, if any, is usually a corporate plan that is unrealistic in terms of the company's capabilities, or in terms of company over-all objectives.

Skilled international executives, on the other hand, have learned these two truths:

▶ Strategic planning, coordination, and control can only be carried out properly at corporate headquarters. These responsibilities can never in fact be decentralized, because decisions of a strategic nature (e.g., selecting the countries or businesses to enter, allocating corporate funds, planning the logistic flow of goods from producing points to markets, and programing any research and development projects) necessarily involve the corporation as a whole and must be made by persons in a position to view the total enterprise.

▶ Responsibility for "local" planning and operations must be decentralized to the level of a practical span of control — that is, top management must fix responsibility and commensurate authority down the line for achieving *corporate-approved* objectives within the framework of guidelines (e.g., policies, strategic plans, and resources to be provided) emanating from headquarters. This means that a manager in the field must be given a free hand to run any corporate facilities or activities within his assigned territory or scope of responsibility. In achieving sales objectives, for example, he must be allowed to select his own channels of distribution, marketing strategy, advertising and sales promotion programs, and method of deploying marketing personnel.

MANAGEMENT TECHNIQUES

A world enterprise calls for modifications in many of the management techniques that have become generally accepted in the United States. The extent of modification is often so great that resulting practices seem entirely new and different to the American-bred executive.

EXECUTIVE MOBILITY

One unique feature of truly international companies is executive mobility. According to an official of a world-wide electronics company based in Europe, "All of our top executives go around the world three or four times a year, and spend less than a third of their time in the country where we are based." Our American top executives must, therefore, develop a willingness to follow such a demanding schedule, and an appreciation of the need to have firsthand exposure to economic conditions in primary markets throughout the world.

To some, the prospect of living out of a suitcase and an airplane may seem unpleasant or even unnecessary. But just as there are many reasons for the Queen of England to tour the realm regularly, so are there a number of practical reasons why the top executives of a world-wide company must frequently visit the site of operations. For example:

Among the first of United States corporations to exploit business opportunities throughout the world was the International Telephone and Telegraph Corporation, which during 1958 reported that more than $400 million of its total $700 million volume came from overseas. A recent issue of *Business Week* revealed that General Edmond H. Leavey, then president of ITT, regularly toured plants in Western Europe, one trip often following on the heels of the previous. In this, General Leavey is much like the late Colonel Sosthenes Behn whose wide travels and intimate talks with foreign officials built ITT into what it is today. General Leavey says: "It's as important for the commanding general to be seen as it is to see things for himself."[2]

PROFIT RESPONSIBILITY

Adoption of a world-wide approach requires most American corporations to modify the usual concepts of profit responsibility and other factors that are frequently used as yardsticks for appraising the performance of company executives. Profit responsibility still exists at various levels, but it is of a different nature in an international environment. There are two primary reasons for this:

1. The use of statutory devices to protect and enhance profits often distorts the significance, in any one place, of such operating results as net profit or return on investment.

2. The logistic pattern of research, manufacturing, and sales determined by headquarters executives may in fact restrict the profit or return attainable in certain operating units.

Let us look at the hypothetical situation of a company, based in the United States, which sends goods to Argentina from a production point in the United Kingdom. A sudden shift in the political situation makes it inexpedient to continue this pattern. Accordingly, headquarters management decides to shift production for Argentina to the United States, where production costs are substantially higher than in the United Kingdom. The results:

▶ In the United Kingdom, a loss in production volume and profit leverage.

▶ In Argentina, higher landed costs.

▶ In the United States, added production volume, although the executive in charge of U.S. operations would prefer to utilize this capacity for a market more profitable to *him* than Argentina.

Thus, a single corporate decision—made from the perspective of the company's best overall interests—has reverberations throughout the system, precipitating actions which may seem unfavorable at the local level. Unless executives down the line are confident that local conditions are clearly understood at headquarters, management problems take on dimensions of morale, organizational discipline, and operating effectiveness.

For these reasons, both the chief executive of an international company and his strategic management team cannot shirk their responsibility to appraise performance within the framework which they themselves have established. Thus, they must appraise performance against *plan*, not merely against *a single set of arithmetical indicators*.

MANAGEMENT CONTROLS

The complexities of international trade place totally new dimensions upon the types and amounts of information that management requires to plan, direct, coordinate, and control an enterprise. Thus, it is not surprising to find that leading international companies are often the authors of ingenious systems for maintaining management maneuverability—that is, for: (a) obtaining wanted information from all points of interest in the world and (b) responding to this information so that action initiated by top management flows quickly to the scene of the problem. Such management information and control systems generally have these two outstanding characteristics:

1. *Sensitivity*. This quality is valuable because an international company is likely to be involved in countries with volatile economic and political structures. Recent developments in Cuba, Venezuela, the Middle East, Spain, and even France point up the need for a signaling system that puts corporate management in a position to react quickly to change anywhere in the world. What is needed is a control system that works like an automatic sprinkler system—in short, one that puts out a fire before it really gets started!

Let us return to the Argentina-United Kingdom example. In deciding how to modify its trade pattern, the

---

2. August 9, 1958, pp. 60–61.

company has several basic alternatives from which to choose — (a) to ship into Argentina from a production source other than the United Kingdom, (b) to establish a production base within Argentina, or (c) to discontinue all operations in Argentina. Since this problem must be considered in the light of alternatives throughout the world, it cannot be resolved properly by a single executive responsible either for Argentine or United Kingdom operations. Therefore, the management information and control system must be such that the problem presents itself without delay to corporate management for resolution on the basis of the corporation's best interests.

2. *Simplicity.* This characteristic in information and control reports is important to an international company because of the technical problems entailed in obtaining reliable and timely information. International trade normally involves numerous languages and currencies. Superimposed on these incompatibles is a continually changing complex of variables in the form of trade, tariff, tax, and legal regulations. It is, therefore, the primary task of the information and control systems to translate all these elements into a series of simple, one language, one currency, reports for headquarters. When this is accomplished, many of the "mysteries" of foreign trade are solved. Top executives recognize that they can exercise such responsibilities as setting objectives, approving plans, and appraising performance regardless of national boundaries.

Such characteristics are not easy to achieve; yet the reports of an international company must provide a sound basis on which management can compare results and consider alternatives in various parts of the world. Headquarters must keep informed on a wide range of market and marketing conditions on product-line needs, and on world supplies and costs of labor, raw materials, component parts, capital equipment, finished goods, and essential services.

A further complication arises when the company has a statutory structure that differs from its operational structure—as is the case with most truly international companies. Thus:

An American company produces a line of products at an Italian subsidiary. The company also has a Swiss corporation, set up primarily as a trading company because of the tax advantages available in Switzerland. Much of the Italian output is sold to the Swiss company, to be resold in France or Germany. Profits thus accrue largely to the Swiss corporation. A portion of these profits is then used to support an extensive research effort in Germany, where costs are a fraction of what they would be in the United States. The research results are applied throughout the entire organization.

THREE CASES

The following examples of United States companies' operations abroad may help to clarify the differences between the operations of a world enterprise and those of a company oriented primarily to the United States.

MEETING COMPETITION

U.S. News & World Report recently posed the question, "Is U.S. Pricing Itself Out of Markets?" and went on to answer it by pointing out the impact of foreign-made bicycles on the United States market as a case in point:

"American manufacturers of bicycles have made a mild comeback against their foreign competition. In the past three years they have increased their share of the U.S. market from a low of 60 percent to 71.8 percent. How did they do it? 'We import chains, brakes, spokes, tires and saddles and combine them with American-made frames and rims,' one industry official explained. 'We've cut our prices so that the industry averages only 2 percent return on gross sales. Our wage costs are about $2.30 an hour, compared with 60 to 70 cents in Germany and a little higher in Great Britain. We can't offset the difference by improved machinery and methods. There's nothing open to us in the technique of building bikes that's not open to the world.'"[3]

Obviously, utilizing foreign-made component parts has at least temporarily stemmed the tide of imports, but it is essentially a defensive maneuver. And the impact on profits of the American corporations can hardly be called desirable.

A bicycle company organized to view the world as its market might have seen opportunities in the past to establish its own production abroad (note the comment on technical capabilities in foreign countries) to serve foreign markets. Thus, it would now be in a position to protect itself competitively in two ways: (1) by serving some part of the domestic market from an overseas production base; (2) by having the ability to retaliate competitively in the home markets of foreign bicycle producers. Battling foreign competitors for the U.S. market without a captive or otherwise reliable source overseas is like boxing an opponent, with whom you are normally well matched, with one hand tied.

From this example it can be seen that even in organizations which view themselves as purely domestic, the problems of top management are

---

3. April 27, 1959, p. 55.

no longer confined to the continental limits of the United States; for the United States is, in effect, an "international" market. The horizons of almost every executive group are being widened by two concurrent developments. One is a growing vulnerability to foreign competition. The other is the emergence of significant profit opportunities overseas. Often these two forces are separated only by time; *for an American company or industry that ignores an opportunity may be nurturing its own competition in markets abroad and even at home.* This is a valuable management principle to remember as we evaluate the impact on the United States of rapidly shifting world trade conditions.

PRODUCT-LINE CHANGES

Recently, an American corporation with annual sales slightly under $400 million (98% of which came from customers in the United States) faced this problem:

For three consecutive years, an operating division had lost more than $1 million on its primary product line, a family of large component parts for a consumer appliance. A study was undertaken to determine what the outlook was, short and long term, for achieving a satisfactory level of profitability. The problem was viewed as purely domestic since the entire U.S. market was supplied by U.S. producers, and exports were insignificant.

A study of the problem showed the industry beset by such factors as market saturation, industry overcapacity, severe price competition from local rebuilders, and potential technological obsolescence. Since this company lacked a substantial captive market and had a relatively small share (less than 10%) of the total market, it decided to discontinue manufacturing the product—even though the producing plant was both modern and efficient.

The result of abandoning the product line was twofold: (1) a significant improvement in earnings, and also (2) a noticeable loss in volume of company sales. This decision was the proper one for the company—as it was organized. However, had it been organized as a world enterprise (in spite of the currently minute volume of international sales), it would have been aware that prime overseas markets for this product line were both growing and profitable, because these foreign countries lagged behind the United States in terms of market saturation by several years. Thus, before deciding to liquidate its U.S. operations, the company would have considered and have priced out any opportunities to:

▶ License some of its technological know-how to foreign manufacturers.

▶ Establish a plant overseas to serve these foreign growth markets, and perhaps export to the United States.

▶ Dismantle the production equipment in the United States and ship it abroad where the resale price might have been substantially higher than the domestic traffic would bear.

The principle of management to be learned from this case is that today major strategic product-line decisions, such as adding, dropping, or changing the emphasis on a product line even with respect to U.S. operations, can best be made from a world-wide perspective. In contemplating any such change or in reviewing current practices, a company is well advised, therefore, to evaluate its profit opportunities in the light of such alternatives as these:

▶ Making and selling the product within the United States.

▶ Exporting to foreign markets from the United States.

▶ Importing the product into the United States from a production source (captive or otherwise) in a foreign country.

▶ Making and selling the product within a foreign country.

▶ Making the product overseas, and shipping from there to other foreign countries.

LICENSING ARRANGEMENTS

During World War II, an American company established a leading position in a highly specialized field of military equipment. After the war, peacetime applications began to develop in many foreign industrial centers. The company chose to serve these through exports from the United States. As these overseas markets grew, and the industrial capacity of war-ravaged countries was rebuilt, local production of the commercial equipment was started. Thereafter, foreign needs and the presence of manufacturers local to these needs caused the shape of product demand to change.

Back in the United States, the wartime innovator was so structured (its International Division was merely an export sales department) that it was unable to comprehend and respond to the changing competitive needs, which required it to modify its product line for foreign markets and to improve its world-wide servicing facilities. The company did know, however, that it was experiencing a sudden and substantial loss of sales and profits.

In a desperate effort to recoup, the company

worked out a licensing arrangement with a leading European manufacturer. Extensive provisions for transmitting know-how were incorporated in the agreement. Initially, some profits were restored. But as overseas markets for the product grew substantially greater than the market within the United States, the American company found itself hamstrung in planning any overseas expansion by its agreement to share design and production developments with what would then be its European competitor. Furthermore, the European company had a base of lower production costs and so possessed considerable price leverage with respect to its licensor.

The final blow came when the licensee established his own distribution outlets in the United States and began to compete vigorously for the American market with the very company that had supplied him with the know-how originally.

Licensing certainly has its place, both domestically and overseas.[4] But a company may be igniting the fuse on a time bomb unless it considers a licensing agreement in the light of its short- and long-term implications to the business at home and abroad.

THE TRANSITION

We have looked at but a few of the illustrations that point out the urgent need to organize many enterprises so that virtually all strategic plans and decisions are considered from a world-wide point of view. The need is there when a company contemplates adding or dropping a product line. It is also present when a company seeks an acquisition, requires a new facility, or plans top-executive changes and personnel development programs, even when such issues *appear* to involve U.S. operations alone.

For the American chief executive who sees the advantages of organizing and operating his company as a true world enterprise, the primary problem within his own organization is likely to be one of effecting an orderly transition. How a company "gets there from here," and how long the process takes, will depend on a number of factors: its present form of organization, its financial and other resources, the qualifications of key line and staff executives, the extent and type of present foreign or international activities, and the kinds of businesses in which the company participates now or plans to enter in the short or long term.

The change from a "domestic versus foreign" business perspective to one that is truly world-

wide in scope has an impact on the entire corporation. For this reason, the chief executive must take the lead in hammering out and implementing an action program that unifies the corporate effort throughout the world. The specific steps, timing, and goals of this program of action are, of course, questions to be dealt with individually by each company. There are, however, certain principles to be derived from analyzing the approaches followed by companies which have eliminated the organizational divarication inherent in the domestically oriented business structure.

SETTING OBJECTIVES

The objective of the transitional program of action is straightforward:

To adopt a world-wide management concept in all business affairs; that is, to view the world as the company's market and to resolve all strategic business questions in the light of alternative opportunities in all parts of the world.

The ultimate objective can be stated broadly:

To have the corporation assume all of the previously described organizational and managerial characteristics of a truly international enterprise.

GROUND RULES

The character of each company's approach to international trade is peculiar unto itself, even among successful world traders. Thus, it remains for the chief executive to forge his own company's pattern by establishing the ground rules to be followed by all representatives of the corporation, wherever in the world they may be.

As a case in point, we can look at The National Cash Register Company, which reported as "foreign sales" nearly one half of its total 1958 volume of $394 million. Stanley C. Allyn, NCR's chairman of the board, recently listed the following as "the basic principles" of his company's foreign operations:

(1) When we go into any foreign country, we go in for keeps.

(2) We believe in staffing our overseas operations with nationals of the countries concerned.

(3) We consistently invest part of our profits in the countries where those profits were earned.

---

4. See, for example, Charles Henry Lee, "How to Reach the Overseas Market by Licensing," HBR January–February 1958, p. 77.

EXHIBIT I ORGANIZATION STRUCTURE OF COMPANY A—DOMESTICALLY ORIENTED

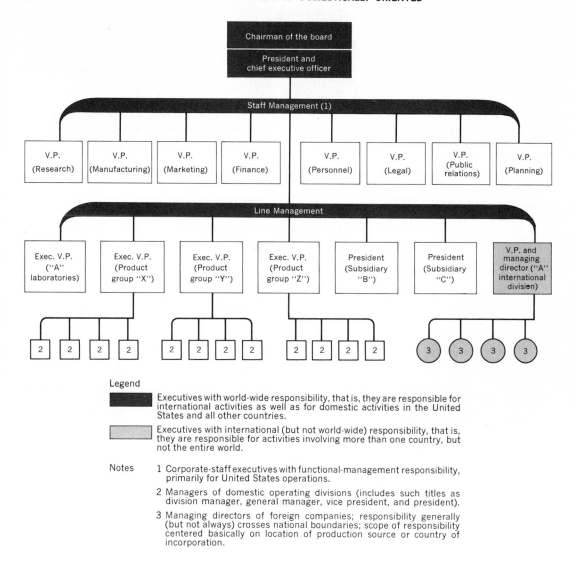

Legend

Executives with world-wide responsibility, that is, they are responsible for international activities as well as for domestic activities in the United States and all other countries.

Executives with international (but not world-wide) responsibility, that is, they are responsible for activities involving more than one country, but not the entire world.

Notes

1 Corporate-staff executives with functional-management responsibility, primarily for United States operations.

2 Managers of domestic operating divisions (includes such titles as division manager, general manager, vice president, and president).

3 Managing directors of foreign companies; responsibility generally (but not always) crosses national boundaries; scope of responsibility centered basically on location of production source or country of incorporation.

(4) We do not treat our overseas employees as step-children. We treat them exactly as we treat our people at home.

(5) We try to give the foreign market the product which the market wants . . . not the product which we think the market ought to have.

(6) We have learned that . . . for us at least . . . service or maintenance of the product comes ahead of sales.

(7) We believe in company operation overseas, instead of general agencies.

(8) We believe in firsthand contacts with our foreign markets, and that means we are constantly traveling.

(9) Finally, we are extremely careful to respect the customs, traditions, religions and sensitivities of foreign peoples.[5]

WORLD-WIDE ORGANIZATION

One vital step in the transitional action program is planning the nature and the sequence of the organization changes needed to build a structure, at headquarters and in the field, suitable for managing a world-wide enterprise. Just as a pilot's navigational efforts are guided by first setting the points of departure and destination, so too will the task of the organizational architect be made easier if he sees clearly the "before" and "after" of his own company's organization plan. Exhibits I and II, included for those American

5. An address entitled "A Philosophy for Doing Business Abroad," delivered on November 19, 1958, at the 45th National Foreign Trade Convention in New York City.

companies which would seek to plot their course toward becoming a truly world-wide enterprise, typify the structural differences that often exist at upper-management levels between a domestically oriented company and an internationally oriented one.

These examples are real. Company A is a large, diversified, decentralized company with corporate headquarters in the United States. Company B is equally large, diversified, and decentralized, but has its corporate headquarters in a European country. Both are in the same general industry,

have similar product lines, have annual sales of nearly $1 billion, and seek to operate in all important world markets. Within this frame of reference, let us consider their respective organizational readiness to deal with strategic business problems and opportunities throughout the world:

▶ *Company A* has assigned responsibility for all its overseas activities to an "international division." Currently, the division accounts for more than 25% of the corporation's sales and investment, and is growing on

EXHIBIT II ORGANIZATION STRUCTURE OF COMPANY B—INTERNATIONALLY ORIENTED

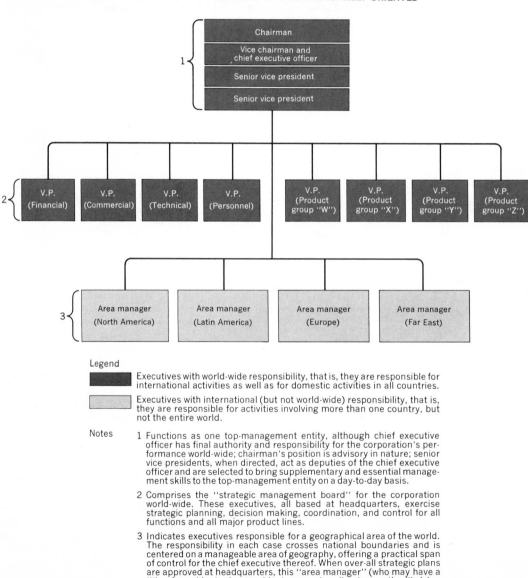

Legend

■ Executives with world-wide responsibility, that is, they are responsible for international activities as well as for domestic activities in all countries.

▢ Executives with international (but not world-wide) responsibility, that is, they are responsible for activities involving more than one country, but not the entire world.

Notes

1 Functions as one top-management entity, although chief executive officer has final authority and responsibility for the corporation's performance world-wide; chairman's position is advisory in nature; senior vice presidents, when directed, act as deputies of the chief executive officer and are selected to bring supplementary and essential management skills to the top-management entity on a day-to-day basis.

2 Comprises the "strategic management board" for the corporation world-wide. These executives, all based at headquarters, exercise strategic planning, decision making, coordination, and control for all functions and all major product lines.

3 Indicates executives responsible for a geographical area of the world. The responsibility in each case crosses national boundaries and is centered on a manageable area of geography, offering a practical span of control for the chief executive thereof. When over-all strategic plans are approved at headquarters, this "area manager" (who may have a title of president, vice president, managing director, or the like) becomes fully responsible for executing the plans, managing company resources and facilities within the geographical area, and achieving operating targets spelled out by the strategic management board.

both these counts more rapidly than almost any domestic unit. To this extent, the chief executive has "delegated" ("abdicated"?) more than a fourth of his responsibility to one man.

Since a chief executive is charged with protecting the total investment made by his stockholders, he is implicitly responsible for distributing his own effort so that he is personally and directly exposed to all of his company's major investment opportunities and situations — and this should mean by country as well as by kind of business. Keeping this in mind, look now at the organizational team that shares responsibility for Company A's interests within the United States. In line management, reporting directly to the president, are three executive vice presidents (each responsible for a group of "autonomous" operating divisions), the presidents of two subsidiary companies (headquartered in the United States), and an executive vice president (in charge of the company's extensive research laboratories in this country). We might ask here, why is it appropriate for the president of Subsidiary B to report on operations directly to the president, but apparently inappropriate for the managing director of an equally large and important European subsidiary so to report?

On the staff, eight functional vice presidents report directly to the chief executive. With the exception of certain legal and financial services provided for the International Division, these executives devote their attention almost exclusively to providing functional management for the U.S. operating groups. Could not the corporation benefit as a whole if the functional-management responsibility (e.g., services, advice, coordination, cross-fertilization) were exercised on a world-wide basis? In such functions as research or manufacturing, is it not logical to provide an organizational device that facilitates the reviewing of techniques used overseas for possible profitable applicability within the United States, and vice versa?

Or consider the ability of Company A's organization to resolve, in the company's best over-all interests, such frequently asked questions as these:

▶ Can our company expand its business in the United States by importing a line of products from an overseas production source?

▶ How can our production bases around the world be utilized so that we maximize market penetration and minimize costs?

▶ Should we acquire in the United States, in Europe, or elsewhere a company that makes products which we desire to add to our line?

▶ *Company B,* in contrast, is organized as a true world enterprise. It has marshaled its management resources so that the company's prime executive skills are regularly brought to bear on business questions and problems, wherever in the world they occur.

The chief executive officer (vice chairman) has cho-

sen in this case to appoint two senior vice presidents. These two men, along with the chairman, share the chief executive's top-management burden and act as "deputy chief executives" when it is appropriate to do so. The final authority for their actions, however, remains clearly and unquestionably in the hands of the vice chairman.

The members of the management board are based at headquarters. They provide the chief executive with a nucleus of top-notch executives whose sole responsibility it is to exercise strategic planning and control (for an assigned field of activity) on a world-wide basis.

Thus, the criterion of centralized strategic planning and control is met by this plan of organization. To our knowledge, all truly international companies have such a "strategic management board," but it takes many different names and forms. In Company B, the board consists of representatives of key functions and of key product lines. In other companies, these kinds of positions are supplemented (or to some extent replaced) by executive or group vice presidents responsible, on a line basis, for company interests in some quarter of the globe. The organizational relationships, within the board and external to it, also vary from company to company.

What is important to recognize here is the principle that this world-wide strategic management board, organized in such a way that all key activities and all kinds of management responsibility are represented, is the vehicle for reviewing, recommending, or deciding — on a world-wide basis — the strategic and logistic questions that have been raised in this article. And it is through this device, therefore, that truly international companies have a significant managerial advantage over domestically oriented competitors such as Company A.

The area manager concept was described earlier. In Company B, these men are stationed in the field; however, in other companies they are sometimes found at headquarters as well. Through these area managers, a world enterprise achieves decentralization of responsibility for local planning and operations, and holds each accountable for his performance against the broader plan formulated by the strategic management board and approved by the chief executive officer.

The organization structure within each area depends on the configuration of the company's business activities there. In Company B's case, for instance, the plan of organization under the area manager for North America might be similar to that shown for the line management of Company A, excluding the "international division," but including any functional executives required at the area level, such as, perhaps, an area controller. In the Far East, the volume of business might warrant only a functional structure; that is, the area manager would have reporting to him an executive responsible for each function (e.g., marketing, manufacturing, personnel, and accounting) for all the company products made or sold within the prescribed Far Eastern area.

CONCLUSION

Companies that are successfully competing as world enterprises find that the factors needed for success in a world-wide business differ from those required in a domestically oriented business. Major revisions in business thinking and methods are needed. Simply stated, the world-wide management concept requires a chief executive (1) to view his own responsibility as global in scope, with the United States as one division thereof, and (2) to organize his corporation in such a way that its major decisions are considered and made in the light of world conditions and opportunities.

Foreign-based companies have, in a manner of speaking, been forced to adopt an international approach to their business planning because of the limited size of their domestic markets—consequently, they often have a head start in the field of international management. N. V. Philips' Gloeilampenfabrieken (the company known here as Philips' Lamps), for example, is based in The Netherlands, a country with a population roughly equivalent to that of metropolitan New York. By treating its domestic operation as just one facet of its world-wide business, this firm has become a recognized world leader in electronics and in other fields. United States businessmen have the advantage of a large domestic market, but can capitalize fully on this advantage only if they see it as the hub of a trade universe.

Many American companies have evolved an organizational structure suitable primarily for carrying on a business within the United States. All activities outside the country are usually managed through a self-contained unit, such as an international division, or a subsidiary international company. Regardless of what it is called, the unit is often treated as a subdivision of the U.S. organization. This alignment of resources and people is being questioned increasingly as industrial capacity and purchasing power build up in other lands. These changing economic conditions require many companies to be organized throughout as truly international enterprises—and to treat the United States as a subdivision of the world-wide organization.

This concept has been expressed well by President Eisenhower, who in an address earlier this year pointed out that there are no longer foreign affairs and foreign policy—the proper term today is world affairs—and concluded, "We have discovered that we cannot separate what we do abroad from what we do at home."[6]

43 – LRP for International Operations

JOHN FAYERWEATHER

"What will be the key policy questions for international managements in the next five to ten years?"

In the past 15 years U. S. business has "gone international" on a truly extraordinary scale. Our overseas investments in manufacturing operations have more than tripled. Whereas foreign operations were essentially the province of a few hundred major concerns before World War II, today an estimated 3,000 U. S. companies of all sizes and descriptions have some interest in overseas production—either through their own investments or licensing agreements. Thus in a multitude of companies one basic policy decision is an accomplished fact—the commitment to move outward from purely domestic business and become an international enterprise. In retrospect, with foreign markets expanding explosively and import controls forcing local production, that decision was an obvious and easy one.

Now come the more difficult problems. The task of shaping the character and policies of a far-flung organization into a unit which can meet effectively the challenges of increasingly tough

6. Address given at St. John's College, Annapolis, May 22, 1959; reported in *The New York Times*, May 23, 1959, p. 14.

"LRP for International Operations," *California Management Review*, III (Fall 1960), 23–35. Reprinted by permission of the author and the publisher. Copyright 1960 by the Regents of the University of California. **John Fayerweather**: Managing Editor, *International Executive*; Director, Research Program, International Advertising Association, New York.

competition and evolving political and social forces. The major aspects of these problems are already apparent and with the knowledge gained from experience and research in the past few years we may outline the thinking which can lead to their effective solution.

At the risk of oversimplification, I will single out three areas which I believe present the critical problems which must be resolved in every company which hopes to have an effective international operation five to ten years hence. A few companies have already gone a long way in the direction of solving these problems but for most international managements these will be major preoccupations for the next few years. The three are:

1. Establishment of operations which are viable in highly nationalistic environments with particular attention to the ownership question and joint ventures.

2. Development of local national executives for senior posts in overseas managements.

3. Welding and molding world-wide operations into an integrated unit.

I. THE THREAT OF NATIONALISM

Through much of the world, especially in the less developed areas, the environment for U. S. business is dominated by two forces:

1. The powerful emotion of nationalism combining patriotic pride and a thrust for independence with negative reactions against racism, colonialism, economic dependence and in general to being "second-class" citizens of the world society.

2. A substantial measure of dependence for rapid economic progress upon the capital and industrial know-how of the economically more advanced nations, especially the United States.

These forces are fundamentally in opposition and it has only been the overriding political and economic importance of the second which has held the first in check. But the balance between the two is by no means static, it is in every sense dynamic and one of the major keys to future planning is recognition that the second, dependence on what U. S. business has to offer, is declining steadily while nationalism shows little signs of abating.

What this means for U. S. business has been spelled out recently from two quite different viewpoints with conclusions, which though different in fact are very similar in implication. Speaking from the perspective of their global study of industrial conditions Professors Harbison and Myers observe:

Eventually the firm is forced to recognize that, in the opinion of the effective political leaders, foreign management and foreign financial control are only temporary instruments for industrial development. In a very real sense, therefore, expatriate managers are expendable, and their power and influence in any rapidly industrializing country will inevitably shrink. Like patrimonial management in the advanced countries, expatriate management too will become an anachronism in modern society. . . . We feel that the wholly owned foreign firm has a limited role to play in the industrializing countries. The future is likely to see an expansion of locally controlled companies which have an affiliation, through licensing, marketing, or consulting arrangements, with large business organizations in the United States, England, and Europe.[1]

Approaching the situation with the eyes of a practicing executive, Harold Solmssen of Schering Corporation perceives the same sort of trend.

As far as we can remember, ours was the most progressive economy and, as a result, we are the leading economic power today. The rest of the world had to adapt itself to our methods if they wanted our money and our products. But this may not always be so and we should guard against considering our views right and those of the others "unfair" or "wrong."[2]

Thus there is a pressing need for U. S. international operations to set their policies so that they will be welcome in countries abroad when the need for our capital and know-how has largely passed. What does this require?

The answer lies essentially in policies that satisfy the major aspirations in the host country falling within the province of the U. S. operations. While the importance of these will vary among countries we may define at least four such aspirations:

1. The quest of individuals, especially at the managerial level for personal opportunity and advancement;

2. The urge of the individual with entrepreneurial instincts to realize them in the creative and financial satisfactions of developing a business venture;

3. The desire of local government and financial circles to retain within their borders a full share of the financial returns of industrial operations; and

4. The drive of governments for economic progress directed in large measure by their plans

---

1. Frederick Harbison and Charles A. Myers, *Management in the Industrial World* (McGraw-Hill Book Company, New York, 1959), p. 391.
2. "Organization Planning for International Operations," *The International Executive*, Winter, 1960, p. 5, summarized from a paper delivered at the American Management Association.

and conceptions of what is in the best national interest.

That the policies of U. S. business may frustrate or at least threaten realization of these aspirations is all too easily documented. A recent study of U. S. subsidiaries in Brazil and Mexico by John Shearer showed that U. S. personnel "dominate most of the top posts. . . . The general manager, and key executives at the second level are non-nationals—usually Americans."[3] Under these circumstances hundreds of foreign executives can only be promoted as U. S. nationals above them are moved and this movement to date has not been notably rapid.

The reactions of local entrepreneurs to U. S. operations are strikingly illustrated in Sanford Mosk's description of the "New Group" of small Mexican manufacturers who gained a foothold during World War II and were the focal point of protective and restrictive policies as they sought shelter from the incursions of bigger, more efficient U. S. companies who they felt, probably correctly, could wipe them out if given free rein.[4] More recently concerted drives among organized commercial interests have threatened Sears, Roebuck and Woolworth as numerous small Mexican merchants have seen a threat to their future in new, mass merchandising methods.[5] They have attempted to curb expansion of such chain firms in various ways.

The classic case of dispute over financial returns from a venture is that of General Motors in Australia. The profits from GM's fully owned Holden operation are running over 30% on its investment, a return in which local investors would like a share and the allocation for GM dividends of $16.8 million of foreign exchange out of total Australian dollar earnings of $173 million in 1959 is a hard fact for the government to swallow. This situation is extreme but in lesser degree the feelings it involves apply to every successful overseas venture making profits and seeking to repatriate them.

Finally, conflicts with government economic planning are found in limitless variety, ranging from major disagreements such as the reluctance of U. S. automobile companies to accelerate manufacture of parts in Brazil a few years ago because they felt it was uneconomic to many lesser problems such as the Indian government's criticism of the "wasteful" expenditures on selling efforts by U. S. tire companies.[6]

"YANKEE FIRM, GO HOME!"

So there is a solid nucleus in frustration of objectives around which the forces of nationalism may be aroused against U. S. foreign operations.

One solution of course is to accept the eventual withdrawal of U. S. companies from abroad. Rejecting this as a defeatist approach, the challenge lies in the conception of policies which give sufficient scope to national aspirations so that U. S. business remains, if not loved, at least accepted as a useful industrial citizen abroad.

Much of the thinking of affected national groups on this subject has coalesced around the concept of the "joint venture." The jointly financed enterprise, especially one in which U. S. interests have a minority position, is seen by government officials, local industrialists and others as the ideal for utilizing United States capital and especially a continuing flow of know-how while still giving full scope to national aspirations. In some instances by legal requirements, but more commonly by administrative pressure and persuasion, new United States ventures are encouraged to move in this direction in many countries.

Reflecting this influence, a research project on joint ventures directed by Professor Wolfgang Friedman at Columbia University, to be published later this year, reveals that there has been a significant increase in interest in joint ventures in the post World War II era. As a percentage of new investments, however, joint ventures still remain a minority and few established investments have been changed from 100% United States ownership to a joint ownership status.

According to the latest census of overseas investments only 26% of subsidiaries had as much as 5% ownership by local capital.[7] United States international managements have not as yet therefore, made any broad shift in policies in the direction of joint venturing. Should they? Or can the pressures of national aspirations be contained without such a policy shift?

GUIDE TO BASIC POLICY

In answer to these questions I propose three basic guides in policy making. Individual situations will vary greatly from company to company and country to country defying universal recommendations. But a general adherence to these guidelines will, I believe, result in enduring policy decisions.

3. "Overseas American Managers—Necessities or Luxuries?", *Management in the Industrial World: An International Analysis.* Princeton University, Industrial Relations Section, p. 17.

4. *Industrial Revolution in Mexico* (University of California Press, Berkeley and Los Angeles, 1950), pp. 32—52.

5. John Fayerweather, *Management of International Operations* (McGraw-Hill Book Co., N.Y., 1960), pp. 222—232.

6. J. Fayerweather (see note 5), pp. 247—248.

7. U. S. Department of Commerce, *Foreign Investment of the United States*, Washington, 1953, p. 23.

1. A joint venture which contemplates a substantial sharing of management control is fundamentally undesirable and to be avoided except in unusual circumstances.

2. A major portion of foreign national aspirations can and should be met by statesmanlike management policies independent of the ownership question.

3. Some sharing with local nations of financial participation in foreign ventures without relinquishing of management control is desirable.

The first point is the most important for it strikes to the heart of joint venturing as many people conceive it. Their idea is that an existing or budding local entrepreneur joins forces with the management of a U. S. firm and, pooling their assets, they form a far stronger enterprise than either could present alone. The local entrepreneur knows his country, he has government contacts and, by giving the venture a strong local flavor, he contributes to the morale of the personnel and the public image of the company. The United States management brings its skills in management and technology and a continuing flow of new know-how from·research.

Competent analysts of this subject like Professor Emile Benoit emphasize the necessity that the partners be compatible.

> Finding the right partner is nine-tenths of the problem. . . . As in marriage, there is nothing so important as mutual confidence, and basic agreement on values.[8]

With this proviso the theory of the marriage of foreign and U. S. managements appears sound and demonstrated successes among the many case studies collected in the Columbia University research indicate that it is feasible.

However, there is clearly another side to the question sharply defined in the difficulties encountered in a number of joint ventures and the ultimate failure of others such as Sears, Roebuck's union with Waltons, Ltd. in Australia which was severed in late 1959 because of disagreement over financial and expansion policies.[9] The significance of these difficulties can be summed up in the question of whether it is reasonable to expect continuing sound and dynamic management to result from a marriage of the entrepreneurial drives and ideas of two managements. This question admits no simple answer and this paper is no place to attempt a full exposition of the subject.

I submit, however, as a general thesis that where success has come out of mergers and other marriages in industry, it has largely come through an unusual coincidence of managerial outlooks or more commonly through the submersion or ultimate elimination of the viewpoints of individuals on one side or the other resulting in dominance of a single partner.

Those who disagree with this thesis should have no difficulty in accepting joint international ventures as a general policy. But, if the thesis is acceptable, it casts grave doubts on joining forces with local national entrepreneurs as a means for satisfying national aspirations. It is important in evaluating this thesis to look more towards the future than the present.

It can be shown quite readily that in the early stages of a joint venture the marriage of assets is of great value. The United States company new to a foreign country profits greatly from the local know-how of its partner and the local partner derives great benefits from American products and technology not otherwise available to him. But these immediate benefits diminish in importance fairly rapidly and then the strengths of the joint venture as with any enterprise begin to depend upon the ability of its management to conceive and execute policies with a unified and persevering direction.

JOINT VENTURES

If the marriage has in fact been between two competent entrepreneurial managements (and that is assumed to be one of the key objectives of joint ventures) then, as·market conditions change, political forces shift, product changes evolve, etc., it is almost certain that there will be significant differences of opinion between the management groups. It is possible that they may work them out and the advantages of the marriage will support effective union. It seems more likely, however, that the venture will either suffer from vacillation and inability to develop effective unified policy or that out of conflict will emerge one dominant management, so that the other loses an effective vehicle for achieving its objectives in the union. Either the entrepreneurial aspirations of the local national are frustrated or the United States company loses effective control over the policies of its foreign unit.

This negative conclusion leads to re-examination of the proposition put forward by many local nationals that joint ventures should be adopted as a means of satisfying the varied national aspirations listed on pp. 281–282. The position of the

8. "When Businesses Marry," *International Management Digest*, October, 1958, p. 20.

9. *Business Week*, November 7, 1959, p. 60.

local nationals is justified today, but primarily for one major reason which need not exist.

If a major share of ownership were in local hands, they could readily force changes in those policies of many United States subsidiaries which currently frustrate national aspirations. For example, they could require the removal of U. S. executives and promotion of local personnel to top positions. However, it is certainly not essential that ownership be shared for such a change to be made.

The success of our most enlightened United States international companies in utilizing local executives, in blending company policies with those of government economic plans, in developing local suppliers, etc., is ample proof that a large portion of the local aspirations can be met without sharing management control.

The critical significance of the strong support of joint venturing from overseas, therefore, lies not so much in a yes or no response as in imaginative and persevering execution of policies which relieve the pressures for sharing management control by undertaking independently those actions which local nationals would foster if they gained control. This objective, we must grant, cannot be fully achieved for much the same reasons that even the most enlightened paternalism is never fully successful. There will always be a residual desire for full control which United States ownership frustrates. But, given a continuance of respect for private property, there seems every reason to assume that United States companies which make a concerted effort to give scope for national aspirations will be able to continue overseas operations indefinitely.

PROFIT SHARING

The third suggested guideline, sharing financial participation with foreign nationals, is essentially part of this approach but it is treated separately because it is a more difficult area of execution than, for example, promotion of local executives. The rates of return on investment earned by American overseas operations are generally no greater than those of local capitalists and the dollars allocated for remission of profits can almost always be justified on sound economic grounds as less than would be required for importation of products made locally as a result of the investment or gains from exports of the products of the U. S. operations. Yet the furor surrounding the Australian General Motors situation cited above is only the most notable expression of a widespread desire by local investors to "have a piece" of the earnings of U. S. companies

and dissatisfaction of government authorities at the allocation of dollars for remission of earnings which might otherwise be used for importing machinery, raw materials, etc.

STOCK SALE IN HOST COUNTRY

Rejecting the concept of shared management in joint ventures, I feel United States managements must still give full consideration to the possibility of limited joint venturing by allowing local capital to invest directly in their operations. A number of companies have already taken steps in this direction by selling common or preferred stock to local investors.

A few are moving in the opposite direction— one major company, for example, recently bought up outstanding common stock rather than face further displeasure from local investors who were dissatisfied with the low dividend payout of the company. Experiences such as this underscore the fact that sharing financial participation is not without significant disadvantages. However, as compared with disputes where management control is shared these disadvantages do not appear to endanger operating success and some concession to the financially oriented nationalistic aspirations seems essential for the continuance of integrated international enterprises.

MUTUAL STOCK EXCHANGE

One approach suggested by *Business International* is the union of companies through mutual exchanges of stock. BI feels such a step "would remove conflicts of interest between majority and minority shareholders. It would create an internationally owned firm that, as it expands and acquires owners of parent stock of an increasing variety of nationalities, can give the only final answer to nationalistic hostilities and the problem of being labeled 'foreign.'"[10]

This solution of course has limited application in that it would involve the marriage of a number of managements but the idea behind it of overcoming hostilities by spreading ownership of the international company all over the world is open to very general application. General Motors stock, for example, could be (and to some degree already is) owned by investors in every continent and in that way they could share in such profits as GM made in their own countries. In fact, however, this solution is currently so impeded by exchange controls and the end result is so far detached from the individual foreign operations

---

10. *Business International*, October 23, 1959, p. 2.

that it is less promising as an immediate solution and more likely as BI suggests to be the "final answer" many years hence.

MUST RETAIN OPERATING CONTROL

Of more immediate promise is the sale of a part of the stock of subsidiaries to the general investing public in individual countries. With such broad sharing of ownership, the U. S. management, even if only retaining a minority interest, can retain operating control. It is by no means essential to sell majority ownership, however, to accomplish the essential objective of giving local capital a chance to share in the venture and to satisfy the desires of local governments. More practical are such efforts as Kaiser Industries' sale of 42% of the equity in its Argentine venture to the public.[11] As a broader investing public emerges through the growth of the middle class and the evolution of security markets in country after country this practice should become increasingly common.

To summarize then, in this first area of policy planning we are confronted with the necessity of satisfying the aspirations which underlie nationalistic drives. Despite pressures to resolve all of these through acceptance of minority positions in joint ventures, United States managements will be wise to adhere to full operating control of overseas ventures seeking to satisfy local national aspirations through statesmanlike operating policies including sharing of some degree of financial ownership through broad sale of company stock.

II. DEVELOPMENT OF LOCAL NATIONAL EXECUTIVES

Today, as Dr. Shearer's study has noted, most of the key executive assignments in the overseas units of most companies are handled by United States executives. But the forces of economics and politics are set against this practice and in favor of the eventual transfer of all management jobs abroad to local nationals. The relatively higher salaries paid to United States executives and the travel and living allowances they require make it appreciably less expensive to employ local nationals in virtually any situation.

Equally important are the pressures of government officials and public opinion in favor of turning management over to local nationals. In some countries these pressures are felt tangibly in the form of laws requiring employment of nationals or refusing entry papers for American executives on the grounds that local personnel are adequate for the work. Such restrictions are not common in the case of senior executives, United States companies generally being legally allowed today to bring in men for top positions.

However, there is strong pressure from government and national opinion directed against those companies which are slow in turning over management to nationals and, conversely, in favor of those who do give responsibility to local executives. These pressures may be expected to grow as the number and capabilities of local executives increase.

Thus a sensible management must adopt a policy of turning over progressively greater management responsibility to local nationals and it must prepare for the day when the senior position in one country after another will be entrusted to a local executive. This thought may be disturbing to some, but it need not be. Some companies have already gone a long way down this road—National Cash Register, for example, has only some half dozen U. S. executives throughout its large and highly effective international organization. But the transition will be effective only if the national executives have been adequately prepared. There have been in recent years cases where management of a foreign unit was turned over to local executives who were not ready and who had subsequently to be replaced by U. S. executives with most unfortunate public relations and organizational repercussions. Thus, it is imperative that a thoughtful plan be evolved for the development of overseas executives.

What are the requisites of such a plan? First, it must be directed to the levels of managerial characteristics at which development is needed. Second, it must foster specific qualities essential for men in senior positions. And third, it must provide experiences which will have a permanent developmental effect. These are fundamentals applicable to all executive development. Our concern here is with the special considerations which enter into their application to overseas executives.

"CONDITIONING" EXECUTIVES

A basic, if usually unstated, assumption of United States executive development plans is that the executives' attitudes are essentially in accord with the codes and objectives expected of men in top management. We assume that they will regard cooperation with other executives as desirable; that they will favor thorough analysis in the formulation of policies, and so on. This is realistic.

---

11. *Business International,* May 23, 1958, p. 6.

Individuals to varying degrees may be deficient in attitudes of this sort. But, by and large, they are an integral part of the personalities of managerial candidates, impressed upon them by a variety of experiences from childhood to maturity.

They are by definition part of our modern managerial culture and, since so many phases of a man's life work toward their development, little explicit attention need be given to them in executive development plans. Accordingly most attention is directed at two less basic phases of men's qualities — technical skills (budgeting, labor negotiations, etc.) and administrative behavior (skill in managerial coordination, approaches to analysis of policy problems, etc.).

In overseas executive development such assumptions about the attitudes of men are not so broadly justified. Research into managerial organizations abroad emphasizes the prevalence of administrative attitudes which are substantially different from those of the U. S. managerial culture. Harbison and Myers, after extensive surveys of management organizations abroad, report:

In each of the countries . . . the conditions generated by the process of industrialization have required increasing attention to managerial organization, attitudes, policies, and development. There are, however, significant differences among countries both in the problems faced and in the types of reactions; these differences reflect various cultural patterns as well as variation in the stage and pace of economic development.[12]

The main theme emerging from my intensive research with management organizations in Mexico was that "the significant difficulties in relations between United States and foreign executives are due to the differences in their national cultures."[13] The codes which govern men's relations with others, the way they approach their work, their motivations, and other attitudes are in many societies significantly different from our own and strongly influence executive performance.

These differences force us to approach overseas executive development at the attitudinal level which is unnecessary in domestic programs. Philosophically one may say that the cultural attitudes of others should be respected and foreign executives should be allowed to evolve administrative patterns consistent with their own culture.

This point of view is however impractical on two counts. First, both research and the practical experience of United States executives confirm that United States managerial attitudes, when applied intelligently, result in more effective management than adoption of local attitudes.

The effectiveness of U. S. subsidiaries abroad is based as much on the efficiency and drive generated by United States administrative attitudes as it is on superior technology and capital.

THE AMERICAN PATTERN

Second, there are strong indications that the evolution of the general administrative attitudes in other countries is in the direction of our own pattern. For all its shortcomings, the United States is the leader among the nations of the world in the evolution of a highly efficient managerial society and the administrative attitudes of our executives are an integral part of that efficiency.

As other nations progress toward a comparable type of society it appears inevitable that they will experience problems similar to ours, and evolve somewhat the same type of culture. Indeed, one finds strong evidence of this trend in the fact that the able and alert managers of Europe, Latin America and Asia have more in common with Americans than do the general run of managers in their societies. Thus it appears that the effectiveness of United States subsidiaries applying United States managerial attitudes is simply evidence that their approaches place them in the lead in a general cultural revolution which will in time envelop the whole society.

While the specific attitudes toward which executive development efforts should be directed will depend upon the nature of each individual, two broad categories emerged from the research reported in *The Executive Overseas* as of widespread importance: attitudes toward interpersonal relations and approaches to work assignments.[14] The attitudes of businessmen in much of the world, especially the less industrialized areas, are strongly influenced (1) by the merchant-trader attitudes characteristic of commercial (as distinguished from industrial) life and (2) by authoritarian social institutions (family, church, schools, etc.).

FOSTER GROUP ATTITUDES

Both of these influences foster individualistic personality characteristics and produce the sort of man who looks on those around him as antagonists and operates as a lone wolf, "dealing-with" and maneuvering around others as best he can. Though such attitudes are highly effective in the bazaar, they are incompatible with the require-

12. F. Harbison and C. A. Myers (see note 1), p. 123.

13. John Fayerweather, *The Executive Overseas* (Syracuse University Press, Syracuse, New York, 1959), p. 6.

14. John Fayerweather (see note 13).

ments of an integrated management team. There is a common need therefore to foster the group-oriented attitudes which are emerging as the small, one-man or family concern gives way to larger, professionally managed industrial units.

The approach of U. S. management to individual work assignments is a lineal descendant of two major forces which spread out of Western Europe in the 16th century: the scientific revolution and the Calvinist "Protestant Ethic." They account in cultural terms for the analytical, disciplined attitude toward managerial responsibilities which is the norm of our industrial society. For the most part these forces scarcely touched the cultures of vast areas of Asia, Africa, the Middle East and Latin America. As a result there is a substantial need in overseas executive development to build disciplined, scientific attitudes.

In considering the development of such attitudes in senior overseas executives it is important to appreciate the need for a real "take" in the personality of the individual and not a superficial acceptance at the behavior level. The latter may result in acceptable performance among junior executives if they work under the strong leadership of an able executive whose own standards set the basic tone of management action. However, when we are considering men to whom the senior leadership position is to be entrusted it is essential that the acceptance of effective management methods be deeply rooted in personal conviction.

THOROUGH INVOLVEMENT A "MUST"

What type experiences are required to achieve this sort of development? The answer lies in two words: *involvement* and *thorough*. The executives must be given experiences in which they become deeply involved personally and which are sustained to the point of thorough absorption.

We must accept as a starting point that changing attitudes is an extremely difficult process and that radical changes are not generally feasible, thus our concern is with gradual changes and in large measure with fostering the development of pre-existing potentials, not injecting new ideas. But even this limited objective can be accomplished only by experiences which have a penetrating and enduring effect on the personality of the individual.

The implications of these generalizations for actual executive development plans are fairly clear. First, because the greater part of a man's experience will come on the job in his own country, it is essential that senior supervising U. S. executives understand the importance of attitu-

dinal development and foster it by their own actions.

Second, extended periods of work experience in the United States should be scheduled at key stages of the development process. Actually living and feeling the various components of the U. S. managerial system has an impact which can never be achieved in a U. S. subsidiary set in the midst of another culture.

American companies have found from experience that local nationals who have gone to college in the United States or worked here for substantial periods often have acquired attitudes which make them good executives. Extended assignments for executives at the formative stage of development can accomplish the same degree of involvement. It is important to emphasize, however, that the visits must be long enough and must immerse the individual deeply in the real functioning of an organization. Companies which have used development of this type effectively have found that periods of several months to a year are the minimum requirement.

A survey by the Institute of International Education indicates that some 5,000 foreign nationals were given training experience in the United States in 1959 but that only 10 percent of these were here for over six months.[15] Doubtless those who were here for brief visits acquired useful technical training but it is only the visits of several months which can be regarded as effective executive development experiences.

A more intensive study of the development practices of 150 U. S. companies by the Council for International Progress in Management to be published soon shows that some companies have given careful thought to design such experiences so that they include extended periods of formal training and working assignments. Taking their policies as harbingers of the future, we may predict that in the next few years other alert managements will develop plans for intensive development experiences in the United States for local national executives.

III. INTERNATIONALIZING MANAGEMENT

There is little doubt that the international operations of most companies will grow in coming years both in absolute terms and in proportion to domestic business. This has been generally true for the past decade and the higher rates of growth of foreign economies suggest a continua-

15. *Open Doors*, Institute of International Education, New York, 1960, p. 14.

tion of the trend. Inevitably the pattern of management will shift to accommodate this change in the nature of corporate business but the manner in which the pattern evolves will require careful thought based on a realistic view of each company's situation.

The general thrust of the change of corporate management has been described in essentially similar terms by several authors in the past year.[16] It starts from the traditionally segregated status of export departments and international divisions which operate with a large measure of autonomy, too often accompanied by ignorance and lack of interest on the part of senior company management and domestic associates. The international side of business draws products, know-how and capital from the rest of the company but structurally its operations are largely independent of the main body of domestic parent company functions. By contrast the emerging new patterns of management involve a high degree of integration between international activities and the rest of the company.

As a general trend this thesis is incontrovertible. It can readily be observed in various stages in many companies today and the growing importance of international business argues for its continuation. The problem of planning lies not, therefore, in establishing the basic direction of change but rather in determining the character it should assume for a specific company. In all probability the result both in operating policies and organizational structure will show many characteristics of the ideal integrated world enterprise, but will retain some of the features of the segregated organizations which are still the dominant pattern today.

OPERATING POLICIES

In the development of *operating policies*, the integration ideal stresses a pattern of activities which renders the optimum economic return. Manufacturing plants are established in countries with low costs, research activities are distributed according to costs and the scientific resources of various areas, financial assets are moved about to maximize return, and so forth. That substantial progress in this direction has already been made is observable on many fronts; for example, in the rapid increase in foreign "sourcing" to supply U. S. markets with goods made in company plants abroad;[17] and in the growth of research facilities in Europe.

The fact that a significant degree of change has occurred does not mean that the process will be carried through to the ideal of the economic op-

timum concept. Its limitations can be best understood by visualizing an extreme, yet not illogical case. It is quite conceivable that, on an economic basis, the most profitable structure for a small electronics company would consist of a single large production unit in Japan, a research organization in Europe, and a sales organization spread around the world.

Such a structure immediately gives one pause. Would any management wish to commit itself so heavily in single separated political areas? In fact, of course, even the economic optimum would rarely call for such an extreme, but the limitations, highlighted by the extreme case, will always be present. Even at the expense of some cost economies a responsible management must plan its operating structure so that it is reasonably secure.

POLITICAL FACTORS

Planning the extent and character of the integration of international and domestic operations becomes therefore a complex problem in which many economic and noneconomic factors must be weighed.[18] Most important undoubtedly are the political forces. The hazards of a global war may be given some weight, though the broader implications of such an eventuality are so catastrophic that probably no plan could really take them into account.

More realistically therefore our concern should be with minimizing the risks from single upheavals and with the evolution of integrated economic areas such as the European and Central American common markets. The former militates against placing a substantial portion of company activities in any but the most stable countries. The latter calls for a substantial segregation of activities on a regional basis.

Indications are, for example, that the European common market will maintain a substantial protective wall which will perpetuate present restrictions on imports from countries like Japan. Projecting this characteristic, we may reasonably assume in our plans that a Latin American common market would be equally, if not more, protective and that current manufacturing plans, to the extent that they attempt to anticipate the development of the Latin American area, will be based on that assumption.

16. For example, John J. Beauvois, "Internationalism: A New Concept for U.S. Business," *California Management Review*, Winter, 1960, pp. 28–37; and Gilbert H. Clee and Alfred di Scipio, "Creating a World Enterprise," *Harvard Business Review*, Nov.–Dec., 1959, pp. 77–89.

17. "Americans Speed Up Foreign Sourcing," *Business Week*, January 2, 1960, pp. 66–68.

18. For a fuller discussion see John Fayerweather, "Logistic Planning" (see note 5), pp. 506–512.

Besides the political factor must be added consideration of the more complex and difficult-to-discern trends of currency restrictions, exchange rates and antitrust laws. When all of these elements are weighed in the balance most companies will find that a significant shift toward the international economic optimum will be in order but that it will also be judicious to hedge their position by a good deal of "uneconomic" dispersion and including retention of a large portion of their activities within the boundaries of the United States.

STANDARD OIL PATTERN

So far as *organization* is concerned, the ideal of the new concepts calls typically for a world headquarters with globally oriented top executives, a line organization divided by areas (North America, Europe, etc.), and staff divisions which serve the whole world in their speciality. Structures along these lines have been characteristic for some time of major international operations like Standard Oil Company (N. J.) and other petroleum companies and of manufacturing companies with large international interests such as National Cash Register, whose Chairman Stanley Allyn is as well known on international rostrums as any international division manager. There is no reason to doubt that, as the international interests of other companies expand, they also will shift their organizations to give greater emphasis and better management attention to overseas operations.

There is another side to this coin, however, which leads me to doubt whether the days of the segregated "international division" are really numbered. It seems more probable that the typical organization a few years hence will be a hybrid, with a substantial degree of internationalization, especially at the very top, but also a good deal of clustering and segregating of international as distinguished from domestic activities in both line and staff personnel.

The essential objective in developing any organization is, of course, to deal effectively with management problems and not to conform to an ideal. The new concept of international organization is an approach to dealing with the problems of an integrated world enterprise. It must be modified, however, to fit those aspects of the enterprise which remain substantially unintegrated or segregated and further to conform to the capacities of individuals.

For the predictable future there will be many aspects of a business for which there is a practical division of approaches between international and domestic, and effectiveness in the management of

each will call for specialized skills of individuals. For example, consider the financial and tax situation. Whether it be through a foreign based tax-haven corporation or a U. S. based international business corporation (the so-called Boggs Bill proposal) it is going to be financially desirable to manage the financing of overseas units so far as possible as a unit independent of the domestic activities.

INTERNATIONAL SPECIALISTS

Thus, regardless of the character of the over-all organization chart, there seems sure to be an executive who has some over-all supervisory responsibility for international financial activities. Furthermore, in the nature of performance of their work it seems quite certain that the men responsible for operations in areas outside the United States will spend a good deal of their time with this international financial supervisor working out the allocation of the international financial resources and that someone will be designated to coordinate and facilitate the efforts of these men as they work as a group. This coordinator may be called, for example, "chairman of the investment committee" but it takes little perception to visualize that such a man will have already assumed much of the role of a "vice president for international operations."

This same line of reasoning may be pursued for personnel, advertising and other aspects of operations. It does not in any way conflict with the basic thesis that organizations must move away from segregation toward integration of international, parent and domestic personnel. It does, however, indicate that the organizational planners have a very difficult task in discerning the exact form that integration should take for any one company at a given stage of its evolution.

The prospect therefore is for steady progress in the evolution of the integrated world enterprise, modified to fit realistically the prospects and requirements of each company situation.

This article has outlined three major areas in which major policy and organization changes are required for satisfactory international operations in the next few years: (1) meeting the threat of nationalism, (2) developing local national executives, and (3) internationalizing management. In each, the general direction of the future is quite clear. The problems lie therefore in the formulation of realistic and effective plans. This will be no small task.

In each area there are conflicting factors to consider and there are, as always, elements of inertia and ignorance to overcome. The hard facts of the tremendous potential of expanding world markets and the increasing competition to capture them should, however, provide ample incentive for U. S. managements to tackle the task realistically and energetically.

44 – Cross-Cultural Perspectives on Management Principles

WINSTON OBERG

The perennial argument between those who hold that management is a science governed by universal principles which can be discovered by research and those who say it is an art whose successful practice is dependent on a lengthy apprenticeship in a specific highly culture-bound situation will probably be intensified as the results of current cross-cultural studies of management become more widely known. Harbison and Myers,[1] for example, in their study of management development practices in twenty-three countries, made a number of generalizations about management and management development which suggested that these did not differ fundamentally from country to country. Bendix[2] compared the management situation in the U.S. today with that of British and Russian management at the turn of the century and management in East Germany today and found many common elements. On the other hand, Gonzalez and Mc-Millan,[3] after serving as consultants on business administration training in Brazil, concluded that management philosophies are highly culture-bound.

An important issue is whether or not the requirements for managerial success and the ground rules under which managers operate are quite similar from country to country or whether they differ so significantly as to make any attempt to generalize meaningless and futile. The study of the ground rules under which managers operate appears to be particularly significant in this analysis. Should the ground rules be the same or similar there would be a presumption that the qualities required and the strategy or "science" involved do not differ too much from country to country. If on the other hand the ground rules are markedly different—or, using an analogy from sports, if the "game" of management is played

according to one set of rules in the United States and quite different rules in France and still other rules in Brazil, it would be as fruitful to study the strategy of baseball in one country, the strategy of soccer in another, and the strategy of cricket in still a third country to derive a set of common principles or generalizations as it would to try to generalize about management when practiced under so many different national conditions.

My own experience in international management leads me to believe that cultural differences from one country to another are more significant than many writers now appear to recognize. For example, the skills that lead to managerial success in the U.S. may not be the skills that lead to managerial success in Brazil, to take the two countries with whose managers I am most familiar. Certainly the problems which managers face in these two cultures differ and the ground rules under which managers operate are almost as unlike in these two countries as the ground rules under which the two countries' national games are played. If, as it appears, the Brazilian manager is playing a form of "soccer" while the U.S. manager is playing "baseball," it is difficult to see how basic generalizations will apply with anywhere equal force to the two situations.

An illustration may clarify this point for the reader. Between August, 1959, and July, 1960, I served as a technical assistant to the University of Rio Grande do Sul (Brazil) under an I.C.A. agreement between my university and the Brazilian government. My role was to help the University of Rio Grande do Sul develop a business administration curriculum and train business administration professors. Part of my responsi-

"Cross-Cultural Perspectives on Management Principles," *Academy of Management Journal*, VI (June 1963), 129 – 143. Reprinted by permission of the author and the publisher. **Winston Oberg:** Graduate School of Business Administration, Michigan State University.

1. Frederick Harbison and Charles A. Myers, *Management in the Industrial World*, (McGraw-Hill Book Company, Inc., New York, 1959).

2. Reinhard Bendix, *Work and Authority in Industry*, (John Wiley & Sons, Inc., New York, 1956).

3. Richard F. Gonzalez and Claude McMillan Jr., "The Universality of American Management Philosophy" *Journal of the Academy of Management*, vol. 4, no. 1, (April 1961) pp. 33–41.

TABLE 1 THE TEN MOST COMMON PROBLEMS MENTIONED BY 51 RIO GRANDE
DO SUL (BRAZIL) TOP MANAGERS IN 1960

Rank		Problem	% Mentioning
1		Shortage of capital	32%
2		Competition with other states	29
3	(tie)	Finding and training high-level executives	26
3	(tie)	Getting good skilled or technical workers	26
5		Inflation	24
6		The farm problem and its effect on business	21
7		Getting good foremen	18
8	(tie)	Tenure	15
8	(tie)	Illiterate or barely literate workers	15
10		The transportation problem	12

bility was to initiate a series of management seminars to demonstrate to the local community the value of the kind of curriculum we were hoping to develop. In preparation for these seminars, I visited a cross-section of businessmen in the state of Rio Grande do Sul (southernmost state in Brazil and the state that holds the dubious distinction of having expropriated more United States-owned businesses than any other in Brazil).[4] In these visits, I attempted to gain an understanding of the main problems or worries that these men were concerning themselves with. Altogether, I visited 34 companies and talked to 51 presidents, vice presidents, or managing directors. Organizations ranged from manufacturing firms to insurance companies and included banks, newspapers, importing and exporting firms, wholesaling and retailing establishments and even one airline. Their size ranged from around 30 to 1,900 employees. (This last company was the largest in that part of Brazil.)

As a cross-section, this was as representative a selection as local businessmen, serving as my advisers, were able to select. The problems which came out of the study can, therefore, be regarded as the typical problems facing top managers in that state in late 1959 and early 1960. These problems will be compared with a subsequent U.S. study designed to get a parallel list of problems from top businessmen in the state of Michigan whose firms compared in size and activity with the Brazilian firms. In early 1962 we sent to some 1,700 small- and medium-sized firms in the state a questionnaire which, among other things, asked for the two or three most difficult problems the small businessman in Michigan was facing. Although the survey was carried out by mail and the approach was in other respects not identical with that used in Brazil, the focus on management problems was quite similar. The size of the companies surveyed was also parallel to that of Brazil. The range was from a low of three employees to a high of 2,000.

Although response to the questionnaire survey was disappointingly low, (less than 10% of the companies responded), there is no apparent reason to feel that the problems which were reported were unrepresentative of the population covered. One hundred and six usable responses to the question about the Michigan small businessman's problems were received. These will be presented immediately following the list of Brazilian managers' problems. Both samples covered predominantly top management. In the Michigan survey, roughly four out of five respondents were at the vice presidential level or higher. In the Rio Grande do Sul survey, three out of four were at that level. A comparison of the problems of these two sets of managers suggests that although some problems are similar a strikingly different total situation exists in Brazil from that in the U.S. The "game" the two sets of managers are playing may conceivably be the same, in some of its fundamentals, but the local ground rules are so different that the reader may well ask how any kind of general strategy, or any set of generalizations or principles can possibly apply to both situations.

THE "GAME" OF MANAGEMENT— PLAYED BY RIO GRANDE DO SUL (BRAZIL) GROUND RULES

Brazilian managers mentioned more than 80 different problems.[5] Since many of them were similar, it was possible to group the problems into some 15 categories. The ten most frequently mentioned categories are reported here in detail. (See Table 1).

4. Between 1959 and 1962, two U.S. owned utilities were expropriated by Leonel Brizolo, governor of the state.
5. Survey results were presented at a conference of Rio Grande do Sul managers held in Porto Alegre, Brazil, and were subsequently published: Winston Oberg, "Como a Universidade Pode Ajudar o Homem de Negocios" *Correio do Povo*, Porto Alegre, Brazil, July 3, 1960, p. 26.

1) The Problem of Raising Money—the Shortage of Capital. Of the fifteen problems mentioned, this one came up most frequently. 32% (11 of the 34 companies) mentioned it in one way or another. Managers complained about the shortage of money, the difficulty of raising capital, the difficulty in financing credit sales. Here are some typical comments:

We buy on 90-day terms and sell on 120- to 300-day terms. It is difficult to finance these long-term sales, but we have to because our competitors do.

Many of our sales are to the government and they take up to three years to pay. This puts a great strain on our capital. It is even worse when a new government takes over. They don't like to pay the bills of the former government.

Seventy-five per cent of the money printed in Brazil is in Rio, Sao Paulo, and Belo Horizonte. There is a real shortage of money down here.

Money is shifted to other states for political reasons. Eight banks in Porto Alegre (capital of Rio Grande do Sul) have only half the assets of one bank in Minas. The president of the country is from Minas and has been favoring that state.

As will be seen, this problem is closely related to several of the subsequent problems. In part, the difficulties are due to the country's galloping inflation and to the consequent flight of money out of the country (the "investment in dollars") or the flight into such inflation hedges as real estate projects.

2) The Problem of Competition with Other States, Particularly Sao Paulo, Minas Gerais, and Rio de Janeiro. 29% of the companies mentioned this problem in different ways. Some sample comments:

Our main markets are in the triangle: Sao Paulo, Minas, Rio. We are at a disadvantage being located down here. Transportation costs to the main market put us at a disadvantage.

We are thinking of moving our headquarters out of Rio Grande do Sul to central Brazil. The future looks better there.

The money that is taken out of Rio Grande do Sul by taxes and spent elsewhere in Brazil makes it difficult for local businesses. Our business down here is discriminated against in favor of some other states.

At the time of these interviews, this problem was probably in its most acute stage. Brazil's new capital, Brasilia, was just being completed. Industrial states nearest to Brasilia—Sao Paulo, Minas Gerais, Rio—had benefited most from the flow of printing press money which had paid for the construction of the new Brazilian capital. Rio Grande do Sul, more than 1,000 miles to the south, had not participated to any great extent in the Brasilia-generated demand for products. Bank deposits and tax money had in large quantities gone north to the states around Brasilia.

3) The Problem of Finding and Training Executives or High-Level Managers. 26% of the companies mentioned this problem in one way or another. Here are some of the comments:

Our businessmen have had no training. In many cases, a man gets to be director because he's the only man available, not because he's well qualified or the best man for the job.

Rio Grande do Sul managements are getting old. They're not keeping up with the progress of the country.

We can't get good management trainees. The universities don't produce them. We tried to get men from the university. They haven't worked out. The people here who are managers have all started as clerks.

We can't replace the directors if they leave. We don't have anybody who can take their places.

We've grown, but our people have not. We've grown too fast for our management.

We need to decentralize but we can't. We don't have any people to give the responsibility to. You can't delegate responsibility. People won't accept it.

Finally, here is a remarkably candid and revealing comment:

The family idea here is strong. You get a young fellow with ability and he works hard expecting to get ahead and then along comes the 20-year old son of the owner and he's boss. It discourages people who aren't relatives. Of course, it's pretty important to have close family control at the top because you need absolute loyalty. No one in Brazil considers it dishonest to cheat the government. But to cheat, you need close family-type management and control. You can't afford to let outsiders in. You have to keep the management in the family. It's possible that this will change now that the government is getting more successful in its tax collection. It's getting quite a bit tougher to cheat.

Tied for 3) The Problem of Getting Good Skilled or Technical Workers. This problem was also mentioned by 26% of the companies. Here are some of the comments:

We can buy machinery easier than we can get good men to run the machinery. It takes up to two years to train a good lathe man.

There is a real shortage of good technical people in the shop and office.

We have to train our mechanics. We can't hire any. Then we have the problem that when you train a man you often lose him. Other companies hire him away from you after you've spent the time and money to train him.

5) *The Problem of Inflation.* In an article published in 1955 on Brazilian economic progress, Spiegel wrote:

Inflation, Keynes quotes Lenin, is the best way to destroy the capitalist system. . . . Inflation tends to confound all values, and its persistence in Brazil may at least in part be held responsible for what Lord Bryce once called 'the habit of mistaking words for facts and aspirations for achievements.' . . . To raise the question whether governmental ideology favors inflation as a means of forcing saving is to inquire whether the government openly favors sin. There are few Brazilian statesmen in responsible positions who have not, time and again, and in the strongest terms, professed profound aversion to inflation and promised prevention or relief. Inflation has progressed notwithstanding. . . .[6]

Spiegel was writing before the 1955 election of President Kubitschek and hence before Brasilia. Even then, inflation was a far more serious problem than anything we in the U.S. have ever faced. By way of illustration, the consumer price index for the city of Porto Alegre computed by the University of Rio Grande do Sul rose nearly 50% in 1954 and another 20% in 1955. Following the election of Kubitschek in 1955, inflation maintained a fairly steady pace, ranging between 10% and 20% per year until 1959. Then the consumer price index began to rise more rapidly, reaching a rate of nearly 40% per year. In the first eight months of 1959, alone, the index rose more than 25%. The index stood at 472 in December, 1958, and by August, 1959, it had reached 588 (1948 prices equal 100).[7] Considering the nature of the inflationary problem, it is somewhat surprising that only 24% of the companies mentioned the problem during the interviews. Possibly there was some censorship of problems during the interview—some limitation of problems to those about which I or the university might be of some assistance; or possibly, inflation generated an appearance of prosperity and high demand which gave it a beneficial appearance to some managers. In any case, the comments of those who realized the problem left no doubt as to its seriousness:

The big problem is how to maintain your capital in the face of inflation. Paper profits aren't real profits.

Some of our competitors don't realize what their real costs and profits are. So they charge unrealistically low prices. They think they're making a profit, but actually they're eating into their capital.

Big farmers and businessmen in general are not putting their money back into the farm or business to produce more but are putting it into city real estate. This cuts down on the amount of things produced and just makes inflation worse.

6) *The Farm Problem and Its Effect on Business.* Rio Grande do Sul historically had been one of the most important agricultural states in Brazil. In 1959, it still accounted for more than two-thirds of Brazil's production of beans, alfalfa, barley, wool, and grapes to mention only a few of the state's agricultural products. However in the years immediately preceding 1959 the government's de-emphasis of agriculture and intensive encouragement of industrialization had sharply decreased some kinds of agricultural production in the state, with resulting dislocations in the economy of Rio Grande do Sul. Several of the businessmen interviewed had been adversely affected by this de-emphasis of agriculture. 21% of them mentioned this problem in one way or another. Here are some of their comments:

Agriculture will always be the main source of income here. We're giving too much attention to industry. We used to feed all of Brazil but now Rio Grande do Sul is even having to import black beans.

Our state is mainly agricultural. Industry should be based on agriculture. Our companies should either be using what the farms produce or making things for the farms to use.

We are trying to do too much and not being realistic. This state should try to improve the quality of its farming first before worrying about industry.

This is an agricultural state. Our money comes from agriculture but we are trying to impose on this an industrial economy. Rio Grande do Sul should concentrate on agriculture. That's where the money is.

7) *The Problem of Getting Good Foremen.* Closely related to the first personnel problem, that of getting good executives, is the problem of finding capable foremen. 18% of the companies mentioned this as a problem:

---

6. Henry William Spiegel, "Brazil: The State and Economic Growth" in Simon Kuznets, ed., "Economic Growth: Brazil, India, Japan" (Duke University Press, Durham, N. C., 1955) pp. 415–416.

7. Statistics reported in "Boletim Informativo" of the Faculdade de Ciencias Economicas, Universidade de Rio Grande do Sul, Ano V, 1958 and Ano VI, 1959.

People don't know how to handle the people working for them, how to get the most out of people. Sometimes they get too friendly with subordinates hoping this will get more cooperation, but just the reverse happens.

There just aren't enough good foremen.

Some good men don't want to be foremen. They don't want to be the boss of their colleagues, don't want responsibility.

This is a family company so we don't have much trouble at the top, but the people below this level — the foremen and sub-foremen — give trouble.

8) The Problem of Tenure. This very interesting problem has no exact U.S. counterpart. Under Brazilian social legislation, companies must give severance pay to anyone who has been employed by them for more than a year. Until a man has ten years of service, a company can discharge him relatively simply by paying him one month's salary for every year of continuous company service. After a man has been employed for more than ten consecutive years, he receives permanent tenure and may not be dismissed except for serious misdemeanor. If the company is successful in getting a labor court to allow it to discharge a man with tenure, the company still must pay the man two months' pay for every year of continuous company service. (This law applies to rank and file workers only. Persons occupying positions of trust and confidence are guaranteed only severance pay in the amount of one month's pay for every year of continuous company service.) The tenure law is a constant source of irritation to many employers. 15% of the companies mentioned it during the interviews:

If you keep a man more than ten years, it's very hard to fire him. Even if he is a very good worker before then, he sometimes starts to loaf once he gets tenure. He knows you won't fire him. So, you generally get rid of your men before they've been with you ten years. This means you lose some good people.

More than 20% of the men we fire are good men who just want to collect severance pay.

The permanent tenure law leads to high turnover. We have to let people go before they get tenure. This is an especially bad thing as far as our mechanics and our salesmen are concerned. You have a real investment in these people and it's expensive to replace them. But you have to.

One of our big problems is what to do about some of our older employees who have got tenure. What can you do to get them to do a good job? Many of them are just trying to get fired to collect severance pay.

Tied for 8) The Problem of Illiterate or Barely Literate Workers. Rio Grande do Sul boasts the highest literacy rate in Brazil. Yet a third of its adult citizens cannot read or write. Only some 18% of its inhabitants have finished primary school (the first four grades), 2½% have finished secondary school (high school), and about one half of 1% have finished the university. The following comments indicate that the lack of good, universal, compulsory, primary education presents serious problems to industrial and commercial managers. 15% of the companies mentioned this problem:

The basic problem in Brazil is the weakness of primary education. It is difficult to get good help. Workers are willing and intelligent but they have had only four years of schooling and they can't do simple arithmetic problems.

Our big problem is the low quality of primary schools in Brazil. Workers can't understand technical orders.

The level of our people is very low. They lack ability to understand mathematics, designs, or drawings. . . .

Our big problem is to reach the rural people who are leaving the farms for industry. They need to be taught to read and do simple mathematics.

10) The Transportation Problem. Another victim of recent government policy, according to businessmen, was the state's transportation system. Although the state has hundreds of miles of navigable rivers, transportation on the rivers has declined in recent years. Highways, many times built along the rivers themselves, were accounting for more and more freight traffic. Even airplanes were taking freight away from river and coastwise shipping. 12% of the businessmen pointed this out and attempted to fix the responsibility for the decline in river and coastwise traffic.

We ship refrigerators to the Sao Paulo market. You will find this hard to believe, but it's true: it costs more to ship them by boat than it does to ship them by air.

The big problem in this state is transportation. We're neglecting our river and coastal shipping, which is the cheapest possible kind of transportation, and building expensive roads that run right alongside the rivers. Social laws have ruined river traffic by requiring so many employees.

We can ship iron by truck to Rio cheaper than by boat. This is completely foolish. The main reason is that when you ship by boat you have to go through customs twice.

The reform that is most urgently needed by this state is a reform in the labor legislation having to do with river and coastal shipping. Without injuring the just rights of the workers, we need to apply common sense to the problem of providing low cost ship transportation.

TABLE 2 THE TEN MOST COMMON PROBLEMS MENTIONED BY 106 MICHIGAN
(USA) TOP MANAGERS IN 1962

Rank	Problem	% Mentioning
1	Competition from larger companies	37%
2	Taxes	31
3	Getting, keeping and motivating employees	27
4	Difficulties with unions	23
5	Government interference and red tape	19
6	Keeping in control of the business — developing records	17
7	Financial problems	15
8	Sales and marketing problems	11
9	Personal shortcomings and inability to afford staff help	10
10	Finding, training, holding executives and foremen	9

The ideal solution would be to transfer all shipping from the control of the government to private companies, giving them special financial help or concessions to encourage them to replace obsolete boats with more modern ones.

This concludes the list of the ten most frequently mentioned problems which came out of my interviews with 51 Brazilian top executives. It should already be obvious that a number of major differences exist between the U.S. situation and that of Brazil. Inflation, inadequate transportation, apparent government favoritism to certain regions of the country, scarcity of managers, scarcity of technicians, a tenure law, featherbedding social legislation, and wholesale evasion of tax laws are virtually unique aspects of the Brazilian businessman's situation. While one or two of these conditions have their counterparts in the U.S., for the most part they present the Brazilian businessman with a very different kind of "game," if we can continue to use our earlier analogy between business and sport, from that in which American businessmen engage.

To examine in detail how little similarity exists between the problems which the Brazilian businessman perceives and the problems U.S. businessmen in comparable-sized companies say that they are facing, we turn now to an analysis of the ten most common problems of the U.S. executives.

THE "GAME" OF
MANAGEMENT — PLAYED BY
MICHIGAN (USA) GROUND RULES

The 106 executives who reported the problems they considered most important to Michigan small businessmen listed a total of 264 different problems.[8] These fell into fourteen major categories. Of the fourteen categories, only ten were reported by 5% or more of the sample. These ten problems are reported here. (See Table 2.)

1. Competition — Especially Competition from Larger Companies. As in Brazil, competition was a major problem. Of the 106 Michigan executives who responded to the questionnaire, 39 men (37%) mentioned this problem. However, instead of complaining as the Brazilians did about competition from companies in other states, nearly half (17) of the Michigan executives referred to the problem of competing with *larger* companies. The size, rather than the location, of the competition was the critical factor. Here are some representative comments.

The large operation today is forcing the small businessman out; however, I feel with education and training he can compete.

The big problem is the constant pressure of big companies to take over small business.

Our big problem is trying to compete with the larger companies. Whereas we can provide local service, apparently most business is done on price.

Others spoke of their "inability to compete with big business in the realms of labor and executive talent," and the "difficulty of competing against the buying advantages of big business." Eight spoke simply of a "profit squeeze" due to increasing competition. Four mentioned specific kinds of competition which they considered unfair, if not actually unethical.

2. Taxes. 31% of the companies mentioned taxes as a problem. More than half of these simply said, "taxes," or "taxation," or "growing taxation" when asked what their major problems were. A few expanded on this theme. One man said,

(A major problem is) the gradual removal of incentive to grow which is necessary if we are to provide

8. This study has been reported in Winston Oberg, "Some Problems Faced by the Small Businessman in Michigan" *The Michigan Economic Record,* vol. 4, no. 11 (December, 1962) pp. 3, 6.

jobs and opportunities for the young people coming into the labor market. If a businessman can overcome the hurdles placed in his way by today's unions and make a profit, the government's share payable in cash doesn't leave him with enough reward to make it worthwhile to extend himself beyond the comfortable point.

Another said, "The tax program could be geared to give a little better break to small business." This point of view was expanded on by another who said the problem was "how to encourage Congress to let small business grow before taxing it the same as giant corporations so that small business can accumulate some capital to buy the latest machinery, hire the best engineers." A slightly contrary view was expressed by another man who said both big and little business were taxed "excessively." "Small industry," he said, "generally is faced with many of the same problems as big industry such as excessive workmen's compensation costs due to the leniency of the commission as well as the courts."

3. Getting, Keeping, and Motivating Employees. 27% of the companies had problems in this area. Most frequently mentioned (9 times) was the problem of getting and keeping good skilled or technically trained help. As one man said, a major problem is "the inability to attract and retain good personnel. If they do show promise, you lose them to larger concerns." One man criticized most newly-hired employees because "their attitude toward customers is one of antagonism rather than one of service." Another spoke of the "disinclination of employees to give of themselves for the company." A third said his major problem was "building an organization of dedicated loyal people who want to earn what they are paid."

4. Difficulties with Unions. 23% of the companies said that their labor relations presented major problems. The most representative expression of this problem is probably this one:

The large corporations set the pattern for wage increases and the unions then expect the same increases and benefits from small business.

Other responses include comments like these:

The small businessman doesn't stand much of a chance to hold his own if a union decides to make an example of him. In too many cases 'bargaining' should be called 'bludgeoning.'

We are in a marginal industry — underground mining — but are nevertheless saddled with basically the same labor agreement as the entire steel industry. This presents problems.

Labor's attitude (is) that the employer should offer security from date of employment until death. This is difficult for a small employer.

5. Government Interference and Red Tape. 19% of the men complained about increasing government interference. One cited as a major problem "how to maintain 'ownership' in face of increasing government pressure to obtain total control of all business activity." Another said,

The problem small businessmen face is, in reality, the broad problem facing our country for some 25 years. It is the problem of an imbalance in the eternal struggle between freedom of the individual and statism. And while this problem is a philosophic one, the struggle will have to be won ultimately on the political level.

Several men complained about "too much government" or "too much government interference" or even the "socialization of everything" and "trying to exist in a socialistic economy." At a less emotional level, others spoke of the great difficulty they experienced in "keeping up with complex state and federal laws affecting . . . business."

6. How to Keep on Top of or in Control of the Business—How to Develop Adequate Records. 17% of the companies mentioned problems in this area. One man, a partner in an insurance company, spoke not of his problems but of the problems of his clients:

(The big problem is) accounting! Too many small businessmen are being led astray or allowed to drift into rough financial seas because of insufficient, inaccurate, unrealistic 'accounting' as done by the so-called accounting and bookkeeping services.

Another said the big problem was how to keep books "so as to be able to determine what financial position (you) are in." Several men mentioned problems with accounting controls; a smaller number talked about problems in interpreting the company's financial data; and a few said they had difficulty knowing what price to charge in order adequately to cover their costs.

7. Financial Problems. This was one of the most difficult problems facing the Rio Grande do Sul executive. In Michigan, although the problem was also important, it was slightly different in its nature. In Rio Grande do Sul the banks didn't even have the money, and the problem was one of providing working capital right now. In Michigan the problem was more one of looking to the future, of which source of money it was best to use, or of how one could get money for R & D work or for company expansion. 15% of the men mentioned this problem. One man said his big problem was "lack of capital, insufficient finances to develop new products (R & D) or to outlast prolonged recessions." Another said his problem was "how to go public with a stock issue." The majority simply commented on growth problems and how to raise capital for growth.

8. Sales and Marketing Problems. Where Brazil and most of Latin America is heavily production oriented—sales will pretty much take care of themselves, there's a shortage of everything—the U.S. executive is being forced to become more marketing oriented.[9] The production problems are largely solved; the problem, even for small business, is becoming how to get rid of what comes off the production line. 11% of the companies mentioned this as a problem. As one man said,

As a small manufacturer in a small town, I think too many of us think of manufacturing as 'making something.' Actually no matter how well a product is made, there is still the big problem of placing it into proper channels.

Another said,

(Too many) businessmen feel that all they need to do is develop a quality product and it will sell itself. To most management, management means production. Sales management is nil or doesn't exist. Marketing and sales promotion is something they've heard big business speak of but doesn't concern them, and advertising . . . is some kind of magic potion that when sprinkled upon the ground produces a genie which will cure all of their sales problems.

The bulk of the problems in this area had to do with getting and keeping and motivating salesmen.

9. Personal Shortcomings of the Top Manager Himself and His Inability to Afford Competent Specialists. 10% of the companies commented about such things as "how to keep informed in areas where big business hires specialists," or lack of "time or ability to analyze business progress or retrogress," or "the need for specialist advice and work and the difficulty because of (low) volume of maintaining specialists on the staff," or the "inability to

handle administrative problems without being able to afford specialists. . . ."

10. Finding, Training, Holding Executives and Foremen. This was the third problem common to the Michigan and Rio Grande do Sul executives. However, here again the similarity was more apparent than real. In the Michigan sample, the problem was not the fact that there was an actual absence of qualified management candidates, it was the competition of other wealthier companies for the available men. 9% of the companies mentioned this as a problem. Here are some typical comments:

Our biggest problem is the very fact that we are small. We find it increasingly harder to compete with larger companies for high caliber personnel as we cannot afford the many fringe benefits nor the opportunities in a large corporation.

Small businessmen do not have the opportunity to hire college trained administrative personnel and usually their administrative heads have come up through the ranks.

(One big problem is the) inability of small corporations to secure high caliber men or men with high potential, due mainly to inability to pay comparable wages due to competition.

This concludes the list of ten most important problems facing these Michigan executives in early 1962. Most of their main problems, for example, competition with large companies both for sales and for people, high taxes, union pressure, government interference, marketing (rather than production) problems, are quite different from those of the Brazilian executives studied.

Table 3 shows that there is actual overlap in the case of only a third of the problems, and the discussion to this point should have made it abundantly clear that much of the overlap is more apparent than real. What these two surveys show is that men can occupy the same position in an organization hierarchy, manage companies of comparable size engaged in parallel lines of economic activity and yet, because the milieus in

---

9. Just how great a cleavage exists between heavily marketing-oriented U.S. managements and the predominantly production-oriented Brazilian managers was indicated by the different responses U.S. and Brazilian executives made to the "Wickersham Mills Case," a fictional account of a company which had to choose a new president. The Brazilians chose the candidate with a production background. U.S. executives preferred the man with the marketing background and orientation. See Winston Oberg, "Re: 'Debate at Wickersham Mills'" *Harvard Business Review*, vol. 39, no. 5 (September–October, 1961) pp. 42, 44, 48.

TABLE 3 PROBLEMS WHICH APPEAR TO BE SIMILAR FOR BOTH RIO GRANDE
DO SUL AND MICHIGAN EXECUTIVES

	Rank		% Mentioning	
Problem	in RGS	in Mich.	in RGS	in Mich.
Competition: from other states	2		29	
from larger companies		1		37
Financial problems/shortage of capital	1	7	32	15
Finding and keeping competent executives	3	(10)*	26	(9)
Finding and keeping competent foremen	7	(10)*	18	(9)

*In the Michigan sample, the problem of finding and keeping competent executives was combined with the problem of finding and keeping good foremen. In Brazil, the two problems appeared to be less closely related and were listed separately

which they operate are highly dissimilar, the two groups of executives concerned can have remarkably few problems in common.

SUMMARY AND CONCLUSIONS

While two small-scale surveys of the kind reported here cannot be made to bear the weight of a set of formal conclusions, the results can at least have some implications for management theory.

1) The first such implication was suggested in the opening paragraph of this report. There it was reported that management theorists are turning their attention to the wealth of research opportunities being opened by the burgeoning U.S. interest in international trade as well as in international economic development. The findings presented here should emphasize that if universal principles do indeed exist they must stand up to rigorous testing in cross-cultural studies far more sophisticated and more adequately designed and controlled than the surveys described here. If management principles are to be truly universal, it is clear that they must face up to the challenge of other cultures and other business climates. This paper suggests the challenge will be a major one.

2) The second implication of this paper is that facile assumptions like that attributed to the 1962 recipient of the Gantt Medal to the effect that,

. . . management is management wherever practiced, a universal profession whose principles can be applied in every organized form of human activity. . . .[10]

are hardly warranted by either evidence or intuition at this stage in the development of management science. What may be equally or even more probable is the conclusion reached by two colleagues of mine after they had spent some years

as technical consultants to a business school in central Brazil. They studied the applicability of U.S. management experience and know-how to the Brazilian situation and concluded that,

American management experience abroad provides evidence that our uniquely American philosophy of management is not universally applicable but rather is a special case.[11]

In any event, the assumption that universal principles exist needs to be examined for what it is — a declaration of faith rather than a proposition established by adequate cross-cultural research.

POSTSCRIPT

The perceptive reader will have seen that the thrust of this paper goes well beyond the comparisons made and the conclusions suggested. If management principles should prove to be limited in their applicability to a particular culture or social climate, as this report suggests, their general applicability within a particular culture will also be open to question. For example, if no principle can be found which applies significantly to both the U.S. and the Brazilian businessman, it may well be questioned whether any principles can be found which apply significantly to such dissimilar U.S. sub-cultures as those of the small rural businessman and the head of a giant corporation. The area of applicability of generalizations, laws, theories or principles of management will thus shrink indefinitely. It is my personal

10. See Harwood F. Merrill, "The Listening Post," *Management News*, vol. 36, No. 1 (January, 1963) p. 4. The words are attributed to Austin Tobin, executive director of the Port of New York Authority. A very similar point of view is found in the introductory management text of Koontz and O'Donnell, *Principles of Management*, (New York, McGraw-Hill Book Company, Inc., 1959).

11. Gonzalez and McMillan, *op. cit.*, p. 41.

belief that such will be the case and that management theorists and teachers in departments of management who still hold what Dale calls the universalist view should take note of recent developments in both the physical and social science fields.[12] It is already more than ten years since Gouldner, for example, surveyed the social science literature on leadership and found that the age-old quest for universal leader traits or attributes had virtually been abandoned.[13] Instead, social scientists had accepted the view that the qualities necessary for leader success were situationally determined and varied from one situation to another. One situation might call for physical prowess, courage, or superior intelligence while success as a leader in another situation might have no relevance at all to physical attributes or courage. Indeed, in some cases scientists found too high an IQ to be a handicap.

Among physical scientists, whose most famous law, $e = mc^2$, has probably served as the model for a generation or more of management scientists showing what a universal principle or law ought to be, some highly significant shifts in orientation are also taking place. In a recent issue of *Science,* Simpson notes that physical scientists are themselves abandoning belief in the existence of absolutes, determinate solutions, or principles that apply to all phenomena.[14]

If the social sciences, in their studies of areas quite closely linked to the theory of management, have adopted a situational point of view, and if the physical sciences are now abandoning faith in the existence of universals, it is hardly likely that those of us operating in such a complex and imprecise field as that of management theory can be justified in continuing to assert our faith in the existence of universal principles, absolutes or determinate solutions. Instead, we might be well-advised to concern ourselves more with a study of variants of what Mary Parker Follett once called the "law of situation."[15] A search for generalizations which are simply situationally valid and admittedly situationally limited in their applicability, although more modest than the quest for universal truth, may well turn out to be a good deal more fruitful and hence, in the long run, more significant.

45 — The Anthropology of Manners

EDWARD T. HALL, JR.

The Goops they lick their fingers
and the Goops they lick their knives;
They spill their broth on the table cloth —
Oh, they lead disgusting lives.
The Goops they talk while eating,
and loud and fast they chew;
And that is why I'm glad that I
am not a Goop — are you?

In Gelett Burgess' classic on the Goops we have an example of what anthropologists call "an enculturating device" — a means of conditioning the young to life in our society. Having been taught the lesson of the goops from childhood (with or without the aid of Mr. Burgess) Americans are shocked when they go abroad and discover whole groups of people behaving like goops — eating with their fingers, making noises and talking while eating. When this happens, we may (1) remark on the barbarousness or quaintness of the "natives" (a term cordially disliked all over the world) or (2) try to discover the nature and meaning of the differences in behavior. One rather quickly discovers that what is good manners in one context may be bad in the next. It is to this point that I would like to address myself.

The subject of manners is complex; if it were not, there would not be so many injured feelings and so much misunderstanding in international circles everywhere. In any society the code of manners tends to sum up the culture — to be a frame of reference for all behavior. Emily Post goes so far as to say: "There is not a single thing that we do, or say, or choose, or use, or even think, that does not follow or break one of the exactions of taste, or tact, or ethics of good manners, or etiquette — call it what you will." Unfortu-

12. Ernest Dale, *The Great Organizers,* (McGraw-Hill Book Company Inc., New York, 1960).

13. Alvin Gouldner (ed.) *Studies in Leadership,* (Harper & Bros., New York, 1950).

14. George G. Simpson, "Biology and the Nature of Science," *Science,* vol. 139, no. 3550 (January 11, 1963) pp. 81 – 88.

15. H. C. Metcalf and L. Urwick (eds.) *Dynamic Administration: the Collected Papers of Mary Parker Follett,* (Harper & Bros., New York, 1940).

"The Anthropology of Manners," *Scientific American,* CXCII (April 1955), 84 – 88, 90. Reprinted by permission of the author and the publisher. Copyright © 1955 by Scientific American, Inc. All rights reserved. **Edward T. Hall, Jr.:** Department of Anthropology, American University; formerly with the Foreign Service Institute of the State Department.

nately many of the most important standards of acceptable behavior in different cultures are elusive: they are intangible, undefined and unwritten.

An Arab diplomat who recently arrived in the U.S. from the Middle East attended a banquet which lasted several hours. When it was over, he met a fellow countryman outside and suggested they go get something to eat, as he was starving. His friend, who had been in this country for some time, laughed and said: "But, Habib, didn't you know that if you say, 'No, thank you,' they think you really don't want any?" In an Arab country etiquette dictates that the person being served must refuse the proffered dish several times, while his host urges him repeatedly to partake. The other side of the coin is that Americans in the Middle East, until they learn better, stagger away from banquets having eaten more than they want or is good for them.

When a public-health movie of a baby being bathed in a bathinette was shown in India recently, the Indian women who saw it were visibly offended. They wondered how people could be so inhuman as to bathe a child in stagnant (not running) water. Americans in Iran soon learn not to indulge themselves in their penchant for chucking infants under the chin and remarking on the color of their eyes, for the mother has to pay to have the "evil eye" removed. We also learn that in the Middle East you don't hand people things with your left hand, because it is unclean. In India we learn not to touch another person, and in Southeast Asia we learn that the head is sacred.

In the interest of intercultural understanding various U.S. Government agencies have hired anthropologists from time to time as technical experts. The State Department especially has pioneered in the attempt to bring science to bear on this difficult and complex problem. It began by offering at the Foreign Service Institute an intensive four-week course for Point 4 technicians. Later these facilities were expanded to include other foreign service personnel.

The anthropologist's job here is not merely to call attention to obvious taboos or to coach people about types of thoughtless behavior that have very little to do with culture. One should not need an anthropologist to point out, for instance, that it is insulting to ask a foreigner: "How much is this in real money?" Where technical advice is most needed is in the interpretation of the unconscious aspects of a culture—the things people do automatically without being aware of the full implications of what they have done. For example, an ambassador who has been kept waiting for more than half an hour by a foreign visitor needs

to understand that if his visitor "just mutters an apology" this is not necessarily an insult. The time system in the foreign country may be composed of different basic units, so that the visitor is not as late as he may appear to us. You must know the time system of the country to know at what point apologies are really due.

Twenty years of experience in working with Americans in foreign lands convinces me that the real problem in preparing them to work overseas is not with taboos, which they catch on to rather quickly, but rather with whole congeries of habits and attitudes which anthropologists have only recently begun to describe systematically.

Can you remember tying your shoes this morning? Could you give the rules for when it is proper to call another person by his first name? Could you describe the gestures you make in conversation? These examples illustrate how much of our behavior is "out of awareness," and how easy it is to get into trouble in another culture.

Nobody is continually aware of the quality of his own voice, the subtleties of stress and intonation that color the meaning of his words or the posture and distance he assumes in talking to another person. Yet all these are taken as cues to the real nature of an utterance, regardless of what the words say. A simple illustration is the meaning in the tone of voice. In the U.S. we raise our voices not only when we are angry but also when we want to emphasize a point, when we are more than a certain distance from another person, when we are concluding a meeting and so on. But to the Chinese, for instance, overloudness of the voice is most characteristically associated with anger and loss of self-control. Whenever we become really interested in something, they are apt to have the feeling we are angry, in spite of many years' experience with us. Very likely most of their interviews with us, however cordial, seem to end on a sour note when we exclaim heartily: "WELL, I'M CERTAINLY GLAD YOU DROPPED IN, MR. WONG."

The Latin Americans, who as a rule take business seriously, do not understand our mixing business with informality and recreation. We like to put our feet up on the desk. If a stranger enters the office, we take our feet down. If it turns out that the stranger and we have a lot in common, up go the feet again—a cue to the other fellow that we feel at ease. If the office boy enters, the feet stay up; if the boss enters and our relationship with him is a little strained at the moment, they go down. To a Latin American this whole behavior is shocking. All he sees in it is insult or just plain rudeness.

Differences in attitudes toward space—what

would be territoriality in lower forms of life—raise a number of other interesting points. U.S. women who go to live in Latin America all complain about the "waste" of space in the houses. On the other hand, U.S. visitors to the Middle East complain about crowding, in the houses and on the street cars and buses. Everywhere we go space seems to be distorted. When we see a gardener in the mountains of Italy planting a single row on each of six separate terraces, we wonder why he spreads out his crop so that he has to spend half his time climbing up and down. We overlook the complex chain of communication that would be broken if he didn't cultivate alongside his brothers and his cousin and if he didn't pass his neighbors and talk to them as he moves from one terrace to the next.

A colleague of mine was caught in a snowstorm while traveling with companions in the mountains of Lebanon. They stopped at the next house and asked to be put up for the night. The house had only one room. Instead of distributing the guests around the room, their host placed them next to the pallet where he slept with his wife—so close that they almost touched the couple. To have done otherwise in that country would have been unnatural and unfriendly. In the U.S. we distribute ourselves more evenly than many other people. We have strong feelings about touching and being crowded; in a streetcar, bus or elevator we draw ourselves in. Toward a person who relaxes and lets himself come into full contact with others in a crowded place we usually feel reactions that could not be printed on this page. It takes years for us to train our children not to crowd and lean on us. We tell them to stand up, that it is rude to slouch, not to sit so close or not to "breathe down our necks." After a while they get the point. By the time we Americans are in our teens we can tell what relationship exists between a man and woman by how they walk or sit together.

In Latin America, where touching is more common and the basic units of space seem to be smaller, the wide automobiles made in the U.S. pose problems. People don't know where to sit. North Americans are disturbed by how close the Latin Americans stand when they converse. "Why do they have to get so close when they talk to you?" "They're so pushy." "I don't know what it is, but it's something in the way they stand next to you." And so on. The Latin Americans, for their part, complain that people in the U.S. are distant and cold—*reraídos* (withdrawing and uncommunicative).

An analysis of the handling of space during conversations shows the following: A U.S. male brought up in the Northeast stands 18 to 20 inches away when talking face to face to a man he does not know very well; talking to a woman under similar circumstances, he increases the distance about four inches. A distance of only eight to 13 inches between males is considered either very aggressive or indicative of a closeness of a type we do not ordinarily want to think about. Yet in many parts of Latin America and the Middle East distances which are almost sexual in connotation are the only ones at which people can talk comfortably. In Cuba, for instance, there is nothing suggestive in a man's talking to an educated woman at a distance of 10 inches. If you are a Latin American, talking to a North American at the distance he insists on maintaining is like trying to talk across a room.

To get a more vivid idea of this problem of the comfortable distance, try starting a conversation with a person eight or 10 feet away or one separated from you by a wide obstruction in a store or other public place. Any normally enculturated person can't help trying to close up the space, even to the extent of climbing over benches or walking around tables to arrive within comfortable distance. U.S. businessmen working in Latin America try to prevent people from getting uncomfortably close by barricading themselves behind desks, typewriters or the like, but their Latin American office visitors will often climb up on desks or over chairs and put up with loss of dignity in order to establish a spatial context in which interaction can take place for them.

The interesting thing is that neither party is specifically aware of what is wrong when the distance is not right. They merely have vague feelings of discomfort or anxiety. As the Latin American approaches and the North American backs away, both parties take offense without knowing why. When a North American, having had the problem pointed out to him, permits the Latin American to get close enough, he will immediately notice that the latter seems much more at ease.

My own studies of space and time have engendered considerable cooperation and interest on the part of friends and colleagues. One case recently reported to me had to do with a group of seven-year-olds in a crowded Sunday-school classroom. The children kept fighting. Without knowing quite what was involved, the teacher had them moved to a larger room. The fighting stopped. It is interesting to speculate as to what would have happened had the children been moved to a smaller room.

The embarrassment about intimacy in space applies also to the matter of addressing people by name. Finding the proper distance in the use of names is even more difficult than in space, because the rules for first-naming are unbelievably complex. As a rule we tend to stay on the "mister" level too long with Latins and some others, but very often we swing into first-naming too quickly, which amounts to talking down to them. Whereas in the U.S. we use Mr. with the surname, in Latin America the first and last names are used together and señor (Sr.) is a title. Thus when one says, "My name is Sr. So-and-So," it is interpreted to mean, "I am the Honorable, his Excellency So-and-So." It is no wonder that when we stand away, barricade ourselves behind our desks (usually a reflection of status) and call ourselves mister, our friends to the south wonder about our so-called "good-neighbor" policy and think of us as either high-hat or unbelievably rude. Fortunately most North Americans learn some of these things after living in Latin America for a while, but the aversion to being touched and to touching sometimes persists after 15 or more years of residence and even under such conditions as intermarriage.

The difference in sense of time is another thing of which we are not aware. An Iranian, for instance, is not taught that it is rude to be late in the same way that we in the U.S. are. In a general way we are conscious of this, but we fail to realize that their time system is structured differently from ours. The different cultures simply place different values on the time units.

Thus let us take as a typical case of the North European time system (which has regional variations) the situation in the urban eastern U.S. A middle-class businessman meeting another of equivalent rank will ordinarily be aware of being two minutes early or late. If he is three minutes late, it will be noted as significant but usually neither will say anything. If four minutes late, he will mutter something by way of apology; at five minutes he will utter a full sentence of apology. In other words, the major unit is a five-minute block. Fifteen minutes is the smallest significant period for all sorts of arrangements and it is used very commonly. A half hour of course is very significant, and if you spend three quarters of an hour or an hour, either the business you transact or the relationship must be important. Normally it is an insult to keep a public figure or a person of significantly higher status than yourself waiting even two or three minutes, though the person of higher position can keep you waiting or even break an appointment.

Now among urban Arabs in the Eastern Mediterranean, to take an illustrative case of another time system, the unit that corresponds to our five-minute period is 15 minutes. Thus when an Arab arrives nearly 30 minutes after the set time, by his reckoning he isn't even "10 minutes" late yet (in our time units). Stated differently, the Arab's tardiness will not amount to one significant period (15 minutes in our system). An American normally will wait no longer than 30 minutes (two significant periods) for another person to turn up in the middle of the day. Thereby he often unwittingly insults people in the Middle East who want to be his friends.

How long is one expected to stay when making a duty call at a friend's house in the U.S.? While there are regional variations, I have observed that the minimum is very close to 45 minutes, even in the face of pressing commitments elsewhere, such as a roast in the oven. We may think we can get away in 30 minutes by saying something about only stopping for "a minute," but usually we discover that we don't feel comfortable about leaving until 45 minutes have elapsed. I am referring to afternoon social calls; evening calls last much longer and operate according to a different system. In Arab countries an American paying a duty call at the house of a desert sheik causes consternation if he gets up to leave after half a day. There a duty call lasts three days—the first day to prepare the feast, the second for the feast itself and third to taper off and say farewell. In the first half day the sheik has barely had time to slaughter the sheep for the feast. The guest's departure would leave the host frustrated.

There is a well-known story of a tribesman who came to Kabul, the capital of Afghanistan, to meet his brother. Failing to find him, he asked the merchants in the market place to tell his brother where he could be found if the brother showed up. A year later the tribesman returned and looked again. It developed that he and his brother had agreed to meet in Kabul but had failed to specify what year! If the Afghan time system were structured similarly to our own, which it apparently is not, the brother would not offer a full sentence of apology until he was five years late.

Informal units of time such as "just a minute," "a while," "later," "a long time," "a spell," "a long, long time," "years" and so on provide us with the culturological equivalent of Evil-Eye Fleegle's "double-whammy" (in *Li'l Abner*). Yet these expressions are not as imprecise as they seem. Any American who has worked in an office with someone else for six months can usually tell within five minutes when that person will be back if he says, "I'll be gone for a while." It is simply a matter of learning from experience the individual's system of time indicators. A reader who is interested in communications theory can fruitfully speculate for a while on the very wonderful way in which culture provides the means whereby the receiver puts back all the redundant material that was stripped from such a message. Spelled out, the message might go somewhat as follows: "I am going downtown to see So-and-So about the Such-and-Such contract, but I don't know what the traffic conditions will be like or how long it will take me to get a place to park nor do I know what shape So-and-So will be in today, but taking all this into account I think I will be out of the office about an hour but don't like to commit myself, so if anyone calls you can say I'm not sure how long I will be; in any event I expect to be back before 4 o'clock."

Few of us realize how much we rely on built-in patterns to interpret messages of this sort. An Iranian friend of mine who came to live in the U.S. was hurt and puzzled for the first few years.

The new friends he met and liked would say on parting: "Well, I'll see you later." He mournfully complained: "I kept expecting to see them, but the 'later' never came." Strangely enough we ourselves are exasperated when a Mexican can't tell us precisely what he means when he uses the expression *mañana*.

The role of the anthropologist in preparing people for service overseas is to open their eyes and sensitize them to the subtle qualities of behavior—tone of voice, gestures, space and time relationships—that so often build up feelings of frustration and hostility in other people with a different culture. Whether we are going to live in a particular foreign country or travel in many, we need a frame of reference that will enable us to observe and learn the significance of differences in manners. Progress is being made in this anthropological study, but it is also showing us how little is known about human behavior.

SECTION **X**

EDP, MODELS, GAMES, PERT, AND AUTOMATION

As noted in the introduction to Part Three, the computer has had far-reaching effects on management thought and practice. Kraut (#46) explores the important research on electronic data processing and its effects on workers and organizations; his article points out the importance of this new technology as well as the problems it creates and the ways in which management might cope with them. The article by Katz, Knight, and Massey (#47) presents a synthesis of the views of an administrator, a behavioral scientist, and a statistician regarding the present capabilities and implications of the computer, as well as its future impact. Shull (#48) discusses the realm of models, the development of which has been greatly facilitated by the computer; the management model, as Shull explains it, takes into consideration empirical evidence from a variety of disciplines that can contribute to effective administration.

Business games, which provide opportunities to practice the process of management, have become very sophisticated with the advent of the computer. Jensen (#49) discusses two noncomputer games; however, his guidelines to the use of business-simulation exercises are useful in this important field of training, whether used in conjunction with computers or not. As in the case of business-simulation exercises, the technique of PERT has also benefited significantly through the use of computers. Avots (#50) discusses the managerial aspects of the technique and shows how it makes possible new breakthroughs in the art and science of management.

The last two articles deal with automation. Drawing on past knowledge and present achievement, Diebold (#51) projects into the future regarding the effect of automation on society in general and on management in particular. Whisler and Shultz (#52) indicate, among other things, the impact of technological changes on the environment of the manager.

46 – How EDP Is Affecting Workers and Organizations

ALLEN I. KRAUT

Office automation made its first major appearance less than a dozen years ago with the installation of a large-scale computer by the Bureau of Census. Within a decade, more than 2,000 computers were in use in business and government offices. In 1959, sales and rentals of electronic data-processing equipment amounted to an estimated total of $1.5 billion.[1] It's expected that by 1970 the EDP market will grow to $8 billion.

The spectacular growth of this dramatic technological innovation has naturally aroused intense interest—coupled with no small amount of concern—among legislators, social scientists, businessmen, and many others, all of whom want to know, for one reason or another, what its effects are likely to be. It is already obvious that office automation is bound to have far-reaching consequences in many segments of our industrial society. At the very least, it is clear that the number of people affected will be very large, for clerical workers now represent nearly one-seventh of the nation's total labor force, and much of the work they do is well suited for electronic data processing.

Paradoxically, while the sudden maturing of office automation has made it imperative to gauge its wider implications as quickly as possible, its rise has been so meteoric that there has not yet been much time for systematically studying its effects.

Several excellent empirical studies have already been completed, however, and from them we can learn a good deal about the impact of automation on the individual employee and the organization as a whole. It may therefore be worthwhile to review the findings of some of these studies insofar as they throw light on both these questions.

LAYOFFS AND ATTRITION

The one question that has so far generated the greatest amount of concern and speculation is how many clerical workers are going to lose their jobs because of automation. The research evidence on this question presents what at first seems to be a paradox: Though EDP makes many employees redundant, there are very few layoffs.

To begin with the first half of this statement, it is obvious that the introduction of EDP equipment permits the same amount of work to be done with fewer people than before or the same number of people to handle more work. A striking but not unusual illustration of this is the experience of the U.S. Treasury Department, where the transfer of certain operations to an electronic computer allowed a 14 per cent increase in the work load at the same time as the number of operating employees was decreased by 48 per cent.[2]

"How EDP Is Affecting Workers and Organizations," *Personnel*, XXXIX (July–August 1962), 38–50. Reprinted by permission of the author and the American Management Association, New York. **Allen I. Kraut:** Ph.D. candidate, Social Psychology, University of Michigan.

1. F. Bello, "The War of the Computers," *Fortune*, Oct., 1959.

2. *Office Automation and Employee Job Security* (Hearings Before the Subcommittee on Census and Government Statistics of the Committee on Post Office and Civil Service). U.S. Congress, 86th Congress, Second Session, Washington, D.C., 1960.

In effect, output per employee increased by 120 per cent.

Why, then, should dismissals and layoffs be infrequent? The explanation lies in two factors—normal attrition and the absorption of excess personnel in ways that make layoffs unnecessary. Studying the introduction of automation in 20 offices employing a total of about 2,800 people in the groups affected by the change, the Bureau of Labor Statistics found that only 13 employees had been discharged and 9 laid off during the year following the conversion to EDP and the half year preceding it.[3] This represented 0.5 and 0.3 per cent of all employees in the units whose work would be done by the computers.

Normal attrition, the Bureau discovered, accounted for a sizable amount of turnover among the office employees in these units. Of all the employees who were separated during the 18-month period—an average of 15.2 per cent of the total work-forces of the units—more than three quarters had quit voluntarily. Many were young women who left their jobs in order to become housewives or mothers. Most of the other separations during this time were accounted for by retirements, death, and leaves of absence.

The effect of normal attrition on the problem of employee redundancy is also shown by a study conducted in an insurance company by H. F. Craig.[4] The rate of clerical turnover in the affected unit, it found, was 15 per cent in the year immediately preceding the conversion to EDP and 21 per cent in the year before that. Over the four-year conversion period, the number of jobs in the affected unit declined 30 per cent from the original total of 529, even though the total work load became slightly heavier. The necessary reduction in clerical staff was accomplished almost entirely by continuously high turnover.

As has already been suggested, normal attrition is not the only factor accounting for the infrequency of layoffs. A study by Ida Russakoff Hoos suggests two reasons why the impact of automation on job opportunities is often imperceptible at the beginning.[5] First, the adoption of EDP is generally confined to expanding companies, whose new operations can absorb most of the "excess" personnel. Second, the dual system that most companies run during the conversion period requires additional personnel, thus helping to take up much of the slack.

It has also been suggested that insurance companies and utilities, both major users of EDP equipment, can afford to take a fairly long time for the changeover—more time, at least, than can be taken by manufacturing companies, whose competitive situation has a somewhat more urgent cast—and can therefore rely on prolonged normal attrition to reduce the number of superfluous employees.[6]

WORK CONTENT AND SETTING

At all events, most employees in the office affected by automation remain in their jobs, but find that their work has changed. Professor Hardin, of Michigan State University, found that 93 per cent of the employees of an insurance company were still in their old jobs six months after the installation of a computer.[7] But 70 per cent of the employees in the "computer area" reported sizable changes in their work as did only 19 per cent of those in the other units. The greatest changes reported by the affected employees were in the amount of work they had to do, the variety of their tasks, and the amount of skill, responsibility, and judgment required of them, all of which had increased significantly.

Changes of quite a different sort have been noted by Professors Mann and Williams, of The University of Michigan.[8] Work routine and pace, their case study found, become closely tied to the machines, and the company becomes less tolerant of errors, which can now be traced to individual employees. In addition, the rationalization of the system puts a premium on regular attendance and imposes specific deadlines and work quotas. The result of all this, Mann and Williams say, is that employees and supervisors often complain that they have lost some of their autonomy.

An increased similarity between office work and factory work has also been reported by Hoos and others.[9] It has been found, for instance, that with the advent of EDP, key-punch operators, who increase in number, are subjected to production quotas and to a considerable amount of pressure for maintaining accuracy. Many of them

3. *Adjustments to the Introduction of Office Automation* (Bulletin No. 1276). Bureau of Labor Statistics, U.S. Department of Labor, Washington, D.C., 1960.

4. H. F. Craig, *Administering a Conversion to Electronic Accounting.* Division of Research, Graduate School of Business Administration, Harvard University, Boston, Mass., 1955.

5. I. R. Hoos, "The Impact of Office Automation on Workers." *International Labour Review,* Oct., 1960, pp. 363–388.

6. F. C. Mann, "The Impact of Electronic Accounting Equipment on the White Collar Worker in a Public Utility Company," in *Man and Automation* (The Technology Project). Yale University, New Haven, Conn., 1956, pp. 32–39.

7. E. Hardin, "The Reactions of Employees to Office Automation," *Monthly Labor Review,* Sept., 1960.

8. F. C. Mann and L. K. Williams, "Observations on the Dynamics of a Change to Electronic Data Processing Equipment," *Administrative Science Quarterly,* Sept., 1960.

9. "Effects of Mechanisation and Automation in Offices," *International Labour Review,* Feb., 1960, pp. 154–173; Mar., 1960, pp. 255–273; and Apr., 1960, pp. 350–369.

develop psychosomatic symptoms because of this stress, and many complain of being "chained to the machine." The "factory-like atmosphere" of their work is further heightened by the noise of the key-punching equipment and other machines. And to complete the picture, office automation makes it economically desirable to run the office on two shifts, so that some employees have to accept shift work. (Because of legal and cultural proscriptions on the assignment of such work to women, it goes chiefly to male employees.)

UPGRADING OF JOBS

But what about the much-debated question of upgrading? Is the trend toward a factory-like atmosphere in some automated units counterbalanced by a widespread raising of job grades? There is a good deal of conflict in the findings on this question but taken as a whole, the available research seems to support the conclusion that Van Auken drew from a case study he conducted some years ago. Though there was very little upgrading among the employees whose work was taken over by the computer, he reported, the indirect effects of the change to EDP created new avenues of upgrading and new jobs, with a higher skill content for a select group of people in other segments of the company.[10]

In the unit studied by Mann and Williams, the least interesting and most menial types of clerical jobs were eliminated, but so were a number of high-level nonsupervisory jobs. The net effect on the organization's average job grade was negligible. On the other hand, a study of an insurance company by the Bureau of Labor Statistics found that with the conversion to EDP the proportion of employees in low- and medium-wage brackets declined from 91 per cent to 73 per cent and the proportion in higher-paid grades grew from 8 per cent to 27 per cent.[11]

A considerable amount of upgrading was also uncovered in the Bureau's 20-office survey. Of all the employees who remained with their companies during the 18 months covered by the study, about 31 per cent were promoted to higher-grade positions and only 1 per cent were downgraded. However, fewer than 2 per cent of the employees whose work was affected by the installation of computers were transferred to positions in the newly created EDP units. These positions ranged in number from 9 to 200, with a median of 29, and were generally in considerably higher grades than the other positions in the offices studied. Though about 80 per cent of them were filled from within,

only 6 per cent went to employees whose work had been directly affected by the change.

The reason for this, according to Mann and Williams, is that the new jobs usually require either new skills or new combinations of skills, and many of the dislocated employees simply cannot meet these qualifications.[12] Most of the new jobs are given to men rather than women and, more specifically, to men who are generally younger and more highly educated than other clerical workers, and have some related work experience.

VULNERABLE GROUPS

The converse of this is that, as Hoos has pointed out, supervisors and older workers are particularly vulnerable to the adverse effects of office automation. Many a supervisor's value to his company stems primarily from his knowledge of the company's traditional paper-handling procedures. When these are drastically altered by the advent of EDP, the supervisor becomes far less valuable an employee than he was, and may even become totally expendable, in which case he will probably find that other companies are not much interested in his specialized knowledge either. Even if he keeps his job, he is likely to suffer a serious loss of prestige, for the conversion to EDP may well reduce the number of people on his staff.

Like the supervisor, the older worker may find automation destroying his special advantage over other employees — his familiarity with the company's traditional systems. In addition, the premium on speed commonly associated with machine operations appears to exclude older workers from many of the new office jobs. Employers' prejudices, traditional hiring patterns, and educational limitations of many older workers make it all the more unlikely that they will be transferred to, or hired for, the newly created jobs.

Many older workers have high seniority, however, and therefore have a better chance of being allowed to keep their old jobs than do their younger co-workers. Older workers who have to be reassigned within the company, even to jobs that are much like their old ones, often find the readjustment difficult, for their own lack of con-

---

10. K. G. Van Auken, Jr., "A Case Study of the Impact of Automation on Skills and Employment," in *Man and Automation*.

11. *The Introduction of an Electronic Computer in a Large Insurance Company* (Studies in Automatic Technology, No. 2). Bureau of Labor Statistics, U.S. Department of Labor, Washington, D.C., 1955.

12. F. C. Mann and L. K. Williams, "Organizational Impact of White Collar Automation," *Proceedings of the 11th Annual Meeting* (Publication No. 22). Industrial Relations Research Association, Madison, Wisc., 1959, pp. 59–69.

fidence in their learning capacity, together with habits of long standing, tends to make them less adaptable than their younger counterparts, and many older workers are reluctant to break long-established ties.

In sum, then, office automation seems to have several kinds of important occupational consequences: Though it does not commonly result in a great many layoffs, it does permit a reduction in the size of the workforce and thus makes many employees redundant. Those employees who remain in their jobs when their work units become automated usually find the content and setting of their work changing markedly—most often, in the direction of factory-like methods and atmosphere. There is a substantial amount of upgrading throughout the organization as a whole, but not very much among the employees whose work is directly affected by the change to EDP, relatively few of whom are given positions in the newly created EDP units. Finally, supervisors and older workers are likely to be especially hard hit by these changes, and find it more difficult to adjust to them than do other employees.

What, then, are the effects of automation upon organizational structure and practice? What administrative problems are raised by the introduction of EDP, and how are they solved?

To begin with, it might be noted that all companies that decide to install EDP equipment do so for essentially the same reasons. Basically, what they are interested in is increasing their productivity and their data-handling capacity. The insurance company studied by Craig, for example, changed to EDP in order to cope with an increasing volume of work, a shortage of suitable clerical personnel, and a need to keep costs down. Similar objectives were reported by the 20 companies surveyed by the Bureau of Labor Statistics. In descending order, the five most important objectives were: (1) savings in the use of clerical labor (though not necessarily involving reductions in the size of the clerical workforce); (2) savings in the amount of equipment, space, and time needed for data processing; (3) greater accuracy; (4) the solution of clerical labor shortages; and (5) the provision of new information.

Once having decided to use EDP, the organization must embark on a fairly long-term process of planning and change before the new system is in smooth working order, for EDP itself is usually a major innovation for the organization, and the changeover to automated operations is an equally weighty undertaking. The various steps involved in the changeover generally proceed in a certain sequence, the research evidence shows, so that the questions and problems generated by the change-over probably present themselves to all organizations in roughly the same order.

Mann and Williams have identified seven phases in the changeover to a computer system: (1) relative stability and equilibrium before the change; (2) preliminary planning; (3) detailed preparation; (4) installation and testing; (5) conversion; (6) stabilization; and (7) new equilibrium after the change.

Analyzing the process in roughly the same terms, the Bureau of Labor Statistics reports that the 20 companies it studied took an average of nearly three years to make the change. The four steps given in its analysis, and the average time for accomplishing each, are as follows: (1) intensive study of the feasibility of the new equipment—16 months; (2) planning and preparing for computer applications (and awaiting delivery of the equipment)—15 months; (3) installation and testing—no specific time given; and (4) normal operation, sometimes preceded by several months of parallel operations.

ORGANIZATIONAL CHANGES

The installation of the new system often leads to changes in the organization's structure, some of them very far reaching. One of the best descriptions of the organizational effects of a change to EDP is given by Mann and Williams.

The introduction of automatic operations, they point out, provides an opportunity for a reappraisal of the basic aims of the organization's various segments and of their performance. Management may find it possible not only to review the distribution of work within specific segments but also to redesign the organization structure as a whole, taking advantage of the climate of change to cut across old divisional and functional lines. If the planning that precedes the installation of EDP is wide in scope (that is, if it takes a broad "systems approach"), the conversion to the new system may be accompanied by several major structural changes in the organization, as it was in the company that Mann and Williams studied.

As this company's record-keeping procedures were altered through consolidation, centralization, and other changes made during the five-year changeover period, there were also "extensive transfers of functions and employees from one major division to another, and a *major reorganization* within the accounting division. Work section and departmental lines were reorganized, new departments were created, and a level of management was added."

Mann and Williams also observed certain nonstructural changes. The various organizational units became more interdependent, losing some of their former autonomy and flexibility, and the relations between them became more formal.

Departmental reorganization, along with the centralization and integration of functions previously performed by individual units, has also been reported by Craig. Much of this reorganization, he notes, stemmed from the need to accommodate to the capacities of the new equipment and use it as efficiently as possible.

One form of organizational change that is especially common is the transfer of data-handling functions from branch offices to the particular office — usually the company headquarters — where the EDP equipment has been installed. Hoos notes that this happened among many of the companies she studied and that it resulted in a great deal of employee displacement and relocation. Stieber, too, indicates that work tends to gravitate to wherever the computer happens to be located.[13] In a large insurance company, he reports, computers were installed in the regional offices and got work from both the home office and the smaller branch offices.

CONFLICT AND DISCONTENT

The advent of EDP has still other effects on the organization's structure and workings. It may reduce promotional opportunities by cutting down the number of middle-management positions. It may lead to destructive conflicts among managers who feel that the distribution of power within the company will henceforth depend mainly on who controls the EDP system, its work, and its staff. As Miller has pointed out, managers or groups of managers who believe that their power or status or opportunities for advancement are threatened by the new equipment will probably be reluctant to cooperate in its installation and may develop negative attitudes toward the whole business.[14]

At a lower level, unfavorable attitudes may well arise among the employees who are shifted to new work groups and must therefore adjust to new tasks and relationships. If, however, the tasks to which they are transferred seem more desirable to them than their former ones, they will of course respond with favorable attitudes.

THE TRANSITION

Several studies have found that the conversion from the old system to the new is a time of great organizational strain. Mann and Williams give an extensive description of the problems experienced during this period by the utility company they studied, where the conversion phase was marked by the parallel operation of three systems — the old, the transitional, and the new.

Needless to say, the use of three systems required both employees and supervisors to put in a great deal of physical effort and many hours of overtime work. There were, naturally, quite a few complaints about the strain. It might be noted here that complaints of excessive overtime work over an extended period of time have been reported in other studies as well, for most companies that run parallel operations fill their additional manpower needs partly by hiring temporary personnel and partly by having their regular staff (chiefly the male employees) work more overtime.

A concomitant strain during this period arises from the necessity of transferring many employees to new positions, some of which are only transitional, and training them for the work of these positions. In the company studied by Mann and Williams, many supervisors and employees had only a vague idea of what the new work would be like. Since operations were switched over to the new system piecemeal, the conversion took a full year. At times, unrealistically short deadlines placed added stress on the employees.

The transition made still other demands. Managers spent a great deal of time at meetings. Employees had to adjust to new sources, as well as new forms, of information. Errors occurred often, and repeatedly, in the early phases, and resulted in hard feelings among departments and a general mistrust of the new system, so that the computer was blamed for many human errors.

COMMUNICATIONS AND JOB SECURITY

Turning to the administrative problems that confront management, it may be well to begin with the question of how to tell the employees about the forthcoming installation of EDP and particularly about what effects this will have on job security. The practices of the companies surveyed by the Bureau of Labor Statistics appear to be typical. Most of the companies informed their employees of the impending change several months before the computer was installed, using the existing channels of communication — em-

13. J. Stieber, "Automation and the White-Collar Worker," *Personnel*, Nov.–Dec., 1957, pp. 8–17.

14. B. Miller, *Gaining Acceptance for Major Methods Changes* (Research Study 44). American Management Association, Inc., New York, N.Y., 1960.

ployee periodicals, bulletin boards, supervisors, employee meetings, and the like. Where employees were organized, the unions were the channel for communications.

A majority of the firms assured their employees that no one would be laid off or would suffer a loss in pay because of the computer, and some of the other companies, while not offering such firm assurances, told their employees that layoffs and pay cuts seemed to be unlikely. Similar statements were made by the companies Miller studied.

Many of these statements are actually restatements of long-standing company policies. In fact, policies guaranteeing job security to clerical employees seem to be quite common in insurance, banking, and utility companies, which are, of course, prominent users of EDP. In the insurance company studied by Craig, for example, stability of employment had long been a matter of policy, and the company never fired employees whose performance and conduct were satisfactory.

If, however, the organization has never before made a formal statement of employment security, it may well—and indeed, should—do so when announcing the change to an EDP system. As Mann and Williams point out:

> There are a number of forces which lead management to this formalization of its obligation to its permanent work force. These include: (a) the maintenance of the morale of employees directly and indirectly affected by the change; (b) the utilization of the skill potential of existing personnel; (c) the demonstration of the organization's concern for the welfare of its employees; and (d) the meeting or anticipating of union demands where the group is organized or [the reducing of] the likelihood of unionization.

Another problem faced by companies installing EDP is what to do with employees whose positions are eliminated. Again, the survey report by the Bureau of Labor Statistics reveals what seem to be typical practices. Most companies, as has already been suggested, manage to avoid layoffs by allowing normal attrition to reduce the workforce and by filling their new vacancies mainly from within or with temporary employees, particularly married women. This normally involves coordinating the hiring policies of the entire office, including groups not directly affected by the change to EDP.

REASSIGNING DISPLACED EMPLOYEES

Transfers and reassignments are usually made according to the procedures previously followed when particular jobs were eliminated. (In union-

ized firms, these are usually spelled out in the contract.) Some companies engage in a good deal of advance planning aimed at minimizing the number of reassignments any one employee will have to undergo. One company, for example, selected women employees and potential draftees for reassignment to units that would be affected by the computer at some time in the future.

The reassignment of the displaced employees may generate a certain amount of dissatisfaction or conflict, the study found. It is often difficult to find suitable openings for older workers and supervisors and to guarantee promotional opportunities equivalent to those offered by the employees' former jobs. In addition, trouble may arise from the company's attempt to maintain the salaries of employees transferred to lower-rated jobs, and there may be differences of opinion about how to interpret the relevant contract provisions.

Sometimes, moreover, the reassignment program is designed to meet goals that are mutually contradictory. This happened in the utility company studied by Mann and Williams, which wanted on the one hand to minimize losses of pay and promotional opportunities and on the other to maintain a staff capable of operating the new system. In deciding which employee was to be reassigned to which job, the company tried to avoid any placements that might prove unsuccessful, and, where possible, it asked the employees which job they would prefer and then followed their wishes. At times, it also had to consider such limitations as physical disabilities.

The result of all this was that its assignments were "best-fit combinations" rather than attempts to fill each job with the man who could perform it best. Yet the company's considerateness toward its employees does not seem to have relieved them of all anxiety about the change, for some employees were dissatisfied with their transfers, and the prevailing uncertainty about future assignments led to tensions and insecurity throughout the reassignment period.

Not all companies, it has been found, pay sufficient attention to planning for personnel reassignments. Miller notes that in a number of the companies he studied there was "so little organized planning for this form of dislocation . . . as to make it seem an almost universal area of oversight—or even indifference." The result, he says, is that in these companies the computer installation proceeded far more slowly than it should have and at a higher cost. Agencies of the federal government, on the other hand, have developed extensive plans for handling the personnel changes necessitated by the automation of clerical work.

RETRAINING

Since dislocated employees are usually transferred to jobs whose duties and skill requirements closely resemble those of their old jobs, not very many of them have to be given formal training for their new work. Some retraining, however, is generally necessary, and even the relatively short time needed for on-the-job training may be hard to come by when energies are taken up with the other demands of the conversion process. Needless to say, the more the new job differs from the old, the greater the problem is.

As for formal training, this too varies with the nature of the job. Employees reassigned to the job of keypunch operator are commonly given only a small amount of formal training, particularly if they already know how to type. Employees who will become programers or equipment operators receive more extensive instruction (about a month for programers); this involves both classroom and on-the-job training and is most often given by representatives of the equipment manufacturers.

SELECTION FOR THE NEW JOBS

Most companies, as has been mentioned before, fill the new EDP positions mainly from the ranks of their own employees, drawing candidates from the entire office staff and not just from the affected units. Some of them announce that the new positions are open to all employees, while others invite selected employees to apply for them. Testing is quite common, particularly in the selection of programers, and is usually designed to measure learning ability.

The employees considered for the new jobs far outnumber the jobs themselves. One office cited by the Bureau of Labor Statistics study interviewed 125 employees in order to fill 10 EDP openings. And an even higher ratio prevailed in units of the Treasury Department and the General Accounting Office, where 470 employees were tested, and 23 chosen, for the job of programer.

From this brief description of the administrative problems and decisions involved in the change to EDP it should be clear that the introduction of the new system represents a major challenge to management and is in fact a test of the organization's capacity for change. According to the research literature, there are several factors that seem to be critical in determining how well the organization will meet this test.

Focusing on the planning process, Miller says that his study found seven common errors or inadequacies that often lead to conflict:

1. Inept approach of methods analysts in dealing with others.
2. Overdependence on outside methods analysts.
3. Manpower shortage in the changeover.
4. Management pressure for early installation.
5. Lack of participation by supervisory employees.
6. Poor planning for transfers and reclassification.
7. Insufficient communication with the affected employees.

Approaching the matter from the positive standpoint, Craig reports that in the company he studied management handled the conversion with considerable skill and success. In particular, he notes that they took account of the traditions, codes, and expectations of the organization and that rather than sacrifice the equilibrium of the organization's social system for the sake of faster progress with the conversion they made compromises designed to achieve a balance between the two.

The disturbance of the organization's equilibrium and the later achievement of a new equilibrium are also highlighted by Mann and Williams, who point out that management's basic philosophy may be severely tested by the change and that previous experiences with change will have left some units better prepared for the necessary readjustments than others. They also note that the quality of the previous relationship between management and employees may, as it did in the company they studied, provide a fund of good will and trust that can be drawn on in the crises that inevitably arise during the trying period of transition.

In unionized companies, needless to say, the success of the conversion can also be affected by the quality of the labor-management relationship and by the union's attitude toward automation. Most of the research on office automation has been in nonunionized firms, but there is some helpful information about this question. It has been found, for instance, that the position of clerical unions on automation is highly similar to that of nonclerical unions.[15] Generally speaking, they accept automation in principle, but they strongly desire to be given prior notice of its introduction and to play an important part in settling the problems of employee adjustment.

In the unionized companies studied by the Bureau of Labor Statistics, the displacements, promotions, and transfers resulting from automation were governed at least in part by existing contract provisions, as was the establishment of

---

15. A. Braunthal, "The Trade Union Movement Faces Automation," *International Labour Review*, Dec., 1957.

new jobs and wage rates. Thus, for example, the order in which employees were displaced depended largely, and in some cases solely, on their seniority. The unions informed the employees about the change to EDP and acted on their behalf to adjust any problems that arose. In some offices, there were disputes about the union's jurisdiction over the newly created EDP positions and about the transfer of work to nonunion employees.

The introduction of office automation has also been accepted by the unions of government employees, which have recommended a five-point program for avoiding any resulting hardships. Their program calls for: (1) thorough advance planning; (2) retraining programs for the affected personnel; (3) firm reassignment procedures; (4) programs for placement in private industry; and (5) advance information on the changes to be made.

In sum, the research findings now available show that office automation has a tremendous impact both on workers and on the organization, generating a number of serious problems along with certain obvious benefits. The evidence also indicates, however, that these problems can be solved, and the studies that have so far been conducted represent in themselves a valuable fund of knowledge for companies that want to benefit from the experience of others.

47 – The Computer in Your Future

ROBERT L. KATZ,
KENNETH E. KNIGHT,
and WILLIAM F. MASSEY,
with editorial synthesis by
RIDGE L. HARLAN

The corporation president's alleged remark to a junior vice-president "Don't confuse me with the facts, young man!" may be apocryphal, but it does illustrate one facet of an anachronistic species of management fauna now beginning to become extinct – the "pure intuition" species which relies solely on trial-and-error experience, prior management folklore, and just plain hunch for its decision-making.

This management species is being assisted toward eventual extinction by the subject of this article. The intent here is to explore some of the present and probable future effects of high-speed computers on corporate decision-making and implementation, to outline the basic uses of the computer, and to discuss its influence on organization structure, communication patterns, and managerial behavior. Covering such an expanse in one short article is a challenging assignment which can be met only through compression or elimination of detail, for a series of articles could be (in fact, has been) prepared on each of the above areas.

This article, then, can be considered a condensed assessment of the subject "The Abilities and Implications of the Computer," with the hope, on the part of the reader, that he will here obtain a useful overview of a complex and often clouded management tool with a minimum of time and mental effort.

ACCELERATED CHANGES AHEAD

Many people foresee greater changes in the practice of management in the next 20 years than in the past 2,000, with the high-speed computer playing both a dynamic and a catalytic role in these changes. Some view the anticipated changes with great enthusiasm for the efficiencies they will bring and the new vistas they will reveal.

A number of others – perhaps, but hopefully not, including you – look at this whole rolling advance with various degrees of trepidation.

Some worry about what will happen to their jobs. Will some machine "displace" them? Others are concerned about the need to learn new skills. Will they have to be retrained or retreaded? Is their present skill obsolescent?

Others worry about the ethical and moral and social issues: how can an un-person, a cold machine, take account of human values and spiritual objectives?

Still others are simply afraid to have the hard truth about their job performance revealed. They therefore view the act of discovery, of objective fact finding, with negative feelings ranging from

"The Computer in Your Future," *Stanford Graduate School of Business Bulletin*, XXXIII (Winter 1965), 2–9. Reprinted by permission of the authors and the publisher. **Robert L. Katz, Kenneth E. Knight, William F. Massey,** and **Ridge L. Harlan:** Graduate School of Business, Stanford University.

uneasiness to nervousness to distrust to down-right fright.

Most people fear what they do not understand. And, since understanding often depends on your vantage point, it may help to view the computer as simply another entrant in the productive parade of mechanical assists to man's progress. It is admittedly an enormously significant entrant.

It also provides its assistance in a vastly different and largely unoccupied (by machines) environment.

When you analyze the machines which have been invented to aid man, you notice they have been put to work almost entirely in the area of physical assistance. Machines, up to the recent past, have primarily and dominantly been applied to free man from grinding and menial physical labor. They have expanded to a fantastic degree man's physical capabilities. Example: where once he was able to move only at a sustained walking speed of, say, five miles an hour, machines have increased man's physical speeds by 100 times (routinely in a commercial jet plane), or 3,500 times (at escape velocity in a space rocket).

While a strong man can repetitively lift 100 pounds, his invention the gantry crane has no problems with loads 2,000 and more times that weight.

HELP FOR THE MENTAL MAN

No need to belabor the examples of machine assistance to the physical man. But how many kinds of machinery have been brought to the assistance of the mental man?

When you arrive at the printing press, you have an almost complete list of machines providing significant help to man's mind. With this orientation, it can be said that as machines have revolutionized man's use of his muscle, they are now, in the form of the high-speed computer, showing similar promise of revolutionizing the use of his mind. As we begin to come close to the point where an individual is able, with a machine's help, to do ten, or one hundred, times as much mental work, we begin to approach the lower limits of the change from physical labor to that of power-driven machines.

This view may help clarify some of the mystery about the position of the computer today. It also introduces the question: Just what can computers do?

When asked, most people will say that a computer is a device which can do arithmetic accurately, awfully fast, and with laudable economy.

They will say that the computer's real contribution is in performing scientific and engineering calculations and in performing repetitive accounting operations. But this is only a small part of the computer's contributions. Actually, these specific chores can perhaps be classified as among the most primitive of its functions, for computers can do much more than reduce data to manageable form. They actually transform *data* to *information.* Their ability to do this is limited primarily by the ingenuity and experience of the people who set up the control systems rather than by any inherent technological restrictions.

MORE THAN "DATA PROCESSING"

Far more significant than "data processing" are the computer's present and future roles in *analysis, decision-making,* and *experimentation.* In these roles, the computer is used: to analyze information; to provide act-upon (decision-making) information; to act upon its own decisions; to perform synthetic experimentation. Let's take a look at each of these extremely important functions; for in these lie the computer's real implications as a management tool.

Increasing use is being made of the computer's ability to *analyze information* by building statistical models of the firm and its environment. The emphasis here is on statistics and econometrics, since the machines are employed to do sophisticated statistical calculations on empirical information. Examples: statistical analysis of marketing trends, marketing activities, and market demands.

Growing more common is the employment of the computer to provide "recommendations," or even "decisions" which human executives can implement. This area of providing *act-upon information* is currently found most often in repetitive or highly complicated tasks. Examples: scheduling work through job shops; calculating the optimum number of toll booths needed on toll bridges; allocating scarce resources; optimizing transportation schedules. This usage comprises the bulk of what is usually considered "Operations Research."

While most of the decision-making operations of the computer are still under the direct control of human problem-solvers, there are other applications in which the computer *makes its own decisions* and *acts upon them.* In this usage, the computer does more than assist humans in arriving at the "best" answers. It is tied into a total machine—machine system, makes decisions, and directs other machines as the result of these decisions. Examples: uses in automated oil refineries, bakeries, meat packers, aircraft parts plants.

Perhaps the most exciting use of all is *synthetic experimentation*, in which computers can be programmed to simulate the operation of physical, organizational, or market forces in almost any given environment. This is accomplished by setting up, in the computer, a mathematical model of a "real world" situation and trying out, on this model, a variety of alternative strategies or actions. If the model is well designed, the results of the simulation approximate those results found in the real world.

In this use, the computer saves an enormous amount of time, and the costs of the tryout are much less than they would be in the real world (if, indeed, the experiment could be conducted in the real world at all).

An early prominent use of the computer to do synthetic experimentation can be found in the 1960 presidential election, in which the machine was used to help the Democratic party strategists decide how to handle a number of important issues—such as the Catholic issue. The computer was used to collect all of the available information about some 480 separate groups of voters, and then to predict how each group would react to alternative methods of handling the crucial issues. Once the reaction of each group had been predicted, the results could be aggregated to make a prediction for the total electorate.

These are the basic uses of the computer today, in the quantitative areas. A few paragraphs farther along, some non-quantitative and future uses of the computer are examined. But first, some human implications.

HOW COMPUTERS ARE AFFECTING MANAGERS

This important subject can be divided into three parts, corresponding to the three broad levels of management. As will be noted, the implications of the computer for each level are quite different.

LOWER MANAGEMENT

This level can be defined as that of foremen and supervisors. Here *data processing* is relieving this group of managers of much menial and routine mental work, is providing information faster, and is generally providing much more accurate information (assuming the ability of the programmer).

A side benefit seems to be accruing here: Since it is necessary to specify what control information is to be obtained from the computer, the whole question of control is forced right down to the lower levels of management. As a result, the organizational goal structure is being made more explicit.

The ability of the computer to *make decisions* will also be applied with increasing effect at supervisory levels. Questions such as inventory control and manpower scheduling are already being solved by computers in many companies and are being taken out of the control of supervisory staff. There is every evidence that the computer can perform these repetitive tasks faster and better than can the supervisory personnel. Obviously, however, human problem solvers will still have to monitor the output of the computers.

The major challenge of this move toward "automated decision-making" at the lower management level will be the attitudes of the lower management themselves. Many such managers have a strong negative attitude toward the machine, for reasons mentioned earlier.

But the fact that the computer is here to stay should not pose a real threat to the status of lower management. As a tool to give them better, faster information, it will give them more time to concentrate on the more important aspects of their jobs—such as the handling of human relations factors.

MIDDLE MANAGEMENT

While the *data processing* function will always be important for middle management, the role of the computer at this level promises to provide managers with better information on which to judge operating results of subordinates and to give them greater scope of decision in time to take meaningful action.

More significant are the *analysis of information* and *decision* functions of the computer. In fact, there is hardly a problem of major importance to management, which is at all complex, which cannot and will not be assisted by the computer. Therefore, middle managers are learning to get along with the machine in an extremely close relationship. This does not mean that they are becoming involved in the technology of the computer or its programming. (Most will probably never see a computer close up—and won't need to.) But they will increasingly need to grasp the techniques which can be used on the machine, including statistics and operations research, in order to understand what the machine can and cannot do in context with their own problems.

One final point: Modern computers are quite flexible in their data processing and analysis functions, thereby allowing a middle manager to specify the kind of information he wants. This flexibility, it would seem, offers great possibilities for increased creativity.

Many people argue that computers will ruin creativity. But the argument to the contrary seems far stronger: with their ability to provide a new, volume flow of useful information, computers could be the greatest boon in history to creative planning and problem-solving by middle management.

TOP MANAGEMENT

At the general management level, the use of the computer is emphasizing (and will continue to) the *analysis* of data which leads to better understanding of the relationships within the firm and between it and its environment.

The real payout for top management, however, would seem to be in the areas of "real time systems" (discussed a few paragraphs farther along) and *synthetic experimentation*. This is the area, of course, in which the computer can be used to evaluate the effects of broad differences in company's strategy over the long run — without having to risk possible negative, damaging results in actual, experimental changes in strategy-direction.

Simulation can, in principle, provide fairly accurate forecasts of what would happen if the company introduced a new package or new product, changed the location of its headquarters, changed its distribution channels, switched modes of transportation, changed its promotional image and its advertising, or any one of a number of other basic strategic considerations.

The fact that questions like these go to the very heart of the top management function cannot be exaggerated. It may well be that simulation, or synthetic experimentation, is the most promising derivative of computer technology, for top management, developed to date.

COMPLEX INFORMATION PROCESSING

In this article to this point, the emphasis has been on the use of the computer in quantitative areas. Unfortunately or fortunately, depending on your bias, an important portion of the management function is not routine or quantifiable. The next question we must ask ourselves: What will be the impact of computers on that portion which we cannot quantify and specify in a mathematical language alone?

Computers originally evolved from the small hand calculator; as a result, the early systems were little more than large adding machines, and many computers today are still used only in that way.

However, as time passed, and computers developed, and memory systems became more spacious and reliable, we have come to realize that computers can actually be general symbol manipulators. In a limited sense, in this context, they are similar to the human mind, with the capability to handle more than just mathematical problems.

They can be programmed to attack non-mathematical problems using models and concepts that are similar to those of the human mind — heuristic programs. (Heuristics are rules we all use in problem-solving to help find a solution. Example: a heuristic that most people use when feeling ill is: go to a doctor. In most cases, but not all, this heuristic is useful in curing our ailment.)

It is well known that computers have performed a number of interesting feats of "human" quality involving logic — solving college geometry problems, playing chess. These are well-defined, well-structured problems. But what can the computer do with the poorly structured decision problems so often faced by general management?

As a prediction, it seems quite reasonable to hypothesize that one day in the future, perhaps within 20 years, management will employ the computer to solve ill-structured problems by using models and concepts and symbols which the human mind employs. It is, in fact, quite probable that joint "problem-solving systems" will be developed, combining human problem solvers and computers, with computers serving as memory aids, information aids, and general problem-solving assistants.

However, this ultra-sophisticated employment of the computer's capabilities will have to wait for further development in Complex Information Processing (CIP) techniques. This capability may well be available within ten to 20 years and with it will come a spectacular improvement in management effectiveness.

REAL TIME INFORMATION PROCESSING

This improvement should result from complex man-machine systems which are now evolving, systems which will perform *real time information processing*. If you haven't run into this notion before, a word of explanation may help.

A real time information system is one which can receive information at any given point in time, process it, and return the analysis or decision material to an output terminal almost instantaneously. The term "real time" simply means that management gets this information in time to do something with it—make effective, on-the-moment decisions, with the machines providing current-to-the-moment decision-making material.

These real time systems will perhaps involve the entire management of an organization, providing near-instantaneous information from tens and hundreds of terminals and also connecting managers with the CIP computers referred to above.

This may sound esoteric, other-worldly. But the fact is that management today often receives information too late for a decision, good or bad, to make any difference. With real time information systems, management gets the information while something can still be done.

OPPORTUNITIES FOR ENORMOUS IMPROVEMENT

With real time information systems, CIP, and heuristic problem solving, we can expect more than just a ten per cent or 20 per cent improvement in the amount of work done by a human problem solver. It is not unlikely that the systems described here rather crudely could produce increases in the human decision maker of the magnitude of the physical assists to man described early in this article.

It is not unlikely that these "mental improvements" could range from 100 per cent to a fantastic 10,000 per cent.

CHANGES IN ORGANIZATIONAL STRUCTURE AHEAD

As every executive knows, handling machines is one thing; attending to human and behavioral problems quite another. What will happen to the people, and to the organization structure of which they are a part, as we rely more and more on computers for economic decision making?

Two behavioral changes, among many, are illustrative and offer considerable hope for interesting non-economic advances for "the human use of human beings."

First, the real time system may well result in the evolution of a more flexible, more decentralized, organization structure in the future.

With the increasing complexities of manage-

ment and the increases in current knowledge, no one man or small group of men can possibly have the ability, talent, experience, and information to manage in a rigid hierarchical sense. More flexible and fluid organizations are evolving that allow the company to call upon the person or persons most capable of undertaking the task at hand.

The computer, with its memory system, will keep an elaborate file of the people in the company, indicating what each individual likes to do, is doing, has done; will list special skills. This will enable top management and middle management to form work groups, involving a number of different specialists, to address themselves to problems for which their special abilities are needed.

Second, the computer may actually contribute to the solution of some of the human problems created by modern industrial life, by automation, and by the computer itself.

More and more emphasis is being given in our society to some of the emotional difficulties created by the demands placed by today's complex organizations on the human nervous system. The problems here, and their causes, are almost classic examples of ill-structured problems, problems whose solutions may well be aided by the real time, Complex Information Processing systems mentioned earlier.

While our knowledge in the area of mental health is admittedly inadequate, there are already signs that we will be able to use the computer to create healthier relationships among several men and between the computer system and the men who use it.

Just as managers will be able to extend their mental abilities through the computer's capabilities, so will the behavioral scientists employ the computer to expand their own frontiers of knowledge of human relations.

THE COMPUTER IN YOUR FUTURE

As in many of life's other questions, the degree to which the computer is employed in the problem-solving situations outlined here will be decided by good old-fashioned economics. It simply may not be economical (let alone possible) to solve all the world's problems on the computer.

However, an interesting and important fact by which the economic future of computers and real time processing may be judged is the sharply decreasing cost of making a computerized computation.

Measuring performance improvement in terms of the number of calculations per dollar, the internal processing capabilities of our equipment have improved at about 80 per cent per year. If we extrapolate this rate of improvement, as appears quite reasonable, it may be predicted that in 1975, computers will perform some 600 computations for the cost of one computation today.

Combine this with an improvement of 100 per cent to 10,000 per cent in man's mental performance, when aided by the computer, and a startlingly economical decision-cost results.

The large question is how to use this economical decision-making most effectively.

THE HUMAN PERSPECTIVE

To those souls who are made restless by the implications of the computer's power, it is hoped that this article has put some of the machine's implications into manageable perspective.

We have seen some of the ways in which the computer can enhance man's capacity to solve problems where all the input data are known quantities. We have also noted ways in which managers can improve the quality of their decisions when dealing with imprecise data.

In so doing, we have dealt with the computer's function of vastly improving the mechanics of problem-solution, specifically with the machine's ability to process more information to produce faster and more accurate results and to increase the probability of predictable outcomes. We have also viewed the likelihood of computers improving the process of problem-solution by aiding the human to be more systematic and logical in how he thinks about problems.

With these capabilities, the machine may be expected to enhance man's ability to cope with his environment to a degree undreamed of a few years ago. Properly used, the computer should allow man to live with greater certainty, less anxiety, and increased compatibility with physical forces and procedures.

Yet, somehow, many will still feel some lurking concern about the possibilities of devaluing the human, of reducing his opportunities for creativity and contribution, of increasing the possibilities of manipulation by others.

In this context it is important to emphasize that decision-making will be most greatly facilitated in strategic areas—the allocation and movement of resources; financing; definition of markets and channels; selection of product specifications. It is also important to point out that much managerial behavior is not at all involved with problem-solving and decision-making, in the sense those terms have been used in this discussion.

Finally, the important practical interface between man and machine comes at the level of the men who use the machine. Who selects the mathematical models to be used? Who decides how to evaluate the results? Who decides how to implement the results? Who does the implementing? It is obvious that the computer is the servant, that man is the master, and that the results—good and bad—depend on the quality of man's input and man's judgment of the output.

This can possibly all add up to a logical question: What's wrong with the computer? But, then, that's the subject for another article.

In the conclusion of this one, let us note that it may well be said that only a fool would blindly trust the output of his computer in a complicated situation.

But it is rapidly becoming fact that the man who refuses to look at the output of the computer is an even worse fool.

At this writing it seems predictable that the human mind must truly learn how to use the computer as an extension of itself, for neither seems able to cope with the kind of problems being thrown up by an enormously complex modern world without the help of the other.

48 – The Nature and Contribution of Administrative Models

FREMONT A. SHULL, JR.

Controversy over whether or not administration can be a unique discipline with associated facts, principles and theories is barren. In fact,

Hobbes, as early as the seventeenth century, said of (public) administration: "The skill of making, and maintaining Common-wealths consisteth in certain Rules, as doth Arithmetique and Geometry; not (as Tennis-play) on Practice only."[1] Yet the development of administrative science lags

"The Nature and Contribution of Administrative Models," *Academy of Management Journal,* V (August 1962), 124–138. Reprinted by permission of the author and the publisher. Fremont A. Shull, Jr.: School of Business, Indiana University.

behind the evolution of managerial skills. Guided largely by instinct and limited experiences, the practitioner has made tremendous progress. His fulfillment of the struggle hypothesis reinforced by an artificially amplified competitive environment has provided the impetus to development of the art. In addition, early stages in the development of any science enhance the application of the art, e.g., the transfer and assemblage of casual observation.

On the other hand, personal motivation and environmental influences may not have forced administrative skill to high levels of proficiency in an absolute sense. First, competitive pressures may not have had any significant leavening influence upon the level of administrative practice. Second, management by imitation may be widespread, leading to the adoption of inefficient as well as effective methodologies. Therefore, neither expediency attending pragmatic needs nor satisfaction associated with practical success should stifle the evolution of the science: reflection and analysis should progressively supplant intuition and mysticism. The dynamics and complexities of our culture require that practice be based upon intelligent reasoning and scientific exploration, not upon habit, imitation, and superstition.

It is not the role and purpose of the practitioner to evolve and develop a science of administration, except to the degree that he feels a professional obligation. Yet, because of the credence attending conventional wisdom and confidence placed in the practitioner's skill, the pedagog until recently appeared to depend upon, and ally himself with the particularized inductive reasoning and rationale of the pragmatist. This affinity still exists in spite of the fact that: "The stressing of perceptual facts to the exclusion of rules and principles which give order to and explain these facts is a practice which has placed serious limitations on the average person's ability to analyze social behavior."[2] In fact, some contend that "only recently can it be said that the observations of the behavioral scientist are better than those of the practical man in the field."[3]

This disclaimer of the academician is no castigation of the gathering of facts and direct observation by the practitioner. But reflection suggests the fable of the "side-hill" chicken with one short leg, for the scholar knows that contributions from observations of the empiricist and model-building of the theoretician is based upon a continuing and reciprocal relationship. He knows that, "there is nothing intrinsically indubitable, there are no absolutely first principles, in the sense of principles which are self-evident or which must be

known prior to everything else. . . ."[4] The method of science is circular. Evidence is obtained in order to construct principles by appealing to empirical data—to what is alleged to be "fact"; and, in turn, the empirical material is analyzed and interpreted on the basis of principles.

While convention and sentiment have retarded the movement, the growth of controlled and objective research in administrative and organization behavior is a tide that will not be stemmed. Recent literature attests to the fact that there has been a definite shift from a preoccupation with the mechanistic and idealized considerations of conventional management prescriptions to a focus upon managerial reality and organizational behavior for understanding administrative processes. With accepted propositions be-damned, the social scientist is studying the phenomenon known as reality.

A useful science requires the establishment of a theory or principles verifiable by experimentation or observation.[5] In fact, Parsons argues that "the most important index of the maturity of a science is the state of its systematic theory."[6] Thus models or abstractions which provide a manageable framework for investigating, understanding, and either communicating about or dealing with the realities of the discipline must be developed, deductively or inductively. Depending upon its purpose, a model may be designed so as to closely approximate or to grossly abstract from the situation under inquiry. The degree of representation of reality depends upon the desire for manageability of the abstraction and its purpose as well as the complexity and breadth of the actual situation depicted.[7]

In immature disciplines, such as management, models are of a highly transitory nature, making it doubly important that they be employed more for general guidance or exploration than as ends in

---

1. Thomas Hobbes, *Leviathan* (New York: E. P. Dutton & Co., Inc., 1950), p. 176.
2. Richard Dewey and W. J. Humber, *The Development of Human Behavior* (New York: The Macmillan Company, 1951), p. 1.
3. David G. Moore, "Contributions to Management Philosophy from the Behavior Sciences," a paper presented to the Annual Academy of Management Meetings, December, 1960.
4. Morris R. Cohen and Ernest Nagel, *An Introduction to Logic and the Scientific Method* (New York: Harcourt, Brace and Company, 1934), p. 396.
5. Webster defines a science as: "a branch of study concerned with observations and classification of facts, especially with the establishment of verifiable general laws . . ."
6. Talcott Parsons, *Essays in Sociological Theory, Pure and Applied* (Glencoe, Ill.: Free Press, 1949), p. 17.
7. Models may be (1) *physical*, such as templates or model airplanes; (2) *schematic*, graphic representations such as flow-process charts and maps; or (3) *conceptual* (either mathematical or verbal), such as Freud's *id, ego,* and *super-ego* (verbal), or laws for movement of gases (mathematical).

themselves. Nonetheless, their ephemeral quality should not deter model-building, since either disconfirmation or validation can lead to progress in the discipline. Accordingly, there is a strong movement in administration for the development of general hypotheses and principles as well as the discovery of the cause-and-effect relationships and the establishment of validities.[8] Where these statements and concepts are systematically and logically related, a model occurs.

PURPOSES OF MODELS

PRESCRIPTIVE MODELS

While management models may be designed for observation and prediction, their most common purpose historically has been to prescribe for managerial practice. This purpose has been perpetuated by the absence of differing schools of thought based upon credible empirical evidence, the implications associated with supervision and control which are inherent in administrative systems, and the desire to support or disseminate a particular set of values. Accordingly, prescriptive models[9] are generally presented by means of word symbols and are typified by phrases introduced by the words, "should" and "ought."

Notwithstanding the volumes of literature treating them and the precedents found in antiquity that support them, these injunctions or rules of action have been characterized as proverbs and myths. This characterization has been offered in order to emphasize that (1) they are not immutable principles, (2) their value lies largely in rationalizing how people should act or be treated in an organization, and (3) they tend to be empirically vacuous.[10] Roy, for example, quotes a colleague as labeling these "pious instructions as 'votes for virtue'" adding that, "such platitudes are ubiquitous enough but repetition alone is not likely to provide better administrative practice." He admits, however, that management writers are bound to vote for virtue from time to time, "through inadvertence if nothing else," and concludes that "if one is to do more than analyze and diagnose, if one is to prescribe any therapy at all, some measure of 'oughts' is inevitable."[11]

In spite of such criticisms, these dogma are widely endorsed and prescription is the predominant approach in management literature and training programs. Perhaps the conservative prefers to perpetuate and proliferate, but not restructure nor substitute for traditional proposi-

tions. Moreover, attempts at prescription lead naturally to discussions of utilitarian skills and techniques. Such discussions are highly popular because of the practitioner's demands for specific propositions relating to pragmatic requirements. Finally, technique may appear more attractive than interpretation; to prescribe methods may be easier than to analyze relationships, while description may be less subject to criticism than inference.

Prescriptive models gain a moralistic, as contrasted to realistic, cast from the original assumptions upon which they are based as well as from the specific restrictions held for the intermediate interpretations and conclusions at various stages in their derivation. Probably the most significant constraint is the assumption of organizational rationality. If managerial performance is assessed and rewarded according to organization accomplishment, the rational conclusion is that managers should identify with the group's formal objective. To the degree that a member of an organization is rational and sensitive and his decisions are grounded in institutional values and experiences, prescriptive models reflect actual behavior. Nonetheless, man does not completely adapt to, nor meet fully, the dictates of the formal organization. In even the highly structured system, man has some natural proclivity for apathy, emotionalism and personal selfishness which can result in behavior at odds with organizational purpose. Where organizationally irrational values or non-supportive activities exist, conventional prescriptive models are incapable of projecting actual behavior.

In addition, the view of managerial or operative satisfaction as a means, rather than an end, has been subject to criticism from both scholar and practitioner. An officer of the National Association of Manufacturers, for example, said in 1950 that "industry exists for the individual. . . . The human personality, not the organization or any institution, is a paramount and supreme consideration."[12] Yet, Argyris has concluded that if conventional wisdom is used to

---

8. These latter aims may be overly ambitious at this time. It may well be that much empiricism is (should be) still in its observational phases.

9. Some prescriptive "models" are nothing more than crude and incomplete classification schemes or streams of ideas, lacking the rigor generally associated with the concept of model.

10. James G. March and Herbert A. Simon, *Organizations* (New York: John Wiley & Sons, Inc., 1958), p. 30.

11. Robert H. Roy, *The Administrative Process*, (Baltimore: The Johns Hopkins Press, 1959), p. 3–4.

12. Earl Bunting, "Industry Looks at Its Relations with Employees." Address delivered at the 20th NAM Institute on Industrial Relations, Virginia Beach, Virginia, October 30, 1950.

develop "traditional formal principles of organizing . . . to create a social organization, and if one uses as an input, agents who tend toward a mature state of psychological development . . . , one creates a disturbance because the needs . . . of healthy individuals are not congruent with the requirements of situations where they are dependent, passive, and use few and unimportant abilities."[13]

Although the psychological basis of identification and the determination of its strength are obscure, the imposition of organizational aims upon the individual's value structure cannot be contradicted. Socializing is real and effective, while commitment or, at least, cooperation is required for organized effort. The practitioner in his supervisory role is continually involved in evoking supportive behavior on the part of his subordinates. Through indoctrination, training, and counseling he attempts to structure the decision premises of subordinates. Such activities are prescriptive in nature and, unwittingly or not, practitioners encourage educational institutions that accept the responsibility for imparting "proper" value premises as well as analytic and informative exercises to participants.

Nonetheless, prescriptions phrased for executive action solely in terms of the economic-efficiency rationale can be highly functional.[14] Many measures of efficiency or performance are susceptible to some type of quantification, while measures of other survival ends of an organization generally permit only qualitative evaluations. In a sense, then, a prescriptive model can provide a yardstick for measuring other survival criteria. Suppose that efficiency and morale are reducible to some total success criterion, UO; and, assume that efficiency and morale are inversely related over the relevant range. To maximize either efficiency (E) or morale (S) would not necessarily maximize UO, while maximizing UO would not necessarily maximize either S or E. The difference between the maximum E and the attainment of E when UO is maximized is the opportunity cost of attaining the optimum S: That which is given up in profit is the alternative cost of gaining increased morale. Subsuming a measurable type of efficiency, prescriptive models can contribute to the measurement of organizational attainment on many fronts where the relationships among the ends are known.

In addition, to the extent that prescriptive models embody systematized general laws subject to verification and statements of proximate causalities, they enable the professional to perform a significant service. With them, he is empowered to abstract from the prejudices and specifics of a particular situation and to propose model patterns which then can be modified to approximate the immediate situation. However, prescriptive models are limited by the accumulation of experience to date or phrased only in terms of practices and ends currently approved. Therefore, the use of such models designed without reference to actual variables at play in the system and without the ability to predict outcomes of administrative action can be irrelevant or misleading.

PREDICTIVE MODELS

A second purpose of models is prediction, which is essentially the foretelling of the nature, direction, and magnitude of change in a system. Such models simulate the dynamics of the environment and permit a symbolic manipulation of the relevant variables.[15] A model used for prediction, therefore, must encompass the major variables of a system and reflect their interrelationships. Such a model assumes causalities or functional relationships which imply measurement. A prognostication results, but not one necessarily moralistic in nature.

Prediction enhances management's ability to adapt intelligently to a changing environment. But administrators are not passive agents of the system; they create change within their organizations as well as the encompassing and contiguous environments. They may cause change merely for the sake of creating a more dynamic setting, i.e., for strategic purposes, or cause change inadvertently through the normal processes of making adjustments in their organizations. Finally, they may create changes within their organization for their own personal interests. To the extent that change and strategy imply risk and uncertainty, prediction becomes complicated and even incalculable by the compounding of relevant probability sets.

Without predictive accuracy, however, managerial action becomes random and largely after-the-fact while the products of administration stem essentially from foresightful and directive behavior. If, for example, management can be viewed as an overlay upon operations,[16] logic leads to the conclusion that management is not practiced for its own sake: management cannot be

---

13. Chris Argyris, *Personality and Organization* (New York: Harper and Brothers, 1957), p. 233.

14. Efficiency and consumer costs may be the most viable and culturally acceptable standards for the business firm.

15. Because of the ambiguity and unwieldiness of word symbols, predictive models are often presented as mathematical analogies and formulations.

16. Although it is useful to distinguish conceptually between administration and operations, the two activities are so inter-related that they are, in reality, an organic whole.

justified in terms of elaborate control systems or organization charts. (Consider the courtroom lawyer who defends his courtroom presentation in terms of the mechanical perfection of his brief.) The value of managerial techniques and strategies lies in the degree of goal-accomplishment implemented primarily by operations. Since operational behavior is largely a product of administration, management must be practiced, not merely understood. Here, as with most fields of endeavor, the ultimate purpose of knowledge is effective action; understanding without art is sterile.[17] It is for the art to "accomplish concrete ends, effect results, produce situations, that would not come about without the deliberate efforts to secure them"[18]—the serving of management art rests upon planning outcomes, the value of which rests upon prediction.

Yet many conventional models are incapable of describing or predicting various actualities of individual and organizational behavior. Consider, for example, the utility of the traditional framework in forecasting an individual's promotion because of low performance in his present assignment; or, predict the personal and organizational energies dissipated in political maneuvering among members of a hierarchy.

Furthermore, many traditional models assume unilinear stimulus-response relationships between phenomena within an organization which has caused considerable frustration on the part of the practitioner. The very techniques prescribed to him for increasing the predictability of subordinate behavior have had unintended and organizationally dysfunctional repercussions. The formally explicated performance standards, for example, may bind perception and motivation to them, resulting in a rigid or habitual type of behavior. Following the dicta springing from the economy-efficiency rationale, the practitioner has engaged in job specialization and standardization. In his efforts to achieve vertical specialization, for example, he has created a hierarchy of communication centers in the organization-system; and, in the feedback of information, each center has tended to de-emphasize data inconsistent with that with which it is primarily concerned or to distort information that will reflect unfavorably upon it. This behavior has caused much consternation in administration because either incomplete or fallacious information impair the factual premises employed in decision-making.[19]

Certain presuppositions about means-ends relationships contained in conventional models have precluded prediction. A case in point is the proposition that an increase in morale resulting from increased employee satisfaction creates a propor-

tionate increase in productivity and, thereby, results in greater organizational effectiveness. To date, empirical evidence does not validate this proposition.[20] In summarizing the pertinent research findings, Miller found that a four-celled matrix is needed to describe the relationships that exist between (high or low) efficiency and (high or low) morale.[21] Employees, for example, may receive a high (low) level of satisfaction and/or work at a high (low) level of performance under conditions of: (1) highly routinized work, (2) close supervision, and (3) great pressures and conflict. If such findings are valid it can be concluded that many prescriptive statements are incomplete, inaccurate, and when applied become organizationally, if not personally, dysfunctional.

DESCRIPTIVE MODELS

The basic distinction stressed thus far has been the difference between a model that prescribes what management should do and a model that aids the prediction of actual behavior. The latter purpose suggests a third use of models: A framework designed to enhance research, description, and measurement. Few would deny that there has been a paucity of research, especially pertaining to administrative practice, or that much research has concentrated upon isolated instances on an *ad hoc* basis. Moreover, most empirical findings appear to have been treated as additives to some prescriptive model only after screening for appropriateness in terms of that model.

Although subject to various types of observation for years, especially as a bureaucracy, recent organizational research has been criticized. Relating to the inadequacies found in much of the research, Clark and Ackoff, commenting on approaches which emphasize experimental control, said: "The results have been rigorous but limited and, in the main, are incapable of being used for extrapolation to problems in real on-going organizations." On speaking of observational studies of particular organizations, they state that the associated findings are "rich in detail, but lack the generality required in the development of theory

---

17. Knowledge for its own sake as well as its artistic application offer certain intrinsic satisfactions.
18. Chester I. Barnard, *The Functions of the Executive* (Cambridge, Mass.: Harvard University Press, 1951), p. 290.
19. Cf. R. M. Cyert and J. G. March, "Organization Structure and Pricing Behavior in an Oligopolistic Market," *The American Economic Review*, XLV (March, 1955) pp. 129–39.
20. Arthur H. Brayfield and Walter H. Crockett, "Employee Attitudes and Employee Performance," *Psychological Bulletin*, LII (September, 1955), p. 421.
21. Delbert C. Miller, "Efficiency, Leadership, and Morale in Small Military Organizations," *American Sociological Review*, (July, 1955).

and methods for solving problems in organizations other than the ones studied."[22]

All of this is not to argue that research has been unfruitful, because only from existing evidence and thought can new ideas be born. However, to paraphrase Roethlisberger, human behavior has been observed since time immemorial, but only as it is observed under more accurate hypotheses is its real significance seen.[23] "The administrator or student who feels that he has acquired through some natural process all of the insights and skills that he needs to understand human behavior and make judgments about others is fooling himself. Indeed, most people are completely unaware of the limitation of their personal experiences and the highly subjective, class-bound, culture-bound nature of their observations and judgments. Yet, because they have had to come to grips with human relations throughout their lives, they somehow develop a certainty of judgment which they would never feel in the considerably less complex physical sciences."[24]

Thus, improvements in, and refinements of, research design and implementation hold great promise for the student of management. Three general fronts for improvement suggest themselves: First, greater administrative acceptance of the cost, nature, and purpose of research, especially "pure" research, would create a climate within which the researcher could ruminate and innovate, and perhaps fail to develop tangible results immediately. Moreover, the opportunity for field study could be greatly improved; for example, management tends to keep the behavioral scientist ". . . in the cloister, immunizing themselves by such adjectives as ivory tower (and) long hair. Such management attitude is today's equivalent of the barber resistance to physiology two hundred years ago. It is attitude and not logic. Any inadequacy of the behavorial sciences is logically an argument for rather than against their use."[25]

Second, working hypotheses for research can be improved by discarding their moralistic flavor—the framework can be restructured or extended so as to include propositions concerning the way people and systems actually behave in real situations rather than the way they should behave. Here, models can be merely suggestive and speculative. Game theory, for example, has provided this service and stimulated substantive research in the behavioral sciences. Models which ignore the prescriptive purpose have permitted the development of a theory of role conflict and its empirical exploration.

A third front pertains to an incorporation of recent findings and theories of the "pure" sciences. The empirical data resulting from psychological investigations into learning behavior, for example, give insight into actual business decision making. It is through merging of the multiple pure sciences with the applied—as in medical schools—that progress will be most accelerated. Heuristic programming, for example, draws upon logic, learning theory, and certain aspects of managerial planning.

Yet the behavorial scientist has been charged with the criticism that he is more concerned with disorganization than with healthy organizational behavior. Given his predisposition for pure, versus applied, research and granting the fact that he takes human behavior and intrinsic latent characteristics of the organization as data, his total area of concern does include individual and organizational pathology; but such a focus does not necessarily reflect his values nor his major interest.

Although such criticisms may be valid in certain instances, the practitioner gains generally from the resulting information. Accepting traditional prescriptions, less organizational irrationality (greater purity of human inputs) brought about by, for example, more effective "indoctrination" could contribute to higher quality of performance. If, indeed, the values espoused by convention set the proper orientation, exposure of non-supportive predilections are prerequisite to preventative or remedial action; knowledge of such "impurity" enhances their treatment and correction.

Nothing is gained by not attending to the conflict between the traditionalist and the behavioralist. First, the conflict does exist and, second, behavioral research is a tangential outgrowth of traditional prescriptions. Easton, for example, in discussing· this dichotomy in political science, states that the traditionalist does assume that it is possible to discover certain uniformities of behavior, but that a "persistent and vocal minority . . . continues to argue that since hu-

22. Donald F. Clark and Russel L. Ackoff, *A Report on Some Organizational Experiments*, Case Institute of Technology, May 1959, p. 2.

23. Fritz J. Roethlisberger, "A 'New Look' for Management," *Worker Morale and Productivity* (General Management Series No. 141; New York: American Management Association, 1948), p. 13.

24. Moore, op. cit., p. 4.

25. F. F. Bradshaw, "Social Sciences—'Natural' or 'Unnatural'," *Advanced Management*, Vol. XXI, No. 5 (May, 1956), p. 4. An interesting point of view concerning the role of the behavioral scientist in business is offered by: Loren Baritz, *The Servants of Power: The Use of Social Science in Industry* (Middletown, Conn.: Wesleyan University Press, 1960). He suggests that the social scientist has become the hired hand of management, purveying the conventional dogma, and playing and instructing in the manipulative role made more insidious by his training and education.

man behavior is fundamentally indeterminate and since each situation is essentially unique, there is little real utility in expending enormous intellectual and material resources in pursuing a goal that is in principle unattainable." In contrast, he states that "for the behavioralist, the question of indeterminacy poses no insuperable barriers. Whether one asserts ineffable free will or some antiquated notion of absolute determinism, at most one is presenting a hypothesis to be tested in research."[26]

If generalizations are not forthcoming from behavioral research, the tested designs still can be used by the practitioner for diagnostic study. If the researcher does establish certain universals, they will offer differing vantage points for the model-builder. First, it may be established that organizational irrationality and conflict are not significant features of administration. If so, management behavior can be predicted upon the basis of institutional rationality. Second, if non-supportive behavior is pervasive and significant, these variables may be viewed as "impurities" in the human resource — either the unwillingness of subordinate management to identify or the inability of superordinates to gain identification with group goals. The disclosure and examination of these factors will enhance the development of sanction systems and organizational techniques for overcoming such imperfections. Third, if the view is that non-supportive predilections are not merely impurities — that they are real and desirable human needs which should be met by the organization — they should be identified and the effects of their fulfillment upon the economy should be investigated.

The orientation of the researcher and the breadth of the system under observation determine the character of the model and its presentation. Whether management is viewed as the behavior or role of an individual manager or as an operating and control system is a case in point. Certainly, the behavioralist has described administrative behavior more because of a desire to understand reality than because of an attempt to prescribe.[27] In fact, the writer of fictional essays on management often gives more insight into administrative reality than the work of many traditionalists.[28] Thus pedagogs, researchers, and practitioners must consider the nature and extent of the model which they employ.

MODELS OF THE PEDAGOG

The pedagog, especially, having a many-faceted obligation, must reflect upon the ends, substance,

and taxonomy employed in the model that he imparts. A model used to enhance elementary understanding of the subject may require a highly simplified framework and a rigorous classification of elements which is analogous to the classical economic model of perfect competition. Such models may not be designed to incorporate the reciprocating influences among the functions nor be dynamic in character. On the other hand, a quantitative model may be highly abstract but, if not just normative in nature, must facilitate the imposition of a measurement system. Furthermore, the major variables must be incorporated in such a way that their inter-relationships are reflected in the model.

The academician, also, has an obligation to consider his purpose through the needs and abilities of his students. He may teach management as a set of activities associated with a managerial role in a structured system, recognizing that this role varies according to the hierarchical level and the environment within which it is played. The differences that exist between the small group and the bureaucracy and between military and hospital organizations illustrate the necessity for differentiating among different structured systems. The contrast between activities associated with operative supervision and those relating to policy-making exemplify hierarchical distinctions.

If thought of as a supervisory role, primary attention can be given to such activities as delegation, reporting, and disciplinary action. In contrast, management can be viewed as a total hierarchical or intelligence and control system. The implication here is that a "system" of management, viewed holistically, is something more than the sum of the roles performed and cannot be described in terms of any particular role. This approach suggests the development of a comprehensive and integrated framework which typically finds its purpose in prediction and control. Here, attention is given not to the particularized activities of an effector or receptor but to the set of linkage systems that connect the role-players. The differences between rules-administration and disciplinary action depict the dichotomy implied. Management can also be viewed as a set of activities which any individual should consider as he attempts to control his own destiny, i.e., "manage his own affairs."

26. David Easton, "Traditional and Behavioral Research in American Political Science," *Administrative Science Quarterly*, Vol. 2, No. 1 (June, 1957), pp. 112–13.

27. See, for example, Melville Dalton, *Men Who Manage* (New York: John Wiley & Sons, 1959).

28. Cf. William Scott, *The Social Ethic in Management Literature*, Studies in Business and Economics Bulletin No. 4, Bureau of Business and Economic Research, Georgia State College of Business Administration, 1959.

The pedagogical approach then depends upon the place and purpose of "management" in the academic curriculum which, in turn, reflects the career aspirations and educational accomplishments of the student. The choice of approach is not a simple one because managerial attainments depend upon proficiency in a complex of skills.[29] Combination of any part of the following classification could provide the focus of a course in management. Although the classification is crude and proximate, the proficiencies relate to:

I. Technical and managerial activities dealing with:
   A. Functional areas: e.g., production or finance,
   B. Administrative requirements: e.g., delegation and training,
   C. Operational duties: e.g., public and governmental relations;
II. Human skills necessitated by behavior in the:
   A. Social environment: e.g., communication and counseling,
   B. Political climate: e.g., bargaining and strategic maneuvers,
   C. Economic system: e.g., rational and optimizing behavior;
III. Conceptual and cognitive proficiencies in:
   A. Perception and learning: including storage and innovation,
   B. Abstraction and insight: including reformulation and integration,
   C. Problem-solving: including analysis and decision-making.

The aspirations and vocational opportunities of the student will determine to a large extent the emphasis given to the level and the exhaustiveness with which the model is presented. Student aspirations and potential for policy-making would emphasize conceptual skills. Staff positions, on the other hand, require considerable attention to political behavior. The intellectual capabilities and educational maturity of the student will influence the degree of realism offered, for it appears that the greater the realism the more complexity and thus the higher the intellectual capacities required.[30]

LEVELS OF REALISM

Nonetheless, the pedagog has alternative models available to him. There appear, for example, to be at least four levels of realism offered currently. The first level is highly static in nature and, focusing upon the managerial role, assumes behavior to be organizationally rational. This view, largely prescriptive in nature, presents the subject of organizing as a set of highly formalized roles and relationships. From the underlying presuppositions, a system of rather unchanging but idealized authority relationships is drawn, wherein the informal or latent features of organizations are viewed, if considered at all, as phenomena attending the formal structure, but as very insignificant (and often undesirable) forces. At this level, then, both managers and operators are treated in a highly mechanistic fashion—as passive and completely adaptive agents of the system. Accordingly, the formal (legal) explanation of authority is given exclusive attention and little, if any, recognition given to the (psychological) acceptance concept of authority.

This description is not intended to decry abstraction, for an engagement in initial tutelage requires that complexity be reduced to a workable format. Furthermore, "Centuries of scientific experience should have taught us that remoteness of a theory from a particular content area is no indication of its relevance or irrelevance."[31] Without a doubt, the pedagog encounters considerable difficulty in explaining task-behavior structured to enhance specialization by means of a sociometric diagram. Abstraction, on the other hand, does not mean ignoring basic and ubiquitous variables of a system; and Pfiffner and Sherwood state that "the classic approach . . . will decline in significance. By 1960, . . . very little of the research of reputable scholars depended for its theoretical design on the traditional dogma. At the practicing and the teaching levels, however, the classic dicta were still strong. They still formed the basis for most applied management research and consulting. The most popular textbooks were firmly rooted in these approaches."[32]

The second level is also prescriptive in nature. Here again, managerial behavior is viewed as approximating very closely prescribed roles defined by formal positions. This approach, however, is more dynamic and detailed than the first level and might be termed the *avant-garde* of traditionalism. Dynamics, in terms of organizational growth, for example, is imputed to the model by encompassing the concept of functional differentiation. Although sanctioned largely upon expediency, limited informality of relationships is introduced by admitting to cross-functionalization. This level implies that the informal organi-

29. Cf. Robert L. Katz, "Skills of an Effective Administrator," *Harvard Business Review*, Vol. XXXIII, No. 1 (January-February, 1955), pp. 33–41.

30. See, for example, the chapter entitled "The Concept of Overlays" in John M. Pfiffner and Frank P. Sherwood, *Administrative Organization* (Englewood Cliffs: Prentice-Hall, Inc., 1960), pp. 16–23.

31. A. Rapoport, "Various Meanings of Theory," *American Political Scientist*, December, 1958, p. 30.

32. Pfiffner and Sherwood, *op. cit.*, p. 462.

zation is largely detrimental to enterprise success, but cannot be legislated out of existence.

Although not a major departure from the previous approach, the second level is somewhat more sophisticated but, nonetheless, is founded upon "classical" assumptions. In this respect, March and Simon offer the following limitations: (1) the motivational assumptions are incomplete and consequently inaccurate; (2) little appreciation is exhibited for intra-organizational conflict; and (3) the limitation of a human being as an information-processing center is given little attention.[33] As such considerations are incorporated in the model, greater realism is gained; but, the intellectual manageability of the model becomes more difficult. Managers are concerned, for example, with subordinates' allegiance to the organization. Yet the individual's commitment seldom coincides over the full range of his preference field because at least three variables are at play: (1) the constraints imposed by the employment contract and its enforcement; (2) the inducements offered for conformity; and (3) the direction and strength of the individual's self-image.[34] Incorporating such considerations in a model permits closer approximations to reality, but complexity is thereby increased.

The third level of realism conceives of a multiplicity of group and individual relationships in the organization. It implies that certain roles and relationships can be formalized and some channeled; but some can be manipulated (e.g., through spatial relocation) only to a minor extent. Leadership, for example, can be structured but not completely prescribed. The eventual success of an organization, according to this view, may well rest upon the direction and intensity of the informal phenomena at play in the system. These unchartered relationships and activities are viable features of any organization, including (1) decisions based upon the information and values of the informal group (e.g., through rumors transmitted by the "grapevine"); and (2) decision-making transferred informally to "unauthorized" individuals.

This level partakes of a holistic point of view and recognizes the sensitized nature of man with his incomplete and subjective perceptions. Recognition of the social sensitivity of man has cast attention to leadership as a social role. This holistic approach, moreover, enhances adherence to the structure-functional concept of the behavioral scientist. This concept reduces the reliance upon naive unilinear assumptions about behavior while admitting to unintended responses to any particular managerial technique. Suppose the formal organization is a normative abstraction, but the

exercise of formal authority can guarantee performance equal only to membership maintenance. If higher performance is necessary for successful operations, the disclosures revealed by the approach of the third level are significant to both understanding and practice.

The approach of the fourth level largely ignores the previous classification. Concern here is directed toward the general characteristics and influences of social affinities and goals. Attention is given to reference groups and field theory. It suggests that sub-groups, in order to maintain integrity, are likely to be in rivalry and competition with other sub-units of the same, as well as other, organizations. Penetrating analyses will show that a business firm can be viewed as a political system—the business firm is rife with political power-plays and propaganda.[35] The mere delegation of authority, for example, is a political phenomenon. Wherever allocation of scarce resources or issue conflicts exist in an organization, bargaining and strategy arise.

This level, on the other hand, is speculative and exploratory in nature. Propositions underlying traditional and conventional prescriptions are opened to examination. The supposed desirability of, and means used in establishing, a formal structure designed to perpetuate the organization beyond the life-span of the current members are reviewed. The assumptions dealing with and the methods for over-coming the "natural" chaos and disorganization inevitably involved in group effort are subjects of controversy. Beer, for example, contends that "Many people dimly realize that an existing system of human relationships . . . is to be regarded as self-organizing, as ordered already . . . (They, for example,) say about a new project: 'We must carry everyone with us.' By this they mean that they ought not to fight the system. (But) . . . when they say 'the system,' they almost certainly do not mean the naturally ordered (real) system . . . ; they mean the *official* system, the one constructed as an artificial order—out of the alleged 'chaos' which is in fact the *real* system . . . If these people were talking

---

33. March and Simon, *op. cit.*, p. 33.

34. If a range of discretion exists wherein private motives may be exercised without loss of membership rights, two aspects of the reward system may further reduce commitment: first, organizational inducements may not be representative of the individual's goals; or, second, his private rewards may not be maximized through greater individual effort. For further elaboration, see Daniel Katz and Robert L. Kahn, "Some Recent Findings in Human-Relations Research in Industry," in Guy D. Swanson, Theodore M. Newcomb, and Eugene L. Hartley (eds.), *Readings in Social Psychology* (New York: Henry Holt and Company, 1952), p. 658.

35. Cf. Robert A. Dahl, "Business and Politics: A Critical Appraisal of Political Science," in Dahl, Haire and Lazarsfeld (eds.), *Social Science Research on Business* (New York: Columbia University Press, 1959), pp. 3–44.

about the real system, they would say instead: Let us use the (natural) system to amplify this project into effect."[36]

A second contribution of this level reflects the maturity of the discipline, that the actual working of an organization is not clearly known. Therefore, since a servo-mechanism cannot be directly applied and completely trusted, some uncertainty attends managerial actions. Since absolute reliance upon a particular technique can create disorganization and failure, administrative practices should allow flexibility, exploration, and learning. Certainly, human behavior cannot be predicted from relatively few general principles, especially as they exist today.

If phenomena not included in the first and second levels are as pervasive and significant as evidence indicates and if the potential of the higher levels can be realized, neither the practitioner nor the teacher can ignore them. The entire spectrum of managerial behavior and interaction lies within the purview of the discipline. An unorthodox point of view may contribute to both social and organizational attainments. No longer can realism and broadening perspectives be discarded from the discipline because they are the province of the behavioral scientist or relate only to operative employees; and, significantly, kindred theoretical concepts and empirical findings are becoming increasingly available.[37] Without a doubt, effective teaching is intimately related to empirical research.

CONCLUSION

Two characteristics determine the nature of the administrative model employed: (1) the role that a set of values is to play and the purpose for which the model is presented and (2) the level of realism and degree of exhaustiveness with which the system is to be attacked. For example, long-run profits or clientele needs may (should) continue to be the predominant, if not single, criterion of business performance. Nonetheless, each of the survival ends of an organization requires definition and priorities assigned, especially if the hypothesis concerning the diverse relationships among them proves to be true. The distinction between morale and productivity, for example, is useful in arriving at evaluations concerning macro as well as micro problems. The social desirability of attempts to meet membership needs at the expense of an economic objective can be determined only if the dichotomy between the two criteria is perceived, which is impossible if admin-

istrative theory and research findings are deleted of actual managerial and organizational behavior. In this respect, Mee has said: "We should learn more about how people behave and why they behave as they do. We may now be working under false assumptions about human motivation and organizational behavior. There is needed more analysis of human motivations and the construction of models for the prediction of human behavior."[38]

Traditional management prescriptions appear particularly vulnerable to criticism from the standpoint of prediction. At least two major weaknesses are apparent. First, the traditionalist may have become so enamored with his preconceived scheme that unprejudiced observation and measurement are impeded. Second, published dogma may have imparted to the practitioner a "way of life" to which he feels he should conform and, whether or not he does, he rationalizes or conceals his actual behavior and aims. To such a degree, reality is not represented in the model and its predictive capacity is destroyed. To this extent, then, prescription becomes a set of moralistic bromides or clichés.

Certainly, an elaborated descriptive system of management must account for, and deal with the major dysfunctional or non-supportive behavior involved in group effort. The first step is to develop a system that permits their explanation and observation, and thus assess their importance. Until real administrative behavior and its environment are understood, new propositions cannot be adequately integrated nor can the model be related to a larger conceptual system. Nonetheless, increased realism imposes greater difficulties for the academician in his attempt to communicate to the uninitiated. In addition, change will come slowly, because the pedagog, who forms the bridge between practice and research, "is caught by two opposing demands. One is to prepare young people for their roles in the future. The other is to help them operate effectively here and now. . . . We cannot easily cast aside our classic categories until we have a new theory which satisfies at least three criteria: (1) is easily communicated and therefore is amenable to considerable over-simplification without disastrous distortion; (2) has greater proven validity

36. Stafford Beer, "Below the Twilight Arch," *General Systems*, Ludwig Von Bertalanffy and Anatol Rapoport (eds.), Society for General Systems Research, Vol. V, 1960, p. 13.

37. See, for example, Albert H. Rubenstein and Chadwick J. Haberstroh, *Some Theories of Organization* (Homewood, Illinois: Richard D. Irwin, 1960).

38. John F. Mee, discussant, "Issues for the Future," Industrial Relations Research Association annual meetings, December 28, 1960.

than the categories we now utilize; and (3) perhaps most importantly, gains relatively universal acceptance. . . . Despite all these handicaps, it seems inevitable that there can be only one direction of change—toward the researcher."[39]

Given this direction, the empirical findings can offer a better balanced and more complete view of man, including the anthropological, political, and sociological aspects of his behavior. This enlarged framework should increase the practitioner's ability in sizing-up the general nature and specifics of a problem-area or offer insight into the general configuration of the problem not previously held. The researcher can provide differing sets of research techniques and tools. Each behavioral area can lay claim to different research methodologies which enable the manager to increase his proficiency in collecting information. Of major importance here would be the discovery

of relationships, especially causalities, not readily observable. Empiricism should result in aids to the development of certain skills in dealing with individuals and groups. Since the manager's behavior ultimately determines the satisfactions and performance of his subordinates, his social and political posture is vital to organizational success and morale. To the extent that the behavioral sciences provide guides to effective management action, organizational accomplishment can be enhanced. As Argyris has said, once understanding is gained, "it is an easy matter to *predict* and *control* behavior. Prediction and control of behavior are the fruits of understanding. . . ."[40] But, and prescriptively stated, the discipline needs the understanding that controlled research can offer. This contribution, however, is bounded by the encouragement given to the researcher and the hypotheses built into his investigations.

49—Business Games for Executive Training

BARRY T. JENSEN

In recent years, considerable time and money have been spent in the development and the subsequent use of games designed to simulate business situations for executive training or development purposes. Some of these games, such as the ones that use computers, are complex; others are more simple.

Occasionally someone asks about the usefulness of the games, but few evaluations result. In this article, I shall contend that while simulation can be used effectively as a training aid, the simple games and devices do have some advantages when compared with the complex ones.

Simulation is an ancient way of providing training. More recently, the army has employed simulated fire and simulated tanks to exercise troops. In a way, target practice is a form of simulation, as was the jousting of knights in days of yore. In a broad sense, simulation refers to the representation of a situation to permit trainees to act in an environment in which they might sometime find themselves. Teachers hope this experience will enable the students to take appropriate actions when faced with similar situations on the job.

For transfer of training to occur through simulation, actual duplication of a situation is unnecessary. However, the more the simulated situation resembles the real one, the greater the transfer of training is likely to be. If the learners see the close similarity between the real and the simulated situation, the trainer can utilize settings that are objectively quite different, yet call upon the participants to take the same action they should take in a real case. In management development, for example, this action might be one of assigning responsibilities to subordinates—or what might be called functional representation.

As an aid in training, simulation has great potential. For one thing, this method permits alteration of the environment and, thus, eliminates the need for dependence upon random events. Time elements may be altered and, at the trainer's discretion, many variables can be used as input.

The great advantage of the games that use computers lies in the complexity of the environment with which the machines can deal. In a typical computer game, for example, the participants are divided into groups constituting the managements of several companies that sell similar products, each group representing a different company. Periods of about 15 minutes are allotted for

39. Pfiffner and Sherwood, *op. cit.*, pp. 462–63.
40. Argyris, *op. cit.*, p. 5.

"Business Games for Executive Training," *Advanced Management—Office Executive*, II (June 1963), 13–14, 16, 18. Reprinted by permission of the author and the publisher. *Barry T. Jensen*: Head of Management Training, System Development Corporation, Santa Monica, California.

the groups to make decisions on matters such as investing capital; hiring, training, and transferring personnel; determining prices of goods and advertising policies; and establishing inventory control.

INTERACTION OF DECISIONS

In these situations, a computer can provide information on the interaction of the decisions made, not only for one company but also among the several companies. The machine makes the calculations in a fraction of the time that humans can, thus permitting knowledge of results almost immediately.

As with all simulation devices, the "adequacy of the world" represented by the computer program affects the direct transfer of skill from the game to the real world. As with all simulation, discrepancies become of little importance (1) *if* the purpose of the game is to illustrate principles and approaches to general problems rather than to teach specific skills and (2) *if* the situation has been presented in such a way the participants accept the functional representation. (Verisimilitude is not necessary if the simulation has not been advertised as duplication.)

Whether the game uses a computer or not, is not the significant factor to consider. At System Development Co. (SDC), for example, we use a game called Staff Training Exercise for Programming Supervisors (STEPS), which comes in both programmed and manual forms.[1] Of more importance than the computer aspect is the question of what the game can illustrate and what the participant can learn. For many purposes, a simple noncomputer game serves well, and it is easy to conduct.

Consider, for instance, a noncomputer game called the block game. The origin of this game is unknown, but we use it regularly in our management training program at SDC.

TRAINEES TO BUILD IDENTICAL OBJECT

In our version of this game, we show several trainees an object made of Lok-A-Blocks.[2] The object roughly represents a bridge or a bird. We tell the trainees that they are to build an identical object as rapidly as possible; that each will be given some blocks, but that they must not exchange blocks before the signal to go is received; and that they may have all the time they wish for

planning. Whenever the team says it is ready to build, a count down starts and, at the signal to begin, time is in.

Ordinarily, the planning period runs about 45 minutes; the construction of the object takes less than a minute. The critique of performance takes from two to four hours (other trainees serve as observers).

The critique may deal with diverse matters such as how the group allocated responsibilities, planned for redistribution of materials, assessed resources before planning construction, planned for contingencies, analyzed individual capabilities, and developed a work plan, and also matters such as social behavior, individual feelings, and management principles illustrated by the activity.

After the class starts suggesting how the work might have been improved, another group is formed from among the observers, and this group begins construction of a different model, with critique. Variations of the game include ways in which the teams are chosen (for example, one person is named project manager, and he chooses his own staff) and changes in personnel or instructions during the course of the exercise.

GAME UTILIZES AN IN-BASKET

Another game we play utilizes an in-basket. We give each participant a package of memos, notes of phone calls, and letters, with the instruction that he is to assume he has just taken over a new job or that he has returned to his office and has looked at the materials in his mail tray.

Sometimes we have each participant write out his responses, and sometimes we have him demonstrate by interacting with others in roles of the persons represented by the items in the in-basket. Action on each item becomes the focal point of considerable discussion, in which the leaders try to identify contrasting views and to generate critical examination of the responses.

These two games—the block and the in-basket—are similar in that both serve as stimuli for encouraging additional participation in learning activities. If, then, in addition to receiving this encouragement, a participant learns something about conducting his affairs by playing the game, he has received a bonus. In neither case is the game alleged to represent the job the participant

---

1. R. Boguslaw, H. Richmond, and W. Pelton, STEPS—*Staff Training Exercise for Programming Supervisors, Model I.* TM-321. (Santa Monica, California: System Development Corp.; 1959).
2. Trade Name.

really has or one he might expect to have. But the game does present a situation requiring the same kind of thinking and planning that might take place on the job.

When evaluated in terms of their function as stimuli, both games are highly successful. That they fulfill our requirements is evident in the lengthy and often heated discussion which follows the play; in the extensiveness of topics or problems which the participants see illustrated; and in the fact that in subsequent weeks the participants refer back to the block or in-basket experience when trying to illustrate a point.

In addition, we find that the child's play of assembling blocks is particularly good for reducing barriers that prevent communication and, therefore, good for starting off a new class.

When using games as stimuli to further learning activities, we find that the simple games have several advantages over the more complex ones which use computers. First, the simple games are relatively inexpensive, for they require no computer time. However, this advantage is reduced as one gets into those activities which simulate business activities, such as the work of a management committee. To provide feedback in these activities within a reasonable time, more and more persons must be added to the simulation crew as the game increases in complexity.

Second, simple games are easy to modify; the rules can be changed during the course of a play. Although Kibbee, Craft, and Nanus[3] point out that computer games are more easily modified than many persons believe, the fact remains that simple games can be changed with a minimum of preplanning, or none, for that matter.

THE GAME CAN BE MODIFIED

The two advantages previously mentioned make possible the major advantage of the simple game —that is, the game can be modified to respond to the topic of the moment or to teach, test, or emphasize some characteristic of the action taken by the playing team.

We cannot say, however, that computer games are better than noncomputer games or vice versa. We can only point to the advantages of each and admonish the user to consider the purpose of his simulation activity before selecting a game. To be noted, too, is that the conditions associated with a play of a game are not necessarily effects of either computer or noncomputer games.

For example, when Steinmetz[4] surveyed 303 executives who had participated in games, he found that the computer game group, as compared with the noncomputer game group, reported less orientation before the game, less individual critique, and less ability to apply the principles learned. He states that the computer games tended to be more concerned with top management problems, while the players were members of middle management.

Orientation and individual critique are more likely to be characteristic of specific training situations and of the trainers than of the game itself, although with the beautiful printouts from the computer, one could easily fall into the habit of utilizing automated analysis and report instead of dealing with individual problems.

Since the effectiveness of simulation as a teaching aid depends on how the game is planned and organized, here are a few sound principles to keep in mind.

1. *Make certain the game and the instructions are appropriate.* The less information given in advance, the more time the players must spend in learning the system. Conceivably, the participants might spend so much time in learning how to play the game and learning the relationship between what they do and the way in which the environment responds, they do not learn what was intended to be learned. And, if no structure is given to the relationships among individuals in the group, the participants have an organization task to perform.

What the participants learn will depend, too, upon the problems presented to them by the game. For some purposes (such as illustrating how much we take for granted or the need to learn about the environment) instructions may be minimal. If the aim is to teach management principles, the game should be such that attention is directed to these principles. In this case, the players may have to be told in advance what they are supposed to learn.

2. *Do not try to duplicate real life.* This admonition may seem unnecessary, but we have seen training settings sold as a duplication, only to find the trainees concentrating on the discrepancies and almost rejecting the program because of the lack of face validity.

In any simulation situation, we should omit facets of the real world. That is, the game is not "for real." As mentioned earlier, reality is unnecessary as long as the situation is advertised as representative or as intended to illustrate the kind of

3. J. M. Kibbee, C. J. Craft, and B. Nanus, *Management Games* (New York; Reinhold Publishing Corp.; 1961).

4. L. L. Steinmetz, "Management Games — Computer Versus Non-Computer," *J. Amer. Soc. Training Directors* (Sept. 1962), pp. 16, 38–45.

problem that might arise. When using the block game, for example, we have had no participants who said the simple tasks failed to illustrate management problems and have never had any one reject the activity, simple as it was.

3. *Involve the trainers in the game by making them observers and reporters.* Automatic techniques of feedback may be of great help in analyzing and reducing data for immediate feedback. But no system yet devised has been able to replace a sensitive observer in detecting the nuances of actions or in inferring the motivations of individuals.

An important area of potential learning concerns interpersonal relationships as well as individual problem-solving techniques, and we doubt that counting responses of each person in the group gives half the data that good observers can marshal. Therefore, we believe the training staff should be active as observers and as sources of critique rather than as merely administrators who set the game in motion.

4. *Provide for "reinforcing value."* The game should be intrinsically interesting; it should present a challenge to the players, in that it has problems which can be solved during the play; and it should be "rational." A good game has internal consistency (for example, railroad cars do not fly, and in a railroad game, travel time must be relative). If the rules do not apply to similar situations or if other aspects of the game change without the players' knowledge, the game will appear to be irrational and become unattractive.

The procedures provided in the game should enable the participants to obtain information about the effects of their actions fairly soon after the actions take place or certainly before the participants have to deal with the same kind of situation again. Steinmetz, in the article cited earlier, reported that 83 per cent of those involved in a computer game wanted to participate again and that more than 50 per cent of them gave as their reasons the belief they could do better the next

time and the feeling that the game was fun and was entertaining. These statements suggest that the game had reinforcing value.

5. *Provide for feedback and discussion.* The game itself is not as important as what is done with it. Discussion outside the decision-making period, when the pressure is off, permits the trainees to look at their problems differently or to plan what can be done the next time. The discussion may become more profitable if the team receives information about its performance, because the participant tends to learn those principles and to solve those problems which he perceives.

An observer can see much in action and can, by his reports, make the problems visible to the trainees. We call this information "feedback." The observer need not report after each game on every aspect of behavior, for feedback should be appropriate to the level of development of the team. Inexperienced players, for example, might become aware of so many things during the first exercise or play that comments from the observer at that time might interfere with their learning to work better.

In some games the feedback consists of computer printouts showing the simulated company profit picture in more or less detail, and the crew immediately begins to make decisions on expenses for the next period. In such instances, the team may never be effective because it might not organize well or might not understand some of the group rules. In other words, before the decisions must be in, the team may need time to discuss its behavior. Feedback from the observers might help the participants in getting started on the organizational problem posed.

We regard management games as a means of providing stimuli for additional participation in learning activities. For this purpose, simple games can serve well, *if* they are part of a package which adequately provides for orientation, feedback, and discussion.

50 — The Management Side of PERT

IVARS AVOTS

No management technique has ever caused so much enthusiasm, controversy, and disappointment as PERT. Within the past two years PERT or, to use its full name, Program Evaluation and Review Technique, developed originally for the United States Navy as part of the Polaris program as a mathematical method for defining the minimum time for completion of a complex project, has moved from the realm of production theory to the solid status of becoming a contract requirement in the nation's major defense programs.

It has also entered the business world where it is referred to not only as PERT but sometimes as "network analysis" and "critical path planning," depending upon the industry in which it is employed. Specific aspects of the PERT theory have become items of controversy and concern in management circles. In addition, hundreds of thousands of dollars have been spent only to find in some cases that a given approach to PERT was not feasible within the context in which its use was planned.

What are the reasons which have caused PERT to make an impact unlike that of any other management technique? What has management learned about the application and limitations of this technique? What can be expected of PERT in the future? These are some of the questions managers need answered if they are to avoid the cost of experimentation. This article attempts to provide these answers with particular attention to problems of implementation on large programs.

PERT burst upon the management horizon in 1958 when it became part of the Polaris program. It was developed by the firm of management consultants, Booz, Allen & Hamilton for the Navy in order to coordinate the thousands of activities and individual processes required to bring to completion the complex project of creating a missile which could be fired under water.

The Air Force also adopted this technique. Its initial name for its program was PEP (Program Evaluation Procedure). Now it uses the same terminology as the Navy for its program evaluation technique. In the construction industry this method of networking time and procedures is called the Critical Path Method.

Despite the dissimilarity in nomenclature, all perform essentially the same logistical function of getting each of the components of a complex procedure completed at the precise time and delivered to the exact proper place to be smoothly integrated into the final fabrication and launching of the product. The obvious advantages of such a technique, its streamlining of production, its essential tidiness and economy, its promise of optimum use at all times of men and material have made it a "natural" for business use wherever and whenever practicable. It is these very factors which have contributed to management's enthusiasm for PERT and also provided background for some of its controversies.

Foremost among them is the change in basic management philosophy which characterizes PERT against other management techniques. While it is true that considerable attention has been given in their day to bar charts, improvement curves, and other techniques, all of these were deterministic in nature. Planning resulted in a static system against which status was measured.

Introduction of PERT suddenly brought a change in traditional management thinking. The new technique did not look forward to meeting a schedule, but accepted uncertainty as part of the system. The effects of this change can be identified both in the enthusiasm for the technique as well as in resistance to it. Both conditions are often observed side by side even within the same organization.

THE SELLING POINTS OF PERT

Writers in technical publications have cited a complete line of selling points for the PERT technique. High on the list is the system's ability to predict the impact of schedule status. While other systems record status at a given time and require separate analysis to determine its effect on program objectives, PERT readily provides this information.

Moreover, PERT is primarily an analytical planning rather than a control method, and therefore does not suffer from the stigma associated with some management control techniques. In fact, as much as sixty percent of the benefits of PERT have been ascribed to its planning function rather than to its use as a control media.

This is because PERT forces integration of planning and thereby shows significant benefits even before it is used as a control tool. In the control area, PERT format cuts across organiza-

"The Management Side of PERT," *California Management Review*, IV (Winter 1962), 16–27. Reprinted by permission of the author and the publisher. Copyright 1962 by the Regents of the University of California. Ivars Avots: Operations Planning Staff, Boeing Company, Santa Monica, California; now with Arthur D. Little, Inc., Cambridge, Massachusetts.

tional lines, eliminating the effect of defensive interpretation of reports along the lines of responsibility. At the same time, however, activities selected for the network usually recognize changes in responsibility and form the basis for positive control.

PREDICTIVE QUALITY

As a background for our discussion of PERT limitations, let us take a closer look at each of these selling points. Four features of the PERT technique give it the unique predictive quality which is not shared by other management control techniques. They are

▶ Critical path analysis
▶ Program status evaluation
▶ Slack determination
▶ Simulation

A typical PERT network is shown in Exhibit 1. The critical path is the longest series of activities which must be performed from the beginning to the end of the network. Obviously, there can be more than one critical path for a program, and, depending on the completion status of individual activities, the critical path may change.

The Critical Path. The advantage of the critcal path is not only the fact that it permits determination of the effects of any schedule delays on program completion, but it also brings into use the exception principle focusing management attention to those areas where schedule maintenance is critical. When problems arise, critical

EXHIBIT I TYPICAL PERT NETWORK*

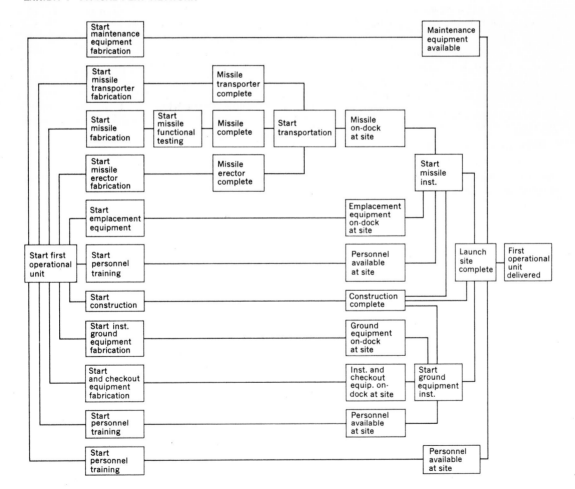

* The PERT network consists of a series of interrelated symbols representing principal events and activities in a program. An event is shown by a box and an activity is indicated by a line or arrow connecting events. When time estimates are assigned to activities, it is possible to compute the critical path of the program, as well as identify activities which have slack time. These may be extended without affecting program schedules.

path analysis highlights the areas where action must be taken to maintain over-all program schedule.

As work progresses and status information is obtained, the PERT technique shows the time required to reach any event in the network. Together with the critical path analysis, this feature permits rapid evaluation of program status. Considering the fact that the status information can be integrated from a large number of sources and cover various levels of program effort, benefits to management can be quite significant.

Time Trade-off. Time estimates are assigned to the activities in a PERT network on the basis of normal manpower assignment and resource allocation. When compared to the concurrent critical path, some activities require less time and therefore possess a certain amount of slack. Listing of activities having slack identifies the area of effort where trade-off in time, resources, or technical performance may improve the schedule along the critical path.

At any time during the program, the effect proposed schedule changes can be easily simulated by the computer. This feature permits management to examine detail activities, especially those critical to the program, for possible adjustments resulting in schedule or cost improvement.

Analytical Planning Method. Observers have rightfully noted that for maximum benefits PERT application must start during or before the planning phase of a new program. The major reason for this is the fact that networking forces integration of planning and helps to discover innumerable conditions which, in a complex program, may easily be overlooked.

Traditional program planners are usually skeptical about any benefits the PERT technique may give them, and quite often there is open antagonism on their part to use of the technique. They maintain that phasing charts and master schedules have been refined to a point where they can sufficiently cover the programming of complex efforts.

However, in some cases where PERT has been applied to a going program, the planning incompatibilities which have been detected have staggered even the proponents of the technique. As a result of networking, one defense manufacturer found that the existing plan called for placing of two missiles on the same launcher on the same day.

PERT has pointed out beyond any doubt the serious weaknesses of traditional scheduling methods when applied to a program such as major missile development, manufacture, and test.

In a PERT network, where each event must be preceded and followed by another event, complex relationships and interdependencies can be identified. It is the discipline of planning logic required to develop a network which forces a planner to take a new look at his task, and in the process, opens to him significant new horizons.

Positive Control. In its entirety, a PERT network normally covers a program from its inception to at least the completion of the first article. Unlike schedules which tend to be related to organizational responsibilities, the network cuts across organizational lines. One week, the design group may be in the line of critical path, another week the line may have shifted, and the test group may be pacing the schedule. Whatever the case, management can readily identify the problem areas and initiate corrective action.

Although the network approach puts emphasis on the total program rather than particular elements, it should be remembered that if the network is sufficiently detailed, each of these elements, described by events and activities, can often be related to a functional organization or even a budget number.

Networking. To permit this, events selected for a network must include those events which represent a change in responsibility for activities within the network. In other words, each activity needs to be identified with a particular organization. By comparison of actuals with activity estimates, the performance of each group can be evaluated, and causes for schedule difficulties can be pinpointed to responsible organizations.

Another contribution and selling point which cannot be overlooked results from the fact that networking requires adoption of positive and unambiguous definitions of all events and activities. Getting everybody in a large organization to talk the same language can be a difficult task, and if this can be accomplished as a side effect of PERT networking, it certainly deserves consideration.

Early in the development of PERT, statisticians recognized that although the technique was superior to existing flow and bar charting techniques for program planning and control, it had basic mathematical weaknesses. They also recognized that because of these weaknesses, careful decisions would have to be made as to the scope and method of application of the technique.

This recognition is well illustrated by the present PERT applications in the Boeing Company. Dictated by specific program characteristics and customer requirements, the applications on Minuteman, Dyna-Soar, and Bomarc programs are basically different in their approach and coverage, highlight different problems of application, and also show different degrees of success.

LIMITATIONS OF PERT TECHNIQUE

Some of the limitations of PERT application are very rudimentary. For example, because of its "time to completion" variable, PERT cannot be used when it is not possible to estimate the occurrence of events. This is true of any project in which there is a reasonable expectancy that a break-through in the state-of-the-art may change the sequence of events at any given stage of development. Alternate routes or paths are therefore required, both of which need to be followed to a point of no return.

Similarly, PERT cannot be used on activities which are under a recurring cycle, such as in manufacturing. PERT networks usually stop with the completion of the first production article, at which point the traditional scheduling techniques or the line-of-balance method takes effect. This range of applicability is very real, and should be kept in mind throughout development of a PERT program.

MILITARY PROJECT EXPERIENCE

From the standpoint of limitations, it is of particular interest that PERT has never been implemented on a total weapon system. For example, on the Polaris program, certain portions were networked and reported on, but the Navy concedes that at no time did a total Fleet Ballistic Missile System network exist. The reasons for this are several:

1. Accuracy of the Model. The network model does not yield itself to the incorporation of computer checks, and there is no known method for verification of the logic of a network. For this reason, accuracy of the network depends on the process of preparing it. In practice, network development involves cycling through computer runs, progressive evaluation, and detection of possible inaccuracies, followed by revisions.

2. Data Handling. When network size exceeds approximately 5,000 events, it becomes difficult to maintain the purity of computer input and quick system response. A large number of events means that a large number of people are involved in the processing of network data. Consequently, the exposure to error becomes greater. Time required for the PERT cycle also increases.

3. Computing Large Networks. Experience shows that it is almost impossible to manually calculate networks larger than 700 events. Therefore, larger networks, such as those for a major weapon system, require a computer. The number of events which can be economically handled by the computer depends on the amount of data which the computer can process in high-speed memory without extensive use of magnetic tapes. For example, the IBM 7090 computer has a storage capacity of 32,000 words. This capacity provides for approximately 10,000 activities or events. When networks exceed this size, it is necessary to utilize magnetic tape storage. Use of magnetic tape considerably increases the required number of computer passes and the associated cost.

4. Summarization and Integration. Large networks are awkward to handle. There is no known method for summarization or reducing the size of a network to a smaller equivalent net. Also, it is difficult to automatically assemble separate networks into a master network and compute it. This can be accomplished only through a special computer program and extensive cross-referencing.

5. Reporting. As the size of networks increases, the technique of translating computer outputs into management information becomes more difficult. Theoretically, network outputs identify problem areas as well as indicate where trade-offs in resources may be desired. While this information can be visualized when networks are small, reporting techniques have not been developed to the extent that similar use can be made of large networks. This factor limits PERT as a management tool on major programs.

PERT AS A MANAGEMENT PROBLEM

The nature and the far-reaching effects of the limitations of the PERT technique are such that the total problem cannot be left to the program planner or to an operations research man. Any large scale implementation of the technique has to follow careful analysis and soul searching and demands careful attention from top management.

Even when a company is required to adopt PERT by the military customer, it is necessary to keep an objective viewpoint. For example, a degree of enthusiasm would help to accelerate the application of network analysis to routine projects, such as installation of a piece of machinery, design of a generator, or construction of a building. However, it would be foolish to use the same approach to a major weapon system. When exercised apart from experience and existing knowledge of limitations, enthusiasm may cause unsound PERT applications which result in unnecessary cost, adverse psychological effect, and possible delay in the implementation of a workable PERT system.

Must Ride Herd on It. The limitations also make it obvious that active adaptation of PERT in any company will cause a considerable amount of developmental research in the technique and may result in the support of particular approaches by various parts of the organization. For this reason, especially if the company is large, PERT is not a technique which, like most management techniques, can be turned over to the departments for implementation. It requires continuous top management attention and guidance during the implementation period.

If this is not done, time and effort are lost when several departments attempt to solve similar problems, and the situation is even more serious when, upon implementation, it is discovered that the system will not work in total or includes portions which are incongruous with the over-all system. Top management attention is also important if the use of PERT techniques is required by a military customer or a major military prime contractor. In this case, definitive policy is required regarding the level of detail which will be effectively reported under the system.

Top management involvement in PERT is not restricted to over-all guidance and policy formulation. Whenever more than one PERT application takes place in a company, certain technical problems immediately become apparent which need over-all coordination. For example, the events in a PERT network can be numbered serially, sequentially, or at random. Computer programs are in existence to handle a network of each type. However, once a particular computer program is adapted by a company, it becomes impractical to introduce variations for each internal application. It should be easy to issue a company policy prescribing the use of a particular numbering system; however, such action would not solve the technical problem.

Major PERT networks may be tied into similar networks at other companies and selected data submitted in card form to military services which have their own PERT staffs. Unless the numbering systems are compatible, application of the technique will result in large workload and undue increase in cost. Unless top management is ready to assist subordinates and outside organizations to come to mutually acceptable terms, there will be disagreement, wasted effort, and an unfavorable impression on involved parties outside the company. Typical of the PERT technical problems, on which management attention will continue to be centered, are matters of system networking, scheduling, and reporting to management. Here are some of the facts concerning each of these problems.

SYSTEM NETWORKING

The usual approach to PERT on a major program starts with an overall master network. However, some people feel that this network may never be computed, and would serve primarily as a map for the selection of critical functional or subsystem areas in which detail networks would be developed. The critical path would be computed from the detail networks after practically all elements of the program have been covered. The master network would be adjusted as more definitive information becomes available in the detail networking process.

Another approach, sponsored mainly by the Boeing Company, takes the viewpoint that critical program areas cannot always be determined from a broad master network without actually computing a critical path. If functional areas are selected and networked in detail, interfaces between such functional networks are not readily apparent and integration of such networks may be extremely difficult. Even if integration is accomplished, such networks may not yield correct results and yet, because of the inability to check the network's logic, the computations have to be taken at face value.

An alternative approach recommended by the proponents of this viewpoint is to expand the master network in subsystem areas only and to use the master network for all computations. While such network would not have detail coverage in specific critical areas, it is believed to give a more dependable picture of the overall program.

Although PERT was developed basically as a planning and control tool, attempts have also been made to use it as a scheduling technique. Theoretically, PERT networks are a convenient base for preparation of bar charts and detail schedules. Networking should precede any bar charting of the program from the top down and may, in fact, eliminate the need for most bar charts and master schedules. When networks are established at proper detail, they can be used for end-to-end scheduling.

PERT AS SCHEDULING TECHNIQUE

While this theoretical approach is feasible on relatively simple programs, it breaks down when the complexity of the program is large, as in the case of major missile efforts. To utilize PERT as a scheduling tool on a complex program would require networking of hundreds of thousands of activities. Even at our advanced stage in computer technology, it is not practical to handle such vast networks. As the pressures arise to include more and more detail into the networking effort, management must recognize the limitations of the technique and draw a line.

A definition as to what PERT application should accomplish must be made and the level of detail to which the technique should be extended must be outlined. The Boeing Company, which unsuccessfully tried the scheduling approach on its Dyna-Soar program, has come to the conclusion that in the present state of development, PERT techniques cannot be used for detailed scheduling of large programs, and their application to such programs should be limited to planning and control purposes.

REPORTING TO MANAGEMENT

The principal objective of PERT reports is to call management attention to situations requiring decisions and action. In small, manually computed networks, status information can be reflected on a bar chart or some other easily visualized form. When larger programs are covered, the reporting output necessarily is in machine print-out form which does not have the visibility required for analysis.

The situation is almost paradoxical since large programs which demand quick action by top managers, necessarily generate a greater amount of reporting paper. Since there is no method to summarize networks automatically, the process of extracting data, analyzing, and then displaying these data requires progressive evaluation and permits some defensive interpretation along the way.

THE BIG PICTURE

In approaching any of these problems, management must avoid focusing on a small number of exceptions and give all its attention to the workability of the total program. It should always be kept in mind that one of those features which makes PERT excel over other techniques is the fact that it cuts across organization lines and looks at the total program. Detail logic and accuracy may have to be overlooked in order to arrive at a workable PERT program. The network should not be expected to be perfect in every detail to make it complete. As a mathematical model, the network should be sufficiently true to reality to yield practical solutions through exercise of its predictive quality.

COST OF PERT

Extensive application of PERT techniques obviously is expensive. Skilled technical personnel are required to plan networks, and engineering and operating men must take time to explain activities to planners and to make time estimates. Data processing and computer costs are impressive, to say the least.

The Special Projects Office of the Navy estimated it cost them $200,000 a year in computer time to conduct biweekly analyses of the Polaris program. While one contractor has priced its contractual PERT requirements at $300,000, other firms feel that PERT can replace a portion of the traditional planning tasks and that very little additional cost is involved.

This, of course, depends on the complexity of the program and the level of detail which may be handled within the limitations discussed earlier. The Air Force has estimated that PERT costs average 0.5 per cent of total cost on research and development programs and 0.1 per cent of major programs generally.

LESS COSTLY THAN COFFEE BREAKS

In one instance, the Air Force found that engineering time consumed in contractor's PERT activity was less than a fourth of the time authorized for coffee breaks. This does not sound like much; however, just ten minutes per engineer per day amounts to over $300,000 a year when applied to one of the major missile programs.

To date, insufficient consideration has been given to the costs of large scale PERT applications. There is no doubt that only small applications can claim to offset these costs with savings in planning and scheduling. It is also true that on some programs, especially in construction, critical path planning can yield immediate tangible savings. For example, the Catalytic Construction Company credits network planning with a 25 percent reduction in cost on an $800,000 project. In most applications of PERT, however, the dollar savings are not quite so tangible. Costs, nevertheless, are real and should be considered in determining an optimum level of application for PERT.

OUTLOOK FOR PERT

During the first two years of PERT, discussions on the subject were limited to technical journals and companies where the technique was being applied. Early in 1961, the technique suddenly emerged as a major selling point of several management consultants. Courses on the subject were announced. American Management Association organized a briefing seminar, and the Aerospace Industries Association formed a PERT task group.

The Department of Defense initiated efforts to achieve some standardization in PERT requirements of the military services. All these activities affected the growth of the technique, shaking out some of the marginal features, such as three time estimates and computation of variance, and advancing the extension of PERT to resource factors.

RESOURCE INCORPORATION

Incorporation of resource factors, especially cost and manpower, is currently the immediate problem in PERT development. From a theoretical standpoint, resource incorporation is not a serious problem. However, the issue becomes clouded when the methods of data collection and assignment to activities come under consideration.

To begin with, introduction of resource factors will further limit computer capacity and the number of events which can be economically processed. Resource application, therefore, will be more easily accomplished on some programs than on others. For example, programs differ in the desired level of detail in cost estimating and collection. If the networks were to be maintained at a gross level, the major problem in cost incorporation may well be that of identifying existing accounts with activities in the network, rather than assigning new account numbers to activities.

Until the problems of planning and control nature are successfully solved in PERT applications to large programs, the incorporation of costs, manpower, reliability, etc., cannot take place. These factors should be incorporated only on smaller networks where PERT technology has been sufficiently developed.

GENERAL SYSTEMS THEORY NEEDED

From a long-range standpoint, the potential of PERT extends even beyond resource incorporation. In the past few years, both industry and government have recognized a growing need for a general systems theory which would consolidate the existing scientific management methods and thereby extend the field of management sciences. Russell D. Archibald of Hughes Aircraft Co. has pointed out that PERT may be an important step toward the development of such a theory, at least in the area of project-type programs. When all business is viewed as a system of interrelated and integrated systems and subsystems, PERT networking technique can serve as one of the necessary catalytic agents.

PERT'S WEAKNESSES

The PERT technique is a logical refinement of planning and control techniques. Its theory is deceivingly simple, and the potential appears unlimited. Experience, however, has shown definite limitations of the technique, particularly in regard to application on large programs. Because of the initial success on military contract applications and the enthusiasm over the technique by the military services, PERT has permeated industry at an accelerated rate. As a result, application of the technique has in some cases resulted in disappointment. This has been a reflection of overenthusiasm, lack of sufficient experience, and the basic weaknesses in the technique when applied to large programs.

PERT'S STRENGTHS

Generally, PERT is a superior system for (a) integration of planning, (b) rapid evaluation of program status, (c) identification of potential trouble spots, and (d) reallocation of resources. In its application to large programs, it is one of the first computer techniques in the management field which not only processes data, but actually helps to make decisions. On small programs, it becomes a highly flexible management tool which does not require computer support.

ITS FUTURE IN MANAGEMENT

Until such time when PERT becomes as common as the bar chart, top management attention is required to coordinate those aspects of PERT which have management and broad technical implications. Experience gained in other companies must be translated in relation to the requirements of each new application, keeping in mind the limitations of applicability, size and accuracy of networks, technical approaches, and cost.

As the technique matures and further experimentation takes place, PERT can be expected to include elements of manpower distribution and cost. The resulting tie-in with operating budgets may bring management a decade closer to the overall control system which it has been seeking.

51 — Automation — Perceiving the Magnitude of the Problem

JOHN DIEBOLD

We have yet to perceive the magnitude and the true nature of the momentous change automation is effecting in our lives, in our businesses and in our society.

The potential and the problem are both far greater and *quite different* than yet perceived. The problem is grave and requires far more *private* as well as public, action than has yet been proposed.

The speed of this technological change is so great that we must today do far more than even yet proposed to ascertain:

1. The true nature of the future that is cast for us by today's innovations;

2. The true magnitude and character of the problems posed for mankind by automation; and

3. The alternatives open to us to cope adequately with the changes automation is making in our world.

Automation is perceived only as a manpower problem — involving changes in labor requirements; changes in skill as jobs change; retraining and worker mobility. Managers and workers who have experienced automation in practice know that it is more than this — that it is more often than not introduced to make possible wholly new ways of performing a task, whether that task be controlling a business, a government agency or passenger air traffic.

Automation is all of these things. But my point is that it is much more.

Machines have always been important to us primarily in their role as *agents for social change*. We use the very term *industrial revolution* not because of the revolutionary machines of James Watt and Richard Arkwright, but because they created a whole new environment for mankind — a whole new way of life. What they gave to history was much more than the steam engine and the cotton gin, the railway and the power loom. Their machines gave society a whole new tempo, a whole new outlook.

Today's crop of machines is a far, far more powerful agent for social change than was that of the first industrial revolution. For today's machines result from a new found ability to build systems which: process and communicate information; translate from one language to another; respond to the human voice; devise their own route to goals that are presented to them; machine systems which improve their performance as a result of encountering the environment (machines in other words which learn in the normal sense in which that term is used); machine systems, in short, which deal with the very core of human society — with information, its communication, and use. These are developments which auger far more for mankind than net changes in manpower, more or less employment, or new ways of doing old tasks.

These are developments which mean that mankind will undertake new tasks, not merely perform old tasks in a new way. This is a technology which vastly extends the range of human capability and which will fundamentally alter human society.

The very nature of today's technology, its concern with the building blocks of human society, will in the course of the lifetime of students now graduating from universities — and perhaps in the lifetime of many businessmen today — force us to reconsider our whole approach to work, to society, and to life itself.

The technology of automation casts before it shadows of far greater social change than were brought about by the industrial revolution set in train by James Watt and Richard Arkwright.

Let us look, for example, at automation as perceived from three viewpoints: the individual; the manager; and public policy.

The individual perceives automation as a job threat or, if he be a mathematician, engineer or otherwise situated to benefit, he perceives it as a challenge and an opportunity.

Yet automation is going to force the individual — and all of mankind — to reconsider his very conception of himself. As Professor Herbert A. Simon, of Carnegie Institute of Technology, states: "The definition of man's uniqueness has always formed the kernel of his cosmological and ethical systems. With Copernicus and Galileo, he ceased to be the species located at the center of the universe, attended by sun and stars. With Darwin, he ceased to be the species created and specially endowed by God with soul and reason. With Freud, he ceased to be the species whose behavior was — potentially — governable by rational mind. As we begin to produce mechanisms that think and learn, he

"Automation — Perceiving the Magnitude of the Problem," *Advanced Management Journal*, XXIX (April 1964), 29–33. Reprinted by permission of the author and the publisher. **John Diebold**: President and founder, The Diebold Group, Inc., Management Consultants, New York.

has ceased to be the species uniquely capable of complex, intelligent manipulation of his environment."

Man will find a new way of describing his place in the universe. Machine systems certainly show no signs of many of the fundamental human qualities such as imagination, volition, purposefulness, compassion or love. Yet my point is that man's ability to build machines which learn and which already possess so much of the quality we today call "intelligence" means that we have the most fundamental of changes in store for the individual and for our conception of our role as humans.

The manager, public administrator and private businessman, today perceive automation as a labor saving device and as a means for exercising tighter control on his enterprise and making it more responsive to rapid change. The great theme in today's business literature is that automation represents an opportunity to a better job of managing.

This is all well and good as far as it goes. But in itself it tells only a small part of the story. For the significance of automation to the manager is not so much the new methods it gives him for managing — the new kit of professional tools so to speak — but the fact that the enterprise he manages will change totally due to the changes automation is effecting in our society.

The real potential, and the enormous problem, automation poses to the manager is that the environment in which the enterprise exists is changing, rapidly and completely. As the goals, aspirations, needs and wants of the individual shift, and shift again and again through the human social change induced by automation, the economic realities that sustain the enterprise will change.

In other words, the great meaning of automation to the manager is to be found in the social change induced by automation. This holds a far more profound meaning to the manager and businessman than the procedural revolution taking place today in management methods. For it is in its role of serving human wants that lies the entrepreneurial raison d'être of business and government organizations alike.

Rapid and major social shifts mean an entirely new and more day to day role for strategic planning in guiding the enterprise. It is here that automation is making profound change and it is here that we must look for the essence of the managerial meaning of this new industrial revolution. For here lies the heart of enterprise — ascertaining and filling human need — not the techniques of management, however important the latter may be in today's giant and changing organizations. Vitality and survival are determined by the ability of the organization — whether private or public — to perceive and fulfill these, now rapidly changing, human needs.

Public policy perceives automation as a problem of unemployment, retraining and change in manpower requirements. Altogether correct as far as it goes, and of critical importance. The additional and accurately perceived need for increased productivity occasionally produces in public policy a schizophrenic impression of calling in effect for "more technology — but go slowly!" But the public policy perception of automation is only too clear — if far too limited.

The reality of the public policy question is that the problem is much greater than yet perceived by all but a very few.

International political as well as economic forces will require us to increasingly press for world leadership in these new technologies — which are correctly perceived by the remainder of the world as a tomorrow in which they intend to live. This necessary drive for technological leadership — on which increasingly rests our economically privileged position — will sharpen and intensify the as yet largely unperceived social problems of automation.

It is significant, I think, that with increasing frequency and forcefulness statements of Soviet political and economic theory refer to automation as the means by which mankind will achieve the highest of estates. No shilly-shallying here. No confusion over whether to move forward. Rather a firm determination to lead tomorrow where our country leads today.

Employment shifts and retraining may be easier in the Soviet, but I think we would be foolish to write it off at this. Marxist-Leninist doctrine has long valued technology as a determinant of social change. It is positively *embracing* automation. Premier Khrushchev has stated, "Automation is good. It is the means we will use to lick you capitalists."

But even leaving the Sino-Soviet bloc aside, the international pressure is still there to force us to pursue the technology even more aggressively than we do today. The developing nations as well as the highly developed countries of the world look to the new technology of automation as a major solution to today's problems. In addition — and this is of great significance — many of them correctly perceive automation as the key to a very different kind of tomorrow.

We have no corner on this technology — even though we lead today. We can look forward only to increasing pressure from all parts of the world to move very much more rapidly in order to hold our leadership. The revolution of information technology is a revolution moved by human brains — and there is precious little built-in advantage to us other than our educational system and our major institutions of research. We will feel increasing pressure to keep ahead with both.

The solution to this public paradox is the creation of an environment conducive to technological leadership and rapid change. The first step must be the removal of all reason for fear over individual harm due to technological change. But the problem cannot be solved backwards—the proper role of public policy is to create the conditions necessary to leadership in the human use of this new technology.

The electronic computer—today's crude precursor of the machine systems automation is so rapidly bringing into existence—is important not nearly so much because of the things it does today—however much we have already come to rely upon it in our daily lives—but because it represents a new-found human ability based upon the most powerful of theoretical insights into the nature of information and its uniquely important place in our lives.

As this ability is expressed in machine systems that abstract as well as translate documents; help physicians to diagnose disease, lawyers to prepare briefs, teachers to develop better the capabilities of their students, the world will become a far different place than it is today.

Major *social* innovation seems to me to be called for to cope with such technological innovation. It must be as rapid and as great as is the technological innovation.

Last time we ignored the need for social innovation. One result was Karl Marx. His ideas have had more to do with shaping the lives of all of us than we would care to believe true.

The very magnitude and importance of the problem mean that we should not look to government for *the* solution. It is a task which should involve all of us, our best minds and hearts. It is a problem to be solved by the *private* as well as the public sector.

Pope John XXIII made a notable contribution to showing what must be done by the private sector in his encyclical *Mater et Magistra*. Governments can do much to ameliorate the human toll of transition and to help create an environment that will encourage technological leadership. But the shape of tomorrow's world is surely a problem to which we all can usefully contribute as individuals and working through private organizations as well as through our governments. We have hardly yet begun to face up to these aspects of the problem.

For example, the foundations and professional societies such as the Society for Advancement of Management, nourished in large part by increasingly automated industries, have thus far been conspicuous in their avoidance of interest in what the late President Kennedy characterized as "the major domestic challenge" of the Sixties. The private foundations and the professional societies are institutions to which we might reasonably look for help and guidance as the private sector contemplates these critical problems. The Society for Advancement of Management is to be commended for this present compendium on the critical issues of automation and management. Through such explorations will come more understanding of the problem. From this illumination new insights should be generated by management responsible for organization change.

Let me revert one last time to that upheaval of two centuries ago that we now call the industrial revolution. No one in the middle of eighteenth century England, least of all Richard Arkwright or James Watt, thought that they were changing civilization itself. Yet, for us, looking back, that is precisely what was *revolutionary* about the inventions they made.

They took men off the fields and out of the small shops and put them for the first time into factory life. Hence they gave us mass production, and through mass production the first civilization in history in which luxury was not confined to a few.

Like the pioneers of the industrial revolution of the eighteenth century, we face today a world in which only one thing is certain: change, fundamental change.

But unlike those earlier pioneers, we live in an age of the greatest sense of social responsibility in all history.

Our task today is to wisely use our technology, our knowledge of history, and our compassion to make the age of automation a golden Periclean age in which a society based on the work of the machine—not the human chattel—rises to the full heights of which the human spirit is capable.

52 — Automation and the Management Process

THOMAS L. WHISLER
and GEORGE P. SHULTZ

The impact of automation is not limited to effects on blue-collar and clerical jobs and workers.[1] A key characteristic of this new form of technological change is its relation to the concept of control. In its application to information processing, automation already affects and seems likely to widen its impact on managerial jobs and on the management process.

The characteristic of direct impact on management gives a new twist to the problems of introducing and adjusting to technological change. The familiar issues are present: who is to get the new jobs, how are training opportunities to be allocated, how are the gains to be shared, and so on. Issues of this kind have traditionally been decided by business managers, just as traditionally the people affected by their decisions have been blue-collar or white-collar workers. But, with automation, the managers themselves are directly affected along with others. The decisions made somewhere in the managerial group about automation will have an impact on the individual members of that group in varying degrees. Can a group change itself? What are the contours of the problem, and what issues are of special importance to society generally as well as to managers personally? These are questions that concern us here.

The piece of automation hardware most likely to change management jobs and the management process is the computer, with its ability to receive, store, and process rapidly large volumes of information. Especially when combined with various mathematical and statistical methods and when applied to decision-making, rather than to simple clerical automation, the computer is the basis for a new information technology that may be a vital part of the way organizations are run in the future.

The evidence to date indicates that the craft of management will be changed sharply in some areas, especially those activities related to decision-making. Traditional ideas of how to make an intelligent decision are challenged by the new technology. For example, how much information is it economic (and therefore necessary) to gather and analyze before reaching a decision? Much more in tomorrow's world than today's. How often should the firm refigure plans and strategies? Much more often after the computer arrives. How precisely and specifically is it possible — and necessary — to express a decision? Much more precisely and explicitly with the computer — to the extent that decisions may become almost uncomfortably visible from the manager's point of view.

Information technology built around the computer and focusing upon vital flows of information through an organization will rechannel these flows and, in the process, alter basic organization structure and change managerial jobs. It is here that managers may come face to face with decisions to inaugurate changes which can substantially influence their own lives.

EFFECTS ON ORGANIZATION AND JOBS

As the computer makes alterations in information channels, visible traces appear in the organization structure. In a specific application, it is possible, as some business firms have shown, to forecast the location and nature of organization changes once the new patterns of information flow have been determined.

Although the impress of the computer will vary from firm to firm, the general nature of its impact can be specified. The first wave of this impact will be upon: (1) the existing structure of organization in each firm, (2) the current bundle of jobs at the managerial level, in terms both of number of jobs and job content, and (3) the present structure of authority in the management hierarchy. From these changes we can then deduce some likely effects upon management job holders and upon the practices and activities which make up the art of administration.

"Automation and the Management Process," *The Annals of the American Academy of Political and Social Science*, CCCXL (March 1962), 81–89. Reprinted by permission of the authors and the publisher. **Thomas L. Whisler** and **George P. Shultz:** Graduate School of Business, University of Chicago.

1. Material presented in this article draws heavily on two earlier publications in which the authors were involved, as well as on their more recent research. The earlier publications are Harold J. Leavitt and Thomas L. Whisler, "Management in the 1980's," *Harvard Business Review*, Vol. 36, No. 6 (November — December 1958) and George P. Shultz and Thomas L. Whisler (eds.), *Management Organization and the Computer* (Glencoe: The Free Press, 1960). We treat here only a small segment of the range of issues presented by this topic and dealt with in the writings referred to above. For example, we do not take up such an important topic as the economics of the use of computers for purposes of management decisions.

STRUCTURAL CHANGES

Consider, first, structural changes in the organization. Formal organization structure reflects reasonably well the pattern of information flow necessary to accomplish the work of that organization. We can expect that when a new technique of handling information is introduced — especially one which channels the information into and out of a computer — the grouping of activities which makes up the divisions and levels of an organization structure will be affected. One effect would be to combine some currently separate activities and, perhaps at the same time, to separate other activities that are currently together. However, the first, the combinatorial effect, should be the stronger, since it is the nature of the computer to integrate and to encapsulate information flows. The tendency is to reduce the number of organization links.

In one company, integration has occurred at a high level, tying marketing activities closely into manufacturing. One consequence has been the replacement of the two former vice-presidents individually responsible for these areas, making one responsible for both. In another company, purchasing has been tied in directly with the responsibilities for controlling material flow for production planning. The organization shows a corresponding consolidation. In a third case, a company has brought together the control of warehouse inventories, granting of credit to customers, shipping of goods, and billing of customers, creating a new managerial position and substantially altering some old ones. An executive in still another firm which is moving rapidly into information-technology applications believes that the traditional grouping of activities in business with familiar titles such as sales and manufacturing will be completely replaced with new divisions and new titles which will reflect the kinds of processes, and information flows, which fit neatly into the computer but which would not have been efficient groupings for men to attempt to manage.

Whatever the effect on departments, some effect on the levels of organization can also be anticipated. The number of levels may be reduced as activities are consolidated and the growth process of hierarchical organizations is, in effect, reversed. Remembering that the computer has a direct impact upon information transmission and analysis, we can anticipate that its greatest effect will be felt in those levels of the organization which, receiving information from within the firm and without, try to construct orderly plans of action from this information. In other words, the middle and upper reaches of management, rather than the lower levels and the nonmanagers, will be most affected.

A company in the middle of an extensive application of the computer to certain of its management functions has plotted the organizational changes it anticipates within a matter of months as a result of this application. Although a greater number of clerical than managerial employees will be displaced, the percentages are reversed. More than a third of the managers will be displaced while only about a fifth of the nonmanagers will be so affected.

Since the range of physical, blue-collar operations in a company is little affected by the applications we are discussing and since the volume and variety of information about the outside world relevant to management actions tends to increase through time rather than decrease, any shrinkage effect on the management organization structure will be uneven. While the middle may thin out, the top will burgeon, especially during the transition period when the new technologists of information cluster thickly about headquarters. The general effect, in fact, will be to slide most of the thinking and planning specialists toward the upper levels as their planning spheres become locked together and consolidated.

MANAGEMENT ACTIVITY

A second major change will have to do with the job activities of many individual managers. A currently visible effect of the computer is the introduction into the business firm of individuals with skills unknown a few years ago. A great demand has developed for mathematicians and computer experts. People with strange titles such as "systems analysts" and "operations researchers" now adorn the management structures in many businesses. As a consequence of the activities of these newcomers, many of the traditional management jobs will be affected.

The manager of a newly consolidated (because of the computer) operation, who also had been the manager of some of these same operations under precomputer arrangements, reflected upon the changes in his own job. Much of the hectic day-to-day planning (or, perhaps more appropriately, "adapting") had been taken over by the computer. Certain facets of his job had been slighted previously under the pressure of crisis planning and improvisation. These were activities centering on interpersonal relations, either with customers or with his own staff. He finds that he now spends more time building a good staff and getting to know customers' needs than was possible in previous years, and, incidentally, he believes this to be more what he, as a manager, should be doing.

The new technology of information places increasing pressure upon the quality of information fed into it. By eliminating traditional time lags, misplaced information, conflicting decision rules, and unco-ordinated planning, which formerly necessitated frequent rechecking of information, it greatly enhances the importance of getting correct information into the system in the first place. The importance of feeding in correct information and of visualizing ways for improving the techniques of analysis will be reflected in an emphasis on these activities in the manager's job.

AUTHORITY AND CONTROL

Perhaps even more significant than these visible organizational changes is the consequent alteration of the structure of authority and control. Control is a concept difficult to define and even harder to measure. But considering it as the power to establish decision rules for the organization, and to alter them in light of subsequent events, it is likely that the integrating and rationalizing force of the new technology will lead to a greater centralization of control within the business firm. It is important to keep in mind that the impetus for this centralization lies not simply in an effort to load fully an expensive machine but also in the computer's enormous capacity for very rapidly analyzing a wide range and quantity of interrelated data. It becomes feasible technically and, in many instances, sound economically to consider effects on a wide range of the firm's activities in making "small" planning decisions. To find the prototype of this kind of decision-making, one must look at the very small business in which one manager makes most of the decisions and, as best he can, assesses each decision in terms of its impact on the whole range of the business operations.

The best illustrations of this centralizing effect occur where operations researchers have been at work. In one major steel company, for example, regional managers formerly were charged with the responsibility for maintaining warehouse stocks of finished steel forms in sufficient quantity "not to disappoint our important customers—at least, not too often" and, at the same time, to minimize investment in finished goods inventories. Operations research specialists were able to provide top management of the firm a quantitative description of the relationship between frequency of failures to give service and dollars

invested in inventory. Top management then chose the level of service it could afford to give to various classes of customers and thereby made the decisions on warehouse stocking for the regional managers. In another case, a multiplant manufacturer was able to schedule production and to order materials on a more efficient basis at headquarters, using computer programs, than the individual plants were able to do previously. The computer now generates better schedules than any group of individuals is able to produce and there is no longer any point in asking individual plant personnel to approve these schedules or edit them. Control in this sense has been centralized.

The economic aspects, as contrasted with the technical, is illustrated in another case in which an airline owning a central computer facility nonetheless maintained small decentralized reservations personnel groups because of the high cost of constantly feeding queries by telephone to the computer. When telephone tariffs were substantially reduced, the decision was made to pull all information and decisions to the computer. Control over reservations was thus placed in one spot and the organization was altered in the process of shifting this control.

SOME ISSUES.

A number of problems, many old and some new, are being generated by the appearance of information technology in American business. Most of these problems must be dealt with by business managers themselves, although their willingness and ability to deal intelligently with these problems may determine whether managers retain the authority to cope with them. Some others of a more long-run nature may be problems that society as a whole must face.

In considering both these types of problems, we have been impressed with the degree to which a given technological change, the problems and opportunities it generates, and the general economic and social setting are interrelated. Indeed, our format for studying these issues can be thought of as a large system of relationships and feedbacks, as shown on the accompanying diagram.

Some effects, as in Box 2 of Table 1, are virtual counterparts of the technological change itself; but those in Box 3, including the dimensions of human adjustments to the effects of change, can vary widely. The success with which these adjustments are made feeds back not only on the direct effects in Box 2 but on the workability of technological change itself and on the broader social environment producing and sustaining such

TABLE 1 DIAGRAMMATIC REPRESENTATION OF THE FLOW OF FORCES SURROUNDING TECHNOLOGICAL CHANGE

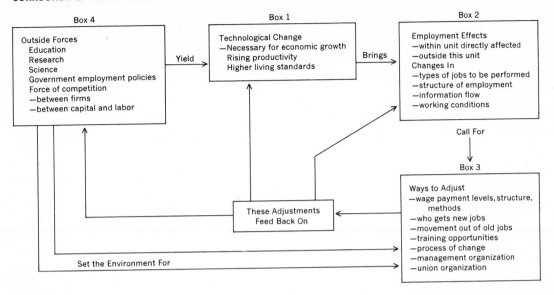

changes. And this environment, of course, is of vital significance to the feasibility of successful adjustments in any individual case. Thus, analysis of the effects of automation on the management process deals with an intricate and far-flung system of relationships. It is vital to recognize these relationships in any analysis of the impact of change. It is also important to recognize that some of the effects are a part of a transition process, while others are of a more enduring nature.

JOBS AND SKILLS

The transitional effects are familiar ones. One, which has occupied a great deal of attention already, is displacement of employees. Curiously, most attention has been centered upon displacement among clerical employees. The evidence indicates that, although clerks undoubtedly will be affected, perhaps the most difficult and persistent problems will arise from displacement of managers. Retraining and relocating those displaced will become someone's responsibility. The retraining problem, with its questions of the kind of training and the distribution of its costs, may be complicated considerably if many firms are feeling displacement effects at about the same time. American business has, by this time, had a great deal of experience in dealing with technologically displaced workers. The applicability to displaced managers of the lessons learned from this experience remains to be tested.

In addition to displacement effects, replacement problems must be expected. Changing job structures and skill patterns deriving from computer applications will shift the pattern of demand in the labor market at the managerial level. The responses of the market and the people in it involve the kinds of adjustments indicated in the right-hand side of our diagram. The fascinating aspect of these transition problems is that the decisions which will have to be made about altered organization structure and altered pay and status relationships will immediately and directly affect those charged with the responsibility for these decisions. Since specialization of labor exists at the management level as well as elsewhere in business, the costs and gains from the decisions made are likely to be unevenly distributed throughout the management structure, with a great deal of resulting organizational tension. The behavioral scientists, no less than the manager, should be closely watching the way in which these changes are actually accomplished.

MANAGEMENT AND DECISION-MAKING

Another source of tension is related to more centralized control over decision-making by managers in the lower and middle ranges of the organization. Historically, this same process swept through American business at lower organizational levels under the impetus of scientific management. The routinization of tasks and centralization of control over blue-collar jobs which this produced during the early decades of the twentieth century is partly responsible for the industrial relations problems of the last twenty or thirty years, including those involving the unhappy foreman whose job has been stripped of much of its content by personnel men and industrial engineers. The planning of one man's work by another has resulted in costs to individuals and to society not usually taken into account by those who accept the scientific-management philosophy. The computer experts seem in many instances to be moving the mistakes as well as the constructive purposes of scientific management to a higher level in the organization. Predictable problems, ignored in the early stages of this development, are sure to take their toll at a later date.

We believe that the kinds of managers to be found in the future business firm will differ from today's managers in important respects. As their skills and job requirements shift, so must their training, both in terms of intensiveness and in terms of particular specialities they choose. We expect that upper-level managers especially will receive substantially more formal education than the average manager today, thereby accelerating a general social trend. This change, along with emphasis upon fundamental theoretical knowledge, will make these men more like today's "staff" man and less like yesterday's boss in terms of behavior, attitudes, and interests. Focusing less upon internal relationships and control problems—thanks to these being taken over to a great degree by the computer—the future manager's orientation would be more that of the professional—outward looking, interested in the problems of others in the profession, more visible to others, and probably more inclined to be mobile. It would be dangerous to apply this description to the whole range of the assumed structure of tomorrow's management, because it is far from clear as to how roles and relationships will be set up. But the emphasis upon rational problem-solving, and the increasing visibility of the decision process associated with the new technology, should doom to extinction most of the "organization men," if such have ever really existed.

SOCIAL IMPLICATIONS

What may turn out to be the most important social effect of the new technology of business management stems from the changing demands placed upon formal training institutions. Business firms have been extremely vague in defining what they expect from colleges and universities, as recent investigations have demonstrated. But information technology should draw the lines more clearly and precisely. A great number of tomorrow's managers will be adequate only if they have the insights and understandings gained from graduate-level university training in physical and social sciences. At the same time, others lower in the hierarachy may need quite different understandings and skills—ones perhaps best gained in specialized training arrangements other than those associated with universities. Whatever the pattern that emerges, it seems likely that institutions outside the business firms will be more likely to be able to provide the individual with the kinds of preparation he needs for a career as a business manager than will the firms themselves. This is largely due to the declining value of low-level work experiences in the firm as preparation for high-level jobs as information technology increasingly centralizes control and differentiates work roles in the management structure.

Society's educational resources, already being shifted more toward professional and scientific training because of other environmental factors, may be expected to have to bear a new load as the business managers—an important group in the labor force—seek new ways of preparing themselves for managerial careers.

Thus, the educational and research institutions, which originally generated the thinking and technical developments resulting in a new technology of information, will themselves be modified as a consequence of the successful application of this technology. In this area, then, as in all the areas discussed above, we see a close pattern of interrelationships among direct effects of new technology, indirect consequences for organizations, and broad implications for important social questions. At the same time, these patterns are presented in new forms by the application of computers to management processes, where the agents of change are also among those directly affected.

Correlation Chart

The majority of textbooks prominent in the field of management, listed below, use the functional approach, either explicitly or implicitly. Generally, they agree in their treatment of the field as a whole, the objectives and strategies, and the functions of planning and decision-making, organizing, motivating, and controlling. The cross references between the sections in this book and the chapters on these topics in the textbooks are therefore quite obvious and relatively simple.

Other sections in this book, however, are not so clearly paralleled in the textbooks. This is true of the sections on innovating, the behavioral sciences, international management, and the final section on EDP, models, games, PERT, and automation.

In these cases, a special effort has been made to correlate the readings with the most appropriate chapter or chapters of the textbooks.

The titles and Roman numerals at the top of each column refer to the sections in this book; the numbers below each heading indicate the relevant chapters in the textbooks cited at the left.

It has been the editor's experience that selected articles from readings books can be used profitably even when complete sections do not readily correspond to textbook chapters and that perceptive students can use a readings book successfully, as a whole or in parts, quite independent of any textbook.

The correlation chart is provided mainly as a guide; it is hoped that each professor, student, and practitioner will find his own best way of using this book.

ALBERS, HENRY H., *Organized Executive Action* (New York: John Wiley & Sons, Inc., 1961).

DALE, ERNEST, *Management: Theory and Practice* (New York: McGraw-Hill Book Company, Inc., 1965).

DRUCKER, PETER F., *The Practice of Management* (New York: Harper & Brothers, 1954).

HAIMANN, THEO, *Professional Management: Theory and Practice* (Boston: Houghton Mifflin Company, 1962).

HART, DONALD J., *Business in a Dynamic Society* (New York: The Macmillan Company, 1963).

HAYNES, W. WARREN, and JOSEPH L. MASSIE, *Management: Analyses, Concepts and Cases* (Englewood Cliffs, N.J.: Prentice-Hall, Inc., 1961).

HODGES, H. G., and R. J. ZIEGLER, *Managing the Industrial Concern* (Boston: Houghton Mifflin Company, 1963).

KOONTZ, HAROLD, and CYRIL O'DONNELL *Principles of Management,* 3rd ed. (New York: McGraw-Hill Book Company, Inc., 1964).

McFARLAND, DALTON EDWARD, *Management: Principles and Practices,* 2nd ed. (New York: The Macmillan Company, 1964).

NEWMAN, WILLIAM H., *Administrative Action,* 2nd ed. (Englewood Cliffs, N.J.: Prentice-Hall, Inc., 1963).

NEWMAN, WILLIAM H., and CHARLES E. SUMMER, *The Process of Management* (Englewood Cliffs, N.J.: Prentice-Hall, Inc., 1962).

NILES, MARY CUSHING, *The Essence of Management* (New York: Harper & Brothers, 1958).

PFIFFNER, JOHN M., and FRANK P. SHERWOOD, *Administrative Organization* (Englewood Cliffs, N.J.: Prentice-Hall, Inc., 1960).

TERRY, GEORGE R., *Principles of Management,* 4th ed. (Homewood, Ill.: Richard D. Irwin, Inc., 1964).

VANCE, STANLEY, *Industrial Administration* (New York: McGraw-Hill Book Company, Inc., 1959).

VILLERS, RAYMOND, *Dynamic Management in Industry* (Englewood Cliffs, N.J.: Prentice-Hall, Inc., 1960).

	I	II	III	IV	V
	The Field	Objectives and Strategies	Planning and Decision-Making	Organizing	Motivating
Albers	1–3	13, 19	7, 10, 12–13	4–8, 18, 21	14–19, 23
Dale	1, 2, 8, 15	22	22, 29	16–21	23–25,
Drucker	1–4, 12, 14, 21	5–7, 11	8, 28	12–14	12–13, 16–17, 23, 27
Haimann	1	6	5–9	4, 10–15, 18	22, 25–30
Hart	5	5, 9	16	4–5	5, 12
Haynes and Massie	1	3	5, 9, 19, 21	3, 5	5, 7
Hodges and Ziegler	1–3, 35	1, 3	3, 5, 8, 25	6, 17, 19	3, 20–21, 35
Koontz and O'Donnell	1–3, 20	6	5, 7–8, 10	11–17, 19	23–27
McFarland	1–3	5–6	4, 7	8–14, 16, 18	17–22, 25
Newman	1	2, 6	2–8	9–17	21–23
Newman and Summer	1	17	12–16, 18–20	2–6, 10	7–11, 21–24
Niles	1–3	4	19, 30	7, 11–14, 18, 20	5, 17, 23
Pfiffner and Sherwood	1, 7	1, 5	6, 13, 21	1–2, 4–5, 7–13	6, 9, 16, 19
Terry	1, 3, 5	1–2, 15, 22, 24–25, 32	6–14	15–19	21–25, 34
Vance	1–2	5	7–8	5–6	6
Villers	1–2, 4	14–15	6, 9, 12, 15	4–5, 7, 12	2, 8, 12–13

	VI Innovating	VII Controlling	VIII Behavioral. Sciences	IX International Management	X EDP, Models, Games, PERT, and Automation
Albers	1, 11–12, 21	2–3, 7, 17	2, 11, 15, 19–20	3, 11, 22	22–23
Dale	27	26	17, 25	30–32	33–35
Drucker	7, 18–19	11, 15	13, 15, 20–22, 25	1–3, 5, 19, 29	3, 14–15, 29
Haimann	18, 26	31–32, 34–35	18, 26, 29	1–2	2, 26
Hart	13–14	5, 16–17	9–12	9, 15	15–17
Haynes and Massie	5	11, 13, 19	1, 5, 7	1	27
Hodges and Ziegler	20–21, 35	3, 8, 10, 12, 17–18, 33	20–21, 25, 32, 35–36	35–36	31
Koontz and O'Donnell	10, 27	27–29, 31	2, 10, 25–27	1–2, 4	2, 8, 10, 27, 29
McFarland	1, 3–6, 11, 14–15, 24	15–16	1–3, 7, 12, 17–19, 22, 25	1	15, 23–24
Newman	4, 6	24–26	21–22, 27	1, 27	6, 8, 27
Newman and Summer	1–2, 6–7, 17, 21	25–28	7–8, 10–11, 13, 20, 22, 27	7	7, 11, 14, 20, 27
Niles	12, 24, 26	22–23	3, 5–9, 15–17, 25	16, 23, 31	5, 27, 29, 31
Pfiffner and Sherwood	13, 18	6	3–4, 6, 8, 12, 14–15, 23	2	5, 22–24
Terry	21, 26, 34	26–30	1, 15, 19, 21–25, 34	3, 5	1, 7–8, 10, 31, 35
Vance	3	9–10	5–6, 17–18	1–2	6, 8, 12, 19
Villers	6–7, 11	10–13	6–7, 12–13, 15	2	3, 11, 15

INDEX OF AUTHORS AND TITLES